Enhanced Microsoft® Office 2013 Fundamentals

ILLUSTRATED

Hunt/Clemens

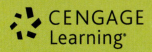

CENGAGE
Learning®

Australia • Brazil • Mexico • Singapore • United Kingdom • United States

Microsoft® Office 2013—Illustrated Fundamentals, Enhanced Edition
Hunt/Clemens

Product Director: Kathleen McMahon

Senior Product Team Manager: Lauren Murphy

Product Team Manager: Brian Hyland

Senior Director of Development: Marah Bellegarde

Product Development Manager: Leigh Hefferon

Senior Content Developer: Christina Kling-Garrett

Product Assistant: Brianna Vorce

Marketing Director: Michele McTighe

Senior Marketing Manager: Eric La Scolla

Developmental Editor: Marjorie Hopper

Senior Content Project Manager: Jennifer Goguen McGrail

Manufacturing Planner: Fola Orekoya

Copyeditor: Mark Goodin

Proofreader: Vicki Zimmer

Indexer: Alexandra Nickerson

QA Manuscript Reviewers: John Freitas, Susan Pedicini, Danielle Shaw, Susan Whalen, Jeff Schwartz

Cover Designer: GEX Publishing Services

Cover Artist: GEX Publishing Services

Composition: GEX Publishing Services

© 2016 Cengage Learning

WCN: 01-100-101

For product information and technology assistance, contact us at
Cengage Learning Customer & Sales Support, 1-800-354-9706

For permission to use material from this text or product, submit all requests online at **www.cengage.com/permissions**
Further permissions questions can be emailed to
permissionrequest@cengage.com

Library of Congress Control Number: 2015930694
ISBN: 978-1-305-49244-8

Cengage Learning
20 Channel Center Street
Boston, MA 02210
USA

Cengage Learning is a leading provider of customized learning solutions with office locations around the globe, including Singapore, the United Kingdom, Australia, Mexico, Brazil, and Japan. Locate your local office at: **www.cengage.com/global**

Cengage Learning products are represented in Canada by Nelson Education, Ltd.

For your course and learning solutions, visit **www.cengage.com**

Purchase any of our products at your local college store or at our preferred online store **www.cengagebrain.com**

Trademarks:
Some of the product names and company names used in this book have been used for identification purposes only and may be trademarks or registered trademarks of their respective manufacturers and sellers.

Microsoft and the Windows logo are registered trademarks of Microsoft Corporation in the United States and/or other countries. Cengage Learning is an independent entity from Microsoft Corporation, and not affiliated with Microsoft in any manner.

Carbonite is a registered trademark of Carbonite, Inc.

Printed in the United States of America
Print Number: 01   Print Year: 2015

Brief Contents

Contents

Windows 8

Office 2013

Word 2013

Excel 2013

Integration 2013

Cloud

Integrated Projects

SAM Projects

Capstone Projects

Preface

Welcome to *Microsoft Office 2013—Illustrated Fundamentals, Enhanced Edition.* This book has a unique design: Each skill is presented on two facing pages, with steps on the left and screens on the right. The layout makes it easy to learn a skill without having to read a lot of text and flip pages to see an illustration.

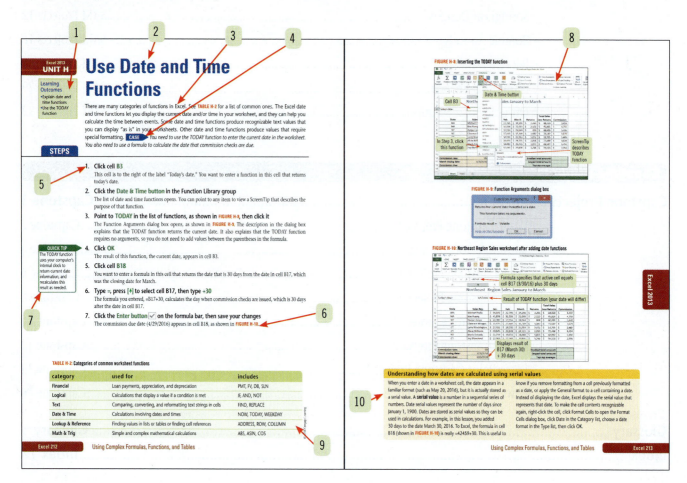

1 **New!** Learning Outcomes box lists measurable learning goals for which a student is accountable in that lesson.

2 Each two-page lesson focuses on a single skill.

3 Introduction briefly explains why the lesson skill is important.

4 A case scenario motivates the steps and puts learning in context.

5 Step-by-step instructions and brief explanations guide students through each hands-on lesson activity.

6 **New!** Figure references are now in red bold to help students refer back and forth between the steps and screenshots.

7 Tips and troubleshooting advice, right where you need it—next to the step itself.

8 **New!** Larger screen shots with green callouts now placed on top keep students on track as they complete steps.

9 Tables provide summaries of helpful information such as button references or keyboard shortcuts.

10 Clues to Use yellow boxes provide useful information related to the lesson skill.

This book is an ideal learning tool for a wide range of learners—the "rookies" will find the clean design easy to follow and focused with only essential information presented, and the "hotshots" will appreciate being able to move quickly through the lessons to find the information they need without reading a lot of text. The design also makes this book a great reference after the course is over! See the illustration on the left to learn more about the pedagogical and design elements of a typical lesson.

About this Edition

- **Streamlined Approach** — This book is the Illustrated Series' shortest book on Microsoft Office 2013. It covers a wide range of skills at a high level so you can cover a lot of ground in a short amount of time.

- **Coverage** — This book features step-by-step instructions on using Microsoft Office 2013—including Word, Excel, Access, and PowerPoint as well as Windows 8 and New! essential computer concepts. New appendix provides eight capstone projects. Working in the Cloud appendix helps students learn to save, share and manage files in the cloud and to use Office Web Apps.

- **New! SAM Projects** — The Word, Excel, Access and PowerPoint units in this new edition map to SAM Projects, which are auto-gradable assignments that students create "live in the application." Please see "Online Learning and Assessment" page for more information about SAM and SAM Projects. (SAM sold separately.)

- **New! Learning Outcomes** — Each lesson displays a green Learning Outcomes box that lists skills-based or knowledge-based learning goals for which students are accountable. Each Learning Outcome maps to a variety of learning activities and assessments. (See the *New! Learning Outcomes* section on page xvi for more information.)

- **New! Updated Design** — This edition features many new design Improvements to engage students — including larger lesson screenshots with green callouts, and a refreshed Unit Opener page.

- **New! Independent Challenge 4: Explore** — This new case-based assessment activity allows students to explore new skills and use creativity to solve a problem or create a project.

Assignments

This book includes a wide variety of high-quality assignments you can use for practice and assessment. Assignments include:

- **Concepts Review** — Multiple choice, matching, and screen identification questions.

- **Skills Review** — Step-by-step, hands-on review of every skill covered in the unit.

- **Independent Challenges 1-3** — Case projects requiring critical thinking and application of the unit skills. The Independent Challenges increase in difficulty. The first one in each unit provides the most hand-holding; the subsequent ones provide less guidance and require more critical thinking and independent problem solving.

- **Independent Challenge 4: Explore** — Case projects that let students explore new skills that are related to the core skills covered in the unit and are often more open ended, allowing students to use creativity to complete the assignment.

- **Visual Workshop** — Critical thinking exercises that require students to create a project by looking at a completed solution; they must apply the skills they've learned in the unit and use critical thinking skills to create the project from scratch.

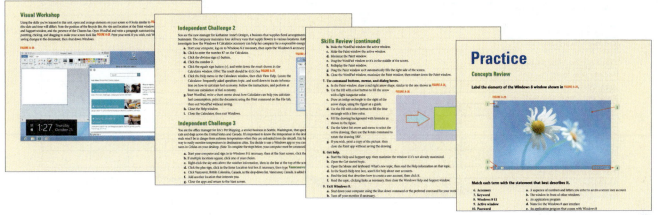

New! Learning Outcomes

Every 2-page lesson in this book now contains a green **Learning Outcomes box** that states the learning goals for that lesson.

- **What is a learning outcome?** A learning outcome states what a student is expected to know or be able to do after completing a lesson. Each learning outcome is skill-based or knowledge-based and is *measurable*. Learning outcomes map to learning activities and assessments.

- **How do students benefit from learning outcomes?** Learning outcomes tell students exactly what skills and knowledge they are *accountable* for learning in that lesson. This helps students study more efficiently and effectively and makes them more active learners.

- **How do instructors benefit from learning outcomes?** Learning outcomes provide clear, measurable, skills-based learning goals that map to various high-quality learning activities and assessments. A **Learning Outcomes Map**, available for each unit in this book, maps every learning outcome to the learning activities and assessments shown below.

Learning Outcomes Map to These Learning Activities:

1. **Book lessons:** Step-by-step tutorial on one skill presented in a two-page learning format
2. **Illustrated Videos:** Videos based on lessons in this book (sold separately on DVD or in SAM as part of e-book)
3. **SAM Training:** Short animations and hands-on practice activities in simulated environment

Learning Outcomes Map to These Assessments:

1. **End-of-Unit Exercises: Concepts Review** (screen identification, matching, multiple choice); **Skills Review** (hands-on review of each lesson); **Independent Challenges** (hands-on, case-based review of specific skills); **Visual Workshop** (activity that requires student to build a project by looking at a picture of the final solution).
2. **Exam View Test Banks:** Objective-based questions you can use for online or paper testing.
3. **SAM Assessment:** Performance-based assessment in a simulated environment.
4. **New! SAM Projects:** Auto-graded projects for Word, Excel, Access and PowerPoint that students create live in the application.
5. **Extra Independent Challenges:** Extra case-based exercises available in the Instructor Resources that cover various skills.

Learning Outcomes Map

A **Learning Outcomes Map**, contained in the Instructor Resources, provides a listing of learning activities and assessments for each learning outcome in the book.

Learning Outcomes Map
Microsoft Office Fundamentals
PowerPoint Unit M: Creating a Presentation

KEY:
IC=Independent Challenge   EIC=Extra Independent Challenge
VW=Visual Workshop

	Concepts Review	Skills Review	IC1	IC2	IC3	IC4	VW	EIC 1	EIC 2	Test Bank	SAM Assessment	SAM Projects	SAM Training	Illustrated Video
Open and view a presentation														
Start PowerPoint		✓	✓	✓	✓	✓	✓				✓	✓	✓	✓
Use presentation views	✓	✓	✓	✓	✓	✓	✓				✓	✓		✓
Create a new presentation														
Create and save a new presentation		✓	✓	✓		✓	✓				✓	✓	✓	✓
Add new slides to a presentation		✓		✓		✓	✓				✓	✓		✓
Apply slide layouts	✓	✓		✓		✓	✓				✓	✓	✓	✓
Enter and format slide text														
Enter slide text		✓	✓	✓	✓	✓	✓				✓	✓	✓	✓
Change font appearance		✓	✓	✓	✓	✓	✓				✓	✓	✓	✓
Apply a theme														
Apply a theme	✓	✓	✓	✓	✓		✓				✓	✓	✓	✓
Apply a theme variation		✓	✓		✓		✓			✓				✓
Add and modify clip art														
Add clip art	✓	✓	✓	✓	✓									✓
Resize cli...			✓											

Online Learning and Assessment Tools

SAM

Get your students workplace-ready with SAM, the market-leading proficiency-based assessment and training solution for Microsoft Office! SAM's active, hands-on environment helps students master Microsoft Office skills and computer concepts that are essential to academic and career success, delivering the most comprehensive online learning solution for your course! Through skill-based assessments, interactive trainings, business-centric projects, and comprehensive remediation, SAM engages students in mastering the latest Microsoft Office programs on their own, giving instructors more time to focus on teaching. Computer concepts labs supplement instruction of important technology-related topics and issues through engaging simulations and interactive, auto-graded assessments. With enhancements including stream-lined course setup, more robust grading and reporting features, and the integration of fully interactive MindTap Readers containing Cengage Learning's premier textbook and video content, SAM provides the best teaching and learning solution for your course. (SAM sold separately; videos available in 2014.)

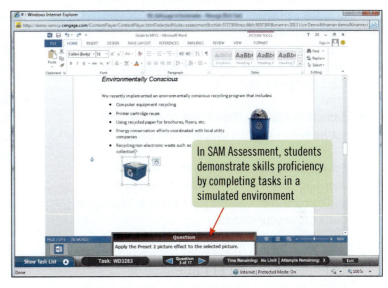

In SAM Assessment, students demonstrate skills proficiency by completing tasks in a simulated environment

Video Companion

Engage your students with videos! The *Video Companion for Microsoft Office 2013 Illustrated Fundamentals* contains more than 100 videos based on the step-by-step lessons in this book. Each video provides a multimedia version of a single two-page lesson in this text and includes a lesson overview along with a demonstration of the steps. Nearly 8 hours of videos provide instructional support. The Video Companion is a great learning tool for all students, and especially distance learning students or students who need help or reinforcement outside of the classroom. (Sold separately on DVD or in SAM MindTap Reader in 2014.)

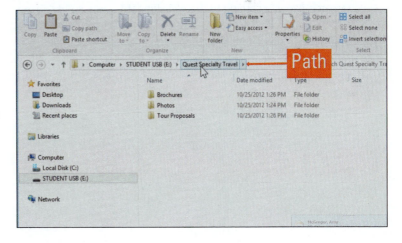

MindTap

MindTap is a fully online, highly personalized learning experience built upon Cengage Learning content. MindTap combines student learning tools—readings, multimedia, activities and assessments—into a singular Learning Path that guides students through their course. Instructors personalize the experience by customizing authoritative Cengage Learning content and learning tools, including the ability to add SAM trainings, assessments, and projects into the Learning Path via a SAM app that integrates into the MindTap framework seamlessly with Learning Management Systems.

Instructor Resources

This book comes with a wide array of high-quality technology-based, teaching tools to help you teach and to help students learn. The following teaching tools are available for download at our Instructor Companion Site. Simply search for this text at *login.cengage.com*. An instructor login is required.

- **New! Learning Outcomes Map** — A detailed grid for each unit (in Excel format) shows the learning activities and assessments that map to each learning outcome in that unit.

- **Instructor's Manual** — Includes lecture notes with teaching tips for each unit.

- **Sample Syllabus** — Prepare and customize your course easily using this sample course outline.

- **PowerPoint Presentations** — Each unit has a corresponding PowerPoint presentation covering the skills and topics in that unit that you can use in lectures, or distribute to your students.

- **Figure Files** — The figures in the text are provided on the Instructor Resources site to help you illustrate key topics or concepts. You can use these to create your own slide shows or learning tools.

- **APA example** — A version of the Formatting a Research Paper lesson provides steps for formatting a research paper according to the APA standard.

- **Solution Files** — These files contain the finished project that students create or modify in the lessons or end-of-unit material.

- **Solutions Document** — This document outlines the solutions for the end-of-unit Concepts Review, Skills Review, Independent Challenges and Visual Workshops. An Annotated Solution File and Grading Rubric accompany each file and can be used together for efficient grading.

- **Test Banks** — Cengage Learning Testing Powered by Cognero is a full-featured, online assessment system that allows instructors to create tests from publisher-provided content as well as write new questions. With the test generator you can:

  - Create tests from publisher — provided question sets

  - Edit publisher questions

  - Write your own questions

  - Tag questions with learning objectives, rubrics, and other meta-information

  - Print tests or deliver them online through a learning management system

Key Facts About Using This Book

Data Files are needed: To complete many of the lessons and end-of-unit assignments, students need to start from partially-completed Data Files, which help students learn more efficiently. By starting out with a Data File, students can focus on performing specific tasks without having to create a file from scratch. All Data Files are available as part of the Instructor Resources. Students can also download Data Files themselves for free at cengagebrain.com. (For detailed instructions, go to www.cengage.com/ct/studentdownload.)

System Requirements: This book was developed using Microsoft Office 2013 Professional running on Windows 8. Note that Windows 8 is not a requirement for the units on Microsoft Office; Office 2013 runs virtually the same on Windows 7 and Windows 8. Please see "Important Notes for Windows 7 Users" on the next page for more information.

Screen Resolution: This book was written and tested on computers with monitors set at a resolution of 1366 x 768. If your screen shows more or less information than the figures in this book, your monitor is probably set at a higher or lower resolution. If you don't see something on your screen, you might have to scroll down or up to see the object identified in the figure.

Tell Us What You Think!

We want to hear from you! Please email your questions, comments, and suggestions to the Illustrated Series team at: **illustratedseries@cengage.com**

COURSECASTS **Learning on the Go. Always Available...Always Relevant.**

Our fast-paced world is driven by technology. You know because you are an active participant—always on the go, always keeping up with technological trends, and always learning new ways to embrace technology to power your life. Let CourseCasts, hosted by Ken Baldauf of Florida State University, be your guide into weekly updates in this ever-changing space. These timely, relevant podcasts are produced weekly and are available for download at http://coursecasts.course.com or directly from iTunes (search by CourseCasts). CourseCasts are a perfect solution to getting students (and even instructors) to learn on the go!

Important Notes for Windows 7 Users

The screenshots in this book show Microsoft Office 2013 running on Windows 8. However, if you are using Microsoft Windows 7, you can still use this book because Office 2013 runs virtually the same on both platforms. There are only two differences that you will encounter if you are using Windows 7. Read this section to understand the differences.

Dialog boxes

If you are a Windows 7 user, dialog boxes shown in this book will look slightly different than what you see on your screen. Dialog boxes for Windows 7 have a light blue title bar, instead of a medium blue title bar. However, beyond this superficial difference in appearance, the options in the dialog boxes across platforms are the same. For instance, the screen shots below show the Font dialog box running on Windows 7 and the Font dialog box running on Windows 8.

FIGURE 1: Font dialog box in Windows 7

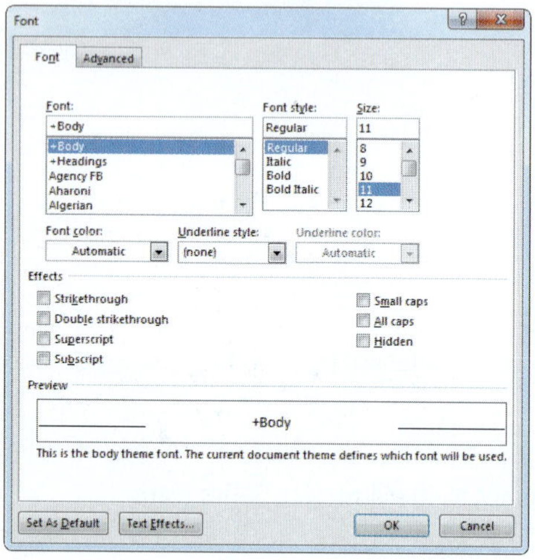

FIGURE 2: Font dialog box in Windows 8

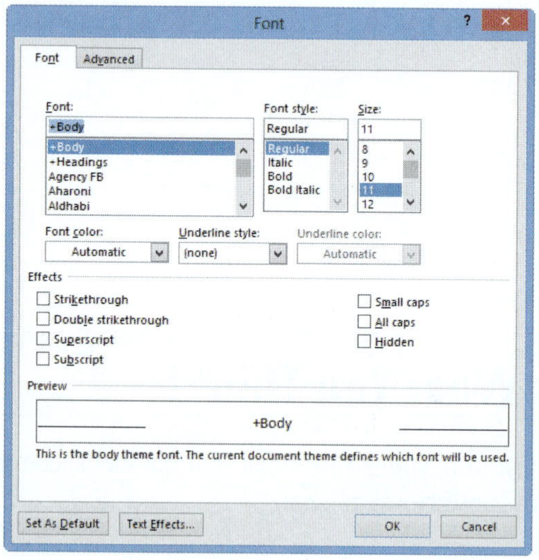

Alternate Steps for Starting an App in Windows 7

Nearly all of the steps in this book work exactly the same for Windows 7 users. However, starting an app (or program/application) requires different steps for Windows 7. The steps below show the Windows 7 steps for starting an app. (Note: Windows 7 alternate steps also appear in red Trouble boxes next to any step in the book that requires starting an app.)

Starting an app (or program/application) using Windows 7

1. Click the **Start button** on the taskbar to open the Start menu.
2. Click **All Programs**, then click the **Microsoft Office 2013 folder**. See Figure 3.
3. Click the app you want to use (such as **Excel 2013**)

FIGURE 3: Starting an app using Windows 7

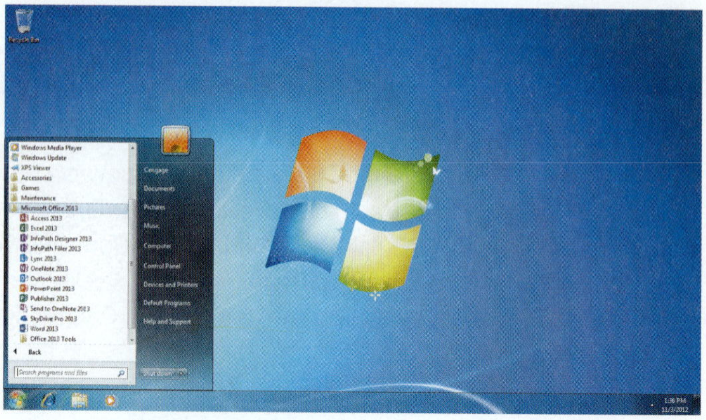

Acknowledgements

Author Acknowledgements

I owe thanks to the fantastic team of people who worked hard to produce this new edition! First off: thank you Barbara Clemens for your excellent authoring work and partnership on this new edition. I also thank Marjorie Hopper, our developmental editor, for her great suggestions and good humor throughout the developmental process. Thank you to our product manager Kim Klasner, who did a great job keeping us on track and handling a wide variety of behind-the-scenes tasks–including managing all the instructor supplements. Amanda Lyons: thank you for assembling our wonderful advisory board and for gathering customer feedback to ensure this new edition reflects the needs of students and instructors. Thank you to our designer Cheryl Pearl at GEX Publishing for her outstanding, beautiful design work for this title and all of our Office 2013 products. Big thanks to our eagle-eyed testers John Freitas, Susan Whalen, Danielle Shaw, Jeff Schwartz, who ensured the quality of all the lessons and exercises and made valuable usability suggestions. Thanks to Marisa Taylor, our content project manager, and all the professionals at GEX Publishing who produced this edition. A big thank you to Brandelynn Perry, our fantastic editorial assistant for the Illustrated team; not only does she provide excellent support to our team every day–but she also came up with the idea for the gorgeous vector art featured on all our Office 2013 covers! Thanks as always to the rest of the Illustrated team for their great work and dedication: Christina Kling-Garrett, Senior Product Manager, and Cathie DiMassa, Senior Content Project Manager.

Thanks as always to Cecil, CJ, and Stephen for their endless patience and constant support during the writing of this edition.

–Marjorie Hunt

Many thanks to Marjorie Hunt for entrusting me with part of this great text; it's always a privilege to work with you. Thanks also to developmental editor Marjorie Hopper for her ideas and corrections. Much appreciation to product manager Kim Klasner, who kept us all on the same page, and our MQA testers, who kept us all on our toes. Thanks to Marisa Taylor and the team at GEX Publishing for their beautiful work, and to Michele Miller (and Bailey) for the bird photo and video. And finally, thanks to Bill Wiley, whose ongoing support and good humor make it all possible.

–Barbara Clemens

Advisory Board Acknowledgements

We thank our Advisory Board who gave us their opinions and guided our decisions as we developed this edition. They are as follows:

Darla Hunt, Kentucky Community and Technical College System

Darenda Kersey, Black River Technical College

Wendy Postles, Wor-Wic Technical Community College

Charmaine Smith, Pitt Community College

Audrey Styer, Morton College

WHAT'S NEW FOR SAM 2013?

Get your students workplace ready with **SAM**

The market-leading assessment and training solution for Microsoft Office

SAM 2013

Exciting New Features and Content

➤ Computer Concepts Trainings and Assessments *(shown on monitor)*

➤ Student Assignment Calendar

➤ All New SAM Projects

➤ Mac Hints

➤ More MindTap Readers

More Efficient Course Setup and Management Tools

➤ Individual Assignment Tool

➤ Video Playback of Student Clickpaths

➤ Express Assignment Creation Tool

Improved Grade Book and Reporting Tools

➤ Institutional Reporting

➤ Frequency Analysis Report

➤ Grade Book Enhancements

➤ Partial Credit Grading for Projects

SAM's active, hands-on environment helps students master Microsoft Office skills and computer concepts that are essential to academic and career success.

CENGAGE Learning®

©2013. Cengage Learning is a registered trademark used herein under license. 13V-TH0056 PM 02/13

On the Path to Success

CASE In this Student Success Guide, you explore tools, techniques, and skills essential to your success as a student. In particular, you focus on planning, time management, study tools, critical thinking, and problem solving. As you explore effective practices in these areas, you will also be introduced to Microsoft OneNote 2013, a free-form note-taking application in the Microsoft Office suite that lets you gather, organize, and share digital notes.

Unit Objectives

- Use Microsoft OneNote to track tasks and organize ideas
- Set and achieve short-term and long-term goals
- Take notes during PowerPoint presentations
- Share OneNote content with others
- Apply critical-thinking strategies to evaluate information
- Follow a four-step process to solve problems

Files You Will Need

No files needed.

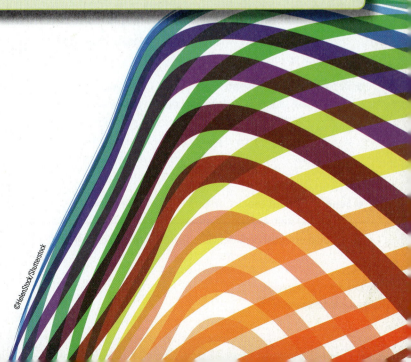

©HelenStock/Shutterstock

Planning Sets You Free

Benjamin Franklin once said, "If you fail to plan, you are planning to fail." When you set goals and manage time, your life does not just happen by chance. Instead, you design your life. Planning sets you free.

Without planning, you simply dig in and start writing or generating material you might use—but might not. You can actually be less productive and busier at the same time. Planning replaces this haphazard behavior with clearly defined outcomes and action steps.

Planning is a creative venture that continues for a lifetime. Following are planning suggestions that flow directly from this point of view and apply to any type of project or activity, from daily tasks to a multiyear career:

● **Schedule for flexibility and fun.** Be realistic. Expect the unexpected. Set aside time for essential tasks and errands, but don't forget to make room for fun.

● **Back up to view a bigger picture.** Consider your longer-range goals—what you want to accomplish in the next six months, the next year, the next five years, and beyond. Ask whether the activities you're about to schedule actually contribute to those goals.

● **Look boldly for things to change.** Don't accept the idea that you have to put up with substandard results in a certain area of your life. Staying open-minded about what is possible to achieve can lead to a future you never dreamed was possible.

● **Look for what's missing—and what to maintain.** Goals are often fueled by problems you need to resolve, projects you need to complete, relationships you want to develop, and careers you want to pursue. However, consider other goals that maintain your achievements and the activities you already perform effectively.

● **Think even further into the future.** To have fun and unleash your creativity while planning, set goals as far into the future as you can.

● **Return to the present.** Once you've stated your longest-range goals, work backward until you can define a next step to take now. Write down the shorter-term goals along the way. Leave some space in your schedule for unplanned events. Give yourself time to deal with obstacles before they derail you from realizing your dreams.

● **Schedule fixed blocks of time first.** When planning your week, start with class time and work time. Next, schedule essential daily activities such as sleeping and eating.

In addition, schedule some time each week for actions that lead directly to one of your written goals.

● **Set clear starting and stopping times.** Set a timer and stick to it. Set aside a specific number of minutes or hours to spend on a certain task. Feeling rushed or sacrificing quality is not the goal here. The point is to push yourself and discover your actual time requirements.

● **Plan for changes in your workload.** To manage your workload over the length of a term or project, plan for a change of pace. Stay on top of your assignments right from the start. Whenever possible, work ahead.

● **Involve others when appropriate.** When you schedule a task that depends on another person's involvement, let that person know—the sooner, the better.

● **Start the day with your Most Important Task.** Review your to-do list and calendar first thing each morning. For an extra level of clarity, condense your to-do list to only one top-priority item—your Most Important Task. Do it as early in the day as possible, impeccably, and with total attention.

● **Plan in a way that works for you.** You can perform the kind of planning that sets you free with any set of tools. What matters above all is clear thinking and specific intentions. You can take any path that leads to your goal.

As you continue through this chapter, you will learn how to use Microsoft OneNote to plan, organize, and maintain the important information and ideas in your life. You will also explore methods for setting and achieving goals, improving study practices, and thinking critically to solve problems.

Quick Tour of Microsoft OneNote

Microsoft OneNote is part of the Microsoft Office suite and provides a single location for storing everything that is important to you, accessible from any device or on the Web. Using OneNote, you store information in a notebook, a collection of electronic pages with text, graphics, and other content, including sound and video recordings. You organize the pages into tabbed sections as you would a tabbed ring binder. In your school notebook, for example, create a section for each of your courses, and then take notes during class on the pages within each section.

Explore the OneNote Interface

As part of the Microsoft Office suite, the Microsoft OneNote 2013 desktop application contains a Ribbon at the top of the window with seven default tabs: FILE, HOME, INSERT, DRAW, HISTORY, REVIEW, and VIEW. See Figure 1.

FIGURE 1: Microsoft OneNote 2013 ribbon

Each tab contains the following types of commands and features:

- **HOME tab:** This tab contains the most commonly used commands and features of Microsoft OneNote, which are divided into six groups: Clipboard, Basic Text, Styles, Tags, Email, and Meetings.

- **INSERT tab:** This tab includes commands for inserting tables, files, images, links, audio and video recordings, date/time stamps, page templates, and symbols.

- **DRAW tab:** This tab includes commands and tools for writing notes on pages, inserting shapes, arranging content, and converting handwritten notes to text or mathematical symbols.

- **HISTORY tab:** This tab includes tools for reviewing unread notes, managing multiple authors in a notebook, and reviewing pages and content in previous versions or pages and content that have been placed in the Notebook Recycle Bin.

- **REVIEW tab:** This tab provides research tools, including a spelling checker and thesaurus, language and translation tools, password-protection options, and links to other notebook sections and pages.

- **VIEW tab:** This tab contains page setup options, zoom tools, and application views, including docking options and the Send to OneNote tool.

Use Page Templates

To get started with OneNote and fill a blank page more quickly and easily, OneNote provides a collection of page templates. A page template is a design you apply to new pages in your notebook to provide an appealing background or to create a consistent layout. The OneNote page templates are organized into five categories: Academic, Blank, Business, Decorative, and Planners.

Additional templates are available on Office.com. After you define a standard way of organizing information, you can also create your own templates.

Time Management

When you say you don't have enough time, the problem might be that you are not spending the time you do have in the way you want. This section surveys ways to solve that time-management problem.

Time is an equal-opportunity resource. Everyone, regardless of gender, race, creed, or national origin, has exactly the same number of hours in a week. No matter how famous you are, no matter how rich or poor, you have 168 hours to spend each week—no more, no less.

As you explore time management in this section, you will learn how to set and achieve goals, how to apply the ABC method to writing a daily to-do list, and how to use technology for effective time management, with a special focus on using Microsoft OneNote to brainstorm ideas, set and achieve goals, and create to-do lists.

Setting and Achieving Goals

You can employ many useful methods for setting goals. One method is based on writing goals that relate to several periods and areas of your life. Writing down your goals greatly increases your chances of meeting them. Writing exposes incomplete information, undefined terms, unrealistic deadlines, and other symptoms of fuzzy thinking.

Write Specific Goals

State your written goals as observable actions or measurable results. Think in detail about what will be different when you attain your goals. List the changes in what you'll see, feel, touch, taste, hear, be, do, or have. Specific goals make clear what actions you need to take or what results you can expect. Figure 2 compares vague and specific goals.

FIGURE 2: Vague and specific goals

Vague Goal	Specific Goal
Get a good education.	Graduate with BS degree in engineering, with honors, by 2017.
Get good grades.	Earn a 3.5 grade point average next semester.
Enhance my spiritual life.	Meditate for 15 minutes daily.
Improve my appearance.	Lose 6 pounds during the next 6 months.
Gain control of my money.	Transfer $100 to my savings account each month.

© 2016 Cengage Learning

Write Goals for Several Time Frames

To develop a comprehensive vision of your future, write down the following types of goals:

- **Long-term goals:** Long-term goals represent major targets in your life. They can include goals in education, careers, personal relationships, travel, financial security, and more—whatever is important to you.

- **Midterm goals:** Midterm goals are objectives you can accomplish in one to five years. They include goals such as completing a course of education, paying off a car loan, or achieving a specific career level. These goals usually support your long-term goals.

- **Short-term goals:** Short-term goals are the ones you can accomplish in a year or less. These goals are specific achievements that require action now or in the near future.

Write Goals in Several Areas of Life

People who set goals in only one area of life may find that their personal growth becomes one-sided. They might experience success at work while neglecting their health or relationships with family members and friends.

To avoid this outcome, set goals in a variety of categories, such as education, career, financial life, family life or relationships, social life, contribution (volunteer activities, community services), spiritual life, and level of health. Add goals in other areas as they occur to you.

Reflect on Your Goals

Each week, take a few minutes to think about your goals. You can perform the following spot checks:

- **Check in with your feelings.** Think about how it feels to set your goals. Consider the satisfaction you'll gain in attaining your objectives. If you don't feel a significant emotional connection with a written goal, consider letting it go or filing it away to review later.

- **Check for alignment.** Look for connections among your short-term to midterm goals and your midterm to long-term goals. Look for a fit between all of your goals and your purpose for taking part in higher education as well as your overall purpose in life.

- **Check for obstacles.** All kinds of complications can come between you and your goals, such as constraints on time and money. Anticipate obstacles and start looking now for workable solutions.

- **Check for next steps.** Decide on a series of small, achievable steps you can take right away to accomplish each of your short-term goals. Write down these small steps on a daily to-do list. Take note of your progress and celebrate your successes.

Take Action Immediately

To increase your odds of success, take immediate action. Decrease the gap between stating a goal and starting to achieve it. If you slip and forget about the goal, you can get back on track at any time by *doing* something about it.

Use OneNote to Set Goals

The versatility of Microsoft OneNote allows you to write ideas anywhere on the page, identify notes with a variety of tags, and organize notes into pages and sections, making it a great tool for writing down your goals, organizing your thoughts and ideas, and building connections among them all.

Brainstorm with Quick Notes

Ideas often present themselves without order, structure, or clear fit in the organization of your existing content. Microsoft OneNote provides a feature called Quick Notes for such ideas. A Quick Note is a small window you can move anywhere on-screen and use to write reminders and other short notes. Getting the ideas on paper (or in your OneNote notebook) can be the first step in using them to define larger ideas and related goals.

Content you create with Quick Notes is initially unfiled within your notebook, but you can easily move or copy it to other sections when you are ready. Think of an electronic Quick Note as you would a sticky note on your desk.

Organize Larger Ideas with Sections and Pages

For larger or more defined ideas, establish an organization system in your OneNote notebook so you can easily locate related information. OneNote provides multiple levels of organization within a notebook.

Most OneNote users store content on pages within sections. As your use of OneNote increases, you can organize related sections into groups or increase the detail of pages by creating subpages for better organization. See Figure 3.

FIGURE 3: OneNote section tabs and Pages pane

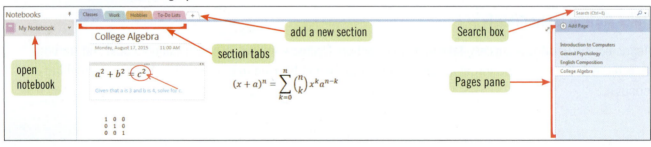

Use Tags to Organize Content in OneNote

OneNote lets you mark notes and other content with tags—keywords that help you find important information—to set reminders, classify information, or set priorities, for example. OneNote provides the following tags by default: To Do, Important, Question, Remember for later, Definition, Highlight, Contact, Address, Phone number, Web site to visit, Idea, Password, Critical, Project A, Project B, Movie to see, Book to read, Music to listen to, Source for article, Remember for blog, Discuss with <Person A>, Discuss with <Person B>, Discuss with manager, Send in email, Schedule meeting, Call back, To Do priority 1, To Do priority 2, and Client request.

You assign a tag to page content by moving the insertion point to the text you want to tag and then selecting an item from the Tags gallery on the HOME tab of the ribbon. You can create custom tags to meet personal needs for organizing OneNote content in your notebooks.

Create an ABC Daily To-Do List

One advantage to keeping a daily to-do list is that you don't have to remember what to do next. It's on the list. A typical day in the life of a student is full of separate, often unrelated tasks—reading, attending lectures, reviewing notes, working at a job, writing papers, researching special projects, and running errands. It's easy to forget an important task on a busy day. When that task is written down, you don't have to rely on your memory.

The following steps present the ABC method for creating and using to-do lists. This method involves ranking each item on your list according to three levels of importance: A, B, or C.

Step 1: Brainstorm Tasks

To get started, list all of the tasks you want to complete in a day. Each task will become an item on a to-do list. Don't worry about putting the entries in order or scheduling them yet. Just list everything you want to accomplish.

Step 2: Estimate Time

For each task you wrote down in Step 1, estimate how long it will take to complete the task. Estimating can be tricky. If you allow too little time, you end up feeling rushed. If you allow too much time, you become less productive. For now, use your best guess. If you are unsure, overestimate rather than underestimate how long you need for each task.

Add up the time you estimated to complete all your to-do items. Also add up the number of unscheduled hours in your day. Then compare the two totals. If you have more time assigned to tasks than unscheduled hours in the day, that's a potential problem. To solve it, proceed to Step 3.

Step 3: Rate Each Task by Priority

To prevent overscheduling, decide which to-do items are the most important given the time you have available. One suggestion for making this decision comes from the book *How to Get Control of Your Time and Your Life*, by Alan Lakein—simply label each task A, B, or C:

- The A tasks on your list are the most critical. They include assignments that are coming due or jobs that need to be done immediately.

- The B tasks on your list are important, but less so than the A tasks. They can be postponed, if necessary, for another day.

- The C tasks do not require immediate attention. C tasks are often small, easy jobs with no set deadline. They too can be postponed.

After labeling the items on your to-do list, schedule time for all of the A tasks.

Step 4: Cross off Tasks

Keep your to-do list with you at all times. Cross off, check, or otherwise mark activities when you finish them, and add new tasks when you think of them.

When using the ABC method, you might experience an ailment common to students: C fever. Symptoms include the uncontrollable urge to drop an A task and begin crossing off C items on your to-do list. The reason C fever is so common is that A tasks are usually more difficult or time consuming to achieve and have a higher risk of failure.

Use your to-do list to keep yourself on track, working on your A tasks. Don't panic or berate yourself when you realize that in the last six hours, you have completed nine Cs and not a single A. Just calmly return to the A tasks.

Step 5: Evaluate

At the end of the day, evaluate your performance. Look for A priorities you didn't complete. Look for items that repeatedly turn up as Bs or Cs on your list and never seem to get done. Consider changing them to A tasks or dropping them altogether. Similarly, you might consider lowering the priority of an A task you didn't complete to a B or C task.

When you're finished evaluating, start on tomorrow's to-do list. That way, you can wake up and start working on tasks productively without panicking about what to do.

Create To-Do Lists in OneNote

The To Do tag in OneNote makes it easy to change any notebook item into a task. When you select an item and then assign the To Do tag to it, a check box appears next to the item. Insert a check mark in the box when you complete the task. You can also use the Planners subcategory of Page Templates in OneNote to generate Simple To Do Lists, Prioritized To Do Lists, and Project To Do Lists quickly and easily—leaving you to merely provide the action items. Figure 4 shows a to-do list based on the Simple To Do List page template.

FIGURE 4: List based on the Simple To Do List page template

When applying the ABC To-Do list practices, you can use the built-in To Do priority 1 and To Do priority 2 tags for A and B items and the standard To Do tag for C items. Another approach is to customize the tags to create your own styles of check boxes from over 25 choices.

Find Time

Good news: You have enough time to accomplish the tasks you want to do. All it takes is thinking about the possibilities and making conscious choices.

Everything written about time management can be reduced to three main ideas:

1. Know exactly *what* you want. State your wants as clear, specific goals. Put them in writing.

2. Know *how* to get what you want. Take action to meet your goals. Determine what you'll do *today* to get what you want in the future. Put those actions in writing as well.

3. Strive for balance. When your life lacks balance, you spend most of your time responding to interruptions, last-minute projects, and emergencies. Life feels like a scramble just to survive. You're so busy achieving someone else's goals that *you* forget about getting what you want.

According to Stephen R. Covey, author of *The Seven Habits of Highly Effective People*, the purpose of planning is to carve out space in your life for tasks that are not urgent but are truly important. Examples are exercising regularly, reading, praying or meditating, spending quality time alone or with family members and friends, traveling, and cooking nutritious meals. Each of these tasks contributes directly to your personal goals for the future and to the overall quality of your life in the present.

Think of time management as time *investment*. Spend your most valuable resource in the way you choose.

Use Technology for Time Management

Time management activities generally fall into two major categories: making lists and using calendars. Today you can choose from dozens of applications for doing both.

You might wonder why you need sophisticated software just to keep lists of stuff to do. That's a fair question, and it has three answers. First, when a to-do list grows longer than an average grocery list, it becomes tough to manage on paper. Second, you probably have more than one list to manage, such as lists of values, goals, to-do items, work-related projects, and household projects. It's easier to keep track of these lists using software. Finally, it's convenient to access your lists from any device with an Internet connection.

The goal is to actually complete tasks. Keep it simple, make it easy, and do what works.

Extend Muscle Reading to Web Pages and E-Books

While reading, skilled readers focus on finding answers to their questions and flagging them in the text. E-books offer features that help with the following steps:

- **Access the table of contents.** For a bigger picture of the text, look for a table of contents that lists chapter headings and subheadings. Click a heading to expand the text for that part of the book.

- **Use navigation tools.** To flip electronic pages, look for Previous and Next buttons or arrows on the right and left borders of each page. Many e-books also offer a Go to Page feature that allows you to enter a specific page number to access the page.

- **Search the text.** Look for a search box that allows you to enter key words and find all the places in the text where those words are mentioned.

- **Follow links to definitions and related information.** Many e-books supply a definition to any word in the text. All you need to do is highlight a word and then click it.

- **Highlight and annotate.** E-books allow you to select words, sentences, or entire paragraphs and highlight them in a bright color. You can also annotate a book by entering your own notes on the pages.

After reading, move the information into your long-term memory by reciting and reviewing it. These steps call on you to locate the main points in a text and summarize them. E-books can help you create instant summaries. For example, the Amazon Kindle allows you to view all your highlighted passages at once. Another option is to copy passages and then paste them into a word-processing file. To avoid plagiarism, include quotation marks around each passage and note the source.

Set Limits on Screen Time

To get an accurate picture of your involvement in social networking and other online activity, monitor how much time you spend on them for one week. Make conscious choices about how much time you want to spend online and on the phone. Don't let social networking distract you from meeting personal and academic goals.

In this section, you will learn ways to effectively use technology to promote positive study habits and successful results. Specifically, you explore ways to integrate Microsoft OneNote with PowerPoint presentations, Web content, and screen clippings, also called screenshots, which are images of your screen that you capture using a OneNote tool. You will also learn techniques for interacting with e-books and for collaborating with others through the sharing features of OneNote and Office Online.

Turn PowerPoint Presentations into Powerful Notes

Some students stop taking notes during a PowerPoint presentation. This choice can be hazardous to your academic health for three major reasons:

- **PowerPoint presentations don't include everything.** Instructors and other speakers use PowerPoint to organize their presentations. Topics covered in the slides make up an outline of what your instructor considers important. Speakers create slides to flag the main points and signal transitions between topics. However, speakers usually enhance a presentation with examples and explanations that don't appear on the slides. In addition, slides will not contain any material from class discussion, including any answers that the instructor gives in response to questions.

- **You stop learning.** Taking notes forces you to capture ideas and information in your own words. The act of writing also helps you remember the material. If you stop writing and let your attention drift, you can quickly lose track of the presentation or topic.

- **You end up with major gaps in your notes.** When it's time to review your notes, you'll find that material from PowerPoint presentations is missing. This can be a major problem at exam time.

To create value from PowerPoint presentations, take notes directly on the slides. Continue to observe, record, and review. Use the presentation as a way to *guide* rather than to *replace* your own note taking.

Prepare Before the Presentation

Sometimes instructors make PowerPoint slides available before a lecture. Scan the slides, just as you would preview a reading assignment. Consider printing the slides and bringing them along to class. You can take notes directly on the printed pages.

If you use a laptop for taking notes during class, then you might not want to bother with printing. Open the PowerPoint presentation file and type your notes in the Notes pane, which appears below each slide.

Create OneNote Page Content from PowerPoint Slides

Use the File Printout button on the OneNote INSERT tab in the Files group to print PowerPoint slides directly to OneNote. You can store the slides where you keep your other notes and then take notes on the same page of your notebook as the slide content.

Take Notes During the Presentation

As you take notes during a presentation, be selective in what you write down. Determine what kind of material appears on each slide. Stay alert for new topics, main points, and important details. Taking too many notes makes it hard to keep up with a speaker and separate main points from minor details.

In any case, go *beyond* the slides. Record valuable questions and answers that come up during a discussion, even if they are not a planned part of the presentation.

Use Drawing Objects, Audio, and Video in Your Notes

On touch interface devices, OneNote makes it easy to handwrite your notes or draw symbols and shapes on the notebook pages. For mouse users, the OneNote DRAW tab contains predefined shapes and pen options for creating notes that are more than just text.

On devices that include microphones or webcams, you can use OneNote to capture audio and video recordings in your notebook pages, ensuring that every moment of an important lecture is captured for later review and study.

Review After the Presentation

If you printed out slides before class and took notes on those pages, then find a way to integrate them with the rest of your notes. For example, add references in your notebook to specific slides. Create summary notes that include the major topics and points from readings, class meetings, and PowerPoint presentations.

If you have a copy of the presentation, consider editing it. Cut slides that don't include information you want to remember. Rearrange slides so that the order makes more sense to you. Remember that you can open the original file later to see exactly what your instructor presented.

Add Links to Other Notebook Content

When creating summary note pages in your OneNote notebook, it is good practice to link text or content on the summary page to the detailed notes elsewhere in your notebook. To do so, select the content you want to use as the link, click the Link button in the Links group on the INSERT tab to open the Link dialog box (shown in Figure 5), and then select the location in the OneNote notebook with the detailed content.

FIGURE 5: Link dialog box in OneNote 2013

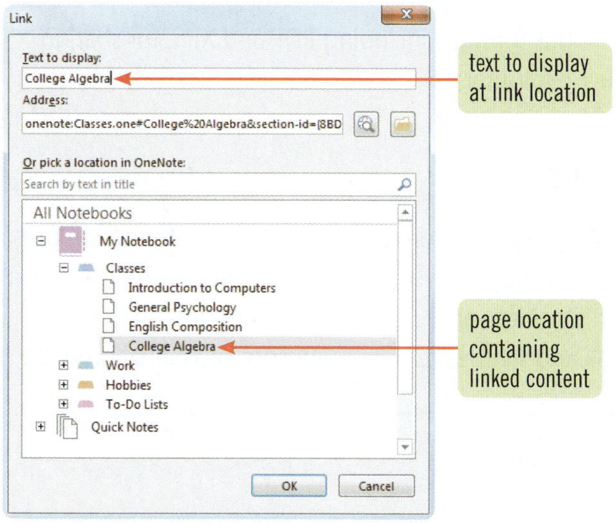

text to display at link location

page location containing linked content

Search Notes and Printouts

You can quickly locate content in your OneNote notebooks using the built-in search features of OneNote 2013. For basic text searches, you can limit the results to content on the current page, current section, current section group, current notebook, or all open notebooks.

After you apply tags to content within the notebook, use the Find Tags button in the Tags group on the HOME tab to locate and filter results based on tags.

Collect Web Content in OneNote

OneNote makes it easy to collect content with notations and links to the original source. When copying content from an electronic source, OneNote adds a reference to the original location below the pasted content. For Web-based resources, OneNote inserts a hyperlink so you can access the source again later.

Insert Screen Clippings

In addition to copying content directly from Web sites, you can use the Screen Clipping tool to collect an image from any open application. To insert a screen clipping into a notebook, display the item you want to capture in another application, switch to OneNote, and then click the Screen Clipping button in the Images group on the INSERT tab. OneNote is minimized and the most recently used application is displayed with a transparent overlay. Draw a box around the area you want to capture to insert the screen clipping into the OneNote page as an image with details of when you collected the screen clipping. You can include additional notes and annotations using other text and drawing tools in OneNote.

 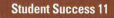

Use Technology to Collaborate

When planning group projects, look for tools that allow you to create, edit, and share documents, spreadsheets, drawings, presentations, and other files. You can find a growing list of applications for these purposes, including Office Online, which includes an online version of OneNote.

When using collaborative technology, your people skills are as important as your technology skills. Set up a process to make sure that everyone's voice is heard during a virtual meeting. People who are silenced will probably tune out.

Function as a professional whenever you're online. Team members might get to know you mainly through emails and instant messages. Consider the impression you're making with your online presence. Avoid slang, idioms, sarcastic humor, and other expressions that can create misunderstanding. A small dose of civility can make a big difference in the quality of your virtual team experience.

Use Office Online

Office Online is the free, online version of Microsoft Word, Microsoft Excel, Microsoft PowerPoint, and Microsoft OneNote available through Office 365, SharePoint Online, and OneDrive accounts. These tools provide basic functionality from the desktop applications directly in a Web browser, giving you the ability to view and edit documents, workbooks, presentations, and notebooks from virtually any device with an Internet connection.

Supported by the cloud storage options associated with Office 365, SharePoint Online, and OneDrive, Office Online makes it easy to do real-time collaborative editing of shared files with classmates, friends, family, and colleagues.

Share Content from OneNote

If you store OneNote notebooks on OneDrive or SharePoint, you can easily share pages, sections, or entire notebooks with others by using the commands in the Share group on the OneNote FILE tab. You can even share individual paragraphs of text on pages by right-clicking selected content and then clicking the Copy Link to Paragraph option on the shortcut menu.

Export pages, sections, or entire notebooks from OneNote in various formats, including PDF and XPS, for sharing with users who don't have access to Microsoft OneNote on their computers.

Use OneNote to Enhance Critical Thinking

Using Microsoft OneNote as a tool for collecting your thoughts and ideas into organized sections of information puts your broad base of knowledge in a single searchable location for retrieval, analysis, and connection. During the critical thinking process, you can create a new section or a new page in OneNote and use the techniques discussed in this chapter to link information from multiple areas of your notebook and synthesize those concepts into a final product.

Critical Thinking and Problem Solving

It has been said that human beings are rational creatures. Yet no one is born as an effective thinker. Critical thinking—the objective analysis and evaluation of an issue in order to form a judgment—is a learned skill. This is one reason that you study so many subjects in higher education—math, science, history, psychology, literature, and more. A broad base of courses helps you develop as a thinker. You see how people with different viewpoints arrive at conclusions, make decisions, and solve problems. This gives you a foundation for dealing with complex challenges in your career, your relationships, and your community.

Thinking Critically as a Survival Skill

Critical thinking helps you succeed in academics and thrive in other parts of your life. Hone your critical thinking skills for the following reasons:

- **Critical thinking frees you from nonsense.** Critical thinkers are constantly on the lookout for thinking that's inaccurate, sloppy, or misleading. Even in mathematics and the hard sciences, the greatest advances take place when people reexamine age-old beliefs.

- **Critical thinking frees you from self-deception.** Critical thinking is a path to freedom from half-truths and deception. One of the reasons that critical thinking is so challenging—and so rewarding—is that people have a remarkable capacity to fool themselves. Master students are willing to admit the truth when they discover that their thinking is fuzzy, lazy, based on a false assumption, or dishonest. These students value facts. When a solid fact contradicts a cherished belief, they are willing to change the belief.

- **Critical thinking promotes your success inside and outside the classroom.** Anytime you are faced with a choice about what to believe or what to do, your thinking skills come in to play. Consider the following applications:

  - Critical thinking informs reading, writing, speaking, and listening. These elements are the basis of communication—a process that occupies most of our waking hours.
  - Critical thinking promotes social change. Critical thinkers strive to understand and influence the institutions in our society.
  - Critical thinking uncovers bias and prejudice. Working through your preconceived notions is a first step toward communicating with people of other races, ethnic backgrounds, and cultures.
  - Critical thinking reveals long-term consequences. Crises can occur when your thinking fails to keep pace with reality.

- **Critical thinking is thorough thinking.** Some people misinterpret the term *critical thinking* to mean finding fault or being judgmental. If you prefer, use *thorough thinking* instead. Both terms point to the same activities: sorting out conflicting claims, weighing the evidence, letting go of personal biases, and arriving at reasonable conclusions. These activities add up to an ongoing conversation—a constant process, not a final product. Almost everything that people call *knowledge* is a result of these activities. This means that critical thinking and learning are intimately linked.

Follow a Process for Critical Thinking

Learning to think well matters. The rewards are many, and the stakes are high. Major decisions in life—from choosing a major to choosing a spouse—depend on your thinking skills.

Following are strategies that you can use to move freely through six levels of thinking: remembering, understanding, applying, analyzing, evaluating, and creating. The strategies fall into three major categories: check your attitudes, check for logic, and check for evidence.

Check Your Attitudes

The following suggestions help you understand and analyze information free from bias and other filters that cloud clear thinking:

● **Be willing to find various points of view on any issue.** People can have dozens of viewpoints on every important issue. In fact, few problems have any single, permanent solution. Begin seeking alternative views with an open mind. When talking to another person, be willing to walk away with a new point of view—even if it's similar to your original idea, supported with new evidence.

● **Practice tolerance.** One path to critical thinking is tolerance for a wide range of opinions. Taking a position on important issues is natural. Problems emerge, however, when people become so attached to their current viewpoints that they refuse to consider alternatives.

● **Understand before criticizing.** The six levels of thinking build on each other. Before you agree or disagree with an idea, make sure that you *remember* it accurately and truly *understand* it. Polished debaters make a habit of doing this. Often they can sum up their opponent's viewpoint better than anyone else can. This puts them in a much stronger position to *apply, analyze, evaluate,* and *create* ideas.

● **Watch for hot spots.** Many people have mental "hot spots"—topics that provoke strong opinions and feelings. To become more skilled at examining various points of view, notice your own particular hot spots. Make a clear intention to accept your feelings about these topics and to continue using critical thinking techniques in relation to them. In addition, be sensitive to other people's hot spots. Demonstrate tolerance and respect before you start discussing highly personal issues.

● **Be willing to be uncertain.** Some of the most profound thinkers have practiced the art of thinking by using a magic sentence: "I'm not sure yet." It is courageous and unusual to take the time to pause, look, examine, be thoughtful, consider many points of view—and be unsure. Uncertainty calls for patience. Give yourself permission to experiment, practice, and learn from mistakes.

Complete Four Steps to Solve Problems

Think of problem solving as a process with four Ps: Define the *problem*, generate *possibilities*, create a *plan*, and *perform* your plan.

● **Define the Problem.** To define a problem effectively, understand what a problem is: a mismatch between what you want and what you have. Problem solving is all about reducing the gap between these two factors. One simple and powerful strategy for defining problems is simply to put them in writing. When you do this, you might find that potential solutions appear as well.

- **Generate Possibilities.** Now put on your creative thinking hat. Open up. Brainstorm as many possible solutions to the problem as you can. As you generate possibilities, gather relevant facts.

- **Create a Plan.** After rereading your problem definition and list of possible solutions, choose the solution that seems most workable. Think about specific actions that will reduce the gap between

what you have and what you want. Visualize the steps you will take to make this solution a reality, and arrange them in chronological order. To make your plan even more powerful, put it in writing.

- **Perform Your Plan.** Ultimately, your skill in solving problems lies in how well you perform your plan. Through the quality of your actions, you become the architect of your own success.

Check for Logic

Learning to think logically offers many benefits: When you think logically, you take your reading, writing, speaking, and listening skills to a higher level. You avoid costly mistakes in decision making. You can join discussions and debates with more confidence, cast your votes with a clear head, and become a better-informed citizen.

The following suggestions will help you work with the building blocks of logical thinking—terms, assertions, arguments, and assumptions:

- **Define key terms.** A *term* is a word or phrase that refers to a clearly defined concept. Terms with several different meanings are ambiguous—fuzzy, vague, and unclear. One common goal of critical thinking is to remove ambiguous terms or define them clearly.

- **Look for assertions.** An *assertion* is a complete sentence that contains one or more key terms. The purpose of an assertion is to define a term or to state relationships between terms. These relationships are the essence of what we mean by the term *knowledge*.

- **Look for arguments.** For specialists in logic, an *argument* is a series of related assertions. There are two major types of reasoning used in building arguments—deductive and inductive. *Deductive reasoning* builds arguments by starting with a general assertion and leading to a more specific one. With *inductive reasoning*, the chain of logic proceeds in the opposite direction—from specific to general.

- **Remember the power of assumptions.** Assumptions are beliefs that guide our thinking and behavior. Assumptions can be simple and ordinary. In other cases, assumptions are more complex and have larger effects. Despite the power to influence our speaking and actions, assumptions are often unstated. People can remain

unaware of their most basic and far-reaching assumptions—the very ideas that shape their lives. Heated conflict and hard feelings often result when people argue on the level of opinions and forget that the real conflict lies at the level of their assumptions.

- **Look for stated assumptions.** Stated assumptions are literally a thinker's starting points. Critical thinkers produce logical arguments and evidence to support most of their assertions. However, they are also willing to take other assertions as "self-evident"—so obvious or fundamental that they do not need to be proved.

- **Look for unstated assumptions.** In many cases, speakers and writers do not state their assumptions or offer evidence for them. In addition, people often hold many assumptions at the same time, with some of those assumptions contradicting each other. This makes uncovering assumptions a feat worthy of the greatest detective. You can follow a two-step method for testing the validity of any argument. First, state the assumptions. Second, see whether you can find any exceptions to the assumptions. Uncovering assumptions and looking for exceptions can help you detect many errors in logic.

Check for Evidence

In addition to testing arguments with the tools of logic, look carefully at the evidence used to support those arguments. Evidence comes in several forms, including facts, comments from recognized experts in a field, and examples.

Think Critically About Information on the Internet

Sources of information on the Internet range from the reputable (such as the Library of Congress) to the flamboyant (such as the *National Enquirer*). People are free to post *anything* on the Internet, including outdated facts as well as intentional misinformation.

Taking a few simple precautions when you surf the Internet can keep you from crashing onto the rocky shore of misinformation.

Between Ideas and Information

To think more powerfully about what you find on the Internet, remember the difference between information and ideas. *Information* refers to facts that can be verified by independent observers. *Ideas* are interpretations or opinions based on facts. Several people with the same information might adopt different ideas based on that information.

Don't assume that an idea is more current, reasonable, or accurate just because you find it on the Internet. Apply your critical thinking skills to all published material—print and online.

Look for Overall Quality

Examine the features of a website in general. Notice the effectiveness of the text and visuals as a whole. Also note how well the site is organized and whether you can navigate the site's features with ease. Look for the date that crucial information was posted, and determine how often the site is updated.

Next, get an overview of the site's content. Examine several of the site's pages, and look for consistency of facts, quality of information, and competency with grammar and spelling. Evaluate the site's links to related Web pages. Look for links to pages of reputable organizations.

Look at the Source

Find a clear description of the person or organization responsible for the website. If a site asks you to subscribe or become a member, then find out what it does with the personal information that you provide. Look for a way to contact the site's publisher with questions and comments.

Look for Documentation

When you encounter an assertion on a web page or another Internet resource, note the types and quality of the evidence offered. Look for credible examples, quotations from authorities in the field, documented statistics, or summaries of scientific studies.

Set an Example

In the midst of the Internet's chaotic growth, you can light a path of rationality. Whether you're sending a short email message or building a massive website, bring your own critical thinking skills into play. Every word and image that you send down the wires to the web can display the hallmarks of critical thinking: sound logic, credible evidence, and respect for your audience.

Forward in Success

Now that you have established a foundation in planning, time management, study tools, critical thinking, and problem solving as it relates to success as a student, apply these skills, concepts, and tools to your personal goals and objectives to find new success in your studies and life.

Understanding Essential Computer Concepts

CASE ▶ Computers are essential tools in almost all kinds of activity in virtually every type of business. In this unit, you'll learn about computers and their components. You'll learn about input and output, how a computer processes data and stores information, how information is transmitted, and ways to secure that information.

Unit Objectives

After completing this unit, you will be able to:

- Recognize you live and work in the digital world
- Distinguish types of computers
- Identify computer system components
- Compare types of memory
- Summarize types of storage media
- Differentiate between input devices

- Explain output devices
- Describe data communications
- Define types of networks
- Assess security threats
- Understand system software
- Describe types of application software

Files You Will Need

No files needed.

Recognize You Live and Work in the Digital World

The Internet, computers, and mobile devices such as smartphones and tablets provide us with a world of information, literally at our fingertips. **CASE** ▶ *You'll look at some ways in which this "always-on" society is transforming your life.*

DETAILS

Over the last 20 years, the Internet has become an indispensable tool for businesses and for people's everyday needs. Just think of all the ways this time-saving technology serves us:

- Instantly communicate with friends and coworkers across town or on the other side of the planet.
- Store music and movies, and access them anywhere.
- Search and apply for jobs without leaving home.
- Quickly access information, instructions, and advice on almost anything.
- Shop for anything from clothing to food to cars to vacation deals.
- Manage your finances or even deposit checks using a mobile device.
- Get directions, view maps, and find nearby restaurants and theaters.

Here are several important ways you can use the Web to get your work done:

- ### Search for information

  Today's search engines are so powerful that you can type in almost anything, from a person's name to a desired flight to a question like, "what should I have for dinner?" and see hundreds or even thousands of results. A **search engine** is an online tool that allows you to enter keywords or terms; the engine then presents a list of sites that match those terms, organized so the most relevant ones appear first. You've probably used search engines such as Google, Yahoo!, or Bing.

- ### Communicate with others

  Email, an electronic message sent from one person to another, is one of the oldest and most basic forms of Internet communication. Your company may provide email service, or you might use a service such as Microsoft's Outlook.com, or Google's Gmail. You can share documents or images with coworkers and friends by sending them as attachments to email messages. **FIGURE CC-1** shows an email being composed in Outlook.com.

  Videoconferencing allows simultaneous two-way transmission of audio and video over the Internet. With a service such as Skype, users can talk to one another directly, as well as send and receive files. For example, the couple in **FIGURE CC-2** is using videoconferencing to stay in touch.

- ### Telecommuting

  One of the biggest changes brought about by the Internet is the ability for a company's employees to work remotely. If you work out of your home office your company doesn't have to spend as much money on office space. As shown in **FIGURE CC-3**, employees can also get to work sooner since they're not sitting in a car during rush hour.

- ### Cloud computing

  This is a friendly term for the way in which data, applications, and resources can be accessed over the Internet (in "the cloud") rather than on your individual computer. Put simply, cloud computing is Internet-based computing. The push toward the cloud has been fueled by reliable high-speed Internet connections combined with less expensive Web-based computing power and online storage. Cloud services such as Microsoft SkyDrive and Dropbox give you access to your documents from any device that has an Internet connection, even your phone.

QUICK TIP

Many computers come with a built-in camera and microphone for use in videoconferencing.

QUICK TIP

Some companies use a virtual private network (VPN) that allows users to log in from a remote location and easily access documents or communicate with coworkers.

FIGURE CC-1: Email being composed in Outlook.com

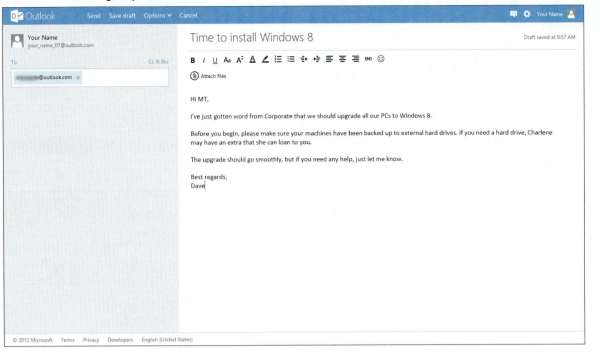

FIGURE CC-2: Couple using videoconferencing to communicate

pressureUA/Photos.com

FIGURE CC-3: Employee telecommuting from home

Comstock Images/Photos.com

How to be a good online citizen

It's important to understand that your Internet activities can have lasting repercussions on your work and life. For instance, while social networks such as Facebook and Twitter let you hang out with your friends online, some employers are known to keep an eye on employee accounts.

Because the Web is an easy source of photos, illustrations, and text, many people assume this content is free to copy for use in their own work. However, if you plan to use an item that you didn't personally create, it's important to know that copyright laws may protect it. For help with understanding copyright issues, and for sources of "public domain" content, visit Creative Commons at creativecommons.org.

Distinguish Types of Computers

Learning Outcomes
- Define a computer
- Distinguish types of computers

A **computer** is an electronic device that accepts information and instructions from a user, manipulates the information according to the instructions, displays the information in some way, and stores the information for later retrieval. Computers are classified by their size, speed, and capabilities. **CASE** *You'll look at the most common types of computers.*

DETAILS

The following list describes various types of computers:

QUICK TIP

In common usage, the term "PC" refers to personal computers running the Microsoft Windows operating system. Computers sold by Apple run the Mac (short for "Macintosh") operating system, and are referred to as Macs.

- **Personal computers (PCs)** are typically used by a single user at home or in the office. Personal computers are used for general computing tasks such as word processing, manipulating numbers, working with images or video, exchanging email, and accessing the Internet. The following are types of personal computers:

  - **Desktop computers** are designed to remain in one location and require a constant source of electricity. **FIGURE CC-4** shows a desktop computer's monitor, CPU, keyboard, and mouse.

  - **Laptop computers** like the one shown in **FIGURE CC-5** have a hinged lid that contains the computer's display and a lower portion that contains the keyboard. Laptops can be powered by rechargeable batteries, and they easily slip into a bag or briefcase. (**Notebook computers** are very similar, but are generally smaller and less powerful than laptops.)

  - **Subnotebook computers**, sometimes called **ultraportable computers** or **netbooks**, are very small and light, and are primarily designed to allow users to access the Internet and check email.

  - **Tablets** are thin computers that do not have an external keyboard or a mouse. To interact with a tablet, the user touches the screen or uses a stylus. Tablets are ideal for surfing the Web, checking email, reading electronic books, watching video, and creating artwork. See **FIGURE CC-5**.

- **Handheld computers** are small computers that usually have more limited capabilities than traditional PCs.

  - **Smartphones**, like the one shown in **FIGURE CC-5**, are used to make and receive phone calls, maintain an address book and calendar, send email, connect to the Internet, play music, and take photos or video. They can also perform some of the same functions as a traditional PC, such as word processing.

  - **MP3 players** are primarily used to store and play music, although some models can also be used to play digital movies or television shows.

- **Mainframe computers** and **supercomputers** like the one shown in **FIGURE CC-6** are used by large businesses, government agencies, and in science and education. They provide centralized storage and processing, and can manipulate tremendous amounts of data.

FIGURE CC-4: Desktop computer

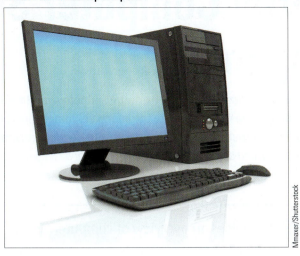

Mmaxer/Shutterstock

FIGURE CC-5: Laptop computer, smartphone, and tablet

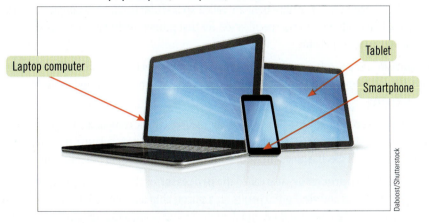

Laptop computer

Tablet

Smartphone

Daboost/Shutterstock

FIGURE CC-6: Supercomputer

senticus/iStockphoto.com

Computers are more personal than ever

Technology is constantly evolving and improving, which means that computer hardware becomes smaller and more powerful. For example, today's desktop PCs are far more powerful than the mainframe computers of a few decades ago, and current handheld smartphones are more capable than the first laptops. As the lines between types of devices become less distinct, consumers may need fewer devices to accomplish their tasks.

Identify Computer System Components

Learning Outcomes
- Define hardware and software
- Define motherboard and processor
- Define input and output

A **computer system** includes computer hardware and software. **Hardware** refers to the physical components of a computer. **Software** refers to the intangible components of a computer system, particularly the **programs**, or data routines, that the computer uses to perform a specific task. **CASE** ▶ *You'll look at how computers work and describe the main components of a computer system.*

DETAILS

The following list provides an overview of computer system components and how they work:

The design and construction of a computer is referred to as its **architecture** or **configuration**. The technical details about each hardware component are called **specifications**. For example, a computer system might be configured to include a printer; a specification for that printer might be a print speed of eight pages per minute or the ability to print in color.

The hardware and the software of a computer system work together to process data. **Data** refers to the numbers, words, figures, sounds, and graphics that describe people, events, things, and ideas. Modifying data is referred to as **processing**.

Processing tasks occur on the **motherboard**, the main electronic component inside the computer. See **FIGURE CC-7**. The motherboard is a **circuit board**, which is a rigid piece of insulating material with **circuits**—electrical paths—that control specific functions. Motherboards typically contain the following processing hardware:

- The **microprocessor**, also called the **processor** or the **central processing unit (CPU)**, consists of transistors and electronic circuits on a silicon chip (an integrated circuit embedded in semiconductor material). The processor is mounted on the motherboard and is responsible for executing instructions. It is the "brain" of the computer. **FIGURE CC-8** shows where the CPU sits in the flow of information through a computer.

- **Cards** are removable circuit boards that are inserted into slots in the motherboard to expand the capabilities of the computer. For example, a sound card translates digital audio information into analog sounds the human ear can hear.

Input is the data or set of instructions you give to a computer. You use an **input device**, such as a keyboard or a mouse, to enter data and issue commands. **Commands** are input instructions that tell the computer how to process data. For example, if you want to enhance the color of a photo in a graphics program, you input the appropriate commands that instruct the computer to modify the data in the image.

Output is the result of the computer processing the input you provide. Output can take many different forms, including printed documents, pictures, audio, and video. Computers produce output using **output devices**, such as a monitor or printer. The output you create using a computer may be stored inside the computer itself or on an external storage device, such as a DVD.

The computer itself takes care of the processing functions, but it needs additional components, called **peripheral devices**, to accomplish the input, output, and storage functions. You'll learn more about these devices later in this unit.

FIGURE CC-7: Motherboard

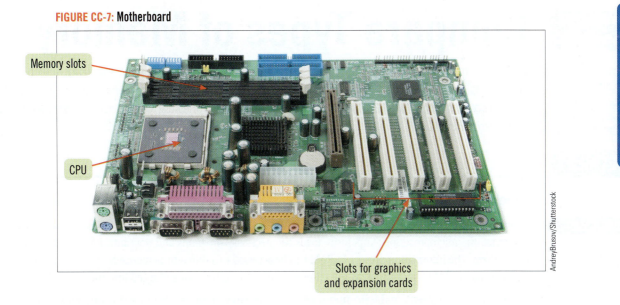

Memory slots

CPU

Slots for graphics
and expansion cards

AndreyBrusov/Shutterstock

FIGURE CC-8: Flow of information through a computer system

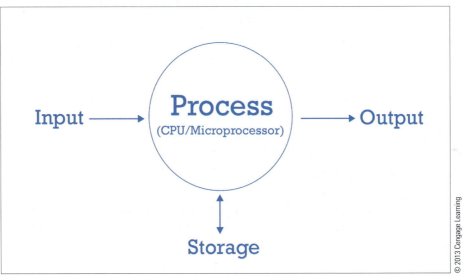

Input → Process (CPU/Microprocessor) → Output

Storage

© 2013 Cengage Learning

About microprocessor speeds

How fast a computer can process instructions depends partially on the speed of the microprocessor. Among other factors, the speed of the microprocessor is determined by its clock speed, word size, and whether it is single or multicore. **Clock speed** is measured in **megahertz (MHz)**, millions of cycles per second, or in **gigahertz (GHz)**, billions of cycles per second. **Word size** refers to the number of bits—the smallest unit of information in a computer—that are processed at one time; for example, a 32-bit processor processes 32 bits at a time. A computer with a large word size can process faster than a computer with a small word size. Most PCs sold today come with 64-bit processors. Finally, a **dual-core processor**, which has two processors on a single chip, can process information up to twice as fast as a **single-core processor**. Likewise, a **quad-core processor**, with four processors on a chip, processes information up to four times as fast as a single-core processor. Other multicore processors, such as hexacore and octacore, are also available.

Compare Types of Memory

One of the most important components of personal computer hardware is the **memory**, which stores instructions and data. **CASE** ▶ *You'll explore the different types of memory found in a typical computer: random access memory, cache memory, virtual memory, read-only memory, and complementary metal oxide semiconductor memory.*

DETAILS

Types of memory include the following:

Random access memory (RAM) holds information only while the computer is on. Whenever you're using a computer, the microprocessor temporarily loads the necessary programs and data into RAM so it can quickly access them. The information present in RAM can be accessed in a different sequence from which it was stored, hence its name. RAM typically consists of chips mounted on cards that are plugged into the motherboard.

- RAM is considered **volatile memory** or **temporary memory** because it's constantly changing or being refreshed. RAM is cleared when the computer is turned off.

- Most personal computers use **synchronous dynamic random access memory (SDRAM)**, which allows faster access to data by synchronizing with the clock speed of the computer's system bus.

- **Memory capacity** is the amount of data the computer can handle at any given time and is usually measured in gigabytes. For example, a computer that has 4 GB of RAM has the capacity to temporarily use more than four billion bits of data at one time.

Cache memory, sometimes called **RAM cache** or **CPU cache**, is special, high-speed memory located on or near the microprocessor itself. Cache memory sits between the CPU and relatively slow RAM and stores frequently accessed and recently accessed data and commands.

Virtual memory is space on the computer's storage devices (usually the hard disk drive) that simulates additional RAM. It enables programs to run as if your computer had more RAM by moving data and commands from RAM to the computer's permanent storage device and swapping in the new data and commands. Virtual memory, however, is much slower than RAM.

Read-only memory (ROM), also known as **firmware**, is a chip on the motherboard that permanently stores the **BIOS (basic input/output system)**. The BIOS is activated when you turn on the computer; it initializes the motherboard, recognizes any devices connected to the computer, and starts the boot process. The **boot process**, or **booting up**, includes loading the operating system software and preparing the computer so you can begin working.

- ROM never changes, and it remains intact when the computer is turned off; it is therefore called **nonvolatile memory** or **permanent memory**.

- Some computers allow ROM to be reprogrammed via a **firmware update**, which allows a manufacturer to fix bugs and add features.

Complementary metal oxide semiconductor (**CMOS**, pronounced "SEE-moss") **memory** is a chip on the motherboard that stores the date, time, and system parameters. Often referred to as **semipermanent memory**, a small rechargeable battery powers CMOS so its contents are saved when the computer is turned off.

FIGURE CC-9 shows the basic relationships between the different types of computer memory.

FIGURE CC-9: Relationships between types of computer memory

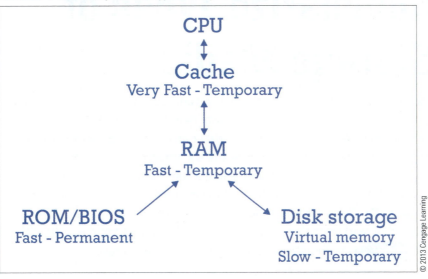

CPU

↕

Cache
Very Fast - Temporary

↕

RAM
Fast - Temporary

ROM/BIOS
Fast - Permanent

Disk storage
Virtual memory
Slow - Temporary

© 2013 Cengage Learning

Upgrading RAM

One of the easiest ways to make your computer run faster is to add more RAM. The more RAM a computer has, the more instructions and data can be stored there. You can often add more RAM to a computer by installing additional memory cards on the motherboard, as shown in **FIGURE CC-10**. Currently, you can buy from 512 MB to 16 GB RAM cards, and usually, you can add more than one card. Check your computer's specifications to see what size RAM cards the slots on your motherboard will accept. Note that if your computer has a 32-bit processor, it can't use more than 4 GB of RAM, even if the computer has places to plug in more cards.

FIGURE CC-10: Installing RAM on a motherboard

Norman Chan/Shutterstock

Understanding Essential Computer Concepts

Summarize Types of Storage Media

Learning Outcomes
- Define storage media
- Distinguish types of storage media

Since RAM retains data only while the power is on, your computer must have a more permanent storage option. As **FIGURE CC-11** shows, a storage device receives data from RAM and stores it on a storage medium, some of which are described below. The data can later be read back to RAM to use again. All data and programs are stored as files. A computer **file** is a named collection of stored data. An **executable file** is a type of computer file that contains the instructions that tell a computer how to perform a specific task; for instance, the files that are used when the computer starts are executable. Another type of computer file is a **data file**. This is the kind of file you create when you use software. For instance, a report that you write with a word-processing program is data, and it must be saved as a data file if you want to access it later. **CASE** *You'll explore some common types of storage media.*

DETAILS

The types of storage media are discussed below:

Magnetic storage devices use various patterns of magnetization to store data on a magnetized surface. The most common type of magnetic storage device is the **hard disk drive (HDD)**, also called a **hard disk** or a **hard drive**. It contains several spinning platters on which a magnetic head writes and reads data. Most personal computers come with an internal hard drive on which the operating system, programs, and files are all stored. You can also purchase external hard drives for additional storage and for backing up your computer.

QUICK TIP

Optical storage devices, such as CDs and DVDs, are much more durable than magnetic storage media.

Optical storage devices use laser technology to store data in the form of tiny pits or bumps on the reflective surface of a spinning polycarbonate disc. To access the data, a laser illuminates the data path while a read head interprets the reflection.

- Originally developed to store audio recordings, the **CD (compact disc)** was later adapted for data storage; the **CD-ROM** then became the first standard optical storage device available for personal computers. One CD can store 700 MB of data.

- A **DVD** is the same physical size as a CD, but it can store between 4.7 and 15.9 GB of data, depending on whether the data is stored on one or two sides of the disc, and how many layers of data each side contains.

- **Blu-ray** discs store 25 GB of data per layer. They are used for storing high-definition video.

QUICK TIP

There is only one way to insert a flash drive, so if you're having problems inserting the drive into the slot, turn the drive over and try again.

Flash memory (also called **solid state storage**) is similar to ROM except that it can be written to more than once. Small **flash memory cards** are used in digital cameras, handheld computers, video game consoles, and many other devices.

- A popular type of flash memory is a **USB flash drive**, also called a **USB drive** or a **flash drive**. See **FIGURE CC-12**.

- USB drives are available in a wide range of capacities, from one to 512 GB. They are popular for use as a secondary or backup storage device.

- USB drives plug directly into the USB port of a personal computer where the device is recognized as another disk drive. The location varies with the brand and model of computer you're using, but USB ports are usually found on the front, back, or side of a computer.

A **solid-state drive (SSD)** is based on flash memory, but is intended as a replacement for a traditional hard disk drive. Per gigabyte, SSDs are still more expensive than hard drives, but use less power and offer much faster data access and increased reliability.

FIGURE CC-11: Storage devices and RAM

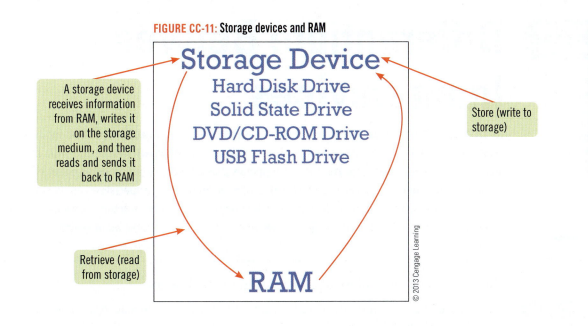

A storage device receives information from RAM, writes it on the storage medium, and then reads and sends it back to RAM

Storage Device
Hard Disk Drive
Solid State Drive
DVD/CD-ROM Drive
USB Flash Drive

Store (write to storage)

Retrieve (read from storage)

RAM

© 2013 Cengage Learning

FIGURE CC-12: USB flash drive being inserted into a laptop

Brian A Jackson/Shutterstock

Rewriting on optical storage

CDs that you buy with software or music already on them are CD-ROMs (compact disc read-only memory)—you can read from them, but you cannot record additional data onto them. To store data on a CD, you need to record it on a **CD-R (compact disc recordable)** or **CD-RW (compact disc rewritable)** drive and a CD-R or CD-RW disc. On a CD-R, after the data is recorded, you cannot erase or modify it, but you can add new data to the disc, as long as the disc has not been finalized. In contrast, you can rerecord a CD-RW. Recordable DVD drives are also available. As with CDs, you can buy a DVD to which you can record only once, or a rewritable DVD to which you can record and then rerecord data. Recordable DVDs come in two formats, **DVD-R** and **DVD+R**, and likewise rerecordable DVDs come in two formats, **DVD-RW** and **DVD+RW.** DVD drives on new computers are capable of reading from and writing to both -RW and +RW DVDs and CDs, as well as DVDs with two layers. **BD-R** are Blu-ray discs that you can record to once, and **BD-RE** are Blu-ray discs that you can record to multiple times. You need a Blu-ray drive to use Blu-ray discs.

Understanding Essential Computer Concepts

Computer Concepts

Learning Outcomes
• Define input device
• Identify various input devices

Differentiate Between Input Devices

To accomplish a task, a computer first needs to receive the data and commands you input. In a typical personal computer system, you provide this information using an **input device** such as a keyboard or a mouse. Most input devices are hardware peripherals that connect to a computer either with cables or wirelessly. Wired devices typically connect with a USB cable, or using a specialized connector. Most wireless input devices connect using radio frequency technology, while some use the same infrared technology found in a television remote control. **CASE** ▶ *You'll look at some common input devices.*

DETAILS

There are many types of input devices, as described below:

QUICK TIP

You may also be able to avoid repetitive motion injuries by taking frequent breaks from computer work and by carefully stretching your hands, wrists, and arms.

The most frequently used input device is a **keyboard**, which allows you to input text and issue commands by typing. The keyboard on the right in **FIGURE CC-13** is a standard keyboard, but the keyboard on the left is **ergonomic**, meaning that it has been designed to fit the natural placement of your hands and may reduce the risk of repetitive-motion injuries. Many keyboards have additional shortcut keys that are programmed to issue frequently used commands.

Another common input device is a **pointing device**, which controls the **pointer**—a small arrow or other symbol—on the screen. Pointing devices are used to select commands and manipulate text or graphics on the screen.

• The most popular pointing device for a desktop computer is a **mouse**, such as the one shown on the left in **FIGURE CC-14**. You control the pointer by sliding the mouse across a surface, and this motion is tracked by either a roller ball or by infrared or laser light. A mouse usually has two or more buttons used for clicking objects on the screen. A mouse might also have a **scroll wheel** that you roll to scroll through the page or pages on your screen.

• A **trackball**, shown in the middle of **FIGURE CC-14**, is similar to a mouse except that the rolling ball is on the top and you control the movement of the pointer by moving only the ball.

• Laptop computers are usually equipped with a touch pad like the one shown on the right in **FIGURE CC-14**. A **touch pad**, also called a **track pad**, detects the motion of your fingers. Buttons are usually located at the bottom of the touch pad, but many also allow you to click by simply tapping the pad.

QUICK TIP

Tablets and smartphones typically feature a "virtual keyboard" for inputting text.

A **touch screen** like the one in **FIGURE CC-15** accepts commands from your fingers (or a stylus), while it simultaneously displays the output. Touch screens are found on ATMs, smartphones, and tablets. Many newer desktop computers running the Microsoft Windows 8 operating system also have hardware that supports touch-screen technology.

A **microphone** can be used to record sound or communicate with others using audio or video conferencing software. Some computers have **voice-recognition software** that allows you to input data and commands with a microphone.

A **scanner** is a device that captures the image on a photograph or piece of paper and stores it digitally. If you scan a text document, you can use **optical character recognition (OCR)** software to translate it into text that can be edited in a word-processing program. If you scan a photo, it can be saved as an image file.

FIGURE CC-13: Ergonomic keyboard and standard keyboard

Dmitry Melnikov/Shutterstock

pav197lin/Shutterstock

FIGURE CC-14: Personal computer pointing devices: mouse, trackball, and touchpad

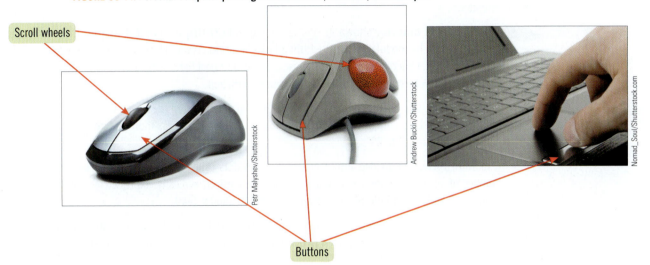

Scroll wheels

Buttons

Petr Malyshev/Shutterstock

Andrew Buckin/Shutterstock

Nomad_Soul/Shutterstock.com

FIGURE CC-15: Touchscreen

vovan/Shutterstock

Understanding assistive devices

Advances in **computer accessibility** mean that people with physical impairments or disabilities can use computers. For example, people who cannot use their arms or hands to operate a mouse may be able to use foot, head, or eye movements to control a specialized assistive device.

Those with poor vision can use keyboards with large keys, screen enlargers that increase the size of objects on a monitor, or screen readers that speak on-screen content aloud. Brain-computer interface technology may soon allow you to control a computer with your thoughts.

Explain Output Devices

Learning Outcomes
• Define output device
• Identify different output devices

An **output device** is any hardware peripheral that communicates the results of data processing. **CASE** ▸ *You'll explore the most commonly used output devices: monitors, printers, and speakers.*

DETAILS

Output devices are described below:

The **monitor**, sometimes called the **display** or simply the **screen**, uses video technology to display the output from a computer.

- The **flat panel monitor** shown in **FIGURE CC-16** uses **LCD (liquid crystal display)** technology to create an image by modulating light within a layer of liquid crystal. LCD monitors require a backlight for illumination. Older monitors typically use a fluorescent backlight, while newer ones use **LED (light emitting diode)** technology, which is more energy efficient.

- Monitor **screen size** is the diagonal measurement from one corner of the screen to the other. In general, monitors on desktop computers range in size from 15" to 30", whereas monitors on laptop computers range in size from 10" to 20".

- A monitor's screen is divided into a matrix of small dots called **pixels. Display resolution** is the number of pixels the monitor displays in each dimension, typically expressed as width x height. Common standard resolutions range from 640 x 480 to 2560 x 1440.

- To display graphics, a computer must have a **graphics card**, also called a **video display adapter** or **video card**, or a built-in **graphics processor** (sometimes called a **built-in graphics card**). The graphics card or processor controls the signals the computer sends to the monitor.

A **printer** produces a paper copy, often called a **hard copy**, of the text and graphics processed by a computer. Print quality, or resolution, is measured by the number of **dots per inch (dpi)** that a printer can produce. The speed of a printer is determined by how many **pages per minute (ppm)** it can output.

- **LED printers** and **laser printers**, like the one shown on the left in **FIGURE CC-17**, are popular for business use because they produce high-quality output quickly and reliably. Each type uses its light source to temporarily transfer an image onto a rotating drum, which attracts a powdery substance called **toner**. The toner is then transferred from the drum onto paper. Laser and LED printers typically feature print resolutions of 600 to 1200 DPI and can print in black and white or color. However, they're generally better at producing sharp text and simple graphics than they are at printing clear photographs.

- **Inkjet printers**, such as the one shown on the right in **FIGURE CC-17**, are popular for home and small business use. These printers spray ink onto paper, producing quality comparable to that of a laser printer, though at much slower speeds. Inkjets can also print on a wide variety of paper types, though use of plain paper may result in fuzzy text. Most inkjets sold today print in color, and they excel at producing photos with smooth color, especially when using special glossy photo paper.

Speakers (and **headphones**) allow you to hear sounds generated by your computer. Speakers can be separate peripheral devices, or they can be built into the computer case or monitor. For speakers to work, a sound card must be installed on the motherboard. The sound card converts the digital data in an audio file into analog sound that can be played through the speakers.

FIGURE CC-16: LCD monitor

Roberts/Shutterstock

FIGURE CC-17: Laser printer and inkjet printer

MalDix/Shutterstock

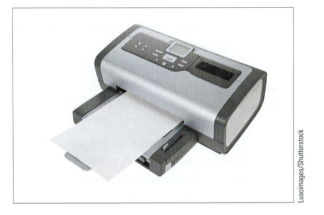

Lusoimages/Shutterstock

About multifunction printers

A **multifunction printer (MFP)** saves office space by combining several devices into one. Most small office/home office (SOHO) MFPs can print, scan, copy, and fax documents. Some MFPs also feature camera card readers and photo printing; this allows the user to print photos quickly without first loading them into a PC. MFPs can be made available to a network when connected to a computer or server. Some MFPs can also connect to a network wirelessly.

Understanding Essential Computer Concepts

Describe Data Communications

Learning
Outcomes
• Define data com-
munications terms
• Identify PC slots
and ports

Data communications is the transmission of data from one computer to another or to a peripheral device. The computer that originates the message is the **sender**. The message is sent over some type of **channel**, such as a telephone or coaxial cable, or wirelessly. The computer or device at the message's destination is the **receiver**. The rules that establish an orderly transfer of data between the sender and the receiver are called **protocols**. A **device driver**, or simply **driver**, handles the transmission protocols between a computer and its peripheral devices. A driver is a computer program that can establish communication because it understands the characteristics of your computer and of the device. **CASE** ➤ *You'll look at some common ways that computers communicate.*

DETAILS

The following describes some of the ways that computers communicate:

The path along which data travels between the microprocessor, RAM, and peripherals is called the **data bus**.

An external peripheral device must have a corresponding **expansion port** and **cable** that connect it to the computer. Inside the computer, each port connects to a **controller card**, sometimes called an **expansion card** or **interface card**. These cards plug into connectors on the motherboard called **expansion slots** or **slots**. Personal computers can have several types of ports, including parallel, serial, USB, MIDI, Ethernet, and Thunderbolt. **FIGURE CC-18** shows the ports on one desktop computer.

A **USB (Universal Serial Bus) port** is a high-speed serial port that allows multiple connections at the same port. The device you install must have a **USB connector**, which is a small rectangular plug. When you plug the USB connector into the USB port, the computer recognizes the device and allows you to use it immediately. USB flash storage devices plug into USB ports. For most USB devices, power is supplied via the port, so there's no need for an extra power supply or cables.

An **Ethernet port**, which resembles a telephone jack, allows data to be transmitted at high speeds over a **local area network (LAN)**. You can use Ethernet to connect to another computer, to a LAN, or to a modem. A **modem** (short for modulator-demodulator) is a device that connects your computer to the Internet via a standard telephone jack or cable connection.

Monitors are connected to computers through HDMI, DVI, or VGA ports. Both **HDMI (high-definition multimedia interface)** and **DVI (digital video interface)** digitally transmit both video and audio. The older **VGA (video graphics array)** only allows analog transmission of video.

FIGURE CC-18: Computer expansion ports

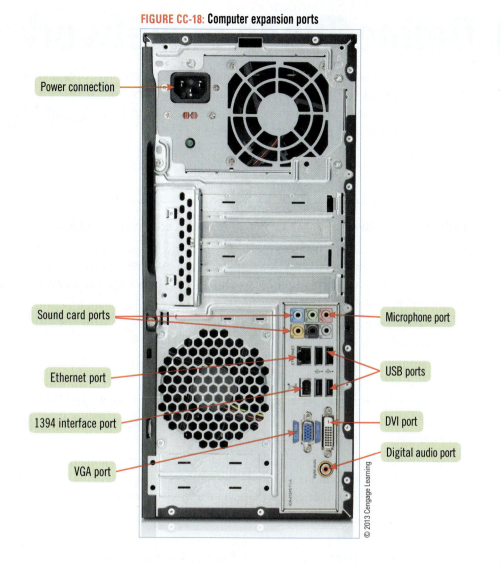

Power connection

Sound card ports

Ethernet port

1394 interface port

VGA port

Microphone port

USB ports

DVI port

Digital audio port

© 2013 Cengage Learning

How computers represent and interpret data

A computer sees the world as a series of **binary digits or bits**. A bit can hold one of two numerical values: 1 for "on" or 0 for "off." You might think of bits as miniature light switches. Of course, a single bit doesn't hold much information, so eight of them are combined to form a **byte**, which can be used to represent 256 values. Integer value 1 equals 00000001 (only 1 bit is "flipped" on), while the byte that represents 255 is 11111111 (all the bits are flipped on). A **kilobyte (KB or K)** is 1024 bytes, or about a thousand bytes. A **megabyte (MB)** is 1,048,576 bytes (about a million bytes). A **gigabyte (GB)** is about a billion bytes, and a **terabyte (TB)** is about a trillion bytes.

Define Types of Networks

Learning Outcomes
- Define networking terms
- Identify network types

A network connects one computer to other computers and peripheral devices, enabling you to share data and resources with others. There is a wide a variety of network types; however, any type of network has some basic characteristics and requirements that you should know. **CASE** ▸ *You'll look at the components that make up some different types of networks.*

DETAILS

Components of networks and the types of networks are described below:

To connect with a network via Ethernet, a computer must have a **network interface card (NIC)** that creates a communications channel between the computer and the network. Most desktop PCs come with a NIC built-in, and an Ethernet cable is used to make the connection to a router or modem. A **router** is a device that controls traffic between network components.

QUICK TIP

The World Wide Web, a subset of the Internet, is a huge database of information stored on network servers.

Network software is also essential, establishing the communications protocols that will be observed on the network and controlling the data "traffic flow."

Some networks have one or more computers, called **servers**, that act as the central storage location for programs and provide mass storage for most of the data used on the network. A network with a server and computers dependent on the server is called a **client/server network**. The dependent computers are the clients.

When a network does not have a server, all the computers are essentially equal, with programs and data distributed among them. This is called a **peer-to-peer network**.

A personal computer that is not connected to a network is called a **stand-alone computer**. When it is connected to the network, it becomes a **workstation**. Any device connected to the network, from computers to printers to routers, is called a **node**. **FIGURE CC-19** illustrates a typical network configuration.

In a **local area network (LAN)**, the nodes are located relatively close to one another, usually in the same building.

A **wide area network (WAN)** is more than one LAN connected together. The **Internet** is the largest example of a WAN.

In a **wireless local area network (WLAN)**, devices communicate using radio waves instead of wires. **Wi-Fi** (short for **wireless fidelity**) is the term created by the nonprofit Wi-Fi Alliance to describe networks connected using a standard radio frequency established by the Institute of Electrical and Electronics Engineers (IEEE). Most Wi-Fi routers can transmit over distances of up to about 200 feet; a technique called **bridging** can be used to increase this range by using multiple routers.

A **personal area network (PAN)** allows two or more devices located close to each other to communicate directly via cables or wirelessly. A PAN can also be used to share one device's Internet connection with another.

Infrared technology uses infrared light waves to "beam" data from one device to another. The devices must be compatible, and they must have their infrared ports pointed at each other to communicate. This is also the technology used in TV remote controls.

Bluetooth uses short range radio waves (up to about 30 feet) to connect devices wirelessly to one another or to the Internet. Bluetooth is often used to connect wireless headsets to cell phones or computers, and for connecting some wireless pointing devices and keyboards.

FIGURE CC-19: Typical network configuration

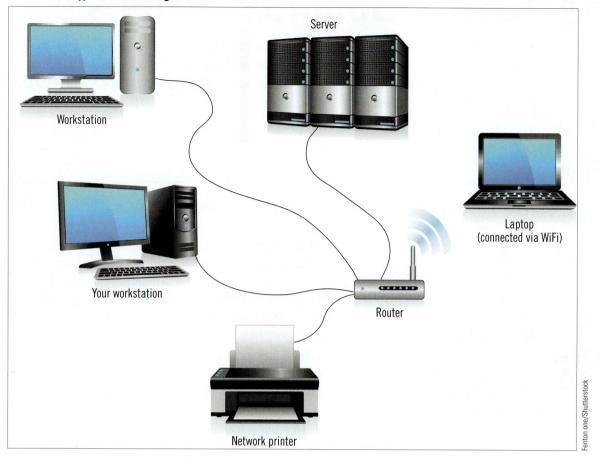

Fenton one/Shutterstock

Workstation

Server

Your workstation

Router

Laptop
(connected via WiFi)

Network printer

Understanding telecommunications

Telecommunications means communicating over a relatively long distance using a phone line or other data conduit. To make this connection, you must use a modem, a device that converts the digital signals that your computer outputs into analog signals that can travel over ordinary phone lines or cable lines. Many desktops and laptops come with a built-in 56K modem that can send and receive about 56,000 **bits per second (bps)** over a phone line. This is slow by modern standards, so many people opt for a high-speed connection using **DSL (digital subscriber line)**, which also operates over a phone line, or using a cable connection. If you go this route, you may need to purchase or rent an external DSL or cable modem. DSL and cable modems typically connect to a computer's **NIC (network interface card)** via an Ethernet cable. High-speed connections are often called **broadband connections**.

Assess Security Threats

Learning Outcomes
- Define types of security threats
- Establish importance of good security

Once a computer is connected to a network, it is essential that it be protected against the threat of someone stealing information or causing malicious damage. **Security** refers to the steps a computer user takes to prevent unauthorized use of or damage to a computer. **CASE** ➤ *You'll look at how important it is to be vigilant about keeping your computers secure and you'll review ways to do this.*

DETAILS

QUICK TIP

Some specific types of viruses are called worms; another type is a Trojan horse. Antivirus software usually protects against both types.

Malware is a broad term that describes any program designed to cause harm or transmit information without the permission of the computer owner.

Unscrupulous programmers deliberately construct harmful programs, called **viruses**, which instruct your computer to perform destructive activities, such as erasing a disk drive. Some viruses are more annoying than destructive, but some can be harmful, erasing data or causing your hard disk to require reformatting. **Antivirus software**, sometimes referred to as **virus protection software**, searches executable files for sequences of characters that may cause harm, and then disinfects files by erasing or disabling those commands. **FIGURE CC-20** shows the dialog box that appears when Windows Defender is scanning a computer for potential threats.

QUICK TIP

Adware is software installed with another program, often with the user's permission, that generates advertising revenue for the program's creator by displaying ads.

Spyware is software that secretly gathers information from your computer and then sends this data to the company or person that created it. Spyware may be installed by a virus, though it may also be installed along with other software without the user's permission or knowledge. **Anti-spyware software** can detect these programs and delete them.

A **firewall** is like a locked door on your computer. It prevents other computers on the Internet from accessing your computer and prevents programs on it from accessing the Internet without your permission.

- A hardware firewall provides strong protection against incoming threats. Many routers come with built-in firewalls.

- Software firewalls, which are installed directly on your computer, track all incoming and outgoing traffic. If a program that never previously accessed the Internet attempts to do so, the user is notified and can choose to forbid access. There are several free software firewall packages available.

Criminals are relentlessly searching for new and aggressive ways of accessing computer users' personal information and passwords.

- A **spoofed** site is a website that's been set up to look exactly like another website, with the intention of convincing customers to enter their personal information. For example, a criminal site developer might create a **URL** (address on the Web) that looks similar to the URL of a legitimate site such as a bank's. If a customer isn't paying attention, he or she may inadvertently enter information such as credit card numbers, Social Security numbers, or passwords. Once a thief has this information, it can be used to steal the customer's money or identity. **FIGURE CC-21** shows the alert displayed in the Internet Explorer browser when a known spoofed site is visited.

QUICK TIP

If you suspect you've received a phishing message, don't click any links in the email. Instead, open your browser and type the correct URL into the address bar.

- **Phishing** refers to the practice of sending email to customers or potential customers of a legitimate website encouraging them to click a link in the email. When clicked, the user's **browser** (the software program used to access websites) displays a spoofed site where the user is asked to provide personal information.

- A **DNS server** is one of the many computers distributed around the world that's responsible for directing Internet traffic. Using a practice called **pharming**, a criminal can sometimes break into a DNS server and redirect any attempts to access a particular website to the criminal's spoofed site.

FIGURE CC-20: Windows Defender scan in progress

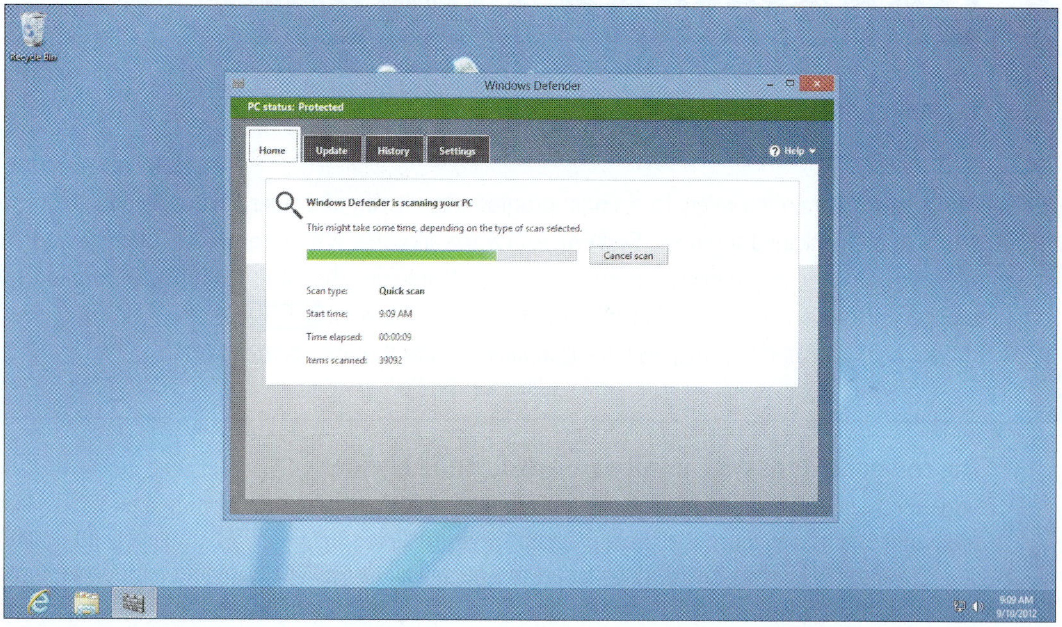

FIGURE CC-21: Internet Explorer browser when visiting a known spoofed site

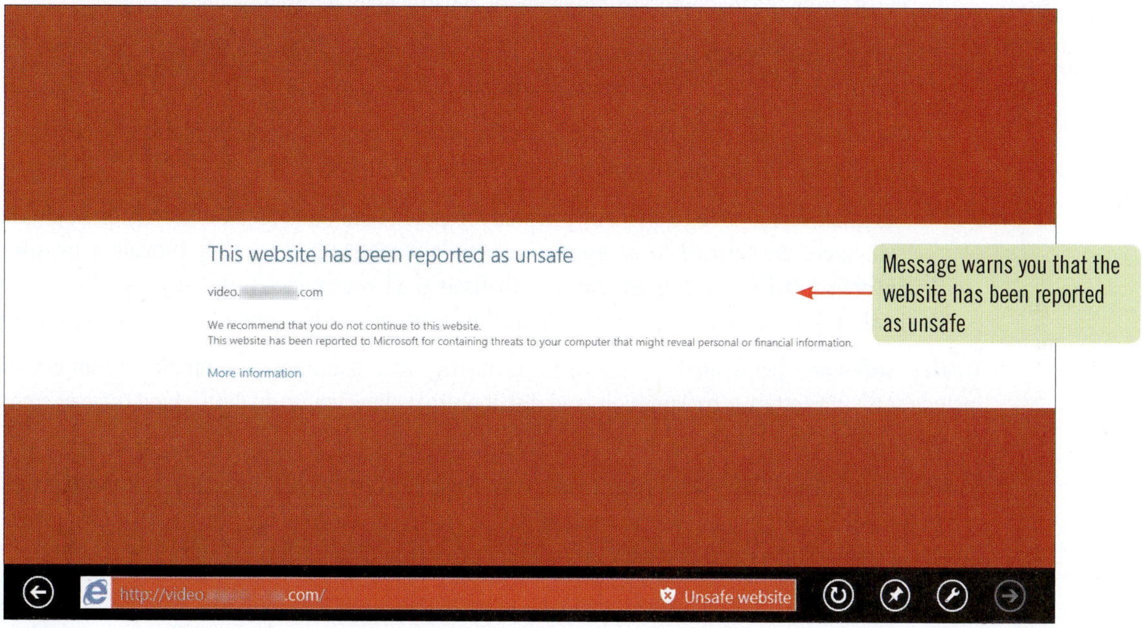

This website has been reported as unsafe

video.████████.com

We recommend that you do not continue to this website.
This website has been reported to Microsoft for containing threats to your computer that might reveal personal or financial information.

More information

> Message warns you that the website has been reported as unsafe

Protecting information with passwords

You can protect data on your computer by using passwords. You can set up multiple user accounts on your computer and require that users sign in with a username and password before they can use it. This is known as **logging in** or **logging on.** You can also protect individual files on your computer so anyone who tries to access a file must type a password. Many websites, especially e-commerce and banking sites, require a username and password to access the information stored there. To prevent anyone from guessing your passwords, always create and use strong passwords. A **strong password** consists of at least eight characters of upper- and lowercase letters and numbers. Avoid using easy to obtain personal information in your passwords, such as birthdays and addresses, and always create different passwords that are unique to each website you use.

Understand System Software

Learning Outcomes
- Define system software
- Identify types of system software

The term *software* often refers to a single program, but it can also refer to a collection of programs and data that are packaged together. **System software** allocates system resources, manages storage space, maintains security, and detects equipment failure. It provides the basic platform for running specialized application software, which you'll learn about in the next lesson. **CASE** ► *You'll look at the components of system software and how they help the computer perform its basic operating tasks.*

DETAILS

The components of system software are described below:

System software (see **FIGURE CC-22**) manages the fundamental operations of your computer, such as loading programs and data into memory, executing programs, saving data to storage devices, displaying information on the monitor, and transmitting data through a port to a peripheral device. There are four basic types of system software: operating systems, utility software, device drivers, and programming languages.

QUICK TIP

As part of its security responsibilities, your computer's operating system may require you to enter a username and password, or it may scan the computer to protect against viruses.

- The **operating system** manages the system resources of a computer so programs run properly. A **system resource** is any part of the computer system, including memory, storage devices, and the microprocessor. The operating system controls basic data **input and output**, or **I/O**, which is the flow of data from the microprocessor to memory to peripherals and back again.

- The operating system also manages the files on your storage devices. It opens and saves files, tracks every part of every file, and lets you know if any part of a file is missing.

- The operating system is always on the lookout for equipment failure. Each electronic circuit is checked periodically, and the user is notified whenever a problem is detected.

- Microsoft Windows, used on many personal computers, and OS X, used exclusively on Apple's Macintosh computers, are referred to as **operating environments** because they provide a **graphical user interface** (**GUI**, pronounced "goo-ey") that acts as a liaison between the user and all of the computer's hardware and software. **FIGURE CC-23** shows the Start screen on a computer using Microsoft Windows 8.

Utility software helps analyze, optimize, configure, and maintain a computer. Examples of utilities include anti-virus software, backup tools, and disk tools that allow you to analyze a hard drive or compress data to save space.

As you learned in the discussion of hardware ports, device drivers handle the transmission protocol between a computer and its peripherals. When you add a new device to a computer, the installation process typically involves loading a driver that updates the computer's configuration.

While most of us have no contact with them, it's important to know that computer **programming languages** allow a programmer to write instructions, or code, that a computer can understand. Programmers typically write software in a particular language and then compile the code to create a program that the computer then executes. Popular programming languages include C, C++, Objective-C, Java, and Visual Basic/Basic.

FIGURE CC-22: Relationships between system software and other system components

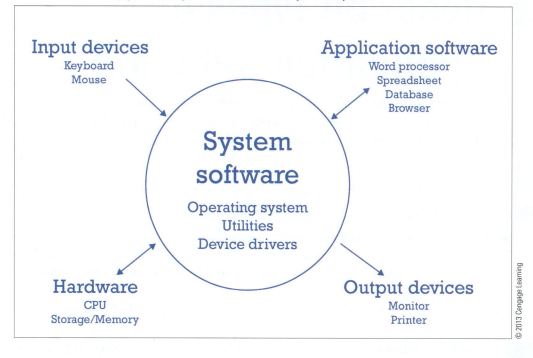

© 2013 Cengage Learning

FIGURE CC-23: Windows 8 Start screen

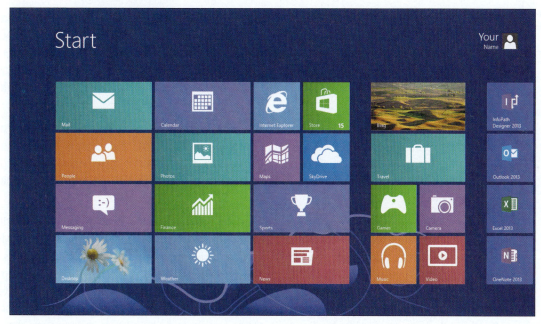

Examining Windows 8 hardware requirements

Windows 8, the newest version of the Windows operating system, requires a computer with at least a 1 GHz processor, 1 GB of RAM for the 32-bit version or 2 GB of RAM for the 64-bit version, a DirectX 9 graphics processor, 128 MB of specialized graphics RAM, and 16 GB of available space for the 32-bit version or 20 GB for the 64-bit version. Keep in mind that these are the minimum recommendations. To prevent your computer from slowing to a crawl, you should consider upgrading the amount of RAM and the processor speed.

Describe Types of Application Software

Learning Outcomes
- Define application software
- Identify types of application software

Application software enables you to perform specific tasks such as writing letters, creating presentations, analyzing statistics, creating graphics, enhancing photos, and much more. **CASE** ▶ *You'll look at some of the most common application software.*

DETAILS

QUICK TIP

To duplicate or move text, document production software allows you to perform copy-and-paste and cut-and-paste operations.

QUICK TIP

In Excel, a workbook is a file made up of multiple worksheets. The terms spreadsheet and worksheet are often used interchangeably.

Typical application software includes the following:

Document production software, which includes word-processing software (such as Microsoft Word) and desktop publishing software (Microsoft Publisher), allows you to write and format text documents. As shown in **FIGURE CC-24**, these tools offer automatic **spell checking** to help you avoid common grammar and spelling errors. You can also customize the look of a document by changing its **font** (the design of the typeface in which text is set) or by adding color, images, and **clip art**, simple drawings that are included as collections with many software packages.

Spreadsheet software is a numerical analysis tool that displays data in a grid of **cells** arranged in columns and rows. This grid is called a **worksheet**. You can type data into the worksheet's cells, and then enter mathematical formulas that reference that data. **FIGURE CC-25** shows a typical worksheet in Microsoft Excel that includes a simple calculation along with a graph that represents the data in the spreadsheet.

Database management software, such as Microsoft Access, lets you collect and manage data. A **database** is a collection of information organized in a uniform format of fields and records. A **field** contains one piece of information, such as a person's first name. A **record** contains multiple fields and can therefore store a person's full name and address. The online catalog of books at a library is a database that contains one record for each book; each record contains fields that identify the title, the author, and the subjects under which the book is classified.

Presentation software allows you to create a visual slide show to accompany a lecture, demonstration, or training session. In Microsoft PowerPoint, each presentation slide can contain text, illustrations, diagrams, charts, audio, and video. Slide shows can be projected in front of an audience, delivered over the Web, or transmitted to remote computers. To supplement a presentation, you can print audience handouts for quick reference.

Multimedia authoring software allows you to record and manipulate digital image files, audio files, and video files. There are several types of multimedia authoring software: **Graphics software**, such as Microsoft Paint, lets you create illustrations, diagrams, graphs, and charts. **Photo-editing software** allows you to manipulate digital photos; you can make images brighter, add special effects, add other images, or crop photos to include only important parts of the image. Examples of photo-editing software include Windows Live Photo Gallery and Adobe Photoshop. **Video-editing software**, such as Windows Live Movie Maker or Adobe Premiere, allows you to edit video by clipping it, adding captions and a soundtrack, or rearranging clips.

Information management software helps you schedule appointments, manage your address book, and create to-do lists. Microsoft Outlook is email software that includes information management components such as a contact list and a calendar. Some information management software allows you to synchronize information between a smartphone and your computer.

Website creation and management software allows you to build websites and mobile apps using technologies that include **HTML (Hypertext Markup Language)** and **CSS (Cascading Style Sheets)**, the primary languages of Web design. Two popular tools, Adobe Dreamweaver and Microsoft Expression Web, allow you to see how the site will appear as you create it.

FIGURE CC-24: Automatic spell checking in Microsoft Word

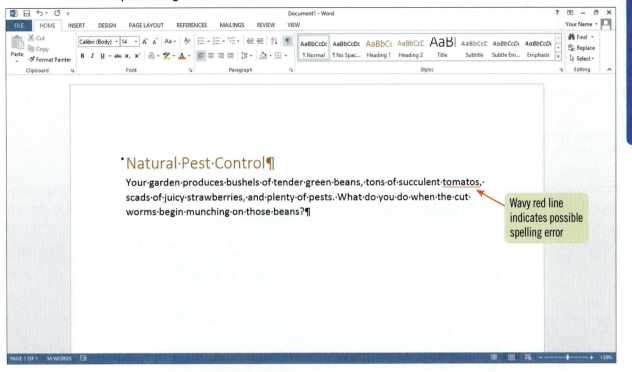

Natural Pest Control¶

Your garden produces bushels of tender green beans, tons of succulent tomatos, scads of juicy strawberries, and plenty of pests. What do you do when the cut worms begin munching on those beans?¶

Wavy red line indicates possible spelling error

FIGURE CC-25: Editing a worksheet in Microsoft Excel

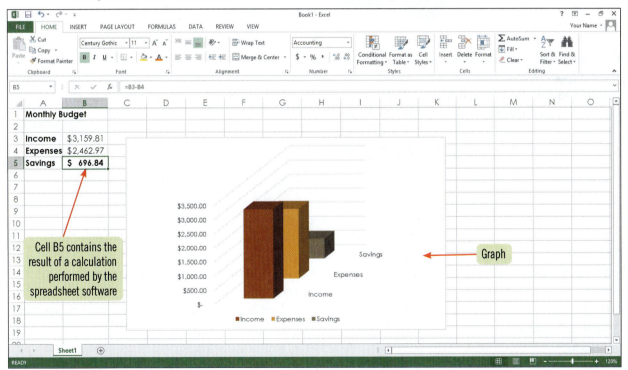

Cell B5 contains the result of a calculation performed by the spreadsheet software

Graph

Practice

Concepts Review

Match the statements with the elements labeled in the screen shown in FIGURE CC-26**.**

FIGURE CC-26

Oleksiy Mark/Shutterstock

1. The component that displays output
2. The component that processes data
3. The component that is used to enter text
4. The component you use to point to items on the screen

Match each term with the statement that best describes it.

5. **Commands**
6. **Spyware**
7. **Virtual memory**
8. **RAM**
9. **Hard disk**
10. **Expansion slot**
11. **Server**
12. **SSD**
13. **Operating system**
14. **Database**

a. Software that allocates resources, manages storage space, maintains security, and controls I/O
b. Space on the computer's storage devices that simulates additional RAM
c. Location on the motherboard into which a controller card for a peripheral device is inserted
d. A collection of information stored on one or more computers organized in a uniform format of records and fields
e. Based on flash memory and intended as a replacement for a traditional hard disk drive
f. Input instructions that tell the computer how to process data
g. Temporarily holds data and programs while the computer is on
h. A program that tracks a user's Internet usage without the user's permission
i. Magnetic storage media that is usually sealed in a case inside the computer
j. A computer on a network that acts as the central storage location for programs and data used on the network

Select the best answer from the list of choices.

15. **Which one of the following would not be considered a personal computer?**
    - **a.** Desktop
    - **b.** Laptop
    - **c.** Mainframe
    - **d.** Tablet

16. **The intangible components of a computer system, including the programs, are called:**
    - **a.** Software
    - **b.** Peripherals
    - **c.** Hardware
    - **d.** RAM

17. **What part of the computer is responsible for executing instructions to process information?**
    - **a.** ROM
    - **b.** Card
    - **c.** Processor
    - **d.** Motherboard

18. **What are the technical details about each hardware component called?**
    - **a.** Configuration
    - **b.** Architecture
    - **c.** Circuits
    - **d.** Specifications

19. **Keyboards, monitors, and printers are all examples of which of the following?**
    - **a.** Peripheral devices
    - **b.** Input devices
    - **c.** Output devices
    - **d.** Data communications

20. **Which of the following is a pointing device that allows you to control the pointer by moving the entire device around on a desk?**
    - **a.** Scroll wheel
    - **b.** Touch pad
    - **c.** Trackball
    - **d.** Mouse

21. **To display graphics, a computer needs a monitor and a:**
    - **a.** Graphics card or graphics processor
    - **b.** Sound card
    - **c.** Network card (NIC)
    - **d.** USB cable

22. **What do you call each 1 or 0 used in the representation of computer data?**
    - **a.** A quark
    - **b.** A bit
    - **c.** A kilobyte
    - **d.** A byte

23. **What is a megabyte?**
    - **a.** About a million bits
    - **b.** About a million bytes
    - **c.** One-half a gigabyte
    - **d.** 10 kilobytes

24. **Which of the following permanently stores the set of instructions that the computer uses to activate the software that controls the processing function when you turn the computer on?**
    - **a.** ROM
    - **b.** RAM
    - **c.** The hard disk
    - **d.** CPU cache

25. **Which of the following is space on the computer's storage devices that simulates additional RAM?**
    - **a.** Solid-state memory
    - **b.** Cache memory
    - **c.** Virtual memory
    - **d.** Volatile memory

26. **Which of the following is considered volatile or temporary memory?**
    - **a.** ROM
    - **b.** CD-ROM
    - **c.** The hard disk
    - **d.** RAM

27. **Which of the following is not a permanent storage medium?**
    - **a.** Hard disk
    - **b.** RAM
    - **c.** DVD
    - **d.** CD-ROM

28. **The transmission protocol between a computer and its peripheral devices is handled by a:**
    - **a.** Driver
    - **b.** Channel
    - **c.** Controller card
    - **d.** Data bus

29. **Which of the following is the data path between the microprocessor, RAM, and the peripherals?**
   a. Cable
   b. Data channel
   c. Data bus
   d. Motherboard

30. **The computer that originates a message to send to another computer is called the:**
   a. Receiver
   b. Sender
   c. Channel
   d. Server

31. **A personal computer that is connected to a network is called a:**
   a. Workstation
   b. Desktop
   c. Laptop
   d. Channel

32. **Which of the following acts as a locked door on a computer?**
   a. Antivirus software
   b. DNS server
   c. Firewall
   d. Browser

33. **A _____ consists of connected computers and peripheral devices that are located relatively close to each other.**
   a. WAN
   b. WLAN
   c. PAN
   d. LAN

34. **When data, applications, and resources are stored on servers rather than on users' computers, it is referred to as:**
   a. Cluster computing
   b. Shared computing
   c. Leased computing
   d. Cloud computing

35. **A website that's been set up to look exactly like another website, with the intention of convincing customers to enter their personal information, is a _____ site.**
   a. spoofed
   b. malware
   c. pharmed
   d. phished

Independent Challenge 1

To run the newest software, many people need to upgrade their existing computer system or purchase a brand new one. But what do you do with your old computer if you buy a new one? Most municipalities have enacted laws regulating the disposal of electronics. Research these laws in your city and state, and write a brief report describing them. *Note: To complete the Independent Challenge, your computer must be connected to the Internet.*

   a. Start your browser, go to your favorite search engine, and then search for information about laws regarding the disposal of electronics in your city and state. Try searching your city's official website for the information, or use **electronics disposal laws** followed by your city name as a search term and then repeat that search using your state's name.
   b. Open each website that you find in a separate browser tab or window.
   c. Read the information on each website. Can some components be thrown away? Are there laws that apply only to display monitors? Are the laws different for individuals and businesses? Does the size of the business matter? Are manufacturers or resellers required to accept used components they manufactured or sold?
   d. Search for organizations you can donate your computer to. How do these organizations promise to protect your privacy? Can you take a deduction on your federal income tax for your donation?
   e. Write a short report describing your findings. Include the URLs for all relevant websites. (*Hint*: If you are using a word processor to write your report, you can copy the URLs from your browser and paste them into the document. Drag to select the entire URL in the Address or Location bar in your browser. Right-click the selected text, then click Copy on the shortcut menu. Position the insertion point in the document where you want the URL to appear, then press [Ctrl][V] to paste it.)

Independent Challenge 2

New viruses are discovered on an almost daily basis. If you surf the Internet or exchange email, it's important to use antivirus software and to keep it updated. Research the most current virus threats, and create a table that lists them along with details about each threat. *Note: To complete the Independent Challenge, your computer must be connected to the Internet.*

a. Use your favorite search engine to go to the Microsoft Malware Protection Center (MMPC) at **www.microsoft.com/security/portal**, and then read about the MMPC and its mission.

b. Under the Recently Published heading, click the links to the five most recent threats, and then read the description of each threat.

c. Open a new word-processing document, and create a table that lists each virus threat, including a description of what each virus does, and how damaging each virus is (the alert level). Also note any steps you can take to prevent getting the virus, along with ways to recover an infected computer.

d. Use your search engine to find three different antivirus programs that can be installed on your computer. In your word-processing document, create a new section that lists the programs you found. Include the benefits and costs of using each program.

Independent Challenge 3

You've decided to buy a new desktop computer to run Windows 8 and Microsoft Office 2013. *Note: To complete the Independent Challenge, your computer must be connected to the Internet.*

a. To help you organize your search, create the table shown below.

	Your Requirements	Computer Retailer 1	Computer Retailer 2	Computer Retailer 3
Windows 8 (Edition)				
Office 2013 (Edition)				
Brand of computer				
Processor (brand and speed)				
RAM (amount)				
Video RAM (amount)				
Hard disk/SSD (size)				
Monitor (type and size)				
Printer (type and speed)				
Antivirus software				
Firewall (software or router with built-in fire-wall)				
System price				
Additional costs				
Total price				

Independent Challenge 3 (continued)

b. Decide which edition of Windows 8 you want, and enter it in the Your Requirements column of the table. To read a description of the available editions, go to **www.microsoft.com** and search the site for information about the different editions (Windows 8, Windows 8 Pro, and Windows RT).

c. Research the hardware requirements for running the edition of Windows 8 you selected. Search the Microsoft website again for the minimum and recommended hardware requirements for running Windows 8.

d. Decide which edition of Office 2013 you want, and enter it in the first column of the table. Search the Microsoft website to find a description of the software included with each edition of Office 2013, and then search for the hardware requirements for running the edition of Office 2013 that you chose. If necessary, change the hardware requirements in the table.

e. Research the cost of your new computer system. To begin, visit local stores, look at advertisements, or search the Web for computer retailers. Most retailers sell complete systems that come with all the necessary hardware, an operating system, and additional software already installed. In the Computer Retailer 1 column of the table, fill in the specifications for the system you chose. If any item listed as a minimum requirement is not included with the system you chose, determine the cost of adding that item and enter the price in the table. Repeat this process with systems from two other retailers, entering the specifications in the Computer Retailer 2 and Computer Retailer 3 columns.

f. If the system you chose does not come with a printer, search the Web for an inexpensive color inkjet printer.

g. If the system you chose does not come with antivirus software, search the Web for the cost, if any, of an antivirus software package. Make sure you look up reviews of the package you chose. Decide whether to purchase this software or download a free one, and enter this cost in the table.

h. If you decide you need a router with a built-in firewall, search the Web for the price of one. Enter this information in the table.

i. Determine the total cost for each of the three systems in your table. If the costs exceed your budget, think about items you can downgrade. Can you get a less expensive printer or share someone else's printer? Would a less expensive monitor still provide the room you need to work? On the other hand, if the total costs come in under your budget, you may be able to upgrade your system; perhaps you can afford a larger monitor with better resolution or a better mouse or keyboard.

Independent Challenge 4: Explore

Cloud storage allows you to store documents and images on remote servers. You then have access to these items from any compatible device that is connected to the Internet. You need to decide which cloud service is best for you. *Note: To complete the Independent Challenge, your computer must be connected to the Internet.*

a. Open your browser and use your favorite search engine to locate the sites for Microsoft SkyDrive, Apple iCloud, Google Drive, and Dropbox. If there is another service you'd like to investigate, include it as well (e.g., Amazon Cloud Drive).

b. To help you compare the different services, create the table shown below.

	SkyDrive	iCloud	Google Drive	Dropbox
Free storage capacity				
Paid storage capacity				
Paid storage cost				
Maximum file size				
Syncs to all your devices? (PC, mobile)				
Supports version tracking?				
Mobile apps provided*				
Additional features/notes				

*List the mobile operating systems the service provides an app for, such as Android, iPhone/iPad, or Windows Phone.

c. Enter details in the table using the information available on each service's website.

d. Search for online reviews and comparisons of each cloud service, and note any additional information that you feel is important. For example, if you have a large music collection on your computer, is it compatible with each service?

e. Based on your research, explain which service would best serve your needs and why.

Getting Started with Windows 8

CASE ▶ You are about to start a new job, and your employer has asked you to get familiar with Windows 8 to help boost your productivity. You'll need to start Windows 8 and Windows 8 apps, work with on-screen windows and commands, look for help, and exit Windows.

Unit Objectives

After completing this unit, you will be able to:

- Start Windows 8
- Navigate the Start screen and desktop
- Point, click, and drag
- Start an app
- Work with a window

- Manage multiple windows
- Use command buttons, menus, and dialog boxes
- Get help
- Exit Windows 8

Files You Will Need

No files needed.

Start Windows 8

Windows 8 is an **operating system**, a type of program that runs your computer and lets you use it. A **program** is a set of instructions written for a computer. When you turn on your computer, the Windows 8 operating system starts automatically. If your computer did not have an operating system, you wouldn't see anything on the screen after you turned it on. The operating system can reserve a special area called a **user account** where each user can keep his or her files. If your computer is set up for more than one user, you might need to **sign in**, or select your user account name when the computer starts, also called **logging in**. If you are the only user on your computer, you won't have to select an account. You might also need to enter a **password**, a special sequence of numbers and letters. Your password lets you enter and use the files in a secured user account area on your computer. Depending on how your user account is set up, your password might also let you access content you have stored online. Users cannot see each other's account areas without the other person's password, so passwords help keep your computer information secure. After you log in, you see the Windows 8 Start screen. You will learn about the Start screen in the next lesson. **CASE** ▶ *You're about to start a new job, so you decide to learn more about Windows 8, the operating system used at your new company.*

STEPS

1. **Press your computer's power button, which might look like ◉ or ▭, then if the monitor is not turned on press its power button**

   On a desktop computer, the power button is probably on the front panel. On a laptop computer it's most likely at the top of the keys on your keyboard. After a few moments, a **lock screen** appears with the time and date. See **FIGURE A-1**. The lock screen appears when you first start your computer and also if you leave it unattended for a period of time.

2. **Press [Spacebar]**

   The sign-in screen shows your Windows user account picture, name, and e-mail address, as well as a space to enter your user account password. The user account may have your name assigned to it, or it might have a general name like "Student" or "Lab User".

3. **Type your password, as shown in FIGURE A-2, using uppercase and lowercase letters as necessary**

   If necessary, ask your instructor or technical support person what password you should use. Passwords are **case sensitive**, which means that if you type any letter using capital letters when lowercase letters are needed, or vice versa, Windows will not let you use your account. For example, if your password is "book", typing "Book" or "BOOK," will not let you enter your account. For security, Windows substitutes bullets for the password characters you type.

4. **Click the Submit button ➡**

   A welcome message appears, followed by the Windows 8 Start screen. See **FIGURE A-3**.

Using touch screens

The Windows 8 style UI was developed to work with touch-screen monitors and tablet computers, in addition to traditional laptops. So if you have a touch-screen device, like the one shown in **FIGURE A-4**, you'll find that many tasks are easier to accomplish because they are designed for use with gestures instead of a mouse. A **gesture** is an action you take with your fingertip directly on the screen, such as tapping or swiping. For example, when you sign into Windows, you can tap the Submit button on the screen, instead of clicking it. In general, mouse users can locate items by pointing to the screen corners, and touch-screen users can swipe from the screen edges. Touch screens are easy to use for many people because they use these same gestures with their other devices, such as mobile phones and tablet computers.

FIGURE A-4: A touch-screen device

vovan/Shutterstock.com.

FIGURE A-1: Lock screen with time and date

FIGURE A-2: Typing your password

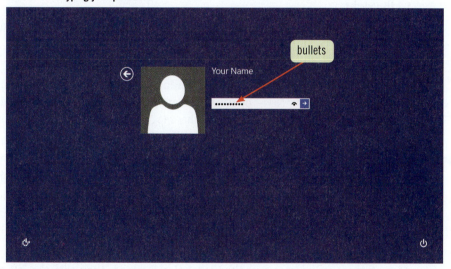

FIGURE A-3: Windows 8 Start screen

Windows 8

Learning Outcomes
- Scroll the Start screen
- Display the Charms bar
- Switch between Start screen and desktop

Navigate the Start Screen and Desktop

Every time you start Windows 8, the **Start screen** appears, containing controls that let you interact with the Windows 8 operating system. These controls are called its **user interface (UI)**. The Windows 8 user interface is called the **Windows 8 UI**. The Start screen contains many shaded rectangles called **tiles**. Each tile represents an **app**, short for **application program**, which lets you perform a certain type of task. For example, the Photos tile represents the **Photos app**, which lets you view and organize your pictures. Your user name and an optional picture appear in the upper-right corner. You can easily switch between the Start screen and the **Windows desktop**, an electronic work area that lets you organize and manage your information, much like your own physical desktop. **CASE** ▶ *To become better acquainted with Windows 8, you decide to explore the Start screen and the desktop.*

STEPS

QUICK TIP

On some computers, you can move the pointer to the right side of the screen to show hidden apps; depending on your mouse, you also may be able to use the scroll wheel.

1. **Move the mouse pointer to the bottom of the screen, then drag the light gray scroll bar to the right**

   If your Start screen contains additional apps that won't fit on the screen, a scroll bar appears when you move the mouse pointer toward the bottom of the screen. See **FIGURE A-5**.

2. **Scroll back to display the left side of the screen**

   The first set of apps reappears. These are **Windows 8 apps**, application programs that have a single purpose, such as Photos, News, or SkyDrive. Some Windows 8 app tiles show updated content using a feature called **live tile**; for example, the Weather app can show the current weather for any city you choose. (Note that the screens in this book do not show live tiles.)

QUICK TIP

You can also open the Charms bar by pointing to the upper-right corner of the screen to display an outline of the bar and then moving down into the bar to display it in full. Touch screen users can sweep inward from the right side of the screen.

3. **Move the mouse pointer to the lower-right corner of the screen, until you see a silhouette of a bar, then slowly move the mouse pointer upward into the bar**

   Pointing to the lower-right corner displays an outline of the Charms bar, and moving up into the outline displays the bar in full. The **Charms bar** is a set of buttons that let you find and send information, change your machine settings, and turn off your computer. When you point to the Charms bar, the time and date appear on the left side of the screen. See **FIGURE A-6**.

4. **Move the mouse pointer over the tile labeled Desktop, then click the left mouse button once**

   The Windows 8 desktop appears. You can use the desktop to manage the files and folders on your computer. A **file** is a collection of stored information, such as a letter, video, or program. A **folder** is a container that helps you organize your files. The desktop is where **desktop apps**, sometimes called **traditional apps**, like the productivity suite Microsoft Office, open in windows. Because desktop apps don't take up the whole screen, you can have several app windows open on the desktop at once, and you can move them around so you can easily go back and forth between them.

5. **If you don't see a blue bar at the bottom of the screen, move the mouse pointer to the bottom of the screen**

   The narrow blue bar, called the **taskbar**, displays icons for apps you use often. See **FIGURE A-7**. By default, the taskbar contains two icons: The 🅔 icon represents the Internet Explorer application program, and the 📁 icon represents an app called File Explorer you can use to view the contents of your computer.

QUICK TIP

You can quickly move between the Start screen and the desktop screen by pressing ⊞ on your keyboard.

6. **Move the mouse pointer back up over the desktop**

   Your desktop contains one or more small images called **icons** that represent items such as the **Recycle Bin**, an electronic wastepaper basket, on your computer. You can rearrange, add, and delete desktop icons. If you're using a new installation of Windows 8, the desktop might show only a Recycle Bin in the upper-left corner of the screen. If you are using a computer in a school or one that you purchased yourself, you might see other icons, files, and folders.

FIGURE A-5: Scrolling to display apps on the Start screen

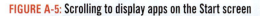

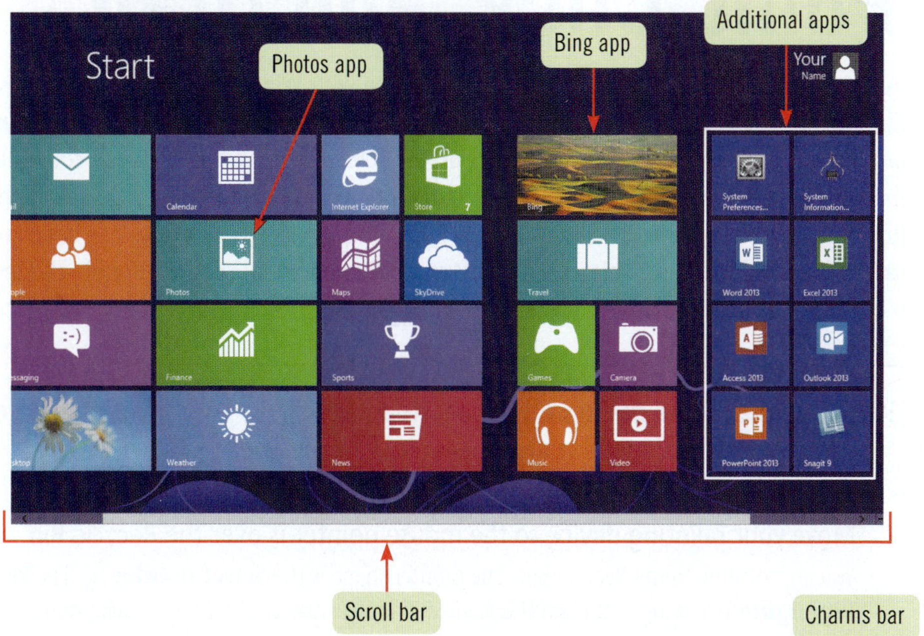

Start
Photos app
Bing app
Additional apps
Your Name
Scroll bar

FIGURE A-6: Displaying the Charms bar

Charms bar
Start
Your Name
Search
Share
Start
Devices
Settings
4:30 Sunday October 16

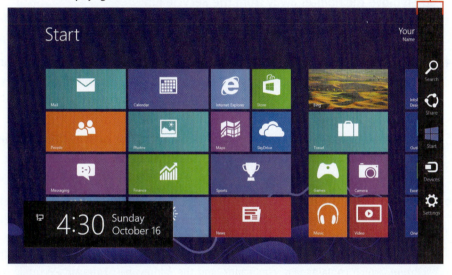

FIGURE A-7: Windows 8 desktop

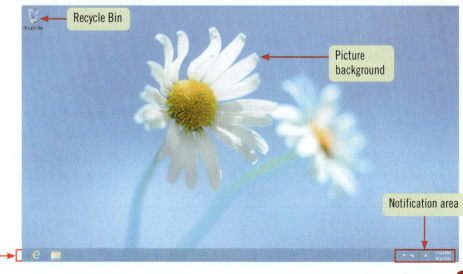

Recycle Bin
Picture background
Notification area
Taskbar

Point, Click, and Drag

Learning
Outcomes
• Point to, select,
  and deselect
  an item
• Move an item

As you learned in the last lesson, you communicate with Windows 8 using a pointing device or, if you have a touch screen, your fingertip. A **pointing device** controls the movement of the **mouse pointer**, a small arrow or other symbol that moves on the screen. Your pointing device could be a mouse, track-ball, touch pad, pointing stick, on-screen touch pointer, graphics tablet, or a touch-enabled mouse or touchpad. **FIGURE A-8** shows some common pointing devices. There are five basic **pointing device actions** you use to communicate with your computer: pointing, clicking, double-clicking, dragging, and right-clicking. **TABLE A-1** describes each action. **CASE** ▶ *You practice the basic pointing device actions.*

STEPS

1. **Locate the mouse pointer on the desktop, then move your pointing device left, right, up, and down (or move your finger across a touch pad)**

   The mouse pointer moves in the same direction as your pointing device.

2. **Move your pointing device so the mouse pointer is over the Recycle Bin**

   You are pointing to the Recycle Bin. The pointer shape is the **Select pointer** ⌖. The Recycle Bin becomes **highlighted**, looking as though it is framed in a box with a lighter color background.

3. **While pointing to the Recycle Bin, press and quickly release the left mouse button once, then move the pointer away from the Recycle Bin**

   You click a desktop icon once to **select** it, which signals that you intend to perform an action. When an icon is selected, its background changes color and maintains the new color even when you point away from it.

4. **Point to (but do not click) the Internet Explorer button** 🅔 **on the taskbar**

   The button border appears and an informational message called a **ScreenTip** identifies the program the button represents. ScreenTips are useful because they identify screen items, helping you to learn about the tools available to you.

5. **Move the mouse pointer over the time and date in the notification area on the right side of the taskbar, read the ScreenTip, then click once**

   A pop-up window appears, containing a calendar and a clock displaying the current date and time.

6. **Place the tip of the mouse pointer over the Recycle Bin, then quickly click twice**

   You **double-clicked** the Recycle Bin. Touch screen users can quickly tap an item twice to double-click it. A window opens, showing the contents of the Recycle Bin, as shown in **FIGURE A-9**. The area at the top of the window is the title bar, which displays the name of the window. The area below the title bar is the **Ribbon**, which contains tabs, commands, and the Address bar. **Tabs** are electronic pages that contain groups of **buttons** you use to interact with an object or a program.

7. **Click any tab**

   The buttons on that tab appear; you can double-click to expand the Ribbon and keep the tab area open. (You'll expand the Ribbon in a later lesson.) Buttons act as commands that perform tasks, and **commands** are instructions to perform tasks. The **Address bar** shows the name and location of the item you have opened. If your Recycle Bin contains any discarded items, they appear in the window.

8. **Point to the Close button** ☒ **on the title bar, read the ScreenTip, then click once**

   Clicking the Close button issues the command to Windows to close the Recycle Bin window.

9. **Point to the Recycle Bin, press and hold down the left mouse button, move the mouse so the object moves right as shown in FIGURE A-10, release the mouse button, then drag the Recycle Bin back to its original location**

   You use dragging to move folders, files, and other objects to new locations.

FIGURE A-8: Pointing devices

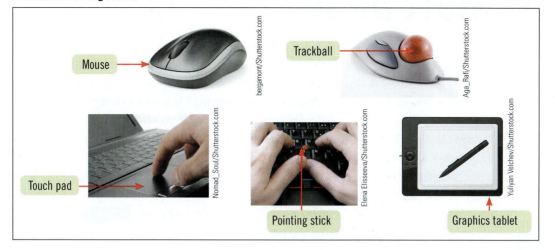

Mouse

Trackball

Touch pad

Pointing stick

Graphics tablet

FIGURE A-9: Recycle Bin window

Tabs

Title bar

Ribbon

Address bar

Any discarded items appear here

FIGURE A-10: Dragging the Recycle Bin

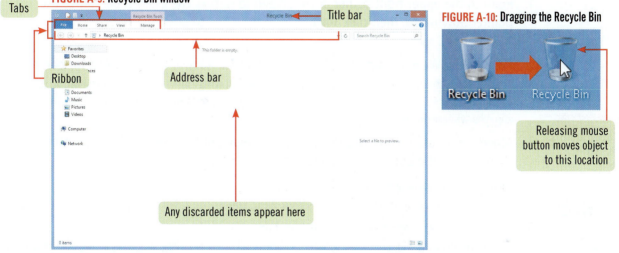

Releasing mouse button moves object to this location

TABLE A-1: Basic pointing device actions

action	mouse action	touch pad action	use to
Point	Move pointing device to position tip of pointer over an item	Move your finger over touch pad to position tip of pointer over an item	Highlight items or display small informational boxes called ScreenTips
Click	Quickly press and release left mouse button once	Tap touch pad surface once	Select objects or commands, opening menus or items on the taskbar
Double-click	Quickly press and release left mouse button twice	Tap twice in quick succession on touch pad	Open programs, folders, or files represented by desktop icons
Drag	Point to an object, press and hold down left mouse button, move object to a new location, then release mouse button	Slide finger over touch pad to point to an object, press and hold left touch pad button, drag across touch pad to move object to new location, then release button	Move objects, such as icons on the desktop
Right-click	Point to an object, then press and release right mouse button		Display a shortcut menu containing options specific to the object

Using newer touch devices

Since the arrival of Windows 8, manufacturers have started releasing new products that incorporate touch technology, such as a touch-enabled mouse and an external touch pad that recognizes gestures such as tapping and swiping. So even if your computer does not have a touch screen, you can still use gestures to take advantage of new Windows 8 features using one of these devices.

Start an App

Learning Outcomes
- Start a Windows Accessory program
- Open the full apps listing
- Run an app

The Windows 8 operating system lets you operate your computer and see the files and folders it contains. But to do your work, you use apps. There are three kinds of apps: Windows 8 apps, desktop apps, and Windows accessories. **Windows 8 apps** fill the screen when you open them and are specially designed so they can stay open as you work without slowing down your computer. Examples include the Photos app, which lets you view your photographs, and the SkyDrive app, which lets you connect to files and programs on the Windows SkyDrive Web site. Windows 8 apps also work well on other devices, such as tablet computers or smartphones. **Desktop apps** such as Microsoft Office let you create letters, financial summaries, and other useful documents, as well as view Web pages on the Internet and send and receive e-mail. Still other apps, called Windows accessories, come with Windows 8. See **TABLE A-2** for some examples of Windows accessories. To use an app, you must start (or open) it so you can see and use its tools. **CASE** ▶ *To prepare for your new job, you start a Windows 8 app and an accessory.*

STEPS

1. **Point to the upper-right corner of the screen to display the Charms bar, move the pointer downward, then click Start**

   The Start screen opens.

2. **Point to the Weather app tile, click once, then click Allow if you are asked for permission**

   The Weather app opens to the weather **app window**, showing the weather for a location, as shown in **FIGURE A-11**. Note that Windows 8 apps are updated regularly, so your app screen may differ. To close the app, you will use dragging.

3. **Move the mouse pointer to the top of the screen, until you see the hand pointer 🖑, then drag to the bottom of the screen to close the app**

4. **Right-click a blank area of the Start screen**

   The App bar appears at the bottom of the screen. Next, you'll open a desktop app called Paint.

5. **Left-click the All apps button in the App bar**

   A list of the apps on your computer appears, as shown in **FIGURE A-12**. The Windows 8 apps are listed alphabetically on the left side of the screen, and all other applications are grouped on the right side.

6. **Scroll to the right until you can see the group called Windows Accessories**

   If you have a lot of apps, Windows categorizes them alphabetically and groups accessories and application suites.

7. **Move the pointer over the Paint accessory, then click once**

   The Paint app window opens on your screen, as shown in **FIGURE A-13**. When Windows opens an application program, it starts it from your computer's hard disk, where it's permanently stored. Then it **loads**, or copies and places, the program in your computer's memory so you can use it.

8. **If your Paint window fills the screen completely, click the Restore Down button 🗗 in the upper-right corner of the window**

Searching for apps and files

If you need to find an app, setting, or file from the Start screen, simply start typing the first few letters of the item you want to find; for example, the letters "P-a-i" for Microsoft Paint. A search box opens, and Windows lists on the left side of the screen all the items that contain the text you typed. Windows lists applications containing your search text, and the Apps category is highlighted below the Search box on the right side of the screen. To see results for a different category, click Settings, Files, or one of the apps in the list, such as Photos, to see matches in that category. For files, you'll also see each file's date, file size, and location. Point to an item in the Results list to see more information, including its location on your computer.

FIGURE A-11: Weather app

FIGURE A-12: Apps list

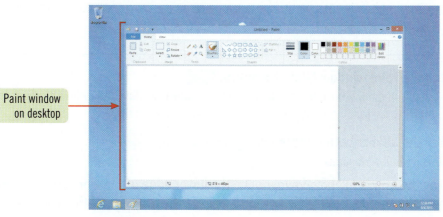

FIGURE A-13: Paint app window

TABLE A-2: Useful Windows 8 accessory programs

accessory name	use to
Notepad	Create text files with basic text formatting
Paint	Create and edit drawings using lines, shapes, and colors
Snipping Tool	Capture an image of any screen area that you can save to use in a document
Sound Recorder	With a computer microphone, make recordings of voice or music
Sticky Notes	Create short text notes that you can use to set reminders or create to-do lists for yourself
Windows Media Player	Play music, videos, recorded TV and show pictures

Work with a Window

Learning Outcomes
- Minimize, restore, and maximize a window
- Scroll a window
- Move a window

When you start a desktop app, its **window**, a frame displaying the app's tools, opens. In many apps, a blank file also opens so you can start creating a new document. For example, in Paint, a drawing app, a blank document opens so you can start drawing right away. All windows in the Windows 8 operating system have similar window elements. Once you can use a window in one app, you will know how to work with windows in many other apps. **CASE** ▸ *To become more familiar with the Windows 8 user interface, you explore elements in the Paint window.*

DETAILS

Many windows have the following common elements. Refer to FIGURE A-14:

- At the top of the window, you see a **title bar**, a colored strip that contains the name of the document and app you opened. This document has not been saved, so it has the temporary name "Untitled" and the app name is "Paint."

- On the right side of the title bar, the **Window control icons** let you control the app window. The **Minimize button** 📏 temporarily hides it, making it a button on the taskbar. The app is still running, but its window is hidden until you reopen it. The **Maximize button** 🔲 enlarges the window to fill the entire screen. If a window is already maximized, the Maximize button changes to the **Restore Down button** 🗗, which reduces it to the last nonmaximized size. Clicking the **Close button** ❌ closes the app.

- Many windows have a **scroll bar** on the right side and/or the bottom of the window. You click the scroll bar elements to show additional parts of your document. See **TABLE A-3** to learn the parts of a scroll bar.

- Just below the title bar, at the top of the Paint window, is the Ribbon, the strip that contains tabs. The Paint window has three tabs, the File tab, the Home tab, and the View tab. Tabs are divided into **groups** of command buttons. The Home tab has five groups: Clipboard, Image, Tools, Shapes, and Colors. Many apps also include **menus** that display words you click to show lists of commands, as well as **toolbars** containing buttons.

- The **Quick Access toolbar**, in the upper-left corner of the window, lets you quickly perform common actions such as saving a file.

STEPS

1. **Click the Paint window Minimize button** 📏
   The app is minimized to a program button with a gradient shading, indicating the app is still open. See **FIGURE A-15**. Taskbar buttons representing closed programs are not shaded.

2. **Click the taskbar button representing the Paint app** 🎨
   The app window reappears.

3. **Drag the gray scroll box down, notice the lower edge of the work area that appears, then click the Up scroll arrow** 🔼 **until you see the top edge of the work area**

4. **Point to the View tab with the tip of the mouse pointer, then click the View tab once**
   Clicking the View tab moved it in front of the Home tab. This tab has three groups, Zoom, Show or hide, and Display, containing buttons that let you change your view of the document window to work more easily.

5. **Click the Home tab, then click the Paint window Maximize button** 🔲
   The window fills the screen, and the Maximize button becomes the Restore Down button 🗗.

6. **Click the window's Restore Down button**
   The Paint window returns to its previous size on the screen.

FIGURE A-14: Typical app window elements

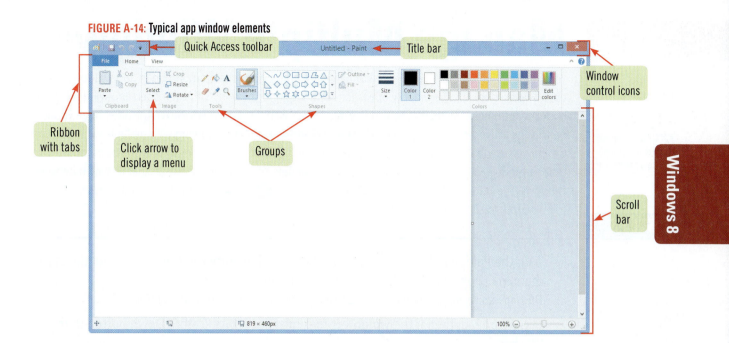

Quick Access toolbar

Title bar

Ribbon with tabs

Click arrow to display a menu

Groups

Window control icons

Scroll bar

FIGURE A-15: Taskbar on the desktop

Icons with solid backgrounds represent programs that are not open

Paint program button with gradient background indicates program is open

Your icons may differ

TABLE A-3: Parts of a scroll bar

name	looks like	use for
Scroll box	(Size may vary)	Drag to scroll quickly through a long document
Scroll arrows	∧ ∨	Click to scroll up, down, left, or right in small amounts
Shaded area	(Above, below, and to either side of scroll box)	Click to move up or down by one screen

© 2014 Cengage Learning

Using the Quick Access toolbar

On the left side of the title bar, the Quick Access toolbar lets you perform common tasks with just one click. The Save button saves the changes you have made to a document. The Undo button lets you reverse (undo) the last action you performed.

The Redo button reinstates the change you just undid. Use the Customize Quick Access Toolbar button to add other frequently used buttons to the toolbar, move the toolbar below the Ribbon, or hide the Ribbon.

Manage Multiple Windows

Learning Outcomes
- Open a second app
- Activate a window
- Resize, snap, and close a window

You can work with more than one desktop app at a time by switching among open app windows. If you open two or more apps, a window opens for each one. You can work with each open app window, going back and forth between them. The window in front is called the **active window**. Any other open window behind the active window is called an **inactive window**. For ease in working with multiple windows, you can move, arrange, make them smaller or larger, minimize, or restore them so they're not in the way. To resize a window, drag a window's edge, called its **border**. You can also use the taskbar to switch between windows. See **TABLE A-4** for a summary of taskbar actions. **CASE** ▶ *Keeping the Paint app open, you open the WordPad app and then work with both app windows.*

STEPS

1. **With the Paint window open, point to the lower-left corner of the screen until the Start thumbnail appears, click the Start thumbnail, then type word**

   The Apps screen appears, displaying apps that have "word" in them, such as WordPad.

2. **Click WordPad, then if the window is maximized, click its Restore Down button in the title bar**

   The WordPad window opens, as shown in **FIGURE A-16**. The WordPad window is in front, indicating that it is the active window. The Paint window is the inactive window. On the taskbar, the gradient backgrounds on the WordPad and Paint app buttons tell you both apps are open.

3. **Point to a blank part of the WordPad window title bar, then drag the WordPad window down slightly so you can see more of the Paint window**

4. **Click once on the Paint window's title bar**

   The Paint window is now the active window and appears in front of the WordPad window. You can make any window active by clicking it, or by clicking an app's icon in the taskbar.

5. **Point to the taskbar, then click the WordPad window button** 🖼️

   The WordPad window becomes active. When you open multiple windows on the desktop, you may need to resize windows so they don't get in the way of other open windows.

6. **Point to the lower-right corner of the WordPad window until the pointer becomes ⬨, then drag up and to the left about an inch to make the window smaller**

   You can also point to any edge of a window until you see the ⟷ or ↕ pointer and drag to make it larger or smaller in one direction only.

7. **Point to the WordPad window title bar, drag the window to the left side of the screen until the mouse pointer reaches the screen edge and you see a vertical line down the middle of the screen, then release the mouse button**

   The WordPad window instantly fills the left side of the screen. This is called the **Snap feature**.

8. **Drag the Paint window title bar to the right side of the screen and release the mouse button**

   The Paint window fills the right side of the screen. Snapping makes it easy to view the contents of two windows at the same time. See **FIGURE A-17**.

9. **Click the WordPad window Close button** ❌ **, click Don't Save if prompted to save changes, then click the Maximize button** ⬜ **in the Paint window's title bar**

   The WordPad app closes, so you can no longer use its tools unless you start it again. The Paint app window remains open.

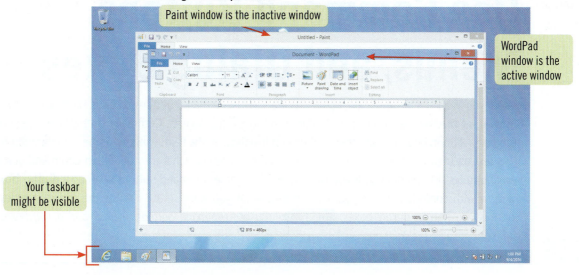

FIGURE A-16: Working with multiple windows

Paint window is the inactive window

WordPad window is the active window

Your taskbar might be visible

FIGURE A-17: WordPad and Paint windows snapped to each side of the screen

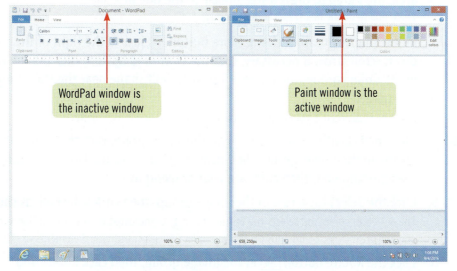

WordPad window is the inactive window

Paint window is the active window

TABLE A-4: Using the Desktop taskbar

to	do this
Add buttons to taskbar	Open an app, right-click its icon on the task bar, then click Pin this program to taskbar
Change order of taskbar buttons	Drag any icon to a new taskbar location
See a list of recent documents opened in a taskbar app	Right-click taskbar app button
Close a document using the taskbar	Point to taskbar button, point to document image, then click its Close button
Minimize all open windows	Click Show desktop button to the right of taskbar date and time
Redisplay all minimized windows	Click Show desktop button to the right of taskbar date and time
See preview of documents in taskbar	Point to taskbar button for open app

© 2014 Cengage Learning

Learning
Outcomes
• Use a command
  button and
  a menu
• Work in a
  dialog box

Use Command Buttons, Menus, and Dialog Boxes

When you work in an app, you communicate using command buttons, menus, and dialog boxes. **Command buttons** let you issue instructions to modify app objects. Command buttons are often organized on a Ribbon into tabs, and then into groups like those in the Paint window. Some command buttons have text on them, and others show only an icon that represents what they do. Other command buttons reveal **menus**, lists of commands you can choose. And some command buttons open up a **dialog box**, a window with controls that lets you tell Windows what you want. **TABLE A-5** lists the common types of controls you find in dialog boxes. **CASE** *You use command buttons, menus, and dialog boxes to communicate with the Paint app.*

STEPS

1. **In the Shapes group, click the More button ⤓ just to the right of the shapes, then click the Five-point star button ☆**

2. **Click the Gold button in the Colors group, move the pointer over the white drawing area, then drag to draw a star similar to the one in FIGURE A-18**
   The white drawing area is called the **canvas.**

3. **In the Shapes group, click the More button ⤓ just to the right of the shapes, click the down scroll arrow if necessary, click the Lightning button, click the Indigo color button in the Colors group, then drag a lightning bolt shape near the star, using FIGURE A-18 as a guide**
   Don't be concerned if your object isn't exactly like the one in the figure.

4. **Click the Fill with color button 🖌 in the Tools group, click the Light turquoise color button in the Colors group, click inside the star, click the Lime color button, click inside the lightning bolt, then compare your drawing to FIGURE A-18**

5. **Click the Select list arrow in the Image group, then click Select all, as shown in FIGURE A-19**
   The Select all command selects the entire drawing, as indicated by the dotted line surrounding the white drawing area. Other commands on this menu let you select individual elements or change your selection.

6. **Click the Rotate button 🔄 in the Image group, then click Rotate 180°**
   You often need to use multiple commands to perform an action—in this case, you used one command to select the item you wanted to work with, and the next command rotated the item.

7. **Click the File tab, then click Print**
   The Print dialog box opens, as shown in **FIGURE A-20**. This dialog box lets you choose a printer, specify which part of your document or drawing you want to print, and choose how many copies you want to print. The **default**, or automatically selected, number of copies is 1, which is what you want.

8. **Click Print, or, if you prefer not to print, click Cancel**
   The drawing prints on your printer. You decide to close the app without saving your drawing.

9. **Click the File tab, click Exit, then click Don't Save**
   You closed the file without saving your changes, then exited the app. Most apps include a command for closing a document without exiting the program. However, Paint allows you to open only one document at a time, so it does not include a Close command.

FIGURE A-18: Star and lightning shapes filled with color

FIGURE A-19: Select menu options

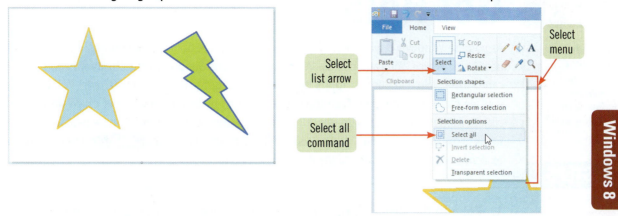

FIGURE A-20: Print dialog box

Print dialog box with General tab, Select Printer area showing Add Printer, Canon MG5300 series (highlighted), Dell 3130cn Color Laser, Fax, Microsoft XPS Document. Status: Ready, Print to file, Preferences, Location:, Comment:, Find Printer..., Page Range (All, Selection, Current Page, Pages:), Number of copies: 1, Collate. Print, Cancel, Apply buttons.

Your default printer will be highlighted here

Specify number of copies to print here

TABLE A-5: Common dialog box controls

element	example	description
Text box	132	A box in which you type text or numbers
Spin box	1	A box with up and down arrows; you can click arrows or type to increase or decrease value
Option button	○ ◉	A small circle you click to select the option; only one in a set can be selected at once
Check box	☑ ☐	A small box that turns an option on when checked or off when unchecked; more than one can be selected at once
List box		A box that lets you select from a list of options
Command button	Save	A button you click to issue a command

© 2014 Cengage Learning

Get Help

Learning Outcomes
- Open the Help app
- Explore and search for help topics

As you use Windows 8, you might feel ready to learn more about it, or you might have a problem and need some advice. You can open the Windows 8 Help and Support to find the information you need. You can browse Help and Support topics by clicking a category, such as "Get started." Within this category, you see more specific topics. Each topic is represented by blue or purple text called **links** that you can click to learn more. You can also search Help and Support by typing one or more descriptive words called **keywords**, such as "taskbar," to find topics related to your keywords. **CASE** *You use Windows 8 help to learn more about Windows and the WordPad accessory.*

STEPS

TROUBLE

If your computer is not connected to the Internet, you will see an alert at the top of the Help window. You can continue with the steps in this lesson.

1. **Point to the lower-left corner of the screen, click the Start thumbnail once to display the Start screen, then type** help

   The Help and Support app is listed in the found items area.

2. **Click** Help and Support, **then click the window's Maximize button** 🔲 **if the window does not fill the screen**

   The Windows Help and Support window opens and is maximized, as shown in **FIGURE A-21**. A search box appears near the top of the window. Three topics appear in blue boxes. Below them, you see text briefly describing each topic.

QUICK TIP

If you are using a mouse with a scroll wheel, you can use the scroll wheel to scroll up and down. If you are using a touch pad, the right side of your touch pad might let you scroll.

3. **Position the** hand pointer 👆 **over** Get Started, **then click once**

   Several categories of Get Started topics appear.

4. **Click** Touch: swipe, tap, and beyond

   Help and Support information appears.

5. **Drag the** scroll box **down to view text and graphics about touch, then drag the** scroll box **back to the top of the scroll bar**

   You decide to learn more about the taskbar.

QUICK TIP

Search text is not case sensitive. If you are searching for help on WordPad, typing "wordpad", "Wordpad", or "WordPad" finds the same results.

6. **Click in the Search text box near the top of the window, type** taskbar, **click the** Search **button** 🔍, **then scroll down and read the topics and descriptions**

   A list of links related to using the taskbar appears. See **FIGURE A-22**.

7. **Click** How to use the taskbar, **scroll down if necessary, then click** To move the taskbar

8. **Read the information, clicking any other** links **that interest you**

9. **When you are finished, click the** Close button ❌ **in the upper-right corner of the Windows Help and Support window**

   The Windows Help and Support window closes.

Finding other ways to get help

The Windows Help and Support Home window includes a variety of resources for learning more about Windows 8 and solving problems. In the More to Explore section, click the **Windows website** link to locate **blogs** (Web logs, which are personal commentaries), downloads, video tours, and other current Windows 8 resources. You'll also find FAQs (Frequently Asked Questions) about current Windows topics. Click the **Microsoft Community website** (formerly called the **Microsoft Answers website**) link to find **forums**, electronic gathering places where anyone can read and add questions and answers on computer issues.

FIGURE A-21: Windows Help and Support window

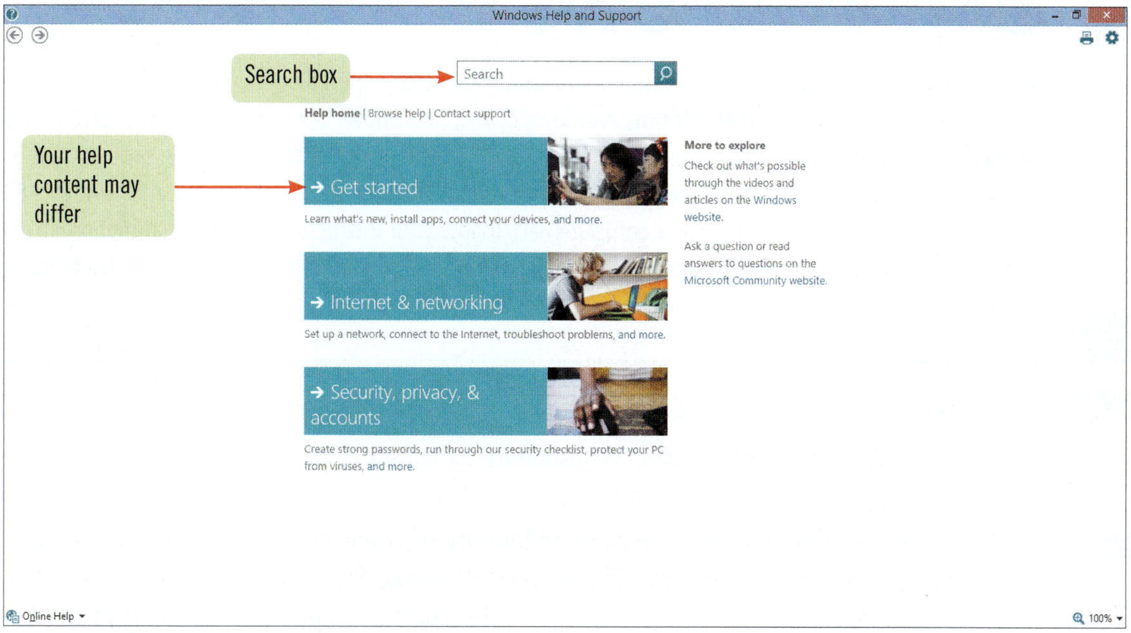

Search box → Search

Your help content may differ →

Help home | Browse help | Contact support

→ Get started
Learn what's new, install apps, connect your devices, and more.

→ Internet & networking
Set up a network, connect to the Internet, troubleshoot problems, and more.

→ Security, privacy, & accounts
Create strong passwords, run through our security checklist, protect your PC from viruses, and more.

More to explore
Check out what's possible through the videos and articles on the Windows website.

Ask a question or read answers to questions on the Microsoft Community website.

Online Help ▾   100% ▾

FIGURE A-22: Getting help on the term "taskbar"

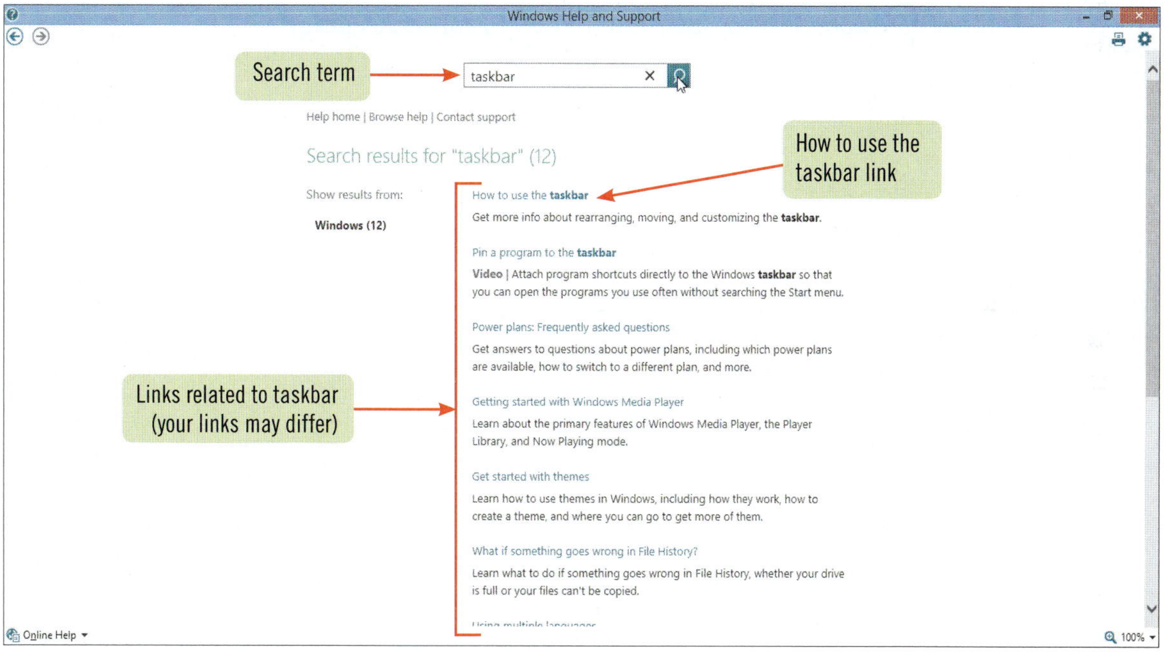

Windows Help and Support

Search term → taskbar   ✕

Help home | Browse help | Contact support

Search results for "taskbar" (12)

Show results from:

Windows (12)

How to use the **taskbar**
Get more info about rearranging, moving, and customizing the **taskbar**.

How to use the taskbar link →

Pin a program to the **taskbar**
Video | Attach program shortcuts directly to the Windows **taskbar** so that you can open the programs you use often without searching the Start menu.

Power plans: Frequently asked questions
Get answers to questions about power plans, including which power plans are available, how to switch to a different plan, and more.

Links related to taskbar (your links may differ) →

Getting started with Windows Media Player
Learn about the primary features of Windows Media Player, the Player Library, and Now Playing mode.

Get started with themes
Learn how to use themes in Windows, including how they work, how to create a theme, and where you can go to get more of them.

What if something goes wrong in File History?
Learn what to do if something goes wrong in File History, whether your drive is full or your files can't be copied.

Using multiple languages

Online Help ▾   100% ▾

Using right-clicking

For some actions, you click items using the right mouse button, known as **right-clicking**. You can right-click almost any icon on your desktop to open a shortcut menu. A **shortcut menu** lists common commands for an object, such as emptying the Recycle Bin. The shortcut menu commands depend on the object you right-click. For example, **FIGURE A-23** shows the shortcut menu that appears if you right-click the Recycle Bin. Then you click (with the left mouse button) a shortcut menu command to issue that command.

FIGURE A-23: Shortcut menu

Open
Pin to Start
Empty Recycle Bin
Create shortcut
Rename
Properties

Getting Started with Windows 8   **Windows 49**

Exit Windows 8

When you finish working on your computer, you should close any open files, exit any open apps, close any open windows, and exit (or **shut down**) Windows 8. **TABLE A-6** shows options for ending your Windows 8 sessions. Whichever option you choose, it's important to shut down your computer in an orderly way. If you turn off or unplug the computer while Windows 8 is running, you could lose data or damage Windows 8 and your computer. If you are working in a computer lab, follow your instructor's directions and your lab's policies for ending your Windows 8 session. **CASE** ▶ *You have examined the basic ways you can use Windows 8, so you are ready to end your Windows 8 session.*

STEPS

1. Press ⊞ [C] to display the Charms bar

2. Click **Settings**, then click **Power**, as shown in **FIGURE A-24**

   The Power button menu lists shut down options.

QUICK TIP

If you are using a Windows 8 tablet, press the lock button on your tablet to bring up the lock screen, swipe the lock screen, then click the shutdown button to power off your computer.

3. **If you are working in a computer lab, follow the instructions provided by your instructor or technical support person for ending your Windows 8 session; if you are working on your own computer, click Shut down or the option you prefer for ending your Windows 8 session**

4. **After you shut down your computer, you may also need to turn off your monitor and other hardware devices, such as a printer, to conserve energy**

Installing updates when you exit Windows

Sometimes, after you shut down your machine, you might find that your machine does not shut down immediately. Instead, Windows might install software updates. If you see an option on your Power menu that lets you update, you can select it to update your software. A window indicating that updates are being installed, do not unplug or press the power switch to turn off your machine. Let the updates install completely. After the updates are installed, your computer will shut down, as you originally requested.

FIGURE A-24: Shutting down your computer

Shut-down options

Power button

TABLE A-6: Power options

option	description
Sleep	Puts computer in a low-power state while keeping any open apps open so you can return immediately to where you left off
Shut down	Closes any open apps and completely turns off the computer
Restart	Closes any open apps, shuts down the computer, then restarts it

Practice

Concepts Review

Label the elements of the Windows 8 window shown in FIGURE A-25.

FIGURE A-25

Match each term with the statement that best describes it.

6. **Accessory**
7. **Keyword**
8. **Windows 8 UI**
9. **Active window**
10. **Password**
11. **Operating system**
12. **App**

a. A sequence of numbers and letters you enter to access a secure user account
b. The window in front of other windows
c. An application program
d. Name for the Windows 8 user interface
e. An application program that comes with Windows 8
f. Descriptive word you use to search Windows Help and Support
g. A program necessary to run your computer

Select the best answer from the list of choices.

13. **You use the Maximize button to:**
    a. Scroll down a window.
    b. Restore a window to a previous size.
    c. Temporarily hide a window.
    d. Expand a window to fill the entire screen.

14. **Which of the following is not a Windows accessory?**
    a. Sticky Notes
    b. Windows 8
    c. Sound Recorder
    d. Paint

15. **Which button do you click to reduce an open window to a button on the taskbar?**
    a. Close button
    b. Minimize button
    c. Restore Down button
    d. Maximize button

16. **The screen controls that let you interact with an operating system are called its:**
    a. Accessories.
    c. User interface.
    b. Application program.
    d. Taskbar.

17. **Which type of program runs your computer and lets you use it?**
    a. App.
    c. Accessory.
    b. Traditional app.
    d. Operating system.

18. **Which Windows 8 feature lets you find and share information, change your machine settings, and turn off your computer?**
    a. Charms bar.
    c. Application program.
    b. Operating system.
    d. Accessory program.

19. **What part of a window shows the name of an open app?**
    a. Scroll bar.
    c. Quick Access toolbar.
    b. Title bar.
    d. Ribbon.

Skills Review

1. **Start Windows 8.**
   a. If your computer and monitor are not running, press your computer's and (if necessary) your monitor's power buttons.
   b. If necessary, click the user name that represents your user account.
   c. Enter your password, using correct uppercase and lowercase letters.

2. **Navigate the Start screen and desktop.**
   a. Examine the Windows 8 Start screen, scroll to the right so you can display any hidden apps, then display the Charms bar.
   b. Display the Windows 8 desktop, and then display the taskbar.

3. **Point, click, and drag.**
   a. Use pointing and clicking to go to the Start screen, then return to the desktop.
   b. On the Windows 8 desktop, use clicking to select the Recycle Bin.
   c. Use pointing to display the ScreenTip for Internet Explorer in the taskbar, and then display the ScreenTips for any other icons on the taskbar.
   d. Use double-clicking to open the Recycle Bin window, then close it.
   e. Drag the Recycle Bin to the lower-right corner of the screen, then drag it back to the upper-left corner.
   f. Click the Date and Time area to display the calendar and clock, then click it again to close it.

4. **Start an app.**
   a. Return to the Start screen, then use the Apps bar to display all the apps on your computer.
   b. Open the Windows 8 accessory of your choice, then close it. (*Hint:* To close, drag from the top of the window all the way to the bottom.)
   c. Scroll if necessary to display the Windows accessories.
   d. Open the WordPad accessory, then if the window fills the screen, restore it down.

5. **Manage a window.**
   a. Minimize the WordPad window.
   b. Redisplay the window using a taskbar button.
   c. In the WordPad window, click the File tab on the Ribbon, then click the About WordPad command.
   d. Read the contents of the window, then close the About WordPad dialog box by clicking OK.
   e. Maximize the WordPad window, then restore it down.
   f. Display the View tab in the WordPad window.

6. **Manage multiple windows.**
   a. Leaving WordPad open, go to the Start screen and use typing to locate the Paint app, open Paint, then restore down the Paint window if necessary.

Skills Review (continued)

b. Make the WordPad window the active window.

c. Make the Paint window the active window.

d. Minimize the Paint window.

e. Drag the WordPad window so it's in the middle of the screen.

f. Redisplay the Paint window.

g. Drag the Paint window so it automatically fills the right side of the screen.

h. Close the WordPad window, maximize the Paint window, then restore down the Paint window.

7. Use command buttons, menus, and dialog boxes.

a. In the Paint window, draw a red right arrow shape, similar to the one shown in **FIGURE A-26**.

b. Use the Fill with color button to fill the arrow with a light turquoise color.

FIGURE A-26

c. Draw an indigo rectangle to the right of the arrow shape, using the figure as a guide.

d. Use the Fill with color button to fill the blue rectangle with a lime color.

e. Fill the drawing background with lavender as shown in the figure.

f. Use the Select list arrow and menu to select the entire drawing, then use the Rotate command to rotate the drawing 180°.

g. If you wish, print a copy of the picture, then close the Paint app without saving the drawing.

8. Get help.

a. Start the Help and Support app, then maximize the window if it's not already maximized.

b. Open the Get started topic.

c. Open the Mouse and keyboard: What's new topic, then read the Help information on that topic.

d. In the Search Help text box, search for help about user accounts.

e. Find the link that describes how to create a user account, then click it.

f. Read the topic, clicking links as necessary, then close the Windows Help and Support window.

9. Exit Windows 8.

a. Shut down your computer using the Shut down command or the preferred command for your work or school setting.

b. Turn off your monitor if necessary.

Independent Challenge 1

You work for Will's Percussion, a Maine manufacturer of drums and drumsticks. The company ships percussion instruments and supplies to music stores and musicians in the United States and Canada. The owner, Will, wants to know an easy way for his employees to learn about the new features of Windows 8, and he has asked you to help.

a. Start your computer, log on to Windows 8 if necessary, then open Windows Help and Support.

b. Search Help for the text **what's new**.

c. Click the Get to know Windows 8 link.

d. Scroll the results window to see its contents, then scroll back to the top.

e. Using pencil and paper, or the WordPad app if you wish, write a short memo to Will summarizing, in your own words, three important new features in Windows 8. If you used WordPad to write the memo, use the Print button to print the document, then use the Exit command on the File tab to close WordPad without saving your changes to the document.

f. Close the Windows Help and Support window, then exit Windows and shut down.

Independent Challenge 2

You are the new manager for Katharine Anne's Designs, a business that supplies floral arrangements to New York businesses. The company maintains four delivery vans that supply flowers to various locations. Katharine asks you to investigate how the Windows 8 Calculator accessory can help her company be a responsible energy consumer.

a. Start your computer, log on to Windows 8 if necessary, then open the Windows 8 accessory called Calculator.

b. Click to enter the number 87 on the Calculator.

c. Click the division sign (/) button.

d. Click the number 2.

e. Click the equals sign button (=), and write down the result shown in the Calculator window. (*Hint:* The result should be 43.5.) See **FIGURE A-27**.

f. Click the Help menu in the Calculator window, then click View Help. Locate the Calculator: Frequently asked questions topic, and scroll down to locate information on how to calculate fuel economy. Follow the instructions, and perform at least one calculation of fuel economy.

g. Start WordPad, write a short memo about how Calculator can help you calculate fuel consumption, print the document using the Print command on the File tab, then exit WordPad without saving.

h. Close the Help window.

i. Close the Calculator, then exit Windows.

FIGURE A-27

Independent Challenge 3

You are the office manager for Eric's Pet Shipping, a service business in Seattle, Washington, that specializes in air shipping of cats and dogs across the United States and Canada. It's important to know the temperature in the destination city, so the animals won't be in danger from extreme temperatures when they are unloaded from the aircraft. Eric has asked you to find a way to easily monitor temperatures in destination cities. You decide to use a Windows app so you can see current temperatures in Celsius on your desktop. (*Note: To complete the steps below, your computer must be connected to the Internet.*)

a. Start your computer and sign in to Windows 8 if necessary, then at the Start screen, click the Weather app.

b. If multiple locations appear, click one of your choice.

c. Right-click the sky area above the weather information, then in the bar at the top of the screen, click Places.

d. Click the plus sign, click in the Enter Location text box if necessary, then type **Vancouver**.

e. Click Vancouver, British Columbia, Canada, in the drop-down list. Vancouver, Canada, is added to your Places Favorites.

f. Add another location that interests you.

g. Close the apps and return to the Start screen.

h. Open WordPad, write Eric a memo outlining how you can use the Windows Weather app to help keep pets safe, print the memo if you wish, close WordPad, then exit Windows.

Independent Challenge 4: Explore

As a professional photographer, you often evaluate pictures. You decide to explore the Windows Photo app so you can access pictures from various online sources. (*Note: To complete the steps below, your computer must be connected to the Internet.*)

a. Start your computer and sign in to Windows 8 if necessary, then click to open the Photos app.

b. Explore any picture that may have been downloaded from your Windows SkyDrive account, Facebook, or Flickr. (*Note:* You might need to sign into your Microsoft account in order to access some locations.)

c. Right-click any area of the Photo app screen, then explore what this allows you to do.

d. Add three pictures to your Pictures library.

e. Click OK.

Visual Workshop

Using the skills you've learned in this unit, open and arrange elements on your screen so it looks similar to **FIGURE A-28** (the date and time will differ). Note the position of the Recycle Bin, the size and location of the Paint window and the Help and Support window, and the presence of the Charms bar. Open WordPad and write a paragraph summarizing how you used pointing, clicking, and dragging to make your screen look like **FIGURE A-28**. Print your work if you wish, exit WordPad without saving changes to the document, then shut down Windows.

FIGURE A-28

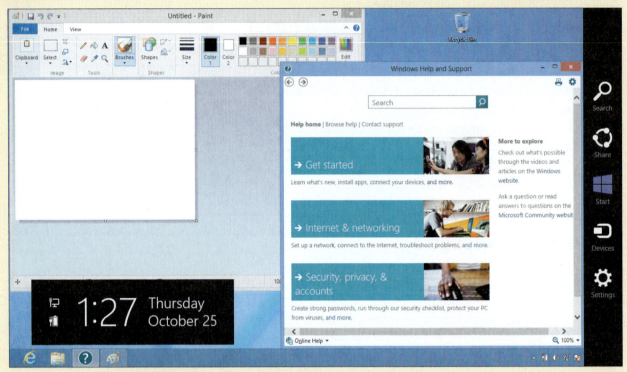

Understanding File Management

CASE ▶ Now that you are familiar with the Windows 8 operating system, your new employer has asked you to become familiar with **file management**, or how to create, save, locate and delete the files you create with Windows application programs. You begin by reviewing how files are organized on your computer, and then begin working with files you create in the WordPad app.

Unit Objectives

After completing this unit, you will be able to:

- Understand files and folders
- Create and save a file
- Explore the files and folders on your computer
- Change file and folder views

- Open, edit, and save files
- Copy files
- Move and rename files
- Search for files, folders, and programs
- Delete and restore files

Files You Will Need

No files needed.

Understand Files and Folders

Learning Outcomes
- Analyze a file hierarchy
- Examine files and folders

DETAILS

As you work with computer programs, you create and save files, such as letters, drawings, or budgets. When you save files, you usually save them inside folders to help keep them organized. The files and folders on your computer are organized in a **file hierarchy**, a system that arranges files and folders in different levels, like the branches of a tree. **FIGURE B-1** shows a sample file hierarchy. **CASE** *You decide to use folders and files to organize the information on your computer.*

Use the following guidelines as you organize files using your computer's file hierarchy:

- ### Use folders and subfolders to organize files

  As you work with your computer, you can add folders to your hierarchy and name them to help you organize your work. As you've learned, folders are storage areas in which you can group related files. You should give folders unique names that help you easily identify them. You can also create **subfolders**, which are folders that are inside other folders. Windows 8 comes with several existing folders, such as My Documents, My Music, My Pictures, and My Videos, that you can use as a starting point.

- ### View and manage files in File Explorer

  You can view and manage your computer contents using a built-in program called **File Explorer**, shown in **FIGURE B-2**. A File Explorer window is divided into **panes**, or sections. The **Navigation pane** on the left side of the window shows the folder structure on your computer. When you click a folder in the Navigation pane, you see its contents in the **File list** on the right side of the window. To open File Explorer from the desktop, click the File Explorer button 📁 on the taskbar. To open it from the Start screen, begin typing File Explorer, and when you see the program name on the Apps screen, press [Enter].

QUICK TIP

The program name "File Explorer" doesn't appear in the title bar. Instead, you'll see the current folder name.

- ### Understand file addresses

  A window also contains an **Address bar**, an area just below the Ribbon that shows the address, or location, of the files that appear in the File list. An **address** is a sequence of folder names, separated by the ▶ symbol, which describes a file's location in the file hierarchy. An address shows the folder with the highest hierarchy level on the left and steps through each hierarchy level toward the right; this is sometimes called a **path**. For example, the My Documents folder might contain subfolders named Work and Personal. If you clicked the Personal folder in the File list, the Address bar would show My Documents ▶ Personal. Each location between the ▶ symbols represents a level in the file hierarchy. The same path appears in the window's title bar, but instead of ▶ between the hierarchy levels, you see the backslash symbol (\ ). If you see a file path written out, you'll most likely see it with backslashes. For example, in Figure B-1, if you wanted to write the path to the Honolulu Sunset photo file, you would write My Documents\Quest Specialty Travel\Photos\Honolulu Sunset.jpg. File addresses might look complicated if they may have many levels, but they are helpful because they always describe the exact location of a file or folder in a file hierarchy.

QUICK TIP

Remember that in the Address bar you single-click a folder or subfolder to show its contents, but in the File list you double-click it.

- ### Navigate up and down using the Address bar and File list

  You can use the Address bar and the File list to move up or down in the hierarchy one or more levels at a time. To **navigate up** in your computer's hierarchy, you can click a folder or subfolder name to the left of the current folder name in the Address bar. For example, in **FIGURE B-2**, you can move up in the hierarchy one level by clicking once on Users in the Address bar. Then the File list would show the subfolders and files inside the Users folder. To **navigate down** in the hierarchy, double-click a subfolder in the File list. The path in the Address bar then shows the path to that subfolder.

- ### Navigate up and down using the Navigation pane

  You can also use the Navigation pane to navigate among folders. Move the mouse pointer over the Navigation pane, then click the small triangles to the left of a folder name to show ▷ or hide ◢ the folder's contents under the folder name. Subfolders appear indented under the folders that contain them, showing that they are inside that folder.

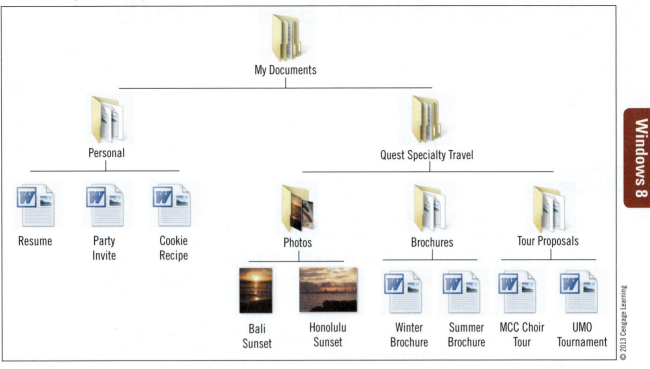

FIGURE B-2: File Explorer window

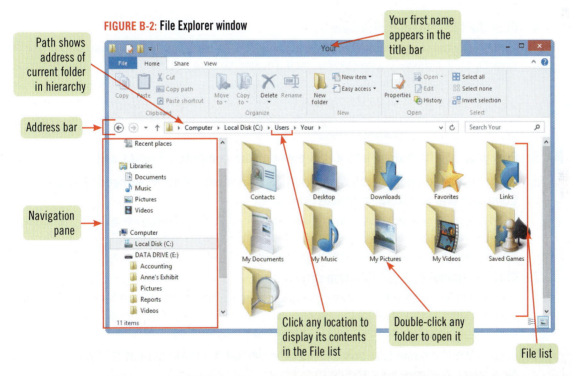

Your first name appears in the title bar

Path shows address of current folder in hierarchy

Address bar

Navigation pane

Click any location to display its contents in the File list

Double-click any folder to open it

File list

Plan your file organization

As you manage your files, you should plan how you want to organize them. First, identify the types of files you work with, such as images, music, and documents. Think about the content, such as personal, business, clients, or projects. Then think of a folder organization that will help you find them later. For example, you can use subfolders in the My Pictures folder to separate family photos from business photos or to group them by location or by month. In the My Documents folder, you might group personal files in one subfolder and business files in another subfolder. Then create additional subfolders to further separate sets of files. You can always move files among folders and rename folders. You should periodically reevaluate your folder structure to make sure it continues to meet your needs.

Understanding File Management

Create and Save a File

Learning Outcomes
- Start WordPad
- Create a file
- Save a file

After you start a program and create a new file, the file exists only in your computer's **random access memory (RAM)**, a temporary storage location. RAM contains information only when your computer is on. When you turn off your computer, it automatically clears the contents of RAM. So you need to save a new file onto a storage device that permanently stores the file so you can open, change, and use it later. One important storage device is your computer's hard drive built into your computer. Another popular option is a **USB flash drive**, a small, portable storage device. **CASE** *You create a document, then save it.*

STEPS

1. **At the Start screen, type word**

   Available apps with "word" in their names are listed. See **FIGURE B-3**.

2. **Click WordPad, then maximize the WordPad window if necessary**

   Near the top of the WordPad window you see the Ribbon containing command buttons, similar to those you used in Paint in Unit A. The Home tab appears in front. A new, blank document appears in the document window. The blinking insertion point shows you where the next character you type will appear.

   TROUBLE
   If you make a typing mistake, press [Backspace] to delete the character to the left of the insertion point.

3. **Type New Tours, then press [Enter] twice, type Thailand, press [Enter], type New Zealand, press [Enter], type Canada, press [Enter] twice, then type your name**
   See **FIGURE B-4**.

4. **Click the File tab, then click Save**

   The first time you save a file using the Save button, the Save As dialog box opens. You use this dialog box to name the file and choose a storage location for it. The Save As dialog box has many of the same elements as a File Explorer window, including an Address bar, a Navigation pane, and a File list. Below the Address bar, the **toolbar** contains command buttons you can click to perform actions. In the Address bar, you can see the Documents library (which includes the My Documents folder) is the **default**, or automatically selected, storage location. But you can easily change it.

   QUICK TIP
   On a laptop computer, the USB port is on the left or right side of your computer.

5. **Plug your USB flash drive into a USB port on your computer, if necessary**

   TROUBLE
   If you don't have a USB flash drive, you can save the document in the My Documents folder or ask your instructor which storage location is best.

6. **In the Navigation pane scroll bar, click the down scroll arrow ⌄ as needed to see Computer and any storage devices listed under it**

   Under Computer, you see the storage locations available on your computer, such as Local Disk (C:) (your hard drive) and Removable Disk (F:) (your USB drive name and letter might differ). These storage locations are like folders in that you can open them and store files in them.

7. **Click the name for your USB flash drive**

   The files and folders on your USB drive, if any, appear in the File list. The Address bar shows the location where the file will be saved, which is now Computer ▸ Removable Disk (F:) (or the name of your drive). You need to give your document a meaningful name so you can find it later.

   TROUBLE
   If your Save As dialog box does not show the .rtf file extension, click Cancel, open File Explorer, click the View tab, then in the Show/hide group, click the File name extensions check box to select it.

8. **Click in the File name text box to select the default name Document.rtf, type New Tours, compare your screen to FIGURE B-5, then click Save**

   The document is saved as a file on your USB flash drive. The filename New Tours.rtf appears in the title bar. The ".rtf" at the end of the filename is the file extension that Windows 8 added automatically. A **file extension** is a three- or four-letter sequence, preceded by a period, which identifies a file to your computer, in this case **Rich Text Format**. The WordPad program creates files in RTF format.

9. **Click the Close button ✕ on the WordPad window**

   The WordPad program closes. Your New Tours document is now saved in the location you specified.

FIGURE B-3: Results list

Apps with "word" in their names are listed here (your list may differ)

Search pane

FIGURE B-4: New document in WordPad

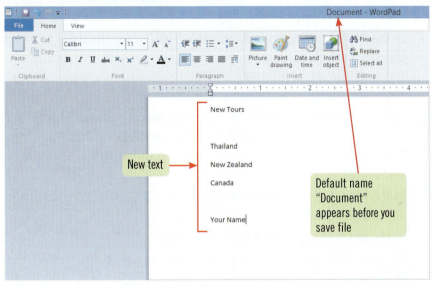

New text

Default name "Document" appears before you save file

FIGURE B-5: Save As dialog box

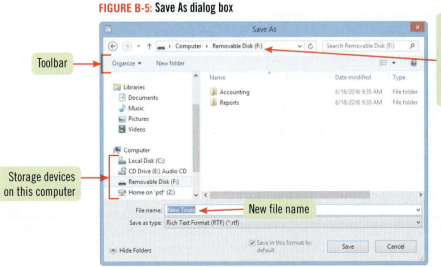

Toolbar

Storage devices on this computer

New file name

After you click Save, your New Tours.rtf document will be saved at this address (your drive name and letter will differ)

Explore the Files and Folders on Your Computer

In a File Explorer window, you can navigate through your computer contents using the File list, the Address bar, and the Navigation pane. Examining your computer and its existing folder and file structure helps you decide where to save files as you work with Windows 8 apps. **CASE** ▶ *In preparation for organizing documents at your new job, you look at the files and folders on your computer.*

STEPS

1. **If you see the Start screen, click the Desktop tile to display the Windows 8 desktop**

2. **On the taskbar, click the File Explorer button ▢, then in the File Explorer Navigation pane, click Computer**

   TROUBLE
   If you don't see the colored bar, click the View tab, then click Tiles in the Layout group.

   Your computer's storage devices appear in a window, as shown in **FIGURE B-6**. These include hard drives; devices with removable storage, such as CD and DVD drives or USB flash drives; portable devices such as personal digital assistants (PDAs); and any network storage locations. A colored bar shows you how much space has been taken up on your hard drive. You decide to move down a level in your computer's hierarchy and see what is on your USB flash drive.

3. **In the File list, double-click Removable Disk (F:) (or the drive name and letter for your USB flash drive)**

   TROUBLE
   If you do not have a USB flash drive, click the Documents library in the Navigation pane instead.

   You see the contents of your USB flash drive, including the New Tours.rtf file you saved in the last lesson. You decide to navigate one level up in the file hierarchy.

4. **In the Address bar, click Computer, or if Computer does not appear, click the far-left list arrow in the Address bar, then click Computer**

   You return to the Computer window showing your storage devices. You decide to look at the contents of your hard drive.

5. **In the File list, double-click Local Disk (C:)**

   The contents of your hard drive appear in the File list.

6. **In the File list, double-click the Users folder**

   The Users folder contains a subfolder for each user account on this computer. You might see a folder with your user account name on it. Each user's folder contains that person's documents. User folder names are the names that were used to log in when your computer was set up. When a user logs in, the computer allows that user access to the folder with the same user name. If you are using a computer with more than one user, you might not have permission to view other users' folders. There is also a Public folder that any user can open.

7. **Double-click the folder with your user name on it**

   Depending on how your computer is set up, this folder might be labeled with your name; however, if you are using a computer in a lab or a public location, your folder might be called Student or Computer User or something similar. You see a list of folders, such as My Documents, My Music, and others. See **FIGURE B-7**.

8. **Double-click My Documents in the File list**

   QUICK TIP
   In the Address bar, you can click ▶ to the right of a folder name to see a list of its subfolders; if the folder is open, its name appears in bold in the list.

   In the Address bar, the path to the My Documents folder is Computer ▶ Local Disk (C:) ▶ Users ▶ *Your User Name* ▶ My Documents.

9. **In the Navigation pane, click Computer**

   You once again see your computer's storage devices. You can also move up one level at a time in your file hierarchy by clicking the Up arrow ⬆ on the toolbar, or by pressing [Backspace] on your keyboard. See **TABLE B-1** for a summary of techniques for navigating through your computer's file hierarchy.

FIGURE B-6: Computer window showing storage devices

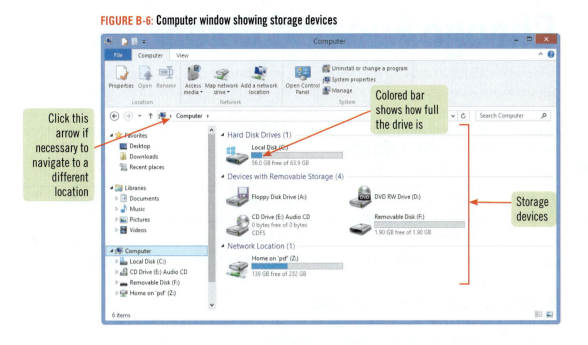

Click this arrow if necessary to navigate to a different location

Colored bar shows how full the drive is

Storage devices

FIGURE B-7: Your user name folder

Path to your user name folder contents

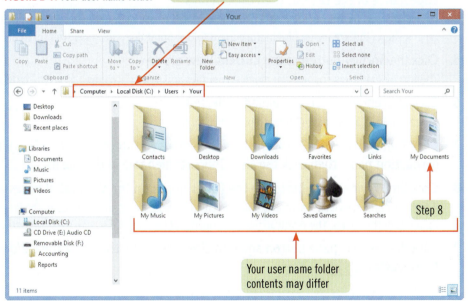

Step 8

Your user name folder contents may differ

TABLE B-1: Navigating your computer's file hierarchy

to do this	Navigation pane	Address bar	File list	keyboard
Move up in hierarchy	Click a drive or folder name	Click an item to the left of ▶ or Click the **Up to** arrow ⬆		Press **[Backspace]**
Move down in hierarchy	Click a drive or folder name that is indented from the left	Click an item to the right of ▶	Double-click a folder	Press ⬆ or ⬇ to select a folder, then press **[Enter]** to open the selected folder
Return to previously viewed location		Click the **Back to** button ⬅ or **Forward to** button ➡		

Change File and Folder Views

Learning
Outcomes
• View files as large
  icons
• Sort files
• Preview files

As you view your folders and files, you can customize your **view**, which is a set of appearance choices for files and folders. Changing your view does not affect the content of your files or folders, only the way they appear. You can choose from eight different **layouts** to display your folders and files as different sized icons, or as a list. You can also change the order in which the folders and files appear. You can also show a preview of a file in the window. **CASE** *You experiment with different views of your folders and files.*

STEPS

1. **In the File Explorer window's Navigation pane, click Local Disk (C:), in the File list double-click Users, then double-click the folder with your user name**

   You opened your user name folder, which is inside the Users folder.

2. **Click the View tab on the Ribbon, then click the More button ⤓ in the Layout group**

   The list of available layouts appears, as shown in **FIGURE B-8**.

3. **Click Extra large icons in the Layout list**

   In this view, the folder items appear as very large icons in the File list. This layout is especially helpful for image files, because you can see what the pictures are without opening each one.

QUICK TIP
You can scroll up and down in the Layout group to see views that are not currently visible.

4. **On the View tab, in the Layout list, point to the other layouts while watching the appearance of the File list, then click Details**

   In Details view, shown in **FIGURE B-9**, you can see each item's name, the date it was modified, and its file type. It shows the size of any files in the current folder, but it does not show sizes for folders.

5. **Click the Sort by button in the Current view group**

   The Sort by menu lets you **sort**, or reorder, your files and folders according to several criteria.

6. **Click Descending if it is not already selected**

   Now the folders are sorted in reverse alphabetical order.

QUICK TIP
Clicking Favorites in the Navigation pane displays folders you use frequently; to add a folder or location to Favorites, display it in the File list, then drag it to the Favorites list.

7. **Click Removable Disk (F:) (or the location where you store your Data Files) in the Navigation pane, then click the New Tours.rtf filename in the File list**

8. **Click the Preview pane button in the Panes group on the View tab if necessary**

   A preview of the selected New Tours.rtf file you created earlier in this unit appears in the Preview pane on the right side of the screen. The WordPad file is not open, but you can still see the file's contents. See **FIGURE B-10**.

9. **Click the Preview pane button again to close the pane, then click the window's Close button ✕**

Snapping Windows 8 apps

If your machine has a screen resolution of 1366 × 768 or higher, you can use snapping to view two Windows 8 apps side by side. Go to the Start screen and open the first app, then return to the Start screen and open the second app. Point to the upper-left corner of the screen until you can see a small square representing the first app, right-click the square, then click Snap left or Snap right. (Or you can drag the square to the right or left side of the screen.) One app then occupies one third of the screen and the other taking up two thirds of the screen. See **FIGURE B-11**.

FIGURE B-11: Using snapping to view Weather and SkyDrive apps

FIGURE B-8: Layout options for viewing folders and files

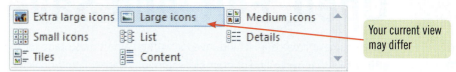

Your current view may differ

FIGURE B-9: Your user name folder contents in Details view

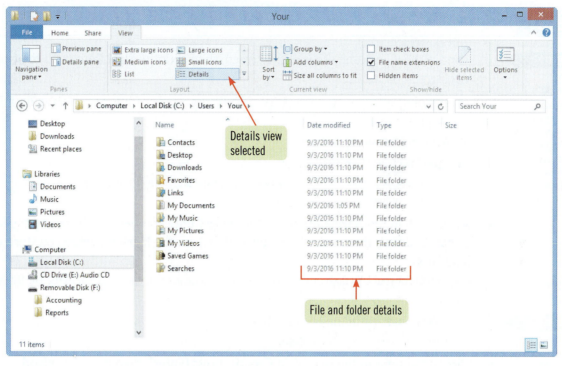

Details view selected

File and folder details

FIGURE B-10: Preview of selected New Tours.rtf file

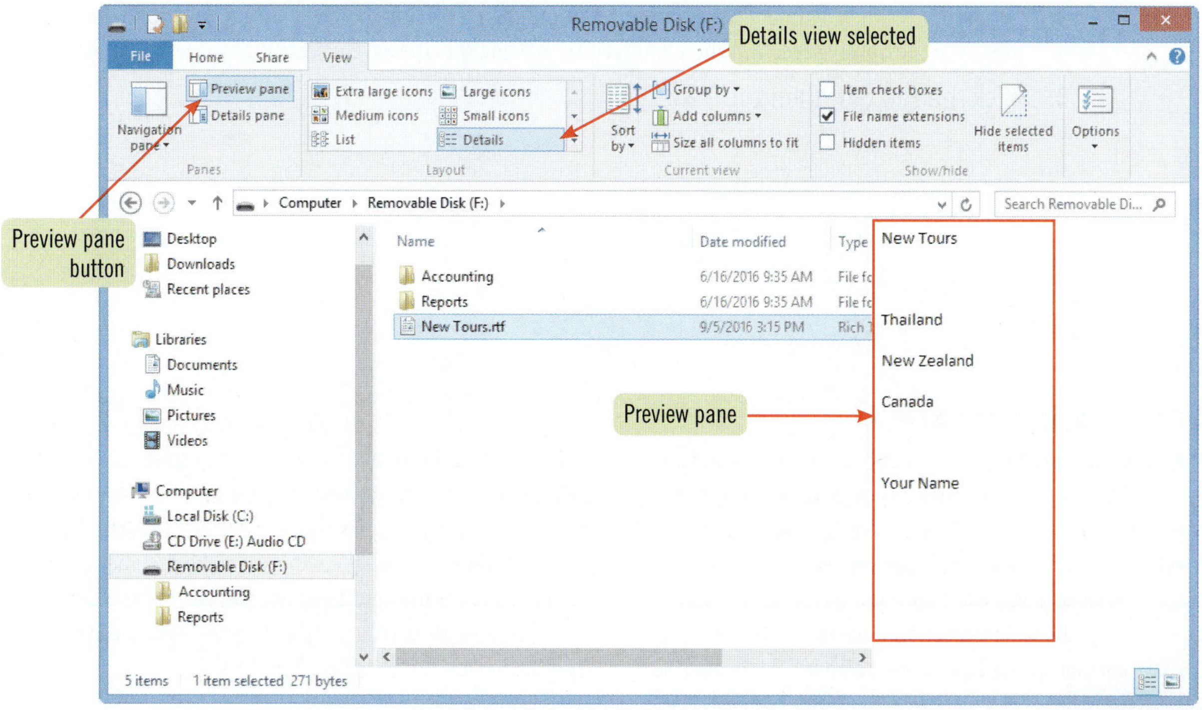

Details view selected

Preview pane button

Preview pane

Open, Edit, and Save Files

Once you have created a file and saved it with a name to a storage location, you can easily open it and **edit** (make changes to) it. For example, you might want to add or delete text or add a picture. Then you save the file again so the file contains your latest changes. Usually you save a file with the same filename and in the same location as the original, which replaces the existing file with the most up-to-date version. To save a file you have changed, you use the Save command. **CASE** ▶ *You need to complete the list of new tours, so you need to open the new Tours file you created earlier.*

STEPS

1. **Point to the lower-left corner of the screen, then click the Start thumbnail to display the Start screen**

2. **Begin typing wordpad, then click the WordPad program if it is not selected or, if it is, simply press [Enter]**
   The WordPad program opens on the desktop.

3. **Click the File tab, then click Open**
   The Open dialog box opens. It contains a Navigation pane and a File list like the Save As dialog box and the File Explorer window.

4. **Scroll down in the Navigation pane if necessary until you see Computer and the list of computer drives, then click Removable Disk (F:) (or the location where you store your Data Files)**
   The contents of your USB flash drive (or the file storage location you chose) appear in the File list, as shown in **FIGURE B-12**.

5. **Click New Tours.rtf in the File list, then click Open**
   The document you created earlier opens.

6. **Click to the right of the last "a" in Canada, press [Enter], then type Greenland**
   The edited document includes the text you just typed. See **FIGURE B-13**.

7. **Click the File tab, then click Save, as shown in FIGURE B-14**
   WordPad saves the document with your most recent changes, using the filename and location you specified when you previously saved it. When you save an existing file, the Save As dialog box does not open.

8. **Click the File tab, then click Exit**

Comparing Save and Save As

The WordPad menu has two save command options—Save and Save As. The first time you save a file, the Save As dialog box opens (whether you choose Save or Save As). Here you can select the drive and folder where you want to save the file and enter its filename. If you edit a previously saved file, you can save the file to the same location with the same filename using the Save command. The Save command updates the stored file using the same location and filename without opening the Save As dialog box. In some situations, you might want to save a copy of the existing document using a different filename or in a different storage location. To do this, open the document, click the Save As command on the File tab, navigate to the location where you want to save the copy if necessary, and/or edit the name of the file.

Understanding File Management

FIGURE B-12: Navigating in the Open dialog box

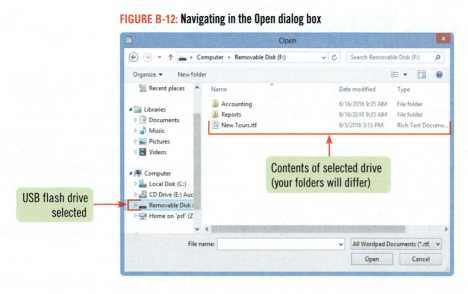

USB flash drive selected

Contents of selected drive (your folders will differ)

FIGURE B-13: Edited document

New Tours

Thailand

New Zealand

Canada

Greenland ◄——— Added text

Your Name

FIGURE B-14: Saving the updated document

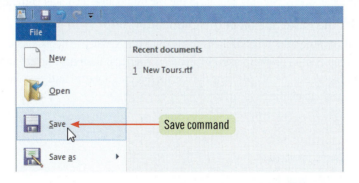

Save command

Using cloud storage

Many users store their files on special file storage locations on the World Wide Web, known as **cloud storage** locations. Examples of cloud storage locations include **Microsoft SkyDrive** and **DropBox**. By storing files in the cloud, your files are automatically updated when you make changes to them on your computer, and you can access them from different devices, including laptops, tablets, and smartphones. Microsoft Office programs such as Word and Excel show SkyDrive as a storage location when you open or save a file, making cloud storage a convenient option.

Copy Files

Learning Outcomes
• Create a new folder
• Copy and paste a file

Sometimes you need to make a copy of an existing file. For example, you might want to put a copy on a USB flash drive so you can open the file on another machine or share it with a friend or colleague. Or you might want to create a copy as a **backup**, or replacement, in case something happens to your original file. You can copy files and folders using the Copy command and then place the copy in another location using the Paste command. You cannot have two copies of a file with the same name in the same folder. If you try to do this, Windows 8 asks you if you want to replace the first one, and then gives you a chance to give the second copy a different name. **CASE** ▶ *You want to create a backup copy of the New Tours document that you can store in a folder for company newsletter items. First you need to create the folder, then you can copy the file.*

STEPS

1. **On the desktop, click the File Explorer button 📁 on the taskbar**

2. **In the Navigation pane, click Removable Disk (F:) (or the drive name and letter that represents the location where you store your Data Files)**
   First you create the new folder you plan to use for storing newsletter-related files.

3. **If you don't see the Ribbon, double-click the Home tab to open the Ribbon**

4. **In the New group on the Home tab, click the New folder button**
   A new folder appears in the File list, with its default name, New folder, selected.

5. **Type Newsletter Items, then press [Enter]**
   Because the folder name was selected, the text you typed, Newsletter Items, replaced it. Pressing [Enter] confirmed your entry, and the folder is now named Newsletter Items.

6. **In the File list, click the New Tours.rtf document you saved earlier, then click the Copy button in the Clipboard group, as shown in FIGURE B-15**
   When you use the Copy command, Windows 8 places a duplicate copy of the file in an area of your computer's random access memory called the **clipboard**, ready to paste, or place, in a new location. Copying and pasting a file leaves the file in its original location.

7. **In the File list, double-click the Newsletter Items folder**
   The folder opens. Nothing appears in the File list because the folder currently is empty.

8. **Click the Paste button in the Clipboard group**
   A copy of the New Tours.rtf file is pasted into the Newsletter Items folder. See **FIGURE B-16**. You now have two copies of the New Tours.rtf file: one on your USB flash drive in the main folder, and another in your new Newsletter Items folder. The file remains on the clipboard until you end your Windows session or place another item on the clipboard.

QUICK TIP
You can also create a new folder by clicking the New Folder button on the Quick Access toolbar (on the left side of the title bar).

QUICK TIP
You can also copy a file by right-clicking the file in the File list and then clicking Copy, or you can use the keyboard by pressing and holding [Ctrl], pressing [C], then releasing both keys.

QUICK TIP
To paste using the keyboard, press and hold [Ctrl] and press [V], then release both keys.

TABLE B-2: Selected Send to menu commands

menu option	use to
Compressed (zipped) folder	Create a new compressed (smaller) file with a .zip file extension
Desktop (create shortcut)	Create a shortcut (link) for the file on the desktop
Documents	Copy the file to the Documents library
Fax recipient	Send a file to a fax recipient
Mail recipient	Create an e-mail with the file attached to it (only if you have an e-mail program on your computer)
DVD RW Drive (D:)	Copy the file to your computer's DVD drive
Removable Disk (F:)	Copy the file to a removable disk drive (F:) (your drive letter may differ)

FIGURE B-15: Copying a file

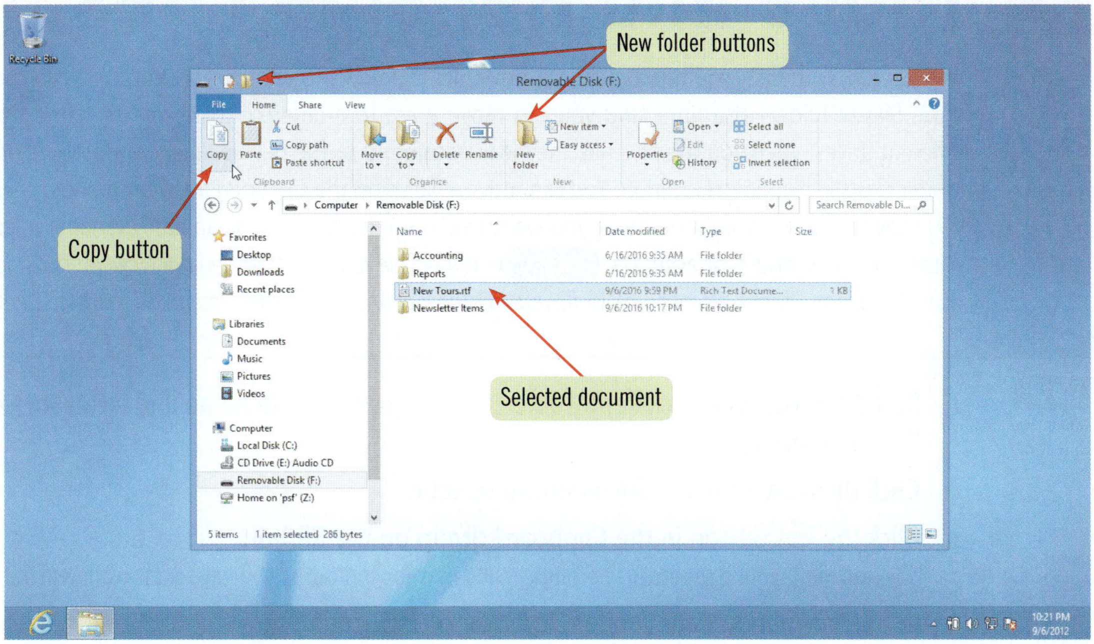

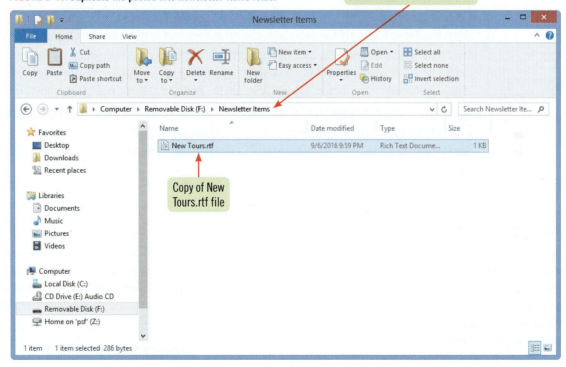

New folder buttons

Copy button

Selected document

FIGURE B-16: Duplicate file pasted into Newsletter Items folder

Copy is pasted in Newsletter Items folder

Copy of New Tours.rtf file

Copying files using Send to

You can also copy and paste a file using the Send to command. In File Explorer, right-click the file you want to copy, point to Send to, then in the shortcut menu, click the name of the device you want to send a copy of the file to. This leaves the original file on your hard drive and creates a copy on the external device. You can send a file to a compressed file, the desktop, a mail recipient, your Documents library, or a drive on your computer. See **TABLE B-2**.

Move and Rename Files

Learning Outcomes
• Cut and paste a file
• Rename a file

As you work with files, you might need to move files or folders to another location. You can move one or more files or folders at a time, and you can move them to a different folder on the same drive or to a different drive. When you **move** a file, the file is transferred to the new location, and unlike copying it no longer exists in its original location. You can move a file using the Cut and Paste commands. Before or after you move a file, you might find that you want to change its name. You can easily rename it to make the name more descriptive or accurate. **CASE** *You decide to move your original New Tours.rtf document to your Documents library. After you move it, you edit the filename so it better describes the file contents.*

STEPS

QUICK TIP
You can also cut a file by right-clicking it in the File list, then clicking Cut, or by clicking it, pressing and holding [Ctrl] on the keyboard, pressing [X], then releasing both keys.

1. **In the Address bar, click Removable Disk (F:) (or the drive name and letter for your USB flash drive)**

2. **Click the New Tours.rtf document to select it**

▶ 3. **Click the Cut button in the Clipboard group on the Ribbon**
   The icon representing the cut file becomes lighter in color, indicating you have cut it, as shown in **FIGURE B-17**.

4. **In the Navigation Pane, under Libraries, click Documents**
   You navigated to your Documents Library.

QUICK TIP
You can also paste a file by right-clicking an empty area in the File list and then clicking Paste, or by pressing and holding [Ctrl] on the keyboard, pressing [V], then releasing both keys.

▶ 5. **Click the Paste button in the Clipboard group**
   The New Tours.rtf document appears in your Documents library and remains selected. See **FIGURE B-18**. Documents you paste into your Documents library are automatically stored in your My Documents folder. The filename could be clearer, to help you remember that it contains a list of new tours.

6. **With the New Tours.rtf file selected, click the Rename button in the Organize group**
   The filename is highlighted. The file extension isn't highlighted because that part of the filename identifies the file to WordPad and should not be changed. If you deleted or changed the file extension, WordPad would be unable to open the file. You decide to add the word "List" to the end of the original filename.

7. **Move the I pointer after the "s" in "Tours", click to place the insertion point, press [Spacebar], type List as shown in FIGURE B-19, then press [Enter]**
   You changed the name of the pasted file in the Documents library. The filename now reads New Tours List.rtf.

8. **Close the window**

Using Windows 8 libraries

The Navigation pane contains not only files and folders, but also libraries. A **library** gathers file and folder locations from different locations on your computer and displays them in one location. For example, you might have pictures in several different folders on your storage devices. You can add these folder locations to your Pictures library. Then when you want to see all your pictures, you open your Pictures library instead of several different folders. The picture files stay in their original locations, but their names appear in the Pictures library. A library is not a folder that stores files, but rather a way of viewing similar types of documents that you have stored in multiple locations on your computer. **FIGURE B-20** shows the four libraries that come with Windows 8: Documents, Music, Pictures, and Videos. To help you distinguish between library locations and actual folder

locations, library names differ from actual folder names. For example, the My Documents folder is on your hard drive, but the library name is Documents. If you save a document to the Documents library, it is automatically saved to your My Documents folder.

FIGURE B-20: Libraries that come with Windows 8

Documents   Music   Pictures   Videos

FIGURE B-17: Cutting a file

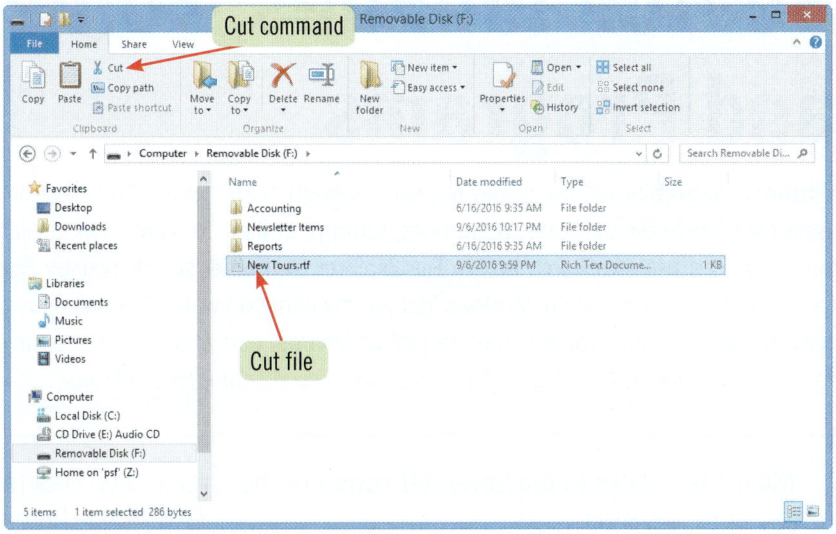

Cut command

Cut file

FIGURE B-18: Pasted file in Documents library

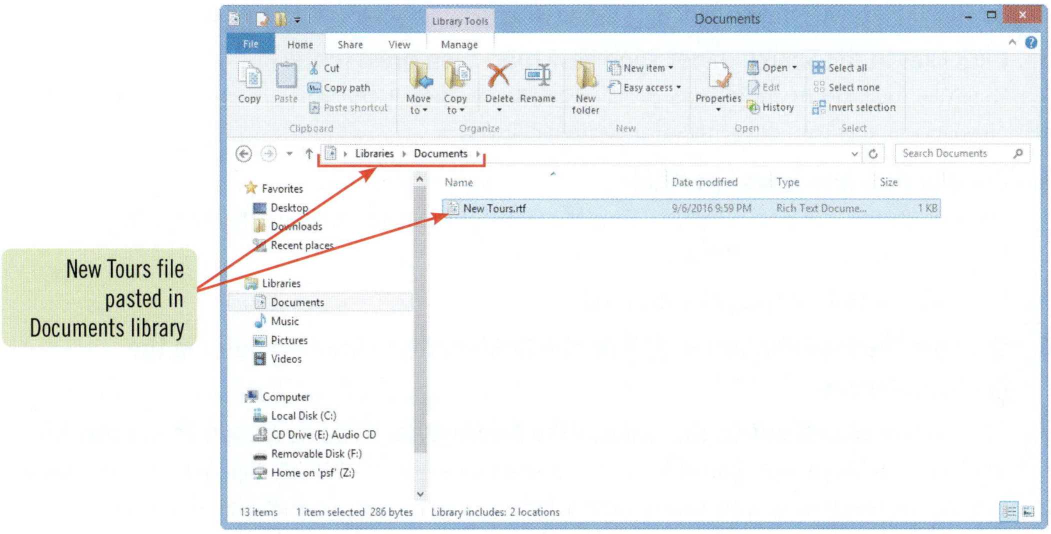

New Tours file pasted in Documents library

FIGURE B-19: Renaming a file

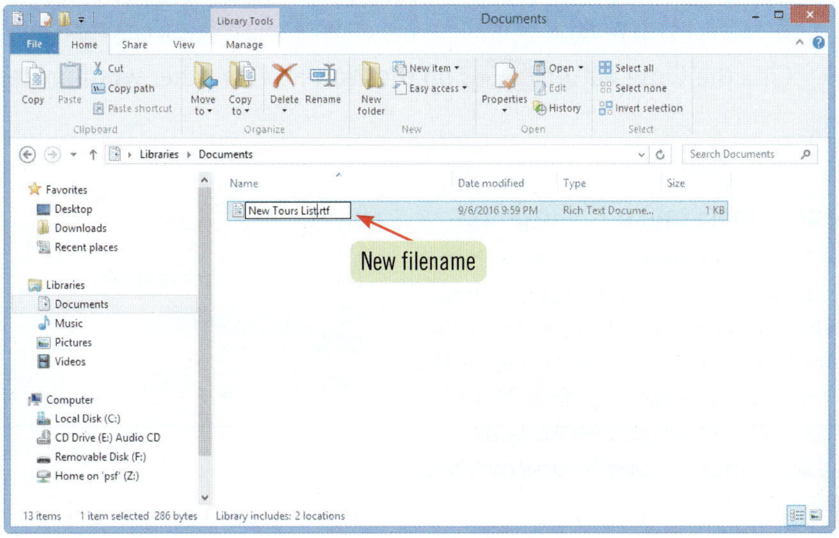

New filename

Understanding File Management

Search for Files, Folders, and Programs

Learning Outcomes
• Search for a file
• Open a found file

Windows Search helps you quickly find any program, folder, or file. You can search from the Start screen using the Charms bar to locate applications, settings, or files. To search a particular location on your computer, you can use the Search box in File Explorer. You enter search text by typing one or more letter sequences or words that help Windows identify the item you want. The search text you type is called your **search criteria**. Your search criteria can be a filename, part of a filename, or any other text. **CASE** *You want to locate the New Tours.rtf document so you can print it for a colleague.*

STEPS

1. **Move the pointer to the lower-left corner of the screen, then click the Start thumbnail**
   The Start screen opens.

2. **Point to the upper-right corner of the screen, then point to and click the Search charm**
   A listing of the apps on your computer appears, along with a Search pane on the right side of the screen. See **FIGURE B-21**. You can search for Apps, Settings, or Files. Apps is selected by default.

   > **QUICK TIP**
   > To immediately open File search in the Search charm, press [⊞] [F].

3. **Click Files in the Search panel, type new tour, then press [Enter]**
   Your New Tours List.rtf document appears under Files. By default, the Search charm finds only files located on your computer hard drive, not on any external drives.

   > **QUICK TIP**
   > If you navigated to a specific folder in your file hierarchy, Windows would search that folder and any subfolders below it.

4. **Point to the New Tours List.rtf file**
   The path in the ScreenTip, C:\Users\Your Name\My Documents, indicates the found file is in the My Documents folder on the C: drive, as shown in **FIGURE B-22**.

5. **Press [⊞] twice to display the desktop**

6. **Click the File Explorer button [📁] on the taskbar, then click Computer in the Navigation pane**

   > **QUICK TIP**
   > Windows search is not case-sensitive, meaning that you can type upper- or lowercase letters when you search, and obtain the same results.

7. **Click in the Search box to the right of the Address bar, type new tour, then press [Enter]**
   Windows searches your computer for files that contain the words "new tour". A green bar in the Address bar indicates the progress of your search. After a few moments, your search results, shown in **FIGURE B-23**, appear. Windows found both the renamed file, New Tours List.rtf, in your My Documents folder, and the original New Tours.rtf document on your removable drive, in the Newsletter Items folder.

8. **Double-click the New Tours.rtf document on your removable flash drive**
   The file opens in WordPad or in another word-processing program on your computer that reads RTF files.

9. **Click the Close button [×] on the WordPad (or other word-processor) window**

Using the Search Tools tab in File Explorer

The **Search Tools tab** appears in the Ribbon as soon as you click the Search text box, and it lets you narrow your search criteria. Use the commands in the Location group to specify a particular search location. The Refine group lets you limit the search to files modified after a certain date, or to files of a particular kind, size, type, or other property. The Options group lets you repeat previous searches, save searches, and open the folder containing a found file. See **FIGURE B-24**.

FIGURE B-24: Search Tools tab

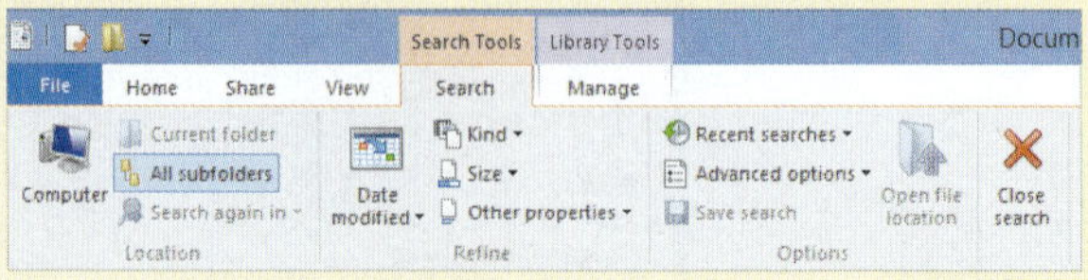

Understanding File Management

FIGURE B-21: Apps screen and search pane

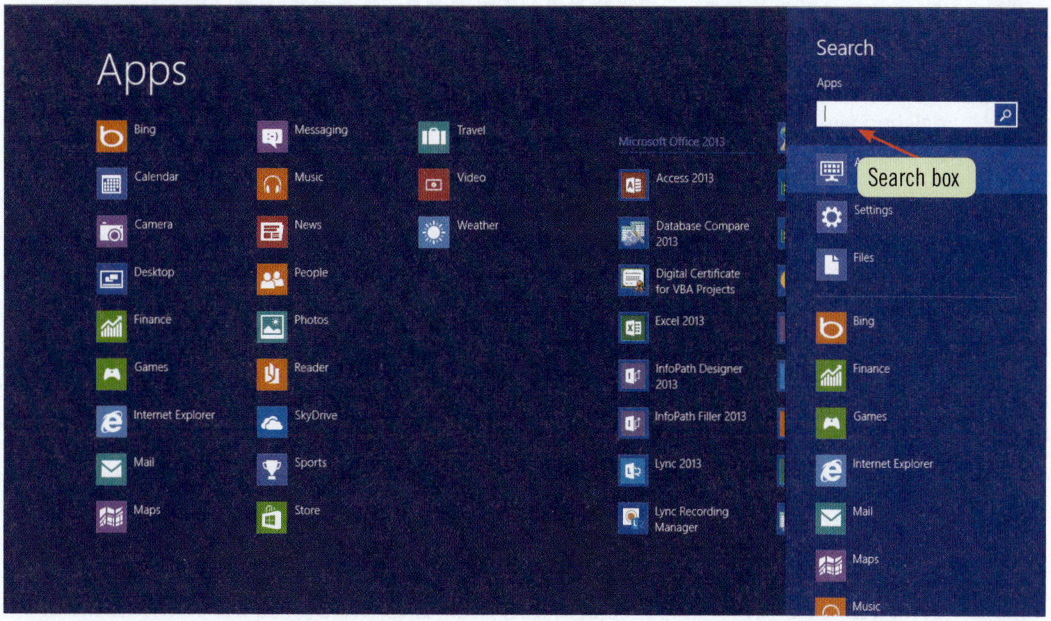

Search box

FIGURE B-22: Viewing the location of a found file

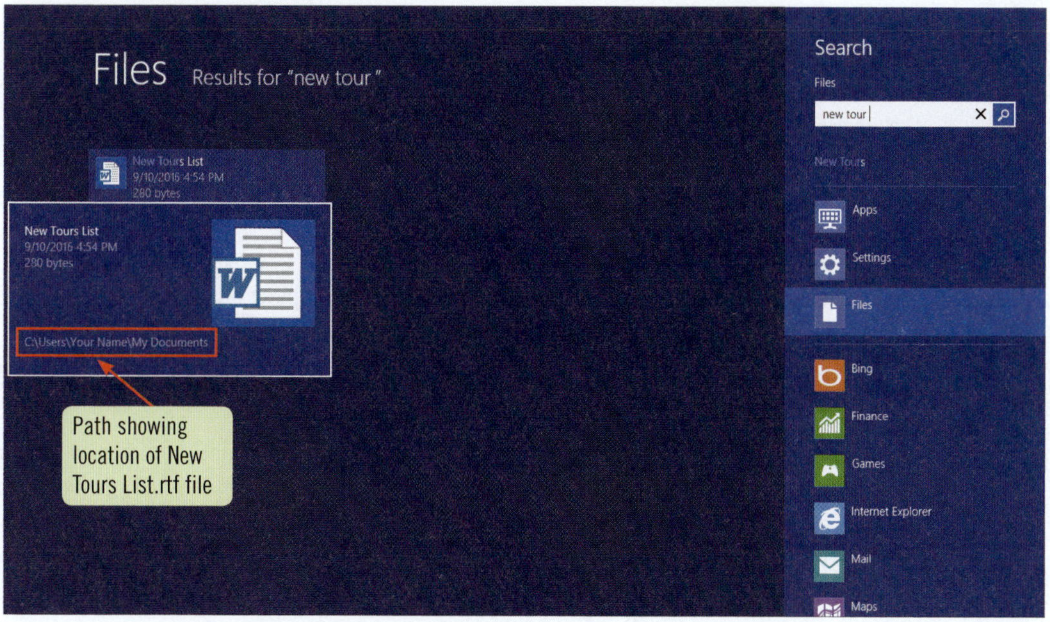

Path showing location of New Tours List.rtf file

FIGURE B-23: Search results in File Explorer

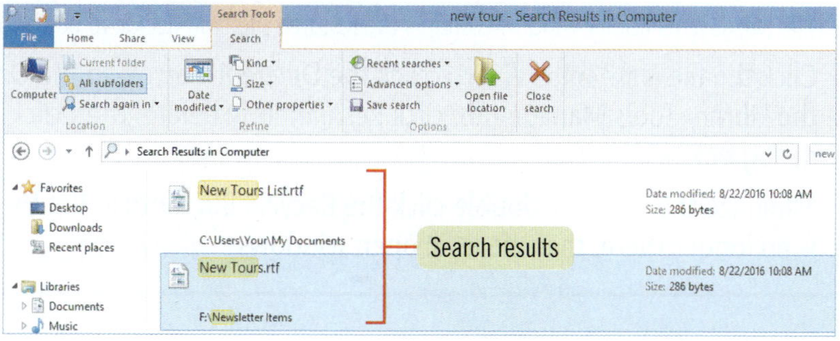

Search results

Delete and Restore Files

Learning
Outcomes
• Delete a file
• Restore a file
• Empty the
  Recycle Bin

If you no longer need a folder or file, you can delete (or remove) it from the storage device. By regularly deleting files and folders you no longer need and emptying the Recycle Bin, you free up valuable storage space on your computer. Windows 8 places folders and files you delete from your hard drive in the Recycle Bin. If you delete a folder, Windows 8 removes the folder as well as all files and subfolders stored in it. If you later discover that you need a deleted file or folder, you can restore it to its original location, as long as you have not yet emptied the Recycle Bin. Emptying the Recycle Bin permanently removes deleted folders and files from your computer. However, files and folders you delete from a removable drive, such as a USB flash drive, do not go to the Recycle Bin. They are immediately and permanently deleted and cannot be restored. **CASE** *You decide to delete the New Tours document, but later you change your mind about this.*

STEPS

1. **Click the Documents library in the File Explorer Navigation pane**

   Your Documents library opens, along with the Library Tools Manage tab on the Ribbon.

2. **Click New Tours List.rtf to select it, then click the Delete list arrow in the Organize group on the Library Tools Manage tab; if the Show recycle confirmation command does not have a check mark next to it, click Show recycle confirmation (or if it does have a check mark, click the Delete list arrow again to close the menu)**

   Selecting the Show recycle confirmation command tells Windows that whenever you click the Delete button, you want to see a confirmation dialog box before Windows deletes the file. That way you can change your mind if you want, before deleting the file.

3. **Click the Delete button ⊠**

   The Delete File dialog box opens so you can confirm the deletion, as shown in **FIGURE B-25**.

4. **Click Yes**

   You deleted the file. Because the file was stored on your computer and not on a removable drive, it was moved to the Recycle Bin.

5. **Click the Minimize button ▬ on the window's title bar, examine the Recycle Bin icon, then double-click the Recycle Bin icon on the desktop**

   The Recycle Bin icon appears to contain crumpled paper, indicating that it contains deleted folders and/or files. The Recycle Bin window displays any previously deleted folders and files, including the New Tours List.rtf file.

6. **Click the New Tours List.rtf file to select it, then click the Restore the selected items button in the Restore group on the Recycle Bin Tools Manage tab, as shown in FIGURE B-26**

   The file returns to its original location and no longer appears in the Recycle Bin window.

7. **In the Navigation pane, click the Documents library**

   The Documents library window contains the restored file. You decide to permanently delete this file.

8. **Click the file New Tours List.rtf, click the Delete list arrow in the Organize group on the Library Tools Manage tab, click Permanently delete, then click Yes in the Delete File dialog box**

9. **Minimize the window, double-click the Recycle Bin, notice that the New Tours List.rtf file is no longer there, then close all open windows**

FIGURE B-25: Delete File dialog box

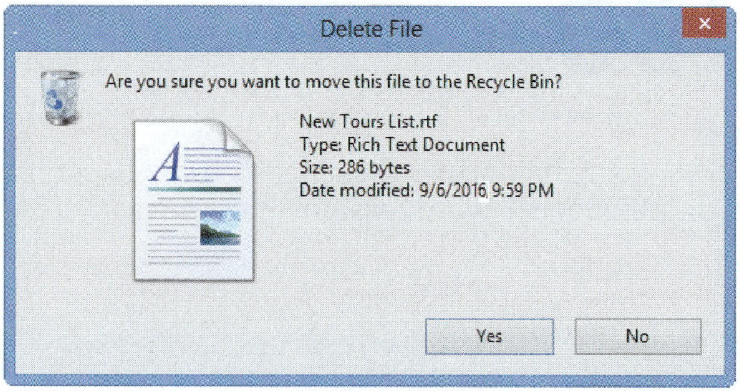

Delete File

Are you sure you want to move this file to the Recycle Bin?

New Tours List.rtf
Type: Rich Text Document
Size: 286 bytes
Date modified: 9/6/2016, 9:59 PM

Yes   No

FIGURE B-26: Restoring a file from the Recycle Bin

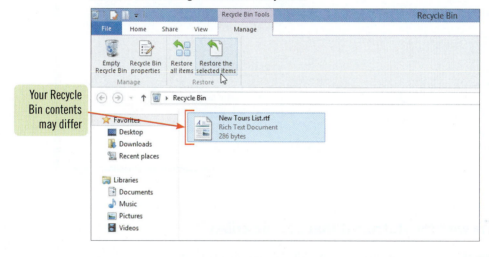

Your Recycle Bin contents may differ

More techniques for selecting and moving files

To select a group of items that are next to each other in a window, click the first item in the group, press and hold [Shift], then click the last item in the group. Both items you click and all the items between them become selected. To select files that are not next to each other, click the first file, press and hold [Ctrl], then click the other items you want to select as a group. Then you can copy, cut, or delete the group of files or folders you selected. **Drag and drop** is a technique in which you use your pointing device to drag a file or folder into a different folder and then drop it, or let go of the mouse button, to place it in that folder. Using drag and drop does not copy your file to the clipboard. If you drag and drop a file to a folder on a different drive, Windows 8 *copies the file*. However, if you drag and drop a file to a folder on the same drive, Windows 8 *moves* the file into that

folder instead. See **FIGURE B-27**. If you want to move a file to another drive, hold down [Shift] while you drag and drop. If you want to copy a file to another folder on the same drive, hold down [Ctrl] while you drag and drop.

FIGURE B-27: Moving a file using drag and drop

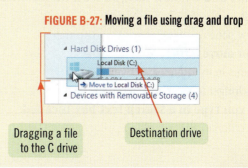

Dragging a file to the C drive

Destination drive

Practice

Concepts Review

Label the elements of the Windows 8 window shown in FIGURE B-28.

FIGURE B-28

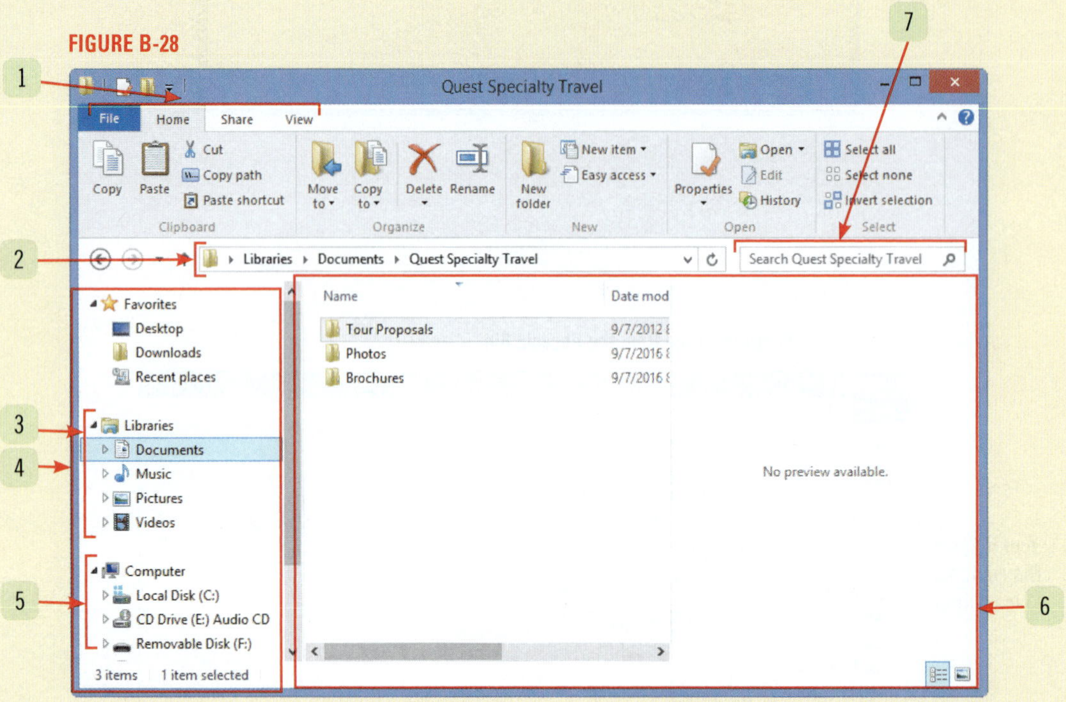

Match each term with the statement that best describes it.

8. File management
9. File extension
10. Address bar
11. Path
12. Library
13. File hierarchy

a. An area above the Files list that contains a path
b. Structure of files and folders organized in different levels
c. A series of locations separated by small triangles or backslashes that describes a file's location in the file hierarchy
d. Skills that help you organize your files and folders
e. A three- or four-letter sequence, preceded by a period, that identifies the type of file
f. Gathers files and folders from different computer locations

Select the best answer from the list of choices.

14. **Which part of a window lets you see a file's contents without opening the file?**
   a. File list
   b. Preview pane
   c. Navigation pane
   d. Address bar

15. **When you move a file:**
   a. It remains in its original location.
   b. It is no longer in its original location.
   c. It is copied to another location.
   d. It is no longer in your file hierarchy.

16. **The text you type in a Search text box is called:**
   a. Search criteria.
   b. RAM.
   c. Sorting.
   d. Clipboard.

17. **Which of the following is not a visible section in a File Explorer window?**
   a. Address bar
   b. File list
   c. Navigation pane
   d. Clipboard

18. **The way your files appear in the Files list is determined by the:**
   a. Path.
   b. View.
   c. Subfolder.
   d. Criterion.

19. **When you copy a file, it is automatically placed in the:**
   a. Preview pane.
   b. My Documents folder.
   c. Hierarchy.
   d. Clipboard.

20. **After you delete a file from your hard disk, it is automatically placed in the:**
   a. USB flash drive.
   b. Clipboard.
   c. Recycle Bin.
   d. Search box.

Skills Review

1. **Understand files and folders.**
   a. Create a file hierarchy for a property management business. The business manages three apartment buildings and two private homes. Activities include renting the properties and managing maintenance and repair. How would you organize your folders and files using a file hierarchy of at least three levels? How would you use folders and subfolders to keep the documents related to these activities distinct and easy to navigate? Draw a diagram and write a short paragraph explaining your answer.
   b. Use tools in the File Explorer window to create the folder hierarchy in the My Documents folder on your computer.

2. **Create and save a file.**
   a. Connect your USB flash drive to a USB port on your computer, then open WordPad from the Start screen.
   b. Type **Tour Marketing Plan** as the title, then start a new line.
   c. Type your name, then press [Enter] twice.
   d. Create the following list:
      Airline co-marketing
      Email blasts
      Web ads
      Adult education partnership
   e. Save the WordPad file with the filename **Tour Marketing Plan.rtf** on your USB flash drive.
   f. View the filename in the WordPad title bar, then close WordPad.

3. **Explore the files and folders on your computer.**
   a. Open a File Explorer window.
   b. Use the Navigation pane to navigate to your USB flash drive or another location where you store your Data Files.
   c. Use the Address bar to navigate to Computer.
   d. Use the File list to navigate to your local hard drive (C:).
   e. Use the File list to open the Users folder, and then open the folder that represents your user name.
   f. Open the My Documents folder. (*Hint:* The path is Computer\Local Disk (C:) \Users \Your User Name\ My Documents.)
   g. Use the Navigation pane to navigate back to your Computer contents.

4. **Change file and folder views.**
   a. Navigate to your USB flash drive using the method of your choice.
   b. Use the View tab to view its contents as large icons.
   c. View the drive contents in the seven other views.
   d. Sort the items on your USB flash drive by date modified in ascending order.
   e. Open the Preview pane, then view the selected item's preview.
   f. Close the Preview pane.

5. Open, edit, and save files.

   a. Open WordPad.

   b. Use the Open dialog box to open the Tour Marketing Plan.rtf document you created.

   c. After the text "Adult education partnership," add a line with the text **Travel conventions**.

   d. Save the document and close WordPad.

6. Copy files.

   a. In the File Explorer window, navigate to your USB flash drive if necessary.

   b. Copy the Tour Marketing Plan.rtf document.

   c. Create a new folder named **Marketing** on your USB flash drive or the location where you store your Data Files (*Hint:* Use the Home tab), then open the folder.

   d. Paste the document copy in the new folder.

7. Move and rename files.

   a. Navigate to your USB flash drive or the location where you store your Data Files.

   b. Select the Tour Marketing Plan.rtf document located there, then cut it.

   c. Navigate to your Documents library, then paste the file there.

   d. Rename the file **Tour Marketing Plan - Backup.rtf**.

8. Search for files, folders, and programs.

   a. Go to the Start screen, and use the Search charm to search for a file using the search text **backup**.

   b. Point to the found file, and notice its path.

   c. Open the Tour Marketing Plan - Backup document from the search results, then close WordPad. (*Hint:* Closing the program automatically closes any open documents.)

   d. Open a File Explorer window, click in the Search box, then use the Data Modified button on the Search Tools Search tab to find a file modified today. (*Hint:* Click the Date Modified button, then click Today.)

   e. Open the found document from the File list, then close WordPad.

9. Delete and restore files.

   a. Navigate to your Documents library.

   b. Verify that your Delete preference is Show recycle confirmation, then delete the Tour Marketing Plan Backup.rtf file.

   c. Open the Recycle Bin, and restore the document to its original location.

   d. Navigate to your Documents library, then move the Tour Marketing Plan-Backup.rtf file to your USB flash drive.

Independent Challenge 1

To meet the needs of pet owners in your town, you have opened a pet-sitting business named CritterCare. Customers hire you to care for their pets in their own homes when the pet owners go on vacation. To promote your new business, your Web site designer asks you to give her selling points to include in a Web ad.

   a. Connect your USB flash drive to your computer, if necessary.

   b. Create a new folder named **CritterCare** on your USB flash drive or the location where you store your Data Files.

   c. In the CritterCare folder, create two subfolders named **Print Ads** and **Web site**.

   d. Use WordPad to create a short paragraph or list that describes three advantages of your business. Use CritterCare as the first line, followed by the paragraph or list. Include an address and a phone number. Below the paragraph, type your name.

   e. Save the WordPad document with the filename **Selling Points.rtf** in the Web site folder, then close the document and exit WordPad.

   f. Open a File Explorer window, then navigate to the Web site folder.

   g. View the contents in at least three different views, then choose the view option that you prefer.

   h. Copy the Selling Points.rtf file, then paste a copy in the Document library.

   i. Rename the copied file **Selling Points Backup.rtf**.

   j. Close the folder.

Independent Challenge 2

As a freelance editor for several international publishers, you depend on your computer to meet critical deadlines. Whenever you encounter a computer problem, you contact a computer consultant who helps you resolve the problem. This consultant has asked you to document, or keep records of, your computer's current settings.

a. Connect your USB flash drive to your computer, if necessary.

b. Open the Computer window so you can view information on your drives and other installed hardware.

c. View the window contents using three different views, then choose the one you prefer.

d. Open WordPad and create a document with the title **My Hardware Documentation** and your name on separate lines.

e. List the names of the hard drive (or drives), devices with removable storage, and any other hardware devices installed on the computer you are using. Also include the total size and amount of free space on your hard drive(s) and removable storage drive(s). (*Hint:* If you need to check the Computer window for this information, use the taskbar button for the Computer window to view your drives, then use the WordPad taskbar button to return to WordPad.)

f. Save the WordPad document with the filename **My Hardware Documentation** on your USB flash drive or the location where you store your Data Files.

g. Close WordPad, then preview your document in the Preview pane.

Independent Challenge 3

You are an attorney at Garcia, Buck, and Sato, a large law firm. You participate in your firm's community outreach program by speaking at career days in area high schools. You teach students about career opportunities available in the field of law. You want to create a folder structure on your USB flash drive to store the files for each session.

a. Connect your USB flash drive to your computer, then open the window for your USB flash drive or the location where you store your Data Files.

b. Create a folder named **Career Days**.

c. In the Career Days folder, create a subfolder named **Nearwater High**, then open the folder.

d. Close the Nearwater High folder window.

e. Use WordPad to create a document with the title **Career Areas** and your name on separate lines, and the following list of items:
Current Opportunities:
Attorney
Paralegal
Police Officer
Judge

f. Save the WordPad document with the filename **Careers.rtf** in the Nearwater High folder. (*Hint:* After you switch to your USB flash drive in the Save As dialog box, open the Career Days folder, then open the Nearwater High folder before saving the file.)

g. Close WordPad.

h. Open WordPad and the Careers document again, add **Court Reporter** to the bottom of the list, then save the file and close WordPad.

i. Using pencil and paper, draw a diagram of your new folder structure.

j. Use the Search method of your choice to search for the Careers document, then open the file, to search your computer using the search criterion **car**. Locate the Careers.rtf document in the list, then use the link to open the file.

k. Close the file.

Independent Challenge 4: Explore

Think of a hobby or volunteer activity that you do now, or one that you would like to start. You will use your computer to help you manage your plans or ideas for this activity.

a. Using paper and pencil, sketch a folder structure with at least two subfolders to contain your documents for this activity.

b. Connect your USB flash drive to your computer, then open the window for your USB flash drive.

c. Create the folder structure for your activity, using your sketch as a reference.

d. Think of at least three tasks that you can do to further your work in your chosen activity.

e. Go to the Windows 8 Start screen, click the Store app tile and scroll to explore the available app categories. Choose a category that might relate to your activity, and click the Top Free tile to see if any of these apps might help you. Click an app name to read its description. (*Note:* You do not need to install any apps.)

f. Close the Store app by dragging its top border to the bottom of the screen.

g. Start a new WordPad document. Add the title **Next Steps** at the top of the page and your name on the next line.

h. Below your name, list the three tasks, then write a paragraph on how Windows 8 apps might help you accomplish your tasks. Save the file in one of the folders created on your USB flash drive, with the title **To Do.rtf**.

i. Close WordPad, then open a File Explorer window for the folder where you stored the document.

j. Create a copy of the file, place the copied file in your documents library, then rename this file with a name you choose.

k. Delete the copied file from your Documents library.

l. Open the Recycle Bin window, then restore the copied file to the Documents library.

Visual Workshop

Create the folder structure shown in **FIGURE B-29** on your USB flash drive (or in another location if requested by your instructor). As you work, use WordPad to prepare a short summary of the steps you followed to create the folder structure. Add your name to the document, then save it as **Customer Support.rtf** on your USB Flash drive or the location where you store your Data Files.

FIGURE B-29

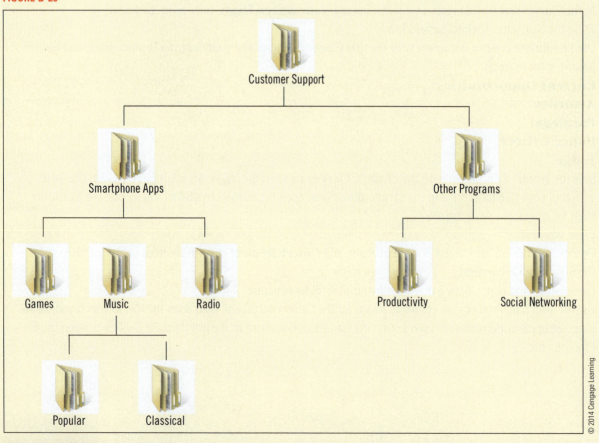

© 2014 Cengage Learning

Getting Started with Microsoft Office 2013

CASE ▶ You have just joined the marketing team at Outdoor Designs, a company that sells outdoor recreational products. You need to familiarize yourself with Microsoft Office 2013 and create a simple task list for your first week on the job.

Unit Objectives

After completing this unit, you will be able to:

- Understand Office Professional Plus 2013
- Start an Office app
- Identify common screen elements in an Office app
- Use the Ribbon and zoom controls

- Use the Quick Access toolbar
- Save a file
- Get Help
- Exit an Office app

Files You Will Need

No files needed.

©HelenStock/Shutterstock

Understand Office Professional Plus 2013

Microsoft Office 2013 is a collection (or **suite**) of programs or **apps** you can use to create documents, analyze data, and complete almost any business task. In this book you will learn how to use the four main productivity apps of the Office suite: Word, Excel, Access, and PowerPoint. Office 2013 is a revolutionary update of the software suite because it is designed for "**the cloud**." In other words, it means you can access the Office work you create from a variety of devices including computers, tablets, and smartphones—as long as they are connected to the Internet. One of the most powerful benefits of Office 2013 is the ability to save your files to **SkyDrive**, a storage location on the Web (or "in the cloud") that you can access from any device. A SkyDrive account is free and includes 7 GB of storage space. SkyDrive also comes with **Office Web Apps**, which are scaled-down versions of Word, Excel, and PowerPoint that you can use with any browser to edit files on your SkyDrive or create new files. For instance, you could create a document on your computer, open it on another computer and make an edit to it, and then reopen it on another device to view the edit. Using Office 2013 and SkyDrive, you can easily share your files with your friends and coworkers and work collaboratively on a single document even if you are in different locations. In addition to the four programs you learn about in this book, Office also includes the apps described in TABLE C-1. **CASE** ▸ *Karen Rivera, marketing director at Outdoor Designs, asks you to familiarize yourself with the apps in Office Professional Plus 2013.*

DETAILS

Microsoft Office Professional Plus 2013 contains the following programs or apps:

*   **Microsoft Word** is a **word-processing program** you can use to create text documents, such as letters, memos, newsletters, and reports. You can also use Word to add pictures, drawings, tables, and other graphical elements to your documents. **FIGURE C-1** shows an Outdoor Designs' annual report created using Word.

*   **Microsoft Excel** is a **spreadsheet program** you can use to manipulate, analyze, and chart quantitative data. Excel is often used to calculate financial information. **FIGURE C-2** shows a quarterly sales report created using Excel.

*   **Microsoft Access** is a **database management program** you can use to store, organize, and keep track of information, such as customer names and addresses, product inventories, and employee information. At Outdoor Designs, you will use Access to create customer and product databases, data entry forms that others can use to input additional data, and reports that staff can use to spot important trends in the data. **FIGURE C-3** shows a form used to input data about Outdoor Designs' distributors.

*   **Microsoft PowerPoint** is a **presentation graphics program** you can use to develop materials for presentations, including slide shows, computer-based presentations, speaker's notes, and audience handouts. **FIGURE C-4** shows one slide from a presentation about Outdoor Designs products.

TABLE C-1: Other Office apps

Office app	what it is	what you use it for
Microsoft Outlook	Information manager	Send and receive email; schedule appointments; maintain to-do lists; store names, addresses, and other contact information
Microsoft Publisher	Desktop publishing program	Create printed documents that combine text and graphics such as newsletters, brochures, and business cards
Microsoft OneNote	Information collection tool and organizer	Store and organize captured information like Web addresses, graphics, notes written by you or others, and research

© 2014 Cengage Learning

FIGURE C-1: Report created in Word

FIGURE C-2: Worksheet and chart created in Excel

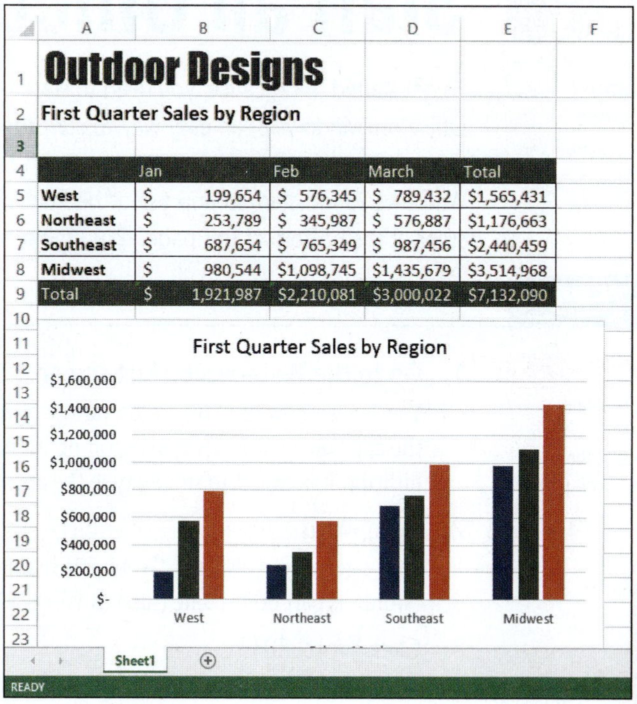

FIGURES C-3 & C-4: Database form created in Access and presentation slide created in PowerPoint

Start an Office App

Learning Outcomes
• Start an Office app
• Explain the purpose of a template

To get started using Office, you need to start, or **launch**, the Office app you want to use. If you are running Office on Windows 8, an easy way to start the app you want is to go to the Windows 8 Start screen, type the app name for which you want to search then click the app name in the Results list. If you are running Windows 7, you start an app using the Start menu. (If you are running Windows 7, follow the Windows 7 steps at the bottom of this page.) **CASE** ▶ *You decide to familiarize yourself with Office by starting Word.*

STEPS

TROUBLE
If you are running Windows 7, follow the steps at the bottom of this page.

1. Go to the Windows 8 Start screen

Your screen now displays a wide variety of colorful tiles for all the apps on your computer. You could locate the app you want to open by scrolling to the right until you see it, but if you have a lot of apps it could be difficult. It is easiest to simply type the app name to search for it.

2. Type word

Your screen now displays "Word 2013" under "Results for "word"" along with any other apps that have "word" as part of its name (such as WordPad). See **FIGURE C-5**.

3. Click Word 2013

Word 2013 launches, and the Word start screen appears, as shown in **FIGURE C-6**. The **start screen** is a landing page that appears when you first start an Office app. The left side of this screen displays recent files you have opened. (If you have never opened any files, then there will be no files listed under Recent.) The right side displays images depicting different templates you can use to create different types of documents. A **template** is a file containing professionally designed content that you can easily replace with your own. Using a template to create a document can save time and ensure your document looks great. You can also start from scratch using the Blank document option.

Follow these steps if you are running Windows 7

1. Click the Start button 🪟 **on the taskbar**
    The Start menu opens, as shown in **FIGURE C-7**.
2. Click All Programs, click the Microsoft Office 2013 folder as shown in FIGURE C-7, then click Word 2013

Office 2013 launches, and the Word start screen appears, as shown in **FIGURE C-6**. The start screen is a landing page that appears when you first start an Office app. The left side of this screen displays recent files you have opened. (If you have never opened any files, then there will be no files listed under Recent.) The right side displays images depicting different templates you can use to create different types of documents. A **template** is a file containing professionally designed content that you can easily replace with your own. Using a template to create a document can save time and ensure your document looks great. You can also start from scratch using the Blank document option.

What is Office 365?

Until the release of Microsoft Office 2013, most consumers purchased Microsoft Office in a traditional way: by buying a retail package from a store or downloading it from Microsoft.com. You can still purchase Microsoft Office 2013 in this traditional way–but you can also now purchase it as a subscription service called Microsoft Office 365 (for businesses) and Microsoft Office 365 Home Premium (for consumers). Office 365 requires businesses to pay a subscription fee for each user. Office 365 Home Premium Edition allows households to install Office on up to 5 devices. These subscription versions of Office provide extra services and are optimized for working in the cloud.

FIGURE C-5: Searching for Word app from the Start screen in Windows 8

Word 2013 app appears as a search result when you type "word"

FIGURE C-6: Word start screen

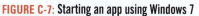
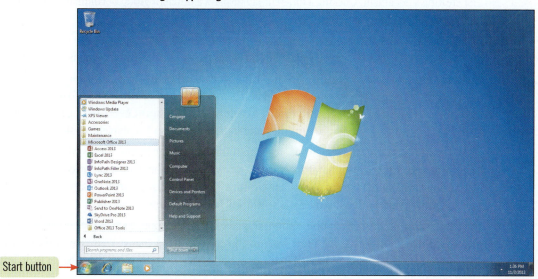

Recently opened documents appear here

Your name will appear here if you signed in using a Microsoft account

Templates let you create a certain type of document fast using professionally designed content you can modify

FIGURE C-7: Starting an app using Windows 7

Start button

Identify Common Screen Elements in an Office App

Office 2013 comes in many different editions, each of which includes a different set of Office apps and services. You can buy Office 2013 by paying a one-time fee, which allows you to install the software on one computer. Or, you could purchase an annual subscription to Office (called Office 365), which lets you install Office on five computers or devices. See TABLE C-2 for a sampling of the different editions that are available. No matter what edition of Office you are using, you will notice that all Office apps share a common user interface. A **user interface** is the collection of buttons and tools you use to interact with a software program. Once you are familiar with the user interface of one app, you will be able to recognize and use them in all of the Office apps. **CASE** *You decide to familiarize yourself with the Word app user interface.*

STEPS

1. **Click Blank document in the Start screen**

   The Start screen closes, and a new blank document appears on screen in the Word app window. See FIGURE C-8.

2. **Read the information below, then refer to FIGURE C-8 to learn the different user interface elements of the Word app, most of which are common to all Office apps**

   - The **title bar** is at the top of the app window. It contains the name of the document (currently the temporary name Document1) and the name of the program (currently Word).The Help icon on the right end of the title bar gives you accesss to the Office Help system. The **Ribbon Display Options button** ⬆ provides commands for hiding or displaying the Ribbon.

   - On the left end of the title bar is the **Quick Access toolbar**, containing buttons for saving a file, undoing an action, and redoing an action. The Quick Access toolbar is always available no matter what tab is active, making it easy to access favorite commands whenever you need them.

   - The **Ribbon** is the band directly below the title bar. It contains commands in the form of buttons, icons, lists, galleries, and text boxes. A **command** is an instruction you give to a computer to complete a task, such as printing a document or saving your changes. You might see your name (or another name) at the right end of the Ribbon. Your name appears if you have signed into your Microsoft account.

   - Across the top of the Ribbon are several **tabs**, each of which contains a different set of commands for completing a particular type of task. At the moment, the **HOME tab** is active, so it appears in front of the other tabs. The HOME tab contains commands for performing the most frequently used commands for creating a document. Clicking a different tab displays a different group of commands related to performing a different type of task.

   - The **FILE tab** contains commands that let you work with the whole document. You use the FILE tab to open, save, print, and close documents. The FILE tab is present in all Office programs.

   - Each tab is organized into **groups** of related commands, such as the Clipboard group, the Font group, and the Paragraph group. You can see these group names at the bottom of each tab. To the right of many group names is a small arrow called a **dialog box launcher**, or **launcher**. Clicking a launcher opens a **dialog box**—a pane where you can enter additional information to complete a task.

   - The **document window** is the work area within the Word app window. This is where you type text into your document and format it to look the way you want. The work area looks different in each Office app based on the type of file you are creating. The **insertion point** is a flashing vertical line in the document window that indicates where text will be inserted when you type.

   - The **status bar** at the bottom of the screen displays key information, such as the current page. At the far right of the status bar are the **View buttons**, which you use to change your view of the document. You can use the **Zoom slider**, located to the right of the View buttons, to set the magnification level of your document.

Getting Started with Microsoft Office 2013

FIGURE C-8: Word app window

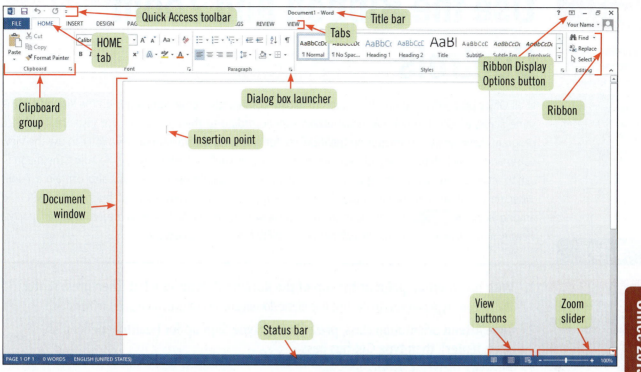

TABLE C-2: Office 2013 product offerings

version	how sold	what it contains
Office Home & Student 2013	One-time purchase; lets you install on one computer	Word, Excel, PowerPoint, OneNote
Office Home & Business 2013	One-time purchase; lets you install on one computer	Word, Excel, PowerPoint, OneNote, Outlook
Office Professional Plus 2013	One-time purchase; lets you install on one computer	Word, Excel, PowerPoint, OneNote, Outlook, Access, Publisher,
Office 365 Home Premium	Requires annual subscription fee; can install and use on five computers/devices	Word, Excel, PowerPoint, Access, Outlook, OneNote, Publisher; also includes 20 GB additional space on SkyDrive and 60 free Skype minutes per month
Office 365 Small Business Premium	Requires annual subscription fee; can install and use on five computers/devices	Word, Excel, PowerPoint, Access, Outlook, OneNote, Publisher; also includes additional tools for running a small business

© 2014 Cengage Learning

Office 2013

Use the Ribbon and Zoom Controls

In all Office programs, you use the Ribbon to initiate commands. Some commands on the Ribbon are the same across all Office programs, while others vary according to the application. For instance, all Office programs have similar commands on the VIEW tab for changing the document view. You can use the View commands to switch to a different predefined view, such as Draft or Web Layout, or to adjust the magnification level so your document appears larger or smaller in size. Many Office apps also contain a Zoom slider on the status bar for changing the magnification level and View shortcut buttons for switching among views. **CASE** ▶ *You decide to create a simple task list for your first week on the job, and then practice viewing it in different ways using the buttons on the VIEW tab and the Zoom slider.*

STEPS

1. **With the insertion point at the top of the document, type Task List, then press [Enter]**

   The text you typed appears in the first line of the document, and the insertion point moves down.

2. **Type Attend orientation class, press [Enter], type Sign up for health benefits plan, press [Enter], then type Get bus pass**

3. **Click the VIEW tab on the Ribbon**

   The VIEW tab is now active. This tab contains commands for changing your view of the document window. Changing your view does not change the document itself; it just lets you see a document differently in order to focus on different stages of the project, such as entering text, formatting, or reading. You are currently working in Print Layout view, which shows you exactly how a document will look when it is printed.

4. **Click the Read Mode button 📖 in the Views group**

   Your task list now appears in a view better for reading on a computer screen, as shown in **FIGURE C-9**. The Ribbon is no longer visible, leaving more room for viewing the document. The commands along the top left of the screen let you open the File tab, search for Information, or change the view.

5. **Click VIEW, then click Edit Document**

   Your task list now appears in the default view—Print Layout—and the VIEW tab on the Ribbon is visible again.

6. **Click the Ribbon Display Options button 🔼 on the title bar, as shown in FIGURE C-10, then click Auto-Hide Ribbon**

   The Ribbon no longer appears on screen; it is hidden. Hiding the Ribbon is helpful when you want to see more of your document.

7. **Click the Ribbon Display Options button 🔼 on the title bar, then click Show Tabs and Commands**

   The Ribbon is fully displayed again.

8. **On the Zoom slider in the lower-right corner of the screen, click the Zoom In button ➕ 10 times until 200% appears to the right of the slider**

   Now the text in your task list appears double its actual size, as shown in **FIGURE C-11**. Each time you clicked the ➕ button, the zoom increased by 10 percent. Note the actual text size in your document has not changed, only the magnification level has. To decrease the zoom level and make the text smaller on screen, you can click the ➖ on the left end of the slider.

9. **Click the 100% button in the Zoom group on the Ribbon**

   Your task list appears again at 100%, the actual size of the document as it would look printed.

FIGURE C-9: Viewing a document in Read Mode view

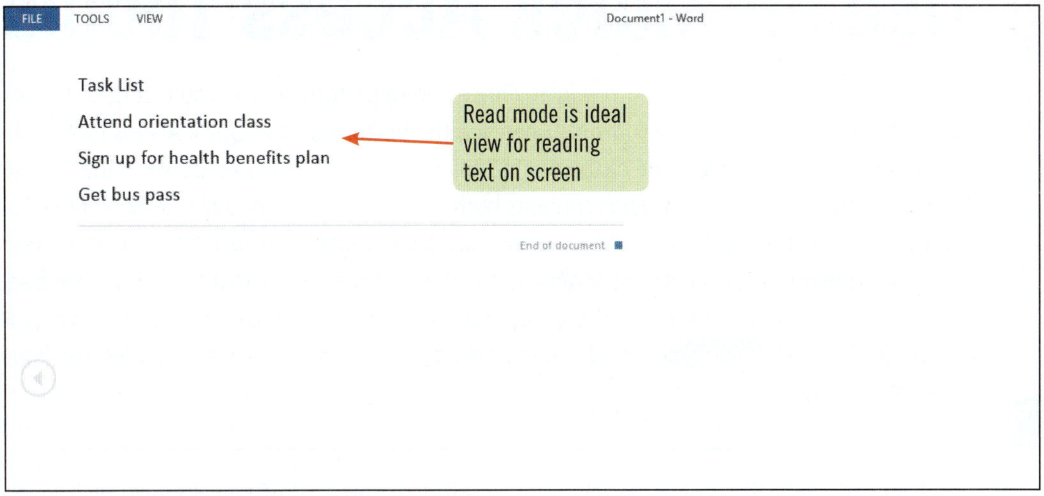

FILE TOOLS VIEW   Document1 - Word

Task List

Attend orientation class ◄———— Read mode is ideal
                                 view for reading
Sign up for health benefits plan   text on screen

Get bus pass

                              End of document ■

FIGURE C-10: Using the Ribbon Display Options button to hide the Ribbon

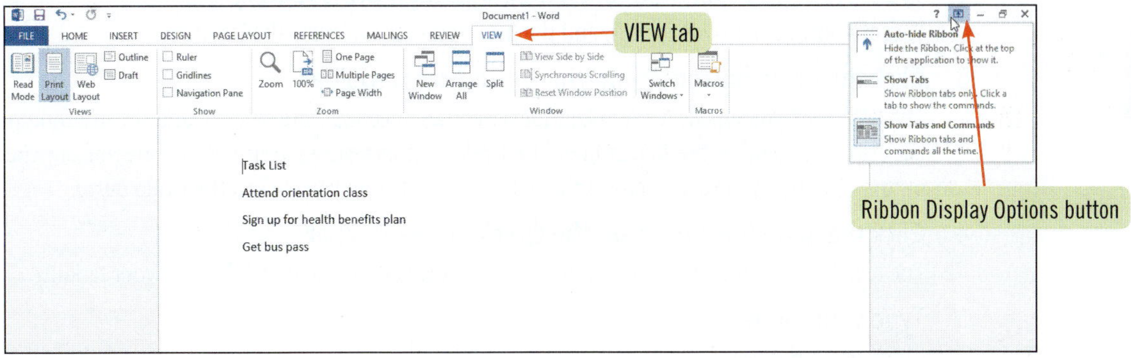

VIEW tab

Ribbon Display Options button

FIGURE C-11: Document with zoom set to 200%

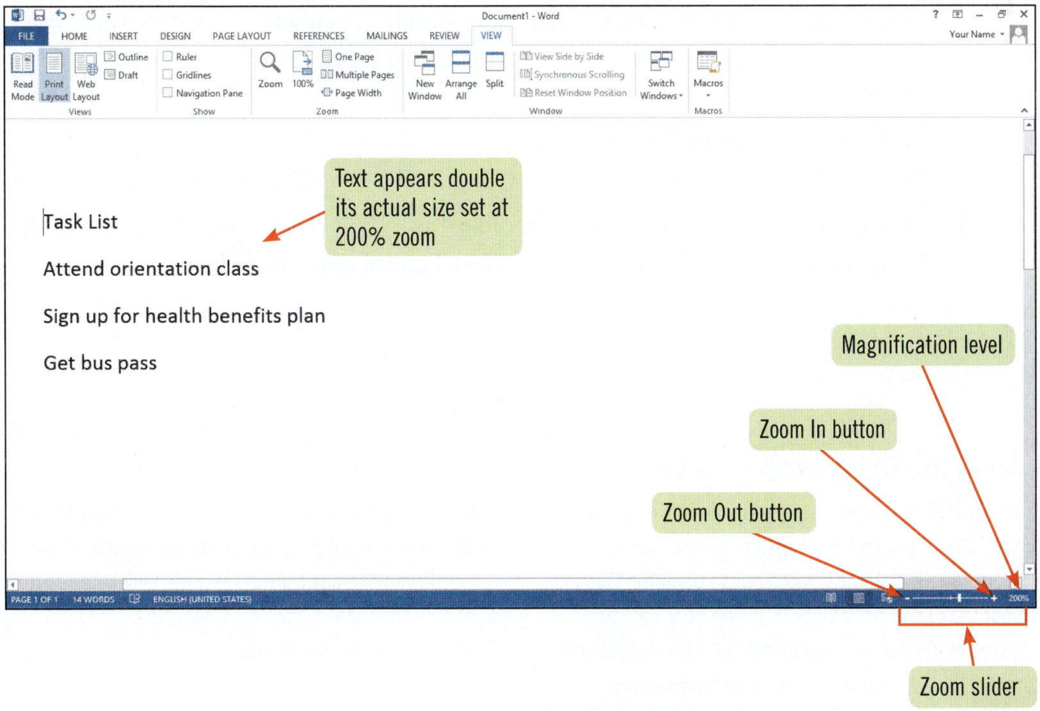

Task List

Attend orientation class

Sign up for health benefits plan

Get bus pass

Text appears double
its actual size set at
200% zoom

Magnification level

Zoom In button

Zoom Out button

Zoom slider

Office 2013
UNIT C

Use the Quick Access Toolbar

Learning Outcomes
• Undo and redo an action
• Move the Quick Access toolbar

If you want to click a particular button in an Office app to perform a task, you first need to make sure the tab that contains that button is in front. However, the buttons on the Quick Access toolbar, located just above the Ribbon on the left side of the screen, are available anytime, except when the FILE tab is active. By default, the Quick Access toolbar contains buttons that let you save a file, undo your last action, and redo the last action you undid. These buttons are also available on other tabs in the Ribbon; having them available on the Quick Access toolbar lets you work faster. You can add buttons you frequently use to the Quick Access toolbar using the Customize Quick Access Toolbar menu, or move its location to below the Ribbon. **CASE** *You continue working on your task list while exploring the buttons on the Quick Access toolbar.*

STEPS

1. **Press [Ctrl][End] to place the insertion point at the end of the document if necessary, then press [Enter]**

   The insertion point is now below the third item in your task list.

2. **Type Order pizza for staff lunch meeting, then press [Enter]**

   Your list now contains four items, and the insertion point is below the last item.

3. **Click the Undo button ⤺ on the Quick Access toolbar**

   The last words you typed, "Order pizza for staff lunch meeting," are deleted, and the insertion point moves back up to the end of the fourth line. The Undo button reverses your last action. You can click the Redo button to restore your document to the state it was in before you clicked the Undo button.

4. **Click the Redo button ⤻ on the Quick Access toolbar**

   The text "Order pizza for staff lunch meeting" is now back as the fourth item in your task list.

5. **Type your name**

   Compare your screen to **FIGURE C-12**.

6. **Click the Customize Quick Access Toolbar button ⯆ on the right side of the Quick Access toolbar**

   A menu opens and displays a list of common commands, as shown in **FIGURE C-13**. Notice that Save, Undo, and Redo all have check marks next to them, indicating these commands are already on the Quick Access toolbar.

7. **Click Show Below the Ribbon**

   The Quick Access toolbar moves, and is now located below the Ribbon, as shown in **FIGURE C-14**.

8. **Click the Customize Quick Access Toolbar button ⯆, then click Show Above the Ribbon**

   The Quick Access toolbar moves back to its default location above the Ribbon.

Customizing the Quick Access toolbar

You can add any button that you use frequently to the Quick Access toolbar. To do this, click the Customize Quick Access Toolbar button, then click More Commands to open the Quick Access Toolbar tab of the Word Options dialog box. Click any command listed in the Popular Commands list, click Add, then click OK. Another way to add a button to the Quick Access toolbar is to right-click the button you want to add on the Ribbon, then click Add to Quick Access Toolbar on the shortcut menu. To remove any button from the Quick Access toolbar, right-click the button, then click Remove from Quick Access Toolbar on the shortcut menu.

FIGURE C-12: Completed Task List

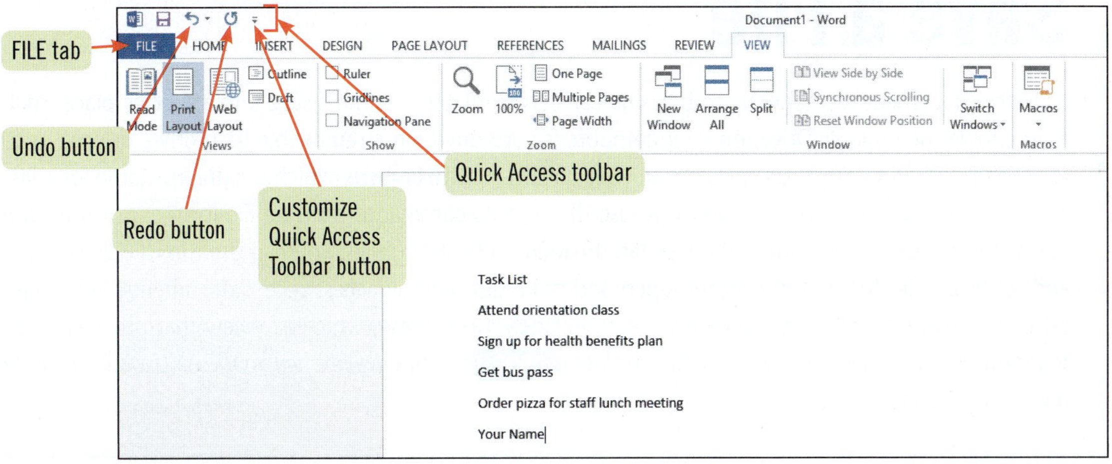

FILE tab

Undo button

Redo button

Customize
Quick Access
Toolbar button

Quick Access toolbar

Task List

Attend orientation class

Sign up for health benefits plan

Get bus pass

Order pizza for staff lunch meeting

Your Name

FIGURE C-13: Customize Quick Access Toolbar menu

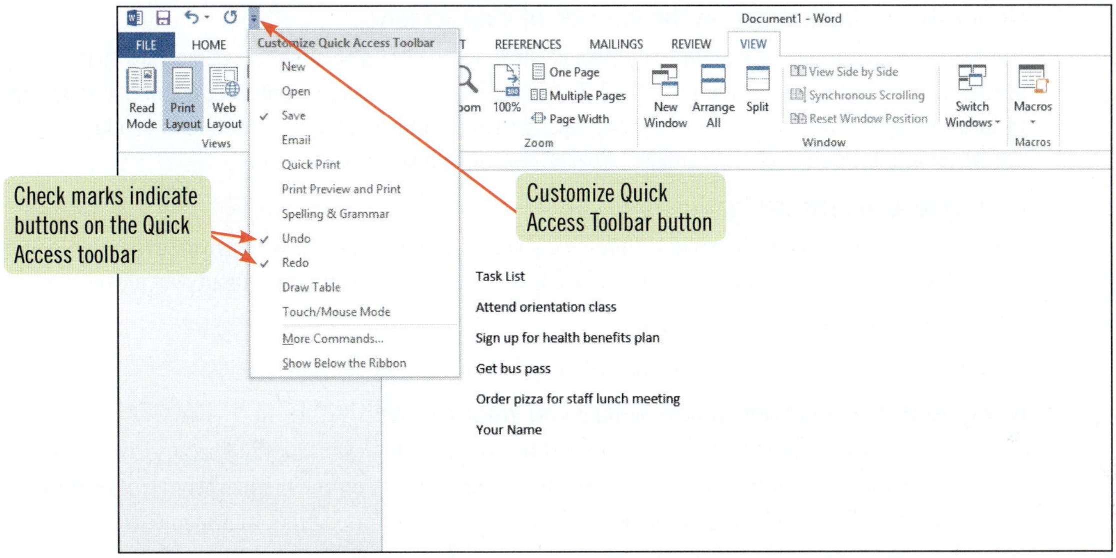

Check marks indicate
buttons on the Quick
Access toolbar

Customize Quick
Access Toolbar button

Customize Quick Access Toolbar
New
Open
✓ Save
Email
Quick Print
Print Preview and Print
Spelling & Grammar
✓ Undo
✓ Redo
Draw Table
Touch/Mouse Mode
More Commands...
Show Below the Ribbon

Task List

Attend orientation class

Sign up for health benefits plan

Get bus pass

Order pizza for staff lunch meeting

Your Name

FIGURE C-14: Moving the Quick Access toolbar

Quick Access toolbar is
now below the Ribbon

Task List

Attend orientation class

Sign up for health benefits plan

Get bus pass

Order pizza for staff lunch meeting

Your Name

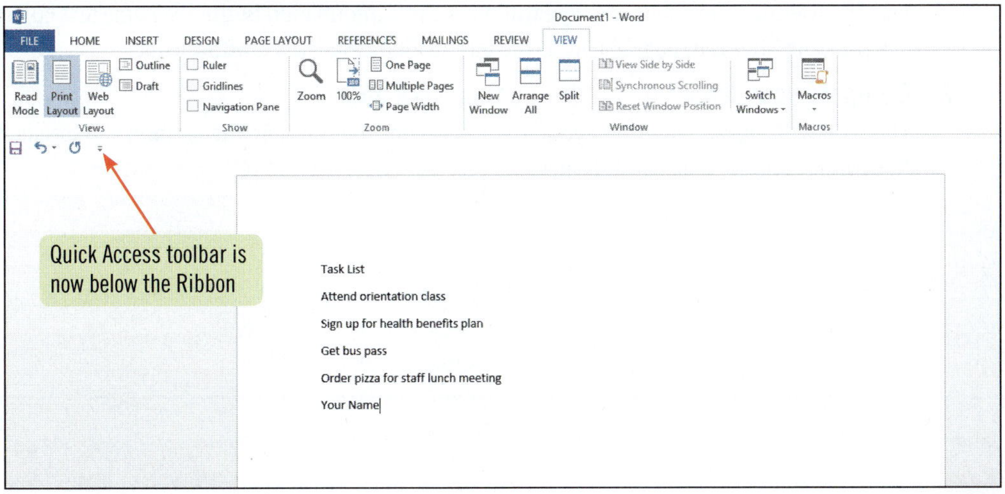

Save a File

To keep a document permanently so that you can access it later, you must save it to a specific place, such as in a folder on your SkyDrive, on your computer's hard drive, on a removable flash drive, or on a drive located on a network. You must also assign your document a **filename**, which is a unique name for a file, so you can identify and access it later. You use the Save As command to save a file for the first time. You access the Save As command on the FILE tab. In addition to saving files, you can use the FILE tab to view and set properties for your document, open and print files, quickly access recent documents, and more. When you open the FILE tab, you are working in **Backstage view**, which is a view that provides commands and tools to help you work with your files. **CASE** ▶ *You have finished your Task List document for now, so you decide to save it.*

STEPS

1. **Click the FILE tab on the Ribbon**

   A large window opens with "Info" at the top. Your document is no longer visible on screen, though you can see its filename in the title bar. You are now in Backstage view, which provides commands for working with files.

2. **Notice the navigation bar on the left side of your screen**

   The FILE tab navigation bar contains commands (such as Open and Save As) as well as tabs that display related commands for a particular task. The Info tab is selected. You use the tools on the Info tab to specify various settings for the open document. The Properties pane on the right shows information about the Task List document, including its size, number of pages, author, and last-modified date.

3. **Click Save As on the navigation bar**

   The Save As screen opens, as shown in **FIGURE C-15**. You use this screen to specify where to save your file. You can specify to save the file on your SkyDrive, on a USB drive, on your hard drive, or anywhere you specify.

4. **Click Computer, then click Browse**

   The Save As dialog box opens, showing the list of folders and files in the current folder.

5. **Navigate to the drive and folder where you want to save the file**

   Now you need to name the file. The File name text box displays the text "Task List" because this is the first line of text in the document; Word always suggests a filename based on the first few words in the unsaved open document. "Task List" is a good name for the file, so you don't need type a new name.

6. **Verify that Task List appears in the File name text box**

   You might see ".docx" at the end of the filename; .docx is the default file extension for this document. When you save a file, the app automatically assigns it a **file extension** to identify the app that created it. Documents created in Word 2013 have the file extension ".docx". Your computer might not be set to display file extensions, in which case you will not see this information in the File name text box or in the title bar of the app; this is not a problem, as the information is still saved with the file.

7. **Compare your screen to FIGURE C-16, then click Save**

   The Save As dialog box closes, and your Task List document is saved in the location you specified. Notice the title bar now displays the new filename.

FIGURE C-15: Save As screen

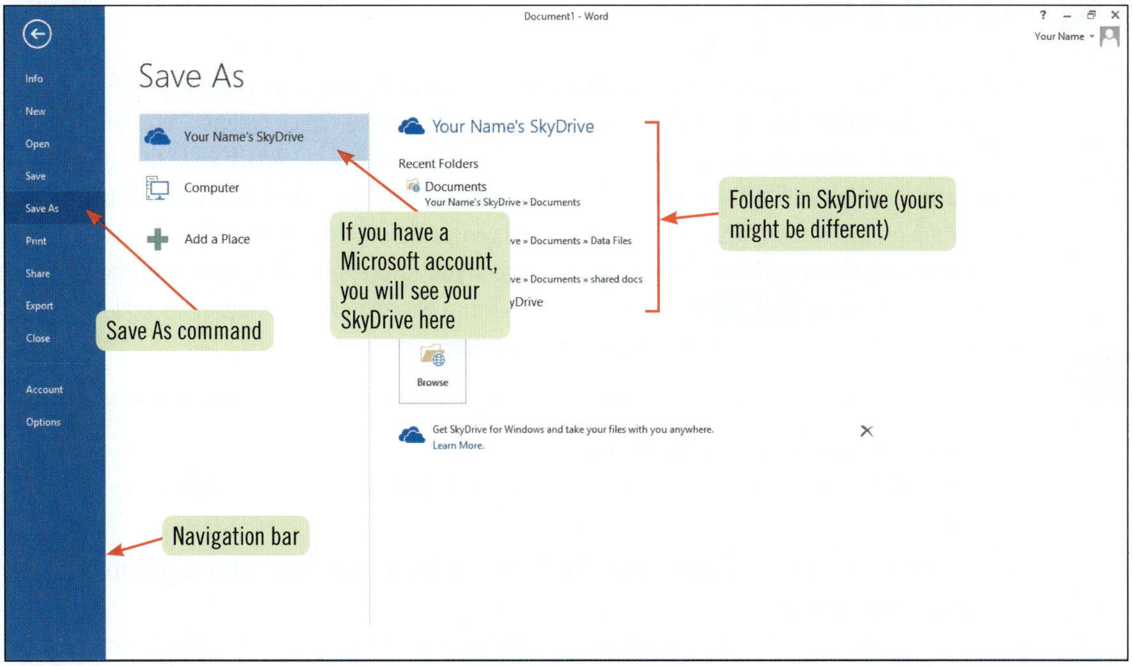

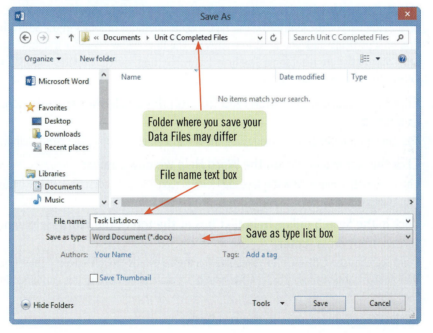

Save As command

If you have a Microsoft account, you will see your SkyDrive here

Folders in SkyDrive (yours might be different)

Navigation bar

FIGURE C-16: Save As dialog box

Folder where you save your Data Files may differ

File name text box

Save as type list box

Using SkyDrive and Web Apps

If you are signed into your Microsoft account, you can easily save your files to SkyDrive and be able to access them on other devices—such as a tablet or smartphone. SkyDrive is available as an app on smartphones, which makes access very easy. If you have the SkyDrive app installed on your phone, you can open files to view them. You can even make edits to documents on SkyDrive using Office Web Apps, which are simplified versions of the apps found in the Office 2013 suite. Because the Web Apps are online, they take up no computer disk space, and you can use them on any computer (as long as it is connected to the Internet). Using SkyDrive, you and your colleagues can create, edit, and store documents in the "cloud" and make the documents available to whomever you grant access. To use SkyDrive, you need a free Microsoft account, which you obtain at http://skydrive.live.com. You can find more information in the "Working in the Cloud" appendix.

Get Help

Office 2013 has a Help system designed to help you complete any task or use any feature in an Office program. The Office Help system is seamlessly integrated with the Office Online Web site and provides a wide range of content to help answer your questions. Help is **context sensitive** in that it displays topics and instructions geared to the specific task you are performing. For example, if you point to a command on any tab on the Ribbon, a ScreenTip opens, displaying a description of what the command does as well as its keyboard shortcut. Many ScreenTips also direct you to press [F1] for more information about that particular command. **CASE** *You decide to familiarize yourself with the Help system. Note: You must be connected to the Internet to perform the steps in this lesson.*

STEPS

1. **Click the INSERT tab on the Ribbon**

   The INSERT tab is now active and displays commands that help you insert shapes, pages, graphics, and other items.

2. **Position the mouse pointer over the Chart button in the Illustrations group until the ScreenTip appears**

   As shown in **FIGURE C-17**, the ScreenTip displays the command name (Add a Chart) and describes its purpose. It also displays a graphic of a chart to give you a visual image of this command.

   QUICK TIP
   You can also open the Help window in any Office application by pressing [F1].

3. **Click the Help button ❓ on the right end of the title bar**

   The Word Help window opens, as shown in **FIGURE C-18**. This Help window provides access to support information to help you use Office. You can type specific questions or topics in the Search box to find information on a particular task you need to complete. The links below "Popular searches" show Help topics that other Word users are requesting. The links below "Getting started" provide information on what's new in Office 2013 and other basic skills.

4. **Click Learn Word basics, then read through the article that appears, scrolling down as needed**

   You can return to the Home screen using the Home icon at the top of the Word Help window.

5. **Click the Home icon 🏠 on the Word Help window toolbar**

   The Word Help window now displays the Home screen. **TABLE C-3** describes all the buttons at the top of the Word Help window.

6. **Click in the Search online help text box at the top of the Word Help window, type touch screen, then press [Enter]**

   Word searches the Office Online Web site for the keywords "touch screen," then lists Help articles from the site that contain those words. A **keyword** is a searchable word that is contained in the Help database. See **FIGURE C-19**.

7. **Click Office Touch Guide in the results list**

   This topic provides a helpful visual reference to using Office on a touch screen device.

8. **Read the topic, scroll all the way down to the end of the article, then click the Close button ✖ in the Word Help window**

   The Help window closes, but your Task List document remains open.

FIGURE C-17: ScreenTip showing purpose of Add a Chart button

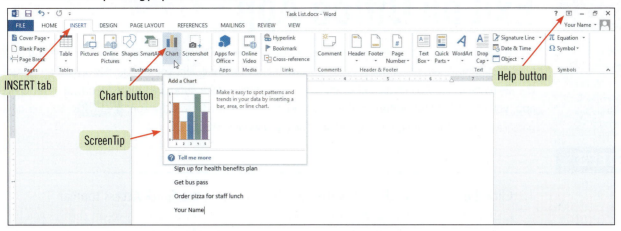

FIGURE C-18: Word Help window

FIGURE C-19: Word Help search results

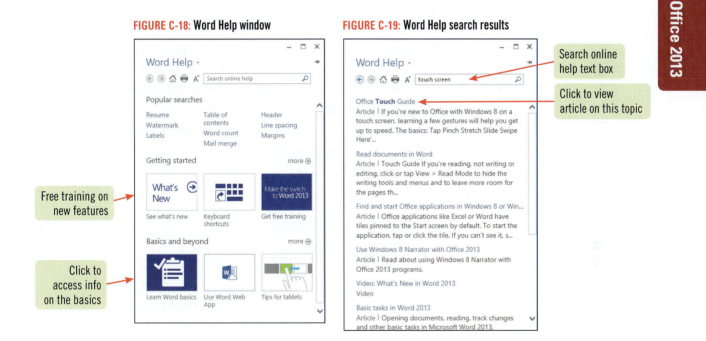

TABLE C-3: Word Help dialog box icons

icon	name	use to
←	Back	Go back to previous screen
→	Forward	Go to next screen
🏠	Home	Go to Home screen
🖶	Print	Print Help topic
A⁺	Use Large Text	Increase size of text in Help dialog box

Exit an Office App

When you complete all the work you want to accomplish in an Office app session, you can save and close your document. Later, when you want to work on the document again, you can quickly open it by clicking the file name in the Recent section of the app's start screen. When you are finished working in an Office app, you click the Close button on the right end of the title bar to exit the app. **CASE** ▸ *You decide to practice opening and closing the Task List file. Then, you will exit Word.*

STEPS

1. **Click the HOME tab, then click the Save button 🖫 on the Quick Access toolbar**

   Clicking the Save button on the Quick Access toolbar is a fast way to save any recent changes you have made to your document. It is a good idea to click the Save button frequently as you work to make sure you do not lose any data if you lose power or your computer crashes.

2. **Click the FILE tab, then click Close**

   The Task List document closes, but Word remains open. The HOME tab is now active. You can quickly locate and open the Task List document by using the FILE tab.

3. **Click the FILE tab**

   The Open screen opens in Backstage view, as shown in **FIGURE C-20**, and the Recent Documents list displays the names of documents opened recently. The Task List document is at the top of the list because it was the most recently opened document. You might see other document names listed below Task List.

4. **Click Task List below Recent Documents**

   The Task List document opens. You are now ready to close the document and end your Word session.

5. **Click the Close button ✖ at the far right end of the title bar, as shown in FIGURE C-21**

   Both the Task List document and the Word app close.

Using Office on a touch screen device

If you are running Office 2013 on a Windows 8 device with a touch screen, you can use gestures instead of mouse clicks to do various tasks including choosing commands. The basic gestures are **tap** (touch screen quickly with one finger), **pinch** (bring two fingers together), **stretch** (move two fingers apart), **slide** (drag an object using your finger), and **swipe** (move your finger from left to right). To choose a command on the Ribbon or in a dialog box, tap the button. To scroll, swipe the screen up, down, left, or right. To zoom in, stretch two fingers apart. To zoom out, pinch your fingers together. To hide the Ribbon, tap the Ribbon Display Options button 🔼 on the title bar, then tap Auto-Hide Ribbon.

FIGURE C-20: Opening a recent document from the Open screen

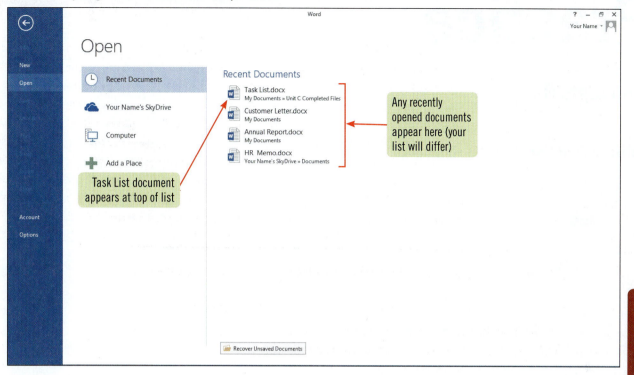

FIGURE C-21: Exiting an app using the Close button

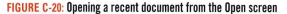

Sharing your saved documents

As you work through this book, you will create many documents that you will need to submit to your instructor. To conserve paper and be more efficient, your instructor might ask you to submit your completed documents electronically. You can email your saved documents easily from within Office using the Share page on the FILE tab. To do this, click the FILE tab then click Share. On the Share page, click Email, then click Send as Attachment. If your file is saved to SkyDrive you can click the Get a Link button to create an email containing a link to where the recipient can download the document. The Share page also lets you fax a document or email a copy of a document in PDF or XPS formats. These formats preserve the content and formatting in the document, but they make the content difficult for others to change or edit.

Office 2013

Practice

Concepts Review

Label each of the elements shown in FIGURE C-22.

FIGURE C-22

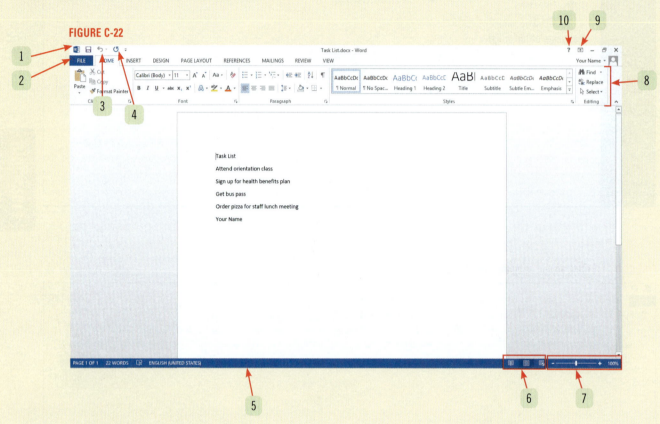

Match each of the following tasks with the most appropriate app for completing it.

11. Create slides for a company-meeting presentation

12. Create a budget

13. Manage a large amount of customer information

14. Create a report containing mostly text with some graphics

15. Store contact information and send email

a. Excel

b. Access

c. Outlook

d. PowerPoint

e. Word

Creating a Document

CASE ▶ Karen Rivera, the marketing director for Outdoor Designs, asks you to finish creating a letter to the winner of the annual Outdoor Designs kite competition. Karen has already created a document that contains part of the letter. You will open Karen's letter; add, edit, and rearrange text in it; proof it for spelling errors; then print it.

Unit Objectives

After completing this unit, you will be able to:

- Create a new document from an existing file
- Enter text in a document
- Select and edit text
- Copy text

- Move text
- Find and replace text
- Format text using the Mini toolbar
- Check spelling and grammar
- Preview and print a document

Files You Will Need

D-1.docx
D-2.docx
D-3.docx
D-4.docx
D-5.docx

©HelenStock/Shutterstock

Create a New Document from an Existing File

Sometimes it is useful to create a new document that uses content from an existing document. For instance, suppose you need to write a memo that will use content from a memo you already wrote. You can use the Open dialog box to open the existing memo. Then, before making any changes to the opened memo, you can use the Save As command to save a copy of it with a new name. This keeps the original file intact in case you want to use it again, while saving you the trouble of creating the new memo from scratch. **CASE** ▶ *You need to complete Karen's letter to the winner of the kite competition. You need to open Karen's document and save it with a different name, to keep Karen's original letter intact.*

STEPS

1. **Go to the Windows 8 Start screen, type Word, then click Word 2013 in the Results list**
   The Word Start screen opens. You want to open an existing file.

2. **Click Open Other Documents at the bottom of the Recent pane on the left side of your screen**
   The Open screen appears in Backstage view and displays Places where files are stored, including Recent Documents (which is currently selected), and Computer (which is your computer as well as any external drives attached to it). If you are signed into a Microsoft account, then you will also see your SkyDrive listed.

3. **Click Computer, click Browse, navigate to the location where you store your Data Files, then double-click the Unit D folder**
   The Open dialog box displays the Data Files for Unit D. See **FIGURE D-1**.

4. **Click D-1.docx, then click Open**
   Karen's partially completed document opens in the document window in Print Layout view.

5. **Click the FILE tab, click Save As to open the Save As screen, click Computer, then click Browse**
   The Save As dialog box opens, as shown in **FIGURE D-2**. You use the Save As dialog box to create a copy of the document with a new name. Notice that the name in the File name text box is **selected**, or highlighted. Because the text is selected—any words you type replace the selected text in the File name text box.

6. **Type D-Kite Winner Letter**
   The File name text box now contains the new title you typed. Because the filename begins with "D-", you will be able to identify it as a file you created for Unit D of this book.

7. **Click Save**
   Word saves the D-Kite Winner Letter file in the drive and folder you specified. The title bar changes to reflect the new name, as shown in **FIGURE D-3**. The file D-1 closes and remains intact.

Creating a new document from a template

If you need to create a certain type of document, you might want to start from a template. A **template** is a file that contains predesigned formatting and text for common business documents such as letters, business cards, and reports. To create a document from a template, click the FILE tab, then click New to open the New screen in Backstage view, then click the template you want. A new document based on the template opens on your screen, ready for you to customize and save. To access a huge variety of templates, you can search online by typing keywords in the search box at the top of the New screen.

FIGURE D-1: Open dialog Box

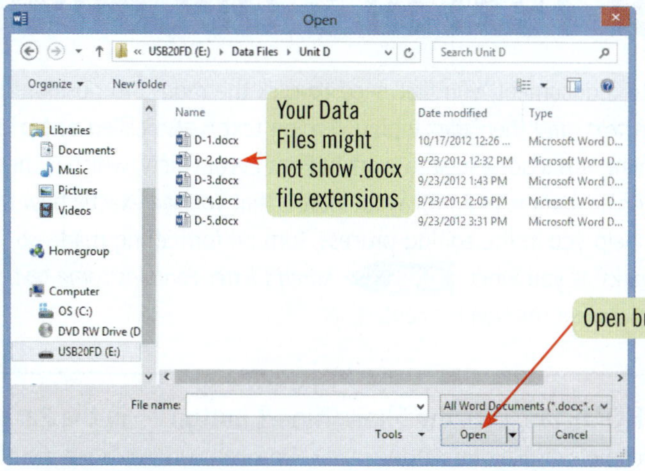
Open
Your Data Files might not show .docx file extensions
Open button
D-1.docx
D-2.docx
D-3.docx
D-4.docx
D-5.docx

FIGURE D-2: Save As dialog box

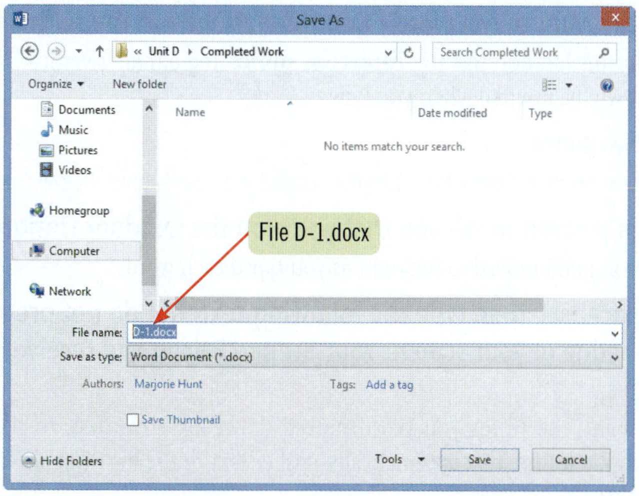
Save As
File D-1.docx
No items match your search.
File name: D-1.docx
Save as type: Word Document (*.docx)

FIGURE D-3: D-Kite Winner Letter open in Print Layout view

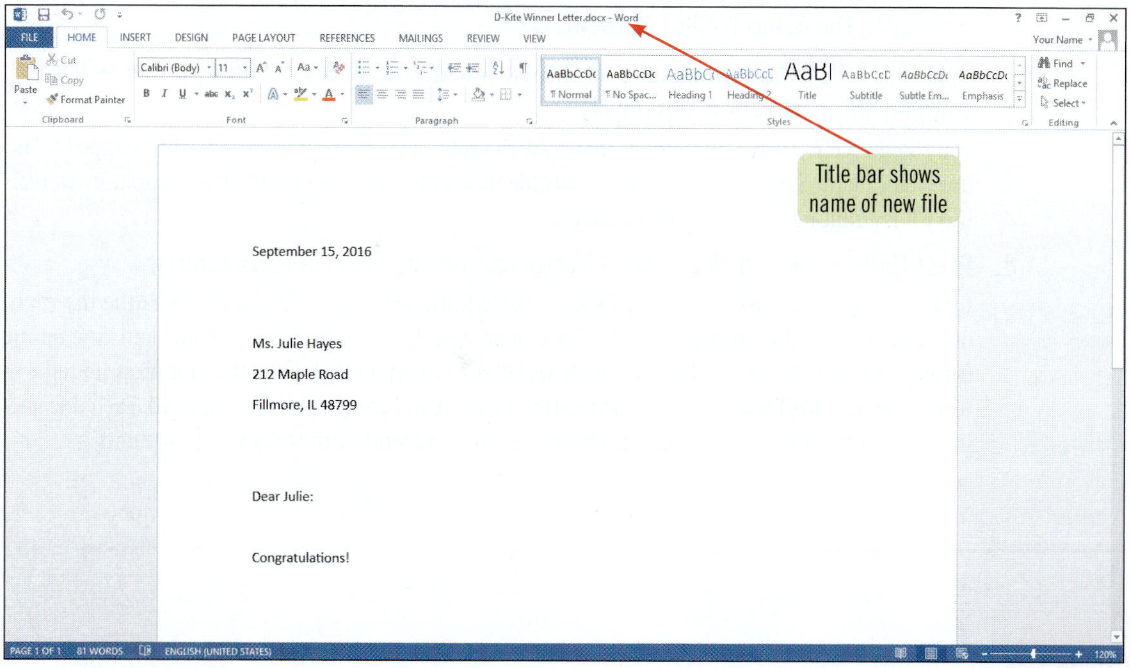
D-Kite Winner Letter.docx - Word
Title bar shows name of new file
September 15, 2016
Ms. Julie Hayes
212 Maple Road
Fillmore, IL 48799
Dear Julie:
Congratulations!

Enter Text in a Document

Learning
Outcomes
• Display formatting
  marks
• Enter text in Print
  Layout view
• Explain
  AutoCorrect

To add text to a document, you first need to click the mouse to position the insertion point where you want to insert text, and then start typing. Typing text is also called **entering** text. When you enter text into a document, it is a good idea to work in Print Layout view, which is the default view for entering and editing text. An advantage of Print Layout view is that you see exactly how the text will look when printed on paper. To help you in the editing process, turn on formatting marks so you can see blank spaces and paragraph marks as you work. **CASE** ▶ *Karen's letter contains some text. You need to add a paragraph informing the recipient she won the contest.*

STEPS

1. **On the HOME tab, click the Show/Hide ¶ button ¶ in the Paragraph group**

   Your screen now displays formatting marks. Dots between words represent spaces, and a paragraph mark) (¶) represents a paragraph return that Word inserts when you press [Enter]. Showing formatting marks when you write and edit makes it easier to see extra spaces, paragraph returns, and other punctuation errors.

2. **Click to the right of the word "Congratulations!" in the sixth line of text**

   Clicking in this location sets the **insertion point**, the blinking vertical line on the screen that controls where text will be inserted when you type.

3. **Press ↓ two times**

   The insertion point is now set next to the second paragraph mark below "Congratulations!".

4. **Type I am pleased to tell you that you won the Outdoor Designs kite competition!**

   The insertion point moved to the right as you typed each word.

5. **Press [Spacebar], then type the following text, but do not press [Enter] when you reach the right edge of your screen: Your Striped Falcon kite received the highest scores from our judges.**

   At some point, the words you typed moved down, or **wrapped**, to the next line. This is known as **word wrap**, a feature that automatically pushes text to the next line when the insertion point meets the right margin.

6. **Press [Spacebar], type teh, then press [Spacebar]**

   Notice that even though you typed "teh", Word assumed that you meant to type "The" and automatically corrected it. This feature is called **AutoCorrect**.

7. **Type the following text exactly as shown (including errors): follong prizes will be shipped shipped to you separately:**

   You should see red wavy lines under the word "follong" and the second instance of "shipped." These red lines indicate the Spell Checker automatically identified these as either misspelled or duplicate words. Green wavy lines indicate possible grammatical errors.

8. **Press [Enter], then click the Save button 🖫 on the Quick Access toolbar**

   Compare your screen to **FIGURE D-4**. Pressing [Enter] inserted a blank line and moved the insertion point down two lines to the left margin. Although you pressed [Enter] only once, an extra blank line was inserted because the default style in this document specifies to insert a blank line after you press [Enter] to start a new paragraph. **Styles** are settings that control how text and paragraphs are formatted. Each document has its own set of styles, which you can easily change. You will work with styles in a future unit.

FIGURE D-4: Letter with new text entered

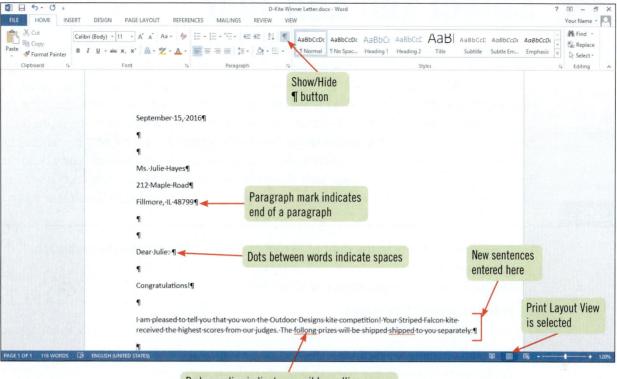

Show/Hide ¶ button

September·15,·2016¶

¶

¶

Ms.·Julie·Hayes¶

212·Maple·Road¶

Fillmore,·IL·48799¶ ← Paragraph mark indicates end of a paragraph

¶

¶

Dear·Julie:·¶ ← Dots between words indicate spaces

¶

Congratulations!¶

¶

I·am·pleased·to·tell·you·that·you·won·the·Outdoor·Designs·kite·competition!·Your·Striped·Falcon·kite·received·the·highest·scores·from·our·judges.·The·follong·prizes·will·be·shipped·shipped·to·you·separately:¶

New sentences entered here

Print Layout View is selected

Red wavy line indicates possible spelling error

Word 2013

Using AutoCorrect

The AutoCorrect feature works automatically to catch and correct incorrect spellings of common words as you type them. For example, if you type "comapny" instead of "company," as soon as you press [Spacebar], Word corrects the misspelling. After Word makes the correction, you can point to the word to make a small blue bar appear under the corrected text. If you place the pointer over this bar, the AutoCorrect Options button appears. Click the AutoCorrect Options button to display a list of options, as shown in **FIGURE D-5**; then click an option.

You can change AutoCorrect settings in the AutoCorrect dialog box. To open this dialog box, click Control AutoCorrect Options on the AutoCorrect menu, or click the FILE tab, click Options, click Proofing in the Word Options dialog box, then click AutoCorrect Options.

FIGURE D-5: AutoCorrect Options menu

The company

↶ Change back to "comapny"

Stop Automatically Correcting "comapny"

⚡ Control AutoCorrect Options...

Select and Edit Text

You can **edit**, or modify, the text in a Word document in several ways. To delete individual letters, first click to the right of the unwanted letters to set the insertion point and then press [Backspace], or click to the left of the letters and then press [Delete]. To delete several words or paragraphs, you must first **select**, or highlight, the unwanted text, then press [Delete]. To select text, drag the I-beam mouse pointer across the text, then release the mouse button. To edit text, you need to move the insertion point around the document. You can do this by pointing and clicking or by using the keyboard. **TABLE D-1** describes other useful methods for selecting text. **TABLE D-2** describes keys you can use to move the insertion point around the document. **CASE** *You need to make some changes to the letter to correct errors and improve wording. You also decide to change the spacing of the document to single spaced, so it is properly formatted for a letter.*

STEPS

1. **Press the ↓ then click to the right of "$100" in the line of text below the paragraph you typed**
   The insertion point is just after the second "0" in "100".

2. **Press [Backspace] three times**
   You deleted "100". Each time you pressed [Backspace], you deleted the character to the left of the insertion point.

3. **Type 250**
   The amount of the prize money now reads $250, the correct amount.

4. **Double-click the second instance of shipped in the second line of the new paragraph you typed**
   The word "shipped" is now selected. Double-clicking a word selects the entire word.

5. **Press [Delete]**
   The second instance of the word "shipped" is removed from the document. You could have deleted either instance of the duplicated word to remove the red wavy line and correct the error. The text after the deleted word wraps back to fill the empty space.

6. **Scroll to the end of the document, place the mouse pointer to the left of "Karen Rivera" (the last line of the document) until the pointer changes to ⟋, then click**
   See **FIGURE D-6**. The entire line of text ("Karen Rivera") is selected, including the paragraph symbol at the end of the line. The area to the left of the left margin is the **selection bar**, which you use to select entire lines. When you place the mouse pointer in the selection bar, it changes to ⟋.

7. **Type your name**
   Your name replaces Karen's name in the letter.

8. **Press [Ctrl][Home] to move the insertion point to the beginning of the document**
   Notice the line spacing of the letter is double spaced after each paragraph mark ¶. So the letter is properly formatted, you want to change the line spacing to be single spaced. To do this, you first need to select all the text in the document.

9. **Press [Ctrl][A] to select the entire document, click the No Spacing button in the Styles group, click anywhere to deselect the text, then save your changes**
   The document is now single spaced after each paragraph mark. Compare your screen to **FIGURE D-7**.

FIGURE D-6: Selecting an entire line of text

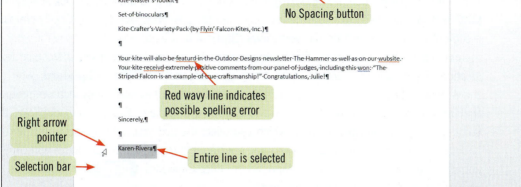

No Spacing button

Red wavy line indicates possible spelling error

Right arrow pointer

Selection bar

Entire line is selected

FIGURE D-7: Document after applying No Spacing style

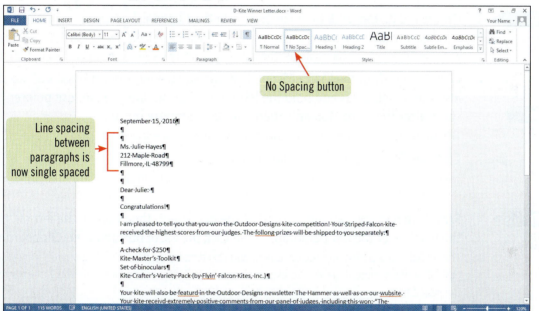

No Spacing button

Line spacing between paragraphs is now single spaced

TABLE D-1: Methods for selecting text

text to select	selection method
One word	Double-click the word
A paragraph	Triple-click in the paragraph
An entire document	Press [Ctrl][A]
A line of text	Position to the left of the line, then click

TABLE D-2: Useful keyboard shortcuts for moving the insertion point

keyboard method	moves insertion point
↑ or ↓	Up or down one line
← or →	To the left or right
[Ctrl]→ or [Ctrl]←	One word to the left or right
[Home] or [End]	To the beginning or end of the line
[Ctrl][Home] or [Ctrl][End]	To the beginning or end of the document

Creating a Document

Copy Text

Learning Outcomes
• Copy and paste text using the Office Clipboard
• Copy text using drag and drop

When editing a document, you often need to copy text from one place to another. **Copying** leaves the text in its original location, and **pasting** moves a duplicate of it to the location you specify. To copy and paste text, you first need to select the text you want to copy. Next, you use the Copy command to place a copy of the selected text on the **Windows Clipboard**, a temporary storage area in your computer's memory for copied or cut items. Finally, you use the Paste command to insert the copied text to a new location. If you need to copy multiple items, you can use the **Office Clipboard**, which works like the Windows Clipboard but stores up to 24 items at a time and is available only in Office programs. To use the Office Clipboard, you need to open the Clipboard task pane. You can also duplicate text using a technique called **drag and drop**, in which you select the text you want to copy, press and hold [Ctrl], and then use the mouse to drag a copy of the selected text to a new location. Items you copy using drag and drop do not get placed on the Windows or Office Clipboard. **CASE** *You decide to make further edits to the letter by copying and pasting text.*

STEPS

1. **On the HOME tab, click the launcher ▣ in the Clipboard group**

   The Clipboard task pane opens to the left of the document window. You use the Clipboard task pane to gather multiple cut and copied items. The task pane is empty because you have not copied or cut any text.

2. **Click to the left of the "S" in "Striped" in the line below "Congratulations!" to set the insertion point, press and hold the left mouse button, drag the mouse pointer to the space after the word "Falcon", then release the mouse button**

   The words "Striped Falcon" and the space that follows are now selected.

3. **Click the Copy button in the Clipboard group**

   The selected text is copied to the Office Clipboard and appears in the Clipboard task pane, as shown in **FIGURE D-8**.

4. **Scroll down so you can see the end of the document, then click to the left of "kite" in the first line of the last paragraph, then click the Paste button in the Clipboard group**

   The copied text is pasted into the document and also remains on the Office Clipboard, from which you can paste it as many more times as you like, as shown in **FIGURE D-9**. The Paste Options button appears under the pasted text.

5. **Click the Paste Options button 🖺 (Ctrl)▼**

   The Paste Options menu opens and displays buttons for applying formatting to the pasted text. By default, the pasted text maintains its original formatting, which in this situation is fine, since it matches the text.

6. **Press [Esc] to close the Paste Options menu**

7. **Select Outdoor Designs and the space after it in the first line of the first paragraph**

8. **Press and hold [Ctrl], drag the selected text to the left of "Kite Master's Toolkit" three lines below the paragraph, release the mouse button, then release [Ctrl]**

   As you drag, the pointer changes to an indicator line that shows where the text will be inserted. This instance of "Outdoor Designs" does not get copied to the Clipboard, as shown in **FIGURE D-10**.

9. **Click the Save button 🖫 on the Quick Access toolbar**

FIGURE D-8: Selected text copied to the Office Clipboard

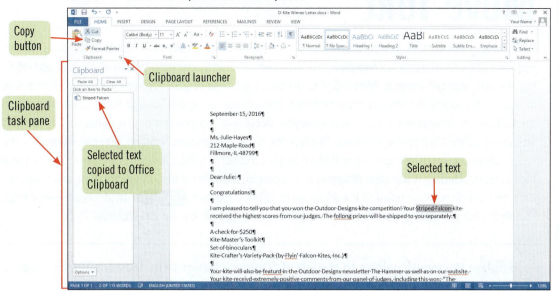

Copy button

Clipboard launcher

Clipboard task pane

Selected text copied to Office Clipboard

Selected text

FIGURE D-9: Text pasted from the Office Clipboard

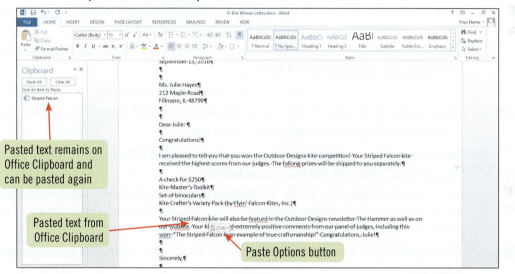

Pasted text remains on Office Clipboard and can be pasted again

Pasted text from Office Clipboard

Paste Options button

FIGURE D-10: Dragged and copied text

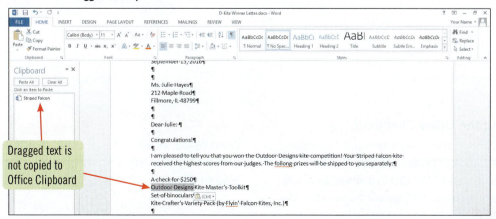

Dragged text is not copied to Office Clipboard

Move Text

While editing a document, you might decide that certain text works better in a different location. Perhaps you want to switch the order of two paragraphs, or two words in a sentence. Instead of deleting and retyping the text, you can move it. **Moving** text removes it from its original location and places it in a new location that you specify. You can move text to a new location using the Cut and Paste commands. Using the **Cut** command removes selected text from your document and places it on the Windows Clipboard as well as the Office Clipboard if activated. To place the cut text in another location, you can either click the Paste button on the HOME tab of the Ribbon or click the item in the Clipboard task pane. You can also move text by selecting it and then dragging it to a new location. Items that you move using the drag-and-drop method do not get copied to the Windows or Office Clipboard. **CASE** ▷ *While checking your letter, you decide that you want to rearrange the list of prizes so they appear in a more logical order.*

STEPS

1. **Position the mouse pointer to the left of "Outdoor Designs Kite Master's Toolkit" until it changes to ⤢, then click**

   The entire line, including the paragraph mark, is selected, as shown in **FIGURE D-11**.

2. **On the HOME tab, click the Cut button in the Clipboard group**

   The text is cut from the document and is now the first item in the Clipboard task pane. The last item you cut or copy becomes the first item in the task pane. If you cut or copy more than 24 items without clearing the task pane, the oldest item is deleted to make room for the new one.

3. **Click to the left of the "K" in "Kite Crafter's Variety Pack", then click the Paste button in the Clipboard group on the Ribbon**

   The text from the Clipboard is pasted to the new location, on the line below "Set of binoculars".

4. **Place the mouse pointer in the selection bar to the left of "Set of binoculars" until it changes to ⤢, then click to select the entire line**

5. **Move the pointer over the selected text, drag it to the left of the "K" in "Kite Crafter's Variety Pack", then release the mouse button**

   As you drag, the pointer changes to ⤢, and an indicator line shows you where the text will be placed. Notice the dragged text does not appear as an item on the Clipboard. Now the prizes are listed in a more logical order, with the best prizes listed first, as shown in **FIGURE D-12**.

6. **Click anywhere to deselect the text, then click the Close button on the Clipboard task pane**

   The task pane closes.

7. **Click the Save button 🖫 on the Quick Access toolbar**

Activating the Office Clipboard

The Office Clipboard stores multiple items only if it is active. Opening the Clipboard task pane automatically makes it active. If you want to activate the Office Clipboard without showing the task pane, click Options on the Clipboard task pane, then click Collect Without Showing Office Clipboard. If the Office Clipboard is not active, you can only copy one item at a time using the Windows Clipboard.

FIGURE D-11: Selecting a line of text

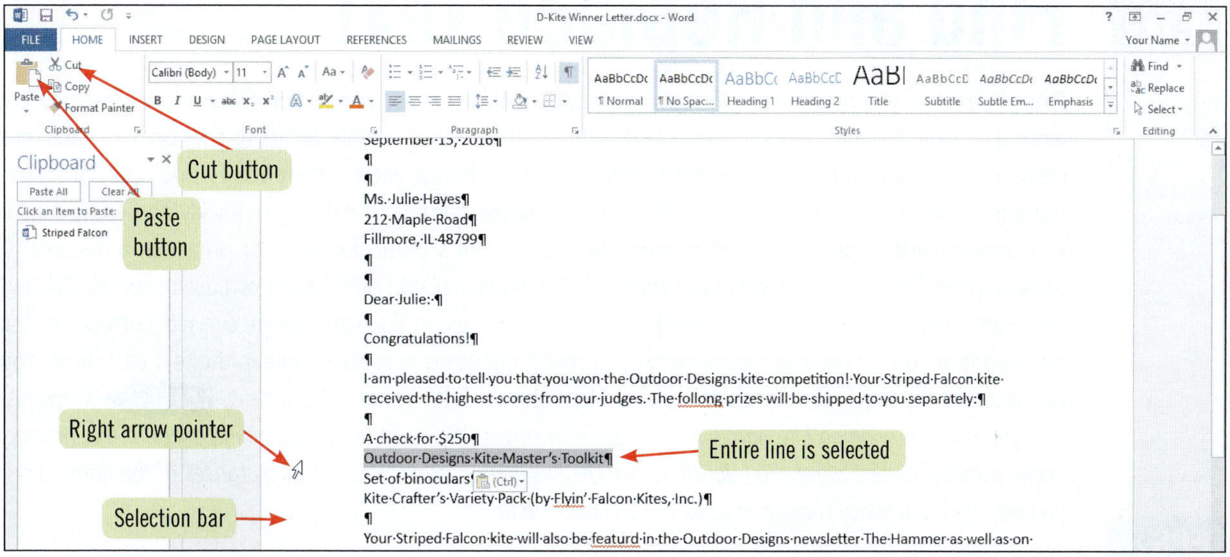

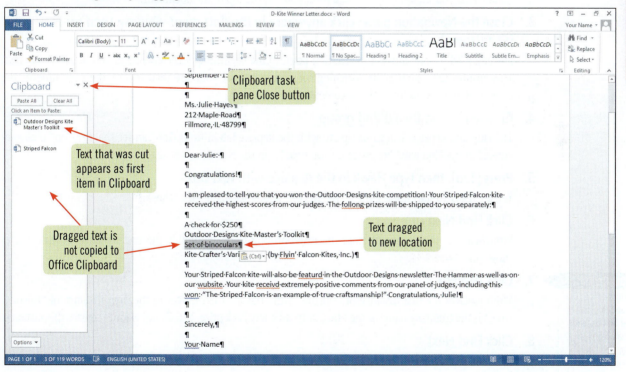

FIGURE D-12: Moving text by dragging it

Find and Replace Text

Once in a while you might need to make a global change in a document. For instance, suppose you are writing a novel about a character named Joe. After writing 50 pages, you decide to change the character's name to Sam. You could manually edit the document to change each occurrence of "Joe" to "Sam", but there is an easier, more automated method. The **Replace** command helps you quickly and easily substitute a new word or phrase for one or more occurrences of a particular word or phrase in a document. Choosing the Replace command opens the Find and Replace dialog box, which you use to specify the text you want to find and the text with which you want to replace it. You can replace every occurrence of the text in one action, or you can review each occurrence, choosing to replace or keep the text each time. You can also use the Navigation pane to quickly highlight all instances of specific text. **CASE** *Karen just told you that the winning kite name in the letter is incorrect. You need to replace all instances of the incorrect name with the correct name. You decide to use the Navigation pane to locate all instances of the name. Then you will use the Replace command to fix the incorrect name.*

STEPS

1. **On the HOME tab, click Find in the Editing group**

   The Navigation Pane opens on the left side of your screen.

2. **Type Falcon**

   All the instances of "Falcon" are now highlighted in yellow. You can quickly see there are four instances of "Falcon" in the document. See **FIGURE D-13**. You can use the Find and Replace dialog box to fix the incorrect names. First you should move the insertion point to the top of the document.

3. **Close the Navigation pane, click anywhere in the document window, then press [Ctrl][Home]**

   Pressing [Ctrl][Home] moves the insertion point to the beginning of the document and deselects any text. This ensures that Word starts searching for occurrences of your specified text at the beginning of the document and checks the entire document.

4. **Click Replace in the Editing group**

   The Find and Replace dialog box opens, with the Replace tab in front. You can see that "Falcon" is already entered in the Find what box, because you typed it in the Navigation Pane.

5. **Press [Tab], then type Hawk in the Replace with text box**

   You are ready to start finding the word "Falcon" and replacing it with "Hawk."

6. **Click Find Next**

   Word searches the document from the insertion point and highlights the first instance of "Falcon", as shown in **FIGURE D-14**.

7. **Click Replace**

   Word replaces the first instance of "Falcon" with "Hawk", then moves to the next instance of "Falcon", which is the company name of the Kite Crafter's Variety Pack prize. You do not want to replace this instance.

8. **Click Find Next**

   Word locates the next instance of "Falcon".

9. **Click Replace two more times, click OK, click Close in the Find and Replace dialog box, then click 🖫 on the Quick Access toolbar**

   Your changes are saved.

FIGURE D-13: Finding text using the Navigation pane

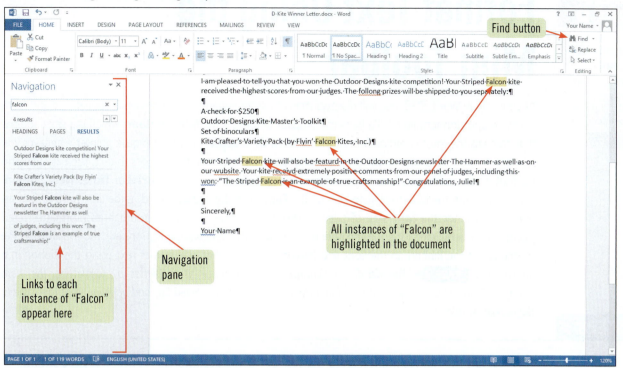

FIGURE D-14: Finding text using the Find and Replace dialog box

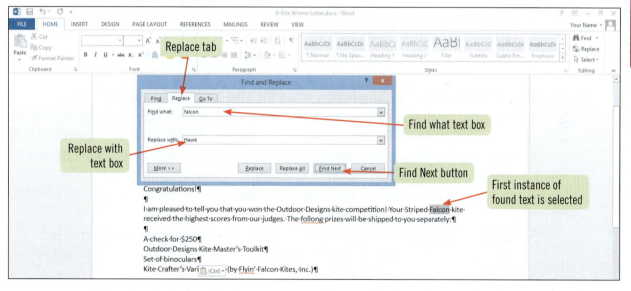

Using research tools

As you create documents in Word, you might want to look up words or information as you work. You can tap into powerful research tools in Word. For instance, you can easily download an online dictionary (such as Merriam-Webster) and look up the definition of any word as you work. To add a dictionary, click the REVIEW tab, click the Define button in the Proofing group, choose the dictionary you want to install in the Dictionaries pane, then click Download. Once a dictionary is installed, you can look up definitions for any word by right-clicking the word, then clicking Define to open the Dictionary pane with the word and definition displayed. To access the built-in thesaurus, click Thesaurus in the Proofing group on the REVIEW tab to open the Thesaurus pane. Type a word in the Search box, then press [Enter] to display a list of synonyms for the word.

Format Text Using the Mini Toolbar

Learning Outcomes
- Explain the Mini toolbar
- Apply formatting to text using the Mini toolbar

As you work in Word 2013, you will discover many tools for enhancing a document's appearance and readability by applying formatting. Perhaps the simplest of these is the **Mini toolbar**, which is a small toolbar that contains the most common formatting commands; it appears near the mouse pointer whenever you select text. The Mini toolbar is useful for making quick, basic formatting changes to text, such as changing the font of selected text. A **font** is the design of a set of characters, such as **Arial** or **Times New Roman**. You can also use the Mini toolbar to change the **font style** by applying bold, underline, or italic formatting, or to change the **font size** of selected text so it is larger or smaller. You can also format selected paragraphs as a bulleted list using the Mini toolbar. All of the Mini toolbar buttons are also available on the HOME tab of the Ribbon, in the Font and Paragraph groups. You will format text using the Ribbon in a future unit. **CASE** ▸ *You decide to enhance the appearance of the letter by formatting the word "Congratulations!" in a larger font size, formatting the prizes as a bulleted list, and applying italic font style to the newsletter title.*

STEPS

1. **Position the mouse pointer ⏴ to the left of "Congratulations!" in the first paragraph, then click**

   The word "Congratulations" and the exclamation point and the paragraph mark (¶) that follow it are selected. The Mini toolbar appears as a ghosted image near the selected text.

2. **Move the mouse pointer toward the Mini toolbar until it appears in a solid form, then click the Bold button B on the Mini toolbar**

   The selected text "Congratulations!" now appears in a darker and thicker font, which sets it apart from the other text in the letter.

3. **Click the Increase Font Size button A˄ on the Mini toolbar three times**

   The selected text grows in size from 11 to 16, as shown in **FIGURE D-15**. The new font size appears in the Font Size box on the Mini toolbar. You measure font size using points. A **point** is 1⁄72", so a font size of 12 is 1⁄6".

4. **Select the four lines of text containing the prizes, starting with A check for $250 and ending with Kite Crafter's Variety Pack (by Flyin' Falcon Kites, Inc.)**

   The four prizes are now selected. You can now apply formatting to the selected text. You decide to make the prizes look more ordered by formatting them as a bulleted list.

5. **Click the Bullets button ☰ on the Mini toolbar, then click outside the selected text**

   Each prize is indented and preceded by a small round dot, or **bullet**. The listed prizes now stand out much better from the body of the letter and help create a more organized appearance.

6. **Select the text The Hammer in the paragraph below the bulleted list, click the Italic button *I* on the Mini toolbar, then save your changes**

   The title of the Outdoor Designs newsletter, *The Hammer*, now appears in italic. Compare your screen to **FIGURE D-16**.

FIGURE D-15: Using the Mini toolbar to format text

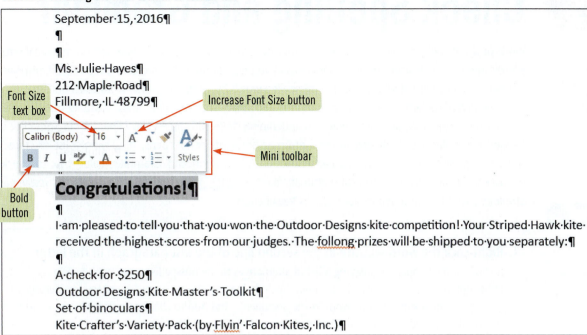

FIGURE D-16: Letter with formatted text and bulleted list

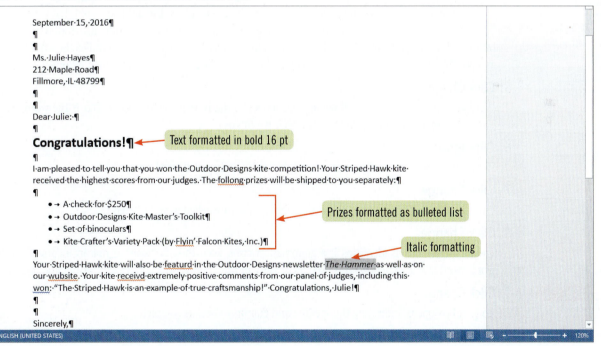

Check Spelling and Grammar

Learning Outcome
• Find and correct spelling and grammatical errors

Word provides tools to help you make sure your documents are free of spelling and grammatical errors. Word's AutoCorrect feature corrects your errors as you type them, but Word cannot correct all mistakes in this way. The program identifies possible misspelled words by comparing each word to its built-in dictionary, then underlines any words that are not in its dictionary with red wavy lines. Word identifies possible grammatical errors such as passive voice by underlining them with green wavy lines. If you right-click the flagged misspelled words or grammatical errors, a shortcut menu opens, displaying a list of correctly spelled or phrased alternatives. You can also open the Spelling and Grammar dialog box to check a document for misspelled words and grammatical errors. **CASE** *You decide to use Word's spelling and grammar checking tools to ensure your letter is free of errors.*

STEPS

1. **Right-click the word wubsite in the second line of the last paragraph in the letter**

   A shortcut menu opens, displaying a list of alternatives to the misspelled word, as shown in **FIGURE D-17**. Other options you can choose in this menu include Ignore All (if you want Word to stop alerting you to the possible misspelling of this word in the document), and Add to Dictionary (if you want Word to add this word as spelled to its built-in dictionary).

2. **Click website from the list at the top of the shortcut menu**

   The shortcut menu closes, and the word "website" replaces the misspelled word.

3. **Click the REVIEW tab on the Ribbon**

   QUICK TIP
   If the correct spelling of the word does not appear in the list, you can edit the text in the top section of the pane, then click Change.

4. **Press [Ctrl][Home] to move the insertion point to the top of the letter, then click the Spelling & Grammar button in the Proofing group**

   The Spelling pane opens, as shown in **FIGURE D-18**. The top text box displays text in red that is flagged as a problem, and the bottom text box displays suggestions for fixing it. The pane also contains an Ignore button, which you can click if you do not want Word to make a change. Word identifies the word "follong" as a possible misspelled word. It suggests changing the spelling to "following," which is correct.

5. **Click Change**

   Word changes "follong" to "following" and moves to the next possible error, which is the word "Flyin'" This is part of a brand name, so you want to leave this as is.

6. **Click Ignore**

   Word advances to the next possible error, which is the misspelled word "featurd."

7. **Click Change**

   Word advances to the next possible error, which is the misspelled word "receivd."

8. **Click Change**

   The next error that is identified is a grammatical error. Even though "won" is not an incorrectly spelled word, Word is able to tell that it is used incorrectly in this context. The correct word should be "one".

   TROUBLE
   If your first or last name is flagged as a possible misspelled word, click Ignore.

9. **Click Change**

   An alert box opens, indicating the spelling and grammar check is complete.

10. **Click OK, then click 🖫 to save your changes**

FIGURE D-17: Spelling shortcut menu with possible alternatives

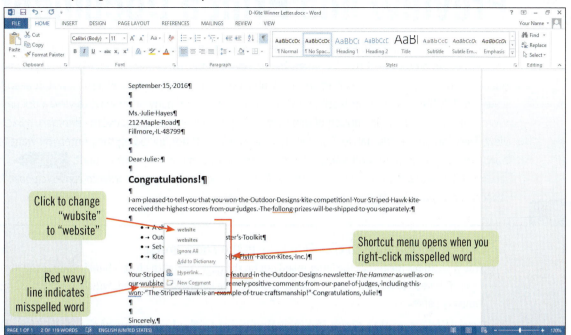

Click to change "wubsite" to "website"

Red wavy line indicates misspelled word

Shortcut menu opens when you right-click misspelled word

FIGURE D-18: Spelling task pane with possible spelling error flagged

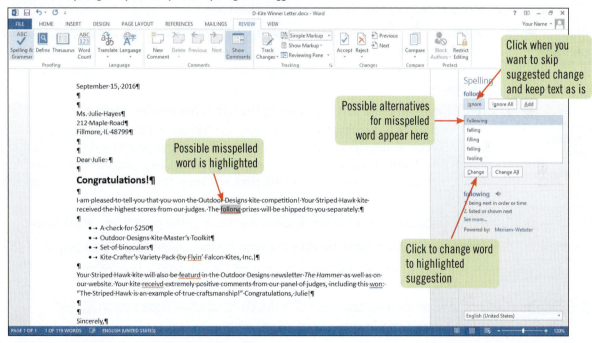

Possible misspelled word is highlighted

Possible alternatives for misspelled word appear here

Click when you want to skip suggested change and keep text as is

Click to change word to highlighted suggestion

Translating documents into other languages

Word 2013 has the ability to translate any word in your document, or even an entire document, into more than 20 different languages. To translate an entire document from one language to another, on the REVIEW tab click the Translate button in the Language group, click Choose Translation Language, specify the Translate from and Translate to languages, then click OK. Once you have specified your language, click Translate in the Language group, then click Translate Document. An alert box opens, telling you the document will be sent over the Internet in unencrypted HTML format. Click Send to send the document, and seconds later your document appears in your browser window fully translated. Use the Views buttons in the Translator window to view the translated text in a separate pane above or beside the original text. To create a new document for the translation, select all of the translated content, copy it to the Clipboard, then paste it into a new Word document.

Creating a Document

Preview and Print a Document

When you finish creating and editing a document, you can preview it to see exactly how it will look when printed. Seeing a preview of the document before printing it is useful and can save paper. If your finished document is going to be viewed primarily on screen (and not printed), you can also view it in Read Mode view, which is the ideal view for reading text on screen. There are many other ways to view a document in Word. See **TABLE D-3** for a description of these views. To print a document, you use the Print tab in Backstage view. The tools on the Print tab let you specify various print settings, including the printer you want to use, how many copies to print, and the specific pages of the document you want to print. **CASE** ▶ *You are ready to preview and print the letter now. (Note: Many schools limit printing in order to conserve paper. If your school restricts printing, skip Step 6.)*

STEPS

1. **Click the VIEW tab, then click One Page in the Zoom group**

   Now you can see the text of the letter is laid out on the page. Notice the text is bunched up at the top of the paper. You need to move it down to make room for the company letterhead, which is preprinted on your company paper.

2. **Press [Ctrl][Home] to move the insertion point to the beginning of the document, then press [Enter] seven times**

   You inserted seven blank lines at the top of the document. See **FIGURE D-19**. The text is now positioned further down the page. You are ready to print the letter now.

3. **Click the 100% button in the Zoom group to restore the default zoom level, click the FILE tab, then click Print**

   The Print tab opens in Backstage view, as shown in **FIGURE D-20**. You can see a preview of the letter in the right pane.

4. **Notice the Printer and Settings areas to the left of the Preview section**

   Use these sections to specify your print settings. The box below Printer shows the default printer. The boxes below Settings let you specify which pages you want to print (if you do not want to print the entire document), the number of copies you want to print, the orientation of the document, the size of the paper on which the document will print, and more. The default settings are appropriate for the letter.

5. **Verify the button below Printer displays the name of the printer you want to use**

6. **If your school allows printing, click the Print button; otherwise, skip to Step 7**

   The document prints, the Print tab closes, and your screen displays your document with the HOME tab open.

7. **Click Save on the FILE tab, then click the Word window close button** ❌

   The letter is saved, and the document and Word both close.

FIGURE D-19: Viewing the entire page of the completed letter

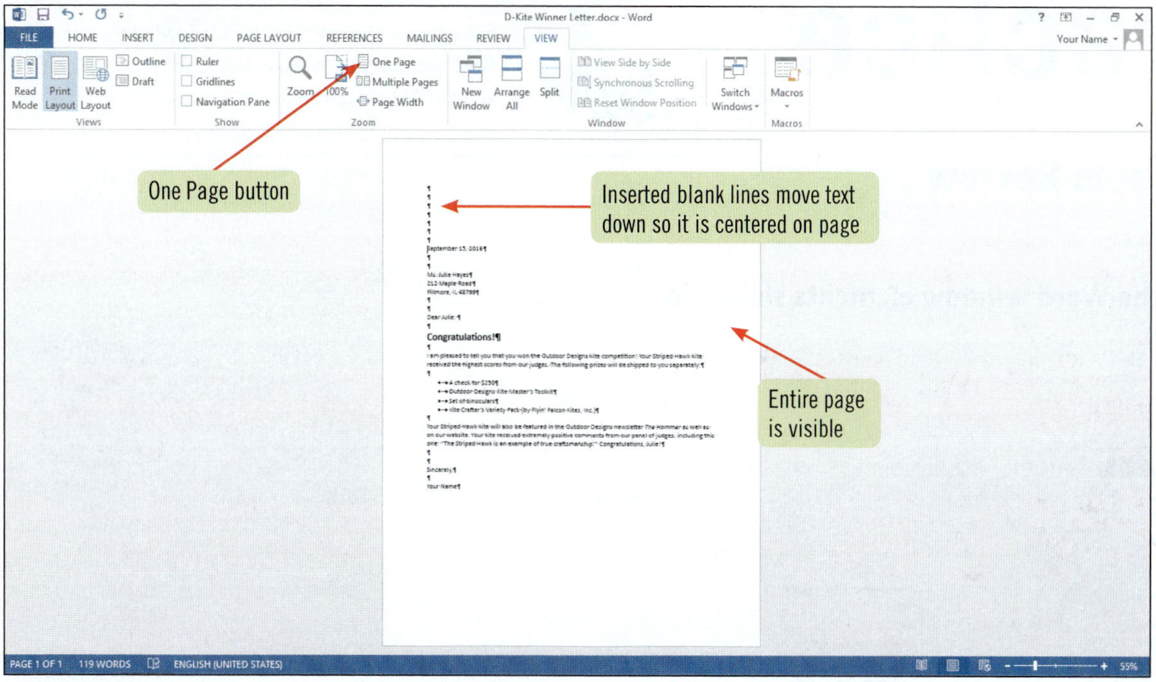

One Page button

Inserted blank lines move text down so it is centered on page

Entire page is visible

FIGURE D-20: Printing the final letter in Backstage view

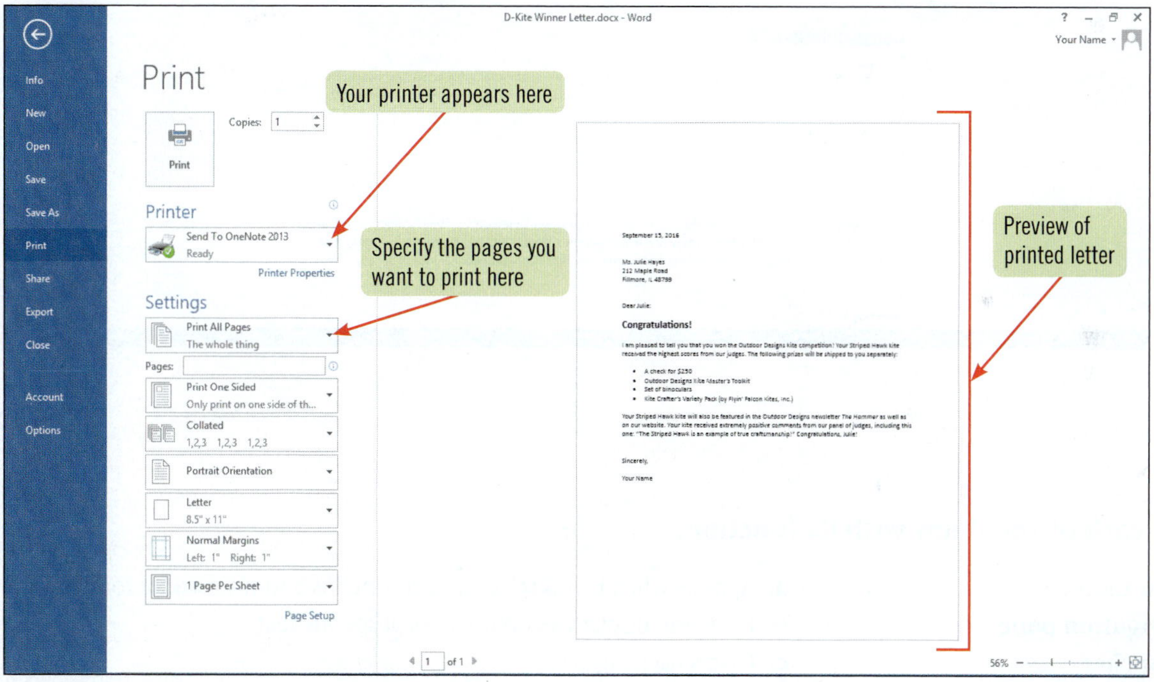

Your printer appears here

Specify the pages you want to print here

Preview of printed letter

TABLE D-3: Available views in Word

view	button	how it displays a document	use for
Print Layout		Shows all elements of the printed page	Previewing the layout of printed page
Read Mode		Optimized for on-screen reading	Reading documents on a computer screen
Web Layout		As it would appear as a Web page	Creating a Web page
Outline		Shows only the headings in a document	Reviewing the structure of a document
Draft		Does not show all page elements	Typing, editing, and simple formatting

Creating a Document

Word 2013

Practice

Concepts Review

Label the Word window elements shown in FIGURE D-21.

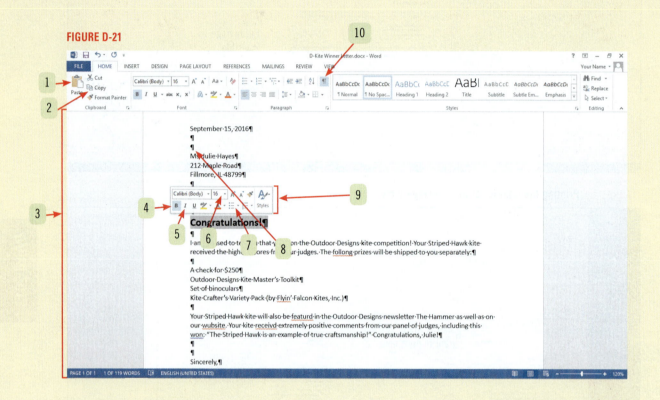

FIGURE D-21

Match each of the items with its function.

11. **Mini toolbar**

12. **Navigation pane**

13. **Launcher**

14. **FILE tab**

15. **Clipboard task pane**

a. Appears when text is selected, and contains buttons used for formatting

b. Finds and displays all occurrences of specific text

c. Opens Backstage view

d. Opens a dialog box or task pane

e. Stores cut and copied items that can be pasted

Creating a Document

Select the best answer from the list of choices.

16. **Which of the following tasks can you complete using the Mini toolbar?**
    a. Changing the document view
    b. Correcting spelling
    c. Formatting text
    d. Editing text

17. **Which of the following tasks can you perform using the Clipboard task pane?**
    a. Pasting text
    b. Printing a document
    c. Formatting paragraphs as a numbered list
    d. Checking the spelling of your document

18. **Which of the following tasks should you perform before copying text from one location and pasting it somewhere else?**
    a. Selecting the text
    b. Clicking the VIEW tab
    c. Opening the Mini toolbar
    d. Clicking the FILE tab

19. **Which of the following keyboard shortcuts selects all the text in a document?**
    a. [Ctrl][Alt][Delete]
    b. [Ctrl][A]
    c. [Ctrl][Home]
    d. [Ctrl][Enter]

20. **Which is the best view for viewing (and not editing) the text of a document on a computer or tablet screen?**
    a. Read Mode view
    b. Print Layout view
    c. Print Preview
    d. Draft

Skills Review

1. **Create a new document from an existing file.**
   a. Start Word, then open the Open screen.
   b. Navigate to the location where you store your Data Files, then open the file D-2.docx.
   c. Save the file as **D-Rosie's Home-Cooked Meals** in the location where you save your Data Files.

2. **Enter text in a document.**
   a. Make sure formatting marks are displayed in the document.
   b. Switch to Draft view.
   c. Move the insertion point to the right of "-9752" (the end of the fax number at the end of line four), then press [Enter] twice.
   d. Type the following text: **About Our Business**. Press [Enter].
   e. Type the following text: **Rosie's Home-Cooked Meals was started with one goal in mind: to provide nutritious home-cooked meals to the working families of Glen City.**
   f. Move the insertion point to the end of the paragraph below the heading "About Our Chef", press [Spacebar], then type **Rosie also contributes weekly recipes to The Glen City Journal.**
   g. Save your changes.

3. **Select and edit text.**
   a. In the paragraph under the heading "About Our Kitchen", replace the text "2000" with **3250**.
   b. In the heading "About Our Chef", delete "Our Chef" and replace it with **Rosie**.
   c. Scroll down if necessary so you can see the paragraph under the heading Our Menus, then use the [Backspace] key to delete the words "five days a week" at the end of that paragraph.
   d. Type **Monday through Friday:** so the last sentence of that paragraph reads "Here are just a few of our best-selling meals, available Monday through Friday:".
   e. Select the entire document, then click the No Spacing button.
   f. Save your changes.

Skills Review (continued)

4. Copy text.

   a. Open the Clipboard task pane. If there are entries on it, clear them.

   b. Select the text "Rosie's Home-Cooked Meals" in the first line of the document, then copy this text to the Clipboard. (*Note*: Be careful not to select the paragraph mark after the word "Meals".)

   c. Delete the words "Our Business" in the heading "About Our Business". (*Note*: Be careful not to delete the paragraph mark at the end of the line.)

   d. Paste the copied text where the deleted text used to be. (*Note*: If a blank line was inserted between the heading and paragraph, delete it before proceeding to Step e.)

   e. Select the text "nutritious" in the first line of text below "About Rosie's Home-Cooked Meals".

   f. Drag a copy of the selected text to the left of "home cooking" three lines below while holding [Ctrl].

   g. Save your changes.

5. Move text.

   a. In the paragraph below the heading "Our Hours", select the text "Stop by or call tonight!" and the space following it, then use the Cut command to move this text to the Clipboard.

   b. Paste the text you cut after the sentence "Or go straight home and call us: we deliver!" at the end of the paragraph.

   c. Scroll down if necessary so the bottom of the document is visible on your screen.

   d. Select the heading "Our Hours", the paragraph below it, and the paragraph mark below the paragraph, then drag the entire selection down to the end of the document.

   e. Close the Clipboard task pane, then save your changes.

6. Find and replace text.

   a. Find all the instances of "Green Beans".

   b. Move the insertion point to the beginning of the document.

   c. Use the Replace command to replace all instances of "Green Beans" with "Broccoli".

   d. Close the Find and Replace dialog box. Close the Navigation pane.

   e. Save your changes.

7. Format text using the Mini toolbar.

   a. Change the view to Print Layout view.

   b. Select "Rosie's Home-Cooked Meals" in the first line of the document, then use the Mini toolbar to apply bold formatting to this text.

   c. With the first line of text still selected, use a button on the Mini toolbar to increase the font size of "Rosie's Home-Cooked Meals" to 22.

   d. Use the Mini toolbar to apply bold formatting to each of the following headings in the document: "About Rosie's Home-Cooked Meals", "About Rosie", "About Our Kitchen", "Our Menus", and "Our Hours".

   e. At the end of the paragraph below the heading "About Rosie", use the Mini toolbar to apply italic formatting to the newspaper title "The Glen City Journal".

   f. Scroll down if necessary so all the text under the heading "Our Menus" is visible, then select the list of meals starting with "Slow-Cooked Beef Stew with Roasted Potatoes" and ending with "Chicken Teriyaki with Fried Rice".

   g. Use the Mini toolbar to format the selected text as a bulleted list.

   h. Save your changes.

8. Check spelling and grammar.

   a. In the paragraph below "About Our Kitchen", correct the spelling of the misspelled word "kitchn" by right-clicking and choosing the correct spelling from the shortcut menu.

   b. Move the insertion point to the beginning of the document.

   c. Click the tab on the Ribbon that contains the Spelling & Grammar button.

   d. Open the Spelling pane.

Skills Review (continued)

   e. Review each spelling and grammatical error that Word identifies, and correct or ignore the errors depending on what seems appropriate for this document.

   f. Save your changes.

9. Preview and print a document.

   a. View the document in Read Mode view. Then close Read Mode view, and view the document in Print Layout view. Finally, click the button in the Zoom group that lets you see the entire page.

   b. Insert two line spaces above the first line of the document.

   c. Move the insertion point to the end of the document, then type your name.

   d. Preview the document again using the Print tab.

   e. Save your changes, then submit your finished document to your instructor. Your final document should look like **FIGURE D-22**.

   f. Close the document, then exit Word.

FIGURE D-22

Rosie's Home-Cooked Meals

44 Washington Street
Glen City, OH 44562
Phone: (773)555-6423 Fax: (773)555-9752

About Rosie's Home-Cooked Meals
Rosie's Home-Cooked Meals was started with one goal in mind: to provide nutritious home-cooked meals to the working families of Glen City.

About Rosie
Rosie Masters knows all about cooking for families; she raised seven children on her nutritious home cooking, and threw a lot of parties as they were growing up. She realized she had a natural talent for cooking, and decided to start her own business, making meals for working families who don't have time to cook. Rosie also contributes weekly recipes to *The Glen City Journal.*

About Our Kitchen
We operate in a facility with a kitchen space of 3250 square feet. Our team includes Rosie (of course) plus four full-time, year-round staff. During the busy times we hire part-time help. We own all cooking appliances and equipment as well as two vans.

Our Menus
We offer a wide variety of main dishes, side dishes, salads, and desserts guaranteed to satisfy any appetite. We purchase all our vegetables locally to ensure their quality and to support our local farmers. Here are just a few of our best-selling meals, available Monday through Friday:

- Slow-Cooked Beef Stew with Roasted Potatoes
- Roasted Chicken with Sweet Potatoes and Broccoli
- Cider-Rubbed Grilled Pork Chops with Garlic Mashed Potatoes
- Rosie's Famous Chicken Pot Pie
- Chicken Parmesan with Pasta and Broccoli
- Sliced Turkey Breast with Stuffing and Gravy
- Chicken Teriyaki with Fried Rice

Our Hours
We are open Monday through Friday from 3:00 to 7:30. Drop by our kitchen and pick up a steaming hot meal tonight! Or go straight home and call us: we deliver! Stop by or call tonight!

Your Name

Independent Challenge 1

As the sales director for Blooms Garden Supply, you are in charge of organizing the winter sales meeting for the sales force. You need to prepare a memo notifying the sales team of the dates and providing basic information so they can make plans to attend. You have already created a partially completed version of this memo, so now you need to make final edits to finish it.

a. Start Word, open the file D-3.docx from the location where you store your Data Files, then save it as **D-Sales Meeting Memo**.

b. Select the entire document, then apply the No Spacing style to the whole document.

c. In the fourth line of text, replace the text "Your Name" with your name.

d. In the sixth line of text (which begins "Our Summer Sales Meeting"), change the word "Summer" to **Winter**.

e. In the heading Dates and Location, delete "Location", then replace it with **Accommodations**.

f. At the end of the paragraph under Dates and Accommodations, type the following text: **Please book your flight home any time after 5:00 on January 7.**

g. In the first line of text under the heading "Trip Planning", move the text "I look forward to seeing you there!" to the end of the paragraph.

h. Increase the font size of the word "Memo" in the first line of the document to 24, then apply bold formatting to it.

i. Apply bold formatting to the following headings in the memo: "Dates and Accommodations", "About the Hotel and Conference Center", "Meeting Information", "Planned Activities", and "Trip Planning".

j. Under the "Planned Activities" heading, format the lines that start with "January 5", "January 6", and "January 7" as a bulleted list.

k. You suddenly learn that the Red Rose Hotel will not be able to accommodate the meeting. Fortunately, you are able to make a reservation at the Pink Diamond Resort, also in Orlando. Replace all instances of "Red Rose Hotel" with **Pink Diamond Resort**.

l. After you enter all the text, check the spelling and grammar, and correct any errors as needed. Ignore any proper names that are flagged as misspelled words.

m. Save your changes, then view the memo in Read Mode. Close Read Mode view, then view the document in Print Layout view, using the setting that lets you see the entire document on one page. Change the view to 100%. Your finished document should look like **FIGURE D-23**.

n. Close the document, then exit Word. Submit your completed documents to your instructor.

FIGURE D-23

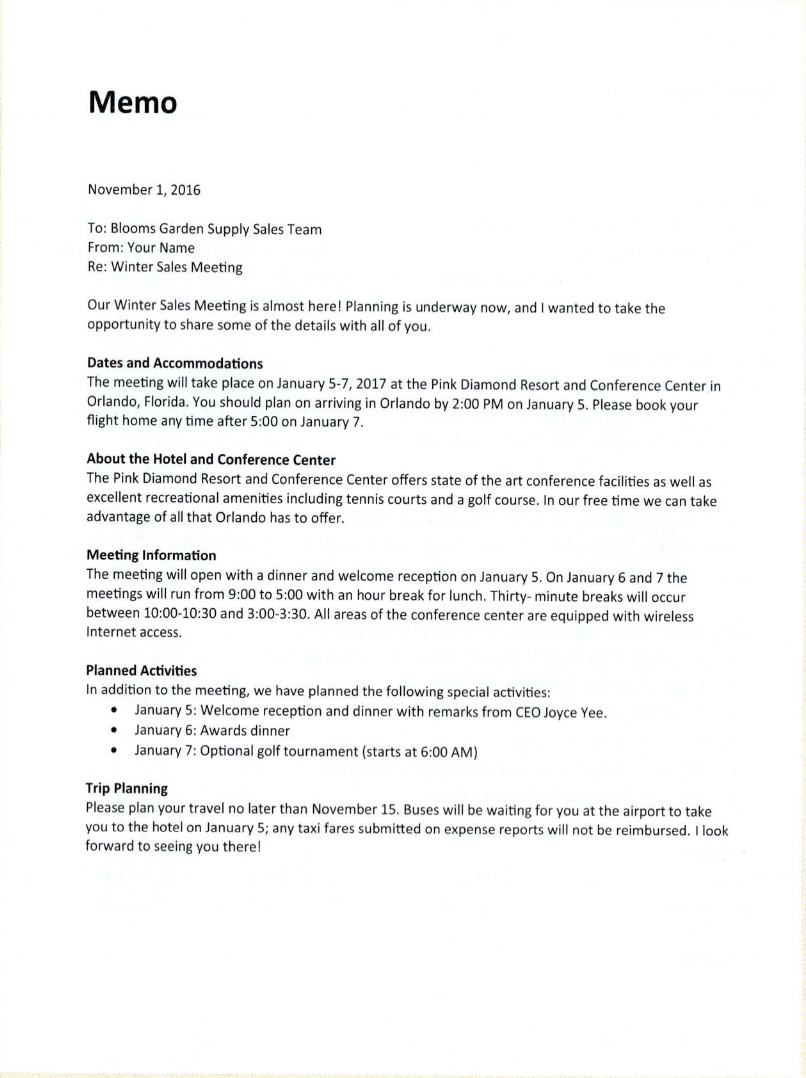

Memo

November 1, 2016

To: Blooms Garden Supply Sales Team
From: Your Name
Re: Winter Sales Meeting

Our Winter Sales Meeting is almost here! Planning is underway now, and I wanted to take the opportunity to share some of the details with all of you.

Dates and Accommodations
The meeting will take place on January 5-7, 2017 at the Pink Diamond Resort and Conference Center in Orlando, Florida. You should plan on arriving in Orlando by 2:00 PM on January 5. Please book your flight home any time after 5:00 on January 7.

About the Hotel and Conference Center
The Pink Diamond Resort and Conference Center offers state of the art conference facilities as well as excellent recreational amenities including tennis courts and a golf course. In our free time we can take advantage of all that Orlando has to offer.

Meeting Information
The meeting will open with a dinner and welcome reception on January 5. On January 6 and 7 the meetings will run from 9:00 to 5:00 with an hour break for lunch. Thirty- minute breaks will occur between 10:00-10:30 and 3:00-3:30. All areas of the conference center are equipped with wireless Internet access.

Planned Activities
In addition to the meeting, we have planned the following special activities:
- January 5: Welcome reception and dinner with remarks from CEO Joyce Yee.
- January 6: Awards dinner
- January 7: Optional golf tournament (starts at 6:00 AM)

Trip Planning
Please plan your travel no later than November 15. Buses will be waiting for you at the airport to take you to the hotel on January 5; any taxi fares submitted on expense reports will not be reimbursed. I look forward to seeing you there!

Creating a Document

Independent Challenge 2

You own and operate a bakery that sells cakes, pies, and cookies. Business is booming, so you would like to expand your product line and offer new types of products and services. You would also like to have a better understanding of what your customers like about your baked goods. You decide to create a simple customer survey that your customers can fill out in the store for a chance to win a prize. You have already started the survey document but need to edit it and improve its appearance before it is ready for distribution.

a. Start Word, open the file D-4.docx from the location where you store your Data Files, then save it as **D-Bakery Survey**.

b. Replace all instances of the name "Grandma" in the survey document with your first name. In the last line of the document, replace the text "Your Name" with your full name.

c. Select all the text in the document, then apply the No Spacing style to all the selected text.

d. In the third line of text in the document, delete "weekly baked treats" and replace it with **one cake per week**.

e. Type **Question 1:** before the first question in the document, press [Spacebar], then apply bold formatting to "Question 1:".

f. Insert **Question 2:**, **Question 3:**, and **Question 4:** to the left of the remaining three questions in the survey, insert a space, and apply bold formatting to the new text.

g. Below each of the four questions, format the list of answers as a bulleted list.

h. Reorder the bulleted items under Question 4 so they are in alphabetical order.

i. Increase the font size of the text in the first line of the document to 20, then apply bold and italic formatting to it.

j. Check the spelling and grammar, and correct all spelling and grammar errors. Ignore flagged words that are spelled correctly—including "Snickerdoodles."

k. Save your changes to the document. Use Print Preview to see how the printed survey will look. Compare your document to **FIGURE D-24**.

l. Submit your work to your instructor.

FIGURE D-24

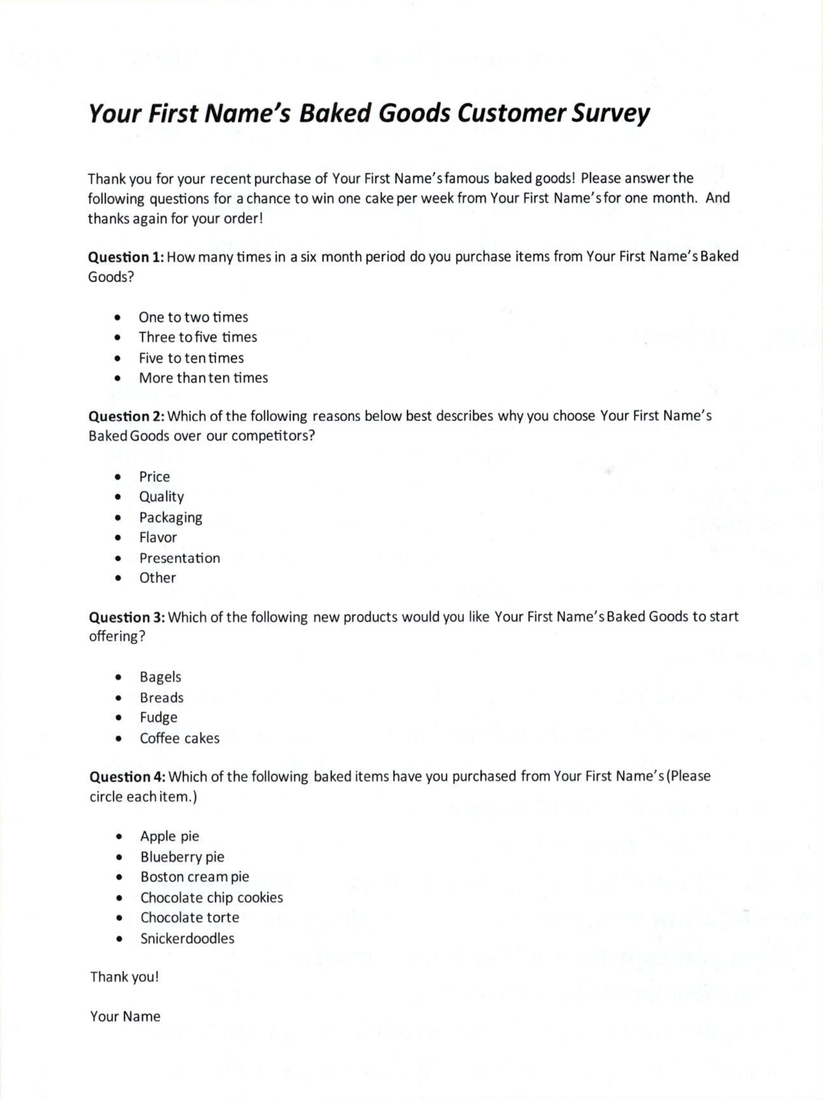

Your First Name's Baked Goods Customer Survey

Thank you for your recent purchase of Your First Name's famous baked goods! Please answer the following questions for a chance to win one cake per week from Your First Name's for one month. And thanks again for your order!

Question 1: How many times in a six month period do you purchase items from Your First Name's Baked Goods?

- One to two times
- Three to five times
- Five to ten times
- More than ten times

Question 2: Which of the following reasons below best describes why you choose Your First Name's Baked Goods over our competitors?

- Price
- Quality
- Packaging
- Flavor
- Presentation
- Other

Question 3: Which of the following new products would you like Your First Name's Baked Goods to start offering?

- Bagels
- Breads
- Fudge
- Coffee cakes

Question 4: Which of the following baked items have you purchased from Your First Name's (Please circle each item.)

- Apple pie
- Blueberry pie
- Boston cream pie
- Chocolate chip cookies
- Chocolate torte
- Snickerdoodles

Thank you!

Your Name

Independent Challenge 3

You work for Eduardo Gomez, director of human resources at a new fitness center. Eduardo needs to recruit candidates to fill the position of fitness program director at the club. Eduardo has asked you to create a document that describes the position and the qualifications that candidates must have.

a. Start Word, open the file D-5.docx from the location where you store your Data Files, then save it as **D-Job Description**.

b. Place the insertion point at the end of the document, type **Reporting Structure**, press [Enter], type **This position reports to the General Manager.**, then press [Enter].

c. In the second line of the document, delete the word "Essential", then type **Required** in its place.

d. In the third line of the document, move the first sentence, "Requires overseeing and managing the fitness budget." so it is the last sentence in that paragraph.

e. Use the Mini toolbar to apply bold formatting to the first line of text in the document, then increase the font size of this text to 24.

f. Use the Mini toolbar to apply bold formatting to each of the following headings in the document: "Required Duties and Responsibilities", "Required Skills", "Work Environment", "Education and Work Experience", and "Reporting Structure".

g. Move the heading "Education and Work Experience" and the paragraph below it so it is located below the "Reporting Structure" paragraph.

h. Check the spelling and grammar in the document, and make all appropriate changes. Ignore any occurrences of sentence fragments that Word identifies. Type your name below the last line of the document.

i. Preview the document, then save and close the document.

j. Submit the document to your instructor, then exit Word.

Independent Challenge 4: Explore

Your French friend, Jacques, who speaks little English, needs help in using Word. Jacques wants to copy some text from the beginning of a document, and place it at the end of the document. He does not know how to do this, so he asks you to send him a document with instructions. You are a good friend, so you agree to create a document that provides the instructions in both English and French. You want the document to look really slick and professional, so you decide to use a template to create the document.

a. Start Word.

b. In the Word Start screen, click in the Search for online templates box at the top of the screen, and type **Facet**. The thumbnail shown in **FIGURE D-25** should appear in the results. Click the thumbnail, read the description, then click Create.

c. Select "Title", then type your name.

d. Select "Heading", then type **How to Copy Text in Word**.

e. Select all the remaining black text in the document, type **Here's how you copy text in Word:**, then press [Enter].

f. Using your knowledge from working through this unit, type three or four steps that provide instructions on how to copy text in Word using the Clipboard. Press [Enter] after each step so there is a paragraph return after each step.

g. Apply bold formatting to any button names in your steps.

h. Format the steps as a bulleted list.

FIGURE D-25

Title

Heading

Facet design (blank)

Independent Challenge 4: Explore (continued)

i. Click the REVIEW tab, click Translate in the Language group, then click Choose Translation Language. Adjust the Translate to: setting to French (France), then click OK.

j. Click the Translate button in the Language group, click Translate document, read the message in the Translate Whole Document dialog box, then click Send.

k. Select the French translated text in browser window, right-click to open a shortcut menu, then click Copy. Close the dialog box.

l. Press [Enter] twice to move the insertion point down two lines, then click the Paste button. Make any formatting adjustments necessary to make the document look good. Preview the document using the One Page zoom setting. Your document should look similar to **FIGURE D-26** (although your steps will be worded slightly differently, since you wrote them).

m. Save the document as **D-Copying Text Instructions.docx** to the location where you store your Data Files.

n. Close the document, then submit it to your instructor.

FIGURE D-26

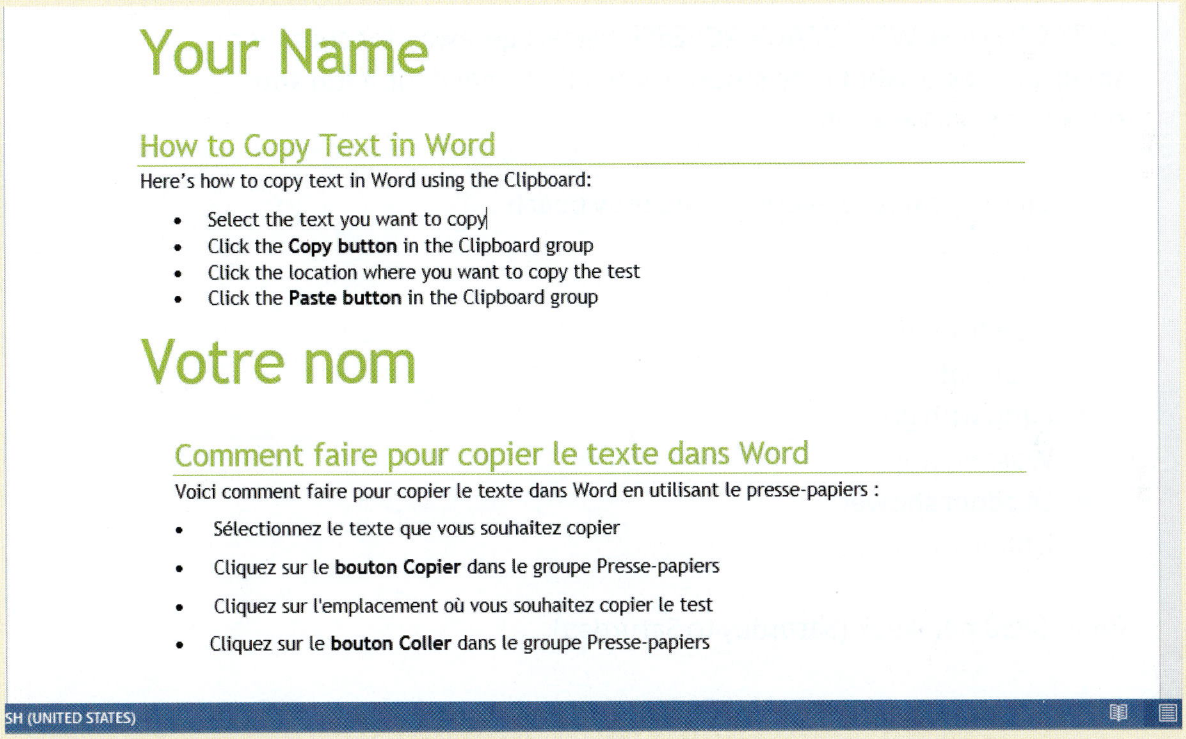

Your Name

How to Copy Text in Word

Here's how to copy text in Word using the Clipboard:

- Select the text you want to copy
- Click the **Copy button** in the Clipboard group
- Click the location where you want to copy the test
- Click the **Paste button** in the Clipboard group

Votre nom

Comment faire pour copier le texte dans Word

Voici comment faire pour copier le texte dans Word en utilisant le presse-papiers :

- Sélectionnez le texte que vous souhaitez copier
- Cliquez sur le **bouton Copier** dans le groupe Presse-papiers
- Cliquez sur l'emplacement où vous souhaitez copier le test
- Cliquez sur le **bouton Coller** dans le groupe Presse-papiers

SH (UNITED STATES)

Visual Workshop

Use the skills you have learned in this unit to create the document shown in FIGURE D-27. Start Word, use the Blank document command to create a new untitled document, then type and format the text as shown. (*Hint*: Click the FILE tab, click New, then click Blank document on the New screen.) Set the font size of the heading text to 26, and set the font size of the body text to 16. Save the document as **D-House Rental Ad** in the location where you store your Data Files. Type your name below the last line of the document. Check the spelling and grammar in the entire document, then save and print it. When you are finished, close the document, then exit Word. Submit your completed document to your instructor.

FIGURE D-27

Beach House for Rent

Description:

COZY COTTAGE WITH BEACH ACCESS! Perfect getaway for couples or small families. Rustic home stocked with all you need for a fun and relaxing beach vacation.

- Charming house overlooking sandy beach
- Fireplace
- Great views of the water
- 2 bedrooms
- 1 full bath
- Patio with grill
- Washer/dryer
- Outdoor shower
- Utilities included

Rent: $850 per week (Saturday to Saturday)

Many weeks are still available! To book your week, call Jose at 555-437-3299

Your Name

Enhancing a Document

CASE   Karen Rivera, marketing director for Outdoor Designs, needs you to finish a fact sheet for a new build-it-yourself boat kit. Karen asks you to format the information on the sheet so it is attractive and easy to read.

Unit Objectives

After completing this unit, you will be able to:

- Change font and font size
- Change font color, style, and effects
- Change alignment and line spacing
- Change margin settings
- Set tabs
- Set indents
- Add bulleted and numbered lists
- Apply Styles

Files You Will Need

E-1.docx	E-5.docx
E-2.docx	E-6.docx
E-3.docx	E-7.docx
E-4.docx	

©HelenStock/Shutterstock

Change Font and Font Size

Choosing an appropriate font is an important part of formatting a document. The fonts you use help communicate the tone you want to set. For instance, if you are creating a report that describes harmful effects of toxins on the environment, you should choose a conservative, traditional font, such as Times New Roman. On the other hand, if you are creating a formal wedding invitation, you should choose a font that conveys a sense of elegance and celebration, such as French Script. **TABLE E-1** shows some examples of fonts available in Word. You can use either the HOME tab or the Mini toolbar to change the font and font size. You can change font and font size before you begin typing, or you can select existing text and apply changes to it. All the text in the boat fact sheet is the same font (Calibri) and size (11 point). **CASE** *You decide to change the font and font size of the first two lines so they stand out from the rest of the text in the document. First, you will open the document and save it with a new name to keep Karen's original document intact.*

STEPS

1. **Start Word, open the file E-1.docx from where you store your Data Files, then save it as E-Boat Kit Fact Sheet**
   The E-Boat Kit Fact Sheet document is now open in Print Layout view.

2. **Place the pointer in the selection bar to the left of Outdoor Designs in the first line until it changes to ⬧ then click to select the entire line**
   To format existing text, you must first select it.

3. **Click the Font Size list arrow in the Font group, then point to 20, as shown in FIGURE E-1**
   Just by pointing to 20, the font size of the selected text increases in size on the page. You might have noticed that pointing to any other font size option instantly caused the selected text to change in size to reflect that point size. This feature is called **Live Preview**, and makes it possible to preview how a formatting option will look on the page before actually choosing that option. Live Preview is available in many formatting lists and galleries.

4. **Click 20**
   The Font Size list closes, and the selected text changes to 20 point. The first line of text is now much larger than the rest of the text in the document.

5. **Select Build-Your-Own Boat Kits in the second line of the document, click the Font Size list arrow, then click 28**
   The second line of text increases in size to 28 point and is now larger than the first line.

6. **Select the first two lines of text ("Outdoor Designs" through "Build-Your-Own Boat Kits")**

7. **Click the Font list arrow in the Font group on the HOME tab, then point to any font to preview it in the document, but do not click**
   Notice that anytime you point to a font in the Font list, the selected text changes to that font.

8. **Scroll in the Font list until you see Impact, click Impact as shown in FIGURE E-2, then click outside the selected text to deselect it**
   The selected text changes to the Impact font. "Impact" appears in the Font list box and will be displayed as long as the insertion point remains in any text with the Impact font applied.

9. **Click the Save button 🖫 on the Quick Access toolbar to save your changes**

FIGURE E-1: Changing the font size of selected text using the Font Size list

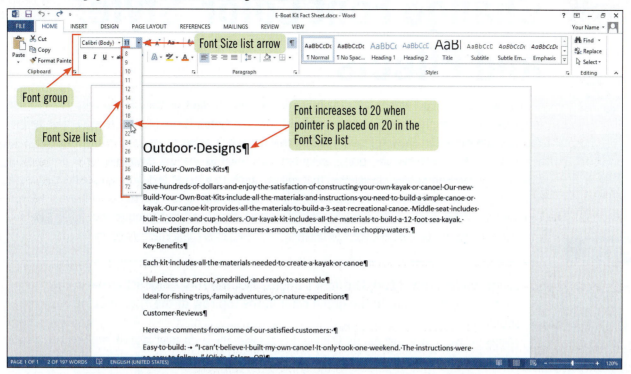

FIGURE E-2: Changing the font type of selected text using the Font list

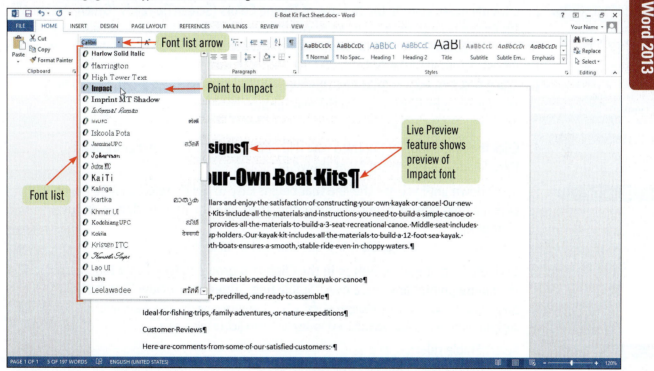

TABLE E-1: Samples of fonts and font sizes

font formats	samples
Font	Times New Roman, *French Script*, **Impact**, ALGERIAN, **Broadway**, Chiller
Size	eight point, twelve point, fourteen point, eighteen point

© 2014 Cengage Learning

Enhancing a Document

Change Font Color, Style, and Effects

Sometimes you want to emphasize certain words, phrases, or lines of text. To do this, you can use font styles, which are font attributes such as **bold** (**darker type**), *italic* (*slanted type*), and underline. You can also make certain words stand out by changing their color, or you can apply font effects to selected text. **Font effects** are special enhancements—such as shadow (**Shadow** looks like this) or strikethrough (strikethrough looks like this) that you can apply to selected text. You can use the buttons in the Font group on the HOME tab to apply font effects and formatting to selected text. To save time, you can use the Format Painter button to copy the formatting of selected text to other text. **CASE** *You continue to format the boat kit fact sheet by applying font styles, colors, and effects to certain words.*

STEPS

1. **Select the first line of text, Outdoor Designs, click the Font Color list arrow in the Font group, then point to the green color in the top row of the Theme Colors, as shown in FIGURE E-3**

   Thanks to Live Preview, you can see Outdoor Designs with the green color applied. Notice that the color palette includes Theme Colors, Standard Colors, and More Colors. A **theme** is a predesigned set of formatting elements, including colors, which you can use to achieve a coordinated overall look in your document. **Standard colors** are the basic hues red, orange, and so on.

   > **QUICK TIP**
   > To remove formatting from selected text, click the Clear All Formatting button in the Font group.

2. **Click the green color in the top row of Theme Colors (ScreenTip reads "Green, Accent 6")**

   The Font Color list closes, and Outdoor Designs is formatted in green. The Font Color button now displays a green stripe, indicating this is the current color. Clicking the Font Color button (not the list arrow) applies the current color to selected text.

3. **Select Build-Your-Own Boat Kits (the second line of text), then click the Text Effects and Typography button in the Font group**

   The Text Effects gallery opens.

4. **Click the first option in the third row (Fill - Black, Text 1, Outline–Background 1, Hard Shadow-Background 1), as shown in FIGURE E-4**

   > **QUICK TIP**
   > To underline text, click the Underline button in the Font group.

5. **Scroll down until you see the line that begins Easy to build:, select Easy to build:, click the Bold button in the Font group, then click the Italic button in the Font group**

   "Easy to build:" is now formatted in bold and italic, and is still selected.

6. **Click the Format Painter button in the Clipboard group on the HOME tab, then place the mouse pointer anywhere over "Stable ride:" three lines below "Easy to build"**

   Notice that the pointer shape changes to when you place it on the document, indicating that you can apply the formatting of the selected text to any text you click or select next.

   > **QUICK TIP**
   > Double-clicking the Format Painter button lets you apply the selected formatting multiple times.

7. **Select Stable ride:**

   The bold and italic formatting is applied to "Stable ride:".

8. **Click outside the selected text, then save your changes**

   See FIGURE E-5.

FIGURE E-3: Font Color list with green color selected

FIGURE E-4: Applying a text effect

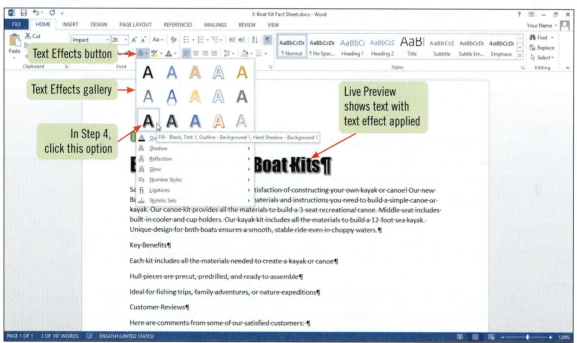

FIGURE E-5: Bold and italic formatting applied to text

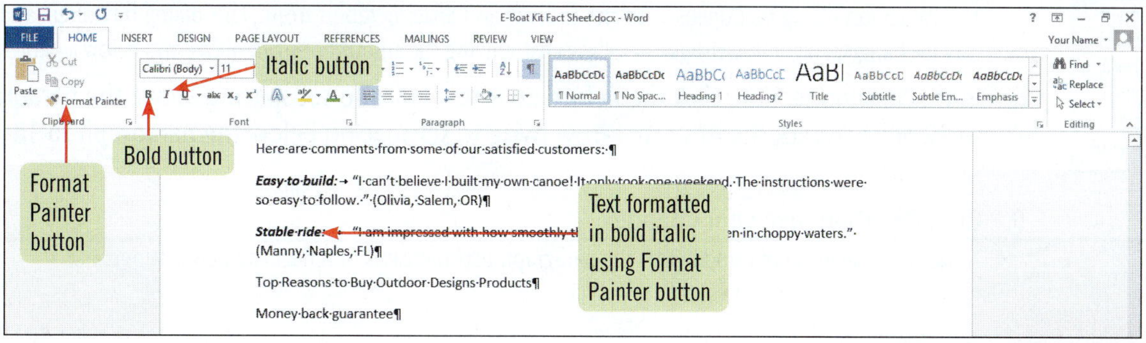

Change Alignment and Line Spacing

Learning Outcomes
- Set paragraph alignment
- Change line spacing in a paragraph
- Adjust line spacing before and after paragraphs

The amount of space between the edge of the page and your document text is called the **margin**. You can change the **alignment**, or position of text within a document's margins, using the alignment buttons in the Paragraph group on the HOME tab. For example, titles are often centered, headings left-aligned, and paragraphs **justified** (aligned equally between the left and right margins). You can also adjust the spacing between lines using the Line and Paragraph Spacing button in the Paragraph group on the HOME tab. **CASE** *All of the text in the boat kit fact sheet is aligned along the left margin. You decide to center the first two lines and justify the descriptive paragraph. You also want to decrease the amount of spacing between the lines in the paragraph so they are single spaced, and increase the amount of space both above and below the paragraph.*

STEPS

1. **Press [Ctrl][Home] to move the insertion point to the beginning of the document**

   Although you need to select text to change character formats such as font size or font style, you can change most paragraph formatting, such as alignment, just by positioning the insertion point anywhere in the paragraph. In Word, a **paragraph** is any text that ends with a paragraph mark (¶) so it can be as short as a one-word title or as long as you like. A paragraph mark is inserted anytime you press [Enter]; this is also called a hard return.

2. **Click the Center button ≡ in the Paragraph group on the HOME tab**

   The text is centered between the two margins.

3. **Click anywhere in the second line of text (Build-Your-Own Boat Kits), then click the Center button ≡**

   See **FIGURE E-6**.

4. **Click anywhere in the paragraph text below "Build-Your-Own Boat Kits"**

   The insertion point is now set in the paragraph. Any paragraph formatting you specify will affect the formatting of the entire paragraph.

5. **Click the Justify button ≡ in the Paragraph group**

   The paragraph's alignment changes to justified. When you select justified alignment, Word adds or reduces the space between each word so the text is aligned along both the right and left margins. This is different from **center-aligning** text, which does not adjust spacing but merely places the text equally between the margins.

6. **Click the Line and Paragraph Spacing button ≡▾ in the Paragraph group on the HOME tab, then click 1.0, as shown in FIGURE E-7**

   The paragraph is now both justified and single spaced.

QUICK TIP
You can also open the Paragraph dialog box by right-clicking a paragraph, then clicking Paragraph in the shortcut menu.

7. **Click the launcher ⌐ in the Paragraph group**

   The Paragraph dialog box opens with the Indents and Spacing tab in front. This dialog box offers another way to change paragraph settings, including customizing the amount of space above and below a paragraph.

8. **In the Spacing section, click the Before up arrow twice to set spacing above the paragraph to 12 pt, then click the After up arrow twice to set spacing below the paragraph to 18 pt**

   See **FIGURE E-8**.

9. **Click OK, then save your changes**

   Notice the spacing above and below the paragraph text increases to reflect the new settings.

FIGURE E-6: Center-aligned text

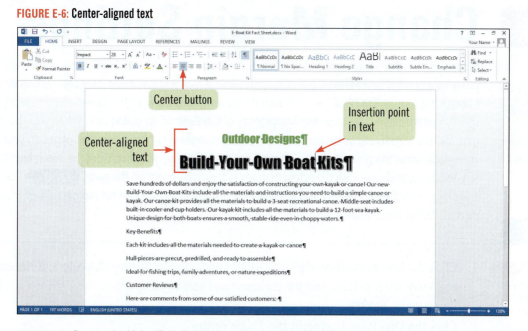

Center button

Insertion point in text

Center-aligned text

FIGURE E-7: Paragraph with justified alignment and line spacing set to 1.0

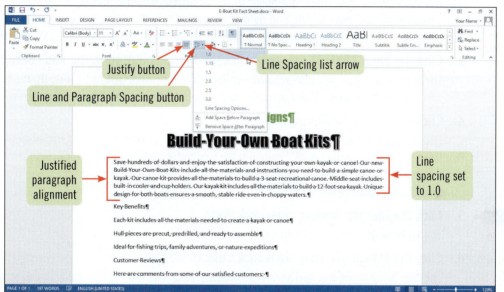

Justify button

Line Spacing list arrow

Line and Paragraph Spacing button

Justified paragraph alignment

Line spacing set to 1.0

FIGURE E-8: Indents and Spacing tab of Paragraph dialog box

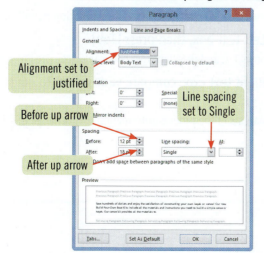

Alignment set to justified

Line spacing set to Single

Before up arrow

After up arrow

Change Margin Settings

By default, Word sets page margins at 1" from the top, bottom, left, and right sides of the page. Word also provides a number of additional preset margin settings that you can easily view and choose by clicking the Margins button on the PAGE LAYOUT tab. If you do not like any of the preset margin settings, you can specify custom settings by using the Margins tab of the Page Setup dialog box. When you change the margins, Word automatically adjusts line wrapping and **repaginates** (renumbers the pages of) your document. To evaluate what margin settings to use in a specific document, you should set the zoom level to One Page so you can see and work with the actual margins as they will appear on the page. **CASE** *The boat kit fact sheet is currently formatted with the default margins. You decide to explore other margin settings to see whether a different setting would make the document look better.*

STEPS

1. **Click the VIEW tab, then click the Ruler check box to display the rulers, if necessary**

   The VIEW tab is in front, and the horizontal and vertical rulers appear along the top and left edge of the document window.

2. **Click the One Page button in the Zoom group**

   You can now see your whole document in the document window, making it possible to see the margin settings at the top, bottom, left, and right of the page. Using the rulers, you can see that the left and right margins are 1". To change the default margin settings, you need to use the PAGE LAYOUT tab.

3. **Click the PAGE LAYOUT tab, then click the Margins button in the Page Setup group**

   The Margins list opens and displays ready-made options for margin settings. Currently, the Normal option is selected, which specifies a 1" margin at the top, bottom, left, and right of the page, as shown in **FIGURE E-9**.

4. **Click Narrow in the Margins list**

   The Margins list closes, and the Narrow margins setting is applied to the document, as shown in **FIGURE E-10**. You can see that there is only a ½" margin at the top, bottom, left, and right. This margin setting is too narrow and makes the text placement look unbalanced; all the text is stretched out at the top of the document, and there is a large blank space at the bottom.

5. **Click the Margins button, then click Wide**

   The Wide margins setting is applied to the document.

6. **Click the Margins button, then click Custom Margins**

   The Page Setup dialog box opens with the Margins tab active. You use this dialog box to set specific margin settings. The first margin text box, Top, is currently selected.

7. **Press [Tab] twice**

   The Left text box is selected. Pressing [Tab] moves the insertion point from one text box to the next.

8. **Type 1.1 in the Left text box, then press [Tab]**

   The Left text box shows 1.1, and the Right text box is selected. The Preview box shows the new left margin.

9. **Type 1.1 in the Right text box, compare your screen to FIGURE E-11, click OK, then save your changes**

   The left and right margins in the product information sheet change to 1.1".

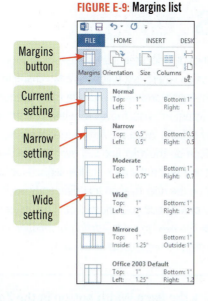

Margins button

Current setting

Narrow setting

Wide setting

FIGURE E-10: Boat Kits Fact Sheet with Narrow margins setting applied

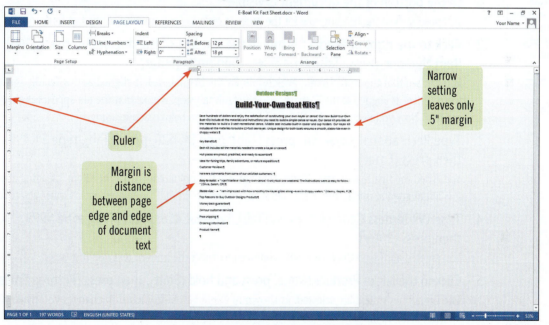

Narrow setting leaves only .5" margin

Ruler

Margin is distance between page edge and edge of document text

FIGURE E-11: Margins tab of Page Setup dialog box

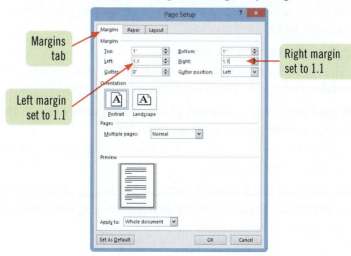

Margins tab

Left margin set to 1.1

Right margin set to 1.1

Enhancing a Document

Word 2013

Set Tabs

You can improve the appearance of a document by using tabs to align text within a line at specific positions on the page. A **tab** is a set position where text following a tab character aligns. (When you press [Tab], Word inserts a tab character—a right-facing arrow—to indicate the presence of a tab.) The ruler makes it easy to set **tab stops** (locations the insertion point moves to when you press [Tab]) and to see immediately how they affect your document. By default, Word sets left-aligned tab stops every 1/2". Any tab stop you add to the ruler will appear as a tab icon on the ruler and will override the default tab stop settings to the left of it. By default, new tab stops that you set on the ruler are left-aligned tab stops and appear as a ⌊ on the ruler. You can use the **tab selector** on the ruler to align text differently, such as to the right or center of a tab stop. When you set tabs, they apply only to text you selected or, if no text is selected, to the paragraph containing the insertion point. **CASE** ▶ *You need to enter ordering information for the boat kit products at the end of the document. You will use tabs to align the information in columns.*

STEPS

1. **Click the VIEW tab, click the Page Width button in the Zoom group, then scroll down so the bottom of the document is visible**

   You need to type the heading row for the product ordering information in the last line.

2. **Click to the right of Product Name in the last line of the document, press [Tab], type Item Number, press [Tab], type Price, then press [Enter]**

   You can see that the word "Item," which follows the first tab, is left-aligned at the default 1" tab stop. The word "Price" is aligned at the 2" mark, also a default tab stop. Notice that the tab appears as a right-arrow in the text. Now you need to enter the product information below each heading.

3. **Type Recreational Kayak Kit, press [Tab], type BK-520, press [Tab], type $1,499, then press [Enter]**

   You typed the first row of data. Notice that "BK-520" is not aligned with the "Item" heading above; instead it is left-aligned at the default 1 1/2" tab stop. However, "$1,499" is aligned with "Price" above it.

4. **Type Wilderness Canoe Kit, press [Tab], type BK-456, press [Tab], type $999, then press [Enter]**

   You entered all the product data; now you need to select the lines of text you just typed.

5. **Click to the left of Product Name, press and hold [Shift], then press [▼] three times**

   The three lines of text are selected, as shown in **FIGURE E-12**. Any tab stop changes you make will apply to all three selected lines.

6. **Notice the tab selector at the top of the vertical ruler**

   The tab selector currently displays an image of a left tab stop ⌊. This means that clicking the ruler will add a left tab stop, which is what you want.

7. **Click the 2 ½" mark on the ruler**

   The left-aligned tab stop appears on the ruler at the 2 ½" mark, and the Item Number heading and the two item numbers below it are now all left-aligned at the 2 ½" mark.

8. **Click the tab selector at the top of the vertical ruler twice so the Right Tab icon ⌟ appears, then click the 5" mark on the ruler**

   The Price heading and the two prices below it are right-aligned. When you arrange numbers in a column, it is a good idea to right-align them.

9. **Select the line of text beginning with Product Name, click the Bold button B on the Mini toolbar, click the document to deselect the text, then save your changes**

   Compare your screen to **FIGURE E-13**.

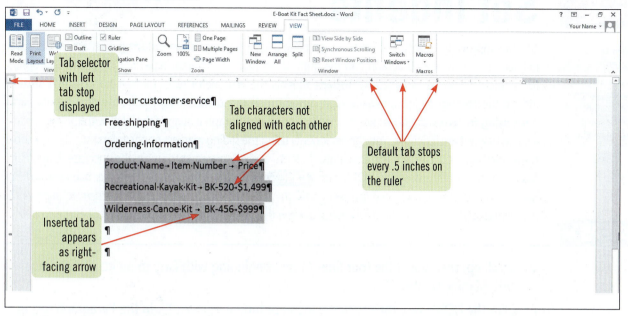

FIGURE E-13: Text arranged in columns with left and right tabs set

Set Indents

You can improve the appearance of text on a page by setting indents. An **indent** is a set amount of space between the edge of a paragraph and the right or left margin. Different types of indents are appropriate for different situations. A **first line indent** indents the first line of text in a paragraph. A **left indent** indents the left edge of an entire paragraph; a **right indent** indents the right edge of an entire paragraph. A **hanging indent** is an indent where the first line of a paragraph is aligned flush left with the margin and all lines below it are indented. You can set indents using the sliding markers on the ruler. **TABLE E-2** describes these markers. You can set left and right indents at 1/2" increments using the Increase Indent and Decrease Indent buttons on the HOME tab. **CASE** *The text containing the customer quotes would look neater if it was aligned under the first word after the tab. You want to set a hanging indent to improve the appearance of this text. You also decide to set a left indent for the paragraph text that describes the product.*

STEPS

1. **Scroll up, then select the four lines of text beginning with** Easy to build: **and ending with** Manny, Naples, FL)

2. **Click the** HOME **tab, then click the** Increase Indent button 🔳 **in the Paragraph group**

3. **Position the pointer over the** Hanging Indent marker △ **on the ruler so the Hanging Indent ScreenTip appears, then click and hold so a vertical dotted line appears on the screen**

   This dotted vertical line helps you position the marker in the desired location on the ruler.

4. **Drag** △ **to the** 1 ½" mark **on the ruler**

   The first line in each of the selected paragraphs remains flush left, and the text below the first line of each paragraph is now aligned at the 1 ½" mark on the ruler, where you dragged the Hanging Indent marker, as shown in **FIGURE E-14**.

5. **Drag the** Right Indent marker △ **to the** 5 ½" mark **on the ruler**

   The text is indented on the right side of the selected paragraphs at the 5 ½" mark. The paragraphs are narrower now.

6. **Select the** last three lines of text **in the document**

7. **Position the pointer over the** Left Indent marker ☐ **on the ruler until the Left Indent ScreenTip appears, then drag** ☐ **to the** ½" mark **on the ruler**

   The product information columns are now indented by ½", as shown in **FIGURE E-15**.

8. **Save your changes**

FIGURE E-14: Setting a hanging indent

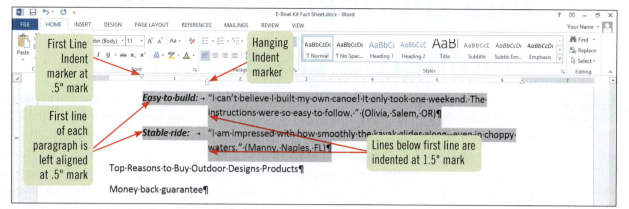

FIGURE E-15: Paragraphs formatted with left indent

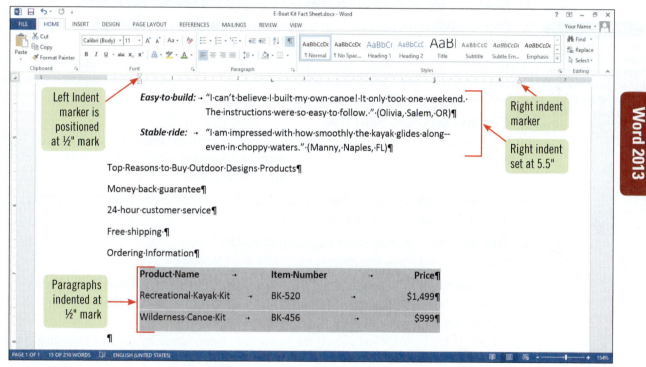

TABLE E-2: Ruler markers used for setting indents

ruler marker name	ruler marker	indents
First Line Indent marker	▽	The first line of a paragraph
Hanging Indent marker	△	The lines below the first line of text in a paragraph
Left Indent marker	☐	The left edge of an entire paragraph
Right Indent marker	△	The right edge of an entire paragraph

© 2014 Cengage Learning

Enhancing a Document

Add Bulleted and Numbered Lists

Word provides many tools for organizing your text into a more orderly format. You can easily organize groups of related paragraphs into bulleted or numbered lists. You already learned how to create a bulleted list using the Bullets button on the Mini toolbar. The Bullets button is also available on the HOME tab. When you apply the bullet format to a paragraph, Word sets off the paragraph with a bullet and automatically formats the text with a hanging indent. Use a numbered (ordered) list when you want to present items in a particular sequence, and use a bulleted (unordered) list when the items are of equal importance. There are many bullet and numbering styles to choose from when using the Bullets list and Numbering list on the HOME tab, or you can create a custom style. **CASE** ▶ *You decide to add bulleted and numbered lists to the canoe kit fact sheet to make it easier to reference.*

STEPS

1. **Scroll up, then select the three lines of text under the heading Key Benefits**

2. **Click the Bullets list arrow ⊞▾ in the Paragraph group on the HOME tab, then point to the Check mark bullet style**
The Bullets list opens and displays bullet formatting options in the Bullet Library. When you point to the Check mark bullet style, the text you selected appears as a bulleted list, with a check mark before each item, as shown in **FIGURE E-16**.

3. **Click the Check mark bullet style**
The bullet list closes. Notice that each bullet in the list is indented and that there is a tab after each check mark. You can see by the ruler that a hanging indent has been automatically set. If any text in the bulleted list wrapped to a second line, it would align with the first line of text, not the bullet.

4. **Click to the right of the third item in the list (after "expeditions"), then press [Enter]**
A fourth check mark bullet appears automatically in the new row.

5. **Type Building it yourself saves hundreds of dollars**
The text you typed is now formatted as a fourth item in the bulleted list.

6. **Scroll down until you can see the bottom of the page, select the three lines of text under the heading Top Reasons to Buy Outdoor Designs Products, then click the Numbering list arrow in the Paragraph group**
The Numbering list opens and displays the Numbering Library, containing different formatting options for a numbered list.

7. **Click the option shown in FIGURE E-17 (the one with the parenthesis after each number), then save your changes**
The selected text is now formatted as a numbered list.

FIGURE E-16: Bullet library

FIGURE E-17: Boat Kit fact sheet with bulleted and numbered lists

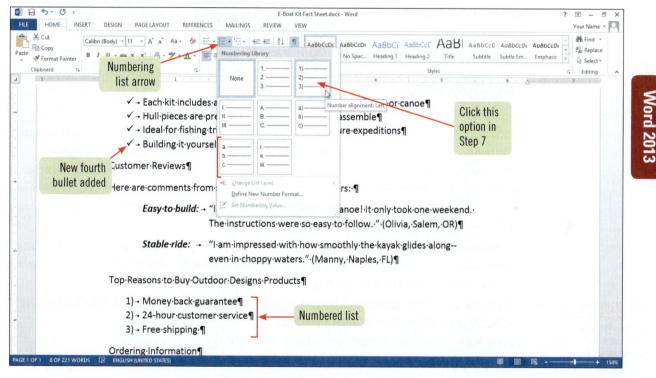

Creating a custom bullet

You can create a custom bullet using an image or symbol. To do this, click the Bullets list arrow in the Paragraph group, click Define New Bullet, then click Picture to open the Insert Pictures dialog box. To choose one of your own images, click Browse next to the From a file or next to your SkyDrive options, navigate to the folder where your image is stored, click Insert, then click OK. Or, to create a bullet using an image from a website, type key words in the Search box next to Bing Image Search, press [Enter], click the image you want, click Insert, then click OK.

Apply Styles

Learning Outcomes
- Explain styles and style sets
- Apply styles to text
- Change the style set and color palette

You can save a lot of formatting time and ensure that your document looks professional by applying styles to your document. A **style** is a set of predefined formatting attributes. For instance, the Normal Paragraph style (which is applied to any text you type in a new document) includes the Calibri 11-point font with 1.15 line spacing. Besides paragraph styles, you can also apply built-in styles for other types of text elements in your document, including headings, titles, and captions. To apply a style to a paragraph, click anywhere in the paragraph, then click the style you want in the Styles gallery, which is in the Styles group on the HOME tab. Once you apply styles to your document, you can then change the look of the entire document in one click by applying a new style set. A **style set** is a group of professionally coordinated styles that look great together; applying a different style set changes all the styles in the document to a different overall look. **CASE** *You decide to use styles to complete the formatting of the boat kit fact sheet.*

STEPS

1. **Scroll up, then click anywhere in Key Benefits in the line below the long paragraph**

   To apply a style to a paragraph, you first click in the paragraph to which you want to apply the style.

2. **In the Styles group on the HOME tab, click the Heading 1 style in the Styles gallery**

   See **FIGURE E-18**. The Key Benefits paragraph now has the Heading 1 style applied to it and is formatted in Calibri Light 16-point blue.

3. **Using the process you followed in Steps 1 and 2, apply the Heading 1 style to the following lines: Customer Reviews, Top Reasons to Buy Outdoor Designs Products, and Ordering Information**

   All of the headings in the document now have the Heading 1 style applied.

4. **Scroll up if necessary to view the text below "Customer Reviews," select the customer quote that begins with "I can't believe I built, then click the More button on the Styles gallery**

   When you want to apply a style to only part of a paragraph, you need to first select the desired text before applying the style; otherwise, the style will be applied to the entire paragraph. The Styles gallery opens and displays all the styles you can apply to paragraphs or characters, as shown in **FIGURE E-19**.

5. **Click the Quote style in the Styles gallery**

   The selected text is now formatted in gray italic, the preset formatting specifications for the Quote style. Because you selected text instead of clicking in the paragraph, the style was applied only to the characters you selected rather than to the whole paragraph.

6. **Select the customer quote that begins with "I am impressed with, click the Quote style in the Styles gallery, then deselect the text**

   Next, you decide to change the style set to change the overall look of the document.

7. **Click the DESIGN tab, click the More button ⊽ in the Document Formatting group to open the Style Set gallery, then click the Lines (Simple) Style Set thumbnail**

   The Lines (Simple) style set is applied to the document. Notice the headings all now have a thin rule under them. Notice, too, that the quotes are no longer formatted in gray, but instead are italic black. You can see that changing a style set immediately changes the overall look of the document.

8. **Click the Colors button in the Document Formatting group, then click the Red Orange color palette**

   The Heading 1 font color is now red, and "Outdoor Designs" is now red. In addition to changing the style set, you can apply a different color palette so the style colors change but remain coordinated for a polished final document.

9. **Press [Ctrl][End], type your name, save your changes, use the zoom slider to set the zoom to 60%, compare your screen to FIGURE E-20, close the document, then exit Word**

   Submit your document to your instructor.

FIGURE E-18: Heading 1 style applied to paragraph

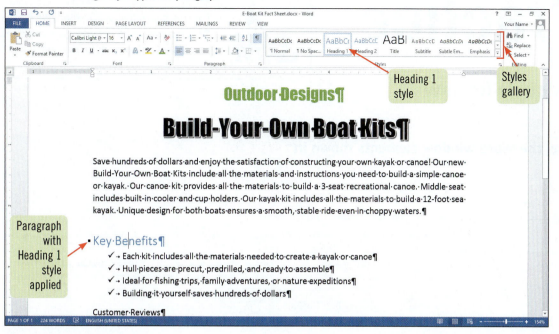

FIGURE E-19: Styles gallery

FIGURE E-20: Completed E-Boat Kit Fact Sheet at 60% zoom

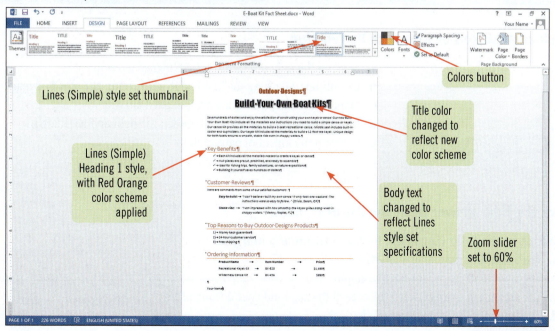

Practice

Concepts Review

Label the Word window elements shown in FIGURE E-21.

FIGURE E-21

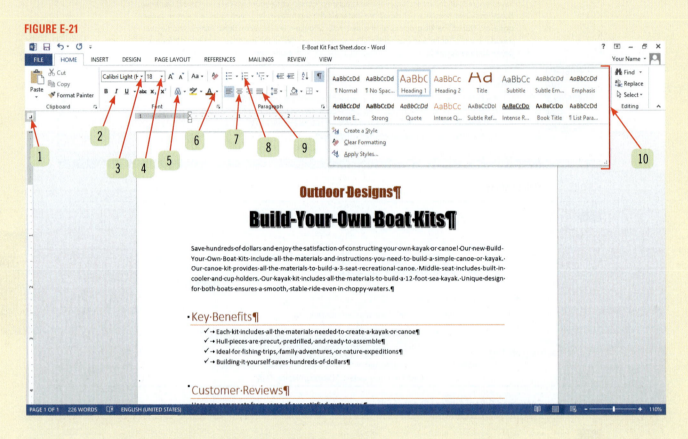

Match each button or icon with its function.

11. ⌐
12. ⌐
13. △
14. ▤
15. ▤

a. Mark on the ruler indicating a right-aligned tab stop
b. Indents text following the first line in a paragraph at a specified mark on the ruler
c. Mark on the ruler indicating a left-aligned tab stop
d. Justifies the current paragraph between the right and left margins
e. Increases the indent of paragraph by ½"

Select the best answer from the list of choices.

16. **Which of the following is the best definition of a margin?**
    a. The amount of space after a tab stop
    b. The amount of space between paragraphs
    c. The amount of space between the edge of the page and your document text
    d. The amount of space between words

Concepts Review

17. Which of the following best describes the purpose of using tabs?

   a. To organize text into columns

   b. To center paragraphs

   c. To adjust the margin

   d. To indent every line in a paragraph

18. Which of the following is the best definition for an indent?

   a. The amount of space between paragraphs

   b. The amount of space between text in a document and the edge of the page

   c. A set amount of space between the edge of a paragraph and the right or left margin

   d. A set amount of space after a tab stop

19. Which of the following tools would you use to copy the formatting of selected text and apply to other text?

   a. Styles gallery

   b. Format Painter button

   c. Font list

   d. Text Effects button

20. Which of the following is not true about using styles?

   a. You apply a style by clicking a thumbnail in the Styles gallery.

   b. You must select all text in a paragraph in order to apply a style to it.

   c. When you click in a paragraph and then click a style in the Styles gallery, the style is applied to the entire paragraph.

   d. Using styles to format a document can save time and ensure your document is formatted consistently.

Skills Review

1. Change font and font size.

   a. Start Word, use the Open command in Backstage view to open the file E-2.docx from where you store your Data Files, then save it as **E-Songwriting Contest**. If necessary, change the view to Print Layout view, with the zoom set to 120%.

   b. Select the entire first line of the document.

   c. Change the font size to 16.

   d. Change the font to Baskerville Old Face.

   e. Select the entire second line of the document, and then change the font size to 24.

   f. Save your changes.

2. Change font color, style, and effects.

   a. Select the first line of the document, then change the font color to dark orange (the sixth color in the last row under Theme Colors).

   b. Format the selected dark orange text in bold.

   c. Select the second line of the document, open the Text Effects gallery, then apply the black option in the top row (first option in top row).

   d. Select the text **Stream City Music Academy** in the third line of the document, then apply bold formatting to the selection. Change the font color to dark orange.

   e. Use the Format Painter to apply the formatting from "Stream City Music Academy" to the other instances of "Stream City Music Academy" in the document. (*Hint*: There are four other instances of it in the document.)

   f. Apply bold formatting to **Janice Brown** (in the 14th line of text) and **Charles Rigdon** (in the 16th line of text).

   g. Save your changes.

3. Change alignment and line spacing.

   a. Change the alignment of the paragraph located below "Songwriting Contest" to justified.

   b. Change the line spacing to 1.15 for the justified paragraph.

Skills Review (continued)

   c. Use the Paragraph dialog box to specify adding 6-point spacing before and after the paragraph.

   d. Center-align the first two lines of the document.

   e. Save your changes.

4. Change margin settings.

   a. Use a command on the VIEW tab to adjust the view so you can see the whole page on the screen.

   b. Verify that the ruler is visible in the document window. (If it is not visible, adjust your settings so it is visible.)

   c. Apply the preset Narrow margins setting to the document.

   d. Apply the preset Wide margins setting to the document.

   e. Open the Page Setup dialog box with the Margins tab displayed, and set the left margin to 1.2 and the right margin to 1.2.

   f. Change the zoom level to Page Width.

   g. Save your changes.

5. Set tabs.

   a. Scroll down until you see the line of text that begins with **Item**.

   b. Select this line and the three lines below it (through the line that begins with **Awards ceremony**).

   c. Set a left tab stop at the 2 ½" mark on the ruler for the four selected lines.

   d. Set a right tab stop at the 5 ½" mark on the ruler for the four selected lines.

   e. Apply bold formatting to the line that contains **Item Description Date**.

   f. Save your changes.

6. Set indents.

   a. Select the four lines of text below Important Dates, then set the left indent to 1/2".

   b. Select the 15th line of text through the 19th line of text (the 15th line of text starts with **Janice Brown** and the 19th line of text ends with **throughout the world.**)

   c. Set a hanging indent at the 1" mark on the ruler for the selected lines of text.

   d. Use a button on the HOME tab to increase the left indent of the selected lines to the 1/2" mark on the ruler. Set the right indent for these lines to the 5 1/2" mark on the ruler.

   e. Save your changes.

7. Add bulleted and numbered lists.

   a. Format lines nine through 12 (**Jazz** through **R&B**) as a bulleted list using the solid black square bullet.

   b. Format the last three lines in the document as a numbered list, choosing the style 1) 2) 3) (a number followed by a parenthesis).

   c. Save your changes.

8. Apply Styles.

   a. Apply the Heading 1 Style to the text **Submissions** (line 7 in the document).

   b. Apply the Heading 1 style to the following headings: **Judges**, **Submission Guidelines**, **Important Dates**, and **How to Enter**.

   c. Open the DESIGN tab, then apply the Basic (Stylish) style set to the document.

   d. Use the Colors button to change the color palette to Red Violet.

   e. Type your name in the last line of the document. (*Note*: Make sure your name is not formatted as a numbered list. If you need to remove the numbered list format from any text in the document, click in the paragraph from which you want to remove it, then click the Numbering button.)

   f. Save your changes.

Skills Review (continued)

g. Preview the document, compare your document with **FIGURE E-22**, then exit Word. Submit your completed document to your instructor.

Independent Challenge 1

You work in the marketing department for the East Riverton Recreation Center. Jamal Michaels, the general manager, needs to create a one-page document that describes the programs and classes offered in September. Jamal has already created a draft with all the necessary information; however, he is not happy with its appearance. He has provided you with his unformatted draft and has asked you to format it so that all the information is presented effectively and looks attractive and professional.

a. Start Word, open the file E-3.docx from where your Data Files are stored, then save it as **E-September Classes**.

b. Center-align the first four lines of the document.

c. Change the font of **September Classes** to Franklin Gothic Medium, and increase the font size to 24.

d. Change the font color of **September Classes** to Blue, Accent 5, then apply bold formatting to it.

e. Increase the font size of **East Riverton Recreation Center** and the two lines below it to 14 points.

f. In the paragraph under "What's New" (lines 6–9), align the paragraph so it is justified, then set the line spacing to 1.5. Increase the space before and after this paragraph to 6 points.

g. Apply the Heading 1 style to the following lines of text: **What's New**, **New Resident Orientation Classes**, **Cooking Classes**, and **Adult Fitness Class**.

h. In the four lines of text that contain tabs below the heading "New Resident Orientation Classes," set two left tab stops—the first at 2" and the second at 4".

i. In the four lines of text that contain tabs below the heading "Cooking Classes," set a left tab stop at 2", a second left tab stop at 3 ½", and one right tab stop at 5 ½".

j. Format the last three lines in the document as a bulleted list. Choose the bullet style that looks like a right-facing arrow.

k. Apply the Shaded style set to the document, then apply the Green color palette.

FIGURE E-22

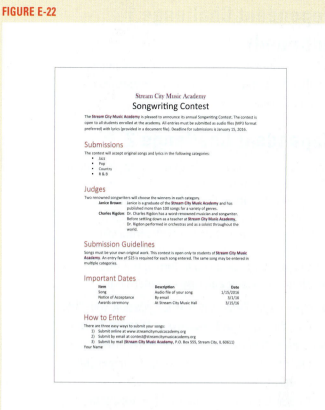

Independent Challenge 1 (continued)

l. Type your name at the end of the document, then right-align it. Compare your finished document to **FIGURE E-23**.

FIGURE E-23

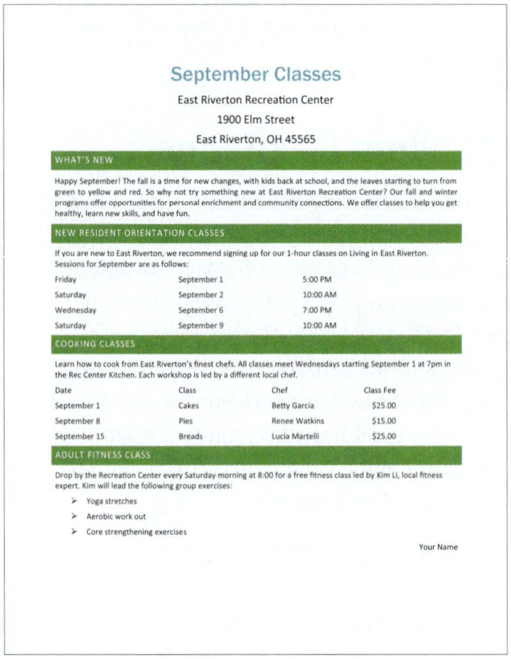

September Classes

East Riverton Recreation Center

1900 Elm Street

East Riverton, OH 45565

WHAT'S NEW

Happy September! The fall is a time for new changes, with kids back at school, and the leaves starting to turn from green to yellow and red. So why not try something new at East Riverton Recreation Center? Our fall and winter programs offer opportunities for personal enrichment and community connections. We offer classes to help you get healthy, learn new skills, and have fun.

NEW RESIDENT ORIENTATION CLASSES

If you are new to East Riverton, we recommend signing up for our 1-hour classes on Living in East Riverton. Sessions for September are as follows:

Friday	September 1	5:00 PM
Saturday	September 2	10:00 AM
Wednesday	September 6	7:00 PM
Saturday	September 9	10:00 AM

COOKING CLASSES

Learn how to cook from East Riverton's finest chefs. All classes meet Wednesdays starting September 1 at 7pm in the Rec Center Kitchen. Each workshop is led by a different local chef.

Date	Class	Chef	Class Fee
September 1	Cakes	Betty Garcia	$25.00
September 8	Pies	Renee Watkins	$15.00
September 15	Breads	Lucia Martelli	$25.00

ADULT FITNESS CLASS

Drop by the Recreation Center every Saturday morning at 8:00 for a free fitness class led by Kim Li, local fitness expert. Kim will lead the following group exercises:

- Yoga stretches
- Aerobic work out
- Core strengthening exercises

Your Name

Independent Challenge 2

You provide administrative help to the owner of Captain Mike's Biking Adventure Tours, a small tour company that offers biking tours in the United States and Europe. Ramon Vasquez, the marketing director, has given you an unformatted document that provides information about the European tours the company will offer in the summer. Ramon has asked you to format the sheet so the information is attractive and easy to understand.

a. Open the file E-4.docx from where you store your Data Files, then save it as **E-Summer Biking Tours**.

b. Center-align the first five lines of text in the document, which include the company name and contact information.

c. Format the Captain Mike's Biking Adventure Tours company name in line 1 of the document using any font, font style, or effects you like to make it look attractive and appropriate for an adventure tour company.

d. Apply italic formatting to the contact information (lines 2 through 5 of the document).

e. Apply the Heading 1 style to the following lines of text: **About Captain Mike's Biking Adventure Tours**, **Summer 2016 Biking Tours**, and **All Adventures Include**.

f. Justify the paragraph of text below the About Captain Mike's Biking Adventure Tours heading, then set line spacing for this paragraph at 1.15. Increase the font size for this paragraph to 14 pt.

g. Select the last four paragraphs below the Summer 2016 Biking Tours heading, beginning with **Bavaria** and ending with **($2295)**. Set a left tab stop for these four selected paragraphs to the 1.5" mark on the ruler.

h. For the same four paragraphs, apply a hanging indent at the 1.5" mark on the ruler, so the paragraph text wraps at the 1.5" mark (the same position of the tab stop that you set in Step g).

i. Apply the Strong style to the text **Bavaria:**, **Tuscany:**, **Normandy:**, and **Scotland:**.

j. Format the last four lines of text in the document as a bulleted list, choosing a bullet style that you like.

k. Apply the Casual style set to the document. Apply the Marquee color palette.

l. Add your name in the last line of the information sheet, then center-align it.

m. Save your changes, preview, and print the information sheet.

n. Close the document, then exit Word.

Independent Challenge 3

You work for Sophie Williams, the marketing director of the Wellspring Day Spa in Utica, New York. Sophie has asked you to create a Day of Beauty Gift Certificate for an upcoming promotion. The gift certificate will be promoted and sold for Mother's Day. Sophie typed the information for the pass in Word and has given the document to you to format.

a. Open the file E-5.docx from where you store your Data Files, then save it as **E-Spa Gift Certificate**.

b. Using the skills you learned in this unit, format the pass using fonts, sizes, styles, and effects that you think are appropriate. Use your creativity to produce an attractive document.

Independent Challenge 3 (continued)

c. Format some of the text on the pass as a bulleted list, choosing whatever style you like.

d. Change the paper orientation to Landscape, and adjust the margins to different settings. (*Hint*: To specify to print the document in landscape orientation, click the PAGE LAYOUT tab, click the Orientation button in the Page Setup group, then click Landscape.)

e. Type your name somewhere on the gift certificate.

f. Save your changes, print the gift certificate, then close the document and exit Word.

Independent Challenge 4: Explore

You work for Stan and Sue's Ice Creamery, a favorite ice cream business in West Overton, New Hampshire. Stan asks you to organize and format their newest menu. You need to open the document that contains all the text for the menu and enhance its appearance using styles, tabs, and other formatting tools and techniques.

a. Start Word, open the file E-6.docx then save it as **E-Ice Cream Flavors.docx**.

b. Apply the Title style to the first line of text (Stan and Sue's Ice Creamery). Apply the Subtitle style to the second line of text (The Most Delicious Ice Cream Anywhere).

c. Apply the Heading 1 style to the following lines of text: **Prices**, **Flavors**, and **Customer Quotes**.

d. Select the Prices heading, then click the Underline button in the Font group. Apply red formatting to the Prices heading. With the Prices heading still selected, right-click the Headings 1 style in the Styles gallery, then click Update Heading 1 to Match Selection. Notice that all the headings in the document are now red and underlined.

e. Select the four lines of text below the Prices heading, then set a right-aligned tab stop at the 6" mark on the ruler. With the text still selected, position the mouse pointer over the selected text, right-click to open a shortcut menu, then click Paragraph to open the Paragraph dialog box.

f. In the Paragraph dialog box, click Tabs to open the Tabs dialog box, click the 2 option in the Leader section, then click OK. Notice the dotted leader lines connecting each scoop option to its associated price.

g. Select all the ice cream flavors below the Flavors heading (Banana through Vanilla). Click the PAGE LAYOUT tab, click the Columns button in the Page Setup group, then click Three. Notice that all the flavors are now formatted into three columns.

h. Apply the Quote style to the three customer quotes and the customer quote names (the last seven lines in the document). Indent the line below each quote (the customer name) at the 1" mark.

i. Open the DESIGN tab then apply the Basic (Elegant) style set to the document. Apply the Blue color palette. Click the Fonts button in the Document Formatting group, scroll down, and then click Arial. Notice that all the fonts in the document are now different. Insert a paragraph return between "Sue's" and "Ice" in the first line of the document (so "Ice Creamery" is on the second line.) Compare your screen to **FIGURE E-24**.

j. Type your name below the last line of the document. Preview, save, and close the document, then submit the file to your instructor.

k. Exit Word.

FIGURE E-24

**STAN AND SUE'S
ICE CREAMERY**
The Most Delicious Ice Cream Anywhere

Prices

Kiddie-sized scoop:	$1.50
One scoop:	$2.50
Two scoops:	$4.00
Three scoops:	$5.50

Flavors

Banana	Coconut	Peppermint Stick
Black Cherry	Cookie dough	Pineapple
Blueberry	Coffee	Raspberry
Butter Pecan	Mint Chocolate Chip	Strawberry
Bubblegum	Orange Sorbet	Vanilla
Chocolate Chip	Pecan	

Customer Quotes

"I've been to ice cream shops all over the country, but Stan and Sue's flavors are the most delicious!"

-Penny Rose, lawyer

"Nothing beats a chocolate cone at Stan and Sue's after a summer baseball game!"

-Bob Fernandez, dad and baseball coach

"If you didn't get your ice cream at Stan and Sue's, then it isn't the most delicious!"

-Ellen Wong, florist

Your Name

Visual Workshop

Open the file E-7.docx from where your Data Files are stored, then save it as **E-Burger Menu**. Format the document so it appears as shown in **FIGURE E-25**. (*Hint*: A different style set has been applied to the document, and the color palette was changed, so you will need to experiment with different combinations of styles, style sets, and color palettes until you find the right mix. If you do not have or cannot find the font used in the title, apply the closest match you can find.) Be sure to set tab stops for all the prices and the Kid's Menu items. Add your name at the bottom of the document, then preview the document. Close the document, then exit Word. Submit the document to your instructor.

FIGURE E-25

Hank's Burger Hut

655 Moreland Avenue
Boulder, CO 80301
630-555-0765

Burgers

BBQ Burger	**$7.75**
Homemade BBQ sauce, bacon, cheddar cheese, onions.	
Turkey Burger	**$5.25**
Ground turkey patty, lettuce and tomato with chutney mayo.	
Veggie Burger	**$6.75**
Portobello patty, Swiss cheese, tomato and lettuce.	
Tuna Patty Melt	**$5.75**
Tuna burger with melted cheddar cheese. Served with a side salad.	
Southwest Burger	**$6.25**
Spicy burger with pepper jack cheese. Served with a side of guacamole.	

Beverages

Lemonade, juices, cola	**$2.00**

Desserts

Hank's Famous Pies	**$4.25**
Top off your lunch with one of Hank's famous pies (pecan, apple, or peach) baked fresh daily.	

Kids' Menu

Any Kids Meal (includes chips and a drink)		**$2.50**
Chicken tenders	Cheese pizza	Macaroni and cheese
Hot dog	Hamburger	Grilled cheese sandwich

Your Name

Adding Special Elements to a Document

CASE ▶ Karen Rivera, marketing director for Outdoor Designs, has asked you to finish a report that recommends a plan for launching green initiatives at Outdoor Designs.

Unit Objectives

After completing this unit, you will be able to:

- Create a table
- Insert and delete table columns and rows
- Format a table
- Add clip art

- Add footnotes and citations
- Insert a header or footer
- Add borders and shading
- Work with themes
- Format a research paper

Files You Will Need

F-1.docx	F-5.docx
F-2.docx	F-6.docx
F-3.docx	F-7.docx
F-4.docx	

©HelenStock/Shutterstock

Create a Table

If you need to include detailed facts and figures in a document, you might want to use a table to organize the information. A **table** is a grid of rows and columns. The intersection of a row and column is called a **cell**. Cells can contain either text or graphics. You can insert a table using the Table button on the INSERT tab. When you create a table, you specify the number of rows and columns; you can also add and delete rows and columns as you modify a table. You can use tabs to organize text into rows and columns, but working with tables is often easier. **CASE** ▶ *Karen gives you a file containing the content for the recommendation report. You begin by inserting a table to present the information about a new task-force organization.*

STEPS

1. **Start Word, open the file F-1.docx from where you store your Data Files, then save it as F-Green Report**

   The report opens in Print Layout view. The status bar indicates that there are four pages. You need to insert the table on page 3. You can use the Navigation pane to help you move to any page quickly.

2. **Click the Find button in the Editing group on the HOME tab**

   The Navigation pane opens. The HEADINGS tab displays links to all headings in the document.

3. **Click the HEADINGS tab on the Navigation pane, then click the Green Teams heading in the Navigation pane**

   The insertion point moves to the Green Teams heading on page 3, as shown in **FIGURE F-1**. You want to insert the table above the heading "Outdoor Designs Vision".

4. **Read the paragraph below the Green Teams heading, then click in the blank line below the last line of the paragraph**

5. **Click the Navigation Pane Close button ✖, click the INSERT tab, then click the Table button in the Tables group**

   The Table menu opens and displays a grid for choosing the number of rows and columns for your table.

6. **Point to the third square in the third row of the grid, as shown in FIGURE F-2, then click**

   A table with three rows and three columns appears below the paragraph, and the insertion point is in the first cell. Notice that two additional tabs now appear on the Ribbon: the TABLE TOOLS DESIGN tab and the TABLE TOOLS LAYOUT tab. These are **contextual tabs**, meaning they appear only when a particular type of object is selected and are not otherwise available.

7. **Type Green Team, then press [Tab]**

   Pressing [Tab] moves the insertion point to the next cell. The symbol in each cell is an **end-of-cell mark**. The marks to the right of each row are **end-of-row marks**.

8. **Type Team Leader, press [Tab], type Department, then press [Tab]**

   Pressing [Tab] in the last cell of a row moves the insertion point to the first cell in the next row.

9. **Type the text shown below in the rest of the table, pressing [Tab] after each entry to move to the next cell, but do not press [Tab] after the last entry**

Waste Reduction	Brad Fitzgibbon	Finance
Recycling	Erica Li	Customer Service

   All the cells in the table have data in them. Compare your screen to **FIGURE F-3**.

10. **Click the Save button 🖫 on the Quick Access toolbar**

    Notice that when you move the mouse pointer over the table, the Table move handle ⊹ appears above the upper-left corner of the table. Clicking this icon selects the entire table.

Adding Special Elements to a Document

FIGURE F-1: Using the Navigation pane to move to Green Teams heading

INSERT tab

Heading 1 style

Navigation pane

Green Teams heading

Insertion point at Green Teams heading

Click here in Step 4

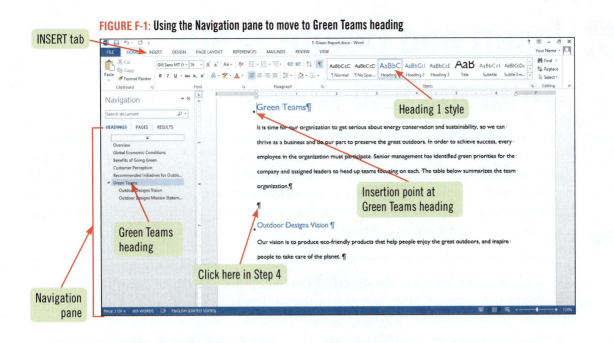

FIGURE F-2: Inserting a 3 x 3 table

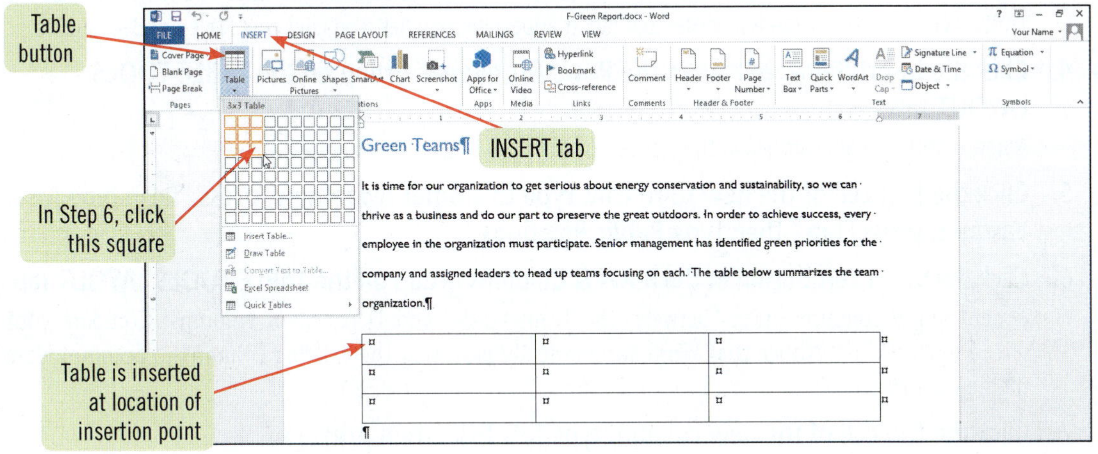

Table button

In Step 6, click this square

Table is inserted at location of insertion point

INSERT tab

FIGURE F-3: Table with all information entered

TABLE TOOLS DESIGN tab

Column

End-of-cell mark

Row

End-of-row mark

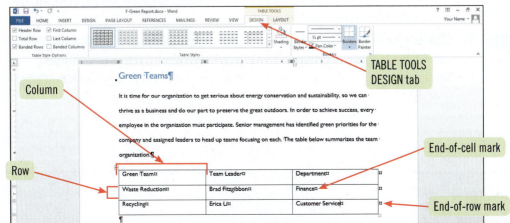

Word 2013

Learning Outcomes
• Insert a table row or column
• Delete a table row or column

Insert and Delete Table Columns and Rows

After you create a table, you might need to add more information or delete existing information. To accommodate the new information, you can add rows to the top, bottom, or middle of a table. You can add columns anywhere in a table, too. You can use commands on the TABLE TOOLS LAYOUT tab to add or delete columns and rows. **CASE** *You need to add a new row in the middle of the table to add information about another team. You also need to add a column to the table that indicates each leader's job title. Finally, you need to delete one of the rows.*

STEPS

1. **Click Customer Service in the last cell of the table if necessary, then press [Tab]**

   Pressing [Tab] in the last cell of a table inserts a new row at the bottom of the table. The table now has four rows, and the insertion point is in the first cell of the new row.

2. **Type Sustainable Package Design, press [Tab], type Rochelle Brown, press [Tab], then type Product Development**

3. **Click any cell in the second row of the table, then click the TABLE TOOLS LAYOUT tab**

   The TABLE TOOLS LAYOUT tab displays tools and commands for adjusting settings in a table. Because the TABLE TOOLS LAYOUT tab is a contextual tab, it appears only when you click in a table or select a table.

QUICK TIP
To insert a row or column using the shortcut menu, right-click a cell in the table, point to Insert, then click an option to insert a row above or below, or a column to the left or right of the current position.

4. **Click the Insert Below button in the Rows & Columns group on the TABLE TOOLS LAYOUT tab**

   A new empty row appears below the second row.

5. **Click the first cell of the new third row, type Customer Awareness, press [Tab], type Jose Vasquez, press [Tab], then type Public Relations**

6. **Click the Insert Left button in the Rows & Columns group on the TABLE TOOLS LAYOUT tab**

   A new empty column appears between the Team Leader and Department columns. Compare your screen to **FIGURE F-4**. Notice that Word automatically narrowed the existing columns to accommodate the new column.

7. **Click the top cell of the new column, type Job Title, then press [↓]**

   The insertion point moves down to the second row in the third column.

8. **Type Manager, press [↓], type Director, press [↓], type Senior Associate, press [↓], then type Vice President**

   You have just learned that the Recycling and Waste Reduction teams will be combined into one. You need to delete the Waste Reduction team row.

QUICK TIP
To delete a column, click in the column, click Delete in the Rows & Columns group, then click Delete Columns.

9. **Click any cell in the row that begins with "Waste Reduction", click the Delete button in the Rows & Columns group, click Delete Rows, then save your changes**

   The entire row is deleted, and the other rows move up to close up the space. Compare your screen to **FIGURE F-5**.

FIGURE F-4: Table with new column and rows added

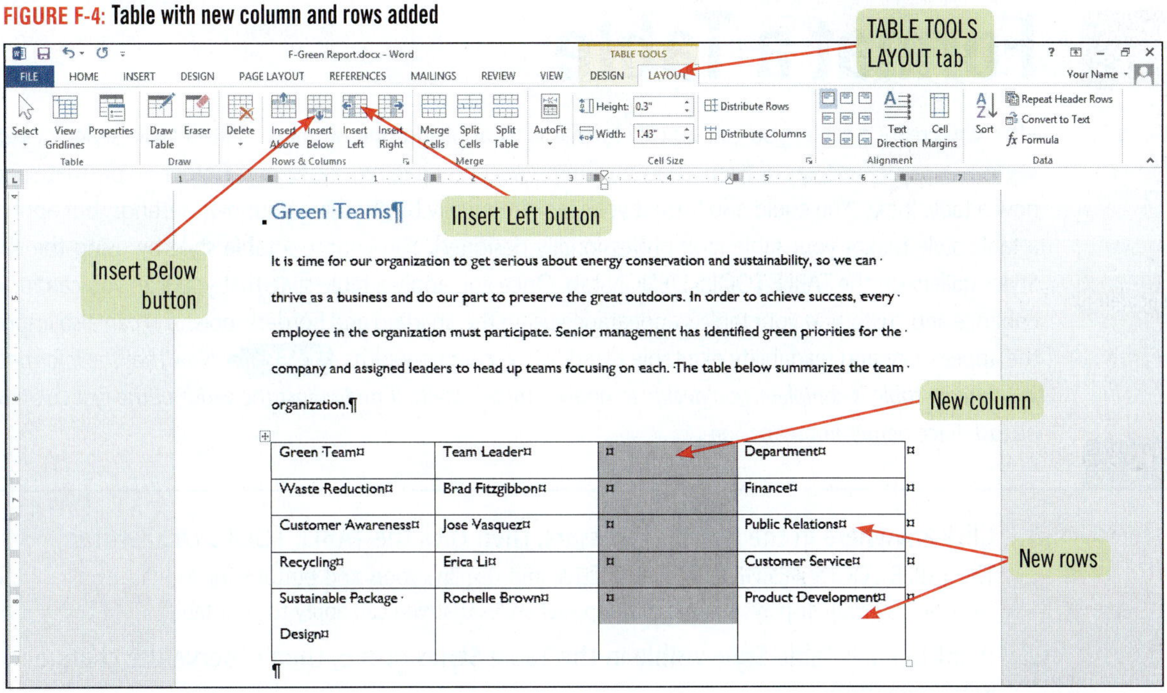

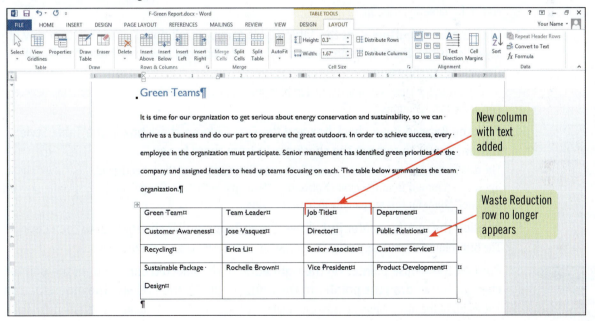

FIGURE F-5: Table after deleting row

Creating a table with the Draw Table button

You can also create a table by drawing using the Draw Table command. To do so, click the INSERT tab, click the Table button, then click Draw Table. This command is also available for drawing new rows and columns in an existing table in the Borders group on the TABLE TOOLS DESIGN tab. The pointer changes to 🖉, which you can drag in a diagonal motion to create the outside border of the table. To create or add columns, drag vertically from the top border down.

To create or add rows, drag horizontally from the right border to the left border. When you are finished drawing the table, press [Esc] to turn off the Draw Table feature. You can use commands in the Borders group on the TABLE TOOLS DESIGN tab to change the pen color or line width and style, or to delete column or row lines. Drawing a table or cells onto an existing table gives you more freedom to create tables with unequal columns, unequal rows, or merged cells.

Format a Table

After you create a table, you can quickly format it by applying one of many built-in table styles. A **table style** is a predefined set of formatting attributes, such as shading, fonts, and border color, that specify how a table looks. You could also format your table manually by choosing your own settings, but applying a table style makes your table look professionally designed. You choose a table style by using the Table Styles gallery on the TABLE TOOLS DESIGN tab. Once you apply a table style that you like, you can further enhance and customize your table's appearance using the Shading and Borders tools. You can also improve the appearance and readability of a table by adjusting column widths. **CASE** ▶ *Now that the information in the team table is complete, you decide to apply a table style to it and adjust the width of the first column so all task-force names fit on one line.*

STEPS

1. **Click anywhere in the table if necessary, then click the TABLE TOOLS DESIGN tab**

   The TABLE TOOLS DESIGN tab is now active and displays tools and buttons for formatting a table. The Table Styles group displays thumbnails of preset styles that you can apply to your table.

2. **Point to each Table Style visible in the Table Styles group, then observe the change in your document**

   With Live Preview, the table in the report changes to display a preview of each style as you move the mouse from one style to the next. You can view all available table styles by clicking the More button ⊽ at the right end of the Table Styles group.

3. **Click the More button ⊽ in the Table Styles group, scroll down so the bottom row of styles is visible, then click the second style in the bottom row (List Table 7 Colorful - Accent 1), as shown in FIGURE F-6**

   All the text in the table is now formatted in blue, and there is a border below the first row and between the first and second columns.

4. **Click the Banded Rows check box and the First Column check box in the Table Style Options group to remove the check marks from these boxes**

   The data in the first column is no longer formatted differently from the other data in these rows. The shading is also removed from the table. Notice that "Sustainable Package Design" in the first column wraps to two lines. You want this team name to fit on one line.

5. **Position the mouse pointer just above Green Team until it changes to ↓, then click**

   The first column is now selected, making it easy to see the right edge of the first column.

6. **Position the mouse pointer on the right edge of the selected column until the pointer changes to ╫, drag the pointer to the right about ¼", then release the mouse button**

   The width of the first column increases, and now the text in each first column cell fits on one line instead of two. The second column is now narrower.

7. **Point to the upper-left corner of the table until the ⊹ pointer appears, then click**

   The entire table is selected. Any formatting settings you choose at this point will be applied to all the cells in the table. You decide that you want to add column gridlines to the table. First you need to choose a blue border style.

8. **Click the Border Styles list arrow in the Borders group, then click the second border style in the first row (Single solid line, 1/2 pt, Accent 1) as shown in FIGURE F-7**

   You chose a blue border style that matches the table color.

9. **Click the Borders button list arrow in the Borders group, then click the All Borders option as shown in FIGURE F-8, then save your changes**

   Blue gridlines now outline all of the cells in the table.

Adding Special Elements to a Document

FIGURE F-6: Applying a table style

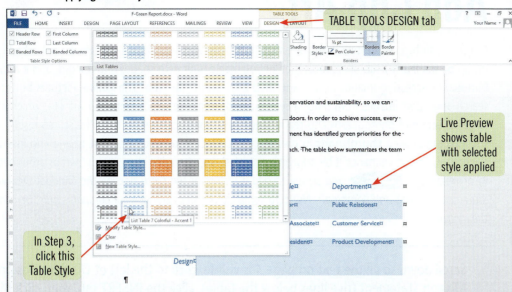

FIGURE F-7: Choosing a Border Style

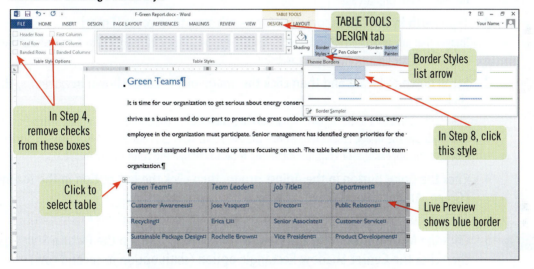

FIGURE F-8: Formatted table with table style and borders added

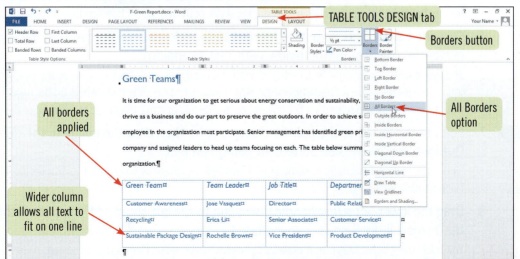

Add Clip Art

Graphics can help illustrate a point or enhance the overall visual appeal of a document. The Illustrations group on the INSERT tab offers tools that let you create your own shapes and images, and it also provides buttons for accessing images from a specified location or the Web. The Online Pictures button lets you search and insert images from Bing, a search site or from the Office.com Clip Art site, which contains a large collection of photographs and ready-made illustrations called **clip art**. The search results appear as small pictures called **thumbnails** in the task pane. Once you select a clip art image and insert it into a document, you can enhance it by applying picture styles, changing the way text wraps around it, moving it, or resizing it. **CASE** *You decide to add a picture of the Earth next to the Outdoor Designs Mission Statement heading and paragraph. Note: To complete the steps below, your computer must be connected to the Internet.*

STEPS

1. **Scroll down so all the text on page 4 is visible, click to the left of Outdoor Designs Mission Statement (five lines below the table), click the INSERT tab, then click the Online Pictures button in the Illustrations group**

   The Insert Pictures dialog box opens, offering different places you can search for images. The top option is the Office.com Clip Art site.

2. **Type earth in the Office.com Clip Art search box, then press [Enter]**

   Images that are associated with the word "earth" appear in the Office.com Clip Art window. These images are fed from the Office.com Clip Art website.

3. **Scroll down to locate and then click the image of the Earth shown in FIGURE F-9, then click Insert**

   The image is inserted in the report. Square **sizing handles** in the corners and square sizing handles on the sides indicate the image is selected. Notice the PICTURE TOOLS FORMAT tab is active. It contains tools to enhance the appearance of graphics including tools to change the color of the image.

4. **Click the Color button in the Adjust group, then click the last option in the second row (Green, Accent color 6 Dark), as shown in FIGURE F-10**

   The image is now all green. You can change the look of the image by applying a Picture Style.

5. **Click the More button ▼ in the Picture Styles group to open the Picture Styles gallery, then click the Center Shadow Rectangle option (sixth option in second row)**

   The image now has soft edges. The image looks awkward because its bottom edge is aligned with top edge of the Outdoor Designs Mission Statement heading. This is known as an **inline graphic**. To fix this so the text flows next to the image, you need to change its wrapping **style**, or the settings for how text flows in relation to a graphic.

6. **Click the Layout Options button 🖾 next to the selected image then click the Square button 🖾 (the first button below With Text Wrapping)**

   The image's left edge should be left-aligned with the paragraph text. Because you set the wrapping style to square, the image is now a **floating image**, which means you can drag it anywhere on the page. The anchor icon next to it indicates it is now a floating image. You decide to move the image to the right of the paragraph.

7. **Point to the image so the pointer changes to 🔁, then drag the image to the right of the Outdoor Designs Mission Statement paragraph text**

   Notice the text automatically rewrapped itself around the image as you moved it. You decide to make the Earth image a little bigger.

8. **Drag the lower-left sizing handle down and to the left about 1/4" to increase the size of the image a little, then save your work**

   You made the graphic larger, so it makes a stronger visual impact. Compare your screen to FIGURE F-11.

Adding Special Elements to a Document

FIGURE F-9: Insert Pictures dialog box with "earth" search results

In Step 3, click this image

Office.com Clip Art search box

FIGURE F-10: Applying a new color to an image using the Color Styles gallery

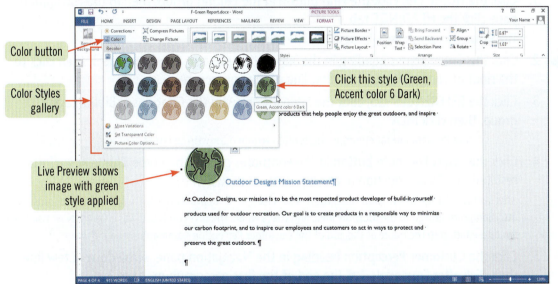

Color button

Color Styles gallery

Click this style (Green, Accent color 6 Dark)

Live Preview shows image with green style applied

FIGURE F-11: Resized earth image with color and picture style applied

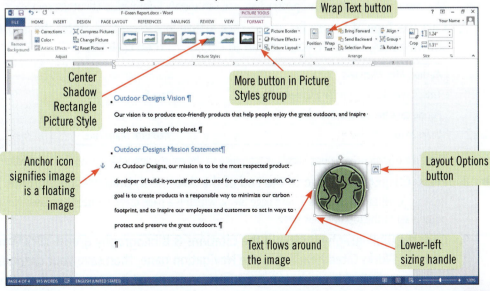

Wrap Text button

Center Shadow Rectangle Picture Style

More button in Picture Styles group

Anchor icon signifies image is a floating image

Layout Options button

Text flows around the image

Lower-left sizing handle

Word 2013

Adding Special Elements to a Document

Add Footnotes and Citations

Learning Outcomes
• Insert a footnote
• Insert a citation and add a new source
• Create a bibliography

If your document includes quotes or paraphrased material from another source, you need to credit that source by inserting a citation. A **citation** is a reference to a source that usually includes the author's name and the page number of the referenced material. There are different styles for using citations; MLA style is often used for research papers. Citations that follow MLA guidelines appear in parentheses after a quote or paraphrase. If a document contains citations, it must also include a **bibliography**, which is a listing of detailed source information for citations in the document. The REFERENCES tab in Word contains tools to manage sources, insert citations, and add a bibliography. You can also use the REFERENCES tab to add footnotes. A **footnote** is a comment that appears at the bottom of a document page; it consists of two linked parts: the reference mark in the body of the document and the corresponding note text. **CASE** ▸ *You need to add a footnote to the report that comments on recent energy savings. You also need to add a new source and citation, and insert a bibliography.*

STEPS

1. **Click the HOME tab, click the Find button in the Editing group, then in the Navigation pane click the HEADINGS tab**

   The Navigation pane shows a listing of all the headings in the document.

QUICK TIP

You can reorganize a document by reordering the headings in the Navigation pane. To move a heading, drag it to where you want it. All the text in that heading's section will move accordingly.

2. **Click the Green Teams heading in the Navigation pane to move to page 3, then click to the right of conservation in the first line of the paragraph**

3. **Click the REFERENCES tab, click the Style list arrow in the Citations & Bibliography group, then click MLA**

   MLA is a popular standard for citations and is often required for writing research papers.

4. **Click the Insert Footnote button in the Footnotes group, then type This year's efforts resulted in a 15% reduction in energy costs. as shown in FIGURE F-12**

   After you clicked the Insert Footnote button, a superscript "1" appears after the word "footprint." Also, the insertion point moved to the footnote area, and that's where the text you typed was entered. Now you need to add a citation to the quote at the end of the Customer Perception paragraph.

5. **Click the Customer Perception heading in the Navigation pane, scroll down a few lines, then click after "materials." at the end of the first paragraph on page 3**

6. **Click the Insert Citation button in the Citations & Bibliography group, then click Add New Source**

   The Create Source dialog box opens, where you can specify information about the source.

7. **Click the Type of Source list arrow, click Article in a Periodical, enter the information shown below, compare your screen to FIGURE F-13, then click OK**

Author: Max Michaels	Month: January
Title: Green Packaging for a Greener Planet	Day: 5
Periodical title: Build-It Monthly	Pages: 22-23
Year: 2016	Medium: Magazine

   The Create Source dialog box closes. A reference to the source you added is inserted as "(Michaels)".

QUICK TIP

To insert a page break using the Ribbon, click the INSERT tab, then click the Page Break button.

8. **Press [Ctrl][End] to move to the end of the document, then press [Ctrl][Enter]**

   Pressing [Ctrl][Enter] inserted a hard page break, which is a page break inserted by a user. Now the insertion point is set at the top of a new page.

9. **Click the Bibliography button in the Citations & Bibliography group, click Works Cited, click the Works Cited heading in the Navigation pane, then save your changes**

   See **FIGURE F-14**. Word inserts the bibliographic information for all the sources cited in the report.

FIGURE F-12: Footnote added to document

Reference mark

Insert Footnote button

HEADINGS tab

Green Teams heading in Navigation pane

Green Team¤	Team Leader¤	Job Title¤	Department¤
Customer Awareness¤	Jose Vasquez¤	Director¤	Public Relations¤
Recycling¤	Erica Li¤	Senior Associate¤	Customer Service¤
Sustainable Package Design¤	Rochelle Brown¤	Vice President¤	Product Development¤

Footnote

This year's efforts resulted in a 15% reduction in energy costs.

FIGURE F-13: Create Source dialog box with source information added

Create Source

Type of Source   Article in a Periodical

Type of Source list arrow

Bibliography Fields for MLA

Author   Max Michaels   Edit

☐ Corporate Author

Title   Green Packaging for a Greener Planet

Title of article in Title text box

Periodical Title   Build-It Monthly
Year   2016
Month   January
Day   5
Pages   22-23
Medium   Magazine

☐ Show All Bibliography Fields

Tag name   Example: Document
Max16

OK   Cancel

FIGURE F-14: Report with bibliography added

Style list with MLA style selected

Insert Citation button

Bibliography button

Navigation

Overview
Global Economic Conditions
Benefits of Going Green
Customer Perception
Recommended Initiatives for Outdo...
Green Teams
    Outdoor Designs Vision
    Outdoor Designs Mission Statem...
Works Cited

New source added

Works Cited

Atkinson, Rob. *America Risks Missing Out in Clean Technology*. 3 February 2010. 2 November 2012.

Kanter, Rosabeth Moss. "Wal-Mart's Environmental Game-Changer." 16 July 2010. http://hbr.org/. 3 November 2012.

Makower, Joel. "The State of Green Business 2010: Green Innovation Becomes a Great Idea." 5 February 2010. http://greenbiz.com/news. 3 November 2012.

Michaels, Max. "Green Packaging for a Greener Planet." *Build-It Monthly* 5 January 2016: 22-23.

Rosenbloom, Stephanie and Michael Barbaro. "Green Light Specials, Now at Wal-Mart." 24 January 2009. http://nytimes.com. 3 November 2012.

Rudolf, John Collins. "White House Awards $2.3 Billion in Tax Credits for Clean Energy." 8 January 2010. http://greeninc.blogs.nytimes.com. 3 November 2012.

Bibliography inserted in MLA style; includes all sources cited in this report

Word 2013

Insert a Header or Footer

When you create a document that contains several pages, you might want to add page numbers and other information to the top or bottom of every page. You can do this easily by adding headers or footers. A **header** is text that appears in the top margin of a page, and a **footer** is text that appears in the bottom margin of a page. Headers and footers usually repeat from page to page. In addition to page numbers, headers and footers often contain such information as the date, the document author's name, or the filename. You add headers and footers using the Header and Footer buttons on the INSERT tab. You can format header and footer text in the same way you format regular text, and you can even add graphics. **CASE** ▶ *You decide to add a header and footer to the report.*

STEPS

1. **Click the Navigation Pane Close button** ☒, **click the INSERT tab, click the Footer button in the Header & Footer group, then click Blank**

   The footer area is now active. The [Type here] placeholder is selected. You want to replace the text placeholder with the current date.

2. **Click the Date & Time button in the Insert group**

   The Date and Time dialog box opens, displaying several preset date formats. The first option in the list is selected, as shown in **FIGURE F-15**, and is the one that is most appropriate for the report.

3. **Click OK, then save your changes**

   The current date now appears left-aligned in the footer.

4. **Click the INSERT tab, click the Header button, then click Blank (Three Columns)**

   The insertion point moves to the header area, which contains three placeholders into which you can click and type text. The HEADER & FOOTER TOOLS DESIGN tab is now open and contains buttons and tools for working with headers and footers. Notice the other text on the Works Cited page is dimmed.

5. **Click the left-aligned [Type here] placeholder, press [Delete], click the center-aligned [Type here] placeholder, then press [Delete]**

   You deleted two of the three placeholders. You can replace the third placeholder with your name and the page number.

6. **Click the right-aligned [Type here] placeholder, type your name, then press [Spacebar]**

7. **Click the Page Number button in the Header & Footer group, point to Current Position, then click Plain Number**

   The header now contains your name and the page number, as shown in **FIGURE F-16**. This header will appear at the top of every page in the report. You do not want it to appear on the first page.

8. **Click the Different First Page check box in the Options group on the HEADER & FOOTER TOOLS DESIGN tab to select it**

   This option applies the header and footer to all pages in the document except the first page.

9. **Click the FILE tab, click Print, then click the Previous Page button** ◀ **at the bottom of the Print Preview pane four times to view each page of the report**

   Notice the header and footer appear on all pages except page 1. **FIGURE F-17** shows page 3.

FIGURE F-15: Date and Time dialog box

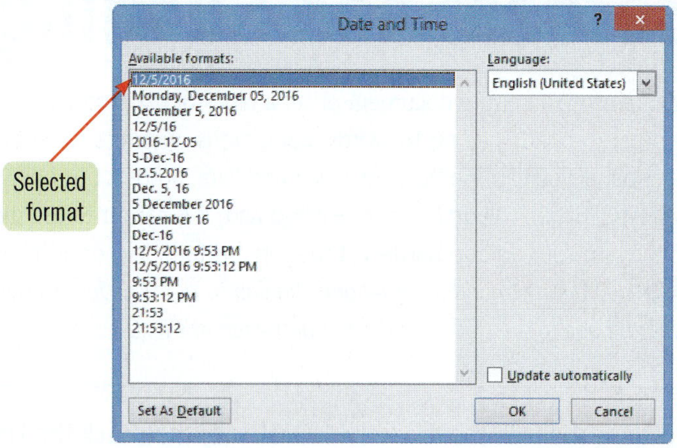

FIGURE F-16: Header with name and page number

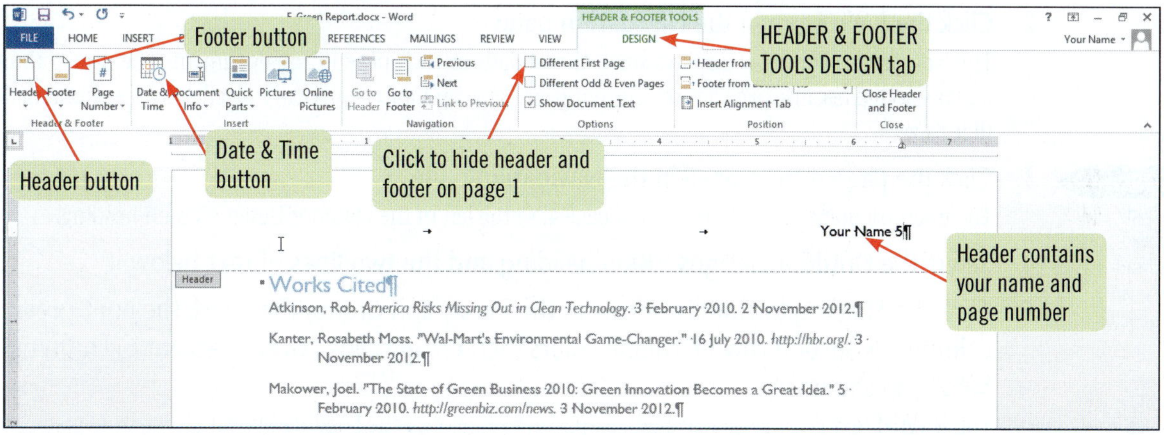

FIGURE F-17: Report in Print Preview showing header and footer on third page

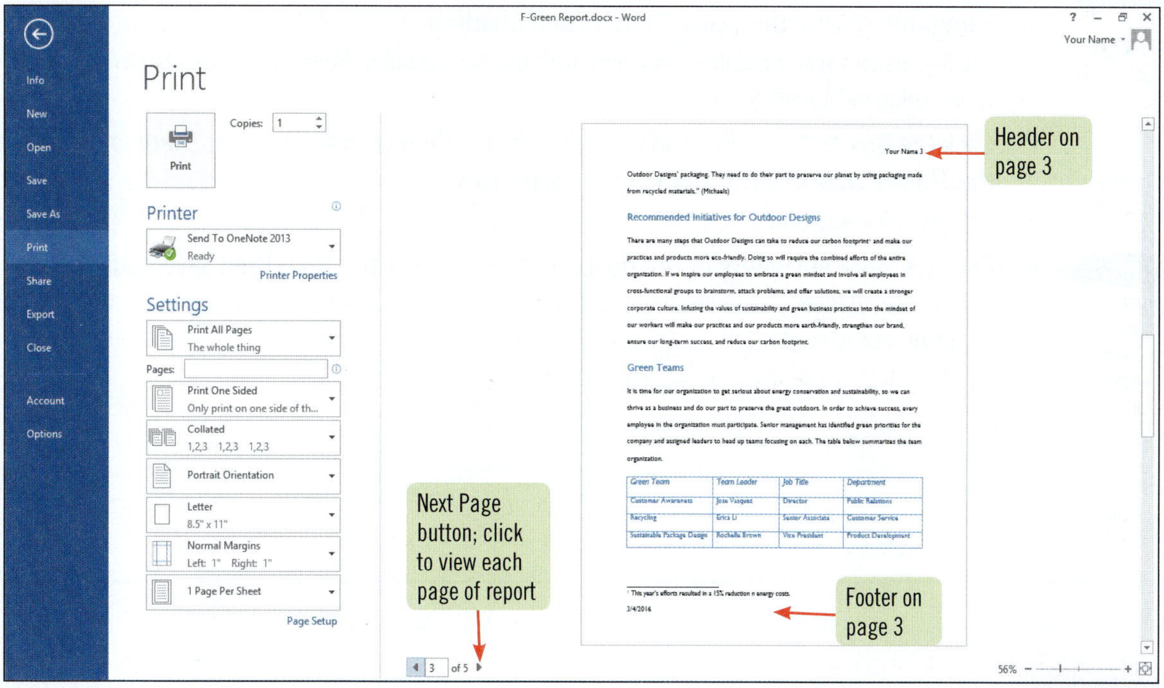

Add Borders and Shading

Learning Outcomes
• Navigate to a page
• Add borders to text
• Add shading to text

You can add visual interest to an entire document or set a block of text apart from the rest of the page by adding borders and background shading to words, paragraphs, graphics, or entire pages. To add these elements to an entire page, you can use the Page Color and Page Borders buttons in the Page Background group on the PAGE LAYOUT tab; to add them to selected text, it is easiest to use the Shading and Borders buttons on the HOME tab. You can add borders at the top, bottom, left, or right edges of text, or around a graphic. **CASE** *You decide to add a border and shading to the "Outdoor Designs Vision" paragraph at the bottom of the fourth page to set it off from the rest of the report's text.*

STEPS

1. **Press [Esc] to close the FILE tab, click the HOME tab, then click the Find button in the Editing group**

   The Navigation pane opens. The PAGES tab in the Navigation pane lets you jump quickly to a specific page in the document.

2. **Click the PAGES tab in the Navigation pane**

   The Navigation pane now displays small thumbnails of each page in the document. The page 5 thumbnail is selected because page 5 is the current page. You can jump to any page by clicking the thumbnail for that page.

3. **Click the page 4 thumbnail in the Navigation pane**

   The insertion point moves to the top of page 4, to the left of the Outdoor Designs Vision heading.

4. **Select the Outdoor Designs Vision heading and the two lines of text below it**

5. **Click the Shading button list arrow in the Paragraph group, then click the light green color in the second row of Theme colors (ScreenTip reads "Green, Accent 6, Lighter 80%"), as shown in FIGURE F-18**

   The selected text now has green shading applied to it. Notice the Shading button displays the green shade you applied. If you wanted to apply this shade of green somewhere else, you could simply select the text and click the Shading button again.

6. **Click the Navigation Pane Close button [X], click the Borders list arrow [▦ ▾] in the Paragraph group, then click Borders and Shading**

   The Borders and Shading dialog box opens, with the Borders tab in front. The Borders tab lets you specify a border color and a style of border.

7. **Click the Box setting, click the Color list arrow, then click the darkest shade of green in the Theme colors (tenth shade in the sixth row)**

   Compare your screen to **FIGURE F-19**.

8. **Click OK, click anywhere in the document to deselect the text, then save your changes**

   The Outdoor Designs Vision heading and paragraph are now shaded in a green box with a green border. Compare your screen to **FIGURE F-20**.

> **QUICK TIP**
> To hide the body text and subheadings below a heading, click the small triangle to the left of the heading. Click the triangle again to redisplay the hidden text.

> **QUICK TIP**
> To apply a border around specific edges of a selected text block, click the Borders list arrow in the Paragraph group, then click the border option you want.

> **QUICK TIP**
> To apply a border around the edge of an entire page, click the Page Border tab in the Borders and Shading dialog box, choose the page border settings you want, then click OK.

FIGURE F-18: Live Preview of paragraphs with light green shading applied

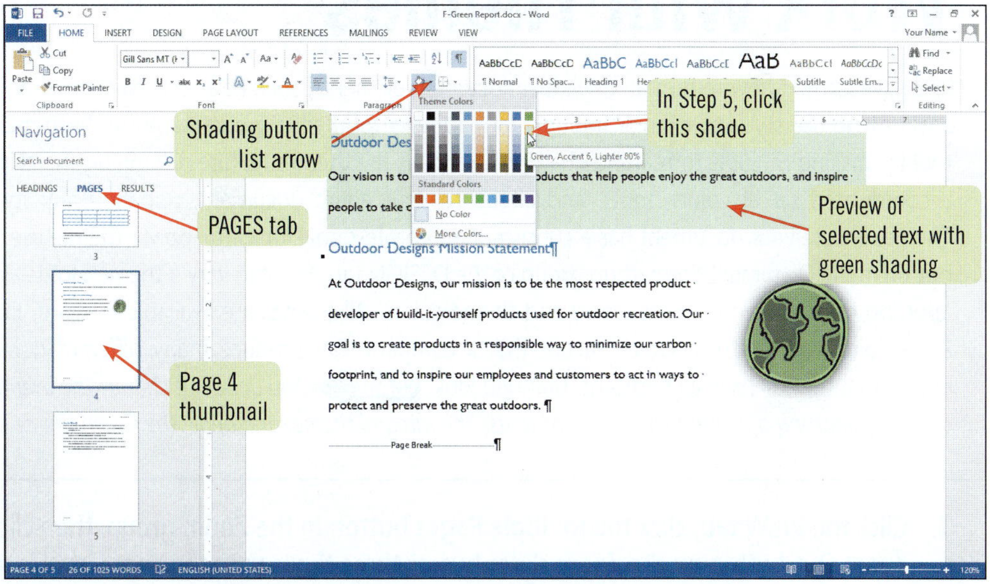

FIGURE F-19: Borders tab of Borders and Shading dialog box

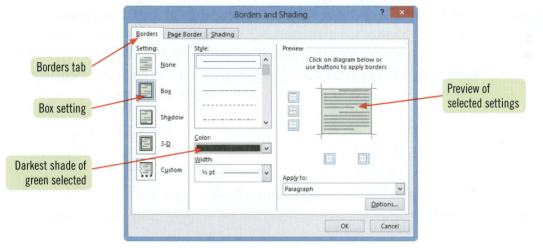

FIGURE F-20: Paragraphs with a box border and shading applied

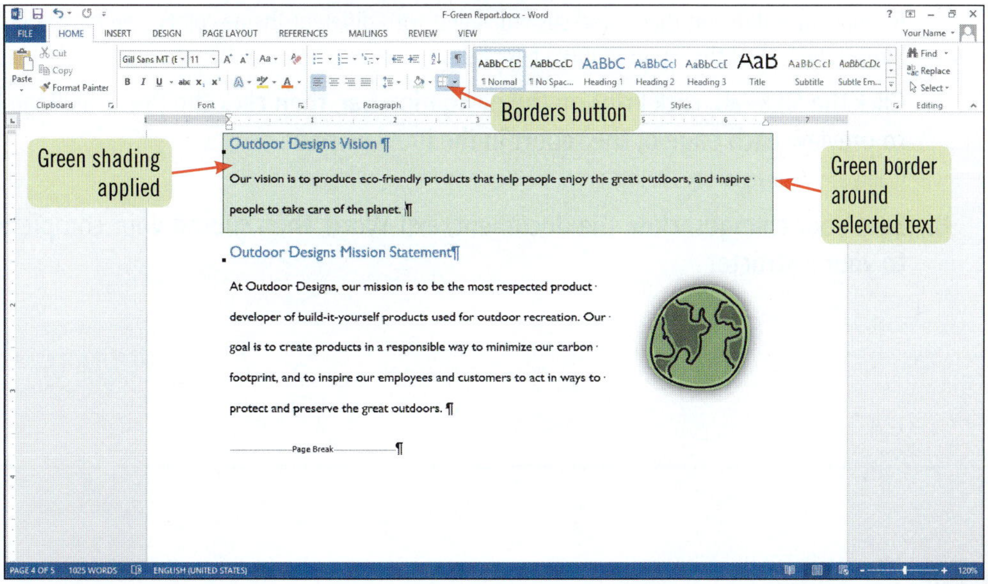

Work with Themes

Learning Outcomes
- Preview and apply a theme
- Apply a new color set

You have learned how to format individual document elements, such as a text selection or an object, and also how to use styles to change multiple formatting attributes in a paragraph. An even more powerful tool for making multiple formatting changes at once is the themes feature. Changing the **theme** applies a coordinated set of colors, fonts, and effects to your entire document, updating any styles applied. Themes ensure your document has a consistent and professional look. To apply a theme, use the Themes button in the Document Formatting group of the DESIGN tab. You can vary a theme's fonts and colors by applying different sets of theme fonts and theme colors. All themes are available in Word, Excel, Access, PowerPoint, and Outlook, which means that a company can produce many different documents and ensure that they all have a consistent, branded look. **CASE** *You decide to change the overall look of the report by applying a theme to it. You want to use the Integral theme, and apply the Green theme colors.*

STEPS

1. **Click the VIEW tab, click the Multiple Pages button in the Zoom group, then click the Zoom Out button on the Zoom slider two or three times until the zoom level is set at 30%**

   With the zoom set at 30%, all five pages of the report are visible on screen, so you can see at a glance how your changes will affect the whole document.

QUICK TIP
Every template has a theme applied to it by default. If you apply a theme to a document but then decide you want to go back to the original template theme, click the Themes button, then click Reset to Theme from Template.

2. **Click the DESIGN tab, then click the Themes button in the Themes group**

   The Themes gallery opens and displays thumbnails of available themes, as well as other options, such as resetting your document to the original theme and browsing for more themes on your computer.

3. **Point to each theme in the gallery, then observe the change in the document window**

   With Live Preview, you can see how the colors and fonts in each theme would affect the document if applied. Notice the change in colors, including the background color in the image, and how the text wraps differently depending on the theme. The Integral theme keeps the report to five pages.

4. **Click the Integral theme**

   The Themes gallery closes, and the Integral theme is applied to the report.

5. **Click the Colors button in the Document Formatting group**

   The Theme Colors gallery opens and displays a list of all the sets of theme colors. You want to apply the Green theme colors to the report.

QUICK TIP
You can create your own customized themes. To do this, change the formatting of any element you want (such as the font used in headings), click the Themes button, click Save Current Theme, type a name for the theme, then click Save. The new theme will appear at the top of the Themes gallery under Custom.

6. **Point to each set of Theme Colors to preview the effect in the report, then click Green, as shown in FIGURE F-21**

   By applying a different theme and customizing it with different theme colors, you have completely transformed the look of the report in just a few clicks.

7. **Click the FILE tab, click Print on the navigation bar, then click the Previous Page button ◄ to preview each page of the report in the Preview pane**

   Compare your report to **FIGURE F-22**.

8. **Save your changes, close the document, exit Word, then submit your completed report to your instructor**

FIGURE F-21: Theme Colors gallery with Green theme colors selected

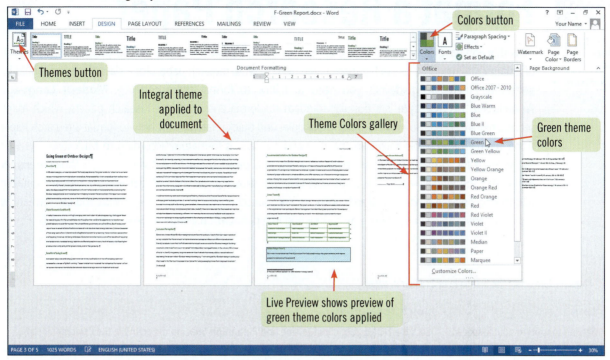

FIGURE F-22: Finished report with Integral theme and Green theme colors applied

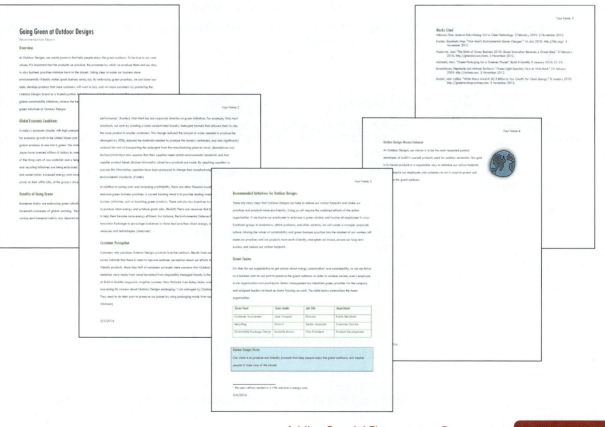

Word 2013

Format a Research Paper

Now that you have completed all the units on Word, you have learned skills to help you create many kinds of documents, including research papers. If you need to write research papers for a class, then you should be aware that there are guidelines you need to follow to format them correctly. **Modern Language Association (MLA) style** is a popular standard for formatting academic research papers, which many schools require. This lesson provides some examples and quick references for how to format a research paper using Word. The example shown in **FIGURE 23** and **FIGURE 24** is formatted according to MLA style. **TABLE F-1** shows steps for formatting the first page of a research paper using MLA style. **TABLE F-2** shows steps for formatting the whole paper. The steps and example shown here will just get you started; for detailed information on MLA guidelines, search online or ask your school librarian for help. (*Note*: You can format the research paper shown in this lesson by completing Independent Challenge 4: Explore for this unit.)

TABLE F-1: Steps for formatting the first page of a research paper

step	task	quick reference
1	Set line spacing to double-spaced	Click the **HOME tab**, click the **Line and Paragraph Spacing list arrow** in the Paragraph group, then click **2.0**
2	Insert header	a. Click the **INSERT tab**, click the **Header button**, then click **Blank** b. Type your name, press **[Spacebar]**, click the **Page Number button**, click **Current position**, then click **Plain Number** c. Click the **HOME tab**, then click the **Align Right button** in the Paragraph group
3	Type your name	At the top of the page (below the header), type your name; make sure it is left-aligned
4	Type your professor's name	Press **[Enter]**, then type your professor's name
5	Type the course number	Press **[Enter]**, then type the course number
6	Type the title	a. Press **[Enter]** then type the title of your paper b. Select the title, then click the **Align Center button** in the Paragraph group
7	Type the body text	Press **[Enter]**, click the **Align Left button** in the Paragraph group, press **[Tab]**, then begin typing the body text of the paper

TABLE F-2: Steps for formatting whole research paper

step	task	quick reference
1	Set line spacing for the entire document	a. Press **[Ctrl][A]** to select all the text in the document b. Click the **HOME tab**, click the **Line and Paragraph Spacing list arrow** in the Paragraph group, then click **2.0**
2	Set margins to Normal (1" on all margins)	Click the **PAGE LAYOUT tab**, click the **Margins button**, then click **Normal**
3	Set indents	Press **[Tab]** at the start of a new paragraph OR Press **[Ctrl][A]** to select the entire document, then drag the first line indent marker to the 1/2" mark on the ruler
4	Specify the font	Click the **HOME tab**, click the **Font list arrow**, then click **Times New Roman**
5	Set the font size	Click the **Font Size list arrow** on the **HOME tab**, then click **12**
6	Insert header	See "Insert header" in Table F-1
7	Insert citations	a. Click where you want to place the citation b. Click the **REFERENCES tab**, click the **Insert Citation button**, then click the **source name** or click **Add New Source** to add source information
8	Insert Works Cited page	a. Click at the end of the document b. Press **[Ctrl][Enter]** c. Click the **REFERENCES tab**, click the **Bibliography button**, then click **Works Cited**

© 2014 Cengage Learning

FIGURE F-23: First page of research paper formatted

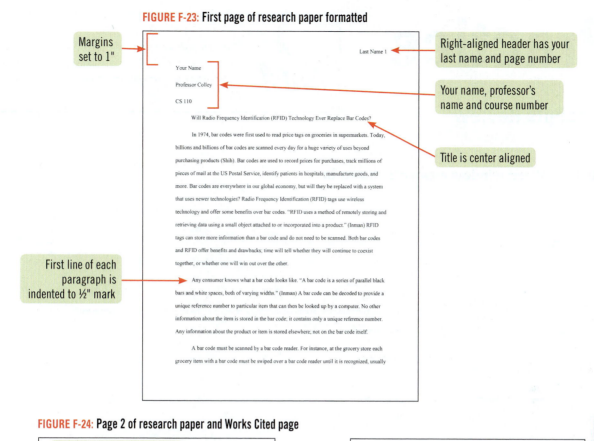

Margins set to 1"
Right-aligned header has your last name and page number
Your name, professor's name and course number
Title is center aligned
First line of each paragraph is indented to ½" mark

Last Name 1

Your Name

Professor Colley

CS 110

Will Radio Frequency Identification (RFID) Technology Ever Replace Bar Codes?

In 1974, bar codes were first used to read price tags on groceries in supermarkets. Today, billions and billions of bar codes are scanned every day for a huge variety of uses beyond purchasing products (Shih). Bar codes are used to record prices for purchases, track millions of pieces of mail at the US Postal Service, identify patients in hospitals, manufacture goods, and more. Bar codes are everywhere in our global economy, but will they be replaced with a system that uses newer technologies? Radio Frequency Identification (RFID) tags use wireless technology and offer some benefits over bar codes. "RFID uses a method of remotely storing and retrieving data using a small object attached to or incorporated into a product." (Inman) RFID tags can store more information than a bar code and do not need to be scanned. Both bar codes and RFID offer benefits and drawbacks; time will tell whether they will continue to coexist together, or whether one will win out over the other.

Any consumer knows what a bar code looks like. "A bar code is a series of parallel black bars and white spaces, both of varying widths." (Inman) A bar code can be decoded to provide a unique reference number to particular item that can then be looked up by a computer. No other information about the item is stored in the bar code; it contains only a unique reference number. Any information about the product or item is stored elsewhere; not on the bar code itself.

A bar code must be scanned by a bar code reader. For instance, at the grocery store each grocery item with a bar code must be swiped over a bar code reader until it is recognized, usually

FIGURE F-24: Page 2 of research paper and Works Cited page

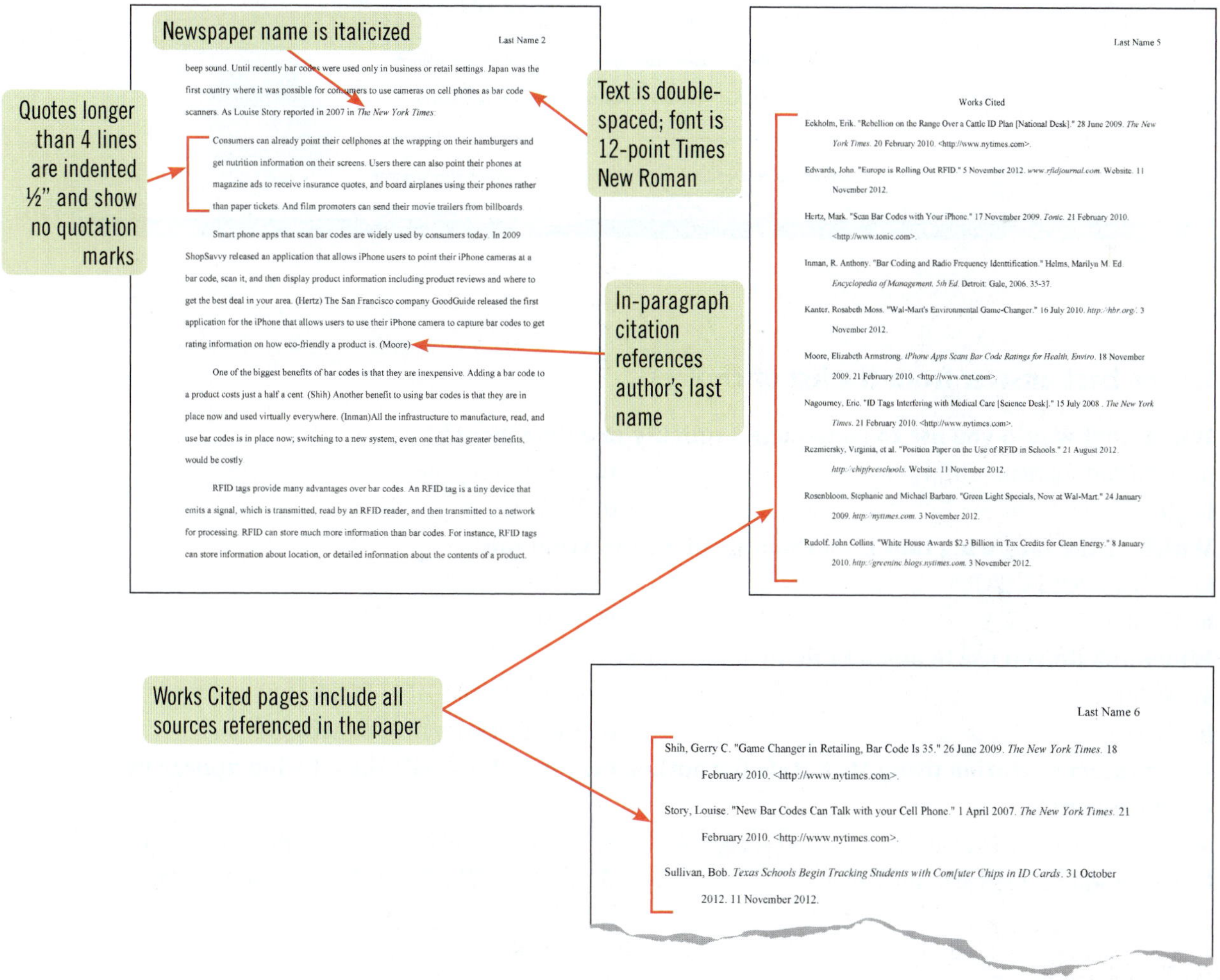

Newspaper name is italicized
Quotes longer than 4 lines are indented ½" and show no quotation marks
Text is double-spaced; font is 12-point Times New Roman
In-paragraph citation references author's last name
Works Cited pages include all sources referenced in the paper

Last Name 2

beep sound. Until recently bar codes were used only in business or retail settings. Japan was the first country where it was possible for consumers to use cameras on cell phones as bar code scanners. As Louise Story reported in 2007 in *The New York Times*:

> Consumers can already point their cellphones at the wrapping on their hamburgers and get nutrition information on their screens. Users there can also point their phones at magazine ads to receive insurance quotes, and board airplanes using their phones rather than paper tickets. And film promoters can send their movie trailers from billboards.

Smart phone apps that scan bar codes are widely used by consumers today. In 2009 ShopSavvy released an application that allows iPhone users to point their iPhone cameras at a bar code, scan it, and then display product information including product reviews and where to get the best deal in your area. (Hertz) The San Francisco company GoodGuide released the first application for the iPhone that allows users to use their iPhone camera to capture bar codes to get rating information on how eco-friendly a product is. (Moore)

One of the biggest benefits of bar codes is that they are inexpensive. Adding a bar code to a product costs just a half a cent. (Shih) Another benefit to using bar codes is that they are in place now and used virtually everywhere. (Inman)All the infrastructure to manufacture, read, and use bar codes is in place now; switching to a new system, even one that has greater benefits, would be costly.

RFID tags provide many advantages over bar codes. An RFID tag is a tiny device that emits a signal, which is transmitted, read by an RFID reader, and then transmitted to a network for processing. RFID can store much more information than bar codes. For instance, RFID tags can store information about location, or detailed information about the contents of a product.

Last Name 5

Works Cited

Eckholm, Erik. "Rebellion on the Range Over a Cattle ID Plan [National Desk]." 28 June 2009. *The New York Times*. 20 February 2010. <http://www.nytimes.com>.

Edwards, John. "Europe is Rolling Out RFID." 5 November 2012. *www.rfidjournal.com*. Website. 11 November 2012.

Hertz, Mark. "Scan Bar Codes with Your iPhone." 17 November 2009. *Tonic*. 21 February 2010. <http://www.tonic.com>.

Inman, R. Anthony. "Bar Coding and Radio Frequency Identtification." Helms, Marilyn M. Ed. *Encyclopedia of Management. 5th Ed.* Detroit: Gale, 2006. 35-37.

Kanter, Rosabeth Moss. "Wal-Mart's Environmental Game-Changer." 16 July 2010. *http://hbr.org/*. 3 November 2012.

Moore, Elizabeth Armstrong. *iPhone Apps Scans Bar Code Ratings for Health, Enviro*. 18 November 2009. 21 February 2010. <http://www.cnet.com>.

Nagourney, Eric. "ID Tags Interfering with Medical Care [Science Desk]." 15 July 2008 . *The New York Times*. 21 February 2010. <http://www.nytimes.com>.

Rezmiersky, Virginia, et al. "Position Paper on the Use of RFID in Schools." 21 August 2012. *http://chipfreeschools*. Website. 11 November 2012.

Rosenbloom, Stephanie and Michael Barbaro. "Green Light Specials, Now at Wal-Mart." 24 January 2009. *http://nytimes.com*. 3 November 2012.

Rudolf, John Collins. "White House Awards $2.3 Billion in Tax Credits for Clean Energy." 8 January 2010. *http://greeninc.blogs.nytimes.com*. 3 November 2012.

Last Name 6

Shih, Gerry C. "Game Changer in Retailing, Bar Code Is 35." 26 June 2009. *The New York Times*. 18 February 2010. <http://www.nytimes.com>.

Story, Louise. "New Bar Codes Can Talk with your Cell Phone." 1 April 2007. *The New York Times*. 21 February 2010. <http://www.nytimes.com>.

Sullivan, Bob. *Texas Schools Begin Tracking Students with Comfuter Chips in ID Cards*. 31 October 2012. 11 November 2012.

Practice

Put your skills into practice with SAM! If you have a SAM account, go to www.cengage.com/sam2013 to access SAM assignments for this unit.

Concepts Review

Label the Word window elements shown in FIGURE F-25.

FIGURE F-25

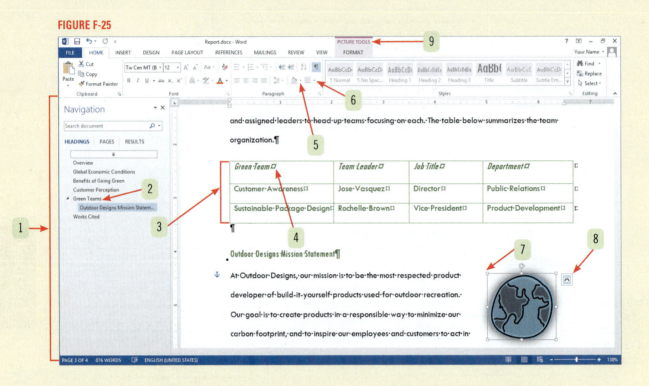

Select the best answer from the list of choices.

10. **Which tool would you use to go to page 3 quickly in a document?**
    a. Keyboard shortcut [Ctrl][Home]
    b. REVIEW tab
    c. Navigation pane
    d. VIEW tab

11. **Which of the following tabs is an example of a contextual tab?**
    a. TABLE TOOLS LAYOUT
    b. HOME
    c. VIEW
    d. DESIGN

12. **Which tab do you use to add a table to a document?**
    a. HOME
    b. INSERT
    c. TABLE TOOLS DESIGN tab
    d. TABLE TOOLS LAYOUT tab

13. **If you insert a citation using MLA style for author Joe Jones, how will the citation appear in the document?**
    a. (Jones) will be inserted at the end of the paragraph.
    b. JONES will be inserted in the footer.
    c. Jones, Joe will be inserted at the insertion point.
    d. (Jones) will be inserted at the insertion point.

14. Which of the following is a good reason for using a table in a document?

  a. You need to insert a reference to a source.

  b. You need to format a paragraph.

  c. You need to organize detailed information.

  d. You need to format a large number of headings quickly and consistently.

15. If you need to change the way text flows around an image, which of the following should you adjust?

  a. The image's text wrapping style

  b. The border style

  c. The margin settings of the whole document

  d. The theme

Skills Review

NOTE: To complete the steps below, your computer must be connected to the Internet.

1. Create a table.

  a. Start Microsoft Word, open the file F-2.docx from where you store your Data Files, then save the new document as **F-New Zealand Report**.

  b. Open the Navigation pane and display the headings of the document in it. Use the Navigation pane to move to the heading "Recommended Tour Dates." Set the insertion point in the blank line above "Classic Walking Adventures" at the bottom of page 2. Close the Navigation pane.

  c. Insert a table that is four columns wide and three rows high.

  d. Enter the information shown in the table below into the table you created.

Tour Name	Start Date	End Date	Price
National Parks	June 15	June 22	$1,499
South Island Strolls	July 1	July 8	$1,199

  e. Save your changes to the document.

2. Insert and delete table columns and rows.

  a. Insert a new row as the last row in the table.

  b. Enter the following information into the cells in the new row:

Kiwi Adventures	July 8	July 15	$2,499

  c. Insert a new row below the row that contains the column headings, then enter the following information into the new cells:

Wellington Walks	June 8	June 15	$1,999

  d. Delete the row that contains the July 1 South Island Strolls.

  e. Insert a new column to the right of the Tour Name column.

  f. Enter the information from the table below into the new column.

Tour Type
Seniors
Family
Hiking and Kayaking

  g. Save your changes.

Skills Review (continued)

3. Format a table.

   a. Format the table by applying the List Table 6 Colorful - Accent 1 style.

   b. Adjust the settings appropriately so there are no banded rows and so the first column is formatted the same as the other columns.

   c. Increase the width of the second column so "Hiking and Kayaking" fits on one line.

   d. Apply borders to all the cells in the table, using the Single solid line, 1/2 pt, Accent 1 style.

   e. Save your changes.

4. Add clip art.

   a. Use the Navigation pane to move to the heading "About New Zealand." Close the Navigation pane. Set the insertion point before the first word in the paragraph text below the heading "About New Zealand" ("New").

   b. Use the Online Pictures button to open the Insert Pictures dialog box. Search for an image of a **kiwi bird** in the Office.com Clip Art search box.

   c. Insert the image shown in **FIGURE F-26**, or a similar one.

   d. Reduce the size of the image so it is approximately 1" wide. (*Hint*: Use the ruler as a guide to help you size it.)

   e. Set the wrapping style of the image to Square.

   f. Drag the image so it is positioned to the right of the paragraph, with the right side of the image at the 6.5" mark on the ruler. Move the image down a little so its top edge is aligned with the top of the first line of paragraph text. The first few lines of the paragraph should flow around the image in a square shape.

   g. Recolor the image with the Blue, Accent color 1 Light.

   h. Apply the Drop Shadow Rectangle Picture Style to the image.

   i. Save your changes.

FIGURE F-26

5. Add footnotes and citations.

   a. Use the HEADINGS tab of the Navigation pane to navigate to the heading "Reasons to Offer Tours in New Zealand."

   b. Set the insertion point to the right of the word "**survey**" in the line below the "Reasons to Offer Tours in New Zealand" heading.

   c. Insert a footnote.

   d. Type the following text as footnote text: **Survey was conducted in May of 2015 and completed by 237 customers.**

   e. Use the Navigation pane to move to the heading "Tourism in New Zealand."

   f. Scroll to the end of the paragraph, set the insertion point after the closing quotation mark that follows the word "**friendly**" at the end of the paragraph, then use the Insert Citation button to add a new source.

   g. Enter the following information in the Create Source dialog box:

Type of Source:	Article in a Periodical
Author:	Joelle Chambers
Title:	New Zealand on Foot
Periodical Title:	The Walking Stick News
Year:	2016
Month:	February
Day:	2
Pages:	3-4
Medium:	Magazine

Skills Review (continued)

h. Close the Create Source dialog box, use the Navigation pane to move to the heading "Recommended Tour Dates," then set the insertion point in the blank line below the table.

i. Insert a page break, then insert a bibliography using the Works Cited style. Use the Navigation pane to move to the "Works Cited" heading.

j. Save your changes.

6. Insert a header or footer.

a. Insert a footer using the Blank option.

b. Replace the [Type text] placeholder with the current date, specifying the format that looks like January 1, 2016.

c. Insert a header using the Blank (Three Columns) option.

d. Delete the left-aligned and the center-aligned [Type text] placeholders. Replace the right-aligned [Type text] placeholder with your name. Insert a space after your name, then insert the page number after the space, choosing the Plain Number style.

e. Specify that the header and footer be different on the first page.

f. Close the header area, then save your changes.

7. Add borders and shading.

a. Use the Navigation pane to move to the "Works Cited" heading.

b. Select the last five lines of text in the document, then apply Blue, Accent 5, Lighter 80% shading to the selection.

c. Use the Borders tab of the Borders and Shading dialog box to apply a box border around the selection that is Blue, Accent 5.

d. Save your changes.

8. Work with themes.

a. Use the Multiple Pages button so all three pages of the report are visible, then use the Zoom slider to set the zoom to 30%.

b. Apply the Organic theme to the document.

c. Apply the Red theme colors to the document.

d. Open the Print screen, then use the Previous button to view each page of the report. Compare your finished report with **FIGURE F-27**, then close the document and exit Word. Submit your report to your instructor.

FIGURE F-27

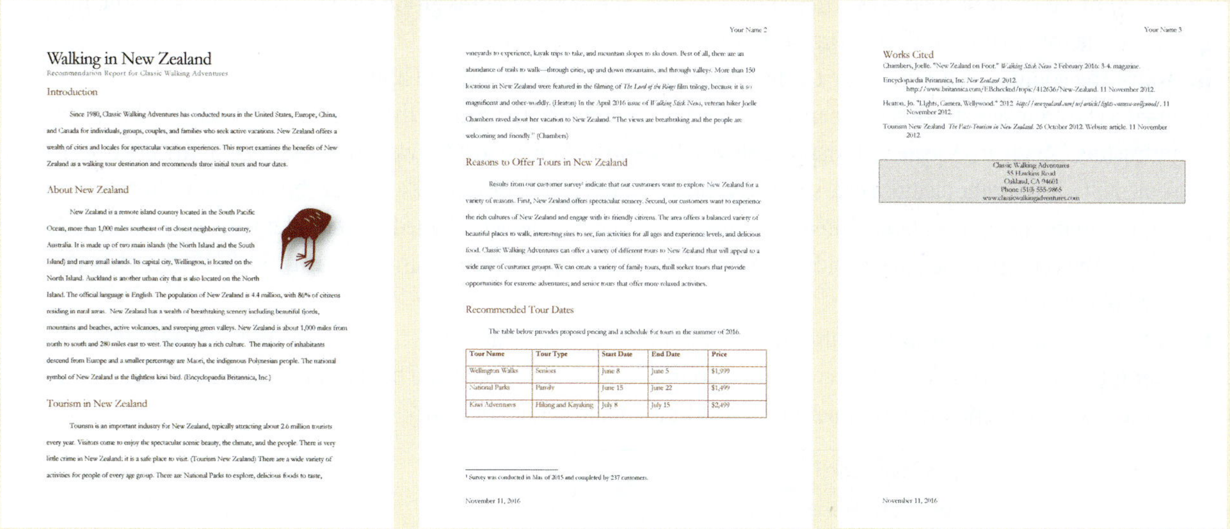

Independent Challenge 1

You are the new manager at The Painted Dog Art Studio, a small art studio in Michigan that offers art classes to the community. You need to create a one-page information sheet for prospective students. You have a partially completed document that you need to finish. You will add a table containing the class schedule and a bibliography that displays information on a book written by one of the instructors.

a. Open the file F-3.docx from where you store your Data Files, then save it as **F-Painted Dog Info Sheet**.

b. Click in the blank line below the heading "Spring Classes," then insert a 4 × 6 table.

c. Enter the information from the table below into the new table.

Class Name	Start Date	Time	Sessions
Oil Paintings	March 1	7:00-9:00	8
Ceramics	March 3	7:00-9:00	6
Digital Media	March 4	7:00-8:30	4
Design	March 8	4:00-6:00	8
Sculpture	March 10	7:00-9:00	6

d. Add a new row below the Sculpture row that contains the following information:

Watercolors Workshop	March 12	9:00-12:00	1

e. Add a column to the right of the Start Date column, then enter the information from the table below into it.

Day
Tuesday
Thursday
Friday
Tuesday
Thursday
Saturday

f. Apply the Grid Table 2 - Accent 4 table style to the table. Make sure the First Column check box, the Header Row check box, and the Banded Rows check boxes in the Table Style Options group all have check marks in them.

g. Delete the row that contains the Digital Media class.

h. Adjust the column width of the first column so each class name fits on one line.

i. Insert a clip art image appropriate for an art studio, and position it to the right of the two paragraphs below "About Our Instructors." Apply the Square text wrapping style to it. Resize the image so it fits well and looks good in the space next to the paragraphs. Recolor the picture a blue shade of your choosing. Apply a picture style of your choosing to the image.

j. Insert a footer using the Blank (Three Columns) style. Replace the left-aligned placeholder with your name, and replace the center-aligned placeholder with today's date, using the format similar to this: 11/3/2016. Delete the third placeholder.

k. In the last line of the document, after the period, insert a citation after the title of Lucy May Frankel's book *Painting for Fun and Profit*. Add a new citation source in MLA style about the book. Click the Type of Source list arrow, click Book, enter the information shown in the table below then click OK.

Author:	Lucy May Frankel
Title:	Painting for Fun and Profit
Year:	2015
City:	Detroit
Publisher:	Canvas Books
Medium:	Book

Adding Special Elements to a Document

Independent Challenge 1 (continued)

l. Press [Enter] after the (Frankel) citation in the last line of the document, then insert the bibliography for the source you entered. (*Hint*: Click the Bibliography button in the Citations & Bibliography group on the REFERENCES tab, then click Bibliography.)

m. Replace the heading Bibliography with **Information on Lucy May Frankel's Book**.

n. Apply Gold, Accent 3, Lighter 60% shading to **Information on Lucy May Frankel's Book** and the line below it. Apply a box border around the shaded text, using Automatic (black) for the border color.

o. Apply the Metropolitan theme to the document. If necessary, resize the clip art image so it fits well on the page with the new theme applied.

p. Apply the Paper theme colors to the document. If there is a paragraph mark on page 2, delete it so the document is only one page.

q. Save your changes, preview the document, and compare your finished document to **FIGURE F-28**. Close the document and exit Word. Submit your completed document to your instructor.

FIGURE F-28

The Painted Dog Art Studio

121 Orchard Road
Grover Creek, MI 56465
(773)555-4466

About The Painted Dog Art Studio

The Painted Dog Art Studio serves the community of Grover Creek and surrounding towns. We offer a wide variety of art classes for a variety of ages and abilities. Our goal is to engage the people of the community through art, and to help them realize a fuller vision of themselves through artistic expression.

Spring Classes

Class Name	Start Date	Day	Time	Sessions
Oil Painting	March 1	Tuesday	2:00-4:00	6
Ceramics	March 3	Thursday	5:00-7:00	6
Design	March 8	Tuesday	7:00-9:00	5
Sculpture	March 10	Thursday	7:00-9:00	8
Watercolors Workshop	March 12	Saturday	9:00-12:00	1

About Our Instructors

Lester Kanter (*Oil Painting, Sculpture, and Design*): Lester started painting when he was just five years old. He is well known in the Midwest for his unusual landscapes and cityscapes. His work has been widely exhibited throughout the United States and Canada.

Lucy May Frankel (*Ceramics, Watercolor Workshop*): Lucy May Frankel is an accomplished artist who won acclaim for her recent exhibit of still life art at the state-sponsored Women and Art exhibition in Lansing. Lucy May's watercolors are featured in the October 2016 issue of *The Brush*. Lucy May is the author of *Painting for Fun and Profit*. (Frankel)

Information on Lucy May Frankel's Book
Frankel, Lucy May. *Painting for Fun and Profit*. Detroit: Canvas Books, 2015. Book.

Your Name   11/11/16

Independent Challenge 2

You are the human resources manager at The Speedy Burrito, a Mexican fast-food chain with headquarters in Raleigh, North Carolina. A new employee, Willa Flanders, starts her first day tomorrow as an associate product manager. You need to create a schedule for Willa that shows the times and locations of her meetings and appointments as well as the contact people with whom she will meet.

a. Open the file F-4.docx from where you store your Data Files, then save it as **F-First Day Schedule**.

b. Set the insertion point in the blank line two lines above "To: Willa Flanders."

c. Insert today's date using the Insert Date and Time dialog box. (*Hint*: Click the Date & Time button on the INSERT tab.) Choose any date format that you like.

d. In the line below "To: Willa Flanders", type your name to the right of "From:".

e. Two lines below the first long paragraph, insert a table containing the information shown in the table below.

When	Where	Contact Person	Description
8:30	Front Desk	Warren Yi	Benefits Review
9:30	Burrito Room	Marco Garvey	Orientation
11:00	Queso Room	Gwen Fisher	PC Setup
12:00	Cafeteria	Ravi Banarjee	Team Lunch
1:30	Taco Room	Helen Jones	Goal Setting

f. Apply a table style of your choosing to the table.

g. Insert a row in the table between the 9:30 and 11:00 time slot. Enter the information shown in the following table into the new row.

10:30	Studio A, 7th Floor	Frank Merino	Get Photo ID

Independent Challenge 2 (continued)

h. Add a border around the Our Mission Statement heading and the paragraph below it using a border setting that you like. Add shading to this text, using a color that looks good with the border you picked. Format the text in this shaded box using fonts, formatting, alignment, and font styles to make it look attractive.

i. Insert a footnote to the right of Ravi Banarjee's name in the table. Type the following text for the footnote: **Ravi will meet you and the rest of the team in the Blue section of the cafeteria.** Format this footnote text so it looks different from the main text in the document.

j. Insert a footer that contains your name, right-aligned.

k. Apply a theme to the document that you think looks good and is appropriate for this type of document.

l. Preview the document, then save your changes.

m. Save and close the document. Submit the document to your instructor.

Independent Challenge 3

Juliette Rodriquez in the Human Resources Department at Dazzle-Star Kitchen Products has asked you to create a one-page flyer for the annual Community Outreach Day event. There are a wide variety of volunteer opportunities that need to be included on the flyer. You have a partially completed document with some of the information already provided. You need to add a table that lists the volunteer activities, the organization that is hosting each, and the location. You also need to enhance the appearance of the document so it is eye-catching and appealing.

a. Open the file F-5.docx from where you store your Data Files, then save it as **F-Outreach Day Events**.

b. Apply shading to the first line of the document (Dazzle Star Kitchen Products) using a fill color and font that look good together.

c. Insert a table containing the information shown in the table below.

Volunteer Activity	Organization	Location
Painting	Veteran's Hospital	760 Main Street
Reading to children	Dr. King Elementary School	12 Elm Street
Animal care	Animal Shelter	44 1st Street
Serving food and restocking shelves	Food Pantry	76 Walker Road
Deliver meals to seniors	Door-to-Door Hot Meals	19 River Road
Sort magazines for Literacy Project	St. Mary's Church	44 Ash Road

d. Resize all the columns of the table so all text fits on one line per cell.

e. Format the table using a table style of your choosing.

f. Format the text in the document so it reflects a friendly and fun mood; you want the flyer to convey that the event will be rewarding and enjoyable. Choose fonts, font sizes, and formatting attributes that make the key information stand out.

g. Insert an appropriate piece of clip art for the event. The image should convey the idea of helping. Apply a text-wrapping style where the text flows around the image. Experiment with different text-wrapping styles to find one that looks good.

h. Insert a footer that contains your name, center-aligned.

i. Apply a theme and theme colors to the flyer.

Independent Challenge 3 (continued)

j. Save your changes, preview the flyer, then close the document. **FIGURE F-29** shows one possible solution; yours will vary depending on the formatting choices you made. Submit your flyer to your instructor.

FIGURE F-29

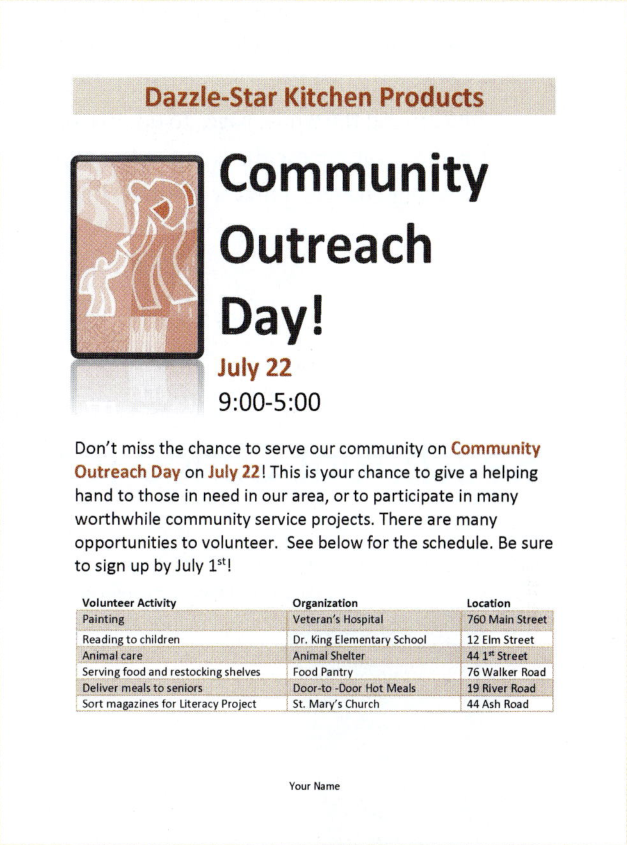

Independent Challenge 4: Explore

Research papers are frequently assigned for history and English classes in college. Knowing how to format a research paper according to standards is extremely important. A common standard used for writing and formatting research papers is MLA. Another popular standard is APA. If your professor assigns a research paper, he or she will probably specify that you write and format your paper according to MLA or APA standards. In this Independent Challenge, you will create a research paper and format it according to MLA guidelines. So you do not have to actually research and write the paper, you will use text from an existing file for the paper. Before completing the steps below, review the lesson Formatting a Research Paper located just before the end-of-unit exercises.

a. Open the file F-6.docx from where you store your Data Files, then save it as **F-RFID Research Paper**.

b. With the insertion point set before the first line of text in the document, type your name.

c. Press [Enter], type **Professor Colley**, then press [Enter].

d. Type **CIS 110**, then press [Enter].

e. Center-align the title of the paper, "Will Radio Frequency Identification (RFID) Ever Replace Bar Codes?"

f. Find "The New York Times" on pages 1 and 2 in the text. Format both of these occurrences in italic.

g. Immediately below *The New York Times*: on page 1, select the four-line quote that begins "Consumers can already…" Set the left indent at the ½" mark on the ruler for this paragraph.

h. Press [Ctrl][A] to select all the text in the document. Set the line spacing to double-spaced (2.0).

i. Change the font for all the selected text to Times New Roman, then change the font size to 12 point.

j. Indent the beginning of each paragraph of body text in the paper to the ½" mark on the ruler. Do not further indent the quote that you indented in Step g. (*Hint*: You can either press [Tab] before the first character in the paragraph or create a first line indent by dragging the First Line Indent marker to the ½" mark on the ruler.)

k. Create a header that contains your last name followed by the page number. Right-align the header. Change the font in the header to 12-point Times New Roman if necessary.

l. Insert a citation to author R. Anthony Inman after the quote in the first paragraph of body text (which ends "… incorporated into a product"). (*Note*: To choose this source, click Insert Citation, then click Inman, R. Anthony.)

m. Move the insertion point to the end of the document. Insert a page break. Insert a bibliography using the Works Cited option. Format all the text in the Works Cited section in 12-point Times New Roman, double-spaced. Center-align the Works Cited heading.

n. Save your changes. Compare your research paper to the one shown in **FIGURES F-23** and **F-24**.

Visual Workshop

Open the file F-7.docx from where you store your Data Files, then save it as **F-Condo Rental Ad**. Use the skills you learned in this unit to create the flyer shown in **FIGURE F-30**. (*Hints*: Apply the Metropolitan theme and the Blue Warm theme colors. For the clip art, search for the image shown by using "palm tree" as the keywords in the search box. Select a different clip art image if the one shown in the figure is not available to you. Apply the picture style shown, and set the wrapping style to Tight. Position the image as shown. Increase the size of the paragraph text to 14 pt, and increase the size of the flyer title to 36 pt. Insert the table, and apply the style shown in the figure. Apply a Box style blue border around the whole page. To do this, open the Borders and Shading dialog box, click the Page Border tab, click the Box style, choose the Blue-Gray Accent 1 for the Color, then click OK.) Type your name in the footer as shown, save your changes, preview the flyer, then submit it to your instructor.

FIGURE F-30

Beachfront Condo for Rent

Enjoy spectacular views in this modern condo on Waikiki Beach! With the Pacific Ocean just steps away, you will feel like you are in paradise as you sip a cold drink from your lounge chair on the lanai. This condo community is situated on ten acres of landscaped grounds, with swaying palm trees and fragrant flowering plants. This cozy 2-bedroom condo features updated appliances, and is fully stocked to ensure you have everything you need while on vacation. Enjoy breathtaking sunsets year round. Prepare meals outside on the propane grill and dine on the lanai. Enjoy swimming, biking, snorkeling, tennis, and windsurfing. Watch humpback whales before they migrate north. World-class restaurants are minutes away!

Property Details

Feature	Description
Location	Waikiki Beach
Weekly rate	$1,549
Bathrooms	2
Bedrooms	2
Outdoor grill	Yes
Beach access	Yes
Air conditioning	Yes
Internet	Yes

For more details, contact:

Felicia Akana 1214 Coco Drive Honolulu, HI 96701 Phone: (773) 555-2090

Your Name

Creating a Worksheet

CASE Karen Rivera, the marketing director for Outdoor Designs, asks you to help her create a worksheet that shows estimated sales for new kite products that will be released in April. You will create a new Excel workbook, enter values and labels into a worksheet, create formulas to make calculations, format the worksheet, and print it.

Unit Objectives

After completing this unit, you will be able to:

- Navigate a workbook
- Enter labels and values
- Work with columns and rows
- Use formulas

- Use AutoSum
- Change alignment and number format
- Enhance a worksheet
- Preview and print a worksheet

Files You Will Need

No files needed.

©HelenStock/Shutterstock

Microsoft® product screenshots used with permission from Microsoft® Corporation.

Navigate a Workbook

Microsoft Excel is a powerful program you can use to organize and analyze data. An Excel **worksheet** is an electronic grid consisting of rows and columns in which you can perform numeric calculations. Similar to a Word table, the intersection of a row and column is called a **cell**. You can use a worksheet for many purposes, such as analyzing sales data, creating a budget, or displaying data in a chart. An Excel file, called a **workbook**, can contain one or more worksheets. Each new workbook you create contains just one worksheet, but you can easily add more. People sometimes refer to a worksheet or a workbook as a **spreadsheet**. **CASE** ▶ *You decide to start Excel, familiarize yourself with the workbook window, and save a blank workbook.*

STEPS

1. **If you are running Windows 8, go to the Start screen, type excel so "Excel 2013" appears as a search result, then press [Enter]**

   Excel starts and the Excel Start screen displays thumbnails of different templates you can create using Excel.

2. **Click Blank workbook**

   A blank workbook opens, as shown in **FIGURE G-1**. Excel contains elements that are in every Office program, including the Ribbon, the FILE tab, the Quick Access toolbar, a status bar, and View buttons.

3. **Look at the worksheet window**

   The cell with the dark border in the upper-left corner of the worksheet is called the **active cell**. The dark border surrounding the active cell is the **cell pointer**. You must click a cell to make it active before entering data. Every cell in a worksheet has a unique **cell address**, which is a specific location of a cell in a worksheet where a column and row intersect. A cell address consists of a column letter followed by a row number (such as B33). When you first start Excel, the active cell in the new workbook (Book1) is cell A1.

4. **Click cell C1**

   Cell C1 becomes the active cell. Clicking a cell selects it and makes it active. **TABLE G-1** lists several methods for selecting cells with the mouse or keyboard. Notice the column and row headings of the active cell (column C and row 1) appear in a contrasting color. The **name box** shows the address of the selected cell, and the **formula bar**, located just above the column headings, shows the contents of the selected cell (it is currently empty). The mouse pointer changes to ✛ when you move it over any cells in the workbook.

5. **Press [→], press [↓], then press [Tab]**

   Cell E2 is now the active cell. You can move to and select a cell by clicking it, by using the arrow keys, or by pressing [Tab] (to move one cell to the right), [Shift][Tab] (to move one cell to the left), or [Enter] (to move one cell down).

6. **Click the New sheet button ⊕ at the bottom left of the worksheet just above the status bar**

   A new worksheet named Sheet2 opens on your screen and is now the active sheet. You can tell it is the active sheet because Sheet2 is in bold on the sheet tab. Notice that cell A1 is the active cell. To work with different sheets in a workbook, you click the sheet tab of the sheet you want to see.

7. **Drag the ✛ pointer from cell A1 to cell C5**

   Cells A1 through C5 are selected as shown in **FIGURE G-2**. A group of selected cells that share boundaries is called a **cell range**. To reference a cell range, use the cell address of the first cell in the range followed by a colon and the cell address of the last cell in the range. The cell range you selected is A1:C5.

8. **Click the Sheet1 sheet tab, then press [Ctrl][Home]**

   Clicking the sheet tab returns you to Sheet1, and the keyboard shortcut returns the cell pointer to cell A1.

9. **Click the Save button 🖫 on the Quick Access toolbar to open the Save As screen, navigate to where you store your Data Files, then save the file as G-Kite Sales Estimates**

Creating a Worksheet

FIGURE G-1: Excel program window

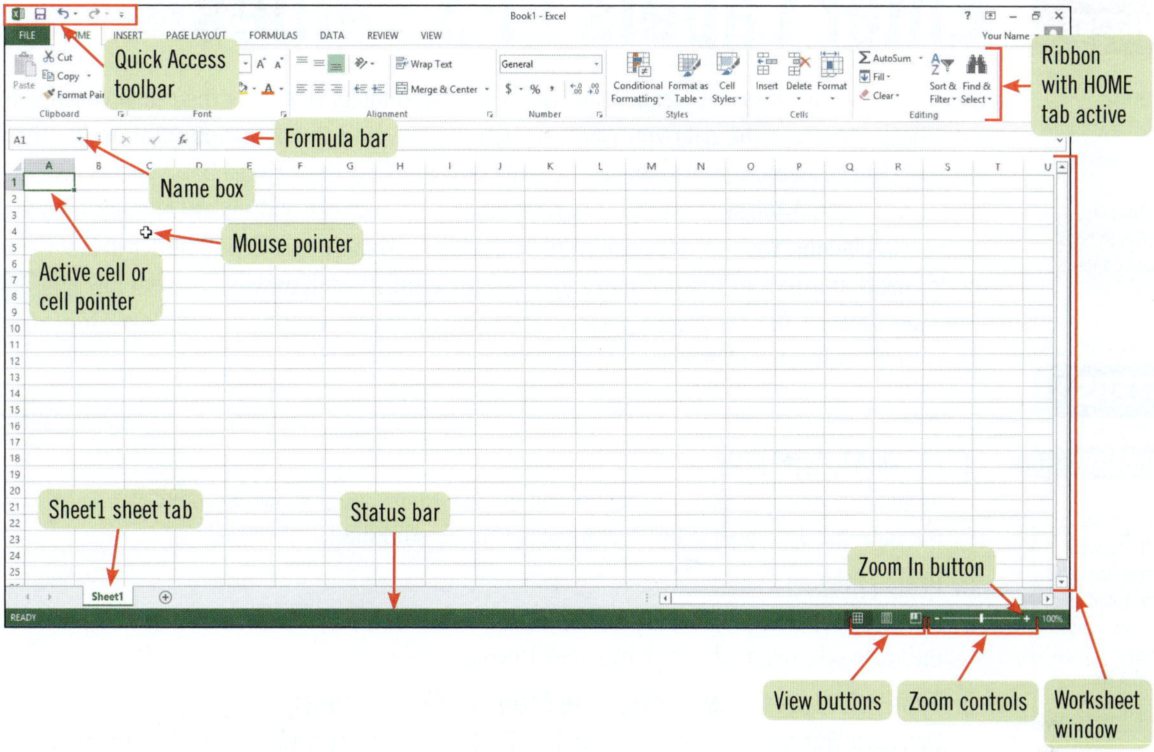

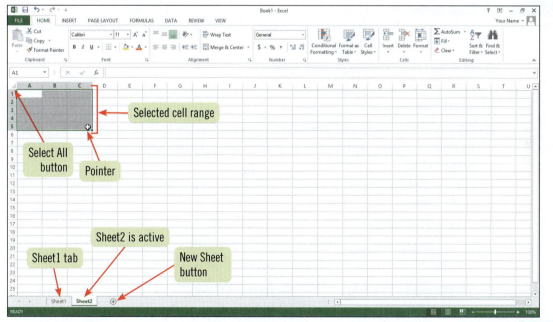

FIGURE G-2: Selecting a range of cells in Sheet2

TABLE G-1: Methods for selecting worksheet cells

to select	with the mouse	with the keyboard
A cell	Click the cell	Use arrow keys
A row	Click the row heading	Select a cell in the row, then press [Shift][Spacebar]
A column	Click the column heading	Select a cell in the column, then press [Ctrl][Spacebar]
A cell range	Drag across the cells	Press [Shift], then press the arrow keys
A worksheet	Click the Select All button to the left of column heading A	Press [Ctrl][A]

Enter Labels and Values

Entering data in a worksheet is similar to typing in a Word table. First, click the cell in which you want to enter data, then type the data you want to enter. After typing the data, you must accept the entry by pressing [Enter], [Tab], an arrow key, or the Enter button f_x on the formula bar. Most worksheets contain labels and values. A **label** is text that describes data in a worksheet. **Values** are numeric data that can be used in calculations. You can edit a cell entry by double-clicking the cell to put the cell in Edit mode. In Edit mode, select the part of the cell entry you do not want, then type your corrections. **CASE** *This worksheet needs to show the names, prices, and estimated first year units for six kites. To get started, you decide to enter the labels first and then enter the values.*

STEPS

1. **In cell A1, type Kite**

   As you type, the text appears in cell A1 and in the formula bar, as shown in **FIGURE G-3**. The text you typed is a label that describes the first column of data in the worksheet.

2. **Press [Tab]**

   Pressing [Tab] accepts your entry and activates the next cell in the row, cell B1. The name box shows B1 as the active cell. You need to type two more labels.

3. **Type Price, press [Tab], then type Estimated Year 1 Units**

   Estimated Year 1 Units is too long to fit in cell C1; although it extends into cell D1, it is actually contained only in cell C1. If cell D1 contained any data, then only the part of the label that fits in C1 would appear.

4. **Press [Enter]**

   Pressing [Enter] moved the cell pointer down to the first cell of the next row. Cell A2 is now the active cell. You need to type a kite product name in this cell.

5. **Type Spiraling Stuntman, then press [↓]**

   Cell A3 is now the active cell. Pressing [down arrow] accepted the cell entry and moved the cell pointer to the cell below.

6. **Type Whirling Hurricane, press [Enter], type Dipping Dragon, press [Enter], type Blazing Bolt, press [Enter], type Typhoon Twirler, press [Enter], type Spinning Goose, then press [Enter]**

   You have typed all the kite names. Cell A8 is the active cell. You need to make an edit to the Typhoon Twirler name.

7. **Double-click cell A6**

   Double-clicking the cell put cell A6 in Edit mode. Notice the insertion point is flashing in cell A6. You can now select part of the cell entry to edit it, just like in Word.

8. **Double-click Twirler, type Spinner, then press [Enter]**

   Cell A6 now contains the label "Typhoon Spinner."

9. **Click cell B2, type 39.95, then press the Enter button ✓ on the formula bar**

   Unlike pressing [Enter] on the keyboard, clicking the Enter button keeps the cell active. Notice that some of Spiraling Stuntman is cut off in cell A2 because cell B2 now contains data.

10. **Press [➡], type 15000, then press ✓**

    You entered the value for Year 1 Units for the Spiraling Stuntman kite in cell C2.

11. **Enter the values shown in FIGURE G-4 for the range B3:C7, then save your changes**

Creating a Worksheet

FIGURE G-3: Worksheet text in active cell and formula bar

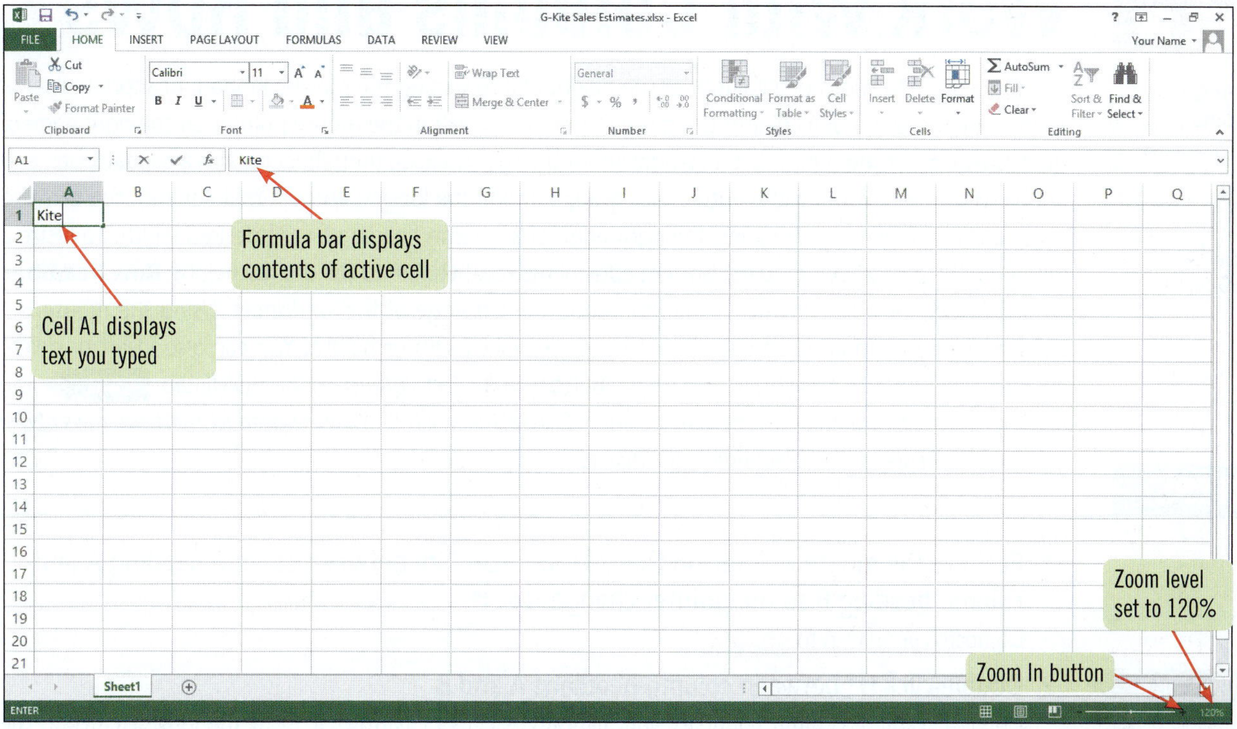

Formula bar displays contents of active cell

Cell A1 displays text you typed

Zoom level set to 120%

Zoom In button

FIGURE G-4: Worksheet after entering labels and values

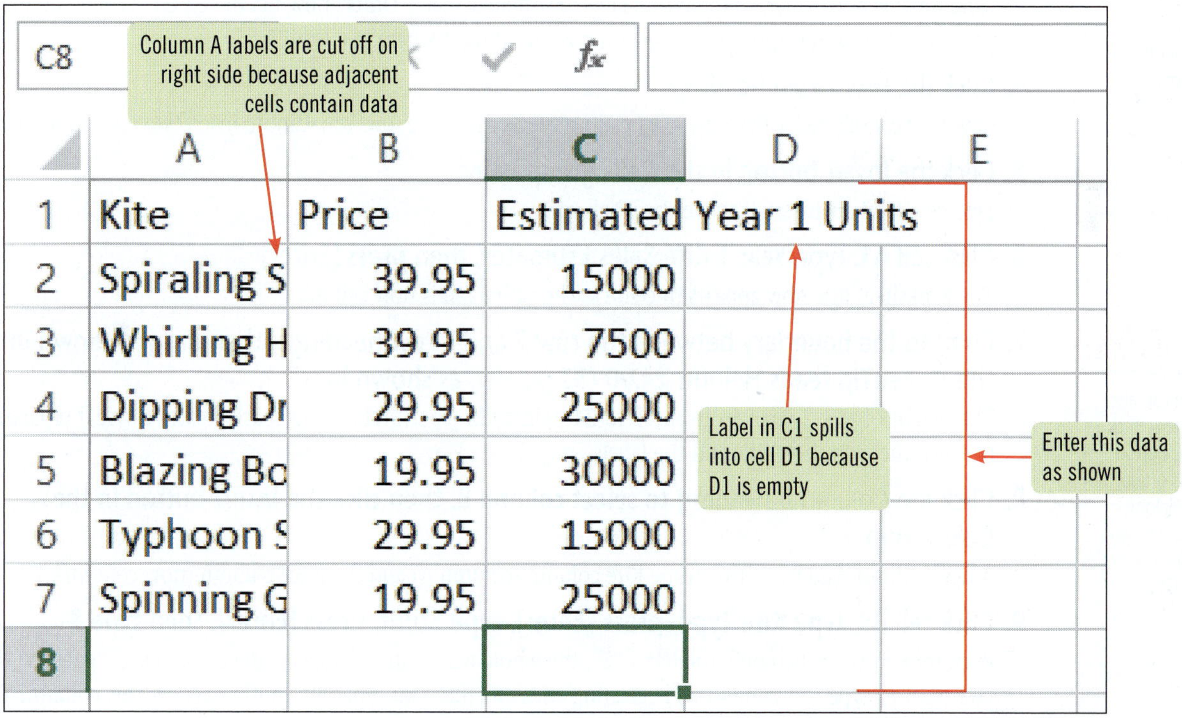

Column A labels are cut off on right side because adjacent cells contain data

	A	B	C	D	E
1	Kite	Price	Estimated Year 1 Units		
2	Spiraling S	39.95	15000		
3	Whirling H	39.95	7500		
4	Dipping Dr	29.95	25000		
5	Blazing Bo	19.95	30000		
6	Typhoon S	29.95	15000		
7	Spinning G	19.95	25000		
8					

Label in C1 spills into cell D1 because D1 is empty

Enter this data as shown

Work with Columns and Rows

You can adjust the width of a column or the height of a row using the mouse, Ribbon, or shortcut menu. To increase the width of a column using the mouse, you position the mouse pointer on the right edge of the **column heading**, which is a rectangle above the worksheet column that contains a capital letter, and double-click. The column width automatically adjusts to fit the longest entry in that column. You can also resize a column width by dragging the right edge of a column heading to the desired width. To resize a row using the mouse, you drag the bottom edge of the row heading to the desired height. **Row headings** are the boxes containing numbers that run along the left edge of the worksheet. Using the mouse is a quick and easy method when you do not need an exact width or height. You can also insert or delete columns and rows using the Insert and Delete buttons in the Cells group on the HOME tab. **CASE** *You need to increase the width of column A and column C so all the labels fit. You also need to insert two rows above the labels and enter a worksheet title in the new top row.*

STEPS

1. **Position the mouse pointer on the column boundary between column heading A and column heading B so the pointer changes to** ✛

   Compare your screen to **FIGURE G-5**.

2. **Double-click** ✛ **between column headings A and B**

   Double-clicking a column boundary automatically widens or narrows it to fit the longest entry in the column using a feature called **AutoFit**. The kite names in cells A2:A7 are now fully visible.

3. **Point to the column boundary between columns C and D, then drag** ✛ **to the right of the "s" in "Units" in row 1**

   Column C is now wider, so the entire label "Estimated Year 1 Units" now fits in cell C1. When you drag a boundary, a dark line appears to help you position it right where you want it.

4. **Click the row 1 row heading**

   Row 1 is now selected. Clicking a row heading selects the entire row. You want to insert two rows above row 1.

5. **Click the Insert button in the Cells group twice**

   Two new rows are inserted above the labels row.

6. **Click cell A1, type Year 1 Kite Sales Estimates, then press [Enter]**

   The worksheet title now appears in cell A1. The active cell is now cell A2.

7. **Point to the boundary between the row 2 and 3 row headings, then drag** ✛ **down until the ScreenTip reads Height: 24.00 (32 pixels), as shown in FIGURE G-6**

   The height of row 2 changes from 15 to 24 points (32 pixels). The extra space creates a visual separation between the worksheet title and the labels.

8. **Click the Column B heading to select column B, then click the Insert button in the Cells group**

   A new column is added between the Kite column (column A) and the Price column (now column C).

9. **Click cell B3, type Kite Type, press [Enter], type Stunt, press [Enter], then type S**

   Even though you typed only the letter "S", the whole word "Stunt" appears in cell B5. Excel "guesses" that you want to type the same word beginning with "S" that you typed in another cell in this column. This feature, called **AutoComplete**, can save you time in entering data in a worksheet.

10. **Press [Enter], type Trick, press [Enter], type Delta, press [Enter], type T, press [Enter], type D, then press [Enter]**

    "Delta" was entered into cell B9 and "Trick" was entered into cell B8, even though you typed only the first letter of each word. Compare your worksheet to **FIGURE G-7**.

Creating a Worksheet

FIGURE G-5: Changing column width in the worksheet

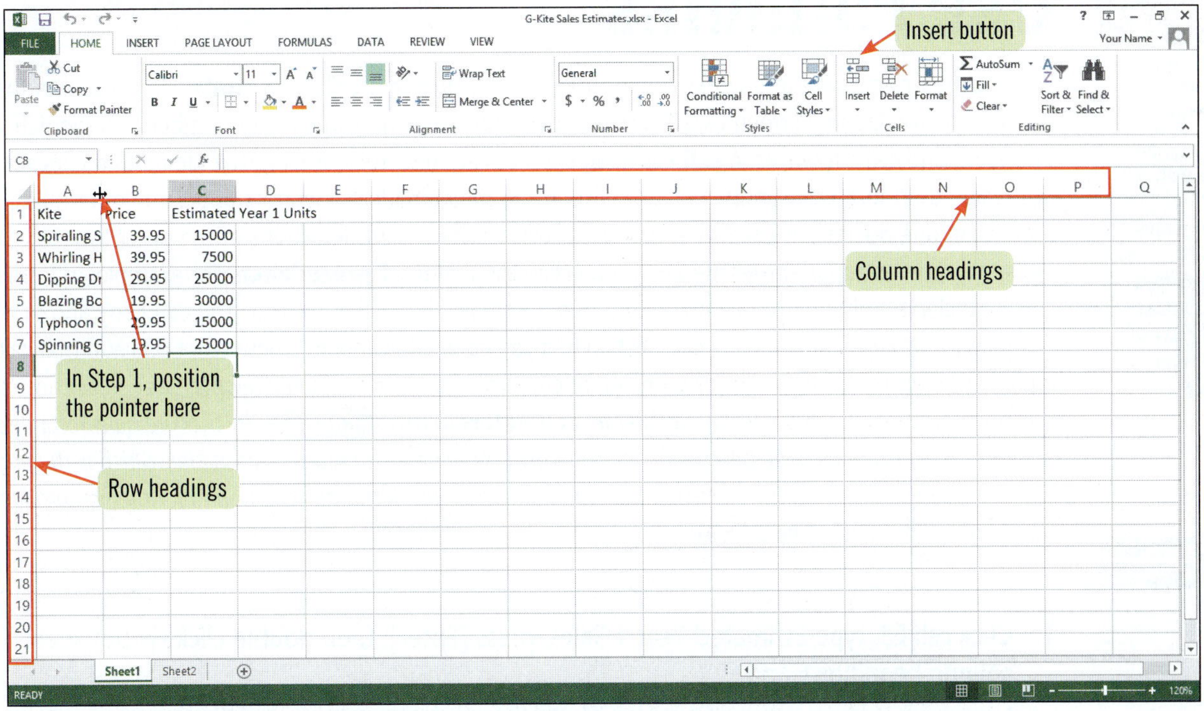

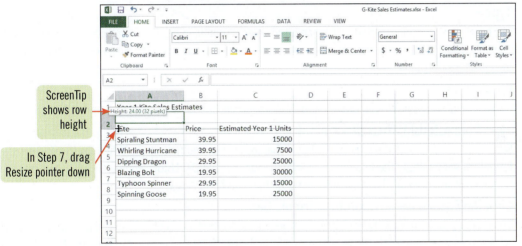

FIGURE G-6: Changing row height in the worksheet

FIGURE G-7: Worksheet with new column and row added

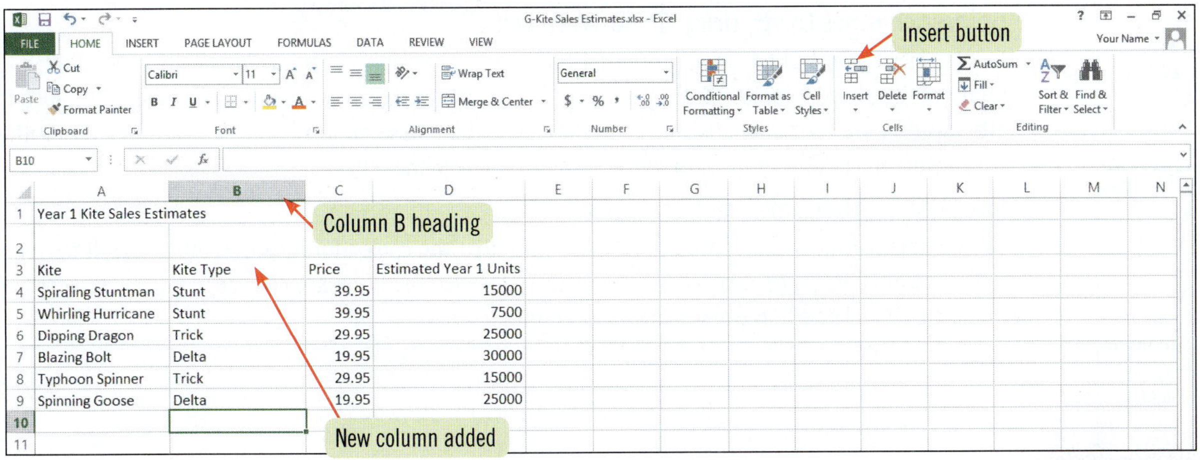

Use Formulas

To perform a calculation in a worksheet, you enter a formula in a cell. A **formula** is an equation that performs a calculation. Formulas start with an equal sign (=) and can contain numbers, mathematical operators, and cell references. A **cell reference** is a cell address, such as E44, that identifies the location of a value used in a calculation. **TABLE G-2** lists some mathematical operators and sample formulas. If more than one operator is used in a formula, Excel performs the calculations in the order listed in the table, which is a standard order used in math called the **order of precedence**. For example, in formulas that include both multiplication and addition, multiplication will occur first. You can copy and move formulas just like other data in a worksheet. When you copy a formula to a new cell, Excel automatically replaces the original cell references with cell references that are in the *same relative position* as those in the original formula. This is called **relative cell referencing**. **CASE** *In the kite sales estimates worksheet, you need to create a formula that calculates the Year 1 estimates for each kite, which is the price multiplied by the year 1 units. You first create a formula that calculates the year 1 sales for the first product, then copy the formula to the other cells.*

STEPS

1. **Click cell E3, type Estimated Year 1 Sales, press [Enter], then double-click ↔ between column headings E and F**

   Estimated Year 1 Sales is now a label in cell E3, and the active cell is now E4. The Estimated Year 1 Sales label fits in cell E3 because you widened the column.

2. **Type =**

   The equal sign (=) indicates that you are about to enter a formula in cell E4. Everything you enter in a cell after the equal sign, including any numbers, mathematical operators, cell references, or functions, is included in the formula.

3. **Click cell C4**

   A dotted border appears around cell C4, and C4 now appears in both the formula bar and cell E4.

   > **QUICK TIP**
   > You can also enter cell references in a formula by typing them, using either uppercase or lowercase letters.

4. **Type * (an asterisk), then click cell D4**

   See **FIGURE G-8**. In Excel, the asterisk symbol is the operator for multiplication. When Excel calculates the formula, it will multiply the value in cell C4 by the value in cell D4. Using cell references ensures that the formula will automatically be updated if the values in C4 and D4 change.

   > **QUICK TIP**
   > You can also double-click the fill handle to Auto Fill a formula to the adjacent cells below. The formula will be copied down to the last cell that is next to a cell containing data.

5. **Click the Enter button ✓ on the formula bar**

   The result of the formula (599250) appears in cell E4. Notice that although the formula's result appears in cell E4, the formula =C4*D4 still appears in the formula bar. To save time, you can copy the formula in E4 to cells E5:E9.

6. **Point to the small dark square in the lower-right corner of cell E4, then when the pointer changes to ➕, drag ➕ down to cell E9**

   Excel copies the amount formula in cell E4 into cells E5 through E9. Notice that cells E5:E9 display the results of the copied formulas, as shown in **FIGURE G-9**. The small dark square that you dragged is called the **fill handle**. The icon that appears after you release the mouse button is the Auto Fill Options button, which you can click to choose additional options when copying cells.

   > **QUICK TIP**
   > If you want your worksheet to display formulas instead of their results in cells, click the FORMULAS tab, then click Show Formulas in the Formula Auditing group.

7. **Click cell E6, then save your changes**

   The formula bar shows the formula =C6*D6. Notice that the copied formula uses different cell references than those used in the original formula. When Excel copied the formula to cell E6, it adjusted the original cell references relative to the new formula location.

FIGURE G-8: Entering a formula

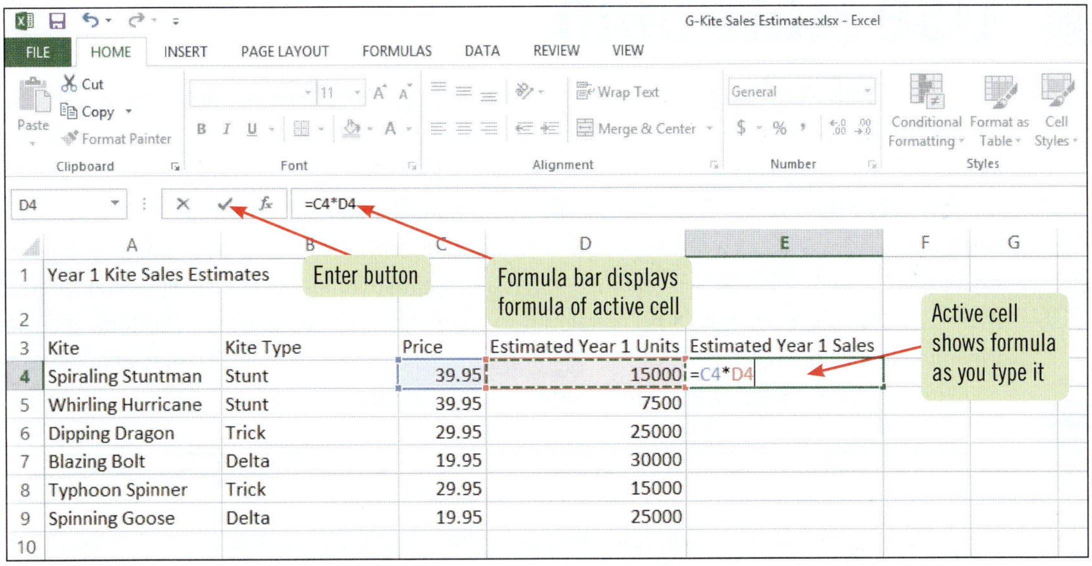

FIGURE G-9: Worksheet after using fill handle to copy formulas to cells E5:E9

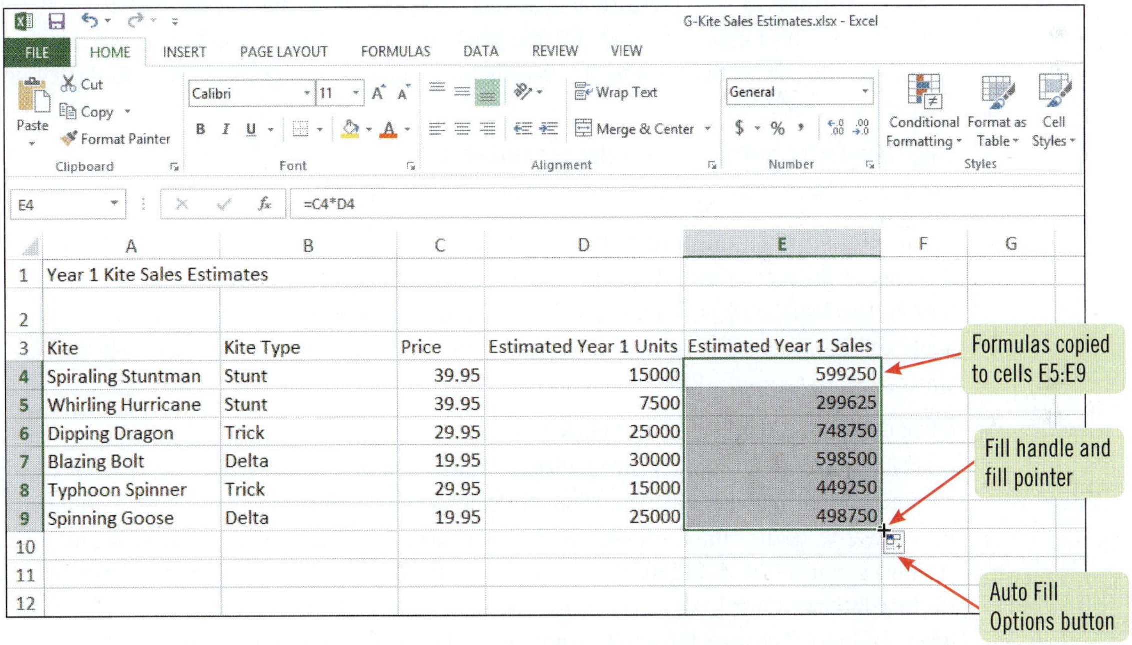

TABLE G-2: Useful mathematical operators and sample formulas listed in order of precedence

operator	description	sample formula	result	sample worksheet (used in sample formulas)		
( )	Parentheses	=(A2*B2)*3	1500		A	B	C
^	Exponent	=B2^2	10,000	1	Price	Quantity	
*	Multiplication	=B2*2	200	2	$ 5.00	100	
/	Division	=B2/2	50	3			
+	Addition	=B2+10	110	4			
–	Subtraction	=B2–20	80				

Creating a Worksheet

Use AutoSum

Learning
Outcomes
• Explain what a
function is
• Identify arguments
in a function
• Calculate totals
using AutoSum

Excel comes with a wide variety of **functions**, which are prewritten formulas designed for particular types of calculations. The most frequently used worksheet function, **SUM**, totals all numbers and cell references included as function arguments. An **argument** is information a function needs to make a calculation, and can consist of values (such as 100 or .02), cell references (such as B3), or range references (such as A9:G16). Functions save time and help ensure accuracy, and they are available for both simple calculations and extremely complex ones. Each Excel function has a name that you usually see in all capital letters, such as AVERAGE or DATE. Because the SUM function is so commonly used, it has its own button— also known as the AutoSum button—on the HOME tab. **CASE** ➤ *You are now ready to add up the Estimated Year 1 Units and Estimated Year 1 Sales columns. You decide to use the AutoSum button.*

STEPS

1. **Click cell D10**

   Cell D10 is now the active cell. You want D10 to display the total year 1 units for all of the kite products, which is the sum of the range D4:D9.

2. **Click the AutoSum button in the Editing group on the HOME tab**

   A moving dotted border appears around the cells in the range D4:D9, as shown in **FIGURE G-10**, indicating that these are the cells that Excel assumes you want to add together. The function =SUM(D4:D9) appears in cell D10 and in the formula bar, ready for you to edit or accept. When you use a function, Excel suggests a cell or range to add. With AutoSum, it is usually the group of cells directly above or to the left of the cell containing the function.

3. **Click the Enter button ☑ on the formula bar**

   Excel accepts the formula and the result, 117500, appears in cell D10.

4. **Click cell E10, click the AutoSum button in the Editing group, then click ☑**

   The sum of the range E4:E9 (3194125) appears in E10. See **FIGURE G-11**. When you clicked the AutoSum button, Excel guessed (correctly) that you wanted to calculate the sum of cells E4:E9, the cells directly above cell E10. You just learned that the price of the Spiraling Stuntman is actually $49.95. You need to correct this.

5. **Click cell C4, type 49.95, then click ☑**

   Changing the value in cell C4 automatically changed the formula results in cell E4 (for the Spiraling Stuntman Estimated Year 1 Sales) and also for the total estimated sales of all the kites in cell E10, as shown in **FIGURE G-12**, because these formulas use the value in cell C4. The Estimated Year 1 Sales for the Spiraling Stuntman increased to $749,250.00, an increase of $150,000.00. This increase is also reflected in cell E10, the total Estimated Year 1 Sales number. See **FIGURE G-12**. You can see what a valuable tool Excel is; changing one value in a cell changes the results in any cell that contains a cell reference to that cell.

6. **Save your changes**

Viewing sum data on the status bar

If you want to know the sum of a range of cells without creating a formula or using AutoSum, you can use the status bar. To do this, select the range of cells that you want to total; the sum of the selected range will appear at the right end of the status bar, along with the average value of the selected range. The status bar also displays a value for Count, which represents the number of cells in the selected range.

FIGURE G-10: Using the AutoSum button

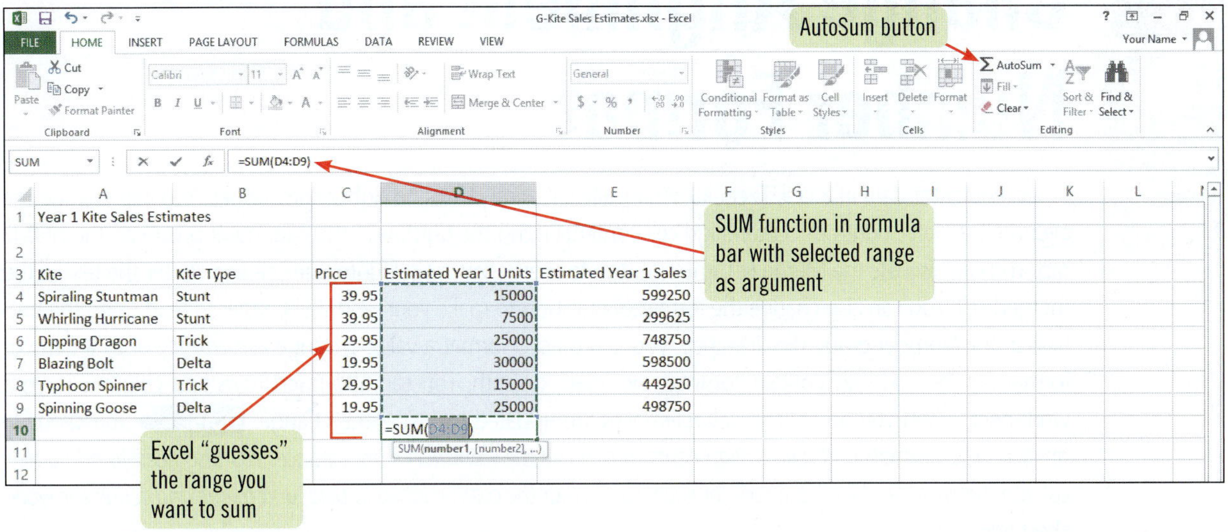

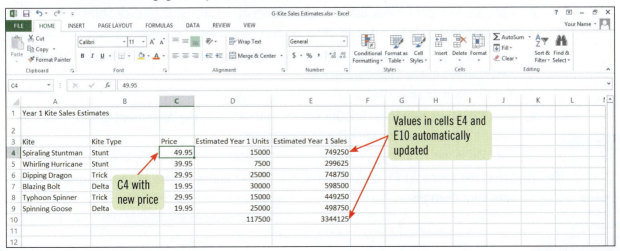

SUM function in formula bar with selected range as argument

AutoSum button

Excel "guesses" the range you want to sum

FIGURE G-11: Worksheet with totals calculated using the SUM function

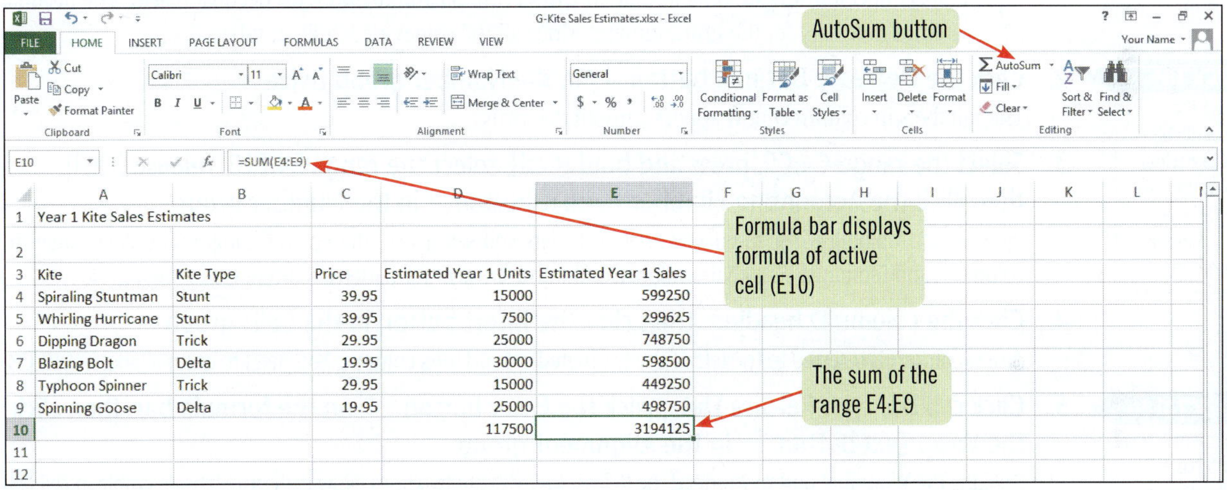

AutoSum button

Formula bar displays formula of active cell (E10)

The sum of the range E4:E9

FIGURE G-12: Worksheet after changing the net price in cell C4

Values in cells E4 and E10 automatically updated

C4 with new price

Excel 2013

Change Alignment and Number Format

When you enter data in a cell, Excel automatically left-aligns text and right-aligns values. You can change the alignment to left-, right-, or center-align cell contents using the buttons in the Alignment group on the HOME tab. You can also use the Merge & Center button to merge several cells into one cell and center the text in the merged cell. You can also change the format of numbers to make your worksheet easier to read using the buttons in the Number group. For instance, you can quickly format a value or range as currency or as a date, or format numbers so they contain commas, decimals, or both. You can also insert rows and columns in your worksheet; when you do so, any cell references are updated to reflect the change. **CASE** *You decide to apply number formats and adjust alignments to improve the worksheet's appearance. You also need to add a new column that includes the release date for each kite, format the column labels in bold, and merge and center the worksheet title.*

STEPS

1. **Select the range D4:D10, then click the Comma Style button** ▼ **in the Number group**
   The numbers in column D are now formatted with a comma and include two decimal places. The decimal places are not necessary for the unit estimates, since all the values are whole numbers.

   > **QUICK TIP**
   > To increase the number of digits following a decimal point, click the Increase Decimal button ◄.0 .00 in the Number group.

2. **Click the Decrease Decimal button** .00 →.0 **in the Number group twice**
   The numbers in column D now appear without decimals.

3. **Select the range C4:C9, press and hold [Ctrl], select the range E4:E10, release [Ctrl], then click the Accounting Number Format button** $ **in the Number group**
   Pressing and holding [Ctrl] when you select cells lets you select nonadjacent cell ranges. The Price values in column C and Estimated Year 1 Sales values in column E are now formatted as currency, as shown in **FIGURE G-13**.

4. **Click the column D heading, then click the Insert button in the Cells group**
   A new column is inserted to the left of the Estimated Year 1 Units column. You need to enter a label in cell D3.

   > **QUICK TIP**
   > The Alignment group also has buttons to align text at the top, middle, or bottom of a cell.

5. **Click cell D3, type Release Date, click the Enter button** ✓ **on the formula bar, then click the Wrap Text button** in the Alignment group
   Clicking the Wrap Text button wrapped the Release Date text to two lines. Now the entire label is visible in cell D3.

6. **Click cell D4, type April 1, 2016, then click** ✓
   Excel recognized that you typed a date in cell D4 and changed the format to 1-Apr-16. You can use the Number Format list in the Number group to change the date format.

7. **Click the Number Format list arrow, as shown in FIGURE G-14, then click Short Date**
   The date format in cell D4 is now 4/1/2016. You can copy this date to the other cells in column D.

8. **Click the Copy button in the Clipboard group, select the range D5:D9, then click the Paste button in the Clipboard group**
   Now all cells in the range D5:D9 display the date 4/1/2016.

9. **Click the row 3 heading, click the Center button** ≡ **in the Alignment group, click the column B heading, then click the Center button** ≡
   Each label in row 3 is now center-aligned, and the kite type values in column B are also center-aligned.

   > **QUICK TIP**
   > The Orientation button in the Alignment group lets you align cell contents at any angle you specify.

10. **Select the range A1:F1, click the Merge & Center button in the Alignment group, then save your changes**
    As shown in **FIGURE G-15**, the worksheet title is centered across the six selected cells, which have merged into one cell. Note that the cell address for this cell is still A1.

FIGURE G-13: Worksheet after using the Accounting Number Format, Comma Style, and Decrease Decimal buttons

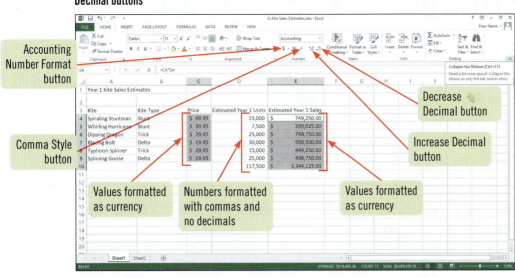

Accounting Number Format button

Decrease Decimal button

Comma Style button

Increase Decimal button

Values formatted as currency

Numbers formatted with commas and no decimals

Values formatted as currency

FIGURE G-14: Applying a date format using the Number Format list

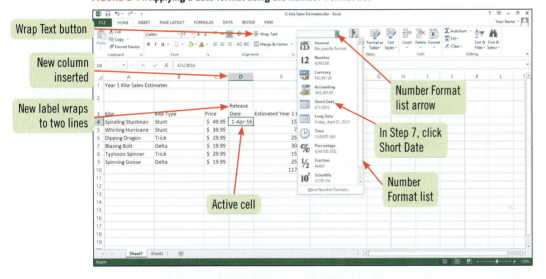

Wrap Text button

New column inserted

New label wraps to two lines

Number Format list arrow

In Step 7, click Short Date

Number Format list

Active cell

FIGURE G-15: Worksheet after changing alignment and number formats

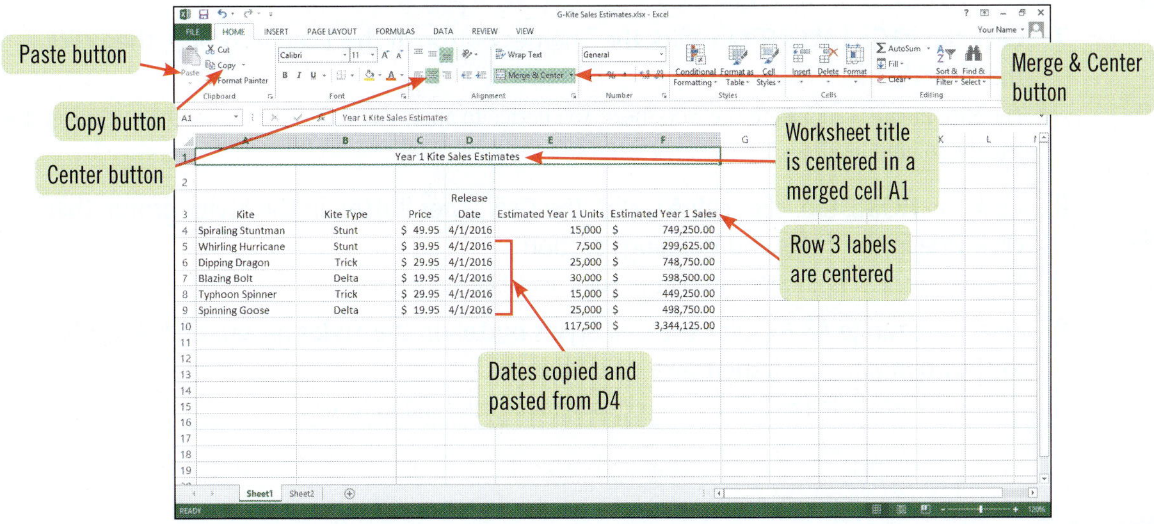

Paste button

Copy button

Center button

Merge & Center button

Worksheet title is centered in a merged cell A1

Row 3 labels are centered

Dates copied and pasted from D4

Creating a Worksheet

Excel 2013

Enhance a Worksheet

Learning Outcomes
- Add a header and footer to a worksheet
- Apply a theme
- Apply cell styles

You can enhance an Excel worksheet to make it look more professional and increase its visual appeal. In Page Layout view, you can add headers and footers containing information that you want to include at the top or bottom of each page. You can apply a new theme to change the colors, fonts, and effects of an entire workbook. You can also apply **cell styles**, which are predefined formatting options to ensure that similar elements in your worksheet are formatted consistently. **CASE** ▶ *You need to add a header that contains your name, and a footer that contains the date and file name. To enhance the appearance of the worksheet, you decide to apply a theme and apply cell styles to the title and the header row.*

STEPS

1. **Click the Page Layout button 🔳 on the status bar, then click the Click to add header placeholder in the header area**

   The worksheet is now in Page Layout view, and the insertion point is above the worksheet title in the middle of the header's three sections. In this view, you can see that the worksheet columns do not all fit on one page; you will fix this later.

QUICK TIP
To apply borders around selected cells, click the Borders list arrow in the Font group, then click a border style.

2. **Press [Tab] to select the right section of the header area, then type your name**

   Your name appears in the right section of the header, right-aligned, as shown in **FIGURE G-16**. The HEADER & FOOTER TOOLS DESIGN tab is now available on the Ribbon.

3. **Click the HEADER & FOOTER TOOLS DESIGN tab, then click the Go to Footer button in the Navigation group**

4. **Click the left section of the footer area, then click the Current Date button in the Header & Footer Elements group**

   Excel inserts the code "&[Date]" into the left section of the footer area. When you click outside of this section, the actual date will appear here.

QUICK TIP
To apply shading to selected cells, click the Fill Color button list arrow in the Font group, then click a color.

5. **Click the right section of the footer area, click the File Name button in the Header & Footer Elements group, then click any cell in the worksheet above the footer**

   The filename appears on the right end of the footer area, and the date is in the left side, as shown in **FIGURE G-17**.

TROUBLE
Some themes use larger font sizes, which might require you to widen columns so all data entries are visible. If a cell is too narrow to fit its contents, you will see ###### instead of numbers.

6. **Click the Normal view button 🔳 on the status bar, then press [Ctrl][Home]**

   Cell A1 is now active, and the worksheet appears in Normal view. The vertical dotted line to the right of column E indicates the page break line. This line is helpful to see if your worksheet contains many columns and you need to fit all columns on one page.

7. **Click the PAGE LAYOUT tab, click the Themes button in the Themes group, then click the Slice theme**

   The Slice theme is applied to the worksheet. You decide to apply cell styles to enhance the worksheet title and the column headings.

TROUBLE
If you do not see the Cell Styles button in the Styles group, click the More button ▼ in the Styles group to open the Styles gallery.

8. **Click the HOME tab, click cell A1, click the Cell Styles button in the Styles group, then click Title in the Titles and Headings section**

   The title in cell A1 is now formatted in 18 point, dark blue.

9. **Select the range A3:F3, click the Cell Styles button in the Styles group, click Accent6 as shown in FIGURE G-18, then save your changes**

   Cells A3:F3 now have a reddish brown cell background color and white text.

FIGURE G-16: Header with text added

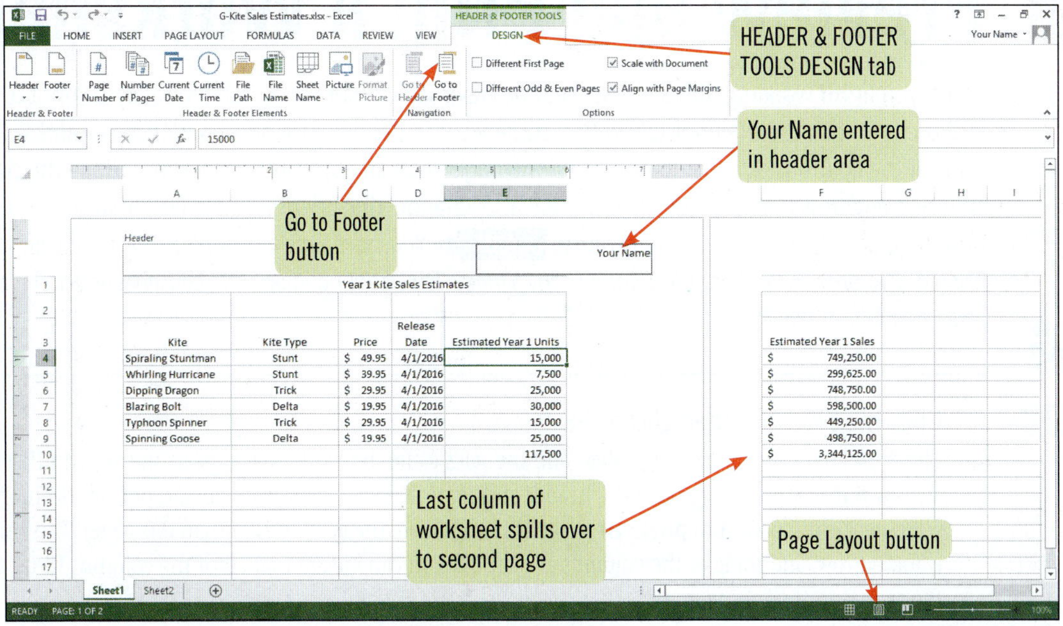

HEADER & FOOTER TOOLS DESIGN tab

Your Name entered in header area

Go to Footer button

Last column of worksheet spills over to second page

Page Layout button

FIGURE G-17: Footer with current date and file name added

Footer area

Current date appears here

Filename replaces &[File] code when you click in the worksheet

Second page of worksheet appears here

FIGURE G-18: Worksheet with Slice theme and cell styles applied

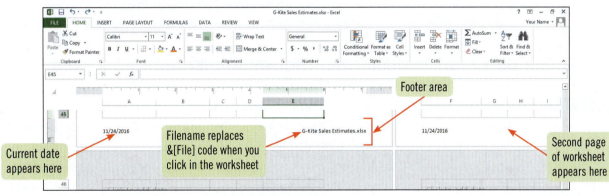

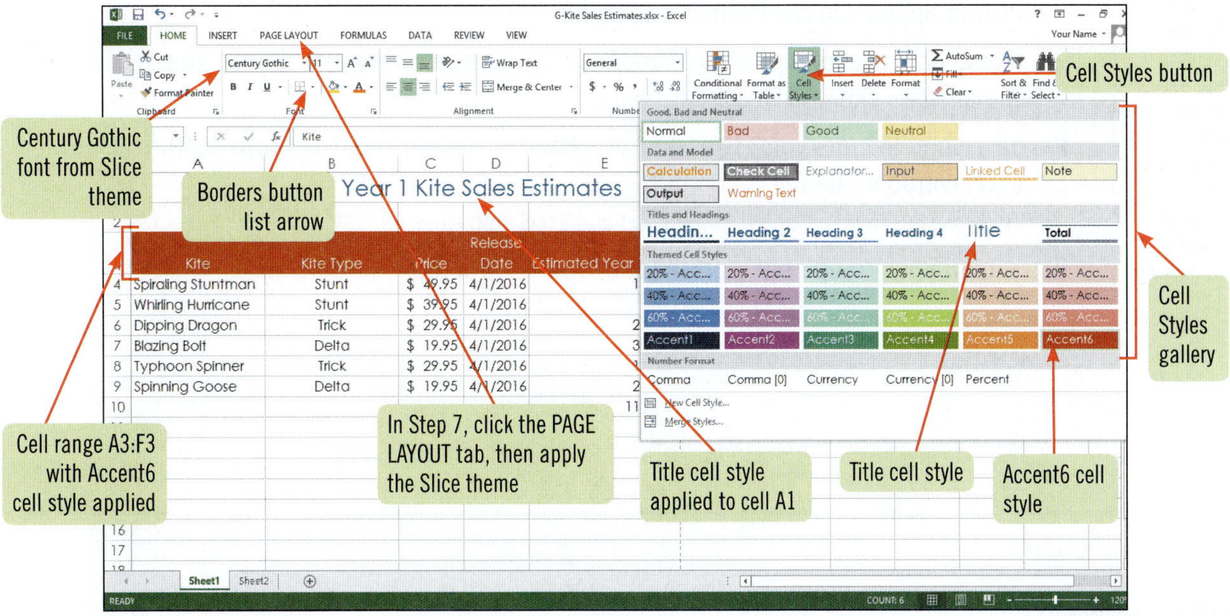

Cell Styles button

Century Gothic font from Slice theme

Borders button list arrow

Cell Styles gallery

Cell range A3:F3 with Accent6 cell style applied

In Step 7, click the PAGE LAYOUT tab, then apply the Slice theme

Title cell style applied to cell A1

Title cell style

Accent6 cell style

Excel 2013

Preview and Print a Worksheet

Learning Outcomes
• Preview a worksheet
• Adjust the scaling and set orientation
• Print a worksheet

When you finish working with a worksheet and have saved your work, you are ready to print it. Just like in Word, you can use the Print tab in Backstage view to preview the printed worksheet and specify settings. If the columns or rows do not fit on one page you can adjust the scaling to reduce the size of the columns and rows enough to fit. You can also change the orientation, adjust margins, specify the printer, specify the paper size, and more. **CASE** ▶ *You have finished working with the worksheet and are ready to preview and print it. (Note: Many schools limit printing in order to conserve paper. If your school restricts printing, skip Steps 6 and 7.)*

STEPS

1. **Click the FILE tab, then click Print**

   The Print tab opens in Backstage view, and the sales estimates worksheet appears in the Print Preview area, as shown in **FIGURE G-19**. Notice the header and footer text appear at the top and bottom of the page. The worksheet is set to print in **portrait orientation** (where the page is taller than it is wide). This orientation is too narrow, and some of the columns are cut off. You can ensure that all of the columns fit by adjusting the scaling in the Settings area.

2. **Click No Scaling at the bottom of the Settings area, then click Fit Sheet on One Page**

   The preview of the worksheet shows the columns all now fit on one page. Adjusting the scaling resulted in squeezing down the width of each column proportionally so all columns fit on one page. You decide to change the orientation to **Landscape** (where the page is wider than it is tall) so there will be more room for all the columns.

3. **Click Portrait Orientation in the Settings area, then click Landscape Orientation**

   The Print Preview area shows the worksheet in landscape orientation, as shown in **FIGURE G-20**.

4. **Click the Show Margins button 🔲 in the lower-right corner of the Print Preview area**

   Lines appear on the worksheet indicating the location of the margins at the Normal setting. The margins look fine at the Normal setting, so there is no need to change this setting.

5. **Click the Zoom to Page button 🔲 in the lower-right corner of the Print Preview area**

   The worksheet appears up close in the Print Preview area, giving you a magnified view of the worksheet data, as shown in **FIGURE G-21**.

6. **Verify that your printer is on and connected to your computer, and that the correct printer appears in the Printer text box**

7. **If your school allows printing, click the Print button, otherwise skip to Step 8**

   The document prints, and the HOME tab opens.

8. **Save your changes, click the FILE tab, click Close, then click the Close button ✕ in the Excel window title bar**

   The worksheet is saved, and the worksheet and Excel both close.

9. **Submit your completed worksheet to your instructor**

FIGURE G-19: Worksheet in Print Preview in Backstage view, portrait orientation

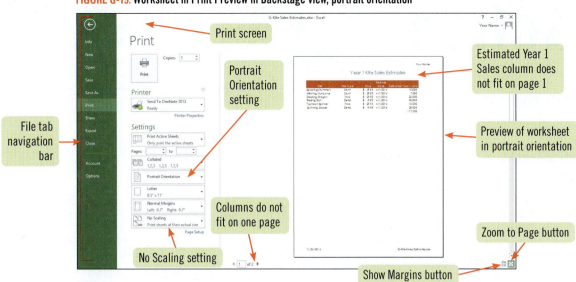

Print screen

Estimated Year 1 Sales column does not fit on page 1

File tab navigation bar

Portrait Orientation setting

Preview of worksheet in portrait orientation

Columns do not fit on one page

Zoom to Page button

No Scaling setting

Show Margins button

FIGURE G-20: Worksheet in Print Preview in Backstage view, landscape orientation

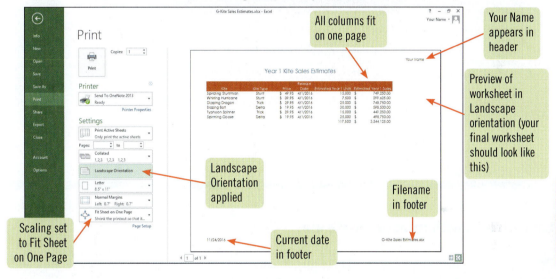

All columns fit on one page

Your Name appears in header

Preview of worksheet in Landscape orientation (your final worksheet should look like this)

Scaling set to Fit Sheet on One Page

Landscape Orientation applied

Current date in footer

Filename in footer

FIGURE G-21: Zooming in on the worksheet in Print Preview

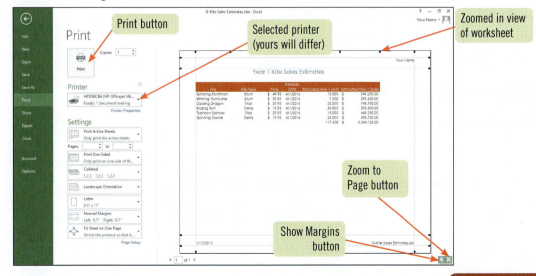

Print button

Selected printer (yours will differ)

Zoomed in view of worksheet

Zoom to Page button

Show Margins button

Creating a Worksheet

Practice

Concepts Review

Label each worksheet element shown in FIGURE G-22.

FIGURE G-22

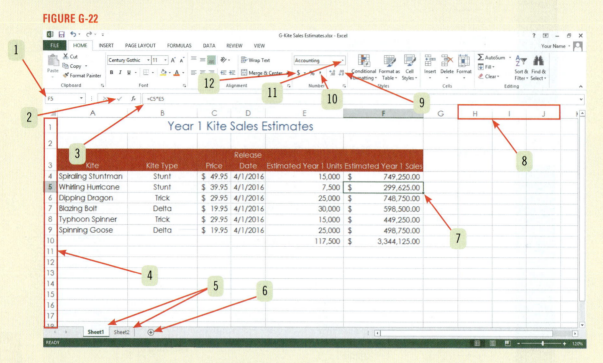

Match each icon with its appropriate use.

13. ✚
14. ✓
15. .00→.0
16. ▣
17. ✛
18. ✚

a. Pointer shape used to resize a column
b. Button used to accept the contents of a cell
c. Button used to decrease the number of decimals
d. Pointer shape when it is placed over a worksheet cell
e. Button used to view the footer in a worksheet
f. Pointer shape when it is positioned over a fill handle

Select the best answer from the list of choices.

19. The name of the cell located in column H and row 114 is:
   a. 114H.
   b. 114.
   c. H114.
   d. HA114.

20. Which of the following formulas is NOT correctly written?
   a. S67*A5=
   b. =A5-B7
   c. =7+B55
   d. =H77*15

21. **Cell C7 contains the formula =A7+B7. If you copy the formula in C7 to cell C8, which of the following formulas will E8 contain?**
   a. =A6+B6
   b. =B7+C8
   c. =A8+B8
   d. =B7+B8

22. **Which of the following actions does NOT accept a formula after you type it?**
   a. Clicking ✓
   b. Pressing [Shift]
   c. Pressing [Tab]
   d. Pressing [Enter]

23. **For which of the following tasks would you NOT use the fill handle?**
   a. Copying a formula from cell E44 to P17
   b. Copying a formula from cell D2 to the range D3:D22
   c. Copying a label from cell D22 to D23
   d. Copying a formula from cell F22 to the range F23:F25

Skills Review

1. **Navigate a workbook.**
   a. Start Microsoft Excel and open a new blank workbook.
   b. Identify the Excel screen elements without referring to the lesson material.
   c. Click cell E14, then click cell C8.
   d. Insert a new sheet, then in Sheet2, select the range B7:G18.
   e. Switch to Sheet1, then use the keyboard to place the cell pointer in cell A1.
   f. Save the workbook as **G-December Sales** in the location where you store your Data Files.

2. **Enter values and labels.**
   a. Starting in cell A1, type the following labels in the range A1:D1:
      Fruit Basket Name   Quantity Sold   Unit Price   Total Sales
   b. Enter the following labels for Fruit Basket Name in the range A2 through A8: **Ultimate Orange**, **Apple Bliss**, **Pineapple Delight**, **Pear Paradise**, **Birthday Berry Bonanza**, **Banana Basket**, **Citrus Sensation**.
   c. Use the table below as a guide to enter the values for Quantity Sold (in the range B2:B8) and the values for Unit Price (in the range C2:C8):

Quantity Sold	Unit Price
490	59.95
2987	49.95
489	39.95
325	49.95
228	39.95
872	29.95
783	29.95

3. **Work with columns and rows.**
   a. Increase the size of column A by dragging the appropriate column boundary so the column is wide enough to fit all the labels in the range A1:A8.
   b. Increase the width of columns B and C by double-clicking the appropriate column boundary for each.
   c. Insert two rows above row 1.
   d. Enter the label **Marley's Organic Fruit Baskets December Sales** in cell A1.
   e. Increase the height of row 2 to 24.75 (33 pixels) using the dragging method. (If you have trouble dragging the row to the exact height, click the Format button in the Cells group, click Row Height, type 24.75, then click OK.)

Skills Review (continued)

f. Insert a new column between column A and column B. Type **Supplier** in cell B3. Enter the following supplier names in cells B4:B10:

Florida Fruit Nation
Jackson Organic Imports
Hawaii Fruit Supply
Jackson Organic Imports
Jackson Organic Imports
Hawaii Fruit Supply
Florida Fruit Nation

g. Adjust the width of column B by double-clicking the column boundary between column B and C.

h. Save your changes.

4. Use formulas.

a. Type a formula in cell E4 that multiplies the value of cell C4 and the value of cell D4, then use a button on the formula bar to accept the entry. When you create the formula, add the cell references to the formula by clicking the cells.

b. Type a formula in cell E5 that multiplies the value of cell C5 and the value of cell D5, then use a keyboard command to accept the entry.

c. Use the fill handle to copy the formula you entered in cell E5 to the range E6:E10.

d. Save your changes.

5. Use AutoSum.

a. Use the AutoSum button to enter a formula in C11 that adds the values in the cell range C4:C10.

b. Use the AutoSum button to enter a formula in E11 that adds the values in the cell range E4:E10.

c. Change the Quantity Sold value for Pineapple Delight to **1188**, then view the changes in cells E6 and E11.

d. Save your changes.

6. Change alignment and number format.

a. Apply the Comma Style number format to the cell range C4:C11. Use a button to remove the decimals for the selected range.

b. Apply the Accounting number format to the cell range D4:E11.

c. Insert a column to the left of column E. Enter the label **Close Date** in cell E3. Format this cell so the label wraps to two lines in the cell.

d. Enter the date **December 31, 2016** in cell E4. Use the Number Format list to apply the Short Date format to this cell. Copy the date in cell E4, and paste it to the range E5:E10. You might see ##### appear in the range E4:E10 because the column is too narrow. If so, widen column E so the full date is visible in E4:E10.

e. Center the labels in the cell range A3:F3.

f. Merge and center cells A1:F1.

g. Save your changes.

7. Enhance a worksheet.

a. Change to Page Layout view.

b. Type your name in the right section of the header.

c. Switch to the footer, then insert the current date in the left section of the footer. Insert a code for the filename in the right section of the footer.

d. Click in any worksheet cell, and look at the footer you entered. Move the cell pointer to cell A1, and change the view to Normal view.

e. Apply the Facet theme to the worksheet. If any of the cells contain ##### characters, then widen the columns by dragging the column heading borders until the cell entries are visible.

Skills Review (continued)

    f. Apply the Title cell style to cell A1.

    g. Apply Accent2 cell style to the labels in row 3 (range A3:F3).

    h. Apply the 20% - Accent1 cell style to the range A4:F10.

    i. Apply the Total cell style to the range C11:F11.

    j. Save your changes.

8. Preview and print a worksheet.

    a. Preview the worksheet using the Print tab in Backstage view.

    b. Change the scaling to Fit Sheet on One Page.

    c. Change the orientation to Landscape.

    d. Use a button to view the margin rules on the worksheet.

    e. Use a button to zoom in on the worksheet.

    f. If your school permits printing, verify that the printer settings are correct, then print the worksheet. Compare your completed worksheet to **FIGURE G-23**.

    g. Save your changes, close the workbook, exit Excel, then submit your completed workbook to your instructor.

FIGURE G-23

Marley's Organic Fruit Baskets December Sales

Fruit Basket Name	Supplier	Quantity Sold	Unit Price	Close Date	Total Sales
Ultimate Orange	Florida Fruit Nation	490	$ 59.95	12/31/2016	$ 29,375.50
Apple Bliss	Jackson Organic Imports	2,987	$ 49.95	12/31/2016	$ 149,200.65
Pineapple Delight	Hawaii Fruit Supply	1,188	$ 39.95	12/31/2016	$ 47,460.60
Pear Paradise	Jackson Organic Imports	325	$ 49.95	12/31/2016	$ 16,233.75
Birthday Berry Bonanza	Jackson Organic Imports	228	$ 39.95	12/31/2016	$ 9,108.60
Banana Basket	Hawaii Fruit Supply	872	$ 29.95	12/31/2016	$ 26,116.40
Citrus Sensation	Florida Fruit Nation	763	$ 29.95	12/31/2016	$ 23,450.85
		6,873			$ 300,946.35

1/25/2016   G-December Sales.xlsx

Independent Challenge 1

You are a sales representative at a small baby food company based in San Antonio. Your manager, Toya Robinson, has asked you to provide her with a worksheet that shows the top five orders in your region for the month of June. The summary needs to include the order number, account name, order date, order total, and payments received. The worksheet also needs to show the monthly sales total and the outstanding balance due.

    a. Open a new workbook, then save it as **G-Top June Orders** in the location where you store your Data Files.

    b. Enter the title **Top Five Orders for June, Midwest Region** in cell A1.

    c. Enter the information shown in the table below, starting in cell A3. (Note that when entering the dates in column C, Excel will automatically change the date format to Day Month-Year format, which is fine.)

Order Number	Account Name	Date	Order Total	Amount Paid
4778	Pink & Blue Care Givers, Inc.	June 10, 2016	17865	14325
4889	Baby City Foods	June 15, 2016	16845	14328
4997	Nathan and Bob's Market	June 17, 2016	6534	5543
5013	Mother Hen's Care Centers, Inc.	June 22, 2016	12259	10954
6024	Jones & Rowley Grocers, Inc.	June 26, 2016	4095	2266

    d. Widen each column as necessary so all the labels and data in the range A3:E8 fit completely in their cells.

    e. Add the label **Balance Due** in cell F3. Widen column F if necessary so the entire label fits in cell F3.

    f. Enter a formula in cell F4 that subtracts cell E4 from cell D4, then use the fill handle to copy the formula to cells F5:F8.

    g. Use the AutoSum button to enter a formula in cell D9 that adds the values in the range D4:D8. Then change the amount in cell D6 to 10966.

    h. Use the fill handle to copy the formula in cell D9 to cells E9 and F9.

    i. Center-align the order numbers in cells A4:A8, then center-align the labels in row 3.

    j. Apply the Accounting number format to cells D4:F9.

Independent Challenge 1 (continued)

k. Merge and center cells A1:F1. Apply the Title cell style to cell A1.

l. Change the date format in the range C4:C8 to the Short Date format.

m. Apply the Total cell style to the totals in row 9 (cells D9:F9). Apply the Heading 1 cell style to the labels in row 3 (A3:F3). Widen columns A through F as needed to accommodate the larger font size of each label with the Heading 1 style applied.

n. Add your name in the left section of the header. Add the filename to the right section of the header. Add the current date to the left side of the footer.

o. Apply the Facet theme to the workbook. *(Note: If any cell is too narrow to fit a number contained in it, you will see ###### instead of a number in that cell. To fix this, widen the column so it is wide enough to display the entire number in that cell.)*

p. Apply 20%-Accent3 style to cells A4:F8.

q. Open the Print tab in Backstage view. Look at the preview of the worksheet, and notice that it does not fit on one worksheet page. Change the orientation to Landscape. Compare your finished worksheet to FIGURE G-24.

r. Save your changes, close the workbook, exit Excel, then submit the workbook to your instructor.

FIGURE G-24

| Your Name | | | | | | G-Top June Orders |

Top Five Orders for June, Midwest Region

Order Number	Account Name	Date	Order Total	Amount Paid	Balance Due
4778	Pink & Blue Care Givers, Inc.	6/10/2016	$ 17,865.00	$ 14,325.00	$ 3,540.00
4889	Baby City Foods	6/15/2016	$ 16,845.00	$ 14,328.00	$ 2,517.00
4997	Nathan and Bob's Market	6/17/2016	$ 10,966.00	$ 5,543.00	$ 5,423.00
5013	Mother Hen's Care Centers, Inc.	6/22/2016	$ 12,259.00	$ 10,954.00	$ 1,305.00
6024	Jones & Rowley Grocers, Inc.	6/26/2016	$ 4,095.00	$ 2,266.00	$ 1,829.00
			$ 62,030.00	$ 47,416.00	$ 14,614.00

7/16/16

Independent Challenge 2

You are the franchise manager for Blackford & Wickes Crafters, a new specialty store business with five craft stores in the Midwest. You need to create a worksheet that analyzes first quarter sales by store. Your worksheet needs to compare third quarter sales of each store to the previous quarter. You also want the worksheet to show how third quarter actual sales compare to the third quarter sales forecast. Because it is a new, growing business, each store was forecast to meet a sales increase of 5% over the prior quarter.

a. Create a new workbook, then save it as **G-Sales Analysis** in the location where you store your Data Files.

b. Enter the company name **Blackford & Wickes Crafters** in cell A1, then enter **Third Quarter Sales Analysis** in cell A2.

c. Enter the information shown in the table below in the worksheet, starting with the **Store** label in cell A4. First type the values, then apply the proper number formatting and adjust decimal places so the data in your worksheet matches the table.

Store	July Sales	June Sales
Madison	$45,090	$39,878
Cleveland	$59,909	$66,476
Detroit	$47,010	$42,767
Naperville	$61,663	$55,590
Lansing	$51,876	$50,989

d. Enter **Change** in cell D4, then enter a formula in cell D5 that calculates the change in sales in July over June for the Madison store. (*Hint*: The formula should subtract cell C5 from cell B5.)

Independent Challenge 2 (continued)

e. Copy the formula in cell D5 to cells D6 through D9. Notice the value in D6 appears in parentheses. This means the value is a negative number; Cleveland's sales in July were lower than they were in June.
f. Enter **July Forecast** in cell E4, then enter a formula in cell E5 that multiplies the June Sales by 1.05. (*Hint*: The formula should use the * operator to multiply cell C5 by 1.05.) Copy this formula to cells E6 through E9.
g. Enter the label **Actual vs. Forecast** in cell F4. Format the label so it wraps to two lines. Enter a formula in cell F5 that subtracts the amount in cell E5 from the amount in cell B5. Copy this formula to cells F6 through F9.
h. Enter **Totals** in cell A10, then use the AutoSum button to enter a formula in cell B10 that calculates the total of cells B5 through B9. Copy this formula to the range C10:F10.
i. Insert a column to the left of column B. Add **State** as a label in cell B4, then add the appropriate states in cells B6:B9. (*Hint*: Madison, WI; Cleveland, OH; Detroit, MI; Naperville, IL; and Lansing, MI). Center align cells B4:B9.
j. Increase the row height of row 3 to 35 pixels. Center-align the labels in row 4.
k. Merge and center cells A1:G1 so the worksheet title is centered in the merged cell A1. Then merge and center cells A2:G2 so the worksheet subtitle is centered in the merged cell A2.
l. Apply the Title cell style to cell A1. Apply the Heading 1 cell style to cell A2.
m. Apply the View theme to the workbook. Apply the Accent 1 cell style to cells A4:G4. Apply the 20% - Accent 1 cell style to cells A5:A9. Apply the Total cell style to cells A10:G10. Apply the Bad cell style to any cells in column E or G that contain negative numbers (numbers in parenthesis). Apply the Good cell style to any cells in columns E or G containing positive numbers.
n. Insert your name in the left section of the header.
o. Preview the worksheet in Backstage view. Set the scaling to Fit Sheet on One Page. Keep the orientation as Portrait. Compare your worksheet to FIGURE G-25. Save your changes, close the workbook, and exit Excel. Submit your completed workbook to your instructor.

FIGURE G-25

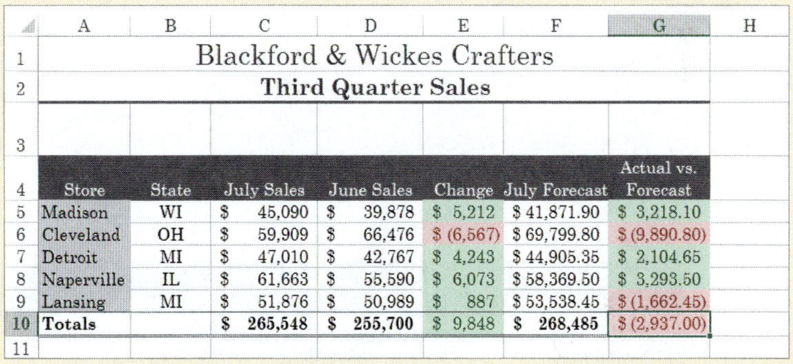

	A	B	C	D	E	F	G	H
1	Blackford & Wickes Crafters							
2	Third Quarter Sales							
3								
4	Store	State	July Sales	June Sales	Change	July Forecast	Actual vs. Forecast	
5	Madison	WI	$ 45,090	$ 39,878	$ 5,212	$ 41,871.90	$ 3,218.10	
6	Cleveland	OH	$ 59,909	$ 66,476	$ (6,567)	$ 69,799.80	$ (9,890.80)	
7	Detroit	MI	$ 47,010	$ 42,767	$ 4,243	$ 44,905.35	$ 2,104.65	
8	Naperville	IL	$ 61,663	$ 55,590	$ 6,073	$ 58,369.50	$ 3,293.50	
9	Lansing	MI	$ 51,876	$ 50,989	$ 887	$ 53,538.45	$ (1,662.45)	
10	Totals		$ 265,548	$ 255,700	$ 9,848	$ 268,485	$ (2,937.00)	
11								

Independent Challenge 3

You own a used car business called Sam's Pre-Owned Cars. You buy used vehicles, pay contractors to fix them up, and then resell them for a profit. You decide to create a spreadsheet to track your profits for cars you have sold in the first quarter.

a. Create a new workbook, and save it as **G-Car Profits** in the location where you store your Data Files.
b. Enter the company name **Sam's Pre-Owned Cars** in cell A1. Enter **Q1 Profits** in cell A2.
c. Enter the labels and data shown in the table below, starting in cell A4. Use Accounting number formatting for the cells that contain dollar amounts.

Car Model	Purchase Price	Cost to Fix	Sale Price	Date Sold
Chevrolet Malibu	$5,200	$ 880	$10,795	January 22, 2016
Subaru Legacy	$9,200	$1,259	$18,095	February 1, 2016
Ford Explorer	$9,500	$1,798	$19,195	February 15, 2016
Mercury Grand Marquis	$3,200	$1,500	$ 9,295	March 1, 2016
Honda Accord	$7,250	$3,250	$15,895	March 7, 2016

Independent Challenge 3 (continued)

d. Adjust the width of the columns as necessary, so that all the data in each cell in the data area is visible.

e. Insert a new column to the left of "Sale Price". Enter the label **Total Investment** in cell D4. Format the label, and adjust the column width so the label wraps to two lines in the cell.

f. Enter a formula in cell D5 that sums cells B5 and C5.

g. Copy the formula in cell D5 to cells D6:D9.

h. Type the label **Profit** in cell G4. Enter a formula in cell G5 that calculates the total profit for the Chevrolet Malibu. (*Hint*: The formula needs to subtract the value in the Total Investment cell from the Sale Price cell.)

i. Copy the formula in cell G5 to cells G6:G9.

j. Add the label **Total** to cell A10. Enter a formula in cell B10 that sums cells B5:B9. Use the Copy and Paste commands to copy this formula to cells C10:E10 and to cell G10.

k. Center-align the labels in row 4. Apply bold formatting to row 10.

l. Change the number format of the Date Sold values to the Short Date format.

m. Format the worksheet by applying a theme, and applying cell styles to enhance its appearance.

n. Add your name to the center section of the header. Add the filename to the right section of the header. Save your changes.

o. Preview the worksheet in Backstage view. Change the orientation to Landscape. Save your changes. FIGURE G-26 shows the completed worksheet with possible formatting options applied.

p. Close the workbook, exit Excel, then submit your completed workbook to your instructor.

FIGURE G-26

Your Name   G-Car Profits.xlsx

Sam's Pre-Owned Cars
Q1 Profits

Car Model	Purchase Price	Cost to Fix	Total Investment	Sale Price	Date Sold	Profit
Chevrolet Malibu	$ 5,200.00	$ 880.00	$ 6,080.00	$ 10,795.00	1/22/2016	$ 4,715.00
Subaru Legacy	$ 9,200.00	$ 1,259.00	$ 10,459.00	$ 18,095.00	2/1/2016	$ 7,636.00
Ford Explorer	$ 9,500.00	$ 1,798.00	$ 11,298.00	$ 19,195.00	2/15/2016	$ 7,897.00
Mercury Grand Marquis	$ 3,200.00	$ 1,500.00	$ 4,700.00	$ 9,295.00	3/1/2016	$ 4,595.00
Honda Accord	$ 7,250.00	$ 3,250.00	$ 10,500.00	$ 15,895.00	3/7/2016	$ 5,395.00
Total	**$ 34,350.00**	**$ 8,687.00**	**$ 43,037.00**	**$ 73,275.00**		**$ 30,238.00**

Independent Challenge 4: Explore

You just got a new job that pays more than your previous position. You have decided to move into a better apartment, without roommates, and you have found a new apartment that looks perfect. However, you are concerned that the new apartment will hurt your ability to save for a house. Not only will the new apartment cost more to rent, but you will need to pay additional money for other living expenses that will be necessary in this new situation. For instance, you currently walk to work, but the new job will require you to lease a car and pay for gas and insurance. You will also have to pay more for utilities and cable TV, since you will not be sharing these expenses anymore. You decide to create a budget spreadsheet that compares your current living expenses to your expected new expenses in the new apartment, and determine what impact this will have on your monthly savings.

a. Start Excel, then save a new workbook as **G-My New Budget** in the location where you store your Data Files.

b. Enter the title **My New Budget** in cell A1.

Independent Challenge 4: Explore (continued)

c. Enter the following labels in cells A3:A5:

New Monthly Salary

Current Monthly Salary

Salary Increase

d. Adjust the width of column A so all labels fit.

e. Enter a formula in cell B3 that calculates your new weekly net salary (which is $950) multiplied by 4.

f. Enter a formula in cell B4 that calculates your current weekly salary (which is $625) multiplied by 4.

g. Enter a formula in cell B5 that calculates the difference between your new monthly salary and your current salary. Apply the Accounting Number format to cells B3:B5.

h. Enter the following labels and values in cells A7 through C17:

Expense	Current Cost	New Cost
Rent	$500	$1,350
Food	$450	$ 450
Utilities	$ 60	$ 150
Car Payment	$ 0	$ 275
Car Insurance	$ 0	$ 125
Gas/Parking	$ 0	$ 100
Student Loan	$150	$ 150
Cable	$ 60	$ 90
Phone	$110	$ 110
Entertainment	$160	$ 160

i. Format all the cells in B8:B17 and C8:C17 with the Accounting number format. Display decimals in the formatting.

j. Enter the label **Change** in cell D7, then enter a formula in cell D8 that calculates the difference between the current cost for rent and the new cost for rent. Copy this formula to cells D9:D17.

k. Add the label **Total Expenses** to cell A18. Enter a formula in cell B18 that calculates the total expenses in the Current Cost column. Copy this formula to cells C18 and D18.

l. Enter the label **Available for Savings** in cell A21. Apply bold formatting to this label.

m. Type the label **Current** in cell A22. Type the label **New** in cell A23.

n. In cell B22, type a formula that subtracts B18 from B4.

o. In cell B23, type a formula that subtracts C18 from B3.

p. Apply a theme of your choosing to the worksheet. Then, format the worksheet using alignment settings and cell styles so it is visually appealing and easy to read. Make sure to use formatting to emphasize the key cells in the worksheet, such as the title, labels, and totals.

q. Insert a header that contains your name centered and the current date left-aligned.

r. Save the worksheet, print it, then exit Excel.

Visual Workshop

Create the worksheet shown in **FIGURE G-27**. Use formulas in the Total column for all the cells with numbers. Use AutoSum to calculate the totals in cells D12, D19, D26, E12, E19, E26 and E29. You will also need to enter a formula in cell D29. Apply the theme shown. Apply the Title cell style to cell A1, then use the Increase Font Size button to increase the font size to 36. Use the Heading 2 style for cell A2. (*Hints*: For the Cookie Baskets label, enter **Cookie Baskets** in cell A5, click the Orientation button list arrow in the Alignment group, then click Rotate Text Up. Next, select A5:A12, click the Merge & Center list arrow in the Alignment group on the HOME tab, then click Merge Cells. Apply the Heading 2 cell style to the selection. Follow the same process to create the Pies and Cakes labels. To apply the borders, select the cells that need borders, click the Borders button list arrow in the Font group, then click All Borders.) Save the workbook as **G-Holiday Sales Summary** in the location where you store your Data Files, with your name in the center section of the footer. Save and preview the worksheet, then submit it to your instructor.

FIGURE G-27

Miss Lexi's Baked Goods
Holiday Sales Summary

	Product	Price	Quantity Sold	Total
Cookie Baskets	Almond Crunches	15.95	559	$ 8,916.05
	Cinnamon Sleds	15.95	1,026	$ 16,364.70
	Coconut Snowmen	19.95	1,598	$ 31,880.10
	Molasses Chews	19.95	2,287	$ 45,625.65
	Raspberry Bells	21.95	787	$ 17,274.65
	Gingerbread Men	21.95	1,065	$ 23,376.75
	Chocolate Delights	25.95	1,076	$ 27,922.20
	Cookie Baskets Subtotal:		8,398.00	$171,360.10
Pies	Mincemeat	15.95	1,087	$ 17,337.65
	Pecan	19.95	3,209	$ 64,019.55
	Pumpkin	15.95	1,044	$ 16,651.80
	Apple	19.95	2,054	$ 40,977.30
	Cherry	15.95	3,423	$ 54,596.85
	Pies Subtotal:		10,817	$193,583.15
Cakes	Chocolate	18.95	1,096	$ 20,769.20
	Vanilla	18.95	543	$ 10,289.85
	Lemon	17.95	227	$ 4,074.65
	Apple Cinnamon	19.95	2,377	$ 47,421.15
	Maple Pumpkin	17.95	4,311	$ 77,382.45
	Cakes Subtotal:		8,554	$159,937.30

Total Holiday Sales: 27,769 $524,880.55

Your Name

Using Complex Formulas, Functions, and Tables

CASE Serena Henning, director of sales for Outdoor Designs, has given you a worksheet that shows sales for the company's northeast region for January, February, and March. She has asked you to perform some calculations on the data, highlight certain information, sort the information in a certain way, and filter it to show only information that meets specific criteria.

Unit Objectives

After completing this unit, you will be able to:

- Create complex formulas
- Use absolute cell references
- Understand functions
- Use date and time functions
- Use statistical functions
- Apply conditional formatting
- Sort rows in a table
- Filter table data

Files You Will Need

H-1.xlsx	H-4.xlsx
H-2.xlsx	H-5.xlsx
H-3.xlsx	H-6.xlsx

©HelenStock/Shutterstock

Create Complex Formulas

Learning Outcomes
- Define complex formula
- Create a complex formula using two operators
- Copy a complex formula to adjacent cells

When you create worksheets that contain many calculations, you might need to create formulas that contain more than one mathematical operator. For instance, to calculate profits for a particular product, a formula would first need to calculate product sales (product price multiplied by number of products sold) and then subtract costs from that result. Formulas that contain more than one operator are called **complex formulas**. When a formula contains multiple operators, Excel uses the **order of precedence** rule to determine which calculation to perform first. Calculations in parentheses are always evaluated first. Next, exponential calculations are performed, then multiplication and division calculations, and finally addition and subtraction calculations. If there are multiple calculations within the parentheses, they are performed according to this same order. **TABLE H-1** lists the common mathematical operators and the order in which Excel evaluates them in a formula. **CASE** *Serena provides you with a worksheet showing January through March sales and returns for the northeast region. She asks you to add a new column that calculates the adjusted sales total for all three months.*

STEPS

1. **Start Excel, open the file H-1.xlsx from where you store your Data Files, then save it as H-Northeast Region Sales**

   A copy of Serena's partially completed worksheet is open and saved with a new name.

2. **Click cell G6**

   You need to enter a formula in this cell that calculates total sales for Michael Parks for January (cell C6), February (cell D6), and March (cell E6), then subtracts Michael's returns (cell F6).

3. **Type =, click cell C6, press +, click cell D6, press +, click cell E6, press -, click cell F6, then click the Enter button ✓ on the formula bar**

   See **FIGURE H-1**. The formula bar displays the formula =C6+D6+E6-F6, and cell G6 displays the formula result, $68,320. This formula added the values in cell C6 (Michael Parks's January sales), D6 (Michael's February sales) and E6 (Michael's March sales), then subtracted the value in cell F6 (the returns). In effect, Excel added $14,565, $22,765 and $34,256, and then subtracted $3,266. Now you need to copy the formula to the range G7:G13, to calculate the Total Sales Less Returns for the other sales reps.

4. **Drag the cell G6 fill handle pointer ✛ down through cell G13 to copy the formula in G6 to the range G7:G13**

   The results of the copied formula appear in cells G7 through G13, as shown in **FIGURE H-2**.

5. **Click the Save button 🔲 on the Quick Access toolbar**

   Excel saves your changes to the workbook.

FIGURE H-1: Complex formula and its returned value

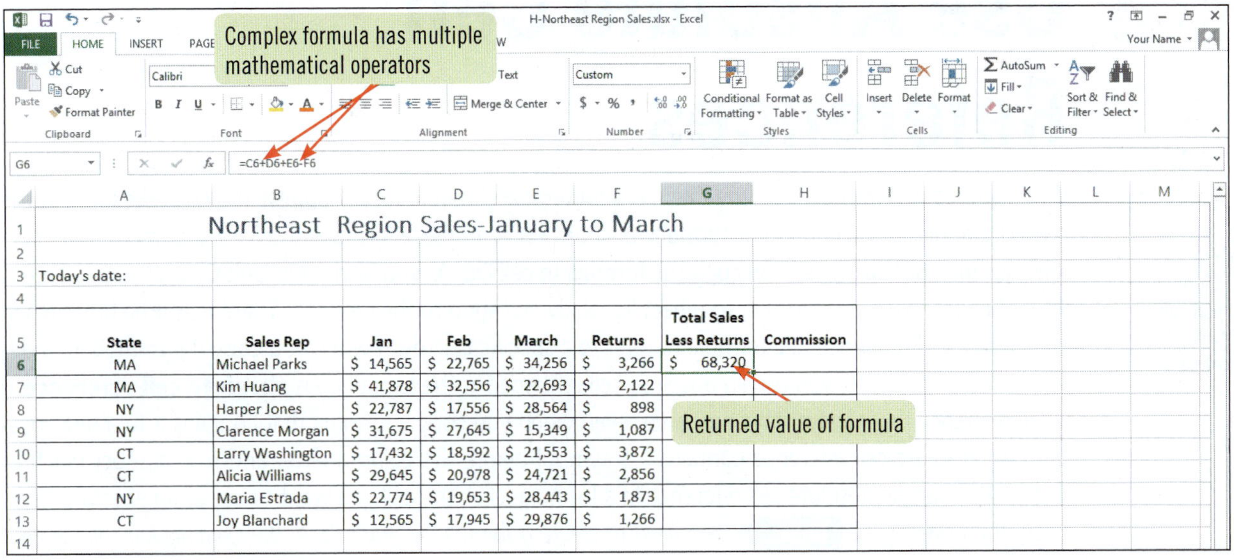

FIGURE H-2: Copying a formula to a range of cells

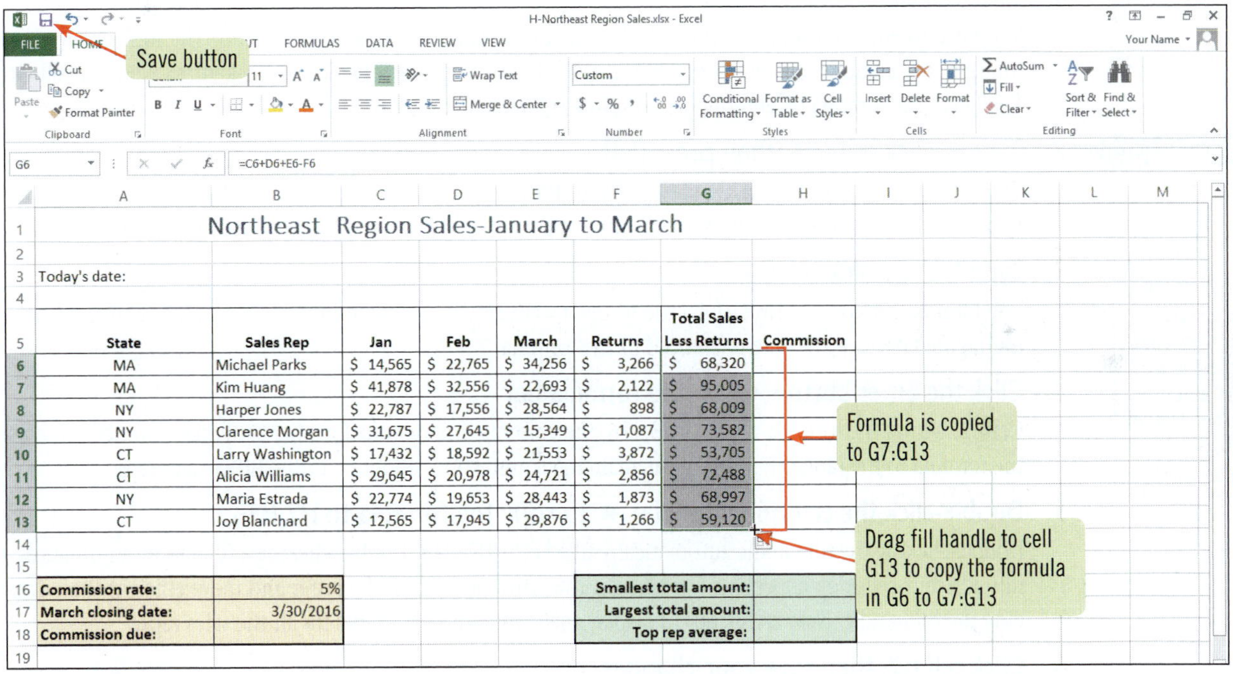

TABLE H-1: Review of order of operations

order of operations	operators
1. Calculate items in parentheses	( )
2. Calculate exponents	^
3. Multiply or divide (from left to right)	* or /
4. Add or subtract (from left to right)	+ or -

Use Absolute Cell References

Learning Outcomes
- Explain absolute cell reference
- Create a formula using an absolute cell reference
- Copy a formula with an absolute cell reference to adjacent cells

When you copy a formula from one cell to another, Excel automatically adjusts the cell references in the copied formula to reflect the new formula location. For example, a formula in cell D5 that reads "=B5*C5" changes to "=B6*C6" when you copy the formula to cell D6. As you learned in Unit G, a relative cell reference changes when you move it, to reflect its relative location to the new cell. There might be times when you want a cell reference in a formula to refer to a specific cell, even when you copy the formula to a different cell. In this case, you use an absolute cell reference in the formula. An **absolute cell reference** is a cell reference that always stays the same, even when you copy a formula that contains it to a new location. An absolute cell reference contains a $ symbol before the column letter and row number (such as $A$1). To insert an absolute cell reference in a formula, click the cell you want to use as an absolute reference, then press [F4]. **CASE** *You need to create a formula for the cells in the Commission column that multiplies the commission rate (5%) in cell B16 by the Total Sales Less Returns value in column G. You need to use the absolute cell reference $B$16 for the commission rate in the formula.*

STEPS

1. **Click cell H6**

   You need to enter a formula in this cell that calculates Michael Parks's commission. The formula needs to multiply the commission rate contained in cell B16 (5%) by the Total Sales Less Returns value in cell G6. You begin the formula by entering the absolute cell reference $B$16.

2. **Type =, click cell B16, then press [F4]**

   The formula bar and cell H6 display =$B$16. Pressing [F4] automatically added two $ symbols to the B16 cell reference to format it as an absolute cell reference. Now you need to complete the formula.

3. **Type *, then click cell G6**

   The formula bar and cell H6 display the formula =$B$16*G6, as shown in **FIGURE H-3**. Cells B16 and G6 are highlighted because they are referenced in the formula.

4. **Click the Enter button** ✓ **on the formula bar**

   Cell H6 shows the formula result of $3,416, the commission amount for Michael Parks. You need to copy the formula to the range H7:H13, to calculate the commission amounts for the other sales reps.

5. **Double-click the cell H6 fill handle** ■ **to copy the formula to H7:H13**

   Double-clicking the fill handle automatically filled cells H7:H13. Double-clicking a fill handle automatically fills adjacent cells down a column or across a row; this method can be faster and more efficient than dragging the fill handle. Now cells H6:H13 display the commission amounts for all the sales reps.

6. **Click cell H7, then save your changes**

   As shown in **FIGURE H-4**, the formula bar displays =$B$16*G7, which is the formula for cell H7. Notice that the formula contains the absolute cell reference $B$16; it was copied exactly from cell H6. The other cell reference in the formula, G7, is a relative cell reference, which changed when the formula was copied to cell H7. Cell H7 displays the value $4,750, the commission for Kim Huang.

FIGURE H-3: Using an absolute cell reference in a formula

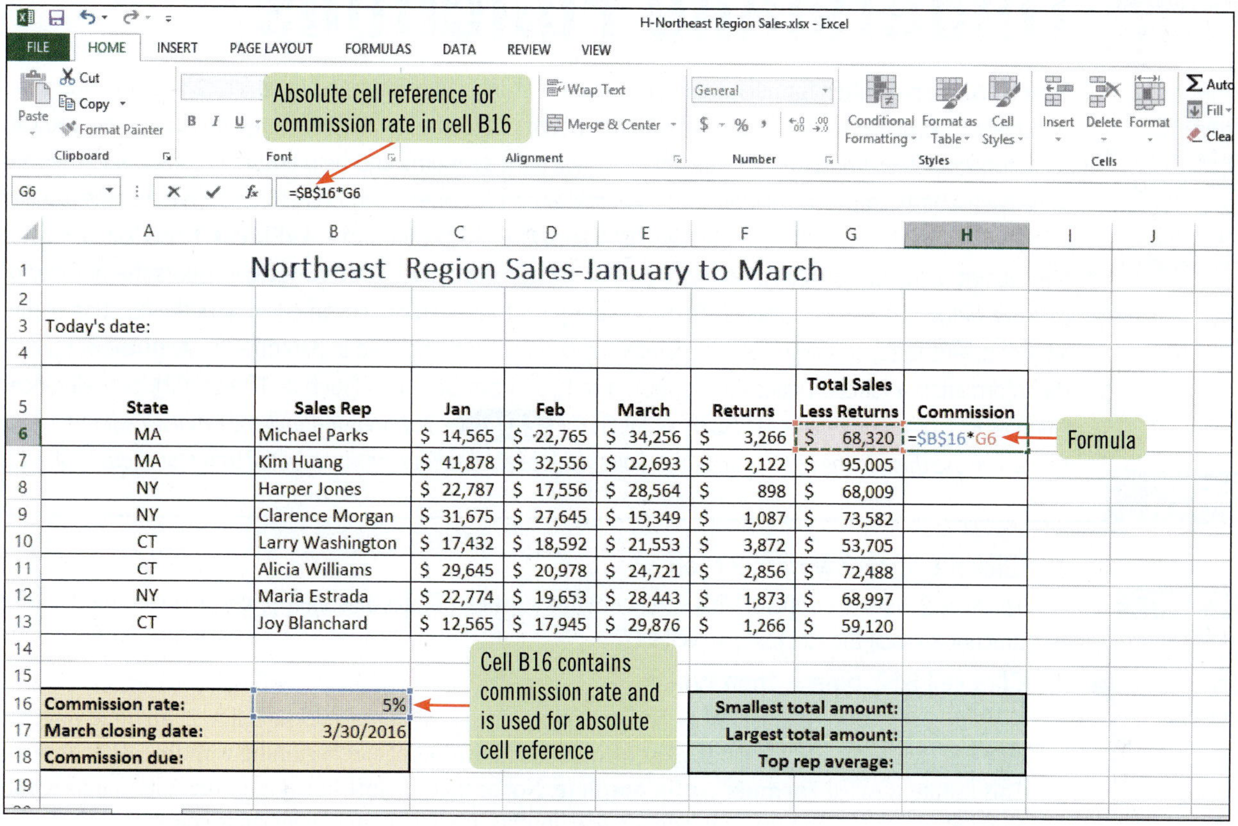

	A	B	C	D	E	F	G	H
1		Northeast Region Sales-January to March						
3	Today's date:							
5	State	Sales Rep	Jan	Feb	March	Returns	Total Sales Less Returns	Commission
6	MA	Michael Parks	$ 14,565	$ 22,765	$ 34,256	$ 3,266	$ 68,320	=$B$16*G6
7	MA	Kim Huang	$ 41,878	$ 32,556	$ 22,693	$ 2,122	$ 95,005	
8	NY	Harper Jones	$ 22,787	$ 17,556	$ 28,564	$ 898	$ 68,009	
9	NY	Clarence Morgan	$ 31,675	$ 27,645	$ 15,349	$ 1,087	$ 73,582	
10	CT	Larry Washington	$ 17,432	$ 18,592	$ 21,553	$ 3,872	$ 53,705	
11	CT	Alicia Williams	$ 29,645	$ 20,978	$ 24,721	$ 2,856	$ 72,488	
12	NY	Maria Estrada	$ 22,774	$ 19,653	$ 28,443	$ 1,873	$ 68,997	
13	CT	Joy Blanchard	$ 12,565	$ 17,945	$ 29,876	$ 1,266	$ 59,120	
16	Commission rate:	5%			Smallest total amount:			
17	March closing date:	3/30/2016			Largest total amount:			
18	Commission due:				Top rep average:			

FIGURE H-4: Viewing an absolute cell reference in a copied formula

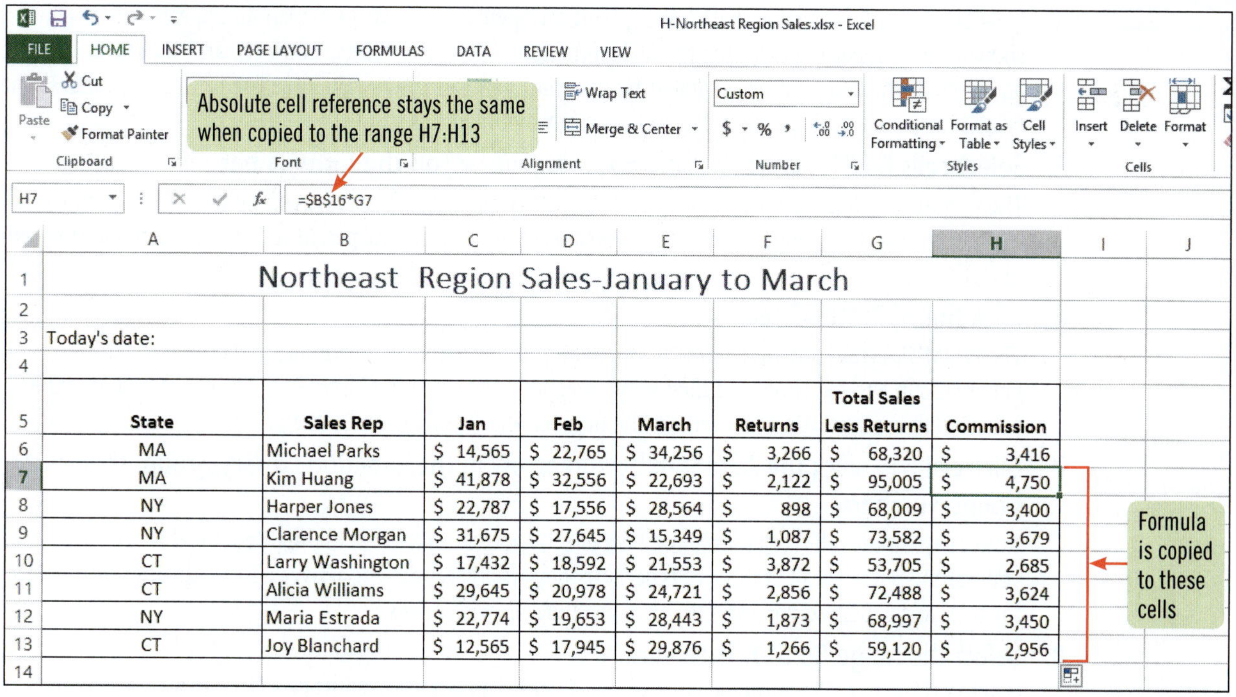

	A	B	C	D	E	F	G	H
1		Northeast Region Sales-January to March						
3	Today's date:							
5	State	Sales Rep	Jan	Feb	March	Returns	Total Sales Less Returns	Commission
6	MA	Michael Parks	$ 14,565	$ 22,765	$ 34,256	$ 3,266	$ 68,320	$ 3,416
7	MA	Kim Huang	$ 41,878	$ 32,556	$ 22,693	$ 2,122	$ 95,005	$ 4,750
8	NY	Harper Jones	$ 22,787	$ 17,556	$ 28,564	$ 898	$ 68,009	$ 3,400
9	NY	Clarence Morgan	$ 31,675	$ 27,645	$ 15,349	$ 1,087	$ 73,582	$ 3,679
10	CT	Larry Washington	$ 17,432	$ 18,592	$ 21,553	$ 3,872	$ 53,705	$ 2,685
11	CT	Alicia Williams	$ 29,645	$ 20,978	$ 24,721	$ 2,856	$ 72,488	$ 3,624
12	NY	Maria Estrada	$ 22,774	$ 19,653	$ 28,443	$ 1,873	$ 68,997	$ 3,450
13	CT	Joy Blanchard	$ 12,565	$ 17,945	$ 29,876	$ 1,266	$ 59,120	$ 2,956

Excel 2013

Understand Functions

Learning Outcomes
- Define function
- Describe the four parts of a function
- Use the SUM and COUNT functions

Functions are prewritten formulas that come with Excel. Instead of figuring out which calculations you need to achieve a particular result—and what order in which to type them so the final result is accurate—you can use a function to compose the formula for you. Functions save time and help ensure accuracy, and they are available for both simple calculations and extremely complex ones. Each Excel function has a name, usually written in capital letters. For example, the **SUM function** adds values, the **AVERAGE function** calculates the average value of a specified range of cells or values, and the **COUNT function** counts the number of cells in a range containing numbers. There are four parts to every function: an equal sign, the function name, a set of parentheses, and arguments separated by commas and enclosed in parentheses. **Arguments** are all the information a function needs to perform a task, and can be values (such as 100 or .02), cell references (such as B3), or range references (such as A9:G16). **CASE** ▶ *You need to familiarize yourself with functions so you can use them in the Northeast Region Sales worksheet. In this lesson you practice using functions in Sheet2.*

STEPS

1. Click the Sheet2 worksheet tab

The Sheet2 worksheet opens. This sheet contains a listing of kites and their prices. You can use the SUM function to total the kite prices in cell B12.

QUICK TIP

When using Formula AutoComplete to enter a function, you can type either capital or lowercase letters; the feature is not case sensitive.

2. Click cell B12, type =, then type s

See **FIGURE H-5**. A list of functions beginning with the letter "S" appears below cell A12. Anytime you type an equal sign followed by a letter, a list of valid functions and names beginning with that letter appears. This feature is called **Formula AutoComplete**. Notice that the first function in the AutoComplete list, SEARCH, is selected, and that a description of it appears in a ScreenTip to help guide you.

QUICK TIP

You can also insert a function from the list by first selecting the function you want, then pressing [Tab].

3. Type u

Typing the letter "U" shortens the list, so only the functions beginning with "SU" are listed. The SUM function is one of the most commonly used functions.

4. Double-click SUM in the list of functions

Now SUM is entered into cell B12 along with an open parenthesis. A ScreenTip appears below cell B12 showing the proper structure for the SUM function. The placeholders, number1 and number2, indicate arguments, which should be separated by commas; you can insert values, cell references, or ranges. The ellipsis (...) indicates that you can include as many arguments as you wish.

5. Select cells B6:B11, then click the Enter button ☑ on the formula bar

The formula bar displays the function =SUM(B6:B11), and cell B12 displays the value $189.70, which is the result of the function. Notice that Excel automatically added a closing parenthesis for the formula, as shown in **FIGURE H-6**.

6. Click the FORMULAS tab

The FORMULAS tab contains commands for adding and working with formulas and functions. The Function Library group lets you choose a function by category or by using the Insert Function command. In cell B13, you need to use a function that returns the number of cells that contain kite prices.

7. Click cell B13, click the AutoSum button arrow in the Function Library group, then click Count Numbers

Notice that all the cells containing numbers directly above cell B13 are highlighted. Excel is "guessing" that you want to reference all of these cells because they are adjacent to the active cell. You do not want to select the total in cell B12, so you need to select just the cells with prices.

8. Select the range B6:B11, then click ☑

Cell B13 displays 6. The formula bar contains the formula =COUNT(B6:B11). See **FIGURE H-7**.

9. Click the Sheet1 tab, then save your changes

The Sheet1 worksheet containing the northeast region sales information is open on your screen.

FIGURE H-5: Entering a formula using Formula AutoComplete

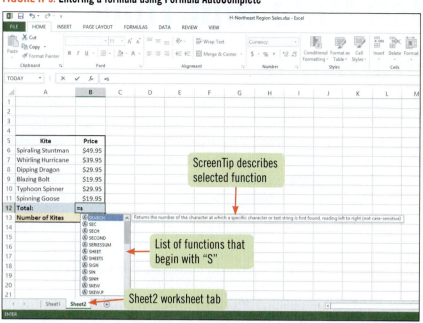

ScreenTip describes selected function

List of functions that begin with "S"

Sheet2 worksheet tab

FIGURE H-6: Completed formula containing the SUM function

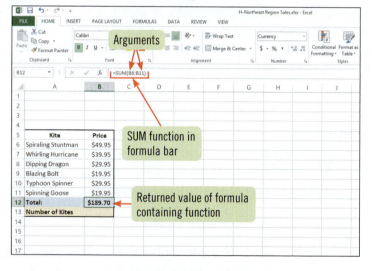

Arguments

SUM function in formula bar

Returned value of formula containing function

FIGURE H-7: Completed formula containing the COUNT function

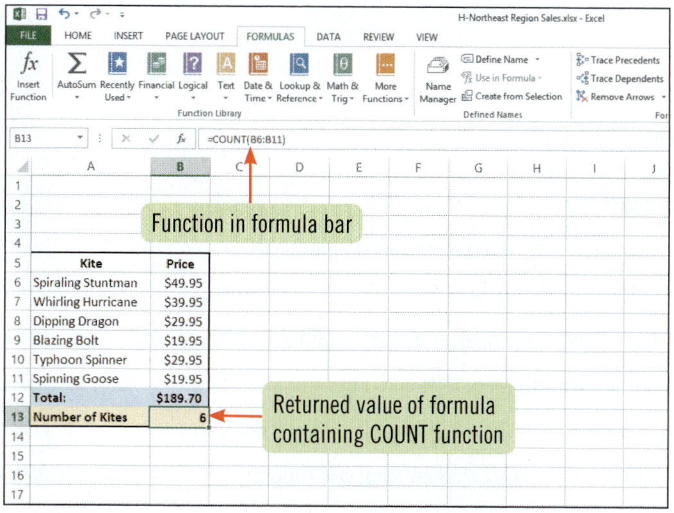

Function in formula bar

Returned value of formula containing COUNT function

Using Complex Formulas, Functions, and Tables

Use Date and Time Functions

Learning Outcomes
- Explain date and time functions
- Use the TODAY function

There are many categories of functions in Excel. See **TABLE H-2** for a list of common ones. The Excel date and time functions let you display the current date and/or time in your worksheet, and they can help you calculate the time between events. Some date and time functions produce recognizable text values that you can display "as is" in your worksheets. Other date and time functions produce values that require special formatting. **CASE** ▶ *You need to use the TODAY function to enter the current date in the worksheet. You also need to use a formula to calculate the date that commission checks are due.*

STEPS

1. **Click cell B3**

   This cell is to the right of the label "Today's date." You want to enter a function in this cell that returns today's date.

2. **Click the Date & Time button in the Function Library group**

   The list of date and time functions opens. You can point to any item to view a ScreenTip that describes the purpose of that function.

3. **Point to TODAY in the list of functions, as shown in FIGURE H-8, then click it**

   The Function Arguments dialog box opens, as shown in **FIGURE H-9**. The description in the dialog box explains that the TODAY function returns the current date. It also explains that the TODAY function requires no arguments, so you do not need to add values between the parentheses in the formula.

   QUICK TIP
   The TODAY function uses your computer's internal clock to return current date information, and recalculates this result as needed.

4. **Click OK**

   The result of this function, the current date, appears in cell B3.

5. **Click cell B18**

   You want to enter a formula in this cell that returns the date that is 30 days from the date in cell B17, which was the closing date for March.

6. **Type =, press [↑] to select cell B17, then type +30**

   The formula you entered, =B17+30, calculates the day when commission checks are issued, which is 30 days after the date in cell B17.

7. **Click the Enter button ✓ on the formula bar, then save your changes**

   The commission due date (4/29/2016) appears in cell B18, as shown in **FIGURE H-10**.

TABLE H-2: Categories of common worksheet functions

category	used for	includes
Financial	Loan payments, appreciation, and depreciation	PMT, FV, DB, SLN
Logical	Calculations that display a value if a condition is met	IF, AND, NOT
Text	Comparing, converting, and reformatting text strings in cells	FIND, REPLACE
Date & Time	Calculations involving dates and times	NOW, TODAY, WEEKDAY
Lookup & Reference	Finding values in lists or tables or finding cell references	ADDRESS, ROW, COLUMN
Math & Trig	Simple and complex mathematical calculations	ABS, ASIN, COS

Using Complex Formulas, Functions, and Tables

FIGURE H-8: Inserting the TODAY function

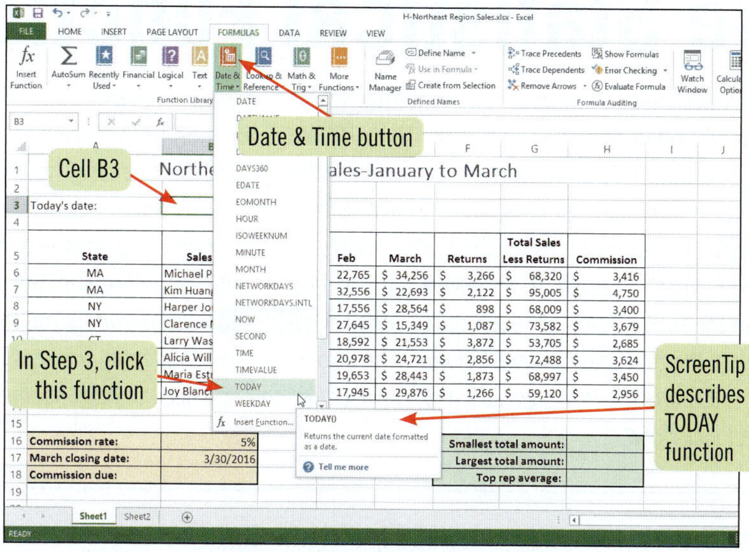

FIGURE H-9: Function Arguments dialog box

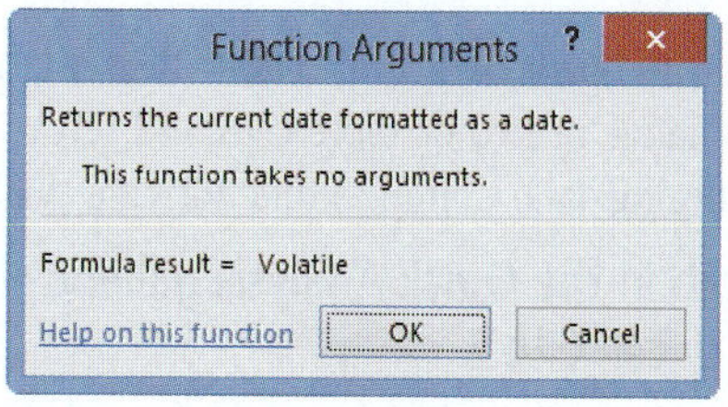

FIGURE H-10: Northeast Region Sales worksheet after adding date functions

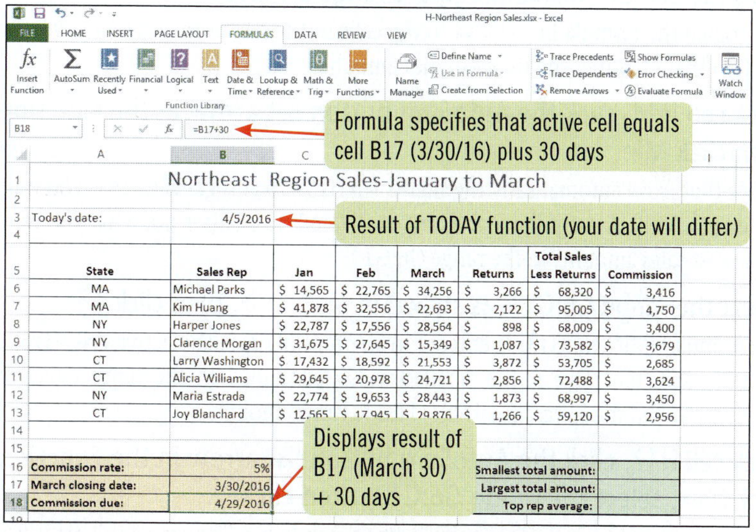

Understanding how dates are calculated using serial values

When you enter a date in a worksheet cell, the date appears in a familiar format (such as May 20, 2016), but it is actually stored as a serial value. A **serial value** is a number in a sequential series of numbers. Date serial values represent the number of days since January 1, 1900. Dates are stored as serial values so they can be used in calculations. For example, in this lesson, you added 30 days to the date March 30, 2016. To Excel, the formula in cell B18 (shown in **FIGURE H-10**) is really =42459+30. This is useful to

know if you remove formatting from a cell previously formatted as a date, or apply the General format to a cell containing a date. Instead of displaying the date, Excel displays the serial value that represents that date. To make the cell contents recognizable again, right-click the cell, click Format Cells to open the Format Cells dialog box, click Date in the Category list, choose a date format in the Type list, then click OK.

Use Statistical Functions

Excel includes many statistical functions that let you analyze numeric data. Three common statistical functions are AVERAGE, MIN, and MAX. The **AVERAGE** function lets you calculate the average of a range of cells. The **MIN** function returns the smallest value in a range of cells. The **MAX** function returns the highest value in a range of cells. You can access these functions quickly using the AutoSum list menu on the FORMULAS tab, or by using the Quick Analysis gallery, which provides easy access to common functions and formatting tools. To access all statistical functions, click More Functions in the Function Library group on the FORMULAS tab, then click Statistical. **CASE** *Serena wants you to insert formulas in row 14 to calculate the averages for each column. She also wants you to identify the reps who had the biggest and smallest totals and the top sales rep's monthly average. You also need to add shading and borders to make the worksheet look good.*

STEPS

1. **Type the label Average: in cell B14, click the Enter button ✓ on the formula bar, select the range C6:C13, then click the Quick Analysis button 📧 that appears just below and to the right of cell C13**

   The Quick Analysis gallery opens, with the FORMATTING tab active. The Quick Analysis button appears whenever you select a range of two or more cells and gives you easy access to frequently used tools for formatting cells or analyzing data. Common functions are available on the TOTALS tab.

2. **Click the TOTALS tab in the Quick Analysis gallery, click the Average button as shown in FIGURE H-11, then click cell C14**

   The value $24,165 now appears in cell C14, and the formula bar contains the function AVERAGE(C6:C13).

3. **Drag the cell C14 fill handle to the range D14:H14**

   You copied the formula in cell C14 to the cells in the rest of the row. Now you need to enter a formula in cell H16 that identifies the smallest sales amount.

4. **Click cell H16, click the AutoSum button list arrow in the Function Library group, then click Min**

   Notice that Excel automatically highlights H6:H15. Excel is guessing that you want to look for the smallest value in the cells directly above the active cell (H6:H15). This is not what you want to do; you want to find the lowest sales amounts in the range G6:G13.

5. **Select the range G6:G13, as shown in FIGURE H-12, then click ✓**

   The formula =MIN(G6:G13) is entered in the formula bar. The active cell (H16) displays the result of the formula ($53,705). This is the smallest value contained in the range G6:G13 and tells us that Larry Washington had the lowest Total Sales Less Returns amount.

6. **Click cell H17, click the AutoSum button list arrow in the Function Library group, click Max, select the range G6:G13, then click ✓**

   The formula =MAX(G6:G13) appears in the formula bar. The active cell H17 displays the formula's result ($95,005). This amount, found in cell G7, is the Total Sales Less Returns amount for Kim Huang. Next you need to enter a function in cell H18 that calculates the monthly average of the top rep (Kim Huang).

7. **Click cell H18, click the AutoSum button list arrow in the Function Library group, click Average, select the range C7:E7, then click ✓**

   Cell H18 displays the formula's result ($32,376), which is Kim Huang's average sales amount.

8. **Click the HOME tab, select the range A14:H14, click the Fill Color button list arrow in the Font group, click the lightest shade of green (second row, 10th color), click the Borders button list arrow in the Font group, click All Borders, click cell H18, then click 💾**

   Row 14 now has light green shading and borders around each cell. Compare your screen to FIGURE H-13.

Using Complex Formulas, Functions, and Tables

FIGURE H-11: Inserting the AVERAGE function using the Quick Analysis gallery

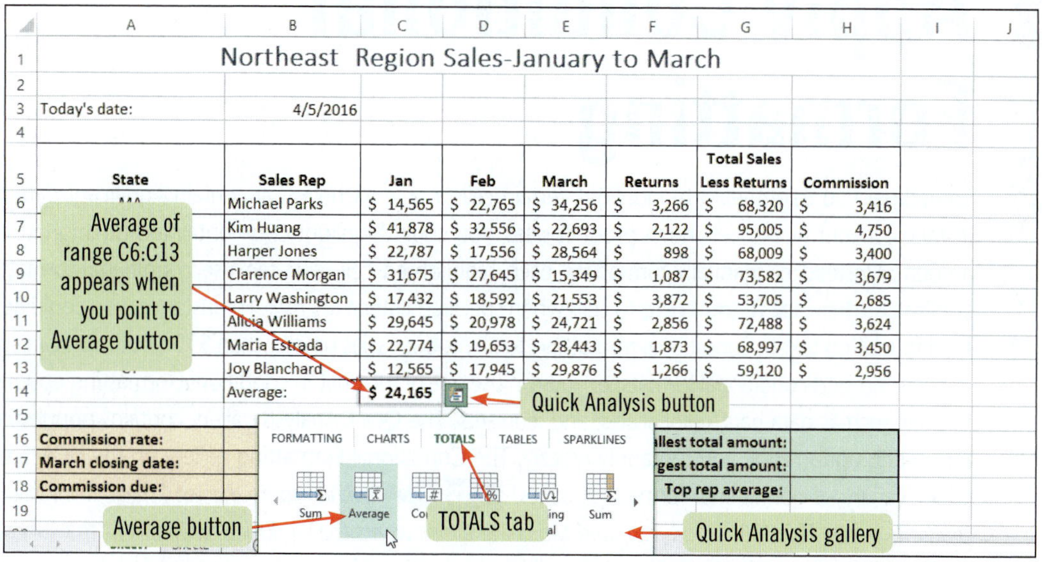

FIGURE H-12: Using the MIN function

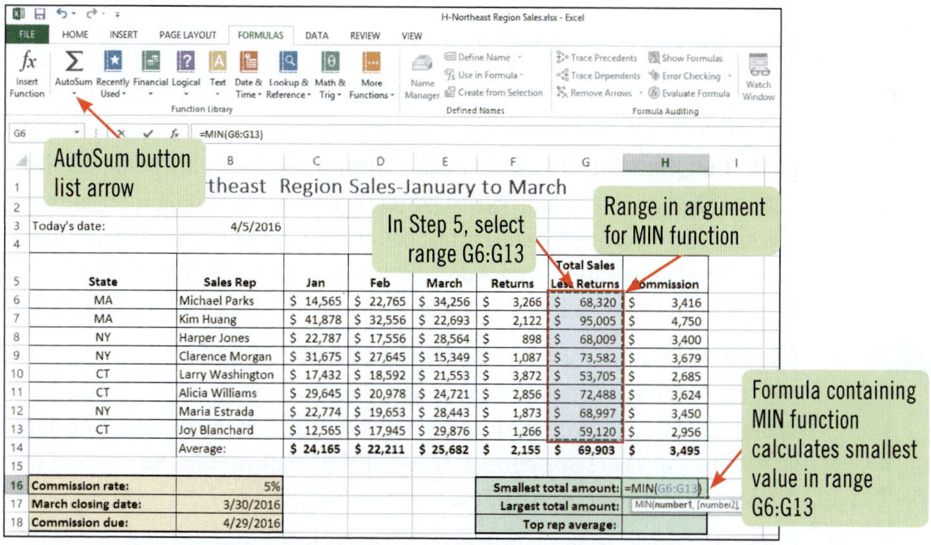

FIGURE H-13: Worksheet with functions added and borders and shading applied

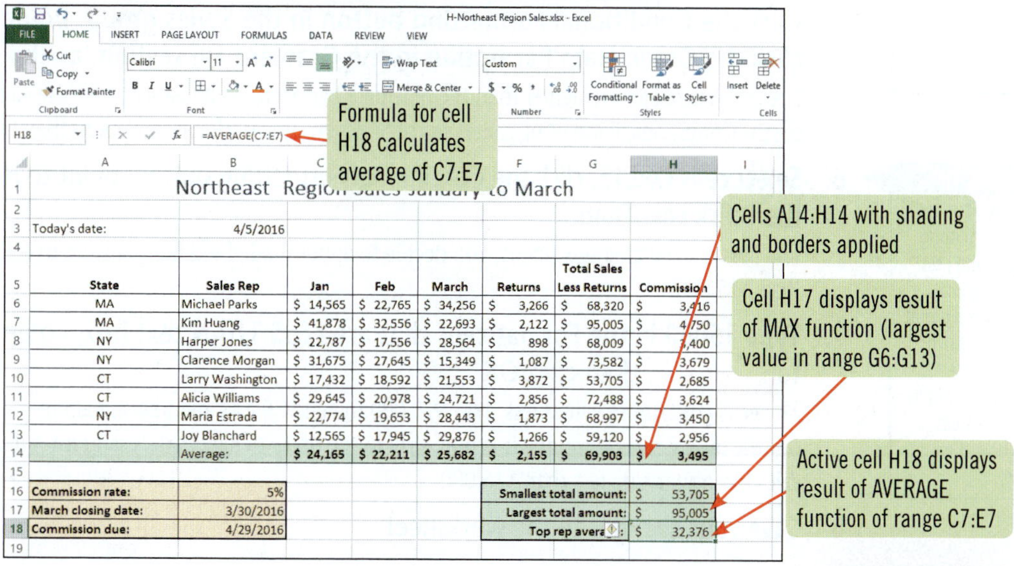

Using Complex Formulas, Functions, and Tables

Apply Conditional Formatting

Sometimes you might want to highlight certain cells in a worksheet that contain significant data points. For instance, if your worksheet shows product sales, you could highlight cells containing the highest and lowest amounts. Instead of manually formatting each highlighted cell, you can use conditional formatting. Excel applies **conditional formatting** to cells when specified criteria are met. For instance, you could apply green, bold formatted text as conditional formatting to all product sales greater than $100,000. You can specify your own customized conditional formats, or you can use one of the built-in conditional formatting options available in Excel such as data bars, color scales, and icon sets. The Quick Analysis gallery contains popular conditional formatting options that you can apply quickly. The Conditional Formatting gallery on the HOME tab offers a wider variety of conditional formatting styles. **CASE** *Serena wants the worksheet to highlight all sales amounts below $15,000 for Jan, Feb, and March. She also wants the worksheet to highlight the varying values in the Total Sales Less Returns cells. You explore different conditional formatting options to find the right effect.*

STEPS

1. Select the cell range G6:G13

You selected the cells in the Total Sales Less Returns column. These cells display the total sales amounts for each rep (minus returns).

2. Click the Quick Analysis button 📧, then point to Color Scale as shown in FIGURE H-14

Color scales are shading patterns that use two or three colors to show the relative values of a range of cells. The selected cells now contain shading gradations of different red and green shades. The green shades highlight the values that are above average; the red shades highlight the values that are below average. The darkest shades are the highest and lowest values. You decide to remove this shading so you can explore other conditional formats.

3. Click the Data Bars button in the Quick Analysis gallery

The cells in the selected range now contain blue shading. The cells with the highest values have the most shading, and the cells with the lowest values have the least. **Data bars** make it easy to quickly identify the large and small values in a range of cells and also highlight the relative value of cells to one another. You decide to clear the blue data bars and explore other options.

4. Click the Quick Analysis button 📧, then click Clear Format

With the conditional formatting rules cleared, the blue data bars no longer appear in the selected cells.

5. Click the Conditional Formatting button in the Styles group, point to Data Bars, then click the Green Data Bar option in the Gradient Fill section, as shown in FIGURE H-15

The green data bars are lighter than the blue data bars were, so it's easier to see the values in each cell. You can see the Conditional Formatting gallery in the Styles group has a lot more options than the Quick Analysis gallery.

6. Select cells C6:E13, click the Conditional Formatting button, point to Highlight Cells Rules, then click Less Than

The Less Than dialog box opens. You decide to apply shaded red highlighting to cells containing values less than $15,000.

7. Type 15000 in the Format cells that are LESS THAN text box, compare your screen to FIGURE H-16, then click OK

The cells containing values less than $15,000 in cells C6:E13 are now shaded in red, making it easy to pick out the lowest sales amounts. It is now easy to see that Michael Parks's sales for January and Joy Blanchard's sales for January are less than $15,000.

8. Save your changes to the worksheet

Using Complex Formulas, Functions, and Tables

FIGURE H-14: Applying Color Scales conditional formatting using the Quick Analysis gallery

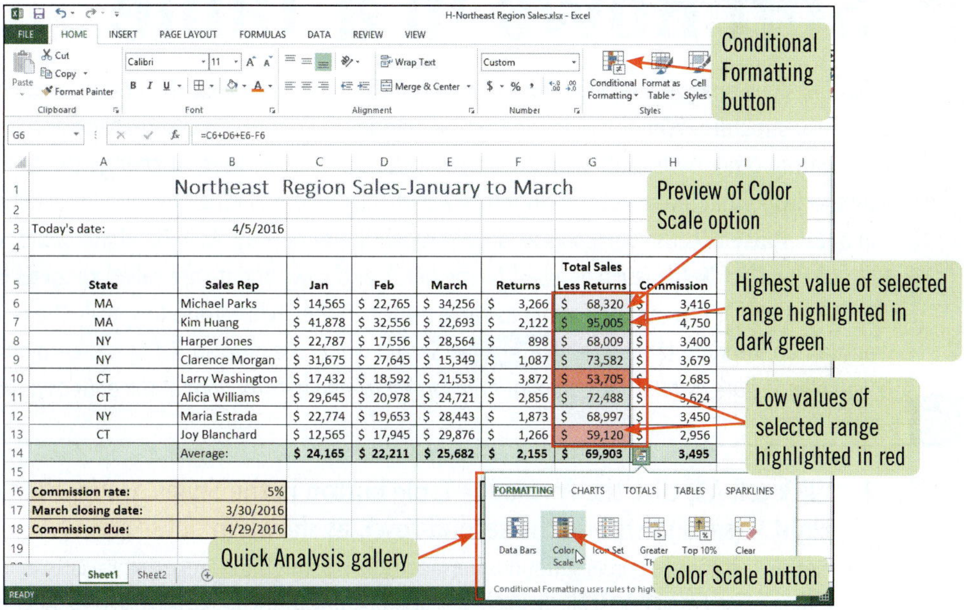

FIGURE H-15: Applying data bars to selected cells

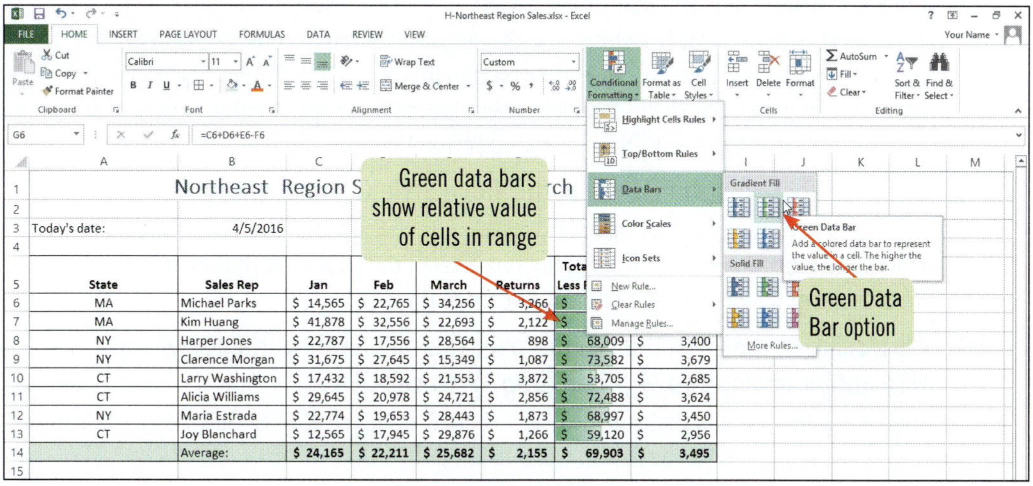

FIGURE H-16: Less Than dialog box with conditional format rules specified

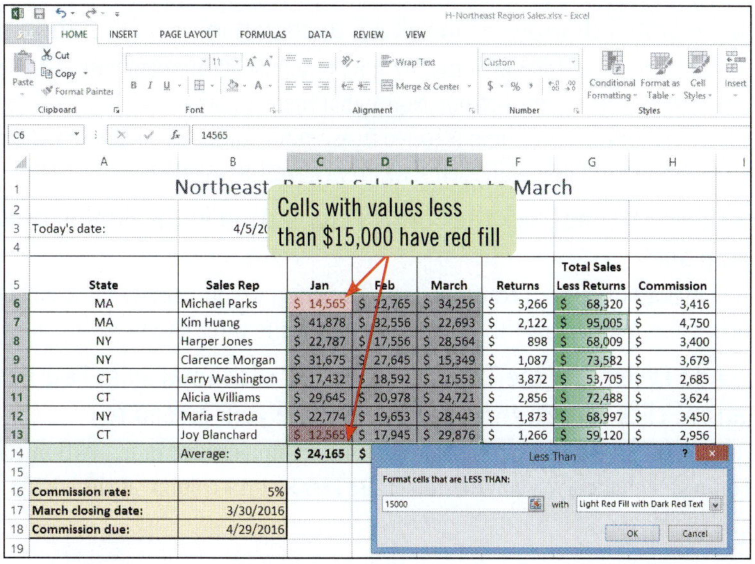

Excel 2013

Sort Rows in a Table

Excel lets you analyze a separate range of worksheet data called a **table**, or rows and columns of data with a similar structure. When you designate a cell range as a table, you can manage and analyze its data separately from other parts of the worksheet. For instance, you can **sort**, or change the order of the table rows, by specifying that the rows be arranged by a particular column in the table. An Excel table is similar to a table in a **database** because you can sort data in much the same way. As in database tables, Excel table columns are often called **fields** (such as a Last Name field), and rows of data are called **records** (such as a record for each customer). You use the Format as Table button in the Styles group to specify the cell range for the table and an appropriate table style. **CASE** ▶ *Serena wants the data sorted by state—alphabetically—and then within each state by total sales amount from largest to smallest. You format the data as a table in order to sort it.*

STEPS

1. **Click cell A5, click the Format as Table button in the Styles group, then click Table Style Light 9 (second style in the second row), as shown in FIGURE H-17**

   Notice that a dotted border surrounds the range A5:H13; this is the range that Excel assumes you want to format as table. The Format As Table dialog box is also open, with the range $A$5:$H$13 specified. The My table has headers check box is selected. In a table, the **header row** is the row at the top that contains column headings.

2. **Click OK, then click any cell in the table**

   The Format as Table dialog box closes, and the range you selected is now defined as a table. Notice that each cell in the header row contains a list arrow on its right edge. On the TABLE TOOLS DESIGN tab in the Table Style Options group, notice the Total Row check box is deselected. A **total row** is an extra row at the bottom of a table that Excel adds. You want to add a Total row to the table.

3. **Click the Total Row check box in the Table Style Options group**

   Row 14 now contains a Total label (in cell A14). By default, the last cell in the Total row contains the SUBTOTAL function, which calculates the sum total of the table's last column of data. Cell H14 now shows the subtotal of the Commission cells (for the range H6:H13).

4. **Click cell H14, position the pointer over the fill handle in the lower-right corner of cell H14 until it changes to ✛, then drag ✛ to cell C14**

   You copied the formula that summed cells H6:H13 from cell H14 to cells C14:G14. Now cells C14:G14 display the sum totals for the data in columns C through G.

5. **If row 14 contains cells that display ##### in them, widen the columns so all the values in those cells are visible**

6. **Click the State list arrow ⊡ in cell A5, as shown in FIGURE H-18, then click Sort A to Z**

   The items in the table are now sorted by state in alphabetical order, with the Connecticut reps at the top and the New York reps at the bottom. Notice that there is now a small Up arrow to the right of the list arrow in cell A5, indicating this column is sorted in ascending order (or smallest to largest). Serena also wants the list to be sorted by totals within each state, from largest to smallest.

7. **Click the HOME tab, click the Sort & Filter button in the Editing group, then click Custom Sort**

   The Sort dialog box opens. Because you already performed one sort on this data, your sort criteria is listed in the dialog box. You can use this dialog box to sort up to three levels.

8. **Click Add Level, click the Then by list arrow, click Total Sales Less Returns, click the Order list arrow, click Largest to Smallest, compare your screen to FIGURE H-19, then click OK**

   The list is now sorted first by the State column in alphabetical order. Within each State listing, the cells containing the highest value in the Total Sales Less Returns column are listed first, as shown in FIGURE H-20.

9. **Save your changes**

Using Complex Formulas, Functions, and Tables

FIGURE H-17: Choosing a table style and defining a table range

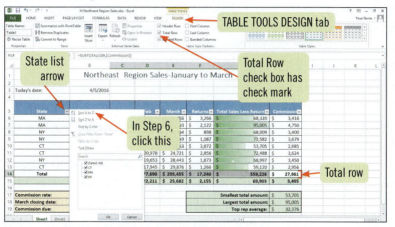

FIGURE H-18: Sorting a list from A to Z

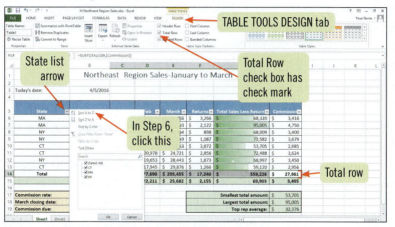

FIGURE H-19: Sort dialog box

FIGURE H-20: Table sorted by two sort criteria

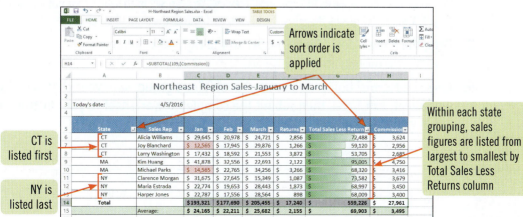

Filter Table Data

If your Excel table contains a large amount of data, you might want to **filter** it to display only the data you need. Applying a filter tells Excel to show only those rows that meet specific requirements, such as customers with a particular zip code, or orders that exceed a certain dollar amount. When you tell Excel which rows in a table you want to see, you are specifying the **criteria** for your filter. Just as when you sort data in a table, you can apply a filter to a table by using the filter list arrows that appear to the right of each column heading. Unlike a sort, a filter does not change the order of the items in your table; instead, it temporarily hides the rows that do not meet your criteria. **CASE** *Serena wants you to filter the table data so it shows only the sales reps for New York and Connecticut whose sales amounts are less than $70,000.*

STEPS

1. **Click the State list arrow** ▾ **in cell A5**

   The filter drop-down list opens and displays the list of available filters for this column. Excel creates filters for each of the values in the column, plus filters to automatically select all values, custom values, specified text, or numeric values. You can even filter a table by cell color.

2. **Click the (Select All) check box**

   The check marks are now removed from all the check boxes. You want to check the CT and NY check boxes, to specify that rows containing CT and NY in the States column be displayed.

3. **Click the CT check box, click the NY check box, compare your screen to FIGURE H-21, then click OK**

   You have applied a filter that shows only the rows that contain the values CT and NY in the State column (six rows). You can tell that the table is filtered because the arrow in the column header contains a filter icon ⎙, and the row numbers have breaks in their numeric sequence.

4. **Click the Total Sales Less Returns list arrow in cell G5, point to Number Filters, then click Less Than**

   The Custom AutoFilter dialog box opens. You use this dialog box to specify one or more criteria for a filter. The list box below Total Sales Less Returns displays "is less than," and the insertion point is in the box where you need to specify an amount.

5. **Type 70000, compare your screen to FIGURE H-22, then click OK**

   The table is filtered to show sales reps whose Total Sales Less Returns amounts are less than $70,000, as shown in **FIGURE H-23**. Now the table displays only four rows. By using the filter drop-down arrows in succession like this, you can apply more than one criterion to the same data in your table.

6. **Type your name in cell A22, then click** ✓

7. **Click the VIEW tab, then click Page Break Preview**

   The worksheet now appears in Page Break Preview. You can see in this view that not all the columns fit on page 1. You can fix this by dragging the blue dotted line to the right of column H.

8. **Drag the Page 1 dotted blue border to the right of column H**

   Now all of the columns fit on one page. See **FIGURE H-24**.

9. **Click the Normal button in the Workbook Views group, save your changes, close the worksheet, exit Excel, then submit the completed worksheet to your instructor**

FIGURE H-21: Applying filters to the State column

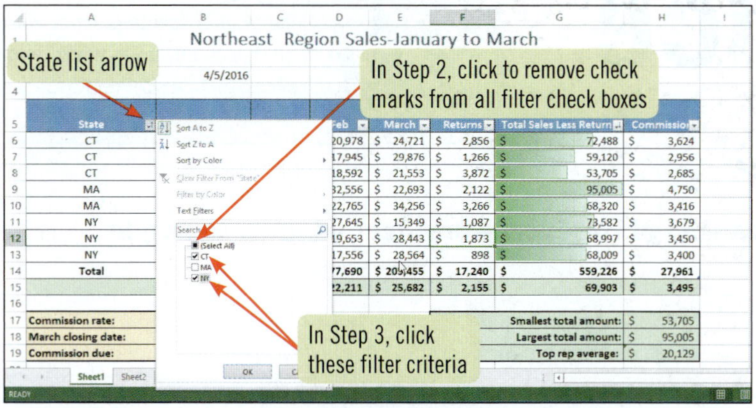

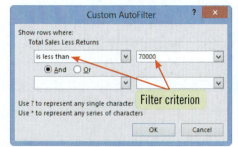

State list arrow

In Step 2, click to remove check marks from all filter check boxes

In Step 3, click these filter criteria

FIGURE H-22: Custom AutoFilter dialog box

Filter criterion

FIGURE H-23: Worksheet with two filters applied

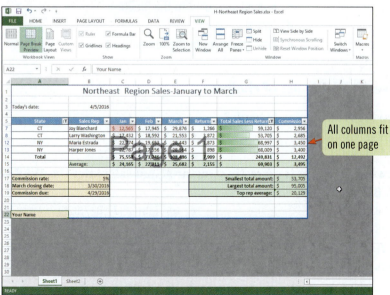

State column header list arrow (icon indicates filter is applied)

Only items with CT and NY in column A appear

Total Sales Less Returns list arrow (icon indicates filter is applied)

Row headings have breaks in their numeric sequence

All amounts are less than 70,000

FIGURE H-24: Worksheet in Page Break Preview

All columns fit on one page

Using Complex Formulas, Functions, and Tables

Practice

Put your skills into practice with SAM! If you have a SAM account, go to www.cengage.com/sam2013 to access SAM assignments for this unit.

Concepts Review

Label each of the elements of the Excel worksheet window shown in FIGURE H-25.

FIGURE H-25

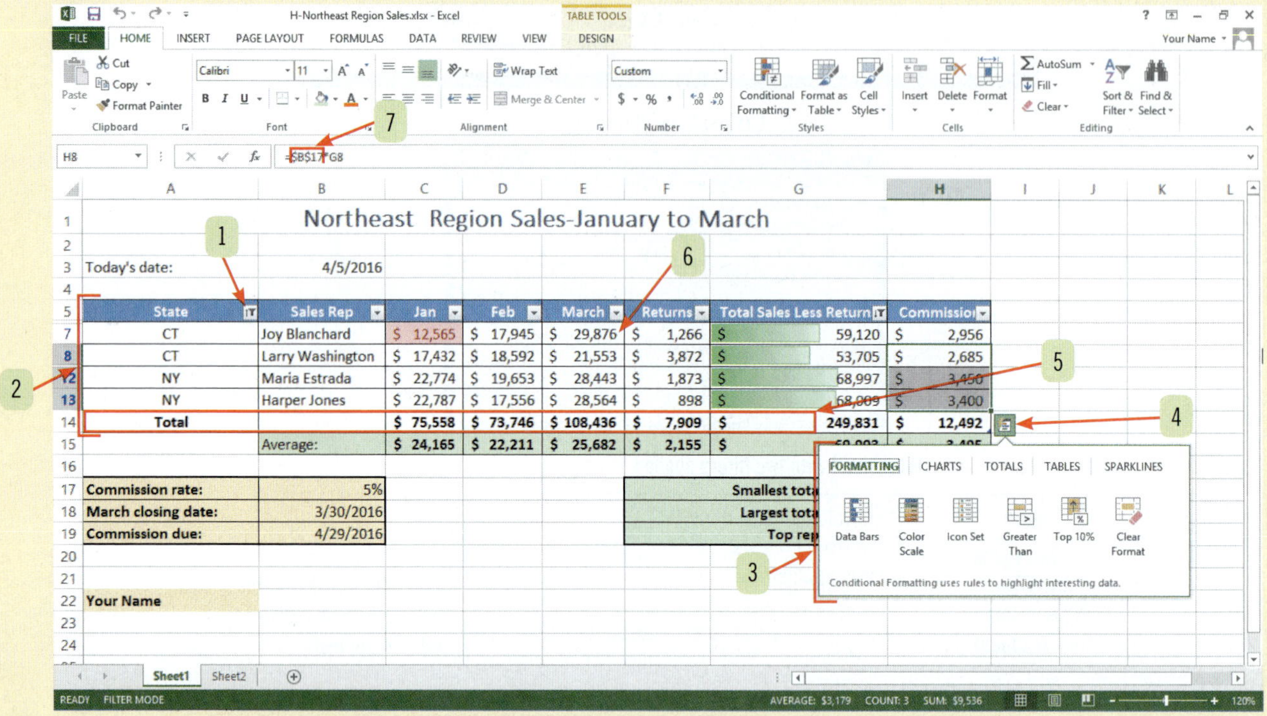

Match components of the formula =SUM(B4:H8,K2:L9) with their descriptions.

8. ,
9. =
10. B4:H8
11. SUM
12. K2:L9

a. Symbol that separates arguments in functions
b. Symbol that indicates beginning of a formula
c. Second argument in the function
d. Function name
e. First argument in the function

Select the best answer from the list of choices.

13. Which of the following is a complex formula?

a. =COUNT(H123:H124)
b. =B7+7844
c. =(E2*E3)+.88
d. =MAX(D47:H224)

14. Which of the following functions is correctly structured and calculates the AVERAGE of 88 plus the values in cells B27, B28, and B29?

a. =AVERAGE(88,B28,B29)
b. =AVERAGE(88,B27:B29)
c. =AVERAGE(77,B27:B29)
d. =AVERAGE(88,B27,B29)

15. In the formula =COUNT(H25:H26, J8:J10), which of the following are the arguments?

a. H25, H26, H28, and J10
b. H25 and J8
c. J8:J10, H25
d. H25:H26 and J8:J10

16. **In a complex formula, which of the following is evaluated first?**
   - **a.** * Multiplication
   - **b.** () Items in parentheses
   - **c.** - Subtraction
   - **d.** + Addition
17. **Which of the following functions returns the value 1776?**
   - **a.** =MIN(41,1776,176,1670)
   - **b.** =AVERAGE(176,107,106)
   - **c.** =MAX(176, 1776,1676)
   - **d.** =SUM((40*2)-10)
18. **What value would Excel return in calculating the formula =SUM(10,MAX(2,3,4))?**
   - **a.** 40
   - **b.** 20
   - **c.** 13
   - **d.** 14
19. **What value would Excel return in calculating the formula =MIN(8,(2*2),100,(40+2),10)?**
   - **a.** 4
   - **b.** 42
   - **c.** 10
   - **d.** 2

Skills Review

1. **Create complex formulas.**
   - **a.** Start Excel, open the file H-2.xlsx from where your Data Files are stored, then save it as **H-June Orders**.
   - **b.** Enter a complex formula in cell G6 that calculates the sum of cells D6 and E6 minus the value in cell F6.
   - **c.** Copy the formula from cell G6 to the range G7:G14, then save your changes.

2. **Use absolute cell references.**
   - **a.** In cell H6, enter a formula that multiplies the value in cell D6 by the value in B17, using an absolute cell reference for B17.
   - **b.** Use the fill handle to copy the formula in cell H6 to cells H7:H14.
   - **c.** Click cell H7. Look at the formula bar and notice the absolute reference to cell B17 is in the formula.
   - **d.** Change the value in cell B17 to **8%**, then click the Enter button. Notice that all values in the range H6:H14 that contained the absolute cell reference $B$17 increased to reflect the new percentage in B17.

3. **Understand functions.**
   - **a.** Click the Sheet2 worksheet tab. Notice the list of June specials with the list of Items and prices.
   - **b.** Click cell B11, type **=**, type **su** to display a list of functions beginning with "su", then double-click SUM.
   - **c.** Select cells B5:B10, then click the Enter button on the formula bar. Notice the Total amount of all the prices in cell B11.
   - **d.** Click the FORMULAS tab, then click cell B12, which is where you need to enter a formula that counts the number of items in the June Special list.
   - **e.** Click the AutoSum button list arrow in the Function Library group, click Count Numbers, select the range B5:B10, then click the Enter button. Notice the value in cell B12, which tells you how many items are in the June Special list.
   - **f.** Click the Sheet1 tab, then save your changes.

4. **Use date and time functions.**
   - **a.** Use the TODAY function to enter today's date in cell B22.
   - **b.** Enter a formula in cell J6 that calculates the date that is 30 days later than the Order Date for Good Times Coffee Shop.
   - **c.** Use the fill handle to copy the formula in cell J6 to cells J7:J14. Save your changes.

5. **Use statistical functions.**
   - **a.** Enter the label **Average:** in cell C15.
   - **b.** Select the range D6:D14, open the Quick Analysis gallery, then click the Average button on the TOTALS tab. Notice the value for the average order that now appears in cell D15.
   - **c.** Copy the formula in cell D15 to the range E15:G15 using the D15 fill handle.
   - **d.** Enter a formula in J17 that calculates the largest June order in the range D6:D14.
   - **e.** Enter a formula in cell J18 that determines the smallest June order in the range D6:D14.

f. Enter a formula in cell J19 that calculates the average June delivery cost for the range H6:H14.

g. Make the HOME tab active, then apply Blue, Accent 1, Lighter 80% shading to the range C15:G15. Apply borders to the range C15:G15 using the All Borders setting. Apply bold formatting to the Average: label in cell C15.

6. Apply conditional formatting.

a. Select the range D6:D14.

b. Open the Quick Analysis gallery, then preview the Color Scale conditional format.

c. Apply the Data Bars conditional format to the selected range.

d. Clear the Data Bars conditional formatting using a button in the Quick Analysis gallery.

e. Open the Conditional Formatting gallery in the Styles group, then apply the Orange Data Bar conditional format from the Gradient Fill section to the selected range (D6:D14).

f. Select the range G6:G14, then apply conditional formatting to the cells in this range, specifying that all cells containing values greater than 500 be formatted in Light Red Fill with Dark Red Text. Save your changes.

7. Sort rows in a table.

a. Format the cell range A5:J14 as a table, applying Table Style Light 10 (red style in second row of Table Styles gallery).

b. Specify to add a Total row to the table. Delete the value in cell J15 of the Total row (because it is a date). Click cell D15, click the cell D15 down arrow, then click Sum.

c. Drag the cell D15 fill handle to cell H15.

d. Sort the table in alphabetical order by Town.

e. Use the Sort dialog box to sort the list data first by Town in alphabetical order, then by June Order Amount in largest to smallest order. Save your changes.

8. Filter table data.

a. Apply a filter so only the rows containing Channel City and Gulverton appear.

b. Apply a custom filter to the filtered table that displays only those items whose Balance Due amount is greater than $300. Enter your name in cell A25 of the worksheet.

c. Click the PAGE LAYOUT tab, click the Orientation list arrow in the Page Setup group, then click Landscape.

d. View the worksheet in Page Break Preview. Drag the dotted blue bar to the right so all the columns in the table fit on one page.

e. View the worksheet in Print Preview, then adjust the scaling so all columns fit on one sheet.

f. Compare your completed worksheet to **FIGURE H-26**. Save your changes, close the workbook, then exit Excel. Submit your completed workbook to your instructor.

FIGURE H-26

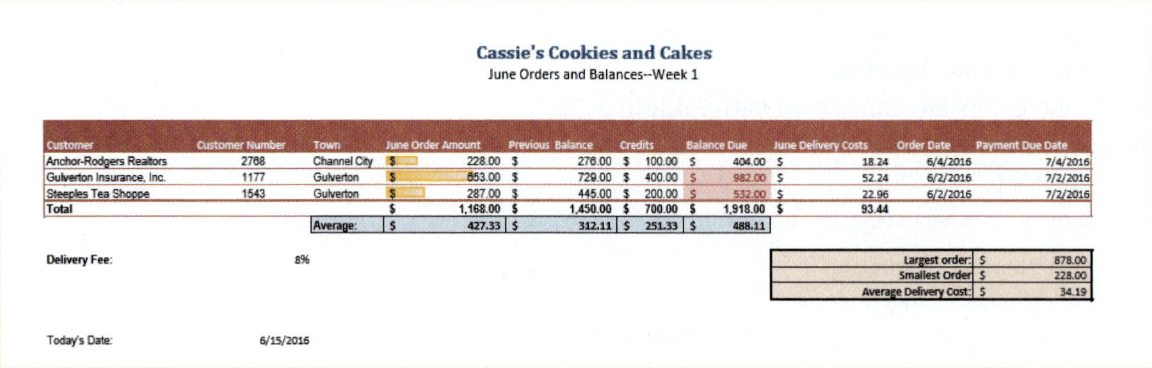

Cassie's Cookies and Cakes
June Orders and Balances--Week 1

Customer	Customer Number	Town	June Order Amount	Previous Balance	Credits	Balance Due	June Delivery Costs	Order Date	Payment Due Date
Anchor-Rodgers Realtors	2788	Channel City	$ 228.00	$ 276.00	$ 100.00	$ 404.00	$ 18.24	6/4/2016	7/4/2016
Gulverton Insurance, Inc.	1177	Gulverton	$ 653.00	$ 729.00	$ 400.00	$ 982.00	$ 52.24	6/2/2016	7/2/2016
Steeples Tea Shoppe	1543	Gulverton	$ 287.00	$ 445.00	$ 200.00	$ 532.00	$ 22.96	6/2/2016	7/2/2016
Total			$ 1,168.00	$ 1,450.00	$ 700.00	$ 1,918.00	$ 93.44		
		Average:	$ 427.33	$ 312.11	$ 251.33	$ 488.11			

Delivery Fee:	8%

Largest order:	$	878.00
Smallest Order	$	228.00
Average Delivery Cost:	$	34.19

Today's Date:	6/15/2016

Independent Challenge 1

You are the sales manager for the West region at Red Condor Coffees and Tea, Inc. You need to complete a worksheet that analyzes sales results for each state in your region. In addition, you need to highlight the total sales, the average sales, and the best and worst performing sales regions. You also need to calculate the bonuses for each sales rep. To calculate the bonus amount, you need to create a formula that multiplies their total sales by 3%.

a. Start Excel, open the file H-3.xlsx from where you store your Data Files, then save it as **H-Red Condor Q1 Sales**.

b. In cell E5, enter a formula that subtracts the value in D5 (Q1 Sales Prior Year) from the value in cell C5 (Q1 Sales). Use the fill handle to copy the formula to cells E6:E15.

c. Enter a formula in cell F5 that calculates the percentage that Q1 Sales increased over Q1 Sales in the prior year. (*Hint*: Your formula needs to divide the value in cell E5 by the value in cell D5.) Use the fill handle to copy the formula to cells F6:F15.

d. In cell B17, use the AVERAGE function to compute the average sales total for all states. (*Hint*: Specify the range C5:C15.)

e. In cell B18, use the MAX function to calculate the maximum (or highest) Q1 sales total for the states.

f. In cell B19, use the MIN function to compute the minimum (or lowest) Q1 sales total for the states.

g. Define the range A4:F15 as a table, and apply table style Table Style Medium 3. Include a Total row. Delete the value in cell F16. Click cell E16, click the down arrow in cell E16, then click Sum. Drag the E16 fill handle to cells D16:C16.

h. Sort the data in the table by the Sales Rep column (column B) in order from A to Z. Using the Custom Sort dialog box, apply a second sort level that sorts by Q1 Sales vs. Prior Year Q1 ($) from largest to smallest.

i. In cell B22, use the AVERAGE function to compute the average Q1 increase (as a percentage) for Carson Johnson's states. (Use the range F5:F8.)

j. In cell B23, use the AVERAGE function to compute the average Q1 increase (as a percentage) for Lila Rivers's states. (Use the range F9:F11.)

k. In cell B24, use the AVERAGE function to compute the average Q1 increase (as a percentage) for Manuel Garcia's states. (Use the range F12:F15.)

l. Apply Blue Data Bar Gradient Fill conditional formatting to the range E5: E15.

m. Enter a formula in cell F22 that calculates Carson Johnson's bonus amount. (*Hint*: The formula needs to multiply cell F19 by the sum of cells C5:C8. Be sure to use an absolute cell reference for F19.)

n. Enter a formula in cell F23 that calculates Lila Rivers's bonus amount. (*Hint*: The formula needs to multiply cell F19 by the sum of cells C9:C11. Be sure to use an absolute cell reference for F19.)

o. Enter a formula in cell F24 that calculates Manuel Garcia's bonus amount. (*Hint*: The formula needs to multiply cell F19 by the sum of cells C12:C15.) Enter your name in cell A26.

p. Preview the worksheet in Backstage view. Change the orientation to landscape. View the worksheet in Page Break Preview and, if necessary, adjust the page breaks so all columns fit on one sheet.

q. Save your changes, close the workbook, then exit Excel. Submit your completed worksheet to your instructor.

Independent Challenge 2

Anna Barstow, the sales director at Plaxco-Perez Windows and Doors, Inc., has just received the raw sales data for the first week of October. She has asked you to finish creating a worksheet that she started. Anna wants you to calculate the commission amount for each rep, which is 5% of the order amount, and then show the order amount less the commission for each order. She also wants you to sort the orders, in alphabetical order by rep and then from highest to lowest within each rep grouping. You also need to highlight orders greater than $10,000 using conditional formatting, and use functions to make key calculations to determine a few statistics for the week, including the highest and lowest individual orders, the averages for each rep who got the highest and lowest orders, and the number of total orders for the week.

Independent Challenge 2 (continued)

a. Open the file H-4.xlsx from where you store your Data Files, then save it as **H-October Sales Rep Report**.

b. Enter a formula in cell E7 that calculates the commission owed to the rep. (*Hint*: Multiply cell D7 by the absolute reference B4.) Use the fill handle to copy the formula to cells E8:E39.

c. Create a formula in cell F7 that subtracts the rep's commission in cell E7 from the order amount in cell D7.

d. Copy the formula in cell F7 to the range F8:F39.

e. Enter the label **Average:** in cell C40. Select the range D7:D39, then use the Quick Analysis gallery to enter a formula in cell D40 that calculates the average of the selected range. Use the fill handle to copy the formula in D40 to E40:F40.

f. Create a table from the range A6:F39. Apply the table style Table Style Light 14 to the table. Include a Total row. Use the fill handle to copy the formula in cell F40 to cells E40:D40.

g. Sort the table first by Sales Rep in alphabetical order and then by Order Amount (Largest to Smallest). Enter a formula in cell C43 that calculates the number of orders for this sales period. (*Hint*: Use the COUNT function and the range D7:D39.)

h. Select cell C44, then enter a formula that uses the MAX function to identify the highest order amount. Apply the Accounting number format to cell C44 with no decimal places. Locate this order amount in the Order Amount column. What is the name of the rep who got this order? Enter his or her name in cell C45.

i. Enter a formula in cell C46 that calculates the average order amounts for the rep who had the highest order (see the name of the rep you entered in cell C45). (*Hint*: The range in this formula should be the range containing the order amounts for this rep.) Apply the Accounting Number format, and remove all decimals.

j. Select cell C47, then enter a formula that uses the MIN function to identify the lowest order amount. Apply the Accounting number format to cell C47 with no decimal places. Locate this order amount in the Order Amount column. What is the name of the rep who got this order? Enter his or her name in cell C48.

k. Enter a formula in cell C49 that calculates the average order amounts for the rep who had the lowest order (see the name of the rep you entered in cell C48. (*Hint*: The range in this formula should be the range containing the order amounts for this rep.) Apply the Accounting Number format, and remove all decimals.

l. Use conditional formatting to highlight in green shading with dark green text all the orders that are above $10,000 in the range D7:D39.

m. Apply light orange shading (Orange, Accent 6, Lighter 80%) to cells C41:F41. Enter your name in cell F1.

n. Preview the worksheet in Backstage view. Adjust the scaling so the whole worksheet fits on one sheet in portrait orientation.

o. Save your changes, close the workbook, then exit Excel. Submit your completed worksheet to your instructor.

Independent Challenge 3

You own and operate a catering business called Rosie's Home-Cooked Meals. You are building an Excel spreadsheet to calculate your profits for the previous year. You have entered sales and most of the expense data in the worksheet. Now you need to enter the necessary formulas to calculate the delivery costs and the profits for each month.

a. Open the file H-5.xlsx from where you store your Data Files, then save it as **H-Catering Profits**. Enter your name in cell A26.

b. Rosie's Home-Cooked Meals pays for food deliveries through a delivery service, which charges a $9.00 flat fee per delivery. The delivery fee is in cell B20. Enter a formula in cell I5 that calculates the cost of deliveries for the month of January. (*Hint*: The formula needs to multiply cell H5—the cell that contains the number of deliveries for January—by cell B20, with B20 as an absolute cell reference.)

c. Enter a complex formula in cell J5 that calculates profits for January. The formula should subtract the sum total of cells C5:G5 and cell I5 from B5 (Sales for January). (*Hint*: Start the formula with B5 followed by the – mathematical operator, followed by the SUM function to add C5:G5 and cell I5.)

Independent Challenge 3 (continued)

d. Select cells I5 and J5, then use the fill handle in cell J5 to copy the formulas down the columns.

e. Enter a formula in cell B21 that identifies the highest profit amount.

f. Enter a formula in cell B22 that identifies the smallest profit amount.

g. Enter a formula in cell B23 that calculates the average monthly profit for the entire year.

h. Apply conditional formatting to the cells J5:J16 to format any cells containing values greater than 35000 with green fill and dark green text.

i. Format the range A4:J16 as a table, choosing any table style you like. Add a Total row. Use the fill handle to copy the formula in cell J17 to cells I17:B17. (*Note*: If any cells display #####, increase column widths until all cells display numbers.) Apply the General number format to cell H17. (*Hint*: Click the HOME tab, click the Number Format list arrow in the Number group, then click General.)

j. Sort the table by the Profits column by Largest to Smallest.

k. Apply shading (your choice) to cells A21: B24. Apply All borders around the shaded cells.

l. Preview the worksheet in Backstage view. Change the orientation to landscape, then adjust the scaling so all columns fit on one sheet.

m. Save your changes, close the workbook, then exit Excel. Submit your completed worksheet to your instructor.

Independent Challenge 4: Explore

You can take advantage of dozens of prebuilt Excel worksheets that are available as templates in the Excel Start screen. These templates provide a wide range of tools for helping you with school, work, and life tasks. For instance, you can find templates for creating invoices, memos, calendars, and time sheets. You can even find templates for helping you plan a party or clean your house. In this Independent Challenge, you use a loan calculator to calculate monthly payments for a car loan. This Independent Challenge requires an Internet connection.

a. Start Excel. The Start screen displays a selection of templates you can download.

b. Click in the Search for online templates text box at the top of the Start screen, type **loan**, then press [Enter]. A large number of loan templates appear on your screen for different types of loans. There is also a Category pane that opens on the right that lists dozens of categories of loans.

c. Look for a loan called "Loan amortization schedule" in the search results area. (It should be in the top row.)

d. Click Loan amortization schedule to open a small window that provides a description of this template and a user rating with a star value assigned to it. Read the description, then click Create.

e. Save the workbook as **H-Car Loan** where you save your Data Files.

f. In cell D5, enter **15000** as the loan amount.

g. In cell D6, enter **5** as the annual interest rate amount.

h. In cell D7, enter **5** for the number of years you want to pay off your loan.

i. In cell D8, enter **12** for the number of payments you want to make in a year.

j. In cell D9, enter a formula that returns today as the result. Leave cell D10 blank.

k. Enter your name in cell C12.

l. Look at the loan summary, and notice the monthly payment you will need to make to pay off the loan. Also, notice the Total interest amount.

m. Now, change the loan period in years amount to **3**. What happens to the Scheduled payment amount in cell J5? What happens to the total interest amount in cell J10?

n. Save your changes, then preview the worksheet in Backstage view. Close the workbook, exit Excel, then submit the workbook to your instructor.

Visual Workshop

Open the file H-6.xlsx and save it as **H-Summer Camps Profits** where you store your Data Files. Modify the worksheet so it contains all the formulas, functions, and formatting shown in FIGURE H-27. The Total Campers Fees cells need to include formulas that multiply the number of campers by the camper fee by the number of sessions. The Coach Cost cells need to include formulas that multiply the number of sessions by the Coach fee ($175.00) in cell B19. (Use an absolute cell reference.) The Profit cells need to subtract the Coach Cost from the Total Camper Fees. Convert the range A4:H16 to a table, then resize column widths to match the figure. Sort and filter the table and add a Total row as shown. Enter appropriate formulas in the range H19:H20. Change alignments to match the figure. Add your name to cell A21. Adjust the print settings to landscape orientation. Save and close the workbook, exit Excel, then submit your finished workbook to your instructor.

FIGURE H-27

	A	B	C	D	E	F	G	H
1				Stride Sports Academy				
2				Summer Camps Profits				
3								
4	Camp	Coach	No. of Sessions	Camper Fee per Session	No. of Campers	Total Camper Fees	Coach Cost	Profit
5	Soccer	Bristol	15	$ 15.00	75	$ 16,875.00	$ 2,625.00	$ 14,250.00
8	Hockey	Flanders	12	$ 18.00	64	$ 13,824.00	$ 2,100.00	$ 11,724.00
9	Fencing	Flanders	9	$ 20.00	21	$ 3,780.00	$ 1,575.00	$ 2,205.00
10	Gymnastics	Masterson	18	$ 22.00	76	$ 30,096.00	$ 3,150.00	$ 26,946.00
11	Swimming	Masterson	20	$ 15.00	87	$ 26,100.00	$ 3,500.00	$ 22,600.00
12	Baseball	Rogers	15	$ 25.00	95	$ 35,625.00	$ 2,625.00	$ 33,000.00
13	Tennis	Rogers	10	$ 10.00	31	$ 3,100.00	$ 1,750.00	$ 1,350.00
14	Football	Zimmer	15	$ 15.00	120	$ 27,000.00	$ 2,625.00	$ 24,375.00
15	Basketball	Zimmer	15	$ 18.00	66	$ 17,820.00	$ 2,625.00	$ 15,195.00
16	Fitness	Zimmer	15	$ 12.00	44	$ 7,920.00	$ 2,625.00	$ 5,295.00
17	Total		144	$ 170.00	679	$ 182,140.00	$ 25,200.00	$ 156,940.00
18								
19	Coach Fee:	$ 175.00					Average Profit:	$ 13,858.17
20							Average No. of Campers	63

Working with Charts

CASE Serena Henning, director of sales for Outdoor Designs, has asked you to create a chart from worksheet data that shows first-quarter sales of kite products by region. You will create and customize two different types of charts for Serena. You will also add sparklines, which are miniature charts, to help illustrate the sales trends for each region in the worksheet.

Unit Objectives

After completing this unit, you will be able to:

- Understand and plan a chart
- Create a chart
- Move and resize charts and chart elements
- Apply chart layouts and styles

- Customize chart elements
- Enhance a chart
- Create a pie chart
- Create sparklines

Files You Will Need

I-1.xlsx	I-4.xlsx
I-2.xlsx	I-5.xlsx
I-3.xlsx	I-6.xlsx

©HelenStock/Shutterstock

Understand and Plan a Chart

Learning Outcomes
- Define chart
- Interpret charts
- Identify chart elements and purpose of each
- Identify common chart types and purpose of each
- Organize a worksheet for a chart

A worksheet is great for presenting and summarizing data, but interpreting numbers in rows and columns takes time and effort. A much more effective way to communicate worksheet data to an audience is to present the data as a chart. A **chart** is a visual representation of worksheet data. For example, a chart can illustrate the growth in sales from one year to the next in a format that makes it easy to see the increase. Excel provides many tools for creating charts to help you communicate key trends and facts about your worksheet data. Before you create a chart, you need to understand some basic concepts about charts. You also need to determine what data you want your chart to show and what chart type you want to use. **CASE** ▶ *Before you create the chart that Serena has requested, you decide to review your data and think about which chart type best represents the information you want to convey.*

DETAILS

In planning and creating a chart, it is important to:

- ### Understand the different parts of a chart

  The chart in **FIGURE I-1** shows sales of Outdoor Designs kites by region for January, February, and March. This chart is based on the range A3:D7 in the worksheet. Like many charts, the one shown here is two-dimensional, meaning it has a horizontal axis and a vertical axis. The **horizontal axis** (also called the **x-axis**) is the horizontal line at the base of the chart that shows categories. The **vertical axis** (also called the **y-axis**) is the vertical line at the left edge of the chart that provides values. The vertical axis is sometimes called the **value axis**. In **FIGURE I-1**, the vertical axis provides values for sales, and the horizontal axis shows months. The **axis titles** identify the values on each axis. The blue and green bars each represent a data series.

QUICK TIP

Some charts also contain a **z-axis**, called the **depth axis**, for comparing data equally across categories and series.

  A **data series** is a sequence of related numbers that shows a trend. For example, the dark blue data series shown in **FIGURE I-1** represents kite sales for the west region. A **data marker** is a single chart symbol that represents one value in a data series. For example, the green data marker on the far right of the chart represents the kite sales in March for the southeast region. A chart **legend** identifies what each data series represents. The **gridlines** in the chart are vertical and horizontal lines that help identify the value for each data series. The **plot area** is the part of the chart contained within the horizontal and vertical axes; in the figure, the plot area is yellow. The **chart area** is the entire chart and all the chart elements.

- ### Identify the purpose of the data and choose an appropriate chart type

  You can use Excel to create many different kinds of charts; each chart type is appropriate for showing particular types of data. Before you create a chart, decide what aspect of your data you want to emphasize, such as making a comparison between two categories, so you can choose the appropriate chart type. **TABLE I-1** provides a listing of common Excel chart types, their uses, and shows a graphic of each. Be sure to study the information in this table so you can identify the appropriate chart types to use for specific needs. As the chart in **FIGURE I-1** demonstrates, column charts are good for comparing values. This chart shows that all regions had increased sales in February. It also shows the west region (represented by the dark blue bars) had the highest overall sales for February, and that both the west region and the southeast region (represented by green bars) had decreased sales in March.

- ### Design the worksheet so Excel creates the chart you want

  Once you have decided on the chart type that best conveys your meaning, you might want to arrange your rows and columns so the chart data illustrates the points you want to make. Serena arranged the data series in the underlying worksheet so the region with the lowest total sales (the northeast) would appear on the left of each cluster, and the region with the highest total sales (the west) would appear on the right.

FIGURE I-1: Example of a column chart

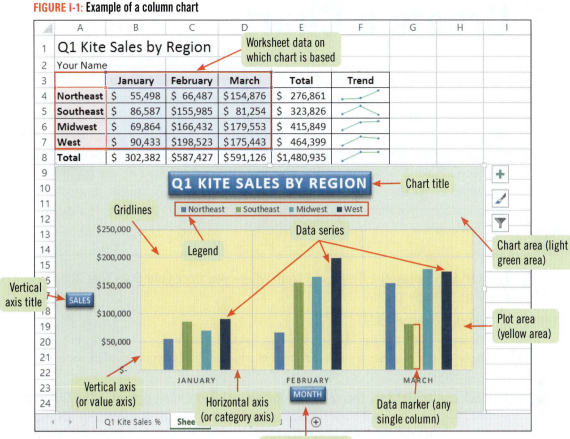

TABLE I-1: Common chart types in Excel

chart type	used for	example
Area	Showing relative importance of values over a period of time	
Bar	Comparing values across categories, with minimal emphasis on time	
Column	Comparing values across categories over time	
Line	Showing trends by category over time	
Pie	Showing the relationship of parts to the whole	
Scatter	Showing the relationship between two kinds of related data	

Interpreting charts

A key reason charts are so useful is they make it easy to see trends and draw conclusions from the underlying worksheet data. Take a moment to look at the chart in **FIGURE I-1** and identify key information it is conveying. See if you can answer the questions below by looking at the chart:

- Which month had the lowest sales for all four regions?
- Which month showed a big jump in sales for the northeast region?

- Which regions had a decrease in sales in March?
- Which region had the lowest sales in February?
- Based on the data in the chart, do you think any of the regions is in trouble? Why do you think so?
- Which region had the most solid sales performance? Why do you think so?

Create a Chart

Learning Outcomes
- Insert a recommended chart in a worksheet
- Change a chart to a different chart type
- Insert a column chart

You can easily create Excel charts based on your worksheet data. Excel provides tools to help you choose the best chart for your data. To create a chart, you first need to select the cells that contain the data you want to chart. Once you have selected the cells in your worksheet, you can then click the Recommended Charts button on the INSERT tab to choose from a selection of chart types, or you can click one of the chart type buttons on the INSERT tab. After you insert a chart, you can easily change the chart type by clicking the Change Chart Type button on the CHART TOOLS DESIGN tab. Any changes you make to the worksheet data are automatically reflected in the chart. **CASE** ▶ *First-quarter sales results for the kite product line just became available at Outdoor Designs. Serena has provided you with a worksheet that shows sales for each month by region. You need to create a chart based on the worksheet data.*

STEPS

1. **Start Excel, open the file I-1.xlsx from where you store your Data Files, then save it as I-Kite Sales by Region**

2. **Select the range A3:D7**

   The range A3:D7 contains the data you want to chart. Notice that you selected the row and column labels but not the column totals. For most charts, you should avoid including totals when selecting worksheet cells.

   QUICK TIP
   You can also quickly insert a chart by clicking a specific chart type button in the Charts group on the INSERT tab.

3. **Click the INSERT tab, then click the Recommended Charts button in the Charts group**

   The Insert Chart dialog box opens as shown in **FIGURE I-2**. The left pane displays thumbnails of recommended chart types for the data you selected. The Clustered Column chart type thumbnail is selected; there is a preview of this chart in the main area of the dialog box. You decide to explore other recommended charts.

4. **Click the second chart thumbnail (Stacked Column)**

   A preview of this chart appears in the main area of the dialog box. Each bar in the stacked column chart represents the total sales for one region, with each colored segment representing a month. On the Northeast column, you can see that the green segment is almost twice as large as the red segment, which tells you that March (represented by green) had the most sales for the northeast region. You decide to insert this chart.

   QUICK TIP
   Depending on your screen resolution, your vertical (value) axis might show different values or number intervals.

5. **Click OK**

   The stacked column chart is inserted into the current worksheet, as shown in **FIGURE I-3**. The double-line border and sizing handles around the chart indicate that the chart is selected. Notice the CHART TOOLS DESIGN and CHART TOOLS FORMAT tabs are available on the Ribbon; these contextual tabs become available when a chart is selected. You decide to try another chart type.

6. **Click the Change Chart Type button in the Type group on the CHART TOOLS DESIGN tab**

   The Change Chart Type dialog box opens. The left pane displays each chart category. The Column category is currently selected because the selected chart is a stacked column chart. You decide to insert the Line chart type.

7. **Click the Line category in the left pane, as shown in FIGURE I-4, then click OK**

   A line chart is inserted into the current worksheet. Colored lines representing the sales data for January, February, and March appear in the chart. This chart type is a little harder to interpret; you decide to change the chart type to a column chart. You can change the chart type using the Column Chart button on the INSERT tab.

8. **Click the INSERT tab on the Ribbon, click the Insert Column Chart button 📊 in the Charts group, click the Clustered Column option as shown in FIGURE I-5, then save your changes**

   The chart in the worksheet changes to a clustered column chart, with three data series (blue, red, green) representing January, February, and March sales for each region.

FIGURE I-2: Insert Chart dialog box

Clustered Column chart type

In Step 4, click this option (Stacked Column)

Left pane displays thumbnails of recommended chart types

Preview of clustered column chart

FIGURE I-3: Stacked column chart in the worksheet

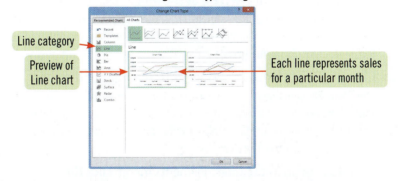

Change Chart Type button

CHART TOOLS DESIGN and FORMAT tabs are available when chart is selected

Sizing handles

Stacked column chart in worksheet

Each column represents total sales for one region

Each colored segment represents a month's sales for a region

FIGURE I-4: Change Chart Type dialog box

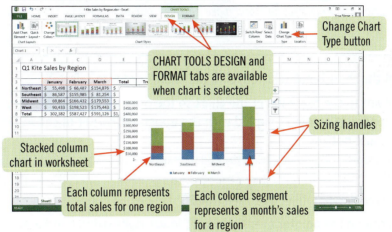

Line category

Preview of Line chart

Each line represents sales for a particular month

FIGURE I-5: Inserting a clustered column chart using the Insert Column Chart button

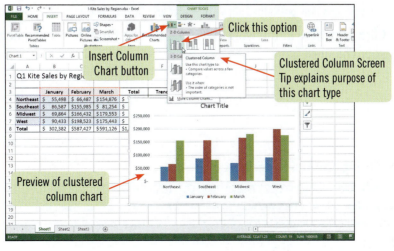

Click this option

Insert Column Chart button

Clustered Column Screen Tip explains purpose of this chart type

Preview of clustered column chart

Excel 2013

Working with Charts

Move and Resize Charts and Chart Elements

You can easily move a chart if it obscures your worksheet data, or resize it if it is too large or too small. You can also move or resize many of the individual components of a chart—called **chart elements** or **chart objects**—such as the chart background or the legend. To move a chart or chart element, select it and drag it to a new location. To resize a chart or chart element, drag one of its sizing handles. The Chart Elements menu lets you choose which chart elements to show or hide; and it also lets you change their locations. **CASE** ▶ *To improve the overall appearance of the worksheet, you decide to move the chart below the worksheet data and make it bigger. You also decide to move the legend so it is at the top of the chart.*

STEPS

1. **If the chart is not selected, click the chart border to select it**

2. **Point to the top edge of the chart so the pointer changes to ⇖, drag the chart so its upper-left corner is aligned with the upper-left corner of cell A9, then release the mouse button**

   The chart is now directly below the worksheet data. As you dragged the chart, an image of the chart moved with the pointer.

3. **Scroll down until you can see row 25**

4. **Position the pointer over the chart's lower-right sizing handle so the pointer changes to ⬉, drag the sizing handle down so the chart's lower-right corner is aligned with the lower-right corner of cell H24, as shown in FIGURE I-6, then release the mouse button**

   The chart enlarges to the new dimensions. If you drag a corner sizing handle, you increase or decrease a chart's height and width simultaneously. To increase or decrease only the height or width of a chart, drag a top, bottom, or side sizing handle.

5. **Click the Chart Elements button ⊞ to the right of the chart**

   The Chart Elements menu opens, listing all the individual chart elements. You use this menu to hide or show chart elements. Elements that have check marks next to their names are showing; elements that are not checked are hidden. You can also use this menu to change the position of elements. You want to move the legend to the top of the chart.

6. **Point to Legend in the Chart Elements menu, click the arrow ▶ that appears on the right, then point to Top as shown in FIGURE I-7, then click Top**

   The legend is now positioned above the chart and below the Chart Title placeholder.

7. **Click anywhere in the worksheet to close the Chart Elements menu, then save your changes**

Creating a chart using the Quick Analysis tool

You can create a chart very quickly using the Quick Analysis tool. To do this, select the worksheet cells on which you want your chart to be based, then click the Quick Analysis button 📄 to open the Quick Analysis tool. Click the CHARTS tab to view recommended chart types, then click the chart you want. The chart is instantly inserted into your worksheet.

FIGURE I-6: Resizing a chart

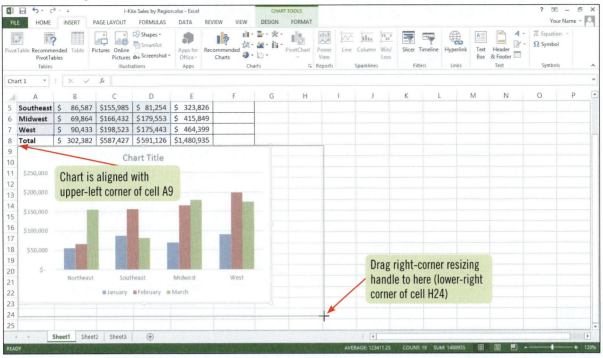

Chart is aligned with upper-left corner of cell A9

Drag right-corner resizing handle to here (lower-right corner of cell H24)

FIGURE I-7: Using the Chart Elements menu to move the legend to the top of the chart

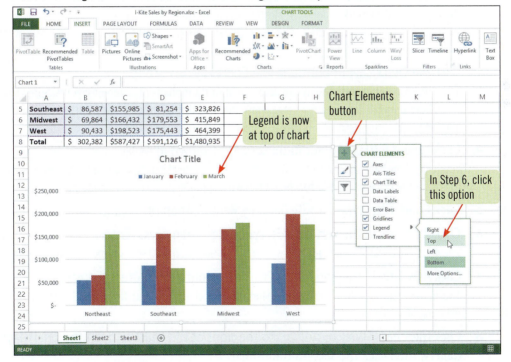

Chart Elements button

Legend is now at top of chart

In Step 6, click this option

Apply Chart Layouts and Styles

Learning
Outcomes
• Switch rows and
  columns in a chart
• Apply a chart
  layout
• Modify chart
  element text
• Apply a chart style

When you create a chart, it has default layout and style settings for the chart type applied. A **chart layout** is a predefined arrangement of chart elements, such as the legend and chart title. A **chart style** is a predefined set of chart colors and fills. Instead of modifying individual chart elements, such as moving the legend or changing the color of a data series, you can instantly change the way chart elements are positioned and whether certain elements are displayed or hidden by choosing a different layout. Chart layouts are available from the Quick Layouts gallery on the CHART TOOLS DESIGN tab. You can change fill colors and textures and fonts by choosing a chart style from the Chart Styles gallery that you can access on the CHART TOOLS DESIGN tab, or by clicking the Chart Styles button to the right of a selected chart. You can also get a different view of your data by reversing the rows and columns. **CASE** ▶ *Serena asks you to change the rows and columns in the chart so the column clusters are grouped by month instead of by region. You also want to improve the appearance of your chart by applying a different chart layout and style.*

STEPS

QUICK TIP
The CHART TOOLS
DESIGN tab is a
contextual tab; it is
available only when
a chart is selected.

1. **Click anywhere in the chart to select it, then click the CHART TOOLS DESIGN tab on the Ribbon**

   The CHART TOOLS DESIGN tab displays commands for changing the appearance of a chart.

2. **Click the Switch Row/Column button in the Data group**

   See **FIGURE I-8**. The chart now shows only three clusters of data series (instead of the original four), one for each month. Each data series now represents the revenue for each region (instead of each month), and there are four data markers for each cluster instead of three. The horizontal axis labels now list the three months of the first quarter (instead of the regions). This view of the data more clearly shows the sales for each month.

3. **Click the Quick Layout button in the Chart Layouts group**

   The Quick Layout gallery displays an assortment of thumbnails of different layouts. Some have gridlines, some have data labels, and a few have chart and axis titles. You want a layout that has a chart title and axis titles.

4. **Click Layout 9 (third layout in third row) as shown in FIGURE I-9**

   Your chart now has placeholder text for a chart title, a vertical axis title, and a horizontal axis title. You need to replace the placeholder text for these titles with appropriate text for your chart.

TROUBLE
When you click
the Chart Title
placeholder and
type text for your
chart title, notice
that the text you
type appears only
in the formula bar
(not in the Chart
Title placeholder).
This can be confus-
ing, but don't be
alarmed—the chart
title text will
appear when you
press [Enter].

5. **Click Chart Title, type Q1 Kite Sales by Region, then press [Enter]**

6. **Click Axis Title in the vertical axis, type Sales, then press [Enter]**

   The vertical axis label now reads "Sales," clarifying that each data series represents sales figures.

7. **Click Axis Title in the horizontal axis, type Month, then press [Enter]**

   The horizontal axis label changes to "Month." The chart and axis titles make it easier to interpret the meaning of the chart.

8. **Click the Chart Styles button 🖉 to the right of the chart to open the Chart Styles gallery, then click the second thumbnail**

   The new style is applied to the chart, as shown in **FIGURE I-10**. This style shows data labels at the top of each data marker, making it easy to see the exact sales amount for January, February, and March for each region.

9. **Click in any worksheet cell to close the Chart Elements menu, then save your changes**

FIGURE I-8: Chart with rows and columns switched

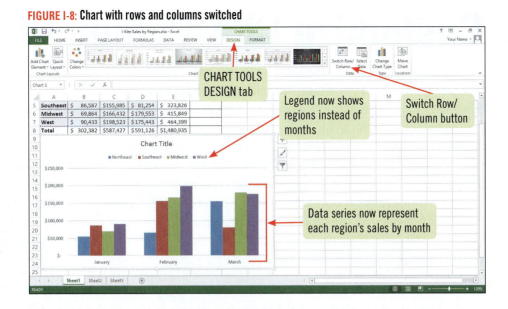

CHART TOOLS DESIGN tab

Legend now shows regions instead of months

Switch Row/ Column button

Data series now represent each region's sales by month

FIGURE I-9: Applying a chart layout

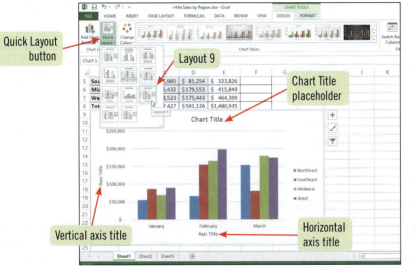

Quick Layout button

Layout 9

Chart Title placeholder

Vertical axis title

Horizontal axis title

FIGURE I-10: Applying a chart style using the Chart Styles gallery

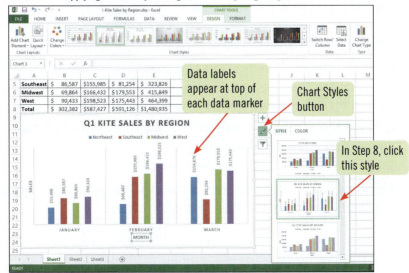

Data labels appear at top of each data marker

Chart Styles button

In Step 8, click this style

Customize Chart Elements

Although Excel's chart layouts and styles are professionally designed and look great, you can still make changes to them to suit your needs. You can add, remove, or change the positioning of chart elements using the Chart Elements menu. If you want to modify the formatting or alignment of a chart element, you can use the Format pane, which displays settings unique to each chart element that you can adjust. To open a chart element's Format pane, right click the chart element, then click Format *chart element name*. Chart elements that can be modified include the chart title, axis titles, legend, data labels, axes, gridlines, plot area, and data table. A **data table** in a chart is a grid containing the chart's underlying worksheet data, which is added below the x-axis in certain types of charts. **CASE** *Serena asks you to remove the data labels from the chart and add the vertical axis values. You also decide to add horizontal gridlines and change the orientation of the title of the vertical axis so it is easier to read. You also decide to explore other options to improve the chart's appearance.*

STEPS

1. **Click the chart to select it, click the Chart Elements button to the right of the chart, then click the Data Labels check box in the Chart Elements menu to remove the check mark**

   The data labels no longer appear on the chart. Next you want the vertical axis to show dollar amounts along its edge.

2. **Point to Axes in the Chart Elements menu, click the arrow ▶ that appears next to it, then click Primary Vertical as shown in FIGURE I-11**

   Dollar amounts in increments of $50,000 now appear along the vertical axis. Now you need to add horizontal gridlines.

3. **Point to Gridlines in the Chart Elements menu, click the arrow ▶ that appears next to it, then click Primary Major Horizontal**

   Horizontal gridlines now appear in the chart, making it easier to identify the estimated sales value for each region's monthly sales. Next you want to experiment by adding a data table.

4. **Click the Data Table check box in the Chart Elements menu**

   See **FIGURE I-12**. A data table is inserted below the chart, with a legend in the first column that identifies the data series in each row. Data tables are helpful when you want to show both the chart and the underlying worksheet data. Because this worksheet already includes the data for the chart, you don't need the data table here; it looks better without it.

5. **Click the Data Table check box in the Chart Elements menu to remove the check mark, then click any cell in the worksheet**

   The data table is removed, and the Chart Elements menu is closed. Next you want to change the orientation of the Sales axis title so it is horizontal. You can do this using the Format pane.

6. **Right-click the SALES vertical axis title, then click Format Axis Title in the shortcut menu**

   The Format Axis Titles pane opens, with options for modifying the fill and border settings. The text alignment settings you need to adjust are not available on this tab.

7. **Click the Size & Properties button 🔠 in the Format Axis Title pane, click the Text direction list arrow, then click Horizontal**

   The SALES vertical axis button is now positioned horizontally. See **FIGURE I-13**.

8. **Click the Close button ✖ in the Format Axis Title pane, click any worksheet cell to close the Chart Elements menu, then save your changes**

FIGURE I-11: Selecting the Primary Vertical axis option on the Chart Elements menu

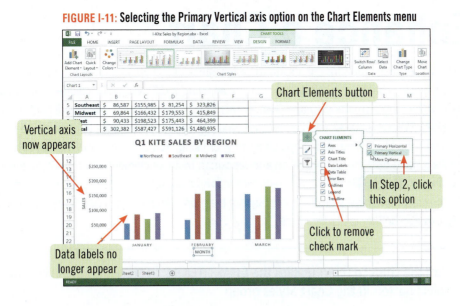

Vertical axis now appears

Chart Elements button

In Step 2, click this option

Click to remove check mark

Data labels no longer appear

FIGURE I-12: Data table in chart

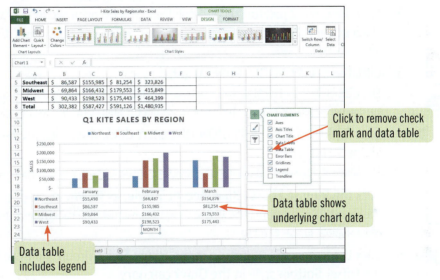

Click to remove check mark and data table

Data table shows underlying chart data

Data table includes legend

FIGURE I-13: Format Axis Title pane with Text direction setting set to Horizontal

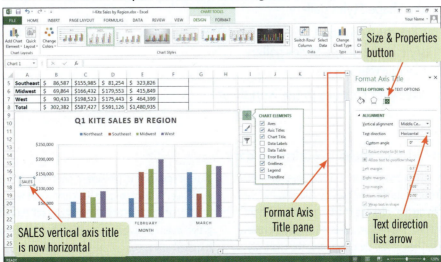

Size & Properties button

Format Axis Title pane

Text direction list arrow

SALES vertical axis title is now horizontal

Excel 2013

Enhance a Chart

Excel provides many tools for enhancing the appearance of a chart so it looks just the way you want it to. You can quickly change the colors in a chart by applying a different color palette. You can apply special effects, styles, and formatting to any chart element by choosing from a wide variety of tools galleries on the CHART TOOLS FORMAT tab. For instance, you can apply a shape style to a chart title or axis title and then adjust the fill, outline, and shape effect to your liking. You can also apply WordArt styles to any text to make it stand out. You can also align and reposition multiple elements. To format an element, you first must select it. **CASE** *You decide to enhance the visual appeal of the chart by applying a different color set to it, and applying a shape style and outline style to the chart title. You also decide to apply the same shape style to the axis titles so they are easier to see.*

STEPS

1. **Click the chart to select it, click the CHART TOOLS DESIGN tab, then click the Change Colors button in the Chart Styles group**

   The Chart Colors gallery opens, showing four Colorful palette options and several other Monochromatic palette options.

2. **Click the Color 2 palette (second palette in the Colorful section) as shown in FIGURE I-14**

   The chart colors change to reflect the new color set you applied. Notice three data series are a shade of blue; the southeast data series is now green.

3. **Click the CHART TOOLS FORMAT tab**

   The CHART TOOLS FORMAT tab is active. This tab contains many buttons and tools for enhancing the appearance of chart elements. You want to format the chart title; first you need to select it.

4. **Click Q1 KITE SALES BY REGION (the chart title), then click the More button ⬇ in the Shape Styles gallery**

   The Shape Styles gallery opens and displays several shape styles you can apply to the selected chart title.

5. **Click the Intense Effect - Blue, Accent 1 style, as shown in FIGURE I-15**

   The chart title is now formatted with a three-dimensional blue background and white font. You decide to add a shadow special effect to it.

6. **Click the Shape Effects button in the Shape Styles group, point to Shadow, then click the Offset Bottom style in the Outer category**

   The chart title now has a shadow along its bottom edge, enhancing the impression that it is three dimensional.

7. **Click the vertical axis title (SALES), then click the Intense Effect - Blue, Accent 1 style in the Shape Styles gallery**

8. **Click the horizontal axis title (MONTH), then click the Intense Effect - Blue, Accent 1 style in the Shape Styles gallery**

   Compare your screen to FIGURE I-16.

9. **Save your changes to the worksheet**

Printing charts with or without worksheet data

If your worksheet contains both a chart and worksheet data, you can preview or print only the chart by itself by selecting the chart before printing it. To do this, click the chart to select it, click the FILE tab, then click Print. The Preview pane will display a preview of the chart by itself. Then, if you click Print, only the chart will print. If you want to preview or print both the chart and the worksheet data, make sure the chart is not selected when you preview or print the worksheet. If any cell (outside of the chart) is active when you preview the chart, both the worksheet data and the chart will appear in the Preview pane.

FIGURE I-14: Changing the color set of a chart using the Change Colors button

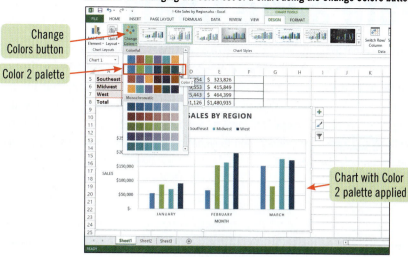

Change Colors button

Color 2 palette

Chart with Color 2 palette applied

FIGURE I-15: Applying a shape style to a chart element

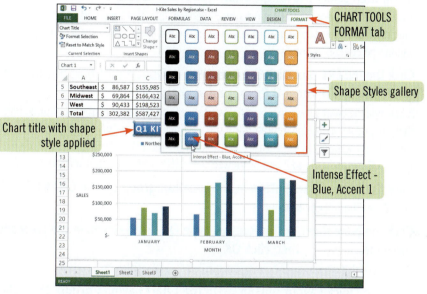

CHART TOOLS FORMAT tab

Shape Styles gallery

Chart title with shape style applied

Intense Effect - Blue, Accent 1

FIGURE I-16: Completed chart with formatting enhancements

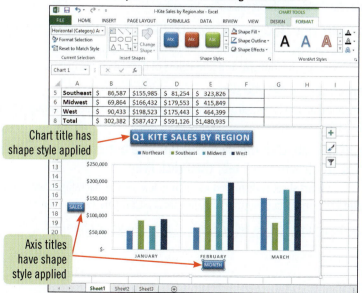

Chart title has shape style applied

Axis titles have shape style applied

Create a Pie Chart

Learning Outcomes
- Select nonadjacent ranges
- Insert a pie chart
- Move a chart to a chart sheet
- Apply a Quick Layout to a pie chart
- Increase the font size of data labels

Column charts are great for comparing values across categories, but they are not very useful for comparing percentages or parts to a whole. For instance, the column chart does not convey the west region's percentage of total first-quarter sales. A pie chart is an effective tool for comparing the relative values of parts to a whole. Just like any other type of chart, you can add it to a worksheet, or you can add it on a separate chart sheet. A **chart sheet** is a sheet in a workbook that contains only a chart; it contains no worksheet cells. **CASE** ▶ *Serena wants you to create a pie chart on a separate chart sheet that compares total first-quarter kite sales by region.*

STEPS

1. **Scroll up so the top of the worksheet is visible, select the range A4:A7, press and hold [Ctrl], then select the range E4:E7**

   You selected two nonadjacent ranges (the region names and total first-quarter sales for each region); this is the only worksheet data you want reflected in the pie chart. You want to create a pie chart that shows each region's percentage of total sales.

2. **Click the INSERT tab, click the Insert Pie or Doughnut Chart button 🥧 in the Charts group, then click the 3-D Pie option as shown in FIGURE I-17**

   A 3D-style pie chart now appears in the worksheet and covers part of the column chart. The pie chart shows that the purple pie wedge (representing the west region) is slightly bigger than the others, and the blue pie wedge (representing the northeast region) is the smallest. You decide to move the pie chart to a new chart sheet in the workbook, so it can be viewed separately from the column chart.

3. **Click the Move Chart button in the Location group on the CHART TOOLS DESIGN tab**

   The Move Chart dialog box opens.

QUICK TIP

You can pull out, or explode, a pie slice from a pie chart to emphasize a particular value. Click the pie chart, click a pie slice, then drag it away from the pie.

4. **Click the New sheet option button, type Q1 Kite Sales % in the New sheet text box as shown in FIGURE I-18, then click OK**

   The pie chart moves to a new chart sheet called "Q1 Kite Sales %."

5. **Click the Quick Layout button 📊 in the Chart Layouts group, then click Layout 1**

   Each pie slice in the chart now contains a label for the region and for the region's percentage of total sales. A chart title placeholder is displayed above the chart.

6. **Click the Chart Title placeholder, type Q1 Kite Sales by Region, then press [Enter]**

   Notice that the data labels are formatted in very small type, and they are hard to read because they are black. You can change the font size and font colors of data labels using buttons on the HOME tab.

QUICK TIP

To add text to a chart sheet, click the CHART TOOLS FORMAT tab, click the Text Box button, click the location where you want to add the text, then type your desired text. Format the text using buttons on the HOME tab.

7. **Click West on the purple pie slice**

   Clicking just one data label selected all of the data labels. Any formatting changes you make will apply to all of the data labels.

8. **Click the HOME tab, click the Increase Font Size button A⁺ seven times to increase the font size to 18, click the FILE tab, then click Print**

   A preview of the chart sheet is displayed in the preview area in Backstage view. Notice that the orientation is set to Landscape, the default setting for chart sheets. Compare your screen to FIGURE I-19.

9. **Press [Esc] to return to the HOME tab, then save your changes**

FIGURE I-17: Creating a pie chart

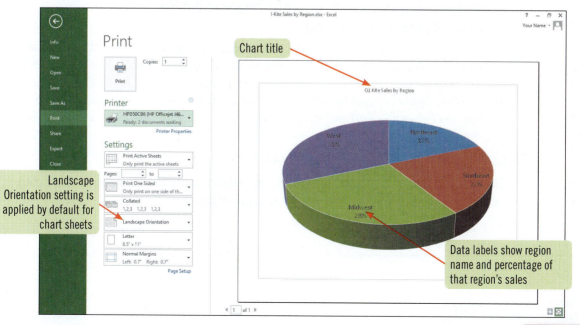

FIGURE I-18: Move Chart dialog box

FIGURE I-19: Preview of completed pie chart in Backstage view

Excel 2013

Working with Charts

Create Sparklines

Learning Outcomes
• Insert a sparkline
• Add sparkline markers
• Apply a sparkline style
• Copy a sparkline from one cell to an adjacent range

In addition to charts, you can also add sparklines to a worksheet to communicate patterns or trends visually. **Sparklines** are tiny charts that fit in one cell and illustrate trends in selected cells. There are three types of sparklines you can add to a worksheet. A **line sparkline** is a miniature line chart that is ideal for showing a trend over a period of time. A **column sparkline** is a tiny column chart that includes a bar for each cell in a selected range. A **win/loss sparkline** shows only two types of bars: one for gains and one for losses. **TABLE I-2** provides descriptions and examples of sparkline types. You should place sparklines close to the cells containing the data they illustrate. **CASE** *You decide to create sparklines next to your worksheet data to illustrate sales trends in the quarter for each of the regions.*

STEPS

1. **Click the Sheet1 sheet tab, click the INSERT tab, then click cell F4**

   This is where you need to insert a sparkline for the range B4:D4, the data series for the northeast region sales from January to March.

2. **Click the Line button in the Sparklines group**

   The Create Sparklines dialog box opens. You need to select the cells for which you want to create a sparkline: the range B4:D4.

TROUBLE
If the Create Sparklines dialog box is blocking the range you want to select, drag it out of the way.

3. **Select the range B4:D4, compare your screen to FIGURE I-20, then click OK**

   Cell F4 now contains a sparkline that starts in the bottom left of the cell and slants upward to the upper-right corner, indicating an increase from cell B4 to C4 to D4. At a glance, the sparkline communicates that sales increased steadily from January to March. You can add markers on the line to indicate values for each cell in the selected range.

QUICK TIP
To change the color of sparklines or sparkline markers for selected cells, click the Sparkline Color arrow or the Marker Color arrow in the Style group, then click the color you want.

4. **Click the Markers check box in the Show group**

   The sparkline now displays three tiny square markers. The left marker represents the northeast region's January sales (B4), the middle marker represents the northeast region's February sales (C4), and the far-right marker represents the northeast region's March sales (D4). You want to change the sparkline to a different color.

QUICK TIP
To change the sparkline type to either column or win/loss, select the cells containing the sparkline, then click the Column button or the Win/Loss button in the Type group.

5. **Click the More button ⊟ in the Style group, then click Sparkline Style Colorful #4 (fourth style in last row)**

   The sparkline color is now green, and the sparkline markers are dark blue.

6. **Drag the cell F4 fill handle to cell F8**

   Cells F5:F8 now contain green sparklines with blue markers that show sales trends for the other regions, as well as the total sales, as shown in **FIGURE I-21**. Notice that the sparkline in cell F5 shows a sharp downward trend from the second to third marker. Notice, too, that the sparkline in cell F7 (for the west region) also shows a slight downward trend from the second to third marker. All other sparklines show an upward direction. You can see how sparklines make it easy to see at a glance the sales performance of each region for the quarter.

7. **Enter *your* name in cell A2, then save your changes**

TROUBLE
If the chart is selected when you preview the worksheet in Backstage view, only the chart will appear in the Preview pane. Click any cell in the worksheet outside of the chart to preview and/or print the worksheet with the chart.

8. **Click the FILE tab, click Print, preview the worksheet, close the worksheet, exit Excel, then submit your completed workbook to your instructor**

Working with Charts

FIGURE I-20: Create Sparklines dialog box

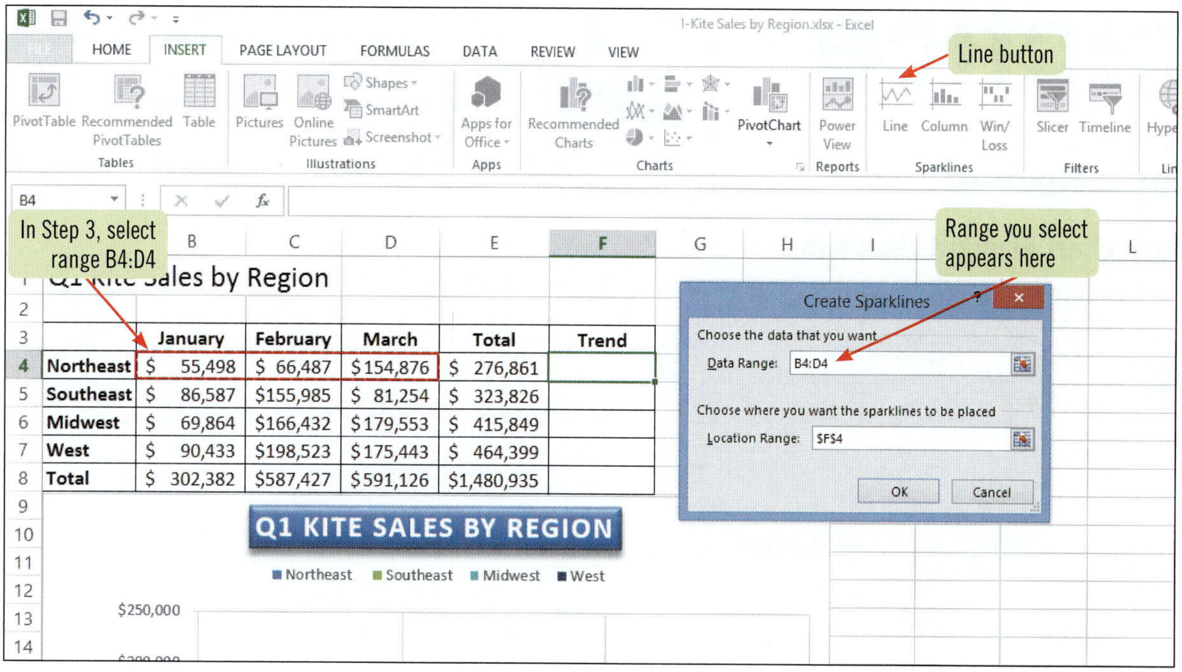

FIGURE I-21: Completed worksheet with sparklines added

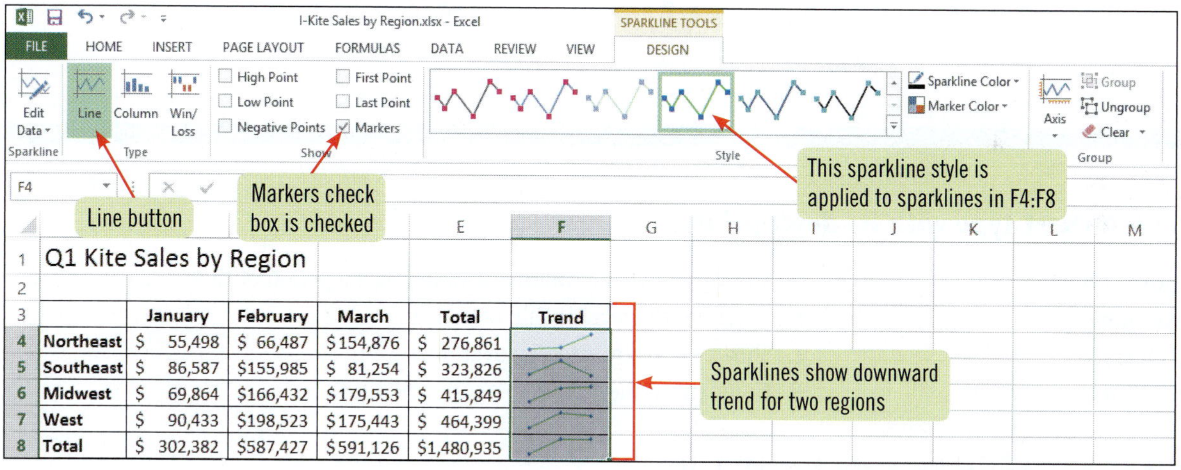

TABLE I-2: Sparkline types and their uses

sparkline type	used for	example
Line	Showing trends over time	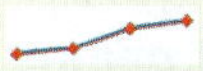
Column	Comparing values over time	
Win/Loss	Showing gains and/or losses over time	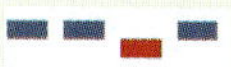

Excel 2013

Practice

Put your skills into practice with SAM! If you have a SAM account, go to www.cengage.com/sam2013 to access SAM assignments for this unit.

Concepts Review

Label each chart element shown in FIGURE I-22.

FIGURE I-22

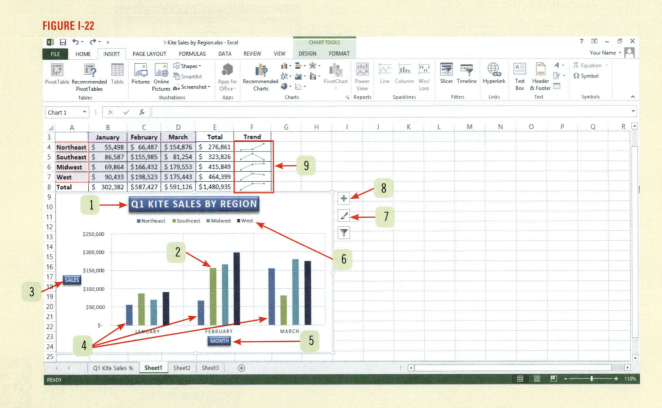

Match each chart type with its description.

10. Column chart
11. Area chart
12. Pie chart
13. Line chart

a. Shows relative importance of values over a period of time
b. Describes the relationship of parts to a whole
c. Shows trends by category over time
d. Compares values across categories over time

Select the best answer from the list of choices.

14. **Which of the following axis titles would most likely be shown on a horizontal axis in a chart?**
    a. Sales
    b. Costs
    c. Temperature
    d. Months

15. **In a chart, a single chart symbol that represents one value in a data series is called a(n):**
    a. Axis.
    b. Chart area.
    c. Legend.
    d. Data marker.

16. **You just finished an 8-week diet program, in which you lost weight every week. You want to create a chart that shows the number of pounds you lost for each week. Which of the following charts would NOT be a good choice for your chart?**
    a. Column chart
    b. Bar chart
    c. Pie chart
    d. Line chart

17. **Which of the following tools do you use to add a chart legend?**
   a. Chart Elements menu
   b. INSERT tab
   c. CHART TOOLS FORMAT tab
   d. Format Chart Title pane

18. **You want to insert a sparkline to show the increase in costs in the range A4:G4. In which of the following locations would it be best to place your sparkline?**
   a. In cell H4
   b. In cell G5
   c. In cell H3
   d. In any cell on a separate chart sheet

Skills Review

1. **Understand and plan a chart.**
   a. Open the file I-2.xlsx from where you store your Data Files, then save it as **I-Solar Panel Sales**.
   b. Examine the worksheet data, then consider what Excel chart types would best present this type of information.
   c. Is the worksheet designed in such a way that it will be easy to create a chart? Why or why not?

2. **Create a chart.**
   a. Select the range A4:D9.
   b. Display the tab on the Ribbon that contains commands for inserting charts, then choose a command on this tab that recommends chart types for the selected range.
   c. Examine the different chart types that are recommended, then insert a Stacked Column chart.
   d. Change the chart type to a Line chart using a button on the CHART TOOLS DESIGN tab.
   e. Change the chart type to a Clustered Column chart, using the INSERT tab.
   f. Save your changes to the workbook.

3. **Move and resize charts and chart elements.**
   a. Drag the chart so the upper-left corner of the chart is aligned with the upper-left corner of cell A12.
   b. Use the lower-right corner sizing handle to align the lower-right corner of the chart with the lower-right corner of cell G28.
   c. Move the legend to the top of the chart, using the Chart Elements menu.
   d. Save your changes.

4. **Apply chart layouts and styles.**
   a. Open the CHART TOOLS DESIGN tab, if necessary.
   b. Use a button on the CHART TOOLS DESIGN tab to reverse the columns and rows and get a different view of the data. Examine the chart, and identify what new meaning this new structure conveys.
   c. Apply the Layout 9 Quick Layout to the chart.
   d. Replace the chart title placeholder with **Solar Panels Sales, 2014-2016**.
   e. Replace the vertical axis title placeholder text with **Sales**.
   f. Replace the horizontal axis title placeholder text with **Region**.
   g. Apply the Style 4 chart style to the chart.
   h. Save your changes.

5. **Customize chart elements.**
   a. Display the Chart Elements menu, then remove the data labels from the chart.
   b. Adjust the settings to specify that the Primary Vertical Axis shows on the chart.
   c. Add primary minor horizontal gridlines to the chart.
   d. Display a data table on the chart. Notice how this looks on the chart; then remove the data table from the chart.
   e. Open the Format Axis Title pane. Change the alignment of the vertical axis title (Sales) so the text direction is horizontal. Close the Format Axis Title pane.
   f. Save your changes.

Skills Review (continued)

6. Enhance a chart.

a. Select the chart, then display the CHART TOOLS DESIGN tab.

b. Change the color palette to the Color 2 palette (under the Colorful category).

c. Select the chart title, then open the CHART TOOLS FORMAT tab, and apply the Moderate Effect - Olive Green, Accent 3 shape to the chart title.

d. Apply a Glow shape effect to the chart title, using the Olive Green, 8 pt glow, Accent color 3 effect.

e. Save your changes.

7. Create a pie chart.

a. Select cells A5:A9, then press and hold [Ctrl] while selecting cells E5:E9.

b. Insert a pie chart, choosing the 3-D Pie option.

c. Move the pie chart to a new sheet in the workbook. Name the sheet **Sales by Region**.

d. Apply the Layout 6 chart layout to the chart.

e. Increase the font size of the percentage amounts on the pie slices to 24. Select the legend, then increase the font size of the legend to 12.

f. Click the chart title placeholder, type **Solar Panels Sales by Region, 2014-2016**, then press [Enter].

g. Preview the chart in Backstage view. Press [Esc] to exit Backstage view and return to the HOME tab. Save your changes.

8. Create sparklines.

a. Click the Sheet1 sheet tab to return to the worksheet.

b. Add a line sparkline to cell F5 that is based on the data range B5:D5.

c. Specify to add markers to the sparkline.

d. Apply Sparkline Style Dark #6 to the sparkline.

e. Use the fill handle to copy the sparkline in cell F5 to the range F6:F10.

f. Enter your name in cell A30. Save your changes.

g. Preview the worksheet in Backstage view. Change the scaling setting to Fit Sheet on One Page, then save your changes. Compare your completed worksheet and chart sheet to **FIGURE I-23** and **FIGURE I-24**. Close the workbook, exit Excel, then submit your completed workbook to your instructor.

FIGURE I-23

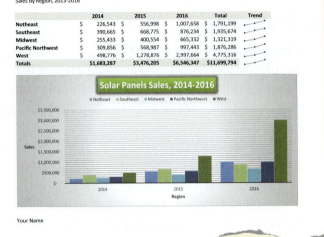

FIGURE I-24

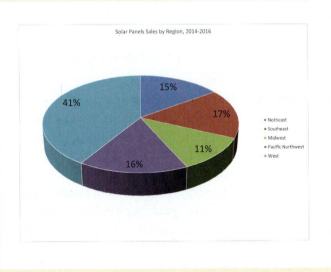

Independent Challenge 1

You work for a dog day care company called Uncle Ruff's Dog Care Services, located in the Pacific Northwest. The company offers many services for caring for dogs, including overnight boarding, obedience training, day care, grooming, and in-home services (such as dog walking and dog sitting). Audrey Wilson, the general manager, has created a worksheet that contains revenue data for the five categories of services that Uncle Ruff's offers. She has asked you to create a chart using the worksheet data to show the results for each month.

a. Open the file I-3.xlsx from where you store your Data Files, then save it as **I-Dog Care Monthly Revenue**.

b. Create a stacked area chart based on the data in the range A4:E9.

c. Change the chart type to a stacked column chart. (*Hint*: Click the Column category in the Change Chart Type dialog box, click the Stacked Column button at the top of the dialog box, click the first Stacked Column thumbnail, then click OK.)

d. Make sure the months (June, July, August, and September) appear on the x-axis. (If the months do not appear along the x-axis, then click the Switch Row/Column button.)

e. Move the chart so it is positioned directly below the worksheet data, then enlarge it so the bottom-right corner of the chart is aligned with cell G29.

f. Apply the Layout 3 chart layout to the chart, then apply Chart Style 7. Add data labels to the chart.

g. Remove the Primary Vertical axis.

h. Replace the chart title placeholder with **Revenue, June-September**.

i. Add the vertical axis title **Revenue** and the horizontal axis title **Month**.

j. Apply the Moderate Effect - Aqua, Accent 5 shape style to the chart title and axis titles.

k. Change the colors of the chart to the Color 9 palette (the lighter blue palette in the Monochromatic section).

l. Open the Format Plot Area pane. (*Hint*: Right-click anywhere on the plot area, then click Format Plot Area.) Adjust the Fill Settings to specify a solid fill. Set the fill color to White, Background 1, Darker 5%.

m. Insert a line sparkline in cell G5 for the range B5:E5; choose the Sparkline Style Dark #5. Add markers to the sparkline. Copy the sparkline to the range G6:G10.

n. Create a 3-D pie chart by selecting the noncontiguous ranges A5:A9 and F5:F9. Move the pie chart to a separate chart sheet named **Revenue by Service Type**. Apply the Layout 2 chart layout to the pie chart. Apply Style 2 to the chart. Change the chart title to **Revenue by Service Type**. Increase the font size of the percentage amount labels on each pie slice to 16. Increase the font size of the chart title to 20.

o. Open Sheet1, then type your name in cell A31.

p. Preview the Sheet1 worksheet in Backstage view. Change the scaling settings to Fit Sheet on One Page, then save your changes. Compare your finished chart to **FIGURE I-25**.

q. View Sheet1 and the Revenue by Service Type chart sheet in Backstage view. Close the workbook, exit Excel, then submit your completed workbook to your instructor.

FIGURE I-25

Independent Challenge 2

You work for Clarissa Monroe Watson, the owner of an online bakery. Clarissa has created an Excel worksheet showing product sales for December and the sales generated by each product category. She has asked you to create a chart in the worksheet that shows the percentage of total sales each category represents.

a. Open the file I-4.xlsx from where your Data Files are located, then save it as **I-December Sales**.

b. Create a pie chart using the data in the range A4:B9. Choose the 2-D Pie option.

c. Move the chart below the worksheet data.

d. Resize the chart so its lower-right corner is aligned with the lower-right corner of cell G29.

e. Change the value in cell B6 (the number of pies sold) to **759**. Observe the change in the chart.

f. Apply the Layout 1 Quick Layout to the chart. Apply Chart Style 5. Change the chart title text to **December Sales by Product**. Apply a shape style that you like to the chart title.

g. Right-click in the chart area (the white space outside the pie), then click Format Chart Area to open the Format Chart Area pane. Click Fill to display fill options, then click Solid Fill. Click the Color button list arrow, then click Aqua Accent 5, Lighter, 80%. Close the Format Chart Area task pane.

h. Increase the size of the labels and percentage amounts in each pie slice to 12.

i. Format the worksheet data and worksheet title using fonts, font sizes, borders, alignments, and shading to make the worksheet look professional, visually pleasing, and easy to understand. Choose formatting options that are complementary to the colors and style of the chart. Make any other formatting enhancements to the chart and to the worksheet data to make it attractive and more professional looking. Enter your name in cell A31 in the worksheet.

j. Preview the worksheet and chart in Backstage view. Close the workbook, exit Excel, then submit your completed workbook to your instructor.

Independent Challenge 3

You work for Alana Ridgeway, the director of a zoo. In July, the zoo opened a new big cat exhibit, featuring lions and tigers. Thanks to an effective ad campaign and increased media exposure, zoo attendance increased dramatically in that month. Alana is preparing to meet with the zoo's board of directors to discuss the increased attendance. She has asked you to create a chart that shows the number of people who visited the zoo from March through July. She also needs the chart to show a breakdown of children, adults, and seniors who attended. The underlying data you need in order to create the chart has already been entered into a worksheet.

a. Open the file I-5.xlsx from where you store your Data Files, then save it as **I-Zoo Visitors**. Enter your name in cell A8.

b. Create a 2D line chart of all three customer categories during the months May through September. Choose the 2-D Line with Markers chart type. Apply Quick Layout 9. Apply Chart Style 11.

c. Replace the chart title placeholder with **Zoo Visitors March-July**. Add axis titles, then replace the vertical axis title with **Number of Visitors**. Replace the horizontal axis title with **Month**.

d. Move the chart to a new chart sheet in the workbook. Name the chart sheet **Zoo Visitors March-July**.

e. Add primary major horizontal gridlines to the chart, then close the Chart Elements menu.

f. Apply a solid color fill to the plot area, choosing the color Olive Green, Accent 3, Lighter 80%. (*Hint*: To do this, right-click the plot area, then click Format Plot Area to open the Format Plot Area pane, click the Solid fill option, click the color button list arrow, then click Olive Green, Accent 3, Lighter 80%.)

Independent Challenge 3 (continued)

g. Apply a shape style of your choosing to the chart title and axis titles. **FIGURE I-26** shows one possible example of the completed chart.

h. Save your changes, preview the worksheet and chart sheet, close the workbook, then exit Excel. Submit your completed workbook to your instructor.

FIGURE I-26

Independent Challenge 4: Explore

Creating a personal budget is a great way to keep your finances in order. In this Independent Challenge, you will create a personal budget for monthly expenses. For the purposes of this exercise, imagine that you earn $3,000 per month. Your budget needs to include categories of expenses and the amounts for each expense. The total expenses in the worksheet must add up to $3,000. Once you enter all your monthly expenses in the worksheet, you will then create a pie chart that shows the percentage of each individual expense.

a. Start a blank Excel workbook, and save it as **I-My Monthly Expenses** where you store your Data Files.

b. Enter **My Monthly Expenses** in cell A1. Format the title so it stands out. Enter *your* name in cell A2.

c. Enter the label **Expense** in cell A3, and enter the label **Amount** in cell B3.

d. Enter the following labels for the expenses in cells A4:A13: **Housing**, **Utilities**, **Car Payment**, **Health and Medical**, **Student Loans**, **Credit Card**, **Food**, **Entertainment**, **Gas**, **Savings**.

e. Enter appropriate amounts for each expense in cells B4:B13.

f. When you have entered all your expenses in the worksheet, enter the label **Total** in cell A14. Enter a formula in cell B14 that totals all the expense amounts in cells B4:B13. If the returning value in the formula cell does not add up to $3,000, then adjust the numbers in your monthly expense amount cells so the total adds up to $3,000.

g. Insert a pie chart based on the data in your chart. (*Hint*: Remember not to include the Total row when you select the data; select only the heading row, the labels, and expense amounts.) Choose any pie chart option that you like. Move the chart so that it is located below the worksheet data.

h. Apply a chart layout and chart style you like. If the chart layout you choose does not include a chart title, add one to the chart using the appropriate options on the Chart Elements menu. Replace the chart title placeholder with the title **My Monthly Expenses**.

i. Select the chart, then click the Chart Filters button to the right of the chart. The Chart Filters menu lets you apply filters to the chart to highlight or show only categories you specify. Point to each category, and observe what happens to the chart. Now click the Housing check box to remove the check mark, then click Apply. The pie chart now shows all expenses except the Housing expense. Notice how all the remaining pie slices got bigger. Click the Housing check box again to add a check mark, then click Apply. Click in a worksheet cell to close the Chart Filters menu.

j. Select the range A3:B13, then click the Quick Analysis button. Click the CHARTS tab, then click the Clustered Bar chart type. Move and resize the chart so it is located to the right of the worksheet data and above the pie chart. Replace the chart title with **My Monthly Expenses**.

k. Save your changes, preview the worksheet with the chart, close the file, then exit Excel. Submit your completed workbook to your instructor.

Visual Workshop

Open the Data File I-6.xlsx, then save it as **I-Volunteer Participation** where you store your Data Files. Make formatting changes to the worksheet so it looks like **FIGURE I-27**, then add the two charts so they match the figure, using the commands and techniques you learned in this unit and previous units. You will need to make formatting changes to both charts so they match the figure. Enter your name in cell A3 as shown. (*Hint*: You will need to merge and center the ranges A1:G1, A2:G2, and A3:G3 so the company name, worksheet title, and your name match the figure.) Save your changes, preview the worksheet and charts, close the file, then exit Excel. Submit your completed workbook to your instructor.

FIGURE I-27

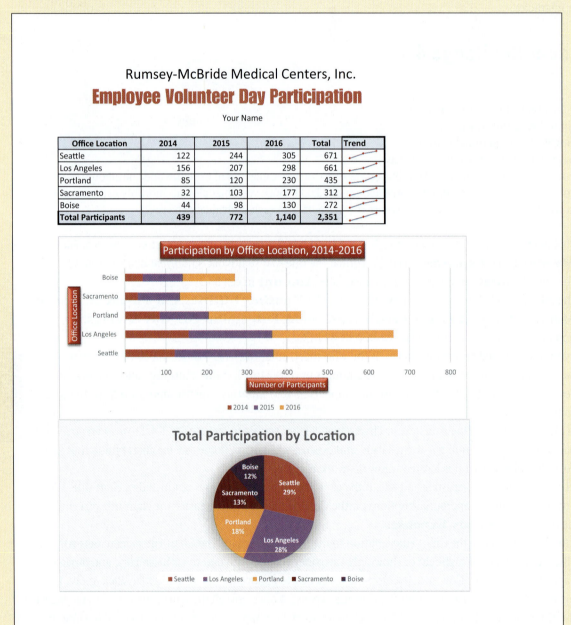

Creating a Database

CASE Karen Rivera, marketing director for Outdoor Designs, has asked you to create a database that helps Outdoor Designs keep track of sales reps and sales managers.

Unit Objectives

After completing this unit, you will be able to:

- Understand databases
- Create a database
- Create a table in Datasheet view
- Create a table in Design view
- Modify a table and set properties
- Enter data in a table
- Edit data in Datasheet view
- Create and use a form

Files You Will Need

No files needed

Microsoft® product screenshots used with permission from Microsoft® Corporation.

©HelenStock/Shutterstock

Understand Databases

You can use Microsoft Access to create a database to help you manage and track a large collection of related data. A **database** is an organized collection of related information. A database can contain information of any kind, such as sales and financial records for a business, products in a warehouse, or employee information. Access is a **database management system** (**DBMS**), a powerful tool for storing, organizing, and retrieving information. **CASE** ▶ *Before you start using Access, you need to know some basic concepts about databases and database management systems.*

DETAILS

Databases can help you:

• **Store information**

A database stores data in one or more spreadsheet-like lists called **tables**. For instance, one table in a database might store all the data about a company's products, another table might store data about the company's customers, and another might store data about the company's orders. A database containing just one table is called a **simple database**, and one that contains two or more tables of related information is called a **relational database**. **FIGURE J-1** shows the Sales Reps table you will create in this unit, which will be used to keep track of sales rep information. Each row in the table is called a **record**. Records consist of **fields**, which contain information about one aspect of a record, such as the rep's last name or the sales goal. The column headings in the table are called **field names**. Because entering data in the rows and columns of a table is tedious, you can create a form to make data entry easier. A **form** is a user-friendly window that contains text boxes and labels that let users easily input data, usually one record at a time. Each text box in a form corresponds with a field in a table. **FIGURE J-2** shows the form you will create in this unit that is based on the Sales Reps table.

• **Retrieve information**

Once you add data to a database, you can use Access queries or reports to retrieve or display all or part of the information in meaningful ways. A **query** extracts data from one or more database tables according to criteria that you set. For instance, at Outdoor Designs, you could create a query that displays all the customers in Ohio. You can also create reports that print selected information from the database. A **report** is a summary of information pulled from the database, specifically designed for printing. Tables, forms, queries, and reports are program components called **objects**. **TABLE J-1** provides a summary of common database objects.

• **Connect information**

As a relational database management system, Access is particularly powerful because you can enter data once and then retrieve information from all or several tables as you need it. For example, **FIGURE J-3** shows a report that contains fields from two related tables, Sales Managers and Sales Reps. Each table has mostly unique information, but they share Manager ID as a common field. Because the Manager ID field is shared by both tables, the tables can be linked, allowing you to pull information from both at once. Also, if you make changes to the data in a particular field in a table, any other object (such as a report or a query) that contains that field will automatically be updated to reflect the new value. For instance, in the example shown in **FIGURE J-3**, imagine that sales rep Sally Fritz changed her name to Sally Greene. If you delete "Fritz" from the Rep Last Name field in the Sales Reps table and replace it with "Greene," the report at the top of the figure would automatically be updated to show the rep's name as "Sally Greene."

FIGURE J-1: Sales Reps table

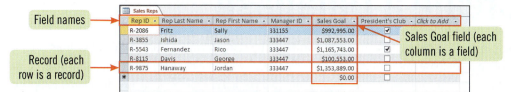

Field names

Record (each row is a record)

Sales Goal field (each column is a field)

Rep ID	Rep Last Name	Rep First Name	Manager ID	Sales Goal	President's Club	Click to Add
R-2086	Fritz	Sally	331155	$992,995.00	☑	
R-3855	Ishida	Jason	333447	$1,087,553.00	☐	
R-5543	Fernandez	Rico	333447	$1,165,743.00	☑	
R-8115	Davis	George	333447	$100,553.00	☐	
R-9875	Hanaway	Jordan	333447	$1,353,889.00	☐	
*				$0.00	☐	

FIGURE J-2: Sales Reps form

Sales Reps

Rep ID	R-2086
Rep Last Name	Fritz
Rep First Name	Sally
Manager ID	331155
Sales Goal	$992,995.00
President's Club	☑

All data in this form is for one record

Fields

Record: 1 of 5 — No Filter — Search

Form View

FIGURE J-3: Report in a relational database containing fields from two related tables

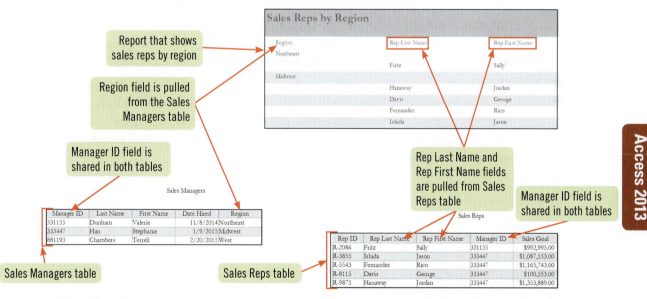

Report that shows sales reps by region

Region field is pulled from the Sales Managers table

Manager ID field is shared in both tables

Rep Last Name and Rep First Name fields are pulled from Sales Reps table

Manager ID field is shared in both tables

Sales Managers table

Sales Reps table

Sales Reps by Region

Region	Rep Last Name	Rep First Name
Northeast	Fritz	Sally
Midwest	Hanaway	Jordan
	Davis	George
	Fernandez	Rico
	Ishida	Jason

Sales Managers

Manager ID	Last Name	First Name	Date Hired	Region
331155	Dunham	Valerie	11/8/2014	Northeast
333447	Han	Stephanie	1/9/2015	Midwest
881193	Chambers	Terrell	2/20/2015	West

Sales Reps

Rep ID	Rep Last Name	Rep First Name	Manager ID	Sales Goal
R-2086	Fritz	Sally	331155	$992,995.00
R-3855	Ishida	Jason	333447	$1,087,553.00
R-5543	Fernandez	Rico	333447	$1,165,743.00
R-8115	Davis	George	333447	$100,553.00
R-9875	Hanaway	Jordan	333447	$1,353,889.00

TABLE J-1: Common database objects in Access

objects	description
Table	A list of data organized in rows (records) and columns (fields)
Query	A set of criteria you specify to retrieve data from a database
Form	A window that lets you view, enter, and edit data in a database one record at a time
Report	A summary of database information designed specifically for distributing or printing

Create a Database

Learning Outcomes
• Start Access
• Create and save a blank database

You can create a database in Access in two ways: by starting with a blank database or from a template. Creating a database from a template can save time, as it contains ready-made database objects, such as tables structured with field names appropriate to a particular type of database. By using a template, you can focus on entering data instead of designing appropriate database objects. When you first start Access, the Start screen opens and displays a variety of templates you can use to create a specific type of desktop database or a database web app that you can use and share using a Web browser To create a database from scratch, you click the Blank desktop database option. **CASE** *You need to create an Outdoor Designs database. You need to start Access, specify a name and location for the database file, and then create the database.*

STEPS

TROUBLE
If you are running Windows 7, click the Start button on the taskbar, click All Programs, click Microsoft Office 2013, then click Access 2013.

1. **Go to the Windows 8 Start screen, type access, then click Access 2013 in the Results list**

   Access starts and displays the Access Start screen as shown in **FIGURE J-4**. The Recent pane lists any recent database files you have opened. The large pane on the right displays thumbnails of different types of templates you can use to create specific types of databases. There is also a thumbnail for creating a custom web app, which allows you to create databases that can be viewed and accessed by others over the Web. (You need a SharePoint server to create a custom web app.) You want to start a new blank database.

2. **Click Blank desktop database**

   The Blank desktop database dialog box opens. You need to specify a name for your new database in it.

3. **Type J-Outdoor Designs**

4. **Click the Browse for a location…button ▣ to the right of the File Name text box**

   The File New Database dialog box opens. Like the Save As dialog box in Excel and Word, you use this dialog box to specify the folder and drive where you want to save the database file.

5. **Navigate to where you store your Data Files, then click OK**

   The dialog box closes. Notice that the path to the database under the File Name text box now in the Blank desktop database dialog box now shows the drive and folder location you specified, as shown in **FIGURE J-5**.

6. **Click Create**

   The Access program window opens in Datasheet view with the TABLE TOOLS FIELDS tab in front, as shown in **FIGURE J-6**. Below the Ribbon are two panes. In the right pane, a blank table datasheet with the temporary name Table1 is open. The left pane is called the **Navigation pane**; this is where all database objects for the open database are listed. Table1 is the only object listed.

Creating databases and database apps from templates

You can create a powerful database quickly by choosing a template from the Access Start screen. Like ready-made templates for Word or Excel, Access templates are database files designed for specific types of tasks, such as managing all your contacts, or tracking inventory, or keeping track of all the tasks in a large-scale project. In a database created from a template, the structure of the database is already set, with tables, queries, forms and reports all prebuilt. All you have to do is name and save the database, then enter the data you want. You can also customize the database by adding additional tables or other objects to suit your needs. In Access 2013, you can also use templates to create Web-based database apps that you can share on the Web with colleagues. The advantage of a Web-based database app is that users can access it from any location using a Web browser. To create a database app, you need a SharePoint server or an Office 365 site to host it.

FIGURE J-4: Access Start screen

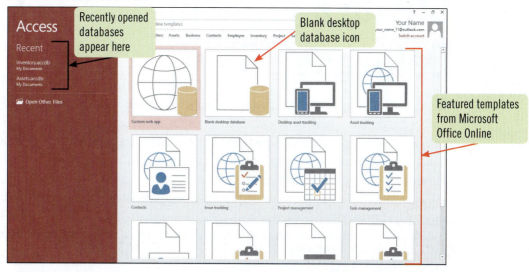

Access
Recent
Inventory.accdb
Assets.accdb
Open Other Files
Recently opened databases appear here
Blank desktop database icon
Your Name
Switch account
Custom web app
Blank desktop database
Desktop asset tracking
Asset tracking
Contacts
Issue tracking
Project management
Task management
Featured templates from Microsoft Office Online

FIGURE J-5: Blank desktop database dialog box showing path to where database file is stored

Blank desktop database
File Name
J-Outdoor Designs.accdb
E:\Unit J\
Create
Browse for a location...button
In Step 3, type the database name here
Location where database will be saved

FIGURE J-6: Blank table datasheet

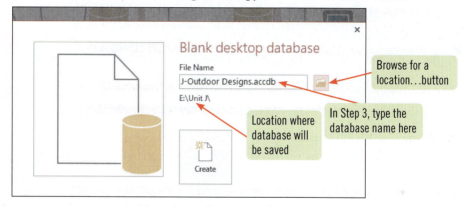

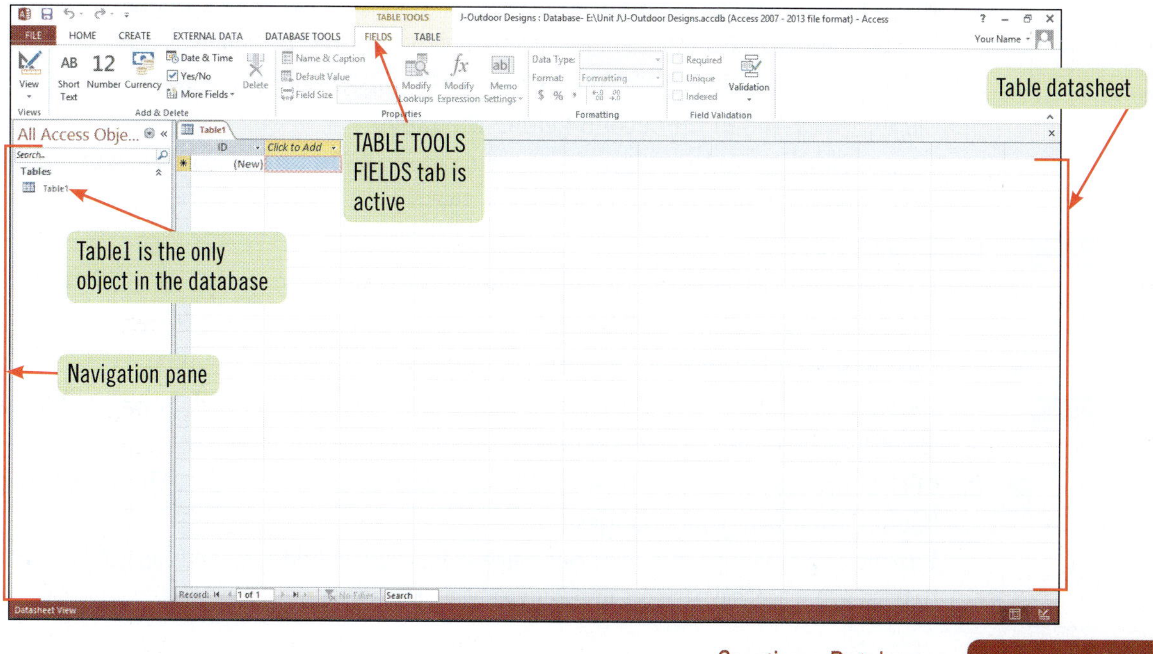

TABLE TOOLS
J-Outdoor Designs : Database- E:\Unit J\J-Outdoor Designs.accdb (Access 2007 - 2013 file format) - Access
FILE
HOME
CREATE
EXTERNAL DATA
DATABASE TOOLS
FIELDS
TABLE
All Access Obje...
Tables
Table1
ID
Click to Add
(New)
Datasheet View
TABLE TOOLS FIELDS tab is active
Table1 is the only object in the database
Navigation pane
Table datasheet

Access 2013

Create a Table in Datasheet View

When you start working in a new database, a blank table opens in Datasheet view. In **Datasheet view**, you can add fields to a table and view any data that the table contains. Before you begin adding fields to the table, it is a good idea to save the table with an appropriate name. Although you already saved the database, you also need to save each object you create within it, including tables. To add a field to a table, you need to specify its data type (such as Date or Currency) and then specify a name. See **TABLE J-2** for a description of field data types you can use. Every table in a database must contain one field that is designated as the **primary key field**, which uniquely identifies each record among all other records in a database. By default, every blank new table in Access includes a blank ID field, which is automatically designated the primary key field. **CASE** ▶ *You need to save the blank table with the name Sales Managers. Then, before you add new fields, you need to change the ID field data type to Short Text. Finally, you need to specify names and data types for new fields in the table.*

STEPS

1. Click the Save button 💾 **on the Quick Access toolbar**

The Save As dialog box opens. You need to specify a name for the new table.

2. Type Sales Managers in the Table Name text box, then click OK

The Sales Managers table is saved to the Outdoor Designs database. The name "Sales Managers" now appears under the Tables heading in the Navigation pane and in the tab above the datasheet. Notice the ID field. In this table, the ID field name can be used to store each manager's ID number.

3. Click ID in the table

The ID field is selected. Notice that the Data Type text box in the Formatting group indicates that the field has the AutoNumber data type applied to it. The **AutoNumber** data type assigns a unique number for each record in the table, starting with 1 and increasing sequentially by 1 for each record. You need to change the data type to Short Text, because Manager ID numbers are unique numbers that need to be entered individually.

4. Click the Data Type list arrow in the Formatting group as shown in FIGURE J-7, then click Short Text

The ID field now has the Short Text data type applied to it. The Short Text data type is appropriate here because it lets you enter text (such as names), numbers that do not require calculations (such as phone numbers), or combinations of text and numbers (such as street addresses).

5. Click Click to Add in the second field in the table

A menu of available field types opens, as shown in **FIGURE J-8**. You want to apply the Short Text data type to this field because it will be used for manager last names.

6. Click Short Text

The Short Text data type is now applied to the second field, and the temporary field name Field1 is selected. You can now type the name for this field.

7. Type Manager Last Name, then press [Tab]

The second field in the table now displays the name "Manager Last Name". The Data Type list is now open for the third field in the table, which you need to use for manager first names.

8. Click Short Text, type Manager First Name, click Click to Add, click Short Text, type Region, then save your changes

You entered the Manager First Name field name and the Region field name and applied the Short Text data type for each. The table now contains four text fields, as shown in **FIGURE J-9**.

Creating a Database

FIGURE J-7: Applying the Short Text data type to the ID field

FIGURE J-8: Specifying a data type for a new field

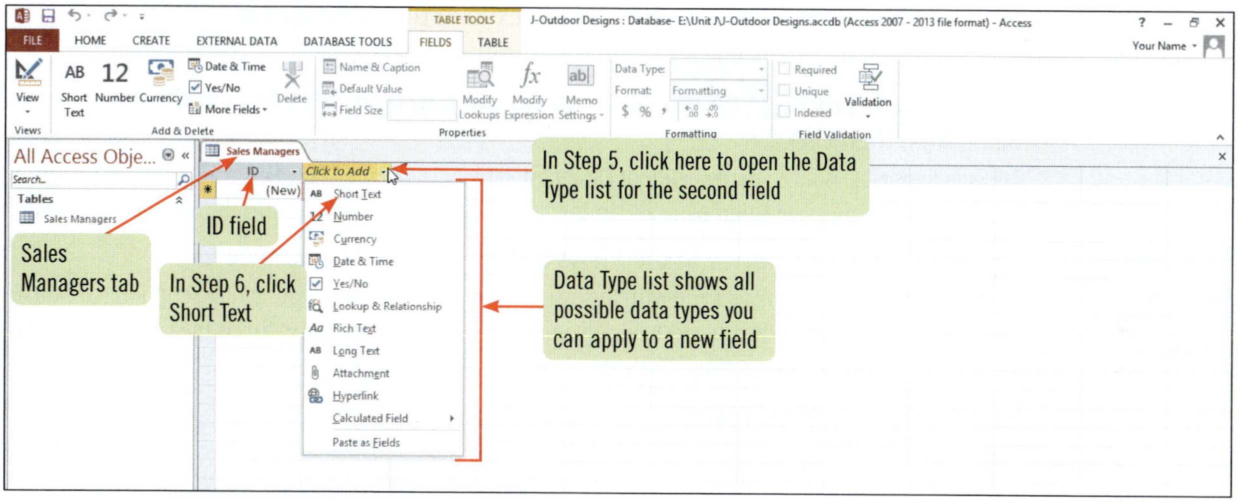

FIGURE J-9: Sales Managers table with four fields

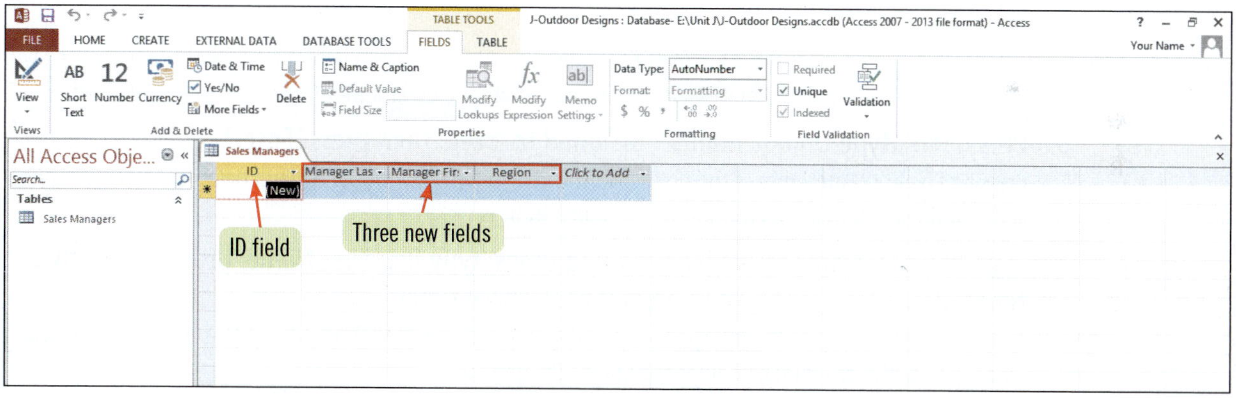

TABLE J-2: Common field data types

data type	description
Short Text	A word or string of words, numbers that do not require calculations, or a combination of text and numbers
AutoNumber	Unique sequential numbers that Access assigns to each new record, which cannot be edited
Number	Numeric data to be used in calculations
Currency	Currency values and numeric data used in calculations
Date/Time	Date and time values
Yes/No	Values that can be only Yes or No; used to identify the presence or absence of specific criteria
Long Text	Lengthy text (which can also contain numbers that do not require calculations)
Calculated	Displays a value that is the result of a formula that includes field values

Create a Table in Design View

Learning Outcomes
• Add fields in Design view
• Specify data types in Design view
• Add field descriptions

Databases usually contain many tables. To add a new table to a database, click the Table button in the Tables group on the CREATE tab. Although you can add fields to a new or existing table using Datasheet view, it is often easier to use Design view. In Design view, you use a grid to enter fields and specify field data types. You can also add field descriptions to fields in Design view. A **field description** identifies the purpose of a field and helps users of the database understand the information that the field is meant to contain. You can also use Design view to view and change the primary key field in a table. **CASE** *You need to create a new table that contains information about the sales reps. You decide to create this table using Design view.*

STEPS

1. **Click the CREATE tab, then click the Table button in the Tables group**
   A new blank table with the temporary name Table1 opens in Datasheet view.

2. **Click the Save button 🔲 on the Quick Access toolbar, type Sales Reps in the Save As dialog box, then click OK**
   The Sales Reps table is saved to the Outdoor Designs database. The name "Sales Reps" now appears under the Tables heading in the Navigation pane and in the tab above the datasheet, next to the Sales Managers tab.

3. **Click the View button arrow in the Views group, then click Design View**
   The main window now displays a grid with the headings Field Name, Data Type, and Description (Optional). The ID field is listed as the first field; the key icon to the left of "ID" indicates this is the primary key field. You want to change the name of the ID field to Rep ID.

4. **Type Rep ID, then press [Tab]**
   The ID field name is changed to Rep ID. This field currently has the AutoNumber data type applied to it. You want to change the data type to Short Text because each rep is assigned a unique Rep ID.

5. **Click the AutoNumber arrow in the Data Type column as shown in FIGURE J-10, then click Short Text**
   The Rep ID field now has the Short Text data type. You need to enter a description for this field, which will appear in the status bar and help users understand what type of data should be entered for this field.

6. **Press [Tab], type Unique number assigned to a rep, then press [Enter]**
   Pressing [Tab] or [Enter] moves the pointer to the next cell in the grid. The blank field below Rep ID is now active and ready for you to type a new field name in it.

7. **Type Rep Last Name, press [Enter] three times, type Rep First Name, press [Enter] three times, type Manager ID, then press [Enter] three times**
   You entered three new fields and specified the data types for each as Short Text. If you specify no particular data type, the Short Text data field is automatically applied.

8. **Type Sales Goal, press [Enter], click the Data Type list arrow, click Currency, then press [Enter] twice**
   You applied the Currency data type to the Sales Goal field. The Currency data type is appropriate because this field will contain the dollar amount of a rep's sales goal for the year. Any numbers entered in this field will automatically be formatted as currency.

9. **Type President's Club, press [Enter], type Y, press [Enter], type Yes if rep met sales goal in prior year, press [Enter], then save your changes**
   Typing the letter "Y" in the Data Type column applied the Yes/No data type for the President's Club field. In Datasheet view, any field with a Yes/No data type will contain a check box; a check mark in a field check box indicates a Yes value for the field. The description you typed in the Description column will let users know to mark this field as Yes if the rep achieved his or her sales goal in the prior year. Compare your screen to **FIGURE J-11**.

FIGURE J-10: Specifying a data type for the Rep ID field in Design view

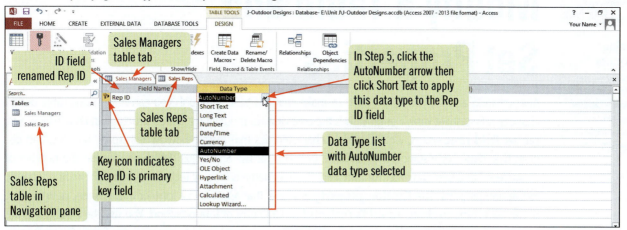

FIGURE J-11: Sales Reps table with six fields in Design view

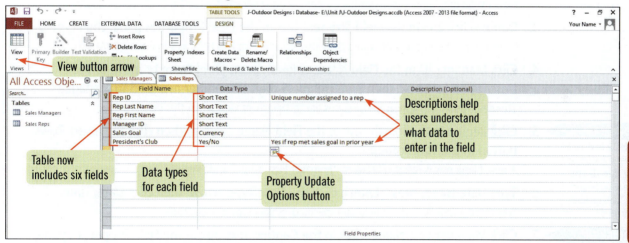

Modify a Table and Set Properties

Learning Outcomes
• Edit field names
• Insert a field
• Specify a caption for a field
• Change field properties

After creating a table, you might need to make changes to it. Although you can make some table design changes in Datasheet view, Design view is the best view for modifying a table's structure. In Design view, you can set **field properties**, which are data characteristics that dictate how Access stores, handles, and displays field data. For instance, the Field Size property for the Short Text data type specifies the number of characters that a user can enter for that field. If a field name is long or technical, you might want to change its Caption property. The **Caption property** is a label that appears in a form or in Datasheet view in place of the field name to clarify the field's contents for data entry or interpretation. You use the Field Properties pane to view and change field properties. **CASE** *You need to make changes to the Sales Managers table. You need to change the name of the ID field, limit its field size to 6, and add a field description for it. You also need to add captions to two fields and insert a new Date Hired field.*

STEPS

1. Click the Sales Managers table tab, click the View button arrow in the Views group, then click Design View

The Sales Managers table opens in Design view. You want to change the name of the ID field to "Manager ID". The ID field is selected, so you are ready to type the new name.

> **QUICK TIP**
> To rename a field, double-click the field name to select it, then type the new name.

2. Type Manager ID

The field name is changed to "Manager ID". The Field Properties pane at the bottom of the screen displays the field properties for the Manager ID field. The settings reflect the default settings for the Short Text data type. By default, Short Text fields have a limit of 255 characters.

3. Double-click 255 in the Field Size text box in the Field Properties pane, then type 6

Users will not be able to enter more than six characters for this field, as shown in **FIGURE J-12**.

4. Click Manager ID in the Field Name column, press [Tab] twice to move to the Description text box, then type Unique 6-digit ID number assigned to manager

This description will appear in the status bar in Datasheet view when this field is active.

> **QUICK TIP**
> To delete a field, click the field you want to delete, then click the Delete Rows button in the Tools group.

5. Click Region in the fourth row of the Field Name column, then click the Insert Rows button in the Tools group

A new, blank row is inserted between "Manager First Name" and "Region".

6. Type Date Hired, press [Enter], click the Data Type arrow, then click Date/Time

You added a new Date Hired field and specified its data type as Date/Time.

> **QUICK TIP**
> The Field Properties pane changes depending on which field is currently selected.

7. Click Manager Last Name, click in the Caption text box in the Field Properties pane, type Last Name, then press [Enter]

The caption for the Manager Last Name field is now "Last Name". This means that only Last Name will be displayed as the field name for this field in Datasheet view and in any form that includes this field.

8. Click Manager First Name, click in the Caption text box in the Field Properties pane, type First Name, then press [Enter]

You specified the caption for the Manager First Name field as "First Name", as shown in **FIGURE J-13**.

> **QUICK TIP**
> You must save changes to an object before switching views.

9. Save your changes, then click the View button in the Views group

The view changes to Datasheet view, as shown in **FIGURE J-14**. Notice that the Manager Last Name and Manager First Name fields now appear as "Last Name" and "First Name".

FIGURE J-12: Changing the Field Size property for the Manager ID field in Design view

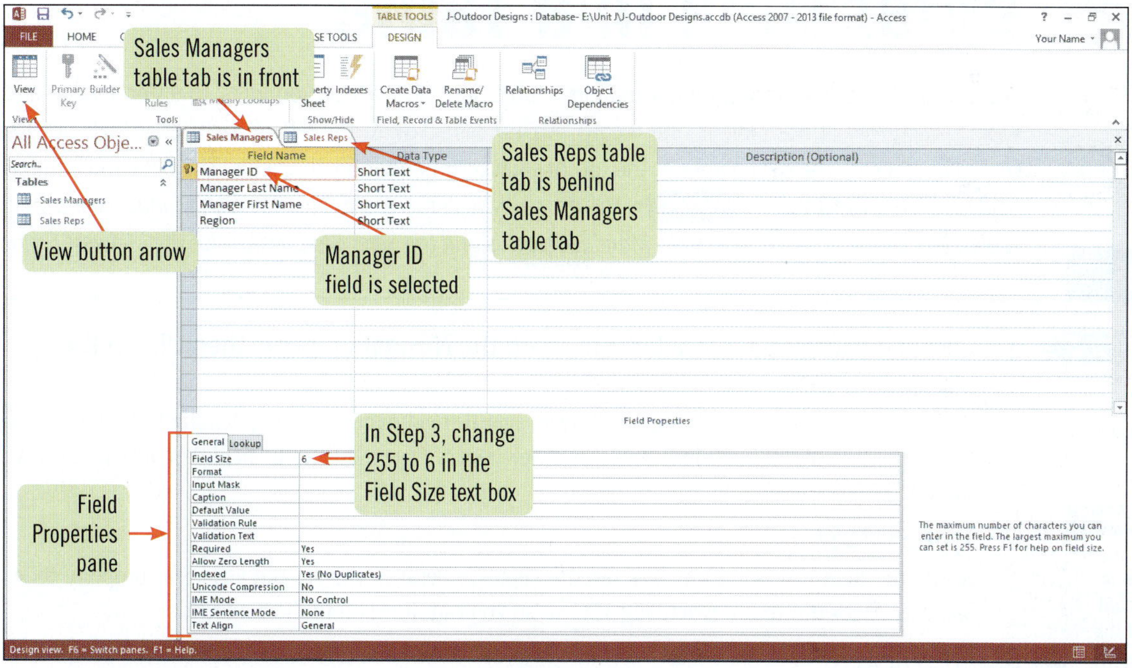

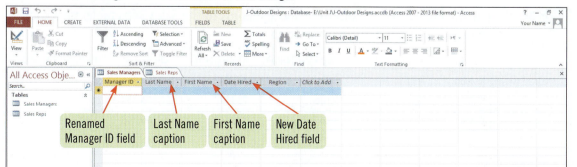

FIGURE J-13: Sales Managers table in Design view after adding a field and changing properties

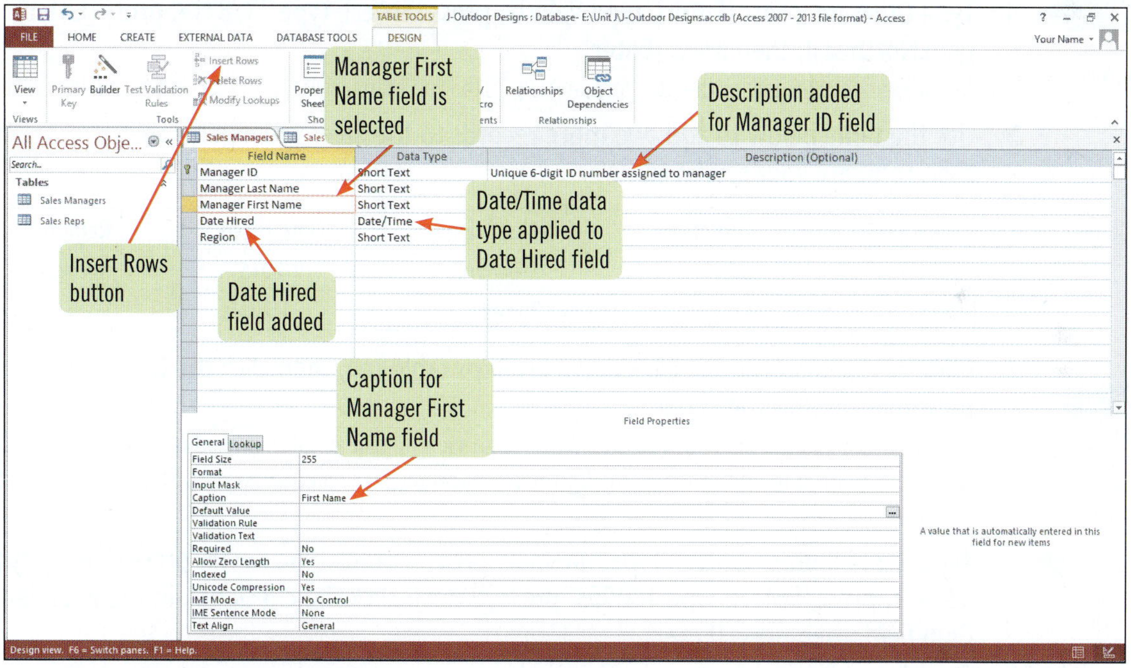

FIGURE J-14: Sales Managers table in Datasheet view after changes

Enter Data in a Table

You can use Datasheet view to enter data in a table; just click where you want to enter a value and start typing. Each row of the table is one record. A **row selector** to the left of each record lets you select a record or records. The field names at the top of each column identify the fields. The data you enter in each field is called a **field value**. **CASE** ▶ *You are ready to enter records into the Sales Managers and Sales Reps tables. You decide to enter three Sales Manager records and the Sales Reps records for the Midwest region.*

STEPS

1. **Click the Shutter Bar Close button ‹‹ on the Navigation pane, then click in the Manager ID field**

   With the Navigation pane minimized, the Manager ID field name is highlighted, indicating it is selected. A star in the first row selector indicates it is a new record. The Manager ID field description appears in the status bar.

2. **Type 3311557**

   Notice the field will not accept the seventh digit (7) because you set the Field Size property to six. The Manager ID for this record is actually 331155, so you can move on to the next field.

3. **Press [Enter]**

   Pressing [Enter] or [Tab] accepts your entry and moves the insertion point to the next field.

4. **Type Dunham, press [Enter], type Valerie, press [Enter], type 11/8/14, press [Enter], type Northeast, then press [Enter]**

   Access changed the date to the date format 11/8/2014. The Manager ID in the second record is now active.

5. **Use the table below to add two more records to the Sales Managers table, press [Enter], then compare your screen to FIGURE J-15**

Manager ID	Last Name	First Name	Date Hired	Region
333447	Han	Stephanie	1/9/2015	Midwest
881193	Chambers	Terrell	2/20/2015	West

6. **Click the Save button 🖫, click the Sales Reps table tab, then click the Datasheet View button ▦ on the status bar**

   In Datasheet view, the six fields you added in Design view appear as column headings, and the Rep ID field is active. You need to enter the records for the reps who report to Stephanie Han. Stephanie's Manager ID is 333447.

7. **Type R-2244, press [Enter], type Marshall, press [Enter], type Kevin, press [Enter], type 333447, press [Enter], type 100553, press [Enter], click the check box in the President's Club field, then press [Enter]**

   The value you entered for the Sales Goal field (100553) is formatted as currency. The check box in the President's Club field indicates a Yes value.

8. **Use the table below to add three more records to the Sales Reps table, save your changes, then compare your screen to FIGURE J-16**

Rep ID	Rep Last Name	Rep First Name	Manager ID	Sales Goal	President's Club
R-2086	Fritz	Sally	333447	$992,118	Y
R-9875	Hanaway	Jordan	333447	$1,353,889	N
R-5543	Fernandez	Rico	333447	$1,165,743	Y

FIGURE J-15: Field values entered in the Sales Managers table in Datasheet view

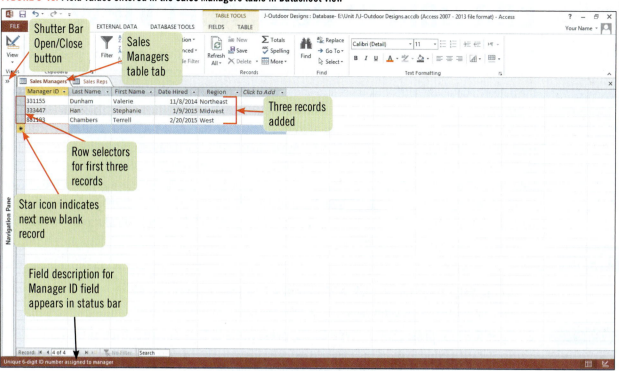

FIGURE J-16: Field values entered in the Sales Reps table in Datasheet view

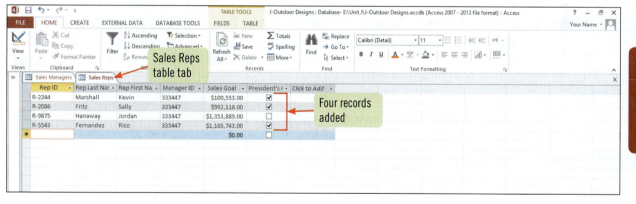

Access 2013

Edit Data in Datasheet View

Learning
Outcomes
• Edit field values in
Datasheet view
• Resize columns in
Datasheet view

The data in a database is dynamic and always changing. Unlike a Word document or an Excel workbook, a database is never "finished"; the data it contains constantly needs updating to reflect changes. To keep the data in a database current, you need to add and delete records and make edits to individual fields on a regular basis. You can edit the data in a table in Datasheet view using the editing skills you learned for Word and Excel. To edit a field value, you need to select either the entire field value or the part of it you want to edit, then type the replacement data. As you make edits in a datasheet, you might find it helpful to resize columns to make the data easier to see. To resize a column to fit its contents, double-click the line between the column headings. To resize a column to a specific width, drag the line between the column headings to the desired width. **CASE** *You just learned that sales rep Sally Fritz moved to New York and now reports to the Northeast sales manager, and that a new rep has taken over Kevin Marshall's territory. You need to edit these records in the Sales Reps table.*

STEPS

1. **In the Sales Reps table, click R-2244 in the first row, then press [F2]**

   Pressing [F2] selects the entire field value R-2244, the Rep ID for Kevin Marshall.

2. **Type R-8115, press [Enter], type Davis, press [Enter], type George, then press [Enter]**

   The text you typed replaced the original field values for the Rep ID, Rep Last Name, and Rep First Name fields for the first record. No other changes are needed for this record.

3. **In the Sales Goal field for the Sally Fritz record, click to the right of $992,118.00, press [Backspace] six times, type 995, then press [Enter]**

   The field value in the Sales Goal field for the second record now reads $992,995.00, the new sales goal for Sally Fritz. Using the [Backspace] key is another useful method for editing field values in a datasheet. You can also edit text by selecting it and then typing new text.

4. **In the Manager ID field for Sally Fritz, double-click 333447, type 331155, then press [Enter]**

   The Manager ID field value for the third record now reads 331155, which is the Manager ID for the Northeast sales manager (Valerie Dunham).

5. **Point to the border between the Rep Last Name field and the Rep First Name field names until the pointer changes to ↔, as shown in FIGURE J-17, then double-click**

   The Rep Last Name column widened just enough to fit the entire field name. The border between the field names that you clicked is called the **column separator**. Double-clicking the column separator automatically resizes a column to make it larger or smaller to fit the widest field name or field contents.

6. **Double-click the column separator ↔ between each of the field names in the field name row**

   Each column is now resized, as shown in FIGURE J-18.

7. **Save your changes to the Sales Reps table, then click the Close 'Sales Reps' button ☒**

   The Sales Reps table closes.

8. **Save your changes to the Sales Managers table, then click the Close 'Sales Managers' button ☒**

   The Sales Manager table closes.

FIGURE J-17: Resizing a column in Datasheet view

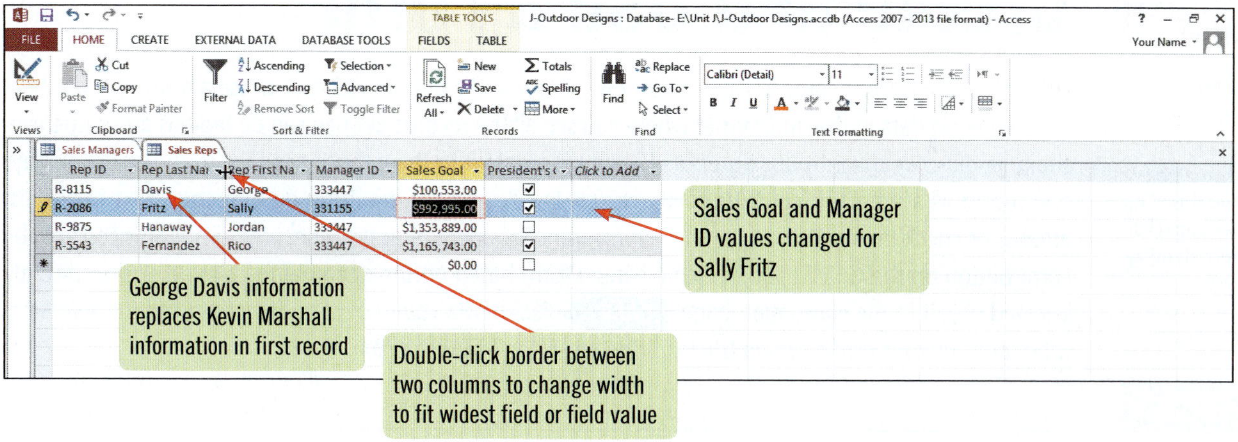

George Davis information replaces Kevin Marshall information in first record

Double-click border between two columns to change width to fit widest field or field value

Sales Goal and Manager ID values changed for Sally Fritz

FIGURE J-18: Edited records in the Sales Reps Table in Datasheet view

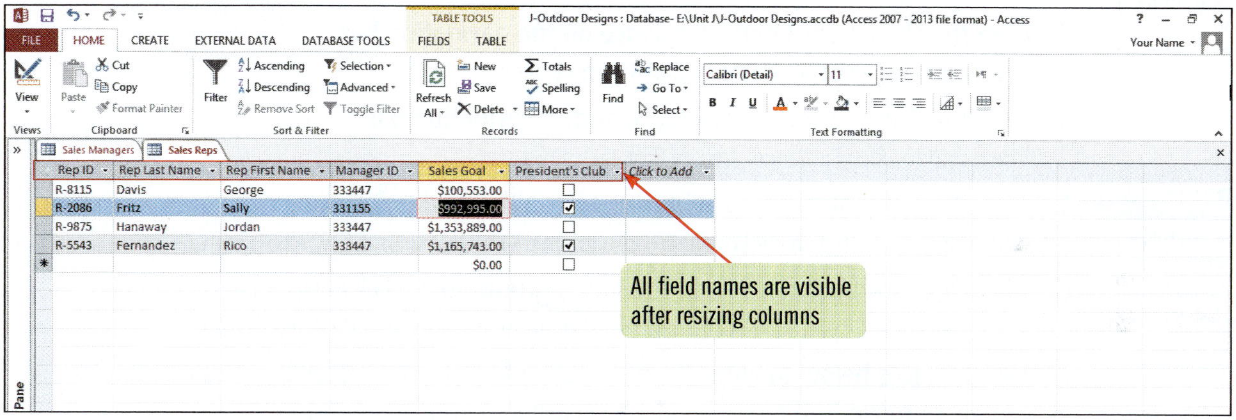

All field names are visible after resizing columns

Printing objects in Access

If you want to print information from a database, you would usually create a report that includes selected fields, then print it. However, there might be times when you want to print a datasheet or form. To print any object in Access, select the object in the Navigation pane, click the FILE tab, then click Print. The Print page opens in Backstage view and displays three print options.

Click Quick Print to print the object using default print settings. Click Print to open the Print dialog box, which lets you adjust print settings. Click Print Preview to preview the object with its default settings. In Print Preview, you can use the tools on the Print Preview tab to adjust settings, then click the Print button when you are ready to print.

Access 2013

Create and Use a Form

Learning Outcomes
- Create a form based on a table
- View records using the navigation bar
- Add records using Form view
- Close a database and exit Access

Entering and editing records in Datasheet view is easy, but it is more efficient to use a form. In Datasheet view, entering data in the grid format where you see all the records at once can be tedious and cause eye-strain, and it may risk introducing errors by entering data into the wrong record. A form usually displays one record at a time and contains **form controls**—devices for inputting data, such as text boxes, list arrows, or check boxes. You can create a form using a variety of approaches; the simplest is to click the Form button on the CREATE tab, which creates a form based on the open database table or the currently selected object in the Navigation pane. **CASE** *Karen asks you to create a form based on the Sales Reps table, and enter a record for Jason Ishida, a new rep in the Midwest region.*

STEPS

1. **Click the Shutter Bar Open button** `»` **in the Navigation pane, then click the CREATE tab**

   The Navigation pane is now open and lists the Sales Managers table and the Sales Reps table. The CREATE tab allows you to add new objects to your database.

> **QUICK TIP**
>
> To apply a theme to a form, click the Theme button in the Themes group on the FORM LAYOUT TOOLS DESIGN tab, then click the theme you want.

2. **Click the Sales Reps table in the Navigation pane, then click the Form button in the Forms group**

   A new form based on the Sales Reps table opens in Layout view, as shown in **FIGURE J-19**. You use Layout view to change the structure of the form. The data for the first record (Sally Fritz) is shown in the form. In Layout view, you can view records but cannot add, delete, or edit records. To view different records, you use the buttons on the **navigation bar**.

3. **Click the Next record button** `▶` **twice on the navigation bar**

   The record for George Davis (record 3 of 4) is now open.

4. **Click the Previous record button** `◀` **on the navigation bar**

   The record for Rico Fernandez (record 2 of 4) is now open.

> **QUICK TIP**
>
> You can also create a new record by pressing [Tab] or [Enter] after the last field in a record.

5. **Click the New (blank) record button** `▶*` **on the navigation bar**

   A blank form for a new record opens. To enter data in a form, you must switch to Form view.

6. **Click the View button arrow in the Views group, then click Form View**

   The form is now displayed in Form view, which you use to add, edit, and delete records.

7. **Use the table below to enter the field values for two new records, pressing [Tab] or [Enter] to move to the next field, then compare your screen to FIGURE J-20**

Rep ID	Rep Last Name	Rep First Name	Manager ID	Sales Goal	President's Club
R-1111	your last name	your first name	331155	$1,000,000.00	Yes
R-3855	Ishida	Jason	333447	$1,087,553.00	No

   If you were to open the Sales Reps table now, you would see the new records you added using the form, with your name appearing as the first record in the table. (It is listed first because records are sorted by the first field in the table in ascending order, and your Rep ID is R-1111.)

> **QUICK TIP**
>
> A **split form** is a form that displays the data entry form above the underlying datasheet. To create a split form, click the CREATE tab, click More Forms in the Forms group, then click Split Form.

8. **Click the Save button** `💾` **on the Quick Access toolbar, click OK in the Save As dialog box, then click the Close 'Sales Reps' button** `✕`

   The Sales Reps form closes. You are now ready to close the J-Outdoor Designs database and exit Access.

9. **Click the FILE tab, click Close as shown in FIGURE J-21, then click the Access window close button** `✕`

   The Outdoor Designs database and Access both close. Submit your database to your instructor.

FIGURE J-19: New form in Layout view

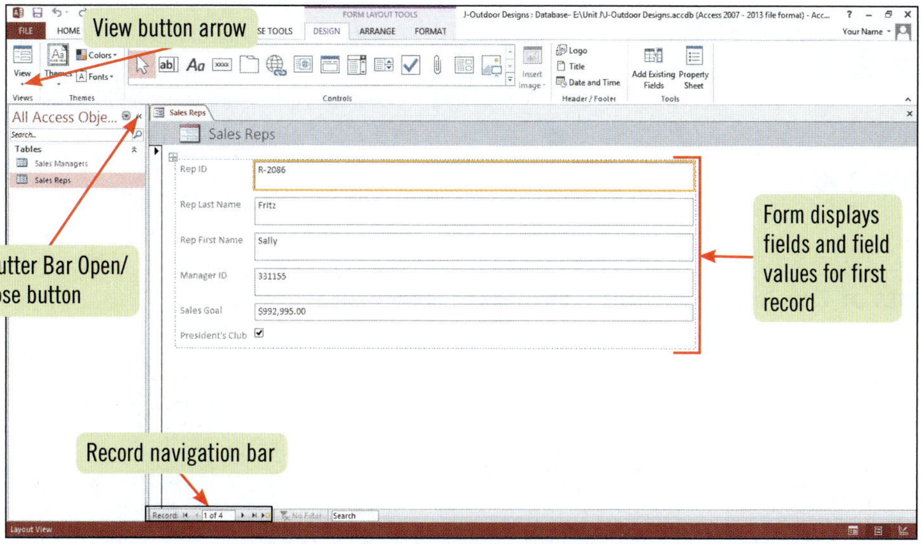

- View button arrow
- Shutter Bar Open/Close button
- Form displays fields and field values for first record
- Record navigation bar

FIGURE J-20: New record added to the Sales Reps form in Form view

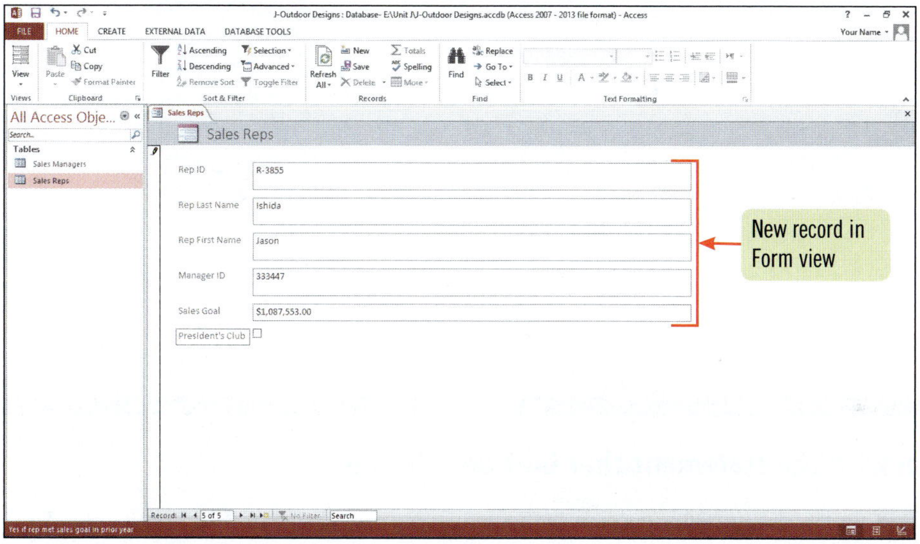

- New record in Form view

FIGURE J-21: Closing the database and exiting Access

- Click to exit Access
- Click to close J-Outdoor Designs database

Creating a Database

Practice

Put your skills into practice with SAM! If you have a SAM account, go to www.cengage.com/sam2013 to access SAM assignments for this unit.

Concepts Review

Label the elements of the Access window shown in FIGURE J-22.

FIGURE J-22

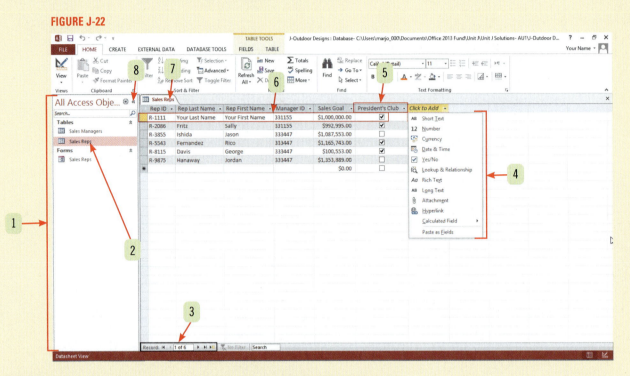

Match each term with the statement that best describes it.

9. **Table**

10. **Record**

11. **Field**

12. **Object**

13. **Database**

14. **Form**

a. Window containing text boxes and labels into which you enter data in a database

b. A collection of information organized in columns and rows and stored electronically in a file

c. A program component, such as a table or form that is saved in a database

d. Information about one item in a particular record in a database

e. A program component in a database that is used to store, view, enter, and edit data in a gridlike format

f. One row of data in a database table

Select the best answer from the list of choices.

15. **In Access, the view that displays information in a rows-and-columns format is _____ view.**

    a. Form

    b. Record

    c. Datasheet

    d. Table Design

16. **Data characteristics that dictate how Access stores, handles, and displays field data are called:**

    a. Field properties.

    b. Field values.

    c. Captions.

    d. Field descriptions.

17. **Which of the following activities is *not* possible to do in Design view?**
    a. Add or edit a record.
    c. Insert a field.
    b. Edit a field name.
    d. Specify the Field Size property.

18. **Which of the following is a not a database object?**
    a. Form
    c. Record
    b. Table
    d. Report

19. **Which of the following activities is possible to do in Datasheet view?**
    a. Add a field description.
    c. Specify the field size.
    b. Add a caption.
    d. Add a record.

20. **Where does a field description appear in Datasheet view?**
    a. In the status bar
    c. In the Navigation pane
    b. In the Field Properties pane
    d. On the CREATE tab

21. **Which of the following is not a data type?**
    a. Short Text
    c. Field
    b. AutoNumber
    d. Currency

22. **Every database must contain one field that is designated as the _____ field, which uniquely identifies each record among all other records in a database.**
    a. Primary key
    c. Key record
    b. AutoNumber
    d. Relational

Skills Review

1. **Understand databases.**
   a. Explain the purpose of Microsoft Access; what type of business tasks is it designed to perform?
   b. Without referring to the lesson material, define database, table, fields, records, forms, reports, and queries.
   c. What are the common database objects in Access? What is the purpose of each?

2. **Create a database.**
   a. Start Access.
   b. Create a new, blank desktop database with the name **J-Party Equipment Rentals**.
   c. Save the new database where you store your Data Files.

3. **Create a table in Datasheet view.**
   a. Save the blank table that is open in Datasheet view with the name **Bounce Houses**.
   b. Use a button on the Ribbon to change the data type of the ID field to Short Text.
   c. Use the table below to add fields to the table.

Field Name	Data Type
Bounce House Type	Short Text
Rental Rate	Currency
Retractable Roof	Yes/No
Data Entered By	Short Text

   d. Save your changes to the table.

4. **Create a table in Design view.**
   a. Create a new table, and save it as **Rental Orders**.
   b. View the Rental Orders table in Design view, then change the name of the ID field name to **Rental ID**. Change the data type for the Rental ID field to Short Text.

c. Use the table below to add fields to the Rental Orders table.

Field Name	Data Type
Rental Date	Date/Time
Customer Last Name	Short Text
Customer First Name	Short Text
Bounce House ID	Short Text
Hours Rented	Number
Data Entered By	Short Text

d. Save your changes to the table.

5. **Modify a table and set properties.**
   a. Open the Bounce Houses table in Design view, then change the ID field name to **Bounce House ID**.
   b. Change the Field Size property for the Bounce House ID field to **5**.
   c. Add a new field between Bounce House Type and Rental Rate. Rename the new field **Date Purchased**, and apply the Date/Time data type to it.
   d. Add the following description to the Rental Rate field: **Rental rate is for one hour of use**.
   e. Change the Caption property for the Rental Rate field to **Rate**.
   f. Add the following description to the Retractable Roof field: **Specify yes if it has a roof that opens and closes**.
   g. Save your changes to the table.

6. **Enter data in a table.**
   a. View the Bounce Houses table in Datasheet view.
   b. Using the table below, enter the three records shown into the Bounce Houses table in Datasheet view, then save the Bounce Houses table.

Bounce House ID	Bounce House Type	Date Purchased	Rate	Retractable Roof	Data Entered By
33511	Castle	5/1/15	$50	No	your name
45612	Obstacle Course	6/1/15	$60	Yes	your name
99113	Sports House	4/1/15	$75	Yes	your name

   c. View the Rental Orders table in Datasheet view.
   d. Using the table below, enter the three records shown into the Rental Orders table in Datasheet view.

Rental ID	Rental Date	Customer Last Name	Customer First Name	Bounce House ID	Hours Rented	Data Entered By
BH-5522	6/1/2016	Bigly	Charles	99113	3	your name
BH-5523	6/2/2016	Allen	Martha	45612	5	your name
BH-5524	6/5/2016	Yi	Holly	33511	3	your name

   e. Save your changes to the Rental Orders table.

7. **Edit data in Datasheet view.**
   a. In the Bounce Houses table, change the Rate field value for the Castle to **$85.00**.
   b. In the Bounce Houses table, change the Bounce House Type field value for the Castle to **King's Castle**.
   c. Adjust all the column widths in the Bounce Houses table datasheet for best fit.
   d. In the Rental Orders table, in the third record, change the Hours Rented field value to **8**.
   e. Adjust all the column widths in the Rental Orders table datasheet for best fit.

Skills Review (continued)

f. Compare the Bounce Houses table to **FIGURE J-23**. Save your changes to the Bounce Houses and Rental Orders tables. Compare the Rental Orders table to **FIGURE J-24**.

FIGURE J-23

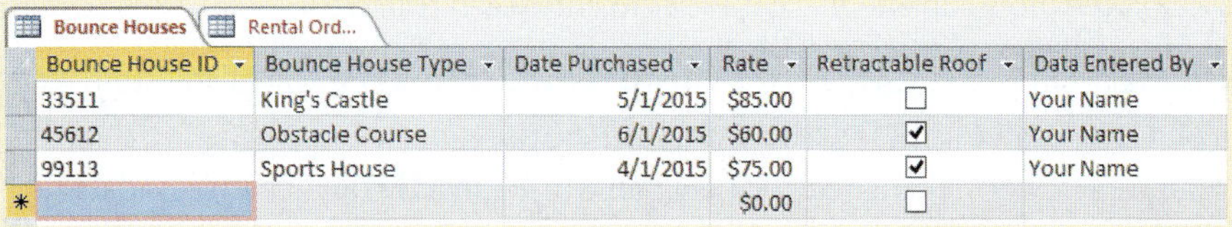

Bounce House ID	Bounce House Type	Date Purchased	Rate	Retractable Roof	Data Entered By
33511	King's Castle	5/1/2015	$85.00	☐	Your Name
45612	Obstacle Course	6/1/2015	$60.00	☑	Your Name
99113	Sports House	4/1/2015	$75.00	☑	Your Name
*			$0.00	☐	

FIGURE J-24

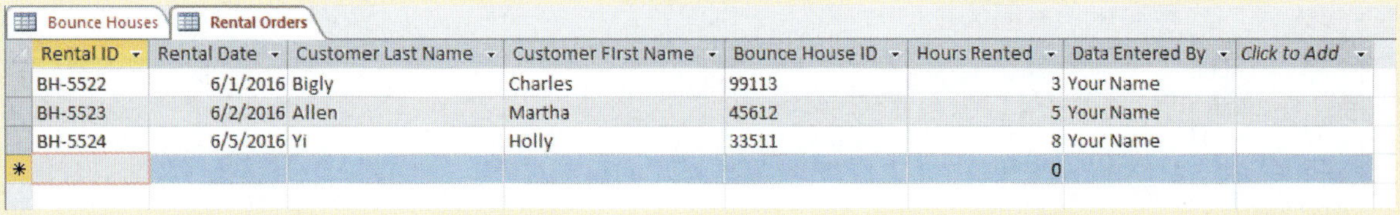

Rental ID	Rental Date	Customer Last Name	Customer First Name	Bounce House ID	Hours Rented	Data Entered By	Click to Add
BH-5522	6/1/2016	Bigly	Charles	99113	3	Your Name	
BH-5523	6/2/2016	Allen	Martha	45612	5	Your Name	
BH-5524	6/5/2016	Yi	Holly	33511	8	Your Name	
*					0		

8. Create and use a form.

a. Create a new form based on the Rental Orders table.

b. In Layout view, view each record one by one using the Previous and/or Next buttons on the navigation bar.

c. Switch to Form view, then add a new record using the information in the table below:

Rental ID	Rental Date	Customer Last Name	Customer First Name	Bounce House ID	Hours Rented	Data Entered By
BH-5525	6/10/16	Hansen	Ian	45612	8	your name

d. Save the form as **Rental Orders**, then compare your screen to **FIGURE J-25**.

e. Close the database, then exit Access.

f. Submit your completed database to your instructor.

FIGURE J-25

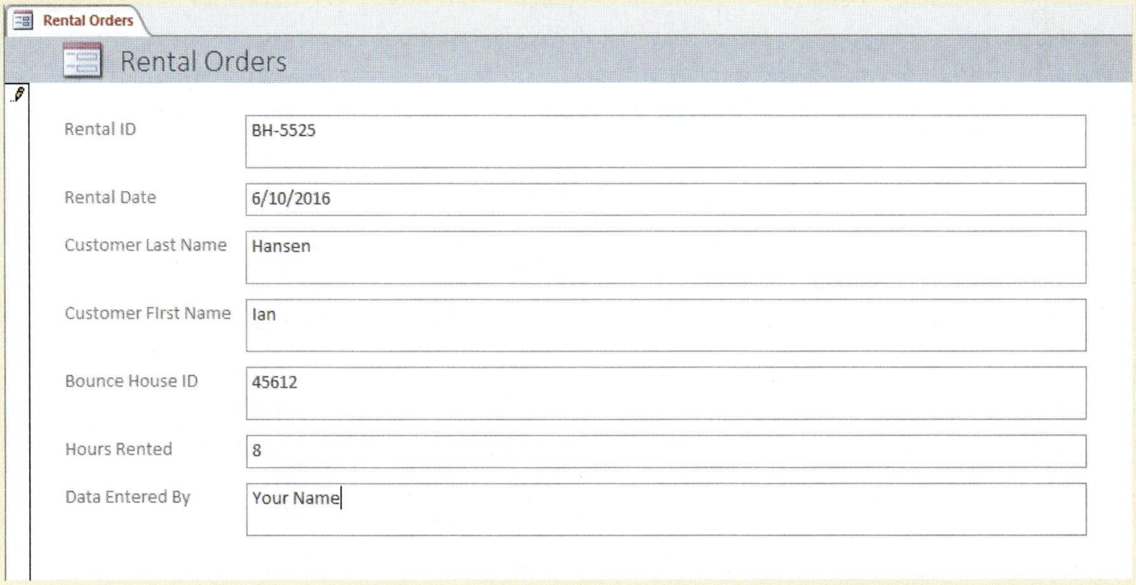

Rental Orders

Rental ID	BH-5525
Rental Date	6/10/2016
Customer Last Name	Hansen
Customer First Name	Ian
Bounce House ID	45612
Hours Rented	8
Data Entered By	Your Name

Independent Challenge 1

You are the prop manager for the Loud Voice Theatre that produces 10 major productions a year. Your job is to obtain props that are needed for every show produced and manage the prop assets that the theatre owns. You decide to create a database to manage all this information. Your database needs to contain a table that includes information about each prop. You will also create a form based on the props table to make it easier to enter each record.

a. Create a new, blank desktop database named **J-Loud Voice Theatre** where you store your Data Files.

b. Save the blank table that appears in Datasheet view as **Props**.

c. View the table in Design view. Change the ID field name to **Prop ID**, and change its data type to Short Text. Use the table below to enter the field names and their data types for the table.

Field	Data Type
Prop Description	Short Text
Date Acquired	Date/Time
Cost	Currency
Purchased?	Yes/No
Data Entered By	Short Text

d. Save your changes. Create a new table, save it as **Prop Suppliers**, then enter the following fields into it in Design view.

Field Name	Data Type
Supplier ID	AutoNumber
Supplier Name	Short Text
Supplier Phone	Short Text
Supplier Contact Name	Short Text
Preferred Supplier?	Yes/No
Data Entered By	Short Text

e. Add the following field description to the Preferred Supplier field: **Yes if supplier offers free shipping and discount**.

f. View the Props table in Design view. Specify the Caption field property as **Acquired** for the Date Acquired field. Add the following description to the Purchased field: **Yes if the prop was purchased; no if the prop was made in house**. Save your changes.

g. View the Props table in Datasheet view, then enter the records shown below into it.

Prop ID	Prop Description	Acquired	Cost	Purchased	Data Entered By
P-4477	Antique telephone	4/7/15	$85.00	Y	your name
P-6588	Pocket watch	5/1/16	$55.00	Y	your name
P-7542	Milk rack with bottles	3/1/15	$25.00	Y	your name
P-6644	Handkerchiefs	2/15/16	$7.00	N	your name

h. Resize the column widths in the datasheet for best fit. Save your changes, then close the table.

i. View the Prop Suppliers table in Datasheet view, then enter the records shown below into it. (*Hint*: Press [Tab] to accept the AutoNumber in the Supplier ID field.)

Supplier Name	Supplier Phone Number	Supplier Contact Name	Preferred Supplier?	Data Entered By
Cassie's Theatre Goods	555-975-1414	Giorgio Carrillo	Yes	your name
Stellar Props, Inc.	555-974-1169	Phil Potter	No	your name
Flanders & Ballard, Inc.	555-865-9800	Lizzy McPherson	Yes	your name

Creating a Database

Independent Challenge 1 (continued)

j. Change the Supplier Contact Name field value for Cassie's Theatre Goods to **Frank Brown**. Adjust the column widths in the datasheet for best fit. Compare your datasheet to FIGURE J-26, then save and close the table.

FIGURE J-26

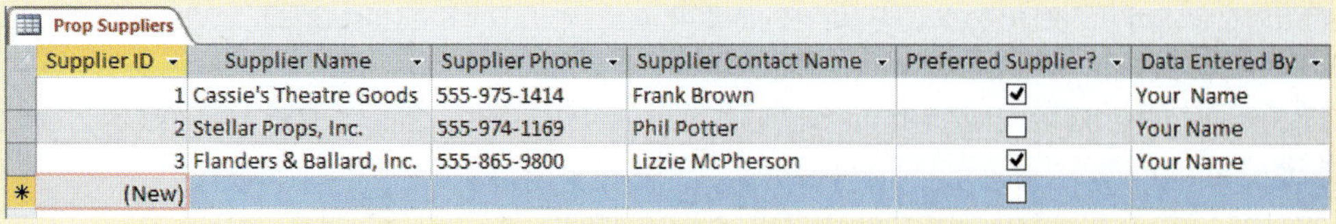

Supplier ID	Supplier Name	Supplier Phone	Supplier Contact Name	Preferred Supplier?	Data Entered By
1	Cassie's Theatre Goods	555-975-1414	Frank Brown	☑	Your Name
2	Stellar Props, Inc.	555-974-1169	Phil Potter	☐	Your Name
3	Flanders & Ballard, Inc.	555-865-9800	Lizzie McPherson	☑	Your Name
(New)				☐	

Prop Suppliers

k. Create a form based on the Props table, then save the form as **Props Form**. View each record using the record navigation bar.

l. Switch to Form view, than add the following record:

Prop ID	Prop Description	Acquired	Cost	Purchased	Data Entered By
P-9955	Old piano bench	7/2/15	$18.99	N	your name

m. Compare your form to FIGURE J-27. Close the database, then exit Access. Submit your completed database to your instructor.

FIGURE J-27

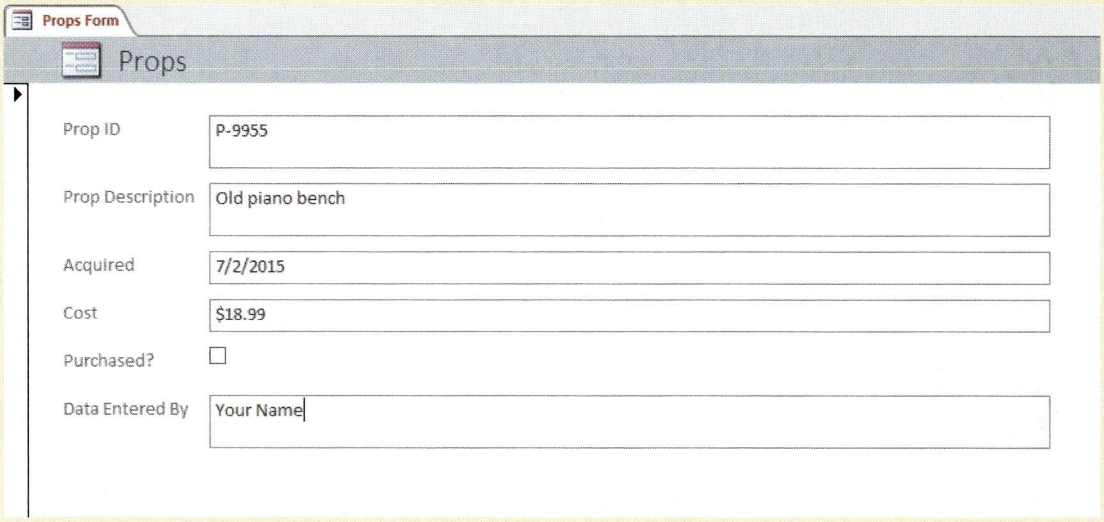

Props Form

Props

Prop ID	P-9955
Prop Description	Old piano bench
Acquired	7/2/2015
Cost	$18.99
Purchased?	☐
Data Entered By	Your Name

Independent Challenge 2

You own a costume rental business that rents costumes for all occasions and age groups. You decide to create a database to keep track of your inventory.

a. Create a new, blank database with the name **J-Costume Rentals**, and save it where you store your Data Files.

b. Save the blank new table as **Costumes**. Switch to Design view, then rename the ID field **Costume ID**. Change the data type for the Costume ID field to Short Text. Then, enter the fields and data types shown in the table below.

Field Name	Data Type
Costume Name	Short Text
Theme	Short Text
Rental Rate	Currency
Times Rented	Number
Size	Short Text
Saleable	Yes/No
Data Entered By	Short Text

c. Add the following description to the Rental Rate field: **Rate is for 72 hours**. Add the following description to the Saleable field: **Yes if Times Rented field value is less than 20. Sale price is three times rental rate**.

d. Set the Caption property to **Rate** for the Rental Rate field. For the Costume ID field, set the Field Size property to **5**. Save your changes to the Costumes table, then close it.

e. Create a form based on the Costumes table using the Form tool. Click the Theme button arrow, then click the Facet theme thumbnail.

f. Save the form as **Costumes**, then switch to Form view.

g. Add the following records to the form:

Costume ID	Costume Name	Theme	Rental Rate	Times Rented	Size	Saleable	Data Entered By
33551	Vampire	Horror	$50	22	Men's Large	No	Your Name
22765	Abraham Lincoln	Historical	$60	18	Men's Medium	Yes	Your Name
88432	Witch	Horror	$45	44	Women's Small	No	Your Name

h. Save and close the form. Open the Costumes table in Datasheet view. Change the Size field value for Abraham Lincoln so it reads **Men's Small**. Resize all the column widths of the table for best fit. Compare your finished datasheet to FIGURE J-28.

i. Close the database, then exit Access. Submit your completed database to your instructor.

FIGURE J-28

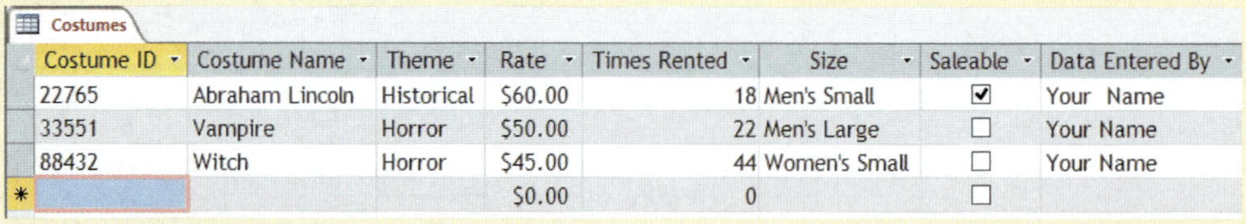

Costume ID	Costume Name	Theme	Rate	Times Rented	Size	Saleable	Data Entered By
22765	Abraham Lincoln	Historical	$60.00	18	Men's Small	☑	Your Name
33551	Vampire	Horror	$50.00	22	Men's Large	☐	Your Name
88432	Witch	Horror	$45.00	44	Women's Small	☐	Your Name
*			$0.00	0		☐	

Independent Challenge 3

As part of a long-term marketing strategy at the Red Onion Cooking School you decide to create a database that contains names, addresses, and other information about people who have participated in your classes. You will use the database to promote future classes.

a. Create a new, blank database named **J-Cooking School**, and save it where you store your Data Files.

b. Save the blank open table as **Students**, then switch to Design view.

c. Use Design view to design your table. Keep the ID field name and data type the same, and keep it as the primary key field.

d. Add at least seven fields that seem appropriate for this type of database. Of those fields, you must include **First Name** and **Last Name**. Include at least one field with each of the following data types: Date/Time and Yes/No.

e. Add a field called **Data Entered By** that has the Short Text data type.

f. Add at least one description for one of the fields.

g. Save the table.

h. View the table in Datasheet view. Resize all columns for best fit. Close the table.

i. Use the Form tool to create a form based on the Students table. In Layout view, apply a theme that you like, then save the form with the name **Students**.

j. Switch to Form view, then add three fictional records. Enter your name in the Data Entered By field. Save and close the form and table.

k. Close the database, then exit Access. Submit your completed database to your instructor.

Independent Challenge 4: Explore

Access comes with a number of ready-made templates that you can use to organize specific types of projects or information. For instance, there is an asset tracker you can use to keep track of business or personal inventory, and there is a task manager template you can use to keep track of projects. In this Independent Challenge, you will create a new database of contacts (people) using the Desktop contacts desktop template. *Note: To complete the Independent Challenge, your computer must be connected to the Internet.*

a. Start Access.

b. Click Desktop contacts on the Start screen. Create a new, blank database named **J-Contacts**, and save it where you store your Data Files.

c. Notice the security warning below the Ribbon. You will see this warning anytime you open a database. Since this database is one that you downloaded from Microsoft you can feel confident that it is safe to use. Click Enable Content. If the Getting Started with Contacts window opens, take a few minutes to watch the two videos that teach how to use the Contacts Management database. When you have finished watching the videos, close your browser to return to the Access program window.

d. Look at the Navigation pane; notice that there are two tables (Contacts, Settings), and three forms (Contact Details, Contact List, and Getting Started). There are also Queries and Reports (which you will learn about in later units) as well as Macros and Modules.

e. Notice that the Contact List form is open now. This form looks more like a table, but you can tell it is a form because the Contact List appears in the Forms area of the Navigation pane.

f. Click New in the first row of the form to open the Contact Details form. Enter the information for Bruce Hubbard, shown in FIGURE J-29, into the form. Specify Business for the Category. (*Note*: You will need to leave some of the fields blank, since the contact information shown in the figure does not have information for some fields.)

FIGURE J-29

Bruce Hubbard, Manager
Blue Square Fitness Center
67 Brook Road
Baltimore, MD 21218
bhubbard@bluesquarefitness.com
301-555-0085

g. Click Save and New to move to a new blank record, then enter the information for Gloria Weber, shown in FIGURE J-30. Notice that when you type the first letter of Blue Square Fitness Center in the Company field, the full name of the company is automatically entered. Access "guesses" that you want to enter the name of the company from an existing contact.

h. Click Save and New, then enter one more contact record. For this record, enter your first name and your last name. Populate the other fields for this contact using the other field values for Gloria Weber or Bruce Hubbard (your choice). Leave the email field blank. Save and close the Contact Details form and the Contact List form.

FIGURE J-30

Gloria Weber, Personal Trainer
Blue Square Fitness Center
67 Brook Road
Baltimore, MD 21218
gweber@bluesquarefitness.com
301-555-0087

i. Double-click Directory in the Navigation pane. The Directory report opens and lists the three contact names in a slick-looking report. Open the Phone Book report; notice that this report shows only the names and phone numbers of Bruce, Gloria, and you. Close the Phone Book report and the Directory report.

j. Close the database and exit Access. Submit your completed database to your instructor.

Visual Workshop

Create the database form shown in FIGURE J-31. (*Hint*: First create a new, blank database called **J-Car Sales Business** where you store your Data Files, then create a table called **Cars** that contains the fields shown in the form. Assign appropriate data types for each field.) Set the Field Size property to **4** for the Year Made field. Add the following field description to the Car ID field: **Unique number assigned at time of purchase**. Create a form based on the table and save it as **Cars**. In Form Layout view, apply the Retrospect theme. Enter the data shown in the figure into the form. Save and close the table and the form, close the database, then exit Access. Submit your completed database to your instructor.

FIGURE J-31

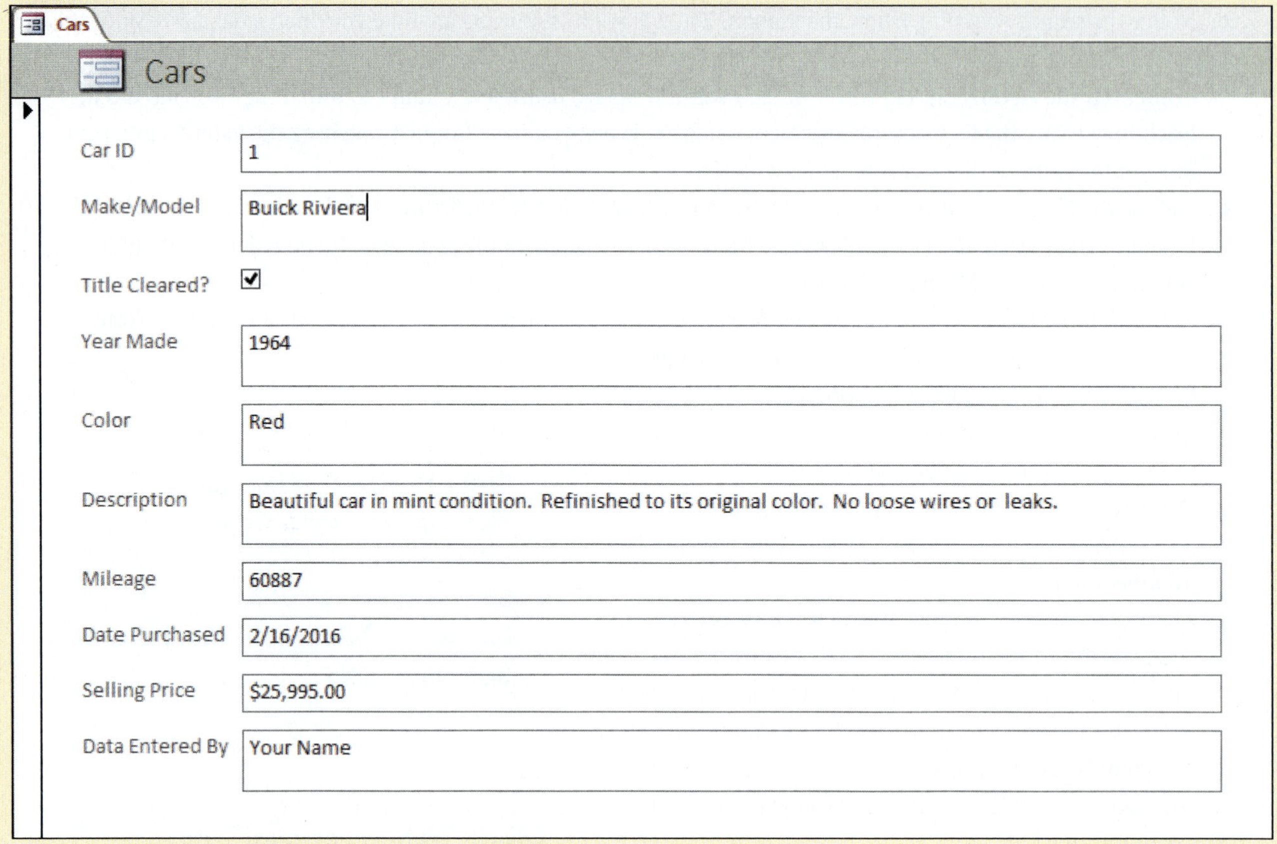

Car ID	1
Make/Model	Buick Riviera
Title Cleared?	✔
Year Made	1964
Color	Red
Description	Beautiful car in mint condition. Refinished to its original color. No loose wires or leaks.
Mileage	60887
Date Purchased	2/16/2016
Selling Price	$25,995.00
Data Entered By	Your Name

Working with Data

CASE   Serena Henning, sales director at Outdoor Designs, has given you a database that contains two tables. She asks you to sort and filter the data so that it is more useful. She also needs you to retrieve some information from these tables by using queries. Finally, she wants you to add a calculated field to one of the tables.

Unit Objectives

After completing this unit, you will be able to:

- Open an existing database
- Sort records in a table
- Filter records in a table
- Create a query

- Modify a query in Design view
- Relate two tables
- Create a query using two tables
- Add a calculated field to a table

Files You Will Need

K-1.accdb	K-5.accdb
K-2.accdb	K-6.accdb
K-3.accdb	K-6a.docx
K-4.accdb	K-7.accdb

©HelenStock/Shutterstock

Microsoft® product screenshots used with permission from Microsoft® Corporation.

Open an Existing Database

Learning Outcomes
- Open a database
- Enable content in a database
- Save a database with a new name

After you enter data into a database, you can pull out information you need by filtering and querying the data and by sorting it in useful ways. In this unit, you will work with an existing database that contains two tables. First you need to open it. Opening an existing Access database is similar to opening a Word or Excel file. From the Access Start screen, you click the Open Other Files command to open the Open screen, navigate to the folder where the file is located, then double-click the file you want. (If you worked with the file recently, you can click its name in the Recent list in the Start screen.) One difference between opening an Access database and opening a file in Word or Excel is that you can only open one Access database file at a time. If you want two databases open at once, you need to start an additional session of Access, then open the additional database in that second session. **CASE** ▶ *To get started on your project for Serena, you decide to open the database and then save it with a new name, so the original database will remain intact. Then, you decide to view the tables it contains in Datasheet view.*

STEPS

1. **Start Access**

   The Access Start screen is displayed on your screen.

2. **Click Open Other Files at the bottom of the Recent list on the Start screen**

   The Open screen opens in Backstage view and displays a list of recently opened files.

3. **Click Computer, click Browse to open the Open dialog box, navigate to the drive and folder where you store your Data Files, click K-1.accdb, then click Open**

   The database opens, as shown in **FIGURE K-1**. Notice the Security Warning in the yellow bar below the Ribbon, which says, "Some active content has been disabled. Click for more details." Unless you change the standard default settings in Access, this security warning appears any time you open an existing database. This warning is Microsoft's way of protecting your computer from potentially harmful files. Because you can trust that this file is safe, you can enable the content for this file and for all data files for this book.

4. **Click Enable Content in the Security Warning bar**

5. **Click the FILE tab, then click Save As**

   The Save As screen opens. Notice that Save Database As is selected in the File Types section and that Access Database (*.accdb) is selected in the Save Database As section. See **FIGURE K-2**. These settings are appropriate; you want to save the file as an Access database file.

6. **Click Save As**

   The Save As dialog box opens.

7. **Type K-Outdoor Designs in the File name text box, navigate to the folder where you save your Data Files, if necessary, then click Save**

   The copy of the database opens with the new name K-Outdoor Designs.accdb. The Security Warning appears below the Ribbon again, as Access recognizes this is a database file you have not opened before.

8. **Click Enable Content in the Security Warning bar, then double-click the Customers table in the Navigation pane**

   The Customers table opens in Datasheet view, as shown in **FIGURE K-3**. You can see in the navigation bar at the bottom of the screen that this table contains 77 records.

9. **Double-click the Sales Reps table in the Navigation pane**

   A new tab opens in the database window and displays the Sales Reps table, as shown in **FIGURE K-4**. This table has only nine records (one for each sales rep) and contains only four fields (Rep ID, Region, Rep Last Name, and Rep First Name). Note that the Rep ID is the primary key field. You will use this table later in the unit, but you do not need it now.

10. **Click the Sales Reps Table Close button ☒ in the database window**

Working with Data

FIGURE K-1: Database open with Security Warning

This database contains two tables

SECURITY WARNING Some active content has been disabled. Click for more details. **Enable Content**

Security Warning appears when you open an existing database

In Step 4, click Enable Content

FIGURE K-2: Save As screen

Save As

File Types

Save Database As

Save Object As

Save Database As

Database File Types

Access Database (*.accdb)
Default database format.

Access 2002-2003 Database (*.mdb)
Save a copy that will be compatible with Access 2002-2003.

Access 2000 Database (*.mdb)
Save a copy that will be compatible with Access 2000.

Template (*.accdt)
Save the current database as a database template (ACCDT).

Advanced

Package and Sign
Package the database and apply a digital signature.

Make ACCDE
File will be compiled into an executable only file.

Back Up Database
Back up important databases regularly to prevent data loss.

SharePoint
Share the database by saving it to a document management server.

Save As

FIGURE K-3: Customers table in Datasheet view

Customers table

Sales Reps table

Customers table contains 77 records

Customer ID	Customer	Address	City	State	Zip	Rep ID	YTD Orders	Prior Year Orders
133212	The Happy Birder	44 West Main	Hartford	CT	06101	R-2086	$7,865.00	$7,543.00
133222	Hiking HQ, Inc.	678 Smithson Road	Chico	CA	95926	R-7754	$5,436.00	$4,532.00
133223	Martin's Mountain Shop	5000 Big Valley Road	Denver	CO	80012	R-6421	$8,986.00	$8,859.00
133267	Wilderness Central	4200 Vintage Highway	Sonoma	CA	95476	R-7754	$9,678.00	$7,564.00
332121	Country Goods	453 Mill Street	Puyallup	WA	98553	R-5876	$53,776.00	$32,445.00
332125	Outside Nation	5365 Chestnut Stree	Detroit	MI	48901	R-9875	$9,875.00	$1,654.00
332134	Fresh Air Mike's Deals	5 Oak Drive	Old Town	IL	66549	R-5543	$2,433.00	$1,454.00
332167	Peppy's Hardware	102 Pine View Way	Portland	OR	97701	R-5876	$7,855.00	$6,543.00
332178	Sully's Surf Shop	2565 Beach Street	Los Angeles	CA	91178	R-7754	$3,432.00	$4,567.00
332180	Backyard Warehousers	345 Sea Breeze Way	Newport Beach	CA	92118	R-7754	$7,866.00	$14,321.00
332190	Nautical Goods, Inc.	254 Main Street	Plywood	AZ	85207	R-6421	$5,532.00	$4,533.00
332198	Foggy Day Gear	342 Branson Street	Newtown	MI	48901	R-9875	$77,654.00	$87,445.00
332232	Kite Nation	100 Sea Breeze Drive	San Diego	CA	92660	R-7754	$543.00	$335.00
332237	Bird Boutique	45 Fire Boulevard	Cleveland	OH	45227	R-3855	$554.00	$1,454.00
332244	Karl and Kevin's Kite Store	147 Sycamore Street	Redmond	WA	45439	R-5876	$9,844.00	$7,755.00
332255	The Canoe Supplier	3463 SE 118th Street	Bellevue	WA	98444	R-5876	$26,755.00	$43,223.00
332256	Jackie's Boating Gear	33 Forest Street	Montpelier	VT	05041	R-2086	$4,422.00	$6,522.00
332257	Mo's Outdoor Warehouse	457 Sparrow Lane	Sandview	WA	98438	R-5876	$77,994.00	$77,422.00
332260	Camping Station	45 Woodchuck Way	Redville	WA	98503	R-5876	$3,360.00	$7,098.00
332265	Stevie's Kites	15 Pond View Drive	High Town	NY	12498	R-2086	$642.00	$1,098.00
332266	s Outdoor Goods	765 Commerce Way	Augusta	ME	04011	R-2086	$1,654.00	$9,953.00
332277	Young Buck's Camping Gear	767 Turnpike Way	Exeter	NH	03675	R-2086	$9,966.00	$6,633.00
332280	Skipper's Camp Depot	44 River Road	Brunswick	ME	05301	R-2086	$4,876.00	$5,963.00
332282	Birdland Warehouse	22 Mountain Way	High Town	VT	05672	R-2086	$4,367.00	$9,456.00
332284	Hank's Outdoor Recreation	16 Oak Street	Concord	NH	03456	R-2086	$6,086.00	$7,834.00
332287	Backyard Warehousers	2 River Way	Portstown	MA	01765	R-2086	$5,986.00	$9,876.00
332288	Petie's Outdoor Goods	17 Scarborough Way	Providence	RI	02886	R-2086	$12,876.00	$9,299.00

Records in Customers table

FIGURE K-4: Sales Reps table in Datasheet view

Rep ID	Region	Rep Last Name	Rep First Name
R-1876	Southeast	Johnson	Martin
R-2086	Northeast	Sally	Fritz
R-3855	Midwest	Ishida	Jason
R-5543	Midwest	Fernandez	Rico
R-5876	West	Chen	Sherwin
R-6421	West	Smedley	Ben
R-7754	West	Abbott	Marcie
R-8115	Midwest	Davis	George
R-9875	Midwest	Hanaway	Jordan

Records in Sales Reps table

Sales Reps table Close button

Sort Records in a Table

You can rearrange, or **sort**, the records in a table in alphabetical or numerical order. To perform a sort, you need to indicate the field on which you want Access to sort, then specify whether to sort the database in ascending order (alphabetically from A to Z or numerically from 0 to 9) or descending order (alphabetically from Z to A or numerically from 9 to 0). For example, in a customer database, you could sort records by the Sales field in descending order to quickly identify the customers who purchased the most products. You might also want to sort records using more than one field. For example, you might wish to sort primarily by state but also by customer name, so that the records for each state are grouped together, with customers listed in alphabetical order within each state grouping. **CASE** *Serena asks you to create a sorted list that groups the records first by Rep ID and then, within each Rep ID grouping, by YTD Orders in descending order. First, you experiment with sorting in different ways.*

STEPS

1. **Click the Shutter Bar Close button ⊲⊲ in the Navigation pane**

   The database window now displays the Customers table with all its fields in view. Just to experiment, you decide to sort the table in ascending order by customer name.

2. **Click any field in the Customer column**

   Before performing a sort, you need to select the field by which you want to sort.

3. **Click the Ascending button in the Sort & Filter group on the HOME tab**

   The table is now sorted by customer name in ascending alphabetical order, with Arnie's Nature Emporium listed first. Notice there is a small upward-pointing arrow to the right of the Customer column header, indicating that the table is sorted in ascending order by this field, as shown in **FIGURE K-5**.

4. **Click the Descending button in the Sort & Filter group on the HOME tab**

   The table is now sorted by customer name in descending alphabetical order (Z to A), with Young Buck's Camping Gear listed first. Notice the downward-pointing arrow in the Customer column heading, indicating the records in the table are sorted in descending order by this field.

5. **Click the Remove Sort button in the Sort & Filter group**

   The table is now ordered in its original order, with The Happy Birder listed first in the Customer column.

6. **Click any field in the YTD Orders column, then click the Descending button in the Sort & Filter group**

   The records are now sorted in descending order by year-to-date order amounts. You see that Mo's Outdoor Warehouse has purchased the most this year, with $77,994.00 in the YTD Orders field value text box.

7. **Click any field in the Rep ID column, then click the Ascending button in the Sort & Filter group**

   The records in the Customers table are now sorted first by Rep ID in ascending order and then, within each Rep ID grouping, by YTD Order amounts in descending order, as shown in **FIGURE K-6**.

8. **Click the Remove Sort button in the Sort & Filter group**

   The table reverts to its original order.

Capturing a screen shot of your sorted table

Your instructor might ask you to capture a screen shot of the sorted Customers table and submit it. To do this, start Microsoft Word, open a new blank document, click the INSERT tab, click the Screenshot button, then click the image of the screenshot in the Available Windows menu. The screen shot of your sorted table is pasted into the new Word document. Save this document as Unit K-Screen Shots, and submit it to your instructor. Click the Access program button on the taskbar to return to Access.

FIGURE K-5: Customers table in alphabetical order by Customer

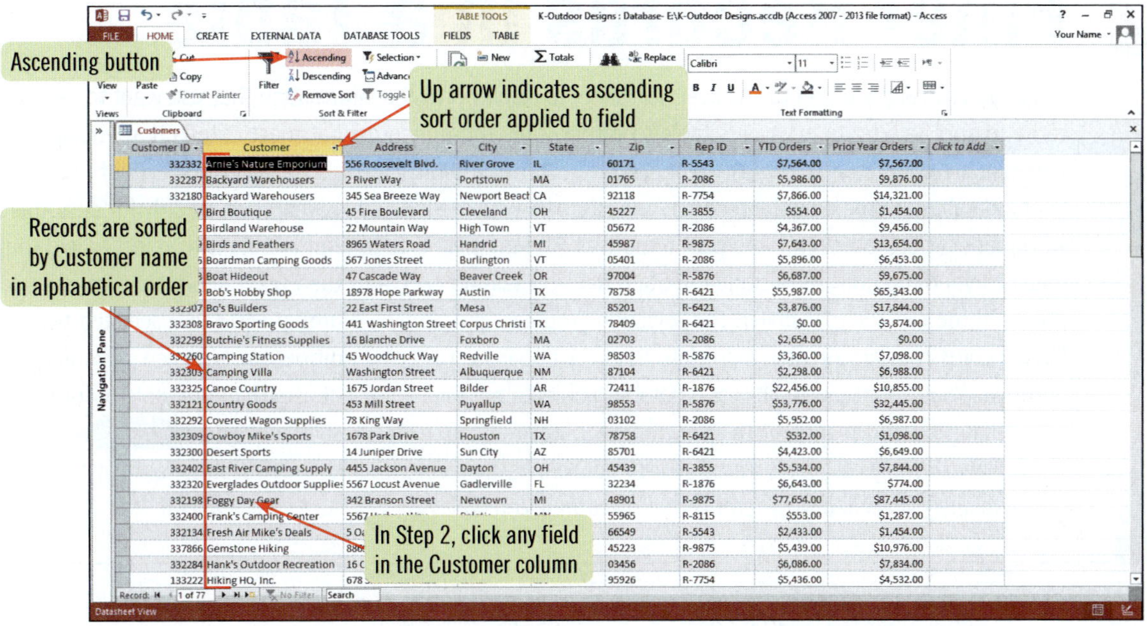

FIGURE K-6: Records sorted by two different fields

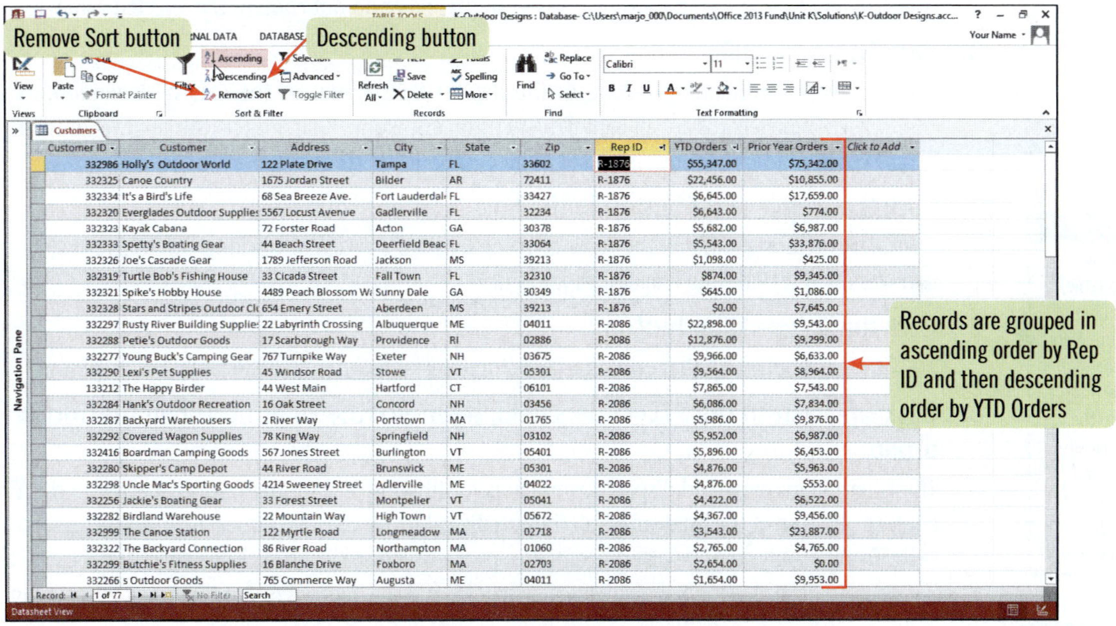

Sorting on multiple fields

Before you sort records in a table by two different fields, you first need to decide which field you want to be the primary sort field and which field you want to be sorted within the primary field grouping. The field that is the primary sort field is called the **outermost sort field**, and the field that is the secondary sort field is called the **innermost sort field**. For example, in **FIGURE K-6**, the Rep ID field is the outermost sort field, and the YTD Orders field is the innermost sort field; the records are first sorted by Rep ID in ascending order, then by YTD Orders in descending order. Ironically, to get the results you want, you need to first sort the records by the innermost field and then sort by the outermost field. This can be confusing because it is counterintuitive; thus, it is important that you understand these rules before you sort on two fields.

Filter Records in a Table

Just as you can apply a filter to an Excel worksheet to display only the information that you want to see, you can also apply a filter to an Access table to display only those records that meet criteria that you specify. **Criteria** are conditions that must be met for a record to be displayed. For example, you might want to filter a database to see only the records for customers who are located in New York, or only for customers who made a purchase within the past 6 months. The simplest way to filter a table is to select a field that matches your criterion (for instance, a State field containing NY), and then use the Equals command to display those records that match the selection. You can also apply a Number Filter to a selected field to filter records that are greater than, less than, or equal to a specific number, or between two different numbers. You cannot save a filter as a database object, but you can save it as part of the table or form you are working on and reapply it the next time. You can also print the results of a filter. **CASE** *Serena needs you to identify customers whose year-to-date orders are greater than $7,500 for sales rep Sally Fritz. You decide to apply filters to display records that meet these criteria.*

STEPS

1. **Click a field in the Rep ID column containing the value R-2086**

   This Rep ID number (R-2086) is the ID number for Sally Fritz, a rep in the Northeast region.

2. **Click the Selection button in the Sort & Filter group**

   The Selection menu opens and displays four commands. These commands let you filter records that are equal or not equal to the selected field value, or that do or do not contain the selected value.

3. **Click Equals "R-2086"**

   Eighteen records containing R-2086 in the Rep ID field appear in the datasheet window, as shown in **FIGURE K-7**. These records are all Sally Fritz's customers. Notice that a filter icon appears to the right of the Rep ID column heading, indicating that a filter is applied to this field.

4. **Click the Toggle Filter button in the Sort & Filter group**

   The filter is removed, and all the records in the table appear again. Clicking the Toggle Filter button once removes the filter; clicking it again reapplies it.

5. **Click the Toggle Filter button**

   The filter is reapplied, so that only the 18 customer records for rep R-2086 (Sally Fritz) appear.

6. **Click any value in the YTD Orders field, then click the Filter button in the Sort & Filter group**

   The Filter menu opens and displays commands for filtering and sorting records specific to the YTD Orders field. The bottom of the list displays all the specific values for the YTD Orders field, with check boxes next to each. To show only records with one of these specific values, you can click the check box next to that value. You want to display records that are greater than $7,500 so you need to use a Number Filter command.

7. **Point to Number Filters in the Filter list, click Greater Than, type 7500 in the Custom Filter dialog box, compare your screen to FIGURE K-8, then click OK**

   The filtered list now shows five records, with two filter criteria applied. All the records contain R-2086 in the Rep ID field, and all the values in the YTD Orders field are greater than $7,500, as shown in **FIGURE K-9**.

8. **Click the Toggle Filter button, then save your changes**

   The filter is removed, and your changes are saved.

FIGURE K-7: Filtered Customers table with one filter applied

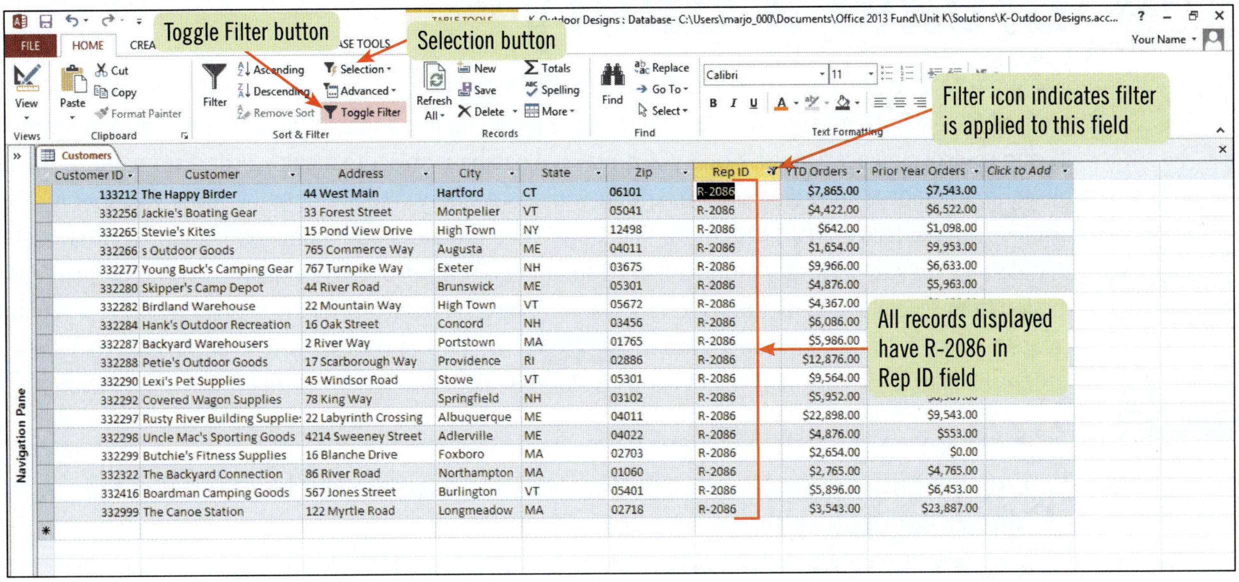

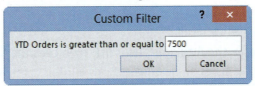

Toggle Filter button

Selection button

Filter icon indicates filter is applied to this field

All records displayed have R-2086 in Rep ID field

Customer ID	Customer	Address	City	State	Zip	Rep ID	YTD Orders	Prior Year Orders	Click to Add
133212	The Happy Birder	44 West Main	Hartford	CT	06101	R-2086	$7,865.00	$7,543.00	
332256	Jackie's Boating Gear	33 Forest Street	Montpelier	VT	05041	R-2086	$4,422.00	$6,522.00	
332265	Stevie's Kites	15 Pond View Drive	High Town	NY	12498	R-2086	$642.00	$1,098.00	
332266	s Outdoor Goods	765 Commerce Way	Augusta	ME	04011	R-2086	$1,654.00	$9,953.00	
332277	Young Buck's Camping Gear	767 Turnpike Way	Exeter	NH	03675	R-2086	$9,966.00	$6,633.00	
332280	Skipper's Camp Depot	44 River Road	Brunswick	ME	05301	R-2086	$4,876.00	$5,963.00	
332282	Birdland Warehouse	22 Mountain Way	High Town	VT	05672	R-2086	$4,367.00		
332284	Hank's Outdoor Recreation	16 Oak Street	Concord	NH	03456	R-2086	$6,086.00		
332287	Backyard Warehousers	2 River Way	Portstown	MA	01765	R-2086	$5,986.00		
332288	Petie's Outdoor Goods	17 Scarborough Way	Providence	RI	02886	R-2086	$12,876.00		
332290	Lexi's Pet Supplies	45 Windsor Road	Stowe	VT	05301	R-2086	$9,564.00		
332292	Covered Wagon Supplies	78 King Way	Springfield	NH	03102	R-2086	$5,952.00		
332297	Rusty River Building Supplie	22 Labyrinth Crossing	Albuquerque	ME	04011	R-2086	$22,898.00	$9,543.00	
332298	Uncle Mac's Sporting Goods	4214 Sweeney Street	Adlerville	ME	04022	R-2086	$4,876.00	$553.00	
332299	Butchie's Fitness Supplies	16 Blanche Drive	Foxboro	MA	02703	R-2086	$2,654.00	$0.00	
332322	The Backyard Connection	86 River Road	Northampton	MA	01060	R-2086	$2,765.00	$4,765.00	
332416	Boardman Camping Goods	567 Jones Street	Burlington	VT	05401	R-2086	$5,896.00	$6,453.00	
332999	The Canoe Station	122 Myrtle Road	Longmeadow	MA	02718	R-2086	$3,543.00	$23,887.00	

FIGURE K-8: Custom Filter dialog box

Custom Filter

YTD Orders is greater than or equal to 7500

OK   Cancel

FIGURE K-9: Customers datasheet with two filters applied

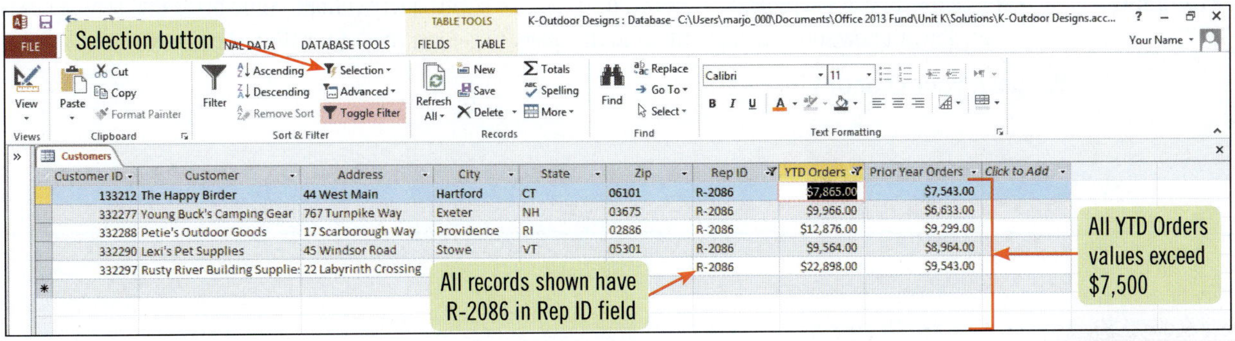

Selection button

Customer ID	Customer	Address	City	State	Zip	Rep ID	YTD Orders	Prior Year Orders	Click to Add
133212	The Happy Birder	44 West Main	Hartford	CT	06101	R-2086	$7,865.00	$7,543.00	
332277	Young Buck's Camping Gear	767 Turnpike Way	Exeter	NH	03675	R-2086	$9,966.00	$6,633.00	
332288	Petie's Outdoor Goods	17 Scarborough Way	Providence	RI	02886	R-2086	$12,876.00	$9,299.00	
332290	Lexi's Pet Supplies	45 Windsor Road	Stowe	VT	05301	R-2086	$9,564.00	$8,964.00	
332297	Rusty River Building Supplie	22 Labyrinth Crossing				R-2086	$22,898.00	$9,543.00	

All records shown have R-2086 in Rep ID field

All YTD Orders values exceed $7,500

Create a Query

Learning Outcomes
• Explain the purpose of a query
• Create a query using the Query Wizard
• View a query in Datasheet view

Filtering data in tables is helpful, but it has some limitations. For one thing, you cannot limit or change the order of the fields Access displays when you apply a filter. You also cannot save a filter. For greater flexibility and control, you need to use a query. A **query** is a database object that extracts data from one or more tables in a database according to criteria that you set. A query displays only the fields you specify. For instance, in a database that contains 10 fields that store product information, you could create a query that displays only the fields for product names and prices. You can also use a query to pull together information from several tables. Because a query is an object, you can save it for later use. The simplest way to create a query is to use the Query Wizard. **CASE** ▶ *Serena wants to see a view of the data that shows customer names, their state, and Rep ID numbers. To accomplish this, you decide to use the Query Wizard.*

STEPS

1. **Click the Customers table Close button ☒ in the database window, then click the Shutter Bar Open button ⏩**

   You need to close a table before creating a query that is based on it. The Navigation pane is now open.

2. **Click the CREATE tab, then click the Query Wizard button in the Queries group**

   The New Query dialog box opens, as shown in **FIGURE K-10**, where you select the type of Query Wizard you want to use. By default, Simple Query Wizard is selected. This wizard creates a **select query**, a query that retrieves or selects data from one or more tables or queries according to your criteria. This is the most commonly used type of query and is the one you want to create.

3. **Click OK**

   If a security Notice dialog box appears, click Open. The Simple Query Wizard dialog box opens. First you need to specify the table or query from which you want to select fields for your query.

4. **Click the Table/Queries list arrow, then click Table: Customers**

   Notice that all the fields from the Customers table are listed in the Available Fields list. You now need to choose the fields you want from this list.

   > **QUICK TIP**
   > You can also select a field by double-clicking its name in the Available Fields list.

5. **Click Customer in the Available Fields list, then click the Select Single Field button ▷**

   The Customer field moves to the Selected Fields list. You can move fields back and forth between the Available Fields list and the Selected Fields list using the buttons shown in **TABLE K-1**.

6. **Click State, click ▷ , click Rep ID, then click ▷**

   Now the Customer, State, and Rep ID fields are listed in the Selected Fields area, as shown in **FIGURE K-11**.

7. **Click Next**

   In this dialog box, you specify a name for the query. Unless you specify otherwise, the Query Wizard will automatically name the query "Customers Query", which is currently in the text box.

   > **QUICK TIP**
   > Records resulting from a query look like a table but are actually a view based on the query.

8. **Select Query in the text box, type by State, then click Finish**

   The Query Wizard closes and the Customers by State query results appear in Datasheet view, showing the Customer, State, and Rep ID fields. Notice that the Customers by State query is now listed in the Navigation pane below the Sales Reps table, as shown in **FIGURE K-12**. This query contains only fields that Serena needs to see. She can now sort and apply filters to the query to get just the information she needs.

9. **Save your changes**

FIGURE K-10: New Query dialog box

FIGURE K-11: Specifying a table and fields for a simple query

FIGURE K-12: Customers by State query results

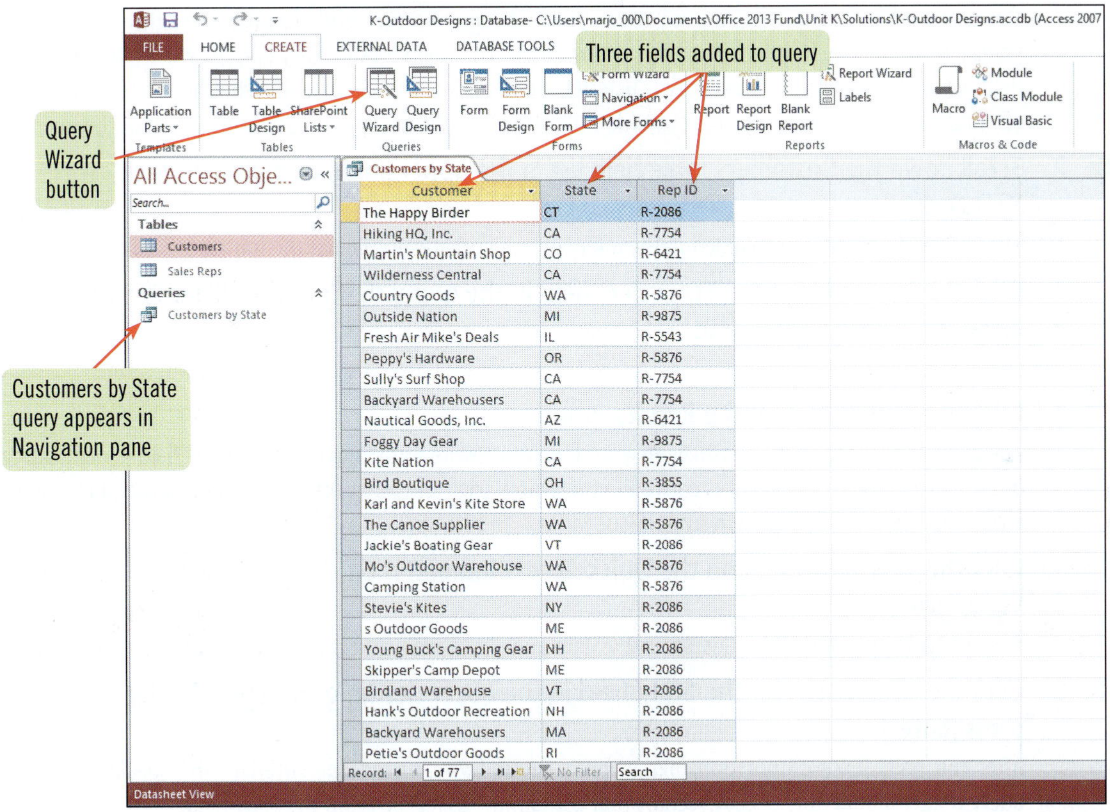

TABLE K-1: Select Field buttons in Query Wizard

button	use to
>	Move a single field to the Selected Fields area
>>	Move all available fields to the Selected Fields area
<	Remove a single field from the Selected Fields area and restore it to the Available Fields list
<<	Remove all fields from the Selected Fields area and restore them to the Available Fields list

Modify a Query in Design View

You can modify an existing query if you need to make changes to it using Design view. In Design view, you can add or delete fields, specify a sort order for one or more fields, or specify criteria for fields. You can also use Design view instead of Query Wizard to create a query. **CASE** ▶ *Serena asks you to modify the Customers by State query so it includes the YTD Orders field. She also wants the results to be sorted by YTD Orders in descending order. In addition, she wants you to create another query based on the Customers by State query that displays customers in the state of Ohio. You decide to create this new query in Design view.*

STEPS

1. **Click the HOME tab, then click the View button in the Views group**

   The database window displays the Customers by State query in Design view, and the QUERY TOOLS DESIGN tab is active. In Design view, the database window is divided into two panes. The upper pane displays the Customers table field list. The lower pane is called the query design grid. You use the cells in this grid to specify fields and their criteria for the current query. The query design grid currently contains the three fields in the Customers by State query (Customer, State, and Rep ID). Notice that the check box in the Show cell under each field contains a check mark, indicating that these fields should be displayed in the query.

2. **Scroll down the Customers table field list in the upper pane, then double-click YTD Orders**

   The YTD Orders field is now added to the query design grid and appears in the fourth column.

3. **Click the Sort cell for the YTD Orders field in the query design grid, click the Sort list arrow, then click Descending**

   See **FIGURE K-13**.

4. **Click the View button in the Results group**

   The query results appear in Datasheet view, and the records are sorted by the YTD Orders field in descending order. As you modify a query, it is convenient to switch back and forth between Design view and Datasheet view to see the modified query results, as shown in **FIGURE K-14**.

5. **Click the Save button 🖫 on the Quick Access toolbar, then click the View button in the Views group**

   The changes you made to the Customers by State query are saved, and the query appears in Design view.

6. **Click the Criteria cell for the State field in the query design grid, type OH, then press [Enter]**

   After you press [Enter], quotation marks appear around your entry. The criteria "OH" specifies that the query results should only display records that contain the letters "OH" in the State field.

7. **Click the View button in the Results group**

   The query results appear in Datasheet view, as shown in **FIGURE K-15**. The results show six records that contain "OH" in the State field. Notice that the records are sorted in descending order by YTD Orders.

8. **Click the FILE tab, click Save As, click Save Object As, click Save As, type Ohio Customers in the Save 'Customers by State' to text box in the Save As dialog box, then click OK**

   The modified query is saved as Ohio Customers and appears in the Navigation Pane below the Customers by State query.

9. **Click the Close 'Ohio Customers' button ✕**

   The Ohio Customers query closes.

FIGURE K-13: Adding a field to the Customers by State query in Design view

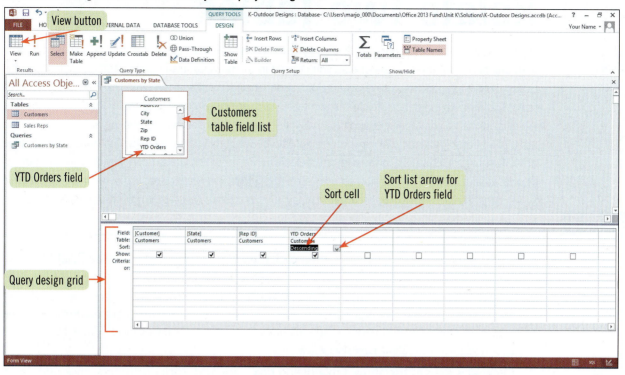

FIGURE K-14: Modified Customers by State query results in Datasheet view

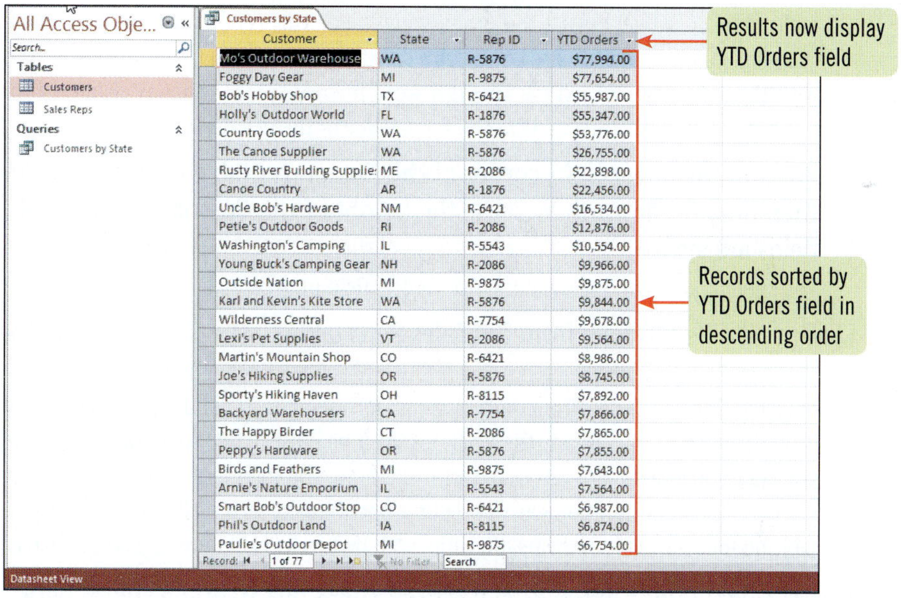

FIGURE K-15: Modified query in Datasheet view

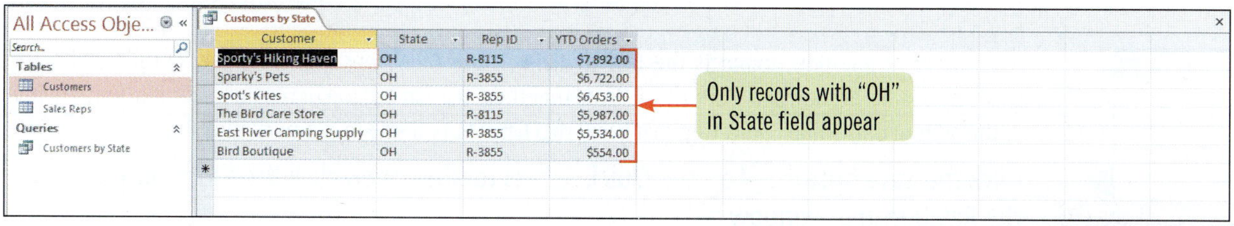

Relate Two Tables

Learning Outcomes
• Set a one-to-many relationship between two fields in two different tables
• Enforce referential integrity
• Define a foreign key

To take advantage of the full power of Access, you sometimes want to create queries that pull fields from more than one table. For instance, the queries you created in the previous lesson pulled from a single table, the Customers table, but it would have been helpful also to include the Rep Last Name field from the Sales Reps table. This is possible if you first relate the two tables, or specify a relationship between them. To do so, your tables must share a common field, and that shared field must be the primary key field in one of the tables. You use the Relationships window to specify a relationship between two or more tables. The most common type of relationship to set up is a **one-to-many relationship**, in which the primary key field in one table is associated with multiple records in a second table. **CASE** ▶ *You need to specify a one-to-many relationship between the Sales Reps table and the Customers table so you can create queries that pull fields from both tables.*

STEPS

1. **Click the DATABASE TOOLS tab, then click the Relationships button in the Relationships group**

   The Relationships window opens. To set up relationships, you first need to choose the tables you want to relate. Notice the Show Table dialog box shown in **FIGURE K-16**. You use this dialog box to add specific tables or queries to the Relationships window so you can specify relationships among them. Notice the Customers table is selected in the Show Table dialog box.

2. **Click Sales Reps in the Show Table dialog box, click Add, click Customers, click Add, then click Close**

   The Show Table dialog box closes, and the Relationships window displays the Sales Reps and Customers tables. Notice that in the Sales Reps table, the Rep ID field is the primary key field, but in the Customers table, the Rep ID field is *not* the primary key field. This is appropriate; in order to relate two tables, the shared field must be a primary key field in *only* the first table. In the second table, the common field shared with the first table is called the **foreign key**. To create a one-to-many relationship, you need to drag the primary key from the first table to the foreign key in the second table.

3. **Point to the lower-right corner of the Customers table until the ↖ pointer appears, then drag ↖ down to increase the height of the Customers table field list until all the fields are visible**

   You should be able to see the Prior Year Orders field in the Customers table now.

4. **Drag the Rep ID field from the Sales Reps table to the Rep ID field in the Customers table**

   The Edit Relationships dialog box opens. The current settings reflect the relationship you just specified by dragging. The Rep ID field from the Sales Reps table is on the left, and the Rep ID field from the Customers table is on the right. At the bottom, the Relationship Type is listed as One-To-Many. These settings are exactly what you want; one sales rep is associated with multiple customers, but each customer is associated with a single sales rep. Therefore, it makes sense to set up a one-to-many relationship with the Rep ID field in the Sales Reps table on the "one" side of the relationship, and the Rep ID field in the Customers table on the "many" side.

5. **Click the Enforce Referential Integrity check box to add a check mark**

   Selecting this check box tells Access to reject any attempts to enter data that would be inconsistent. For instance, if a user entered "777" as a Rep ID number in the Customers table, Access would reject the entry because that Rep ID number does not exist in the Sales Reps table. See **FIGURE K-17**.

6. **Click Create**

   A relationship line now connects the Rep ID field in the Sales Reps table and the Rep ID field in the Customers table, as shown in **FIGURE K-18**. Note that there is a 1 at the top of the line and an infinity symbol at the bottom of the line, indicating that these two fields have a one-to-many relationship.

7. **Click the Save button 🖫 on the Quick Access toolbar, then click the Close button ✕ in the Relationships window**

Working with Data

FIGURE K-16: Show Table dialog box

Show Table

Tables | Queries | Both

Customers
Sales Reps

Available tables in K-Outdoor Designs database

Add | Close

FIGURE K-17: Edit Relationships dialog box

Edit Relationships

Table/Query:	Related Table/Query:
Sales Reps	Customers
Rep ID	Rep ID

Enforce Referential Integrity check box

☑ Enforce Referential Integrity
☐ Cascade Update Related Fields
☐ Cascade Delete Related Records

Relationship Type: One-To-Many

Create | Cancel | Join Type.. | Create New..

FIGURE K-18: Relationships window with a one-to-many relationship established

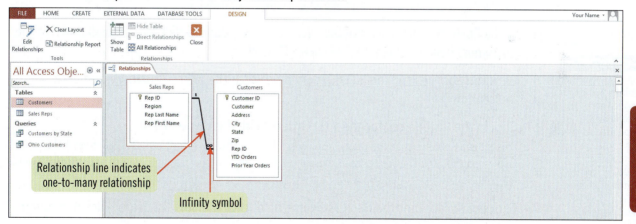

Relationship line indicates one-to-many relationship

Infinity symbol

Understanding good database design

Creating a well-designed database requires careful planning. First, decide on the main goals of the database. What is its purpose? What data will it store? Once you decide this, you need to organize the database into categories of data. For instance, if your database will track information about your sports league, you might have categories called Teams, Players, Coaches, and Games. You can then turn each of these categories into tables in your database. Then, you need to define fields and the data types for each table. Remember that each table must have a primary key field that uniquely identifies each record from any other in the database. Once you have created your tables, you need to decide how each table relates to the others in the database and set up appropriate relationships between them. You might need to add new fields to the tables to create these relationships. Creating a well-designed structure for your database will ensure that your data is easy to access, maintain, and update.

Working with Data

Create a Query Using Two Tables

Learning
Outcomes
• Add tables in
  Query Design view
• Add fields from
  two tables to
  a query
• Use comparison
  operators in
  a query
• Explain benefits of
  referential integrity

Setting up relationships between tables offers many advantages. One is that you can create a query that pulls fields from two or more related tables. Also, if you specify to enforce referential integrity in related tables, any changes you make to fields in one table are instantly reflected in all related tables or queries that contain that field. This is a huge benefit and ensures that the data in your database is consistent. Setting up table relationships also ensures that your data is valid and accurate. Access will prohibit any attempt to enter data in the foreign key field that is not consistent with the data in the primary key field. **CASE** ▶ *Serena would like a view of the data that shows customers whose year-to-date orders exceed $7,500. Because you have set up a one-to-many relationship between the Sales Reps table and the Customers table, you can create a query that contains the information Serena needs.*

STEPS

TROUBLE

If the Show Table dialog box is covering the field lists, drag its title bar to a new location.

1. **Click the CREATE tab, then click the Query Design button in the Queries group**

   A new blank query opens in Design view, and the Show Table dialog box opens with the Customers table selected.

QUICK TIP

To delete a field from a query, click anywhere in the field column in the query design grid, then click the Delete Columns button in the Query Setup group.

2. **On the Tables tab of the Show Table dialog box, click Sales Reps, click Add, click Customers, click Add, compare your screen to FIGURE K-19, then click Close**

   The field lists for the Sales Reps table and the Customers table appear. Notice the relationship you created between the Rep ID field in the Sales Reps table and the Rep ID field in the Customers table is shown.

3. **In the Sales Reps field list, double-click Rep Last Name, then double-click Region**

   The Rep Last Name and Region fields are added to the query design grid.

4. **In the Customers field list, double-click Customer, double-click State, scroll down in the Customers field list, then double-click YTD Orders**

QUICK TIP

To specify multiple criteria for a field, type additional criteria in the Or cell for that field in the query design grid; results will include any records that match either the Criteria cell contents or the Or cell contents.

5. **Click the Sort cell for the YTD Orders field, click the Sort list arrow, then click Descending**

6. **Click in the Criteria cell for the YTD Orders field, then type >7500**

   This criteria specifies that the query results should only display records whose YTD Sales field value is greater than $7,500. The greater than symbol (>) is one type of operator you can use in the Criteria cell to return the query results that you want. **TABLE K-2** displays useful comparison operators.

7. **Click the Sort cell for the Rep Last Name field, click the Sort list arrow, click Ascending, then compare your screen to FIGURE K-20**

QUICK TIP

You can also view query results by clicking the Run button in the Results group in Design view.

8. **Click the View button in the Results group**

   The query results appear in Datasheet view, as shown in **FIGURE K-21**. You can see that the results are grouped first by Rep Last Name in alphabetical order, then by YTD Orders in descending order.

9. **Click the Save button 🖫 on the Quick Access toolbar, type Top Customers by Rep in the Save As dialog box, click OK, then close the Top Customers by Rep query**

   The query is saved as Top Customers by Rep and appears in the Navigation Pane below Queries.

FIGURE K-19: Adding tables in Design view

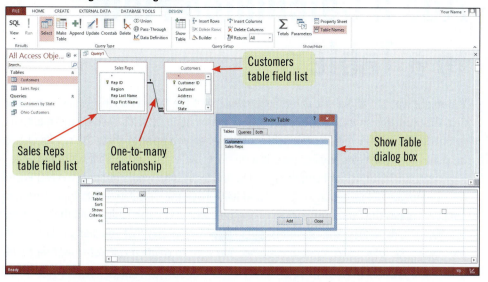

FIGURE K-20: Query with specified fields, sorts, and criteria in Design view

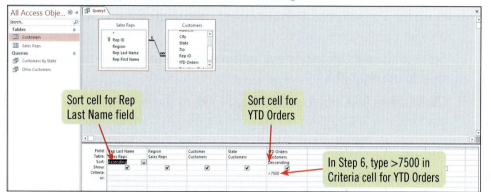

FIGURE K-21: Query results in Datasheet view

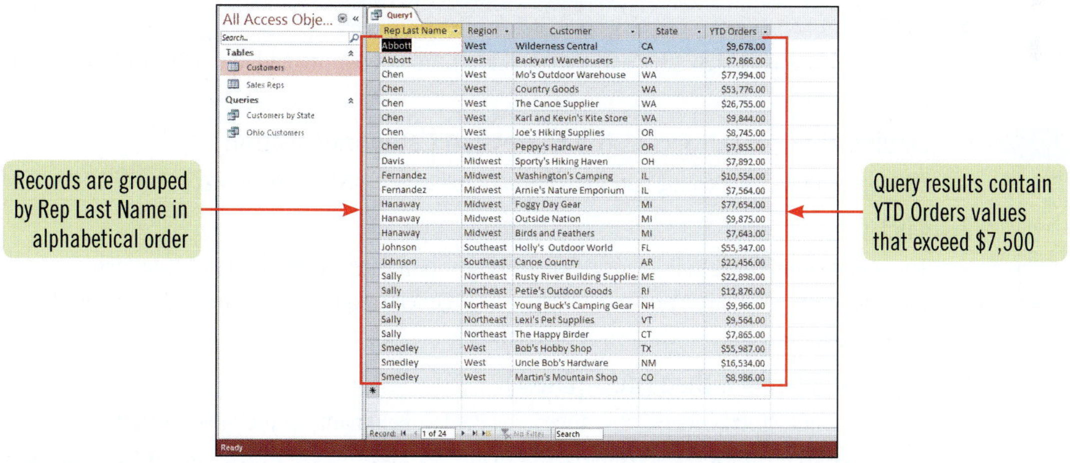

TABLE K-2: Comparison operators

operator	description
>	Greater than
<	Less than
=	Equals
<>	Not equal to

Add a Calculated Field to a Table

You might want to add a calculated field to a table if the table contains values. A **calculated field** is a field that contains an **expression**, which is a combination of fields, values, and mathematical operators (similar to a formula). A calculated field is useful when you want to show the results of calculations based on values in certain fields. For instance, in a products table that contains a field for net price, you could add a calculated field for determining the sales tax; the expression would multiply the Net Price field by .08 (or the appropriate tax percentage). Calculated fields have the Calculated data type. Choosing a Calculated data type opens the Expression Builder dialog box, where you can easily build the expression you want by specifying fields, values, and operators. **CASE** *Serena asks that you add a field to the Customers table that shows the total orders for each customer. You need to create a calculated field that adds the Prior Year Orders field to the YTD Orders field.*

STEPS

1. **Open the Customers table in Datasheet view, then click the Shutter Bar Close button** ⌦
   The Customers table opens in Datasheet view.

2. **Scroll to the right (if necessary) until you see the last field in the table and the blank field to the right of it**

3. **Click Click to Add, point to Calculated Field, as shown in FIGURE K-22, then click Currency**
   The Expression Builder dialog box opens, which lets you build the expression using fields, values, and mathematical operators. You need to build an expression that sums the Prior Year Orders field and the YTD Orders field.

4. **Double-click Prior Year Orders in the Expression Categories section**
   The Prior Year Orders field appears in the top part of the dialog box in brackets. This field is the first part of your expression. Next you need to enter the addition operator.

5. **Type +**
   You typed the plus sign (the addition operator). You can now add the YTD Orders field to complete the expression.

6. **Double-click YTD Orders in the Expression Categories section**
   The top section of the dialog box shows the completed expression, as shown in FIGURE K-23.

7. **Click OK**
   The new column (next to Prior Year Orders) is now populated with currency values, which are the result of the expression you built (Prior Year Orders + YTD Orders). You need to type a label for this field. The placeholder label is selected, so you can type a new label.

8. **Type Total Orders, then press [Enter]**
   The field name "Total Orders" now appears as the last field name in the table, as shown in FIGURE K-24.

9. **Select The Happy Birder (the first customer), type your name, click 🖫, click the FILE tab, click Close, click the Access window Close button, then submit your database to your instructor**
   The Customers table, the database, and Access all close.

Working with Data

FIGURE K-22: Adding a calculated field to a table

In Step 3, click here to add a new field
Field Type list with Calculated Field selected
You can specify that the results of a calculated field have one of these data types
Click to Add
Short Text
Number
Currency
Date & Time
Attachment
Hyperlink
Calculated Field
Text
Yes/No
Date/Time

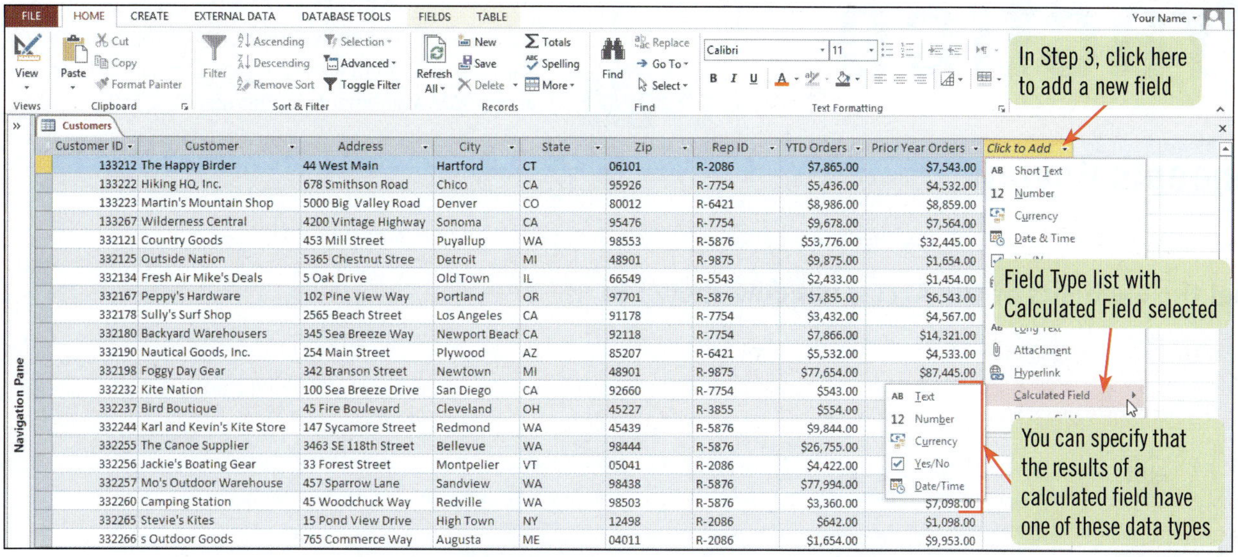

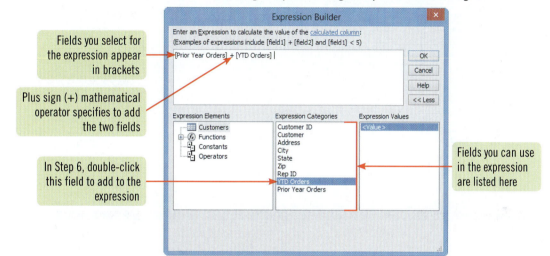

FIGURE K-23: Building an expression using the Expression Builder dialog box

Expression Builder
Enter an Expression to calculate the value of the calculated column:
(Examples of expressions include [field1] + [field2] and [field1] < 5)
[Prior Year Orders] + [YTD Orders]
OK
Cancel
Help
<< Less
Expression Elements
Customers
Functions
Constants
Operators
Expression Categories
Customer ID
Customer
Address
City
State
Zip
Rep ID
YTD Orders
Prior Year Orders
Expression Values
<Value>
Fields you select for the expression appear in brackets
Plus sign (+) mathematical operator specifies to add the two fields
In Step 6, double-click this field to add to the expression
Fields you can use in the expression are listed here

FIGURE K-24: Customers table with new calculated field added

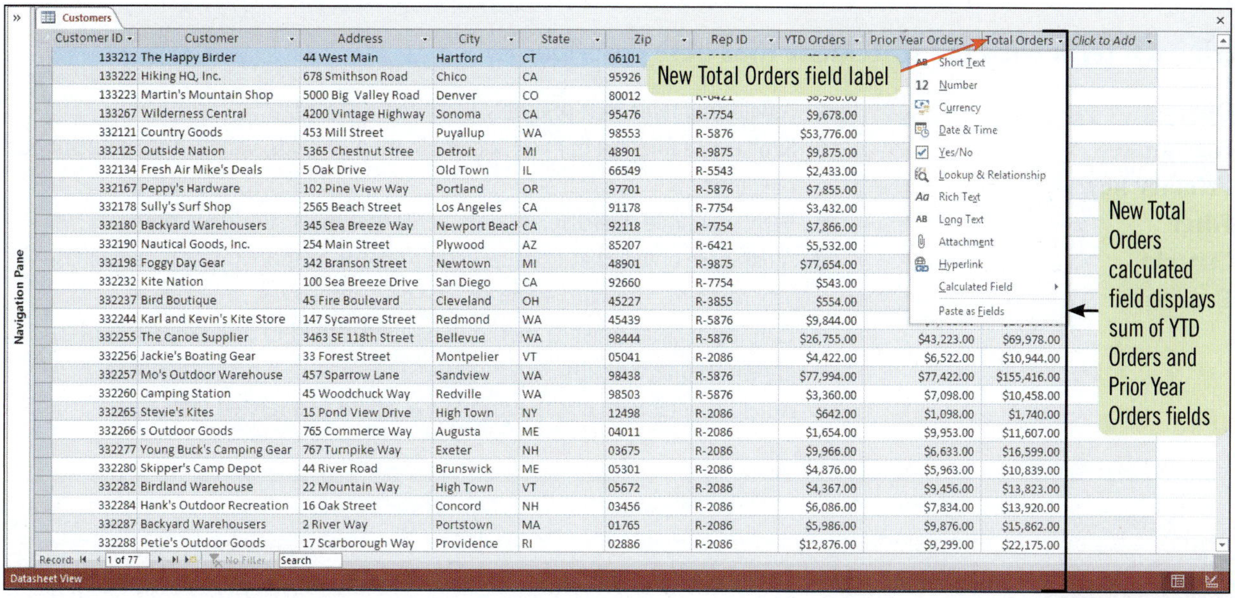

New Total Orders field label
New Total Orders calculated field displays sum of YTD Orders and Prior Year Orders fields
Total Orders
Click to Add

Access 2013

Practice

Concepts Review

Label the elements of the Access window shown in FIGURE K-25.

FIGURE K-25

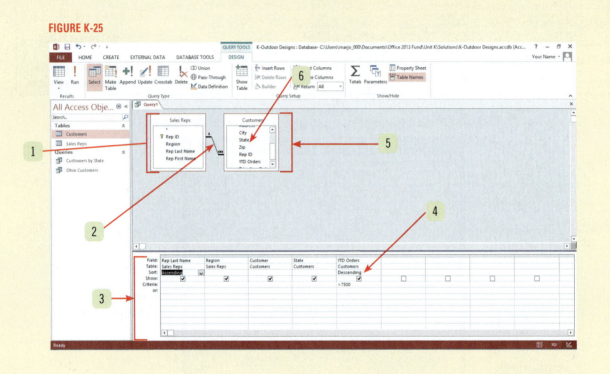

Match each term with the statement that best describes it.

7. Query
8. Foreign key
9. Primary key
10. Filter
11. Criteria
12. Expression

a. A field in a table that uniquely identifies a record
b. Similar to a formula in Excel; a combination of fields, values, and mathematical operators
c. View of a table that displays only fields that meet specified criteria
d. A database object that extracts data from one or more tables in a database according to criteria that you set
e. Conditions that must be met for a particular field in order for a record to appear in query results
f. A field in a table that is the primary key field in a related table

Select the best answer from the list of choices.

13. **Which of the following cannot be saved as an object in Access?**
    a. Query
    b. Table
    c. Form
    d. Filter

14. **Which of the following shows how the Cost field would appear in an expression?**
    a. (Cost)
    b. <Cost>
    c. [Cost]
    d. =Cost

15. **Which of the following actions would you do first when creating a query in Query Design view?**
    a. Add the tables from which you want to pull fields.
    b. Add fields to the query design grid.
    c. Specify a sort order for one of the fields in the query.
    d. Set the criteria for a field cell.

16. **To apply a filter that displays all the records that contain London in the City field, which of the following actions would you take?**
    a. Click the Filter button, then type London.
    b. Click London in the table, click the Selection button, then click Equals London.
    c. Click any field in the table, click the Selection button, then click Equals London.
    d. Click the City field name in the column heading, click the Selection button, then click Equals London.

17. **Which of the following cannot be included in an expression?**
    a. Fields
    b. Mathematical operators
    c. Field descriptions
    d. Values

18. **Johnson Elementary School has a database that contains two tables; one called Teachers and one called Students. Both tables contain one common field: Teacher ID. Which of the following statements about these tables is NOT true?**
    a. In the Teachers table the shared field (Teacher ID) is the foreign key.
    b. In the Teachers table the shared field (Teacher ID) is the primary key.
    c. The Teacher ID field is the foreign key in the Students table.
    d. One record in the Teachers table is related to many records in the Students table.

Skills Review

1. **Open an existing database.**
    a. Start Access.
    b. Open the Data File K-2.accdb from the drive and folder where you store your Data Files. Specify to enable the content in the database.
    c. Save the database as a new database with the name **K-Poster Business**. Enable the content.
    d. Open the Artists table in Datasheet view, and review the fields and records it contains. View the Posters table in Datasheet view, and review its fields and records.
    e. View each table in Design view. Note the number of fields in each table and the data type assigned to each.
    f. Close the Artists table.

2. **Sort records in a table.**
    a. View the Posters table in Datasheet view. Close the Navigation Pane.
    b. Sort the table by the Poster Name field in ascending order. What is the Poster ID of the first record in the sorted list? Reverse the sort order so the records are sorted descending by Poster Name. What is the Poster ID of the first record now?
    c. Clear all sorts, so the records appear in their original order.
    d. Sort the table by the Amount Sold field in descending order. What is the Poster Name of the first record? Then sort the table by the Subject field in descending order. Now what is the Poster Name for the top record in the sorted list?

Skills Review (continued)

e. Select the first Poster ID value (11268), then type your name. Save your changes to the Posters table. If your instructor asks you to provide a screen shot of your sort results, follow the instructions in the yellow box on page 282.

3. Filter records in a table.

a. Apply a filter to the Posters table to show only records that contain the field value **Nature** in the Subject field. How many records are displayed with the filter applied? What is the Poster Name of the first record?

b. Remove the filter using a button on the HOME tab.

c. Apply a Number filter to show only records with values greater than 10,000 in the Amount Sold field. How many records are displayed with the filter applied? What is the Poster Name for the last record?

d. Save your changes. If your instructor asks you to provide a screen shot of your sort results, follow the instructions in the yellow box on page 282. Remove the filter, then save your changes.

4. Create a query.

a. Close the Posters table, then open the Navigation pane. Create a new query using the Simple Query Wizard.

b. Base the query on the Posters table, and include the Poster Name, Subject, and Amount Sold fields in the query. Specify to create a detail query.

c. Name the query **Posters by Subject**, then finish the Wizard and view the query results in Datasheet view.

d. Sort the query in ascending order by the Subject field.

e. Save your changes.

5. Modify a query in Design view.

a. View the Posters by Subject query in Design view.

b. Add the Size field to the query design grid.

c. Set the sort order to Descending for the Amount Sold field.

d. Use the query design grid to enter the criteria **city living** for the Subject field. Set the criteria to **small** for the Size field cell.

e. View the query results in Datasheet view. Save the modified query as **Small City Living Posters Sold**. Compare your datasheet to **FIGURE K-26**.

f. Close the Small City Living Posters Sold query.

FIGURE K-26

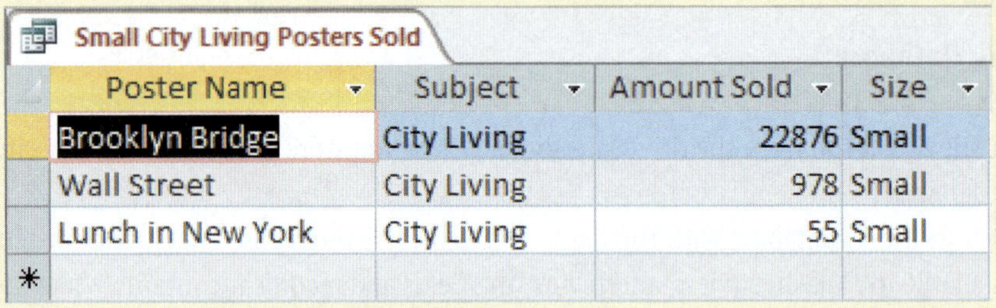

Poster Name	Subject	Amount Sold	Size
Brooklyn Bridge	City Living	22876	Small
Wall Street	City Living	978	Small
Lunch in New York	City Living	55	Small

6. Relate two tables.

a. Open the Relationships window.

b. Add the Posters table to the Relationships window, then add the Artists table to the Relationships window. Close the Show Tables dialog box.

c. Drag the Artist ID field from the Artists table to the Artists ID field in the Posters table.

d. Specify to enforce referential integrity, then create the relationship.

e. View the tables in the Relationships window, and make sure there is a one-to-many relationship set between the Artist ID fields.

f. Save your changes, then close the Relationships window.

7. Create a query using two tables.

a. Create a new query in Query Design view.

b. Use the Show Table dialog box to add the Artists table and the Posters table to the upper pane of the query design window. Close the Show Table dialog box.

c. Notice the relationship line between the Artists table and the Posters table.

d. Add the Poster Name and Amount Sold fields from the Posters table to the query design grid.

e. Add the Artist Name and Phone Number fields from the Artists table to the query design grid.

f. In the Criteria cell for the Amount Sold field, enter an operator and value that will return records with values greater than 15,000.

g. Set the Amount Sold sort order to Descending.

h. View the query results in Datasheet view. Select Faith Jacula in the Artist Name cell for the Tightrope Walker record, type your name, then press [Enter] twice. Notice that your name now appears as the artist name in the first, second and fifth rows in the query. This is because of referential integrity: When you replaced Faith Jacula with your name, all other records containing Faith Jacula in the Artist Name field changed immediately to your name to reflect the edit. Save the query as **Top Posters by Artist**. Compare your datasheet to FIGURE K-27. Close the query.

i. Open the Artists table. Notice that the field value for the Artist Name for the third row is your name. Again, due to referential integrity, your name automatically replaced all instances of "Faith Jacula" in the Artist Name field throughout the database. Close the Artists table.

FIGURE K-27

Poster Name	Amount Sold	Artist Name	Phone Number
Brooklyn Bridge	22876	Your Name	460-555-2867
Tightrope Walker	19654	Your Name	460-555-2867
Football Helmet	17542	Peaceful Johnson	773-555-1543
Pretzel Cart	16554	Adrian Sanchez	773-555-0753
Soloist	16423	Your Name	460-555-2867

8. Add a calculated field to a table.

a. Open the Posters table in Datasheet view, then close the Navigation pane.

b. Add a calculated field to the table with the Currency data type.

c. In the Expression Builder dialog box, enter an expression that multiplies the Price field by the Amount Sold field. (*Hint*: The multiplication operator is *.) Click OK to close the Expression Builder dialog box.

d. Enter the field name **Total Sales** for the new field. Sort the table by the Total Sales field in descending order.

e. Compare the top part of your table to FIGURE K-28. Save your changes, close the Posters table, then close the database. Exit Access. Submit your completed database to your instructor.

FIGURE K-28

Poster ID	Artist ID	Poster Name	Subject	Size	Price	Amount Sold	Total Sales
11250	A-1355	Soloist	Performing Art	Small	$29.95	16423	$491,868.85
11252	A-1355	Brooklyn Bridge	City Living	Small	$19.95	22876	$456,376.20
11253	A-1355	Ballet Dancer	Performing Art	Large	$29.95	14323	$428,973.85
11256	A-1355	Tightrope Walker	Performing Art	Large	$19.95	19654	$392,097.30
11259	A-1299	Football Helmet	Sports	Medium	$19.95	17542	$349,962.90
11279	A-1277	Pretzel Cart	City Living	Medium	$19.95	16554	$330,252.30

Independent Challenge 1

You work for Hannah Bigelow, the director of a summer arts camp. Hannah recently hired you to help manage information about her campers and leaders. Applications for camp have just started coming in for the summer session. Hannah has created a database to manage the data about each leader and camper. She wants you to answer some questions about the campers and leaders so she can make appropriate plans for the summer session.

a. Start Access, then open the Data File K-3.accdb from the drive and folder where you store your Data Files. Enable the content in the database. Save the database as **K-Arts Camp**, and enable the content. Open each table in the database, and review the fields and records of each.

b. View the Leaders table in Datasheet view. Replace "Minson" in the Leader Last Name field with your last name. Replace "Gregory" in the leader First Name field with your first name. Save and close the Leaders table.

c. View the Campers table in Datasheet view, then sort the table by the Age field in ascending order. Then sort the Campers table in ascending order by Leader ID.

d. Apply a filter to the Campers table so only the campers for Leader ID L-101 are displayed. Apply a second filter to show only the campers who are 12 and under. (*Hint*: Use an appropriate number filter.) If your instructor asks you to provide a screen shot of your results, follow the instructions in the yellow box on page 282. Save your changes. Close the Campers table.

e. Create a simple query using the Query Wizard. Base the query on the Campers table, and include the fields Camper First Name, Camper Last Name, and Age. Name the query **Campers by Age**. In Datasheet view, sort the query results in ascending order by the Camper Last Name field, and then by Age. Replace the first name of the first camper with your name. Save your changes.

f. Open the Campers by Age query in Design view. Add the Leader ID field to the query. Add appropriate criteria to one of the cells in the query design grid specifying to show only the records containing L-102 in the Leader ID field. View the query results in Datasheet view, then save the modified query as **L-102 Campers**. Close the query.

g. Open the Relationships window, then add the Leaders table and the Campers table to the window.

h. Drag the Leader ID field from the Leaders table to the Leaders ID field in the Campers table. In the Edit Relationships dialog box, specify to enforce referential integrity, then create the relationship.

i. Save the layout of the relationship, then close the Relationships window.

j. Create a new query in Query Design view. Add the Leaders table and the Campers table to the grid. Use the appropriate tables to add the following fields to the query design grid in this order: Camper First Name, Camper Last Name, Age, Leader Last Name, and Specialty.

k. Set the sort order for the Age field to Ascending. Set the criteria for the Specialty field to **Sculpture**.

l. Save the query as **Sculpture Campers**. View the query results in Datasheet view, compare your screen to FIGURE K-29, then close the Sculpture Campers query.

m. Close the database, then exit Access. Submit your completed database to your instructor.

FIGURE K-29

Camper First	Camper Last	Age	Leader Last Name	Specialty
Christopher	Grady	8	Moore	Sculpture
Maria	Marquez	11	Moore	Sculpture
Billy	Colber	11	Moore	Sculpture
Curtis	Walker	12	Moore	Sculpture

Independent Challenge 2

You are the programs director at a local fitness center. You have created an Access database to manage information about your fitness classes and your students. In preparation for upcoming classes, you want to filter and query the data.

a. Start Access, then open the Data File K-4.accdb from the drive and folder where you store your Data Files. Enable the content in the database. Save the database as **K-Fitness Center**. Enable the content.

b. Open the Students table in Datasheet view, then filter the data to show students who are signed up to take the class with Class Code 3011. Sort the filtered results in alphabetical order by the Last field. Type your name in the Data Entered By field for the first filtered record, then save your changes. If your instructor asks you to provide a screen shot of your results, follow the instructions in the yellow box on page 282. Remove the filter, then close the table.

c. Use the Relationships window to create a one-to-many relationship from the Classes table to the Students table using the Class Code field. Specify to enforce referential integrity in the Edit Relationships dialog box. Save the relationship, then close the Relationships window.

d. Open the Classes table. Add a calculated field to the table that has the Currency data type. Build an expression for this new field that multiplies the Number of Classes field by the Per Class Fee field. Name the field **Total Class Fee**. Close the Classes table.

e. Create a new query in Query Design view. Use the Show Table dialog box to open both the Classes table field list and the Students table field list. Close the Show Table dialog box.

f. Add the following fields to the query design grid: First, Last, Class Name, Start Date, Instructor Last Name, and Total Class Fee.

g. Set the sort order to Ascending for the Class Name field. Use the Save Object As command on the FILE tab to save the query with the name **Classes List**. View the query in Datasheet view.

h. Return to Design view, then set the criteria for the Class Name field as **Cardio Mix**. Set the sort order to Ascending for the Last field. Use the Save Object As command to save the modified query as **Cardio Mix Class List**. View the query results in Datasheet view.

i. Open the Classes table in Datasheet view. Select Watkins in the Instructor Field for the Cardio Mix class, then type your name.

j. Save and close the Classes table. Now look at the Cardio Mix Class List query in Datasheet view, and observe the change in the Instructor Last Name field. Close the Cardio Mix Class List query.

k. View the Classes List query in Datasheet view. Observe your name in the Instructor Last Name field for the Cardio Mix class. Close the Classes List query.

l. Close the database, then exit Access. Submit your database to your instructor.

Independent Challenge 3

You own a small, residential pet-care business called Uncle Ruff's Dog Care Services. You offer boarding and day care services for dogs. You also employ three dog walkers who go to clients' homes and walk their dogs. You have created a database to help you manage information about your dog clients and your dog walkers. You need to create a schedule for your Monday appointments that combines information from two tables in your database. You also need to create some handouts for your dog walkers that list schedule information and service notes. You first need to relate the two tables, then you will use queries to create the schedule and handouts you need.

a. Start Access, then open the Data File K-5.accdb from the drive and folder where you store your Data Files. Enable the content in the database. Save the database as **K-Uncle Ruff's Dog Care**, and enable the content.

b. Open each table in Design view, and review the fields and field types each contains. Note which fields are the primary key fields. Get a sense of the information that each table contains. Close both tables when you have finished reviewing them.

Independent Challenge 3 (continued)

c. Open the Relationships window, then establish a one-to-many relationship between the Dog Walker ID field in the Dog Walkers table and the Dog Walker ID field in the Dogs table. Specify to enforce referential integrity. Save the relationship, then close the Relationships window.

d. Open the Dog Walkers table. Replace Rizzo in the Last Name field for the first record with your last name. Replace Jon in the First Name field for the first record with your first name.

e. Add a calculated field in the Dog Walkers table that has the Currency data type. Build an expression for this field that multiplies the Hours Per Week field by the Hourly Rate field. Name the field **Weekly Pay**. Close the Dog Walkers table.

f. Create a new query in Query Design view. Use the Show Table dialog box to open the field lists for the Dog Walkers table and the Dogs table, then close the Show Table dialog box. Save the query as **Monday Schedule**.

g. Add the following fields in the order listed to the query design grid: Day to Visit, Visit Time, First Name, Last Name, Street Address, Dog Name, Breed.

h. Enter **Monday** as the criteria for the Day to Visit field. Enter your first name as the criteria for the First Name field. Save your changes.

i. View the query results in Datasheet view.

j. Switch back to Query Design view, then save the query as **Darcy's Dogs**. Delete "Monday" in the Criteria cell for the Day to Visit field. Enter **darcy** as the criteria for the First Name field. View the query in Datasheet view, then save and close the query.

k. Create a new query in Design view that pulls from both database tables and contains the following fields: Last Name, Owner Name, Dog Name, Service Notes. Set the criteria for the Last Name field to **Martinez**. Save the query as **Martinez Weekly Service Notes**. View the query results in Datasheet view.

l. Close the database, then exit Access. Submit your database to your instructor.

Independent Challenge 4: Explore

You can use relational databases to help you manage information in your own life. For instance, you could create a database to track your personal expenses or organize your movie collection. In this Independent Challenge, you work with a database to help you keep track of your classes. This database contains three tables for classes, instructors, and assignments. One of these tables contains Attachment and Hyperlink field data types, which you have not worked with before. You will add records to all three tables and set up relationships among them. Then you will create a query that lists your assignments for each class. *Note: To complete the Independent Challenge, your computer must be connected to the Internet.*

a. Start Access, then open the Data File K-6.accdb from the drive and folder where you store your Data Files. Enable the content in the database. Save the database as **K-My Classes**. Enable the content.

b. Open the Classes, Instructors, and Homework tables in Design view, review the fields that each contains, and identify the data types for each field.

c. Add five appropriate records to the Classes and Instructors tables using information for your actual classes and instructors. (*Note*: You may need to make up Instructor ID numbers. Therefore, it is recommended that you enter your Instructors' records first, then enter those made-up Instructor IDs in the Classes table.) When you are done, widen columns as necessary to ensure that all field names and field values are visible on the screen. Save your changes, then close the Instructors table.

Independent Challenge 4: Explore (continued)

d. View the Homework table in Datasheet view. Press [Tab] to enter 1 for the Homework ID (which has the AutoNumber data type), enter your class number for this class in the Class ID field, enter **Unit K exercises** for the Assignment Description field, then enter an appropriate date in the Due Date field. Double-click the paper clip icon in the field to the right of Due Date to open the Attachments dialog box, click Add, navigate to the folder where you store your Data Files, double-click file K-6a.doc, then click OK to close the Attachments dialog box. Double-click the paper clip icon in the first row of the table to open the Attachments dialog box again, click file K-6a, then click Open to open the file in Word. As you can see, this document contains the Concepts Review questions for Unit K. Close the document then close the Attachments dialog box.

e. Click the Online Homework field value cell for the first record, then type **www.cengage.com/sam2013**, then press [Enter]. Notice the blue line under the text you just typed, indicating it is a live link. Click the link to view the page. Close your browser window.

f. Add four more assignments to the Homework table; one for each of your classes. You can use real information or you can make up fictional information. Be sure to enter the appropriate Class ID values from the Classes table for each assignment.

g. Open the Relationships window. Show the Instructors table, the Classes table, and the Homework table (in that order). Create a one-to-many relationship between the Instructor ID field in the Instructors table and the Instructor ID field in the Classes table. Enforce referential integrity. Then create a one-to-many relationship between the Class ID field in the Classes table and the Class ID field in the Homework table. Enforce referential integrity. Save your changes, then close the Relationships window.

h. Create a new query in Design view. Display the Instructors, Classes, and Homework tables (in that order) in the upper pane. Save the query as **My Class Assignments**.

i. Add the following fields to the query design grid in the order specified: Assignment Description, Due Date, Class Name, Class Days, Class Times, Instructor Last Name, Data Entered By. View the query results in Datasheet view, then type your name in the first Data Entered By field. Sort the query results from newest to oldest by the Due Date field. Save your changes.

j. Close all open objects, then exit Access. Submit your completed database to your instructor.

Visual Workshop

Open the Data File K-7.accdb from the drive and folder where you store your Data Files, enable the content, then save it as **K-Dance Charity Event**. Enable the content. Set up the relationships shown in **FIGURE K-30**. Create the query shown in **FIGURE K-31** using fields from the three related tables in the database. Specify the appropriate sort order for the Amount field and the appropriate criteria for the Charity Name field. View the query in Datasheet view, then replace the sponsor name for the first record with your name. Save the query as **United Way Donations**. Close the database, then exit Access. Submit your completed database to your instructor.

FIGURE K-30

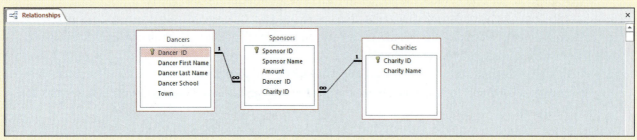

FIGURE K-31

Charity Name	Dancer First Name	Dancer Last Name	Sponsor Name	Amount
United Way	Tiffany	Singer	Your Name	250.00
United Way	Brendan	Bleasdale	Tuckton Woods Bank	250.00
United Way	Rosie	Moss	Woodlands Hospital	200.00
United Way	Ray	Wyatt	Bo's Burgers	100.00
United Way	Alyssa	Farnum	Brickston's Auto Body	100.00
United Way	Stacy	Chu	Valley Dental	100.00
United Way	Millie	Dolan	Strickland Auto Body	100.00
United Way	Ray	Wyatt	Pesky Pest Removal	75.00
United Way	Millie	Dolan	Burrito Hut	75.00
United Way	Brendan	Bleasdale	Pete's Plumbing	60.00
United Way	Mary	Gladstone	Fred's Bowling Alley	50.00
United Way	Tiffany	Singer	Good Bikes, Inc.	50.00

Creating Database Reports

CASE ▶ Karen Rivera, the marketing director for Outdoor Designs, has asked you to
create a series of reports containing information from the customer database.
The first report needs to show customers for each region and year-to-date sales. The second
report needs to show the year-to-date sales for rep Marcie Abbott. You also need to create
some customer mailing labels for an upcoming promotion.

Unit Objectives

After completing this unit, you will be able to:

- Create a report using the Report Wizard
- View a report
- Modify a report
- Add a field to a report
- Apply conditional formatting to a report
- Add summary information to a report
- Create mailing labels

Files You Will Need

L-1.accdb	L-5.accdb
L-2.accdb	L-6.accdb
L-3.accdb	L-7.accdb
L-4.accdb	

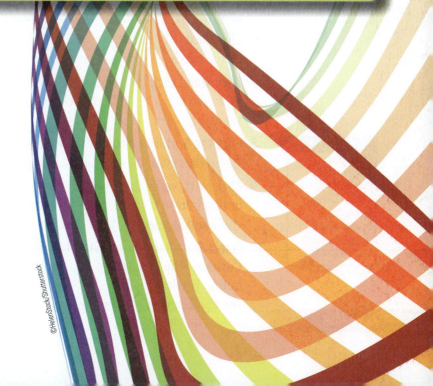

©HelenStock/Shutterstock

Create a Report Using the Report Wizard

Spotting statistical trends in a large database can be difficult. For example, if a sales database contains hundreds of records, it's hard to determine average sales or total sales just by looking at the data. You can solve this problem by creating reports based on table or query data. A **report** is a summary of database information designed specifically for printing. Report data can be from one database object, such as a table, or from multiple database objects. You can create new reports quickly using the **Report Wizard**, which automatically creates a report based on settings that you specify and displays it in Print Preview. You can save reports as objects in a database, so that you can open or print them anytime. All reports are composed of sections, each of which contains specific information. **CASE** ▶ *Karen asks you to create a report that shows customers for each region and year-to-date sales for each customer. You decide to use the Report Wizard to create this report.*

STEPS

1. **Start Access, open the Data File L-1.accdb from the location where you store your Data Files, then save the database as L-Outdoor Designs**

2. **Enable the content, click the CREATE tab, then click the Report Wizard button in the Reports group**

    The first dialog box of the Report Wizard opens. You use this dialog box to choose the **record source(s)**, to select the database object(s) from which a report gets its data, and to specify the fields you want to include in the report.

3. **Click the Tables/Queries list arrow, click Table: Sales Reps, click Region in the Available Fields list, then click the Select Single Field button ▷**

    The Region field now appears in the Selected Fields list.

4. **Click the Tables/Queries list arrow, click Table: Customers, double-click Customer in the Available Fields list, double-click City, double-click State, then double-click YTD Orders**

    The Customer, City, State, and YTD Orders fields are added to the Selected Fields list, as shown in **FIGURE L-1**.

5. **Click Next**

    The next dialog box lets you organize records in the report so they are grouped by a recommended field (in this case, Region) or ungrouped. **Grouping** organizes a report by field or field values. You want to group the customers by Region, which is the current setting.

6. **Click Next**

    This dialog box lets you specify additional grouping levels in the report.

7. **Click State, click ▷, notice that State now appears in blue below the Region grouping as shown in FIGURE L-2, then click Next**

    The records will be grouped by State within each Region grouping. The next dialog box sets the sort order.

8. **Click the Sort list arrow for the first field, then click Customer**

    This specifies to sort the records in ascending order by Customer.

9. **Click Next, verify the Stepped Layout option button is selected, verify the Portrait option button is selected, verify the Adjust the field width so all fields fit on a page check box is selected, then click Next**

10. **Select Sales Reps in the What title do you want for your report? text box, type Customers by Region and State as the report title, verify the Preview the report option button is selected, then click Finish**

    The Report opens in Print Preview, as shown in **FIGURE L-3**.

FIGURE L-1: Report Wizard dialog box

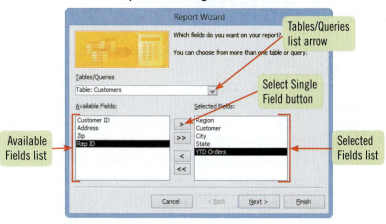

Tables/Queries list arrow

Select Single Field button

Available Fields list

Selected Fields list

FIGURE L-2: Setting a second grouping level

State is now specified as a second grouping level

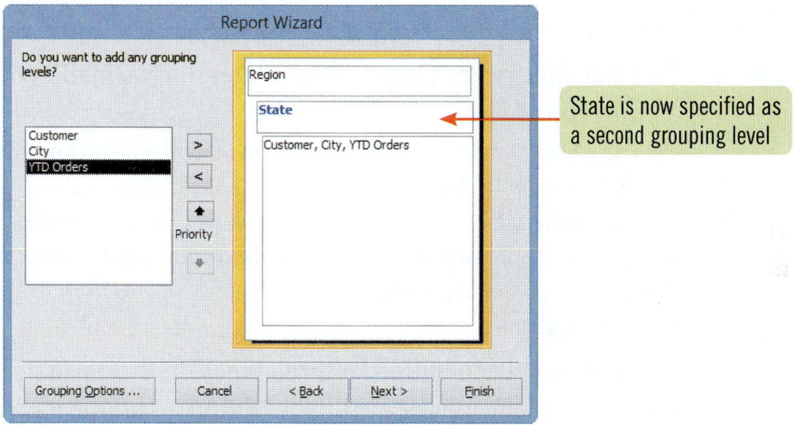

FIGURE L-3: Customers by Region and State report in Print Preview

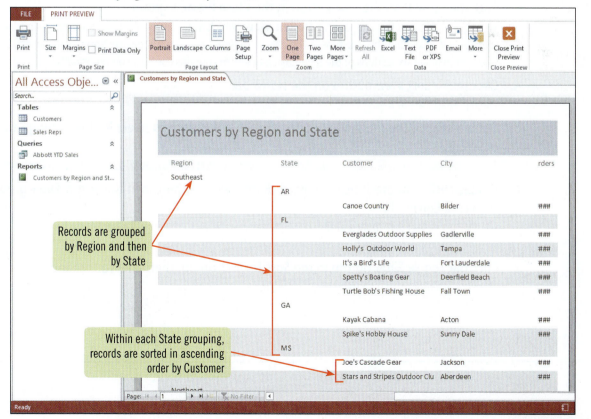

Records are grouped by Region and then by State

Within each State grouping, records are sorted in ascending order by Customer

View a Report

Learning
Outcomes
• View a report in
Print Preview,
Design view, and
Report view
• Apply a filter by
selection in Report
view
• Remove a filter

Access offers several ways to view a report. After you create a report using the Report Wizard, the report opens in **Print Preview**, which shows you exactly how the printed report will look. In Print Preview, you can use the buttons on the record navigation bar to view each page of the report. **Report view** is the default view when you open a report from the Navigation pane. Report view looks similar to Print Preview, except that it displays the report in a continuous flow, without page breaks. If you need to make layout changes to your report, you can use either Design view or Layout view. **Design view** includes many powerful tools for modifying a report; however, it can be a difficult view in which to work because it shows only the structure of the report, not the data contained in it. **Layout view** does not include as many modification tools as Design view, but it shows you report data as you work. TABLE L-1 describes the views that are available for reports. To switch views, click the View buttons on the status bar. **CASE** *You decide to view the Customers by Region and State report in Print Preview, Design view and Report view.*

STEPS

QUICK TIP
Clicking on the
report when the
Zoom In pointer
is active will cause
the view to zoom
in again.

1. **Click the Shutter Bar Close button ≪ on the Navigation pane, then click ⌕ anywhere on the report**

   The Zoom Out pointer ⌕ appears when you place the pointer over the report. Clicking the report when the ⌕ is active will let you see the full page. The first page of the report is now fully visible on the screen in Print Preview, as shown in FIGURE L-4. Notice the title "Customers by Region and State" appears at the top in the **Report Header** section. Below the Report Header, the **Page Header** section contains all the fields you selected in the wizard. Also notice the report is first grouped by Region and then by State in alphabetical order.

2. **Click the Next Page button ▶ three times on the navigation bar to view each page of the report, then click the First Page button ◀ on the navigation bar**

   Notice that each page contains a **Page Footer**, which contains the date and the page number.

3. **Click the Close Print Preview button in the Close Preview group**

   See FIGURE L-5. The report appears in **Design view**, which you can use to make formatting and layout changes and to modify the structure of the report. Design view does not display any records; instead, the screen displays all six sections of the report, each of which contains controls you can modify.

4. **Click the Report View button on the status bar**

   The report appears in Report view.

5. **Double-click Canoe (in Canoe Country) in the first record to select it, then attempt to type Kayak**

   As you can see, it is not possible to edit data in Report view. You can, however, sort and filter in Report view.

6. **Double-click FL in the State column, click the Selection button in the Sort & Filter group, then click Equals "FL"**

   See FIGURE L-6. You just applied a filter to the report specifying to show only records that have "FL" in the State field. You can remove a filter using the Toggle Filter button.

7. **Click the Toggle Filter button in the Sort & Filter group, then save your changes**

   The filter is removed, and all the records reappear.

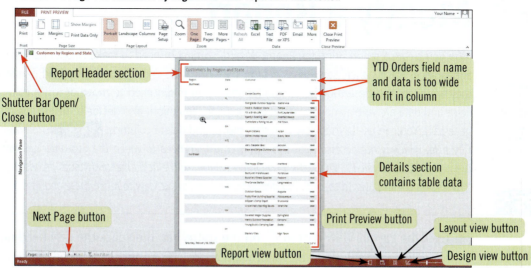

Report Header section

YTD Orders field name and data is too wide to fit in column

Shutter Bar Open/ Close button

Details section contains table data

Next Page button

Print Preview button

Layout view button

Report view button

Design view button

FIGURE L-5: Customers by Region and State report in Design view

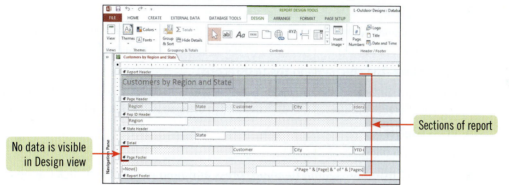

No data is visible in Design view

Sections of report

FIGURE L-6: Filtering a report in Report view

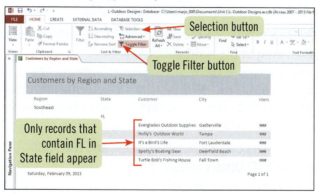

Selection button

Toggle Filter button

Only records that contain FL in State field appear

TABLE L-1: Available report views in Access

button	view	use to
	Print Preview	See exactly how your report will look when printed
	Report view	View records in a report; apply a filter; copy data to the clipboard
	Design view	Add or edit controls; change properties; view the underlying report structure (but not its data)
	Layout view	Add or delete fields; resize, move, or delete columns while also viewing records; add grouping levels; change sort order

Access 2013

Creating Database Reports

Modify a Report

Learning
Outcomes
• View a report in
Layout view
• Resize, move, and
delete report
columns in Layout
view

After you create a report using the Report Wizard, you might need to make layout changes to improve its appearance. For instance, sometimes columns are not wide enough to display field names or values, or they are either too close together or too far apart. You might need to move or resize columns so all the fields and data are visible and look good on the page. You might also decide to delete columns that aren't necessary. You can use Layout view to resize, move, and delete columns. **CASE** *You need to delete the City field, which is not necessary for this report. You then need to widen the Customer column so all names are visible. You also need to widen the YTD Orders column so the field label and values are visible, and move the YTD Orders column over to the left. You decide to work in Layout view to make these changes.*

STEPS

1. **Click the Layout View button ☰ on the status bar, then click the City heading**

   The view changes to Layout view, which at first glance looks very much like Report view. However, you can see a dotted border around the outside edge of the report as well as an orange border around the City column heading indicating that it is selected.

2. **Press [Delete]**

   The City column header is deleted. Notice that the data below the deleted column header is still in the report; you need to select field value cells separately from the column header.

3. **Click Bilder (the city name in the first record)**

   Clicking the first value in this column selected the entire column of City field values, as shown in **FIGURE L-7**. Notice the first cell (Bilder) is outlined in orange and the other cells are outlined in yellow.

4. **Press [Delete]**

   The City data column is deleted from the report.

5. **Click the Customer column heading, press and hold [Shift], then click Canoe Country (the first customer name below the Customer heading)**

   The Customer column heading and all the data in the Customer column are selected. You need to widen this column by dragging its right edge to the right so all customer names are visible.

6. **Position the ↔ pointer on the right edge of the orange border that surrounds Canoe Country, then drag to the right about ½"**

   The Customer column is now 1/2" wider, as shown in **FIGURE L-8**. All of the customer names should now be entirely visible. Notice that the YTD Orders column header (the last column in the report) is only partially visible, and the field values below it appear as ## characters because the column is too narrow. You need to increase the width of the column and column heading.

7. **Click the YTD Orders column heading, press and hold [Shift], then click the first instance of ## below the YTD Orders column header**

   The entire YTD Orders column is now selected.

8. **Position the ↔ pointer over the left border of the orange YTD Orders column header, then drag approximately 1" to the left**

   The YTD Orders column header and all the values in the column are now visible. Now you need to move the YTD Orders heading and column over to the left so it is closer to the Customer column. This will make it easier to see the YTD Orders amounts for each customer.

QUICK TIP
You can also press
[Ctrl][Home] to
move the pointer to
the top of the report.

9. **With the YTD column heading and column values still selected, position the ⬚ pointer over YTD Orders, drag to the left about ½", then scroll up so the top of the report is visible**

   The YTD Orders column is now a 1/2" closer to the Customers column. Compare your screen to **FIGURE L-9**.

10. **Save your changes**

Creating Database Reports

FIGURE L-7: Selecting a field in Layout view

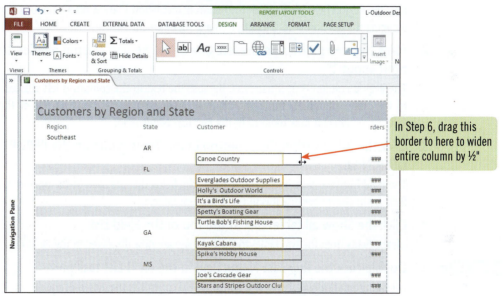

City column heading no longer appears

Clicking any value selects all the values in the column

FIGURE L-8: Report in Layout view after widening the Customer column

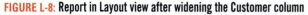

In Step 6, drag this border to here to widen entire column by ½"

FIGURE L-9: Repositioned and resized fields in Layout view

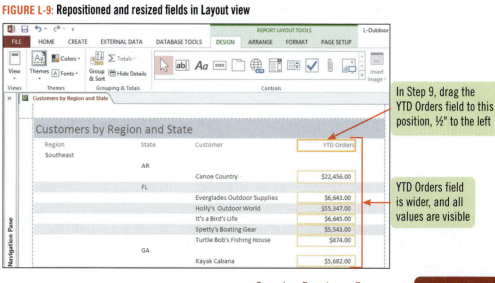

In Step 9, drag the YTD Orders field to this position, ½" to the left

YTD Orders field is wider, and all values are visible

Creating Database Reports

Add a Field to a Report

You can add fields to a report in Layout view. To add a field, open the Field List, then double-click the field you want. Fields are added to the left side of the report, so you might need to make adjustments to the other columns to place the new field where you want it. A field is composed of two parts: the field label, and its associated control. A **control** is an object that displays information in a report. Different controls are used for each data type. For instance, a text box control is used to display field values that have the Text data type; a check box control is used for field values that have the Yes/No data type. When you add a field to a report, the field label is automatically added to a header section, and the control is added to either the Group Header or the Detail section. **TABLE L-2** describes the sections of a report. **CASE** ► *You need to add the Rep Last Name field to the report. Before you can add this field, you need to decrease the width of the Region column to create space for the new field.*

STEPS

1. **Click the Region column header, press and hold [Shift], then click Southeast**

   You selected both the Region field label and the first text box control for the Region field (which displays "Southeast"). Clicking the first text box control in the column selected all the controls in that column. So, now the Region field label and all the region names below it are selected. You can now resize the column by dragging the left border to the right to make room for the new field.

2. **Place the ↔ pointer on the left side of the Region column header, then drag it to the right about 1"**

   The Region column is now narrower. Because the text in the column is left aligned, the text is now closer to the State column. Resizing the column opened up a space on the left of the report, as shown in **FIGURE L-10**. There is now room to fit the Rep Last Name field.

3. **Click the Add Existing Fields button in the Tools group on the REPORT LAYOUT TOOLS DESIGN tab**

   The Field List task pane opens and displays the fields that are used in the open report. The Rep Last Name field is not shown because it is in the Sales Reps table.

4. **Click the Show all tables link at the top of the Field List**

   All the fields from the two tables in the database are now displayed in the Field List.

5. **Double-click the Rep Last Name field in the Field List task pane**

   Access automatically places a new field and field control in the far left of the report. The Rep Last Name field is now the first column in the report. See **FIGURE L-11**.

6. **Click the Field List Close button ✕, then save your changes**

FIGURE L-10: Report after resizing the Region column

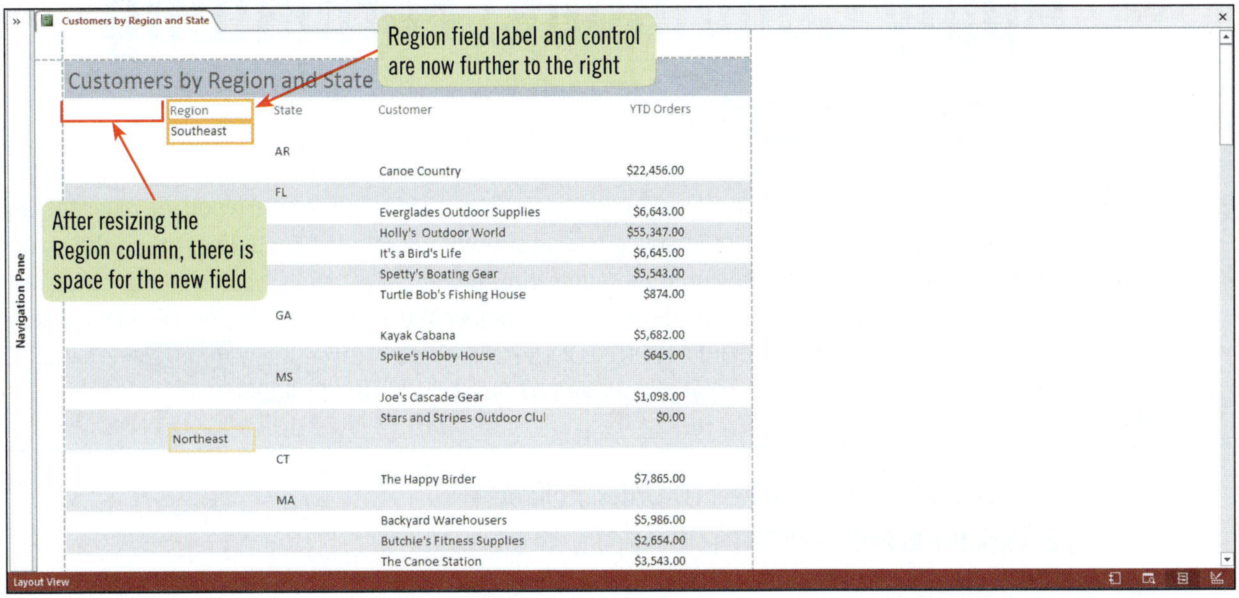

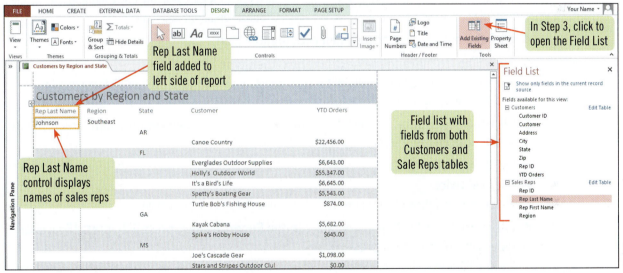

FIGURE L-11: Adding the Rep Last Name field using the Field List

TABLE L-2: Report sections

section	description
Report Header	Contains the report name or company logo and appears only at the top of the first page of the report
Page Header	Contains field labels and appears at the top of every page (but below the Report Header on the first page)
Group Header	Contains the chosen group field name and appears at the beginning of a group of records ("Group" is replaced by the chosen field name)
Detail	Usually contains bound controls and appears once for every record in the underlying datasheet
Group Footer	Contains the chosen group field name and appears at the end of every group of records ("Group" is replaced by the field name)
Page Footer	Usually contains the current date and page number and appears at the bottom of every page
Report Footer	Appears at the end of the last page of the report, just above the page footer

Learning Outcomes
• Apply conditional formatting to a report
• Add text to a report header

Apply Conditional Formatting to a Report

As in an Excel worksheet, you can apply conditional formatting in an Access report to highlight key information. Applying conditional formatting is a great way to draw attention to information that meets specific criteria. For instance, in a report that summarizes product sales results, you could use conditional formatting to highlight in yellow results above a certain number. You access the Conditional Formatting Rules Manager dialog box from the REPORT LAYOUT TOOLS FORMAT tab in Layout view. **CASE** ➤ *You want to apply conditional formatting to the report to highlight YTD Orders that exceed $5,000.*

STEPS

1. **Click any field value in the YTD Orders column**

2. **Click the REPORT LAYOUT TOOLS FORMAT tab**

   The REPORT LAYOUT TOOLS FORMAT tab is now active.

3. **Click the Conditional Formatting button in the Control Formatting group, then click the New Rule button in the Conditional Formatting Rules Manager dialog box**

   The New Formatting Rule dialog box opens. It displays options for specifying one condition and setting a format, but you can click the Add button to set additional conditions and formats.

4. **Click the between list arrow, then click greater than**

5. **Press [Tab] to move to the next text box, then type 5000**

   You have set the conditions for which the conditional formatting will take effect. Now you need to specify formatting to apply if these conditions are met.

6. **Click the Bold button B, click the Font color list arrow, then click the dark green square in the bottom row (Screen tip reads "Green")**

   Compare your screen to FIGURE L-12.

7. **Click OK twice**

   All values greater than $5,000 in the YTD Orders column appear in green bold.

8. **Click Customers by Region and State in the Report header, press [F2], press [Spacebar], type (your name), then press [Enter]**

   Pressing [F2] activated Edit Mode and placed the insertion point after the last character in the Report Header. Your name, enclosed in parentheses, now appears in the report title.

9. **Click the REPORT LAYOUT TOOLS DESIGN tab, click the Themes button, click the Organic theme as shown in FIGURE L-13, then save your changes**

10. **Click the Print Preview button 🔍 on the status bar, click the Next Page button ▶ twice on the Navigation bar to view each page of the report, compare your screen to FIGURE L-14, click the Close Print Preview button, then close the report**

    The Customers by Region and State report closes.

FIGURE L-12: New Formatting Rule dialog box

In Step 4, set this to greater than

In Step 5, type 5000 here

In Step 6, click the Bold button and set the font color to Green

FIGURE L-13: Applying the Organic theme to the report

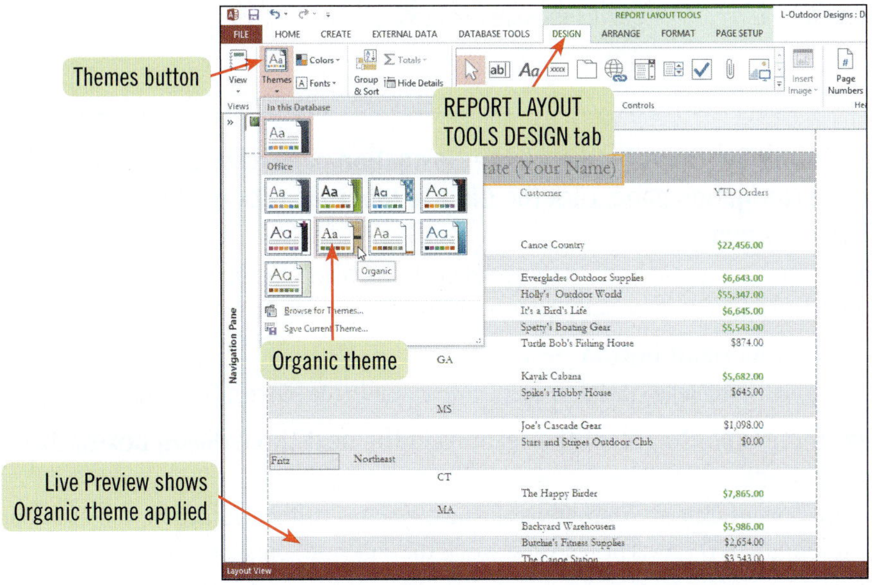

Themes button

REPORT LAYOUT TOOLS DESIGN tab

Organic theme

Live Preview shows Organic theme applied

				Customer	YTD Orders
				Canoe Country	$22,456.00
				Everglades Outdoor Supplies	$6,643.00
				Holly's Outdoor World	$55,347.00
				It's a Bird's Life	$6,645.00
				Spetty's Boating Gear	$5,543.00
				Turtle Bob's Fishing House	$874.00
		GA			
				Kayak Cabana	$5,682.00
				Spike's Hobby House	$645.00
		MS			
				Joe's Cascade Gear	$1,098.00
				Stars and Stripes Outdoor Club	$0.00
	Northeast				
		CT			
				The Happy Birder	$7,865.00
		MA			
				Backyard Warehousers	$5,986.00
				Butchie's Fitness Supplies	$2,654.00
				The Canoe Station	$3,543.00

FIGURE L-14: Customers by Region and State report with Organic theme and conditional formatting applied

Organic theme applied

Field values that are greater than 5000 are formatted in green bold

Access 2013

Add Summary Information to a Report

Learning
Outcomes
• Use the Report
Wizard to add
summary infor-
mation to a report
• Identify summary
values that can be
added to a report
• Resize summary
information
columns

Summary information in a report displays statistics about one or more fields in a database. Summaries can include statistics for the sum, average, minimum, or maximum value in any numeric field. **TABLE L-3** describes the five summary calculations you can use in your database reports. You can add summary infor-mation to a report while creating the report with the Report Wizard. **CASE** ▶ *Karen has asked you to create a new report that shows customer YTD orders by state for Marcie Abbott, a sales rep for the West region. The record source for this report is a query that Karen created.*

STEPS

1. **Click the** Shutter Bar Open button **on the Navigation pane, click the** Abbott YTD Sales **query in the Navigation pane, click the** CREATE tab, **then click the** Report Wizard button **in the Reports group**

   The Report Wizard dialog box opens. "Query: Abbott YTD Orders" appears in the Tables/Queries list box because you selected it in the Navigation pane before starting the Report Wizard.

2. **Click the** Select All Fields button `>>`

   All the fields from the Abbott YTD Orders query now appear in the Selected Fields list.

3. **Click** Next **three times to accept the settings in the next three dialog boxes, then click** Summary Options

   The Summary Options dialog box opens. Of the fields you selected for this report, summary options are available only for the YTD Orders field because this is the only field containing numeric values.

4. **Click the** Sum check box, **click the** Avg check box, **click the** Min check box, **click the** Max check box, **click the** Detail and Summary option button **if necessary, then click the** Calculate percent of total for sums check box

   You specified to include all of the summary values in the dialog box, as shown in **FIGURE L-15**.

5. **Click** OK, **then click** Next **twice to accept the settings in the next two dialog boxes**

6. **Select** Sales Reps **in the What title do you want for your report? text box, type** Abbott YTD Orders (Your Name) **as the report title, then click** Finish

   The report opens in Print Preview. Notice that ## appears in the YTD Orders column because the column is not wide enough to display the values. You need to switch to Layout view and widen this column.

7. **Click the** Layout View button **on the status bar, click any cell containing ## below the YTD Orders column header if necessary, place the** ←→ **pointer over the** left yellow border **of the selected column, then drag to the left about ½"**

   All of the field values in the YTD Orders column are now visible. Notice the summary information you specified in the Report Wizard at the bottom of the report. The ## characters appear in the column contain-ing the summary values. You need to widen each cell that contains these ## characters.

8. **Click the first cell that contains ## at the bottom of the report, press and hold** [Shift], **then click each of the remaining cells containing ##**

   All the cells containing the summary values are now selected, so you can resize all the cells at once.

9. **Position the pointer over the left yellow border of any selected cell, drag approximately 1" to the left, compare your screen to** FIGURE L-16, **save your changes, then close the report**

FIGURE L-15: Summary Options dialog box

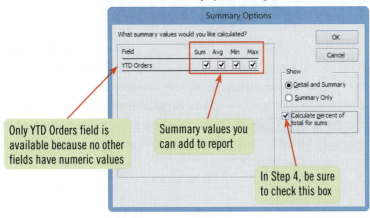

Only YTD Orders field is available because no other fields have numeric values

Summary values you can add to report

In Step 4, be sure to check this box

FIGURE L-16: Report in Layout view after widening columns

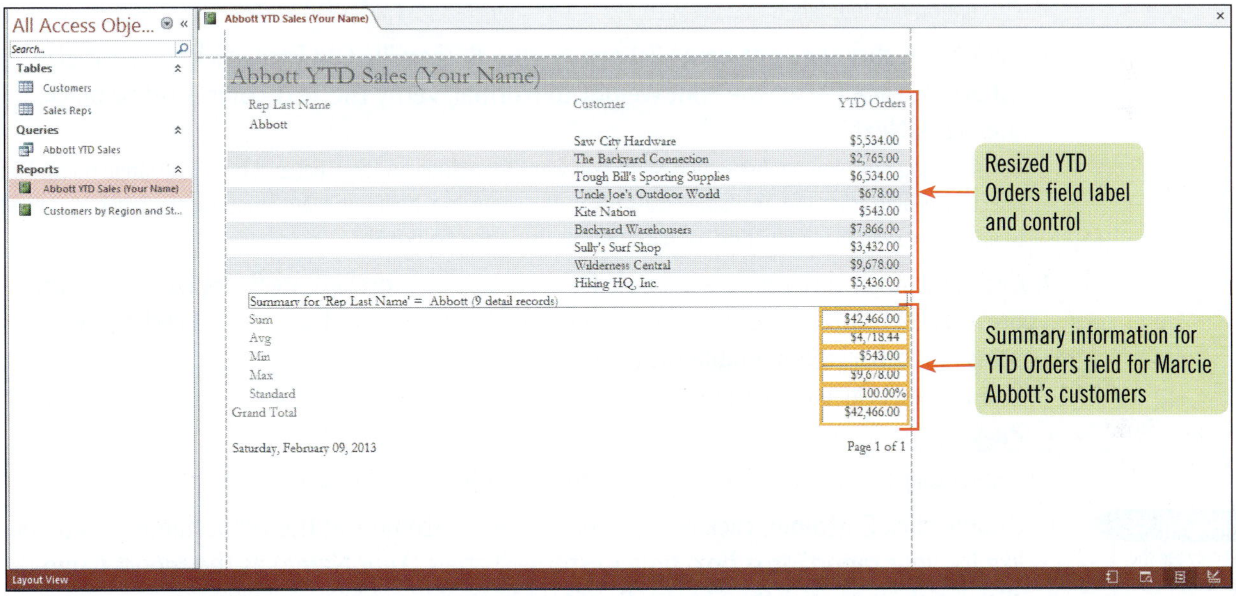

Resized YTD Orders field label and control

Summary information for YTD Orders field for Marcie Abbott's customers

TABLE L-3: Common summary calculations available in database reports

summary	statistic	calculates
SUM	Sum	Total of all values in the field
AVG	Average	Average of all values in the field
COUNT	Count	Number of records in the database
MIN	Minimum	Smallest value in the field
MAX	Maximum	Largest value in the field

© 2014 Cengage Learning

Create Mailing Labels

Learning Outcomes
• Create mailing labels using the Label Wizard
• Resize the Page Footer in Design view
• Add a label to the Page Footer

You don't have to print all reports on sheets of paper. You can use the data in a database to create other forms of printed output, such as labels or envelopes. Access includes a Label Wizard to help you create labels containing data from any fields in a database. As with the reports you have already created, you can create labels based on queries or tables, such as a mailing to all customers in California or all employees in the Marketing Department. **CASE** *Karen has asked you to create labels for a promotional mailing announcing some new product lines. The mailing will be sent to all Outdoor Designs customers. You decide to use the Label Wizard to create the mailing labels.*

STEPS

1. **Click Customers in the Navigation pane, click the CREATE tab, then click the Labels button in the Reports group**

   The first dialog box of the Label Wizard opens.

2. **Click the Filter by manufacturer list arrow, click Avery if necessary, then click C2243 in the Product number list**

   This option has four labels that are each 1½" × 1½" aligned across a sheet.

3. **Click Next, click the Font name list arrow, click Baskerville Old Face, click the Font Size list arrow, click 10, set the Font weight to Normal, verify the Text color is set to black, then click Next**

   In this dialog box, you choose which fields you want to include on the label and how to arrange them. You select each field from the Available Fields list in the order in which you want them on the label. You need to enter any spaces, punctuation, or hard returns using the keyboard.

4. **Click Customer, click the Select Single Field button [>], press [Enter], double-click Address, press [Enter], double-click City, type , (a comma), press [Spacebar], double-click State, press [Spacebar], then double-click Zip**

   Your screen should look similar to **FIGURE L-17**.

5. **Click Next**

   In this dialog box, you specify how you want to sort the records when you print them.

QUICK TIP
You will only see the labels arranged in four columns in Print Preview. If you view the labels report in Report view or Layout view, the labels will appear in a single column.

6. **Double-click Customer, click Next, select Labels Customers in the What name would you like for your report? text box, type Customer Labels (Your Name) as the report name, click Finish, then click the Shutter Bar Close button**

   The labels appear in Print Preview. They are sorted alphabetically by Customer. Notice that the labels are sorted going across the page in rows rather than down the page in columns.

7. **Click the Design View button [icon] on the status bar**

8. **Position the pointer over the bottom of the Page Footer bar until it changes to ↕, drag down ½", click the Label button [Aa] in the Controls group, click the left side of the Page Footer section, type your name, then press [Enter]**

   See **FIGURE L-18**. You added your name as a label to the Page Footer section, which will appear on every page of the report.

9. **Click the Print Preview button [icon] on the status bar, then click the report to zoom out**

   Your name now appears at the bottom of the labels in the Page Footer section. Because it is in the Page Footer section, it will appear on every page. Compare your labels with **FIGURE L-19**.

10. **Save your changes, close the L-Outdoor Designs database, exit Access, then submit your database to your instructor**

FIGURE L-17: Label Wizard dialog box

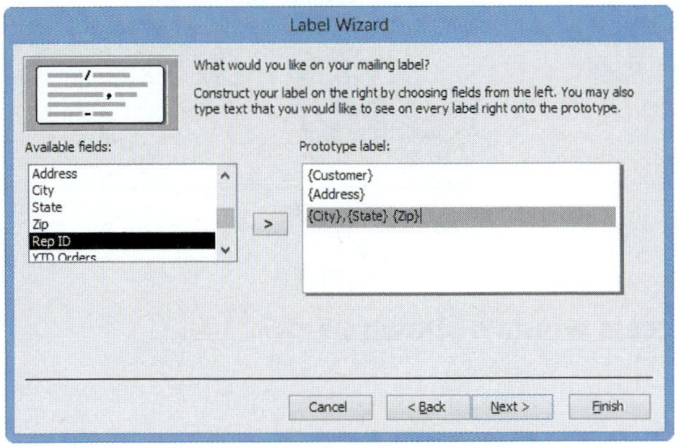

Label Wizard

What would you like on your mailing label?

Construct your label on the right by choosing fields from the left. You may also type text that you would like to see on every label right onto the prototype.

Available fields:
- Address
- City
- State
- Zip
- Rep ID
- YTD Orders

Prototype label:

{Customer}
{Address}
{City}, {State} {Zip}

[Cancel] [< Back] [Next >] [Finish]

FIGURE L-18: Adding a label to the Page Footer section in Design view

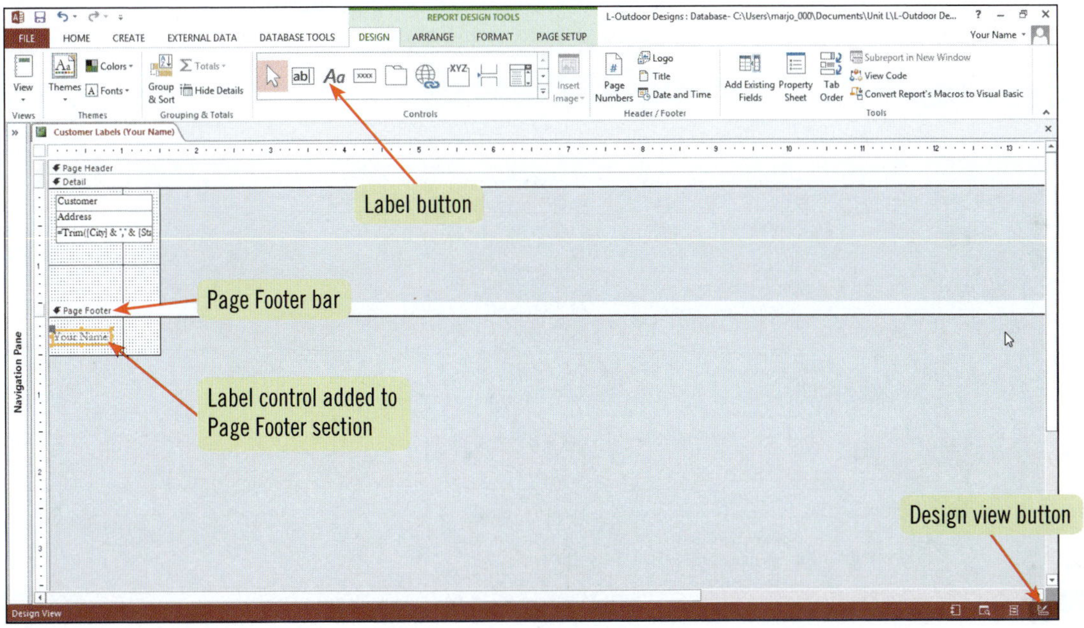

Label button

Page Footer bar

Label control added to Page Footer section

Design view button

FIGURE L-19: Customer Labels report in Print Preview

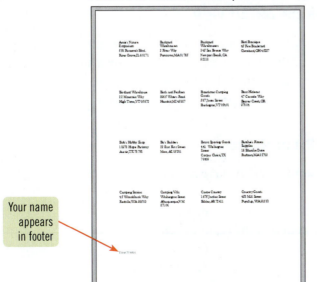

Your name appears in footer

Access 2013

Practice

Put your skills into practice with SAM! If you have a SAM account, go to www.cengage.com/sam2013 to access SAM assignments for this unit.

Concepts Review

Label the elements of the Access window shown in FIGURE L-20.

FIGURE L-20

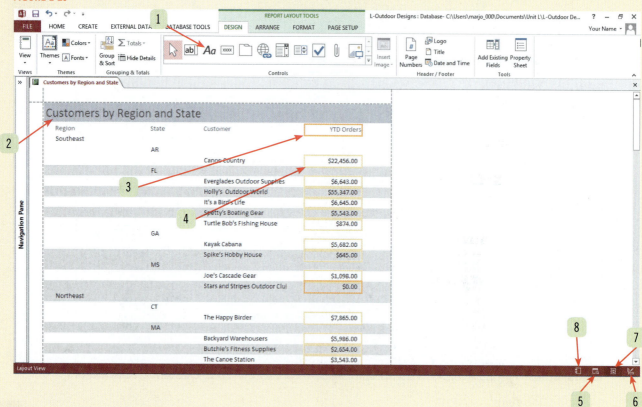

Match each view description with the correct view.

9. Layout view

10. Print Preview

11. Report view

12. Design view

a. Shows records but not individual pages of a report

b. Displays only the structure of a report and not the data in it

c. Shows the individual pages of a report

d. Displays a report with data and lets you make formatting changes

Select the best answer from the list of choices.

13. **Which of the following views is best for seeing page numbers?**
   a. Layout view
   b. Report view
   c. Design view
   d. Print Preview

14. **Which section of a report usually contains the report title?**
   a. Detail
   b. Report Header
   c. Group Header
   d. Report Footer

15. In a report, a field consists of two parts: a _____ and a control.
  a. Shutter bar
  b. Summary option
  c. Record
  d. Field label

16. Summary options can be used in a report for a field that has which of the following data types?
  a. Number
  b. Long Text
  c. Hyperlink
  d. Short Text

Skills Review

1. **Create a report using the Report Wizard.**
  a. Start Access, then open the database L-2.accdb from where you store your Data Files. Save the database as a new database with the name **L-Poster Business**. Enable the content.
  b. Use the Report Wizard to create a new report based on the Artists table and the Posters table. Include the Artist Name field from the Artists table, and the Poster Name, Subject, Size, and Amount Sold fields from the Posters table.
  c. Specify to view the data by Artist Name, then specify to group the data by Subject. Specify to sort in ascending order by Amount Sold. Select the Stepped layout and Portrait orientation.
  d. Type **Posters by Artist** as the report title.
  e. View the report in Print Preview.

2. **View a report.**
  a. Close the Navigation pane, then zoom out in Print Preview to see the full first page.
  b. Close Print Preview to view the report in Design view.
  c. View the report in Report view.
  d. Filter the report to show only records containing **Melvin Cowens** in the Artist Name field. If your instructor asks you to provide a printout of your filtered results, follow the instructions in the yellow box on page 282. Toggle the filter.

3. **Modify a report.**
  a. View the report in Layout view.
  b. Delete the Size field and field values from the report.
  c. Notice the Amount Sold column heading is not fully visible because the column is too narrow for it to fit. You need to resize this column header so it is wider, and you also need to move it to the far right of the page so it is on the right side of the Poster Name column. First, click the Amount Sold column header, press and hold [Shift], then click 675 (the first field value below the Amount Sold column header). Now the entire column is selected. Position the pointer over the selected column, then drag to the right about 3", to the other side of the Poster Name column. Scroll up to the top of the page if necessary.
  d. Increase the width of the Amount Sold column so the entire field name and all the field values are visible.
  e. Increase the width of the Subject column so all of the field values in that column are visible.
  f. Save your changes.

4. **Add a field to a report.**
  a. Select Artist Name and Adrian Sanchez so the entire Artist Name column and all the field values are selected.
  b. Drag the left border of the selected column to the right about an inch to make room for a new field.
  c. Display the Field List if necessary, and show all tables in the list.
  d. Add the Specialty field to the report. Close the Field List.
  e. Save your changes.

5. **Apply conditional formatting to a report.**
  a. Select one of the Amount Sold values in the report.
  b. Open the Conditional Formatting Rules Manager dialog box, then create a new rule.
  c. Set the conditions as greater than 10000, then specify green bold formatting.
  d. Close the Conditional Formatting dialog boxes.

Skills Review (continued)

e. Display the REPORT LAYOUT TOOLS DESIGN tab. Apply the Ion theme to the report. Preview the report in Print Preview. Compare your report to **FIGURE L-21**.

f. Save and close the report.

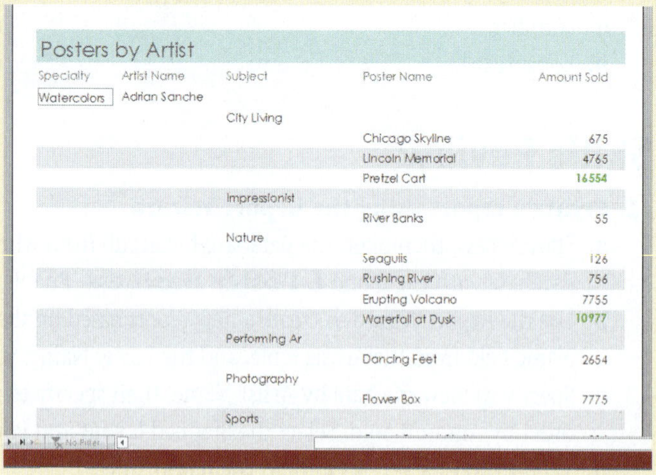

6. Add summary information to a report.

a. Open the Navigation pane. Use the Report Wizard to create a new report based on the Sanchez Sports Posters Sales query.

b. Select all the fields, then specify to view by Artist Name.

c. Open the Summary Options dialog box, then specify to add the Sum, Avg, Min, and Max summary values for the Total Sales field. Also, specify to calculate percent of total for sums.

d. Sort in ascending order by the Total Sales field, choose the Stepped layout, choose Portrait orientation, and type **Sanchez Sports Posters Sales** as the report title.

e. Preview the report. If necessary, use Layout view to adjust the column widths of the field values and the summary information columns so all information is visible and the page looks balanced.

f. Add your name to the Report Header in parentheses, preview and print the report, compare your screen to **FIGURE L-22**, then save and close the report.

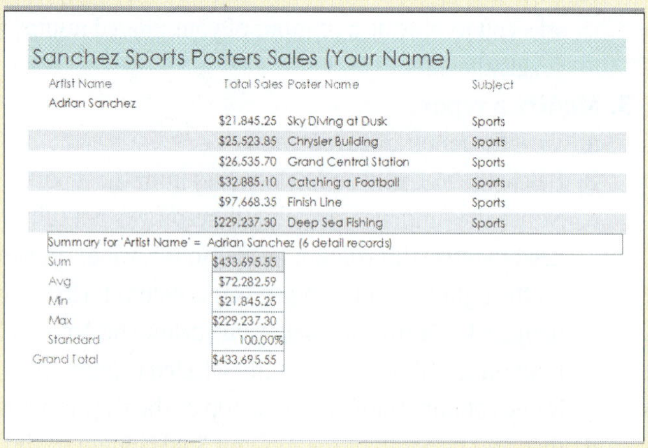

7. Create mailing labels.

a. Create a new report using the Label Wizard, based on the Posters table.

b. Choose Avery in the Filter by manufacturer list, choose the English option button, then choose label C2160.

c. Choose font settings of black 10-point Arial, Normal font weight, with Italic formatting.

d. Set up the label as shown in **FIGURE L-23**. Be sure to type the additional text shown in the figure.

e. Sort the records first by Subject and then by Poster Name. Title the report **Poster Labels**.

FIGURE L-21

FIGURE L-22

FIGURE L-23

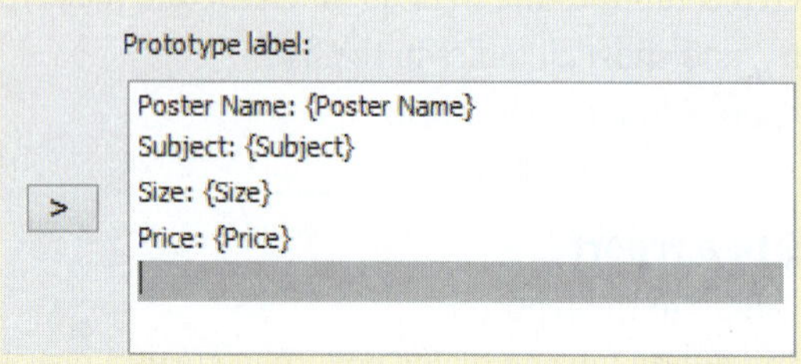

Skills Review (continued)

f. Preview the labels, then switch to Design view. Add your name as a label to the Page Footer section, then preview the first page of labels. Compare the bottom of your first page with **FIGURE L-24**.

g. Save the labels, close the report, then exit Access. Submit your completed database to your instructor.

Independent Challenge 1

You work for Hannah Bigelow, the director of a summer arts camp. Hannah wants to distribute information about this summer's campers to the camp staff. She also would like to have name labels to affix to each camper's locker. You need to create reports to provide her with the information she needs.

a. Start Access, then open the file L-3.accdb from where you store your Data Files. Save the database as **L-Arts Camp**. Enable the content.

b. Create a report using the Report Wizard based on the Leaders and Campers tables. Include the Specialty and Leader Last Name fields from the Leaders table, then include the Camper First Name, Camper Last Name, Camper ID, Age, and Camper Phone fields from the Campers table.

c. Specify to view the data by Specialty and Leader Last Name, then specify to group the data by Age. Sort the records by Camper Last Name in ascending order. Choose the Block Layout style and Landscape orientation. Title the report **Campers By Specialty**.

d. View the report in Layout view. Resize the width of the Age column by about half its original width by dragging its right edge to the left ½". (*Hint:* Select both the Age column header and an Age field value before dragging so the entire column is resized.) Widen the Camper Phone field so the entire field is visible.

e. Delete the Camper ID field and field values. Move the Camper Phone field and field values over to the left by 1".

f. Apply the Integral theme to the report.

g. Add your name after the report title in parentheses. Save your changes. View the report in Print Preview, then compare your finished report to **FIGURE L-25**. Close the report.

h. Create labels for all campers based on the Camper Label query. Use Avery label C2243, and choose Bodoni MT for the font, 10 for the font size, Normal for the font weight, and black for the font color. Place the fields for the label as shown in **FIGURE L-26**. Sort the labels first by Specialty, then by Camper Last Name. Save the report as **Campers Labels**, then preview it.

i. View the labels in Design view, then add your name as a label to the Page Footer section. Save your changes.

j. Preview the first page of the labels, close the Campers Labels report, then exit Access. Submit your completed database to your instructor.

FIGURE L-24

FIGURE L-25

Specialty	Leader Last Name	Age	Camper Last Name	Camper First Name	Camper Phone
Jazz Band	Lynch	9	Crawford	Craig	555-9857
		11	Gaddis	Ian	555-3678
			Miller	Roxanne	555-1785
		13	Chory	Ray	555-2876
			Desantis	Francis	555-0753
		14	Cruz	George	555-7654
Improvisation	Goulet	11	Bright	Paul	555-8977
			Indigo	Debbie	555-2876
		12	Gardiner	Felipe	555-8742
			Smith	Sally	555-4986
		13	Peppers	Stephen	555-3789
Irish Step	Espinosa	9	Gaston	Graham	555-2635
		11	Whipple	Reed	555-1188
		13	Jones	Philippa	555-1985
		14	Scales	Christie	555-2654
Sculpture	Moore	8	Grody	Christopher	555-8903
		11	Colber	Billy	555-2654
			Marquez	Maria	555-1653
		12	Walker	Curtis	555-1879
Music Composition	Han	9	Evans	Roy	555-4637
		12	Garcia	Beth	555-4660
			Jackson	Lavonda	555-1449
		13	Bauman	Rose	555-3627
			Mowder	Jamal	555-7653

Campers by Specialty (Your Name)

FIGURE L-26

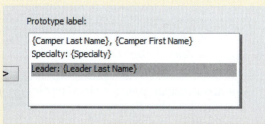

Prototype label:

{Camper Last Name}, {Camper First Name}
Specialty: {Specialty}
Leader: {Leader Last Name}

Independent Challenge 2

You are the programs director at a local fitness center. You recently purchased Access to track information about your students, classes, and instructors. You need to create a report that shows a listing of all your students for the upcoming classes, grouped by class. The report also needs to show the amounts due for each student. You will create this report from existing tables in the database.

a. Start Access, then open the database L-4.accdb from where you store your Data Files. Save the database as **L-Fitness Center**.

b. Use the Report Wizard to create a report based on the Classes and Students tables. Include the Class Name, Instructor Last Name, and Per Class Fee fields from the Classes table, and the Last and First fields from the Students table. Specify to view the data by the Classes table, then group the fields by Class Name.

c. Sort the records by the Last field in ascending order, and choose the Stepped layout with Landscape orientation. Type **Students by Class** as the report title.

d. View the report in Layout view. Move the Per Class Fee field to the right of the Class Name field. Resize and move the Instructor Last Name column and the Class Name column as needed so the field names and field values are all visible and the report looks balanced.

e. Add your name in parentheses to the Report Header after the title, preview the report, save the report, then close the report.

f. Create a report using the Report Wizard based on the query Class Fees Due. Include all the fields from the query in the report. Specify to view by Classes, and do not specify any additional grouping levels. Sort the records by the Last field in ascending order. Set the orientation to Portrait and choose the Stepped layout. Save the report with the name **Class Fees Due (Your Name)**.

g. View the report in Layout view. Apply the Retrospect theme. If necessary, resize any columns so all information is visible and the columns are balanced. View the report in Print Preview, then close the report.

h. Close the database. Exit Access. Submit your completed database to your instructor.

Independent Challenge 3

You own a small, residential pet-care business called Uncle Ruff's Dog Care. You have decided to initiate a Premium Customer program for any customers who purchase $500 or more of services in a calendar year. To manage this program, you decide to create a report based on the tables in your database to track customer payments, and use conditional formatting in the report to identify all customers whose purchases are equal to or greater than $500.

a. Start Access, then open the file L-5.accdb from where you store your Data Files. Save the database as **L-Uncle Ruff's Dog Care**. Enable the content.

b. Use the Report Wizard to create a report based on the Customer YTD Payments query. Specify to include all the fields from the query in the report. Specify to view the data by Dogs. Do not add any grouping levels. Do not specify a sort order. Choose the Tabular layout and Portrait Orientation. Save the report with the name **Customer YTD Payments**, then click Finish.

c. View the report in Layout view. Delete the Last Name field (the last column). Move and resize the other columns so all the field values appear, and so the report looks balanced.

d. Apply conditional formatting to the YTD Payments field. Add a new rule that formats values greater than or equal to 500 in green bold. Add a second rule that formats field values that are less than 200 in red bold. (*Hint*: To add a second condition, click the New Rule button in the Conditional Formatting Rules Manager dialog box, then enter the settings for the new rule.)

e. Type your name in parentheses next to the report title, then save your changes. Preview the report, then close the report.

f. Exit Access. Submit your completed report to your instructor.

Independent Challenge 4: Explore

You can create reports to help you view and understand the information in any personal databases that you create. For instance, if you create a database to track your personal spending, you could create a report that shows the spending for a particular type of expense, like education or holiday shopping. In this Independent Challenge, you will create a report that shows your class information. Then you will save it as a PDF file, which is a format that preserves formatting and allows viewing on multiple devices. (*Note*: If you completed the Independent Challenge 4: Explore in Unit K, you can build on your completed solution from that exercise.)

a. Start Access, then open the database L-6.accdb from where you store your Data Files. (Or, if you completed Independent Challenge 4: Explore in Unit K, you can open your completed solution from that exercise by opening the database K-My Classes.accdb.) Save the database as **L-My Classes**. Enable the content.

b. Open the Classes, Homework, and Instructors tables in Datasheet view. Review the fields contained in each table, and identify the field types for each. If you are using a completed solution file that you created in the Independent Challenge in Unit K, skip Step c.

c. If you did not complete the Independent Challenge in Unit K and are working with the file L-My Classes.accdb, add appropriate records to all three of the tables using information from your classes, homework, and instructors. (*Note*: You will probably need to make up Instructor ID numbers. Therefore, it is recommended that you enter your Instructor records first, then enter those made-up Instructor IDs in the Classes table.) When you are done, widen columns as necessary to ensure that all field names and field values are visible on the screen. Save your changes.

d. Create a report using the Report Wizard that is based on all three tables. Include the following fields: Class Name, Instructor Last Name, Assignment Description, and Due Date. Specify to view the report by the Classes table. Do not specify a grouping level. Choose a layout that you like. Choose Portrait orientation. Save the report with the name **My Homework (Your Name)**.

e. View the report in Layout view. Resize and move the columns if necessary so all the data is visible.

f. Click in the Report Header section (My Homework (Your Name)). Click the REPORT LAYOUT TOOLS DESIGN tab, then click Date and Time in the Header/Footer group. In the Date and Time dialog box, click OK to accept the default settings. Notice that today's date and the current time are added to the Report Header and are right aligned.

g. Apply a Theme that you like to the report. Click the Colors button in the Themes group, then apply a different color palette (any one that you like). Click the Fonts button in the Themes group, then click a different Font set that you like.

h. Adjust the widths of the columns as necessary to ensure all information is visible and the page looks balanced. Save and close the report.

i. Click the My Homework report in the navigation bar, then click the EXTERNAL DATA tab. This tab lets you import data into your database or export it into different formats. You will export your report into a PDF file, which is a file format that is easily viewed on many devices. Click PDF or XPS in the Export group. In the Publish as PDF or XPS dialog box, navigate to the location where you store your Data Files, click Publish, then click Close. *Note*: If the My Homework file opens on your screen after you click Publish, close the file. (Windows 8 users: right click on the screen, click More, then click Close File. Windows 7 users: click the Close button.)

j. Exit Access. Using Windows Explorer, open the folder where you store your Data Files, then double-click the My Homework.PDF file to view your report. Close the file, then submit the PDF to your instructor.

Visual Workshop

Open the database L-7.accdb from where you store your Data Files, then save it as **L-Dance Charity Event**. Enable the content. Create the report shown in FIGURE L-27, based on the United Way Donations query. (*Hint*: In the Report Wizard, choose the fields shown, sort as shown, and be sure to add the Summary Information shown.) Specify the Stepped layout and Portrait orientation. Save the report as **United Way Donations**. Adjust the column widths as needed. Apply the conditional formatting and theme shown. Preview the report in Print Preview, then close the database and exit Access.

FIGURE L-27

United Way Donations			
United Way Donations (Your Name)			
Charity Name	Amount	Sponsor Name	Dancer Last Name
United Way			
	$50.00	Fred's Bowling Alley	Gladstone
	$50.00	Duffy Landscapers	Gladstone
	$50.00	Good Bikes, Inc.	Singer
	$60.00	Pete's Plumbing	Bleasdale
	$75.00	Pesky Pest Removal	Wyatt
	$75.00	Burrito Hut	Dolan
	$100.00	Strickland Auto Body	Dolan
	$100.00	Valley Dental	Chu
	$100.00	Brickston's Auto Body	Farnum
	$100.00	Bo's Burgers	Wyatt
	$200.00	Woodlands Hospital	Moss
	$250.00	Your Name	Singer
	$250.00	Tuckton Woods Bank	Bleasdale

Summary for 'Charity Name' = United Way (13 detail records)

Sum	$1,460.00
Avg	$112.31
Min	$50.00
Max	$250.00
Standard	100.00%
Grand Total	$1,460.00

Creating a Presentation

CASE Karen Rivera, marketing director for Outdoor Designs, has asked you to create a presentation to tell the company's sales reps about the new products the company will introduce in April. It will introduce new products from the watercraft, kite, and lounge chair product lines.

Unit Objectives

After completing this unit, you will be able to:

- Open and view a presentation
- Create a new presentation
- Enter and format slide text
- Apply a theme

- Add and modify clip art
- Add and modify shapes
- Create SmartArt
- Insert tables

Files You Will Need

M-1.pptx	M-3.pptx
M-2.pptx	M-4.pptx

©HelenStock/Shutterstock

Open and View a Presentation

PowerPoint is a **presentation graphics app** that allows you to create dynamic **slides**, which are on-screen pages you use in a slide show. A **slide show** displays a sequence of full-screen slides on a computer. Slides can combine text, graphics, sound, and video. PowerPoint includes several ways to view a presentation. When you start PowerPoint, the workspace opens in **Normal view** and is divided into two **panes**, or areas. The larger pane on the right, the **Slide pane**, shows the full slide, and the smaller **Thumbnail pane** on the left shows **thumbnails**, or small versions, of the slides. You can also switch to other views. **Outline view** shows only the slide text in the left pane, in an indented format, instead of thumbnails. **Slide Sorter view** shows only thumbnails of the entire presentation and is useful for reordering and deleting slides. You can switch to **Slide Show view** to view the slide show as your audience will see it, or **Reading view**, to view it full screen but also see the status bar. PowerPoint also includes a **Notes Page view**, where you can see your slide and any notes you have made, plus three master views you can use to change multiple slides in a presentation. **CASE** *Before you get started using PowerPoint, you view a presentation about Outdoor Designs watercraft products.*

STEPS

TROUBLE
If you are running Windows 7, click the Start button on the taskbar, click All Programs, click Microsoft Office 2013, then click PowerPoint 2013.

1. **Go to the Windows 8 Start screen, type PowerPoint, then click PowerPoint 2013**
   PowerPoint 2013 starts, and the PowerPoint start screen appears, as shown in **FIGURE M-1**.

2. **Click Open Other Presentations on the left side of the screen**
   The Open screen appears, allowing you to open a presentation from your SkyDrive or from your computer.

3. **Click Computer, then click the Browse button**
   The Open dialog box opens.

QUICK TIP
To resize the panes, point to the gray border between the two panes, then when the pointer changes to ⟺ drag the pane border left or right.

4. **Navigate to the location where you store your Data Files, click M-1.pptx, then click Open**
   A presentation about Outdoor Designs watercraft products opens, as shown in **FIGURE M-2**. When you start PowerPoint, the workspace opens by default in Normal view.

5. **Click the Next Slide button ⥥ at the bottom of the vertical scroll bar**
   Slide 2 appears on the screen, and the Slide 2 thumbnail is highlighted in orange. You can move to the next or previous slide by clicking the Next Slide button ⥥ and Previous Slide button ⥣, or by pressing the Up and Down arrow keys or the Page Up and Page Down keys on the keyboard.

6. **Click the VIEW tab, then click the Outline View button in the Presentation Views group**
   The VIEW tab contains buttons that let you change how the presentation appears on the screen. The Thumbnail pane changes to display only the text on each slide, arranged in indented form, like an outline.

QUICK TIP
To move a slide in Slide Sorter view, drag it to a different position.

7. **Click the Slide Sorter button in the Presentation Views group**
   The view changes to Slide Sorter view, as shown in **FIGURE M-3**. The slide thumbnails are arranged in rows across the window. The currently selected slide, Slide 2, is highlighted in orange. The status bar also contains view buttons.

8. **Double-click Slide 1 to return to Outline view, click the Slide Show button 🖵 on the status bar, then press [Spacebar] until you reach the end of the presentation**
   The slide show advances and ends with a black screen. Pressing [Spacebar] again (or clicking the black screen) returns you to Outline view. You can also advance a slide show by clicking the screen, or pressing [Enter], [Page Down], or ▼.

9. **Click the FILE tab, then click Close, clicking No if asked to save your changes**
   The M-1.pptx file closes.

FIGURE M-1: PowerPoint Start screen

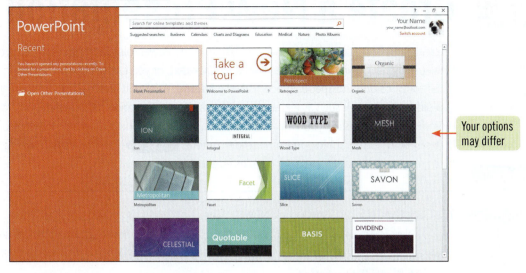

Your options may differ

FIGURE M-2: Presentation open in Normal view

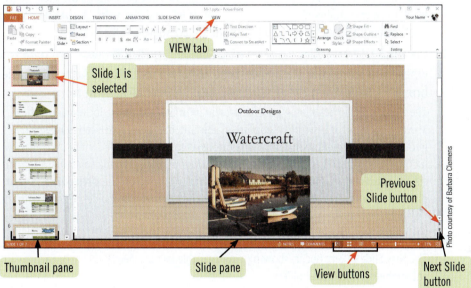

VIEW tab

Slide 1 is selected

Outdoor Designs

Watercraft

Previous Slide button

Thumbnail pane

Slide pane

View buttons

Next Slide button

Photo courtesy of Barbara Clemens

FIGURE M-3: Presentation in Slide Sorter view

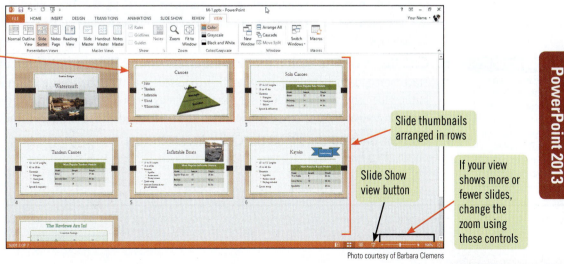

Orange highlight means this slide is selected

Slide thumbnails arranged in rows

Slide Show view button

If your view shows more or fewer slides, change the zoom using these controls

Photo courtesy of Barbara Clemens

Creating a Presentation

Create a New Presentation

Learning
Outcomes
• Create and save a
  new presentation
• Add new slides to
  a presentation
• Apply slide layouts

To create a presentation of your own, you begin at the PowerPoint Start screen. There you can choose a blank presentation, which has white slides and black text, or you can select a presentation that has coordinated fonts, colors, and special effects, called a **theme**. After you create a presentation, you save it, then add slides and content such as text and graphics. A new presentation has one slide, but you can easily add more. For each new slide you add, you can select a **layout**, which is an arrangement of **placeholders** that can hold text, graphics, and other slide content. **CASE** ▶ *You are ready to create the presentation Karen requested. You begin by creating a blank presentation.*

STEPS

QUICK TIP
You can also create a
new presentation
based on a template
that contains con-
tent. See the Apply a
Theme lesson for
more information.

1. **Click the FILE tab, then click New**

   The New screen appears, shown in **FIGURE M-4**. Here you can choose to create a blank presentation or a presentation with a theme. If you choose a blank presentation now, you can easily add a theme later.

2. **Click Blank Presentation**

   A new, blank presentation opens. The Thumbnail pane contains a thumbnail representing one blank slide. Because it is the only slide, it is highlighted. The Slide pane shows the slide's placeholders. The **title placeholder** contains the text "Click to add title", and the **subtitle placeholder** contains the text "Click to add subtitle." You'll add text to these placeholders in the next lesson.

3. **Click the FILE tab, click Save As, click Computer, click Browse, navigate to the location where you store your Data Files, type M-New Products for April in the File name text box, click Save, then click the HOME tab if it isn't already in front**

   The Save As dialog box closes, and the presentation is saved to the location you chose. The new filename, M-New Products for April.pptx, appears in the title bar. The HOME tab is now active, showing the most frequently used presentation command buttons. Before adding slide content, you'll add slides to the presentation. When you add a slide, you can choose a layout. Each layout also contains formatting for placeholders. For example, the slide in your new presentation is based on the **Title slide layout**, which contains a placeholder with larger, centered text for a title, and another placeholder below it with smaller centered text for a subtitle.

4. **Click the New Slide list arrow in the Slides group**

   The New Slide gallery opens, showing nine available layouts. See **FIGURE M-5**. Each layout contains a different arrangement of placeholders.

5. **Click the Two Content layout**

   A new slide thumbnail appears in the Thumbnail pane, under the first slide. The new slide has a title placeholder at the top, and two content placeholders below it. See **FIGURE M-6**. The content placeholders contain text prompts as well as six icons you can click to add other types of content. **TABLE M-1** lists each available content type.

QUICK TIP
To add a new slide
using the keyboard,
press and hold [Ctrl]
and press [M]. To
delete a slide, click it
in the Thumbnail
pane, then press
[Delete].

6. **Click the New Slide button (not the list arrow) in the Slides group three times**

   Three more slide thumbnails appear after the second slide, and the fifth slide is highlighted. As you can see in the Slide pane, the fifth slide has the same layout as the second one. When you click the New Slide button instead of the list arrow, PowerPoint adds a new slide with the same design as the slide before it.

7. **Click the Save button 🖫 on the Quick Access toolbar**

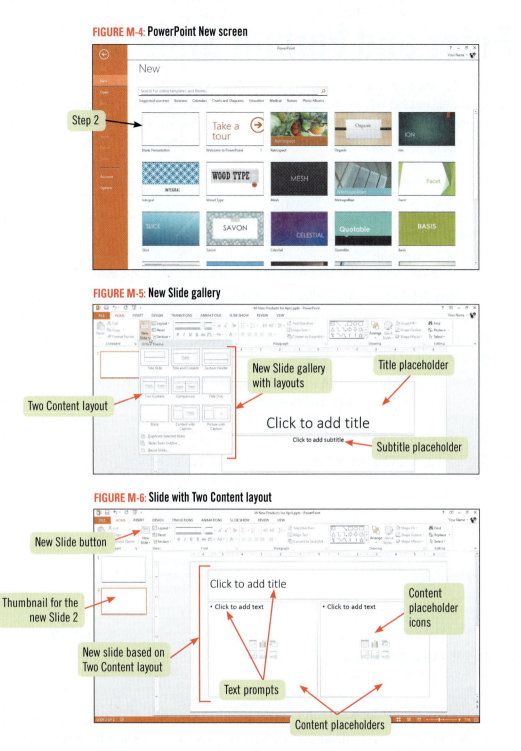

FIGURE M-4: PowerPoint New screen

FIGURE M-5: New Slide gallery

FIGURE M-6: Slide with Two Content layout

TABLE M-1: Content placeholder icons

icon	lets you add
	A table with the number of rows and columns you specify
	A chart using any Excel chart type
	A predesigned SmartArt diagram you can customize
	A picture stored on your computer or on a network location
	A picture from the Office.com website or from the Web using Bing Search
	A video file stored on your computer or from the Web using Bing Search

Enter and Format Slide Text

Learning Outcomes
• Enter slide text
• Change font appearance

You can enter text on a slide in the Slide pane or in Outline view. Working in the Slide pane shows you exactly how the text will look on the slide, while Outline view can be useful when you have a lot of text to edit and rearrange. A placeholder containing text, a graphic, or a table is an editable **object** on the slide that you can move and resize. **CASE** ▶ *You begin the New Products presentation by adding text to the title slide.*

STEPS

QUICK TIP
Clicking a slide thumbnail is another way to move to a slide in the Slide pane. To display a thumbnail that is hidden, use the vertical scroll bar in the Thumbnail pane.

1. **Click the Slide 1 thumbnail, then position the mouse pointer over the title placeholder in the Slide pane until it changes to** ⌶**, then click once**

   A dashed-line **selection box** surrounds the title placeholder, the prompt text is no longer visible, and a blinking vertical insertion point indicates where the new text will be entered, as shown in **FIGURE M-7**.

2. **Type New Products for April, click the subtitle placeholder, then type Outdoor Designs**

   The title text appears in the title font and style, and the subtitle text appears in the subtitle font and style.

3. **Click the Slide 2 thumbnail, click the Click to add title placeholder in the Slide pane, then type Sugarloaf Camp Chair**

4. **Click the prompt text Click to add text in the left placeholder, type Carbon fiber supports, press [Enter], type Lightweight, press [Enter], then type Designed for comfort**

   Each time you press [Enter], the insertion point moves to a new bulleted line. Your slide text appears on the slide, as shown in **FIGURE M-8**. You'll enter content in the right placeholder in a later lesson.

5. **On Slides 3, 4, and 5, enter the text shown in the table below:**

slide #	title	bullets in left placeholder
3	Mercer Racing Canoe	Designed for speed Easy to assemble Patented hull
4	Dipsy Flyer Kite	Basic assembly skills Six-sided Japanese design Plastic and bamboo
5	Projected Sales	[No bullet text on this slide]

   Each completed slide thumbnail displays the added text. The presentation now has five slides.

6. **Click the Slide 2 thumbnail, double-click comfort in the third bullet, then in the Mini toolbar, click the Bold button** Ⓑ

7. **Click Slide 1, click the subtitle Outdoor Designs, click the edge of the subtitle place-holder with the** ⬥ **pointer so that its edges become solid lines, click the Font list arrow in the Font group, scroll down and click Impact, click the Font Size list arrow in the Font group, then click 28**

   Clicking the edge of the placeholder so that its edges become solid lines selects the entire placeholder. Any formatting you apply after that applies to everything inside the placeholder.

8. **Click the Font Color list arrow** 🅐▾ **in the Font group, click More Colors, on the Standard tab in the Colors dialog box click the leftmost green color, then click OK**

   The Outdoor Designs text is now green, the color of the company logo.

9. **Click in the title placeholder, click the Align Text button in the Paragraph group, click Middle, then save your changes**

   Because alignment is a form of paragraph formatting, you don't need to select the entire title text object. You only need to click inside the text. See **FIGURE M-9**.

Creating a Presentation

FIGURE M-7: Entering text in a placeholder

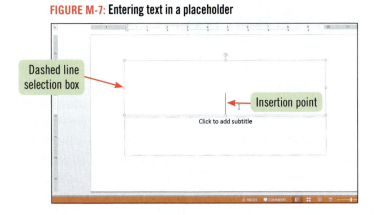

Dashed line selection box

Insertion point

Click to add subtitle

FIGURE M-8: Entering bulleted text

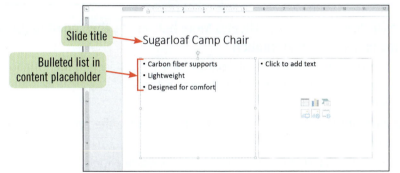

Slide title — Sugarloaf Camp Chair

Bulleted list in content placeholder
- Carbon fiber supports
- Lightweight
- Designed for comfort

Click to add text

FIGURE M-9: Completed title slide

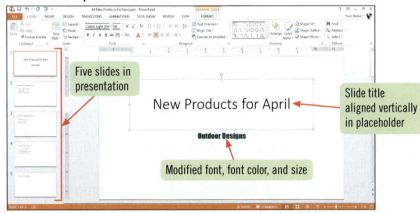

Five slides in presentation

New Products for April

Slide title aligned vertically in placeholder

Outdoor Designs

Modified font, font color, and size

© 2014 Cengage Learning

Indenting and unindenting text

When you enter text in a bulleted list placeholder, it is automatically formatted as a Level 1 bullet, meaning that it starts at the left side of the placeholder. However, you can "demote" a bullet so it is indented from the left side, indicating it is a subbullet of the previous one. To demote a bullet to a Level 2 bullet, click just before the first character in the bullet you want to demote, then press [Tab]. After you type the Level 2 bullet text and press [Enter], the next bullet will also be a Level 2 bullet. To raise a bullet to Level 1, click before the first character if necessary, press and hold [Shift], then press [Tab].

You can also use the ruler to control text indents, just as you do in Microsoft Word. Click the VIEW tab, click the Ruler check box

in the Show group to insert a check mark and display the ruler. The ruler will show the text indents for the placeholder containing the insertion point. Drag the indent markers shown in **TABLE M-2** to set indents for any text placeholder.

TABLE M-2: Indent markers in the PowerPoint ruler

indent marker	controls
▽	First line indent
△	Hanging (second line and following) indent

© 2014 Cengage Learning

PowerPoint 2013

Apply a Theme

Learning Outcomes
• Apply a theme
• Apply a theme variation

A **theme** is a slide design you can apply to any presentation to give it a professional look. A theme contains a professionally designed combination of colors, graphics, fonts, and special effects, such as shadows and reflections. Once you apply a theme to your presentation, you can also choose a color variation for a more distinctive appearance. Choose a theme that matches your presentation content. For example, if your presentation is related to nature, you might want to choose a theme with greens and blues as a suggestion of trees or plants. Although you can choose a theme when you first create a presentation, it is often helpful to first create your slide content, then try out several different themes to see which one looks best with your content. **CASE** *You decide to apply a theme to make your product presentation more appealing to the sales reps.*

STEPS

QUICK TIP

The Themes gallery also contains a Browse for Themes command, which lets you search for saved themes (or a themed document) on your computer or network. For example, your company might have a specific theme for its employees to use, containing the company colors and logo.

1. **Click the DESIGN tab, click the Themes More button ▼, then point to (but don't click) the theme under "This Presentation"**

   The Themes gallery opens. Although you created a blank presentation, the ScreenTip for the highlighted icon at the top part of the gallery shows that this presentation is actually formatted with the Office theme, which is plain, having no special graphics or colors.

2. **Point to each of the themes in the gallery, then observe the presentation after you point to each one**

   See **FIGURE M-10**. As you point to each theme, its name appears in a ScreenTip, which can help you refer to it later. Live Preview shows you what each theme looks like on the slide. The formatting you applied to the Outdoor Designs text on the title slide remains unchanged.

3. **Click the Wisp theme (the ninth one)**

   Your presentation slides are now formatted with the Wisp theme, which has an ivory background, gray and red graphics, and gray text.

TROUBLE

If you see a small pane with the text "Click to add notes" at the bottom of the screen, click the VIEW menu, then click the Notes button in the Show group.

4. **Click the Slide Show button 🖵 on the status bar, view the presentation, then return to Normal view**

   The red arrow graphic provides a nice contrast with the other theme colors. Each theme lets you choose one of several **variants**, which are different color combinations. The first variant in the Variants group has a pink border, indicating it is selected. You decide to experiment with the other three variants of the Wisp theme.

QUICK TIP

When you select a presentation theme when you first start PowerPoint, a dialog box lets you view that theme using miniature slides with placeholder text and sample graphics.

5. **Click the second, third, and fourth variants in the Variants group on the DESIGN tab, observing the title slide and the slide thumbnails**

   The second variant has green text and graphics and a yellow arrow, which are natural colors that seem appropriate for Outdoor Designs.

6. **Click the second variant**

   The background graphics are now green, which goes well with the green in the Outdoor Designs logo. See **FIGURE M-11**.

7. **Save your changes**

FIGURE M-10: Themes gallery

Pointing to theme shows Live Preview on slide

Wisp theme

...cts for April

Outdoor Designs

Company name retains formatting you applied earlier

FIGURE M-11: Theme with second variation applied

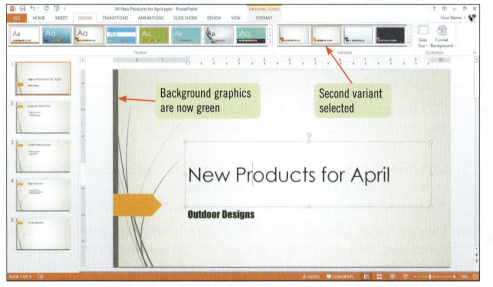

Background graphics are now green

Second variant selected

New Products for April

Outdoor Designs

Using templates

While a theme is a combination of colors, graphics, fonts, and effects that can add visual interest to your presentations, a **template** has all these elements but also content guidance for specific types of presentations you might want to create. You can use a template as a basis for creating your own presentation. Templates, along with themes, are organized into topic categories. For example, the Business category contains over 1,000 themes and templates, including a Business Strategy template with 12 slides. The slides include graphics, text placeholder, and suggested text relating to business strategy. See **FIGURE M-12**. You select templates when you first create your presentation. At the New screen, click a category near the top of the screen, such as Business, Education, or Nature. The templates, as well as the themes, available in that category appear. Click a template or

theme, then in the Preview windows, click the More Images arrows to view that layout with sample text and graphics and content guidance, if any. When you find one you want to use, click Create to create a new presentation based on that template or theme.

FIGURE M-12: Business Strategy template

Creating a Presentation

Add and Modify Clip Art

Learning Outcomes
- Add clip art
- Resize clip art
- Add a shadow to clip art

You can add **clip art**, which are predesigned photos and illustrations, anywhere on a slide. You'll find countless clip art images available online, both in the Office.com Clip Art collection and elsewhere on the Web. To find clip art, you can click the Online Pictures icon in a content placeholder or click the Online Pictures button in the Images group on the INSERT tab. You can search for clip art using **keywords**, words that you type into a search box to locate items related to a topic. The advantage of using clip art from the Office.com website is that the pictures are **royalty free**, meaning you don't need to pay a fee to use them. You can also apply special effects to alter the appearance of clip art. **CASE** ▶ *You decide to add clip art to the camp chair slide, then format the clip art to give it a shadow. Note: To complete the steps below, your computer must be connected to the Internet.*

STEPS

QUICK TIP

If you are signed in with your Microsoft account, you can also find pictures and videos from Flickr, SkyDrive, and other online locations. Be sure to check any online image source to see if you can legally use the image.

1. **Click the Slide 2 thumbnail**

   You'll insert the clip art in the content placeholder on the right side of the slide.

2. **Click the Online Pictures icon** 🖼️ **in the content placeholder**

   The Insert Pictures dialog box opens, as shown in **FIGURE M-13**. You can use this dialog box to search the Office.com website for royalty-free pictures, to search the Web using Bing Image Search, or to select a picture from your SkyDrive. The insertion point is in the Office.com search box, so you can just start typing to enter a keyword.

3. **Type camp chair, then press [Enter]**

   Thumbnail images of camp chairs from Office.com appear in the dialog box. See **FIGURE M-14**.

QUICK TIP

If the clip art image shown in Figure M-14 is not available, click a different image.

4. **Click the brown camp chair, then click Insert**

   The camp chair clip art is inserted on the slide, and the PICTURE TOOLS FORMAT tab appears and becomes active in the Ribbon.

5. **Click the Height text box in the Size group, type 4, press [Enter], then drag the chair image so it is centered in the blank area**

   When you adjust the height, the width adjusts automatically to keep the image's proportions the same.

6. **Click the Picture Effects button in the Picture Styles group, point to Shadow, scroll down if necessary, then click the first effect in the first row under Perspective (the ScreenTip reads "Perspective Diagonal Upper Left"), as shown in FIGURE M-15**

   The camp chair image now has a shadow above and to the left of its base.

7. **Save your changes**

FIGURE M-13: Insert Pictures dialog box

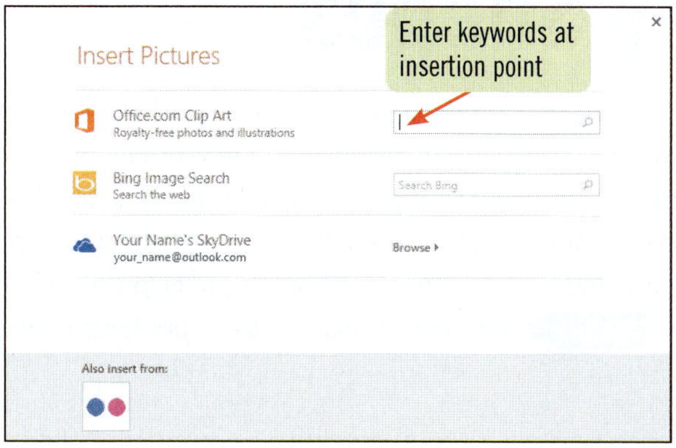

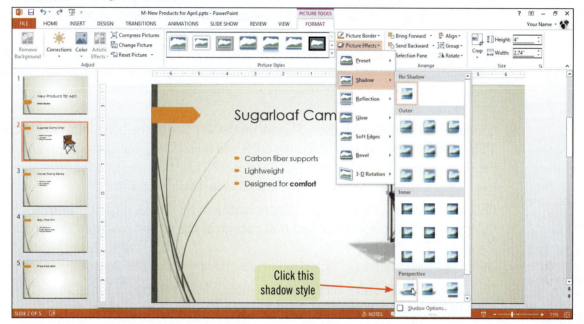

FIGURE M-14: Found images for "camp chair" search

FIGURE M-15: Selecting a shadow effect

Understanding picture effects

PowerPoint contains many editing features that let you change the look of your pictures. First, select the picture to activate the PICTURE TOOLS FORMAT tab. The Corrections button in the Adjust group lets you change the picture's color, brightness, and contrast. The Artistic Effects button lets you make your picture look like a painting or drawing. You can see a Live Preview of each effect before applying it. See **FIGURE M-16**. Not all features are available for each file type.

FIGURE M-16: Viewing picture corrections and artistic effects

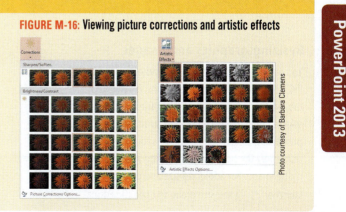

Photo courtesy of Barbara Clemens

PowerPoint 2013

Add and Modify Shapes

PowerPoint has dozens of built-in shapes, such as squares, circles, and stars, which can help add visual interest to a presentation. Once you add a shape to a slide, you can change its appearance by modifying its style, outline, and fill, and by applying shape effects. You can also instantly add text to a shape and format it, just as you do with other presentation text. As you work with shapes, it's often helpful to display the PowerPoint horizontal and vertical rulers above and to the left of a slide, which can help you to insert a shape in the same location on multiple slides. **CASE** ▶ *You want to add a shape to provide excitement on the title slide, so you add a shape and format it.*

STEPS

1. **Move to Slide 1**

2. **Click the VIEW tab, then click the Ruler check box in the Show group to select it**
   The horizontal and vertical rulers appear.

3. **Click the INSERT tab, click the Shapes button in the Illustrations group, then click the 5-Point Star shape ☆ under Stars and Banners in the Shapes gallery, as shown in FIGURE M-17**
   You can select from a variety of shape styles, including Lines, Rectangles, Basic Shapes, Block Arrows, Equation Shapes, Flowcharts, Stars and Banners, Callouts, and Action Buttons. After you click the shape you want, the gallery closes and when you move the pointer over the slide, it changes to + so you can draw the shape on the slide.

4. **Position + so it aligns with the 1.5" mark on the left side of the horizontal ruler and the 3" mark at the top of the vertical ruler, press and hold [Shift], then drag down and to the right to create a star about 2-1/2" wide and 2-1/2" tall**
   A star shape appears on the slide. Holding down [Shift] creates a symmetrical shape.

5. **Click the HOME tab, click the Quick Styles button in the Drawing group, then click the Colored Fill - Green, Accent 6 effect (last column of the second row from the top), as shown in FIGURE M-18**
   The style is applied to the shape. You can type to add text to any selected shape on a slide.

6. **Type 2016, select the text, click the Bold button, click the Increase Font Size button A̅ twice to increase the font size to 24 pt, then click a blank area of the slide**
   The text appears bold and 24 pt on the shape.

7. **Compare your screen to FIGURE M-19, then save your changes**

Resizing graphics and images

You can modify shapes, clip art, and other images using the PICTURE TOOLS FORMAT tab or the DRAWING TOOLS FORMAT tab, which opens whenever an image is selected. To resize a selected image, you can drag its sizing handles: To resize it proportionally, drag a corner sizing handle inward or outward; to resize only the height or width, drag a sizing handle on one side of the image. For additional size and position options, click the launcher ⬛ in the Size group to open the Format pane. In the category list, click ▷ next to Size for options to adjust its size, scale, and rotation. Click ▷ next to Position to see options to enter a specific location on the slide. Use Text Box options to set the text alignment, direction, behavior, and margins. Use Alt Text options to specify the alternate text, or **Alt text**, which is read by Screen reader software, and which appears as the image loads or if the image is missing when you publish the slide show to the Web.

FIGURE M-17: Selecting a shape

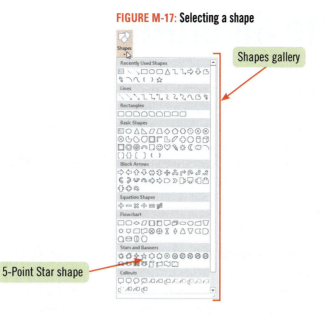

Shapes gallery

5-Point Star shape

FIGURE M-18: Applying a Quick Style

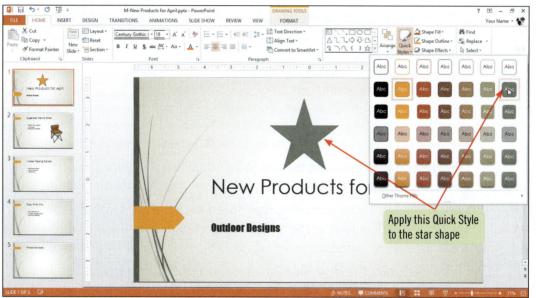

Apply this Quick Style to the star shape

FIGURE M-19: Title slide with formatted star shape

Shape with Quick Style and formatted text

2016

New Products for April

Outdoor Designs

PowerPoint 2013

Create SmartArt

Although text and shapes can help capture a viewer's attention and illustrate a point, there may be times when you need to communicate a concept or a relationship. To do this, you can use **SmartArt** to instantly create professional-looking diagrams. SmartArt includes many layouts from which to choose, organized by category, as listed in **TABLE M-3**. For example, you can show proportional or hierarchical relationships, processes, and directional flows. You can also convert existing text to SmartArt. Once you create a SmartArt graphic, you can modify its style just as you can with any object. **CASE** *You want to emphasize safety on the slide for the Mercer Racing Canoe and decide to use SmartArt to create a diagram to help illustrate this. You then convert new slide text to SmartArt.*

STEPS

1. **Click Slide 3 in the Thumbnail pane, then in the right placeholder, click the Insert a SmartArt Graphic icon**

   The Choose a SmartArt Graphic dialog box opens, as shown in **FIGURE M-20**. The dialog box consists of three panes. The left pane lists the SmartArt categories, the middle pane shows thumbnails of SmartArt layouts in the selected category, and the right pane shows a preview of the selected layout and a description of how to use it.

2. **Click Process, click several Process layouts observing the preview and description of each one, scroll down to and click the Gear process (second row from the bottom, on the far right), then click OK**

   A blank SmartArt object with the Gear process layout appears on the slide, using the current theme colors. The SMARTART TOOLS DESIGN tab is active, as shown in **FIGURE M-21**. The SmartArt object may also show a text pane on its left side that you can use to enter SmartArt text. Depending on your settings, the text pane might open or it might be closed and display only the text pane button on the left side of the object. You'll be entering text directly on the SmartArt objects, instead of using the text pane.

3. **Click the text placeholder in the top SmartArt object, then type Fun**

   The text automatically resizes to fit the text box.

4. **Click the middle text placeholder, type Speed, click the third text placeholder, type Safety, then click outside of the SmartArt object to deselect it**

   The SmartArt object is complete. Next, you'll add a slide to the end of the presentation.

5. **Click Slide 5, click the New Slide list arrow, then click Title and Content**

   A new slide appears at the end of the presentation.

6. **Enter the slide title Ready for Spring?, then enter three bullets in the content box: Learn the products, Work your contacts, and Build sales!**

7. **With the insertion point anywhere in the bulleted list, click the Convert to SmartArt Graphic button in the Paragraph group, click Chevron List (third row, second from left), then click a blank area of the slide**

   The bulleted list is converted into a SmartArt graphic using the Chevron List design, as shown in **FIGURE M-22**.

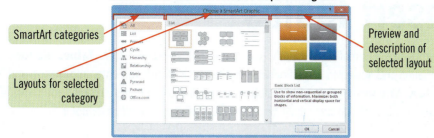

FIGURE M-21: SmartArt inserted on a slide

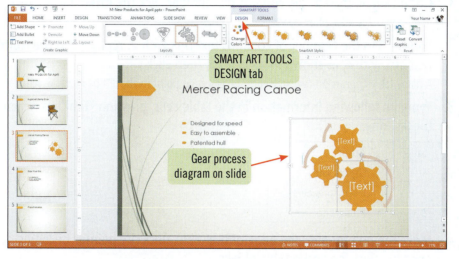

FIGURE M-22: Bulleted list converted to SmartArt

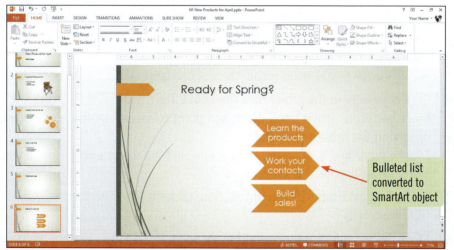

TABLE M-3: SmartArt categories

type	use	type	use
List	Nonsequential information	Matrix	Complex relationships relating to a whole
Process	Directional flow and connections between parts of a process	Pyramid	Proportional or hierarchical relationship
Cycle	Repeating or circular processes	Picture	Highlight photos with or without text
Hierarchy	Decision tree, chain of command, and organizational chart	Office.com	Layouts downloadable online at Office.com
Relationship	Connections between two or more sets of information		

Insert Tables

Learning
Outcomes
• Insert a table
• Format a table

To summarize information efficiently, you can use PowerPoint tables. **Tables** are rows and columns of information and appear in PowerPoint just as they do in Word. You enter information and format them the same way. As in Word, a PowerPoint table is an object you can format, modify, and move. **CASE** *Karen asks you to use a table to show three simple kite assembly steps, and then format it.*

STEPS

1. **Go to Slide 4, then in the content placeholder click the Insert Table icon** ▦

   The Insert Table dialog box opens.

2. **Replace 5 in the Number of columns text box with 2, replace 2 in the Number of rows text box with 4, as shown in FIGURE M-23, then click OK**

   A blank table appears on the page with the insertion point in the left header row cell.

3. **Type the following information in the table cells, pressing [Tab] after each entry, except the last one:**

Step	Action
1	Lay out kite
2	Insert spreaders
3	Attach kite

4. **Move the pointer over the edge of the table, until the pointer becomes** ⬚, **then click once to select the entire table object**

   Now any formatting you select will apply to the entire table, instead of just one part of it.

5. **Click the TABLE TOOLS LAYOUT tab, click the Height text box in the Table Size group, type 3, then press [Enter]; click the Cell Margins button in the Alignment group, then click Wide**

   The cell margins become wider, making the table data easier to read. See **FIGURE M-24**.

6. **Click anywhere in the table, click the TABLE TOOLS DESIGN tab, click the Table Styles More button** ⬚, **then scroll down and point to several table styles in each category, observing the table on the slide**

   To apply a table style, you don't need to select the entire table. As you point to each style in the table styles gallery, the table on the slide shows a preview.

7. **In the Best Match for Document section, click the Themed Style 1 - Accent 2 (top row, third from left)**

8. **Move the pointer slightly above the top edge of the Step cell until the pointer becomes** ⬇, **click once, click the right mouse button, click the Center button on the Mini toolbar, then click outside the table**

   The completed table appears in **FIGURE M-25**.

9. **Create a shape on the first slide with your name on it, save your changes, close the presentation, exit PowerPoint, then submit your presentation to your instructor**

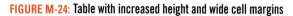

FIGURE M-23: Insert Table dialog box

Insert Table ? ×

Number of columns: 2
Number of rows: 4

OK   Cancel

FIGURE M-24: Table with increased height and wide cell margins

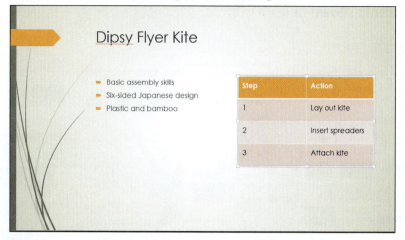

FIGURE M-25: Completed table

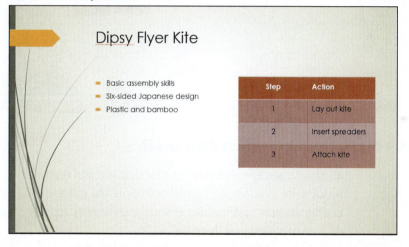

Add slide footers

You can add a **footer** to appear at the bottom of one or more slides, containing such information as the date and time, the slide number, or specific text you enter. If you only want the footer to appear on certain slides, select the first slide, press and hold [Ctrl], then click the others. Click the INSERT tab, then click the Header & Footer button in the Text group. In the Header and Footer dialog box, shown in **FIGURE M-26**, click the Slide tab, and click the check boxes next to the items you want to include. You can select a date that updates automatically every time the presentation is opened, or a fixed date that you enter. Then click Apply to add the footer to the selected slides, or click Apply to All to add it to all the slides in your presentation.

FIGURE M-26: Slide tab in the Header and Footer dialog box

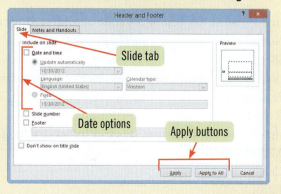

Creating a Presentation

Practice

Concepts Review

Label each of the elements shown in FIGURE M-27.

FIGURE M-27

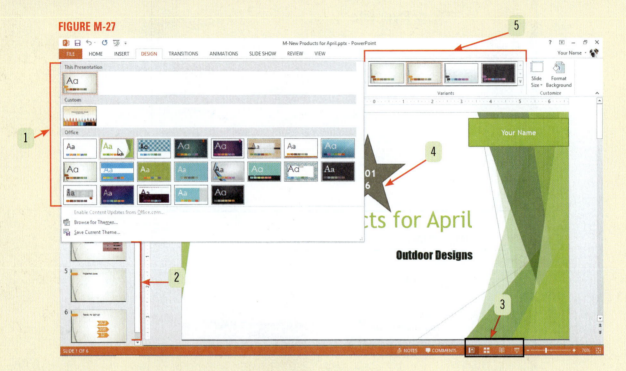

Match each term with the statement that best describes it.

6. **Slide Sorter view**
7. **Placeholder**
8. **Layout**
9. **Themes gallery**
10. **SmartArt**

a. An arrangement of placeholders for slide text and graphics
b. Contains a collection of predefined colors and styles you can apply to a presentation
c. Displays presentation slides as thumbnails in rows, for easy rearranging of slides
d. A set of predesigned diagrams
e. Object in which you can enter text or add graphics

Select the best answer from the list of choices.

11. **Which view allows you to see slide thumbnails arranged in rows?**
    a. Normal view
    b. Slide Sorter view
    c. Slide Show view
    d. Outline view

12. **Which feature allows you to summarize information in a row and column format?**
    a. Reading view
    b. A chart
    c. A placeholder
    d. A table

13. **Which PowerPoint feature lets you insert predesigned pictures and illustrations into your presentations?**
    a. Charts
    b. Tables
    c. Shapes
    d. Clip art

Skills Review

This Skills Review requires an Internet connection.

1. **Open and view a presentation.**
   a. Start Microsoft PowerPoint, then open the presentation file M-2.pptx.
   b. Use the Next Slide button to view the slides in Normal view.
   c. View the presentation in Outline view.
   d. View the presentation in Slide Sorter view.
   e. View the presentation in Slide Show view, viewing each slide in the presentation.
   f. Return to Normal view.
   g. Close the presentation, clicking No if you are asked to save changes.

2. **Create a new presentation.**
   a. Create a new blank presentation, and save it as **M-Adventure.pptx**.
   b. Add three new slides using the Two Content layout.
   c. After the fourth slide, add one new slide with the Title and Content layout.
   d. Save your changes.

3. **Enter and format slide text.**
   a. Go to Slide 1, then type **Raye's Adventure Tours** in the title placeholder.
   b. Type **Let the fun begin!** in the subtitle placeholder.
   c. Type **Coastal Kayaking** in the title placeholder on Slide 2.
   d. Type **Half and full day tours**, **Sunset tours**, **Group tours** as bullets in the left content placeholder.
   e. Add the information in the table to Slides 3, 4, and 5.
   f. Go to Slide 3, and apply bold formatting to the word "Experienced."
   g. Go to Slide 1, and select the title placeholder by clicking its border. (*Hint*: Click once in the placeholder first, then click its edge; verify that its border becomes a solid line.)
   h. Format the selected placeholder text with the Arial Rounded MT Bold font, 60 pt, and the Blue font color.
   i. Change the vertical alignment of the title text to Middle, then save your changes.

slide	title	bullets
3	Hiking	• Beginning to advanced • Experienced guides • Gear provided • Great snacks and meals
4	Horseback Riding	• English or Western • Gentle horses • Gear for all weather
5	Whitewater Rafting	[no bullet text on this slide]

4. **Apply a theme.**
   a. Apply the Slice theme to the presentation. (*Hint:* It has a blue background.)
   b. Apply the fourth variation of the Slice theme to the presentation.
   c. View the presentation in Slide Show view, then save your changes.

5. **Add and modify clip art.**
   a. Go to Slide 2, Coastal Kayaking.
   b. Use the Online Pictures icon to insert the kayak image of your choice from Office.com Clip Art.
   c. Use the Shape Height and Shape Width text boxes in the Size group of the PICTURE TOOLS FORMAT tab to resize the image so it fits well on the slide.
   d. Use the Picture Effects button to apply the Full Reflection 4 pt offset effect to the clip art object.
   e. Save your changes.

6. **Add and modify shapes.**
   a. Go to Slide 3, and click the edge of the right content placeholder to select it.
   b. Press [Delete] to delete the placeholder.
   c. Display the horizontal and vertical rulers, if they are not already displayed.

Skills Review (continued)

   d. Draw an isosceles triangle shape (in the Basic Shapes group of the Shapes gallery) on the right side of the slide, starting at the 1″ mark on the left side of the horizontal rule, and at the 3″ mark at the top of the vertical ruler, so it is approximately centered in the blank area to the right of the bulleted list.

   e. Enter the text **We specialize in mountain hikes**, then format the text in 24 pt bold.

   f. Save your changes.

7. Create SmartArt.

   a. Go to Slide 4, and use the Insert a SmartArt Graphic button to insert a Circle Arrow Process diagram, from the Cycle group (it's also in the Process group).

   b. In the three circular shapes, insert the words **Horse**, **Rider**, and **Leader**.

   c. Drag a corner of the SmartArt object to enlarge it so it fills the right side of the slide.

   d. Click Slide 5, then add a new slide to the end of the presentation, using the Title and Content layout.

   e. Add a slide title **BOOK YOUR TOUR NOW!** to the new slide, and add three bullets to the content placeholder: **Compare our rates**, **Check out our guides**, and **Our 30th year**.

   f. Select the content placeholder, and convert it to SmartArt, using the Pyramid List SmartArt design.

   g. Save your changes.

8. Insert tables.

   a. Go to Slide 5, then insert a table with 3 columns and 4 rows. Enter the following information into the table:

   b. Click the edge of the table to select the entire object, then use commands on the TABLE TOOLS LAYOUT tab to add wide margins and increase the height of the table to 4″.

Location	Length	Difficulty
Moose River	9 miles	Level I
Farm River	15 miles	Level III
Deer River	5 miles	Level II

   c. Verify that the table is selected, then use the HOME tab to increase the font size to 24 points.

   d. Use the TABLE TOOLS DESIGN tab to apply the Themed Style 1 - Accent 5 table style. (*Hint*: The style is in the first row of the Best Match for Document section of the gallery.)

   e. Double-click the right side of each column to fit the cells to the content, then position the table in the center of the blank area. (*Hint*: Move the mouse pointer over the edge of the table and drag it.)

   f. Add a shape with your name in it anywhere on the title slide. Save your changes, go to Slide Sorter view, then compare your screen to FIGURE M-28.

   g. Save your changes, close the presentation, then exit PowerPoint. Submit your completed presentation to your instructor.

FIGURE M-28

Independent Challenge 1

You own Back In Shape, a chain of fitness clubs in your state. The clubs are distinctive because they offer not only exercise equipment and classes, but they also have small cafés serving healthy meals. You have recently expanded your offerings to include healthy cooking classes. To help market your new classes, you create a presentation that will play in the lobby of the clubs.

a. Start PowerPoint, open the file M-3.pptx from the location where you store your Data Files, then save it as **M-Back In Shape**.

b. Apply the Ion theme to the presentation, then apply the third variation of the Ion theme.

c. On Slide 1, change the title to 60 pt bold text.

d. On Slide 1, add the subtitle text **GET COOKING!**, change its font color to white, then apply bold formatting to it.

e. On Slide 2, add the following two bullets to the content placeholder: **You control what you eat** and **You control how it's prepared**.

f. On Slide 3, use the Online Pictures button in the content placeholder to insert clip art. Search Office.com Clip Art, use the search text **cooking**, and choose one of the clip art images that shows pots and pans.

g. Apply the Perspective Diagonal Upper Left shadow to the clip art.

h. Adjust the height of the clip art to 4", then drag it to center it on the right side of the slide.

i. On Slide 4, add the following two bullets to the left content placeholder: **Classes start September 21st** and **Sign up at the front desk**.

j. On Slide 4, use the Insert Table button in the right content placeholder to create a table with the following information:

Class	Starts
Low Fat and High Taste	9/21
Low-Cholesterol Foods	9/25
Who Needs Butter?	9/30
Naturally Healthy Ethnic Foods	10/6

k. Double-click the right border at the top of each column to fit the text.

l. Select the entire table, make the table height 3", set the cell margins to Narrow and the table width to 6".

m. Apply the Themed Style 1 - Accent 5 style to the table. (*Hint*: It's in the Best Match for Document section of the gallery.)

n. Center all of the table text vertically within each cell. (*Hint*: On the TABLE TOOLS LAYOUT tab, use the Center Vertically button in the Alignment group.)

o. Add your name to a shape you insert anywhere on the title slide. Save your changes, view the presentation in Slide Show view, close the presentation, then exit PowerPoint. Submit your completed presentation to your instructor.

PowerPoint 2013

Independent Challenge 2

You work for Look Out, Inc., a manufacturer of replacement windows for the home. You will be attending a home products show next month, and you will be in charge of the Look Out booth. You need to create a PowerPoint presentation that will appeal to homeowners who are considering remodeling. The presentation will summarize the main types of windows the company makes.

a. Start PowerPoint, create a new presentation, then save it as **M-Look Out Windows.pptx** in the location where you store your Data Files.

b. Add four more slides after the title slide, using the Two Content layout.

c. Enter the following slide information:

slide	title text	subtitle text	bullet text in left placeholder
1	See Your World	Look Out, Inc.	
2	Our Product Line		• Picture windows • Sliding windows • Sash windows
3	Picture Windows		• Energy efficient • Low-sun glass • Heavy weather glass
4	Sliding Windows		[no bullet text]
5	Sash Windows		[no bullet text]

d. Insert a new slide at the end of the presentation, using the Title and Content layout, with the title text **Let us help you look out!**, and the bullet text **Please take a fact sheet** and **Free estimates on any home**.

e. Apply the Retrospect theme to the presentation, then view the presentation in Outline View and Slide Sorter view.

f. Return to Slide 1 in Normal view, then view the presentation in Slide Show view.

g. Format the subtitle text on Slide 1 with bold formatting, enlarge the text to 32 pt, and change its font color to Orange, Accent 1. (*Hint*: Click the Font Color list arrow, then under Theme Colors, select the fifth square from the left in the top row.)

h. Click Slide 5, enter the bullet text **Windows you can pull up** in the left placeholder, then in the right placeholder, insert clip art of a window.

i. Resize and reposition the clip art if necessary, then add the picture effect of your choice.

j. Go to Slide 4, enter the bullet text **Windows you can slide sideways**, then insert a SmartArt graphic using the Arrow Ribbon design in the Relationship category. Enter the text **Window 1** in the left SmartArt text placeholder, and **Window 2** in the right one.

k. Go to Slide 3, change the layout to Title and Content, then convert the list to SmartArt, using the Vertical Bullet List design.

l. Select the entire SmartArt object, then drag its right side to the left, so it just contains the text. (*Hint*: Position the pointer over the small square handle on the right side until the pointer becomes a two-pointed white arrow pointer, then drag.)

m. Add a shape with your name in it anywhere on the title slide. Save your changes, view the presentation in Slide Show view, close the presentation, then exit PowerPoint. Submit your completed presentation to your instructor.

Independent Challenge 3

You are the director for Computers for You, a nonprofit organization that recycles computer parts and uses them to offer usable personal computers and training in homeless shelters. You are working on a presentation in which you explain your organization's work to a charitable organization that might offer you funding.

a. Start PowerPoint, open the file M-4.pptx from the location where you store your Data Files, then save it as **M-Computers for You**.

b. Apply the Integral theme, apply the fourth variant, then view the slide show.

c. Format the title slide text using fonts, sizes, and colors of your choice.

d. Add any appropriate clip art to Slide 3. (*Hint*: You can either change the slide layout and use a placeholder, or you can use the Online Pictures button in the Images group on the INSERT tab.)

e. Move or resize the clip art as necessary, and apply the picture effects of your choice.

f. On Slide 6 (Our Proposal), insert a table with the following information:

Year	Amount
2016	$15,000
2017	$25,000
2018	$35,000

g. Resize and move the table as necessary.

h. Format the table font, style, size, and margins using any options you choose, then position the table appropriately on the slide.

i. Go to Slide 7, then insert one or more shapes that reflect the slide content. Add text to a shape, using the formatting of your choice.

j. Add a shape with your name in it anywhere on the title slide. Save your changes, view the presentation in Slide Show view, close the presentation, then exit PowerPoint. Submit your completed presentation to your instructor.

Independent Challenge 4: Explore

You want to get a job with a training company, and you have an interview coming up. The company has asked you to prepare a PowerPoint presentation that instructs someone on how to do something, using any subject matter you like.

a. Start PowerPoint, then create a new presentation based on a template; at the New screen select a template from the Education category. Save the presentation as **M-Training.pptx** in the location where you store you Data Files.

b. Add content to the presentation, creating a presentation of at least four slides. Put your name in the Title slide subtitle. In your slides, supply instructions on how to complete a task or a process. If you have to replace existing text, select the text, press [Delete], then type new text. To create new slides, try copying and pasting existing slides in the Thumbnail pane, then entering new text in the duplicate slide.

c. View the slide in Slide Sorter view, then drag at least one slide to change its position in the presentation.

d. Insert clip art on at least one slide. Move and resize it as necessary. Experiment with the Corrections, Color, and Artistic Effects (if available) until the image looks the way you want it to.

e. View the presentation in Slide Show view, make any necessary corrections, save and close the presentation, then exit PowerPoint. Submit your completed presentation to your instructor.

Visual Workshop

Using the skills you learned in this unit, create and format the slides shown in **FIGURE M-29**. Create a new, blank, presentation with three slides, and save it as **M-Party Ideas.pptx**. Use the Retrospect theme with the fifth variant. The SmartArt is in the Process category; the table font is 24 pt with wide margins. The shape on Slide 3 has a fill of Colored Fill Blue - Accent 2, as well as a shadow. Save the presentation, close it, then exit PowerPoint. Submit your completed presentation to your instructor.

FIGURE M-29

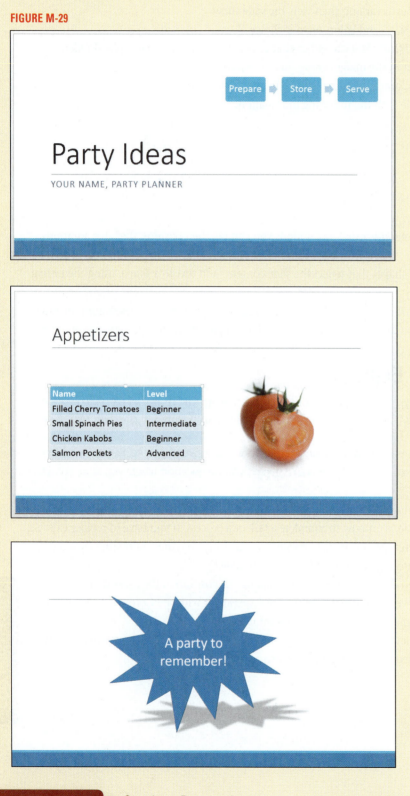

Polishing and Running a Presentation

CASE ▶ Jihong Chen, assistant sales manager, has asked you to create a presentation for the Outdoor Designs sales reps, presenting products in development for the coming year. You will polish the presentation by adding pictures, sounds, and video. Then you will set slide show transitions and animations, add speaker notes, print handouts, then review the presentation for effectiveness.

Unit Objectives

After completing this unit, you will be able to:

- Add pictures
- Add sound
- Add video
- Set slide transitions and timing
- Animate slide objects
- Use speaker notes and slide show commands
- Print handouts and notes pages
- Design effective presentations

Files You Will Need

N-1.pptx	flare.mp4
kite.png	N-4.pptx
bird.jpg	gull.jpg
bailey.wmv	whales1.jpg
N-2.pptx	whales2.jpg
gary.jpg	glacier1.jpg
gary_exploring.wmv	glacier2.jpg
N-3.pptx	N-5.pptx
telescopes.jpg	N-6.pptx

©HelenStock/Shutterstock

Add Pictures

In PowerPoint, a picture might be a photograph, a shape you draw, a piece of clip art, or an illustration created using a graphics app. PowerPoint lets you insert pictures in many different file formats, including JPEG, PNG, GIF, TIFF, and BMP. (Be sure you have written permission to use any file you choose.) After you insert a picture into your presentation, you can use features on the PICTURE TOOLS FORMAT tab to **crop**, or cut off, portions of a picture to keep the parts you want and remove the picture background. **CASE** ▶ *You insert a photograph of an upcoming kite product on a slide, crop it, then modify its background and its position on the slide.*

STEPS

1. **Start PowerPoint, open the file N-1.pptx from the location where you store your Data Files, then save it as N-Upcoming Products**

2. **Go to Slide 2, click the INSERT tab, then click the Pictures button in the Images group**
   The Insert Picture dialog box opens.

3. **Navigate to the location where you store your Data Files, click kite.png, then click Insert**
   A picture of a kite is inserted on top of the slide content, and because the picture is selected, the PICTURE TOOLS FORMAT contextual tab appears on the Ribbon. The picture hides a lot of the slide text, so you decide to crop off some of the area around the kite.

4. **Click the Crop button in the Size group, then drag the upper-left and lower-right cropping handles toward the center, so your graphic looks like FIGURE N-1, then click the Crop button in the Size group again to complete the crop**
   Cropping handles on each corner and each side let you reduce the size of the picture. You have reduced the sky area around the kite. However, you want to make the kite stand out even more, so you decide to remove its background.

5. **Click the Remove Background button in the Adjust group**
   The area behind the kite image turns magenta, which represents the program's best "guess" at the areas to delete, and the BACKGROUND REMOVAL contextual tab appears in the Ribbon, containing tools that let you fine-tune the removal areas if necessary. See FIGURE N-2. For this picture, the entire sky background is magenta, so you know that all of the sky background will be removed and you won't have to fine-tune it. You decide to keep the background changes to the picture.

6. **Click the Keep Changes button in the Close group**
   The background is removed, and only the kite is visible. It needs to be a little smaller.

7. **Move the mouse pointer over the picture's upper-left corner until the pointer becomes the diagonal resize pointer ⬉, then drag down and to the right about 1/2"**
   The picture is smaller, but it would look better if it were centered to the right of the text.

8. **Move the mouse pointer over the picture until the pointer becomes a four-pointed arrow ✣, then drag the picture to the right so it's centered horizontally in the white space**

9. **Click the Align button in the Arrange group of the PICTURE TOOLS FORMAT tab, click Align Middle, click on a blank area of the slide, compare your screen to FIGURE N-3, then save your changes**
   Now the picture is also centered vertically on the slide.

FIGURE N-1: Cropping a picture

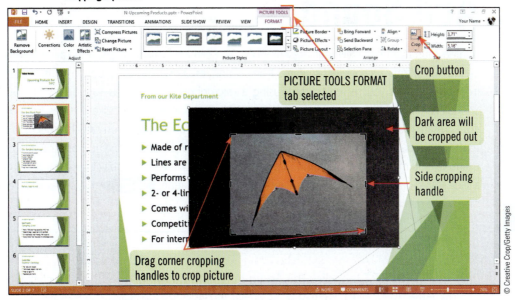

© Creative Crop/Getty Images

FIGURE N-2: Removing a picture background

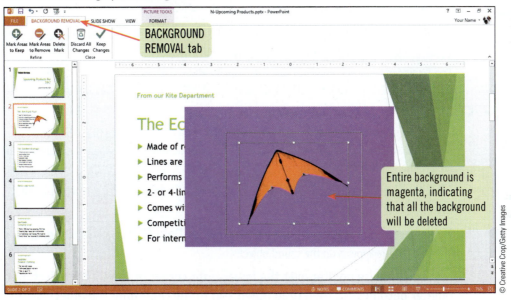

© Creative Crop/Getty Images

FIGURE N-3: Resized and repositioned picture

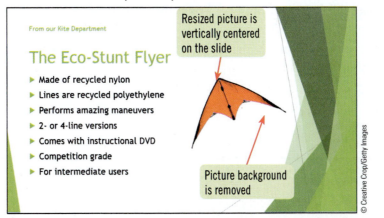

© Creative Crop/Getty Images

Polishing and Running a Presentation

Add Sound

Learning Outcomes
• Insert a sound clip
• Add a picture to an audio clip

Adding sound can enhance your presentations. You can add **sound clips**, also called **audio files**, from online collections such as Office.com, from sound or music files you obtain from other sources, or from sounds that you record yourself using a microphone and save as sound files on your computer. Sounds can include short sound effects or complete musical selections. Like pictures, sounds you add to your presentation are objects on a slide that you can move and modify. You can also specify whether or not to show the sound file icon on a slide, how the icon will appear, and when you want the sound to play—for example, you might want the sound to play when you click the sound object during a presentation, when a slide starts, or to play across all the slides in your presentation. **CASE** ➤ *You add an online sound to the slide about the new birdcage product, and then modify it.*

STEPS

1. **Go to Slide 3**

2. **Click the INSERT tab, click the Audio button in the Media group, then click Online Audio**

   The Insert Audio dialog box opens, as shown in **FIGURE N-4**, letting you enter keywords to help locate royalty-free sound clips on Office.com.

3. **Type bird, then press [Enter]**

   A scrollable list of bird sounds appears.

   QUICK TIP
   To adjust the playback volume, use the volume button in the Audio Options group on the AUDIO TOOLS PLAYBACK tab.

4. **Point to (but don't click) one of the sound file icons, locate and preview the Birdie Sings sound, click the Birdie Sings sound, then click Insert**

   The Birdie Sings sound appears as an object on the slide, as shown in **FIGURE N-5**. Because the sound file is selected, the AUDIO TOOLS FORMAT tab and the AUDIO TOOLS PLAYBACK tab appear on the Ribbon.

5. **Click the Play button ▶ below the icon**

   The Start option in the Audio Options group reads "On Click," indicating that when you run the slide show, the sound will play only when you click the icon, not automatically when the slide appears. Now you'll replace the sound icon with a picture.

   QUICK TIP
   To have a sound play automatically and be invisible on the slide, select the sound, and on the AUDIO TOOLS PLAYBACK tab, set the Start option to Automatically, then select the Hide During Show check box to select it.

6. **Click the AUDIO TOOLS FORMAT tab, click the Change Picture button in the Adjust group, then click Browse**

7. **Navigate to the location where you store your Data Files, click bird.jpg, then click Insert**

   The bird picture appears on the sound object.

8. **Move the mouse pointer over the lower-right corner of the sound object, until the pointer becomes ⬉, then drag down and to the right until the object is about 2" tall and 2" wide**

   QUICK TIP
   To insert your own sound or music files in a presentation, you can use files with many of the common sound file extensions, such as .midi, .mp3, .m4a, .mp4, .wav, or .wma.

9. **Click the Slide Show button on the status bar, move the mouse pointer over the bird image, click the Play button ▶ near the bird image, as shown in FIGURE N-6, press [Esc], then save your work**

   After the slide appears, the sound plays only after you click the Play button under the sound object on the slide.

FIGURE N-4: Insert Audio dialog box

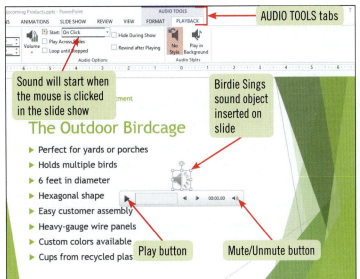

FIGURE N-5: Inserted sound object on the slide

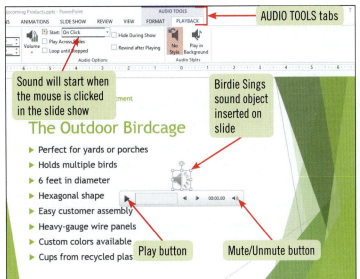

FIGURE N-6: Playing the sound clip during the slide show

Photo courtesy of Michele Miller

Adjusting sound playback during a slide show

You can change the way a sound plays back during the slide show by using the commands on the AUDIO TOOLS PLAYBACK tab. Using the tools in the Editing group, you can trim the beginning or end of an audio clip using the Trim Audio button, or have the sound fade in and out by using the Fade Duration controls. You can also control when and how the audio clip plays during the slide show by using the tools in the Audio Options group. To have a selected sound play in the background of the entire presentation, click the Play in Background button in the AudioStyles group. To reset a clip's playback settings to the default settings, click the No Style command in the AudioStyles group.

Add Video

Learning Outcomes
- Insert a video clip
- Trim a video clip

Adding video to a presentation can help your viewers remember your message. You can insert a video file from an online resource or from a collection you have saved on your computer. After you insert a video into your presentation, you can use features on the VIDEO TOOLS PLAYBACK tab to adjust how and when the video plays during the slide show. **CASE** ▶ *You decide to add a video of a bird to support the information about the outdoor bird cage.*

STEPS

QUICK TIP

You can also insert a video by clicking the Insert Video button in a content placeholder. To change a slide layout so it includes placeholders, on the Home tab click the Layout button in the Slides group, and click a layout with a content placeholder, such as Title and Content or Two Content.

1. Go to Slide 4, click the INSERT tab, click the Video button in the Media group, then click Video on My PC

2. Navigate to the location where you store your Data Files, click bailey.wmv, then click Insert

   The video file appears on the slide, and the VIDEO TOOLS FORMAT tab and the VIDEO TOOLS PLAYBACK tab appear on the Ribbon.

3. Click the Play button ▶ below the video, watch for a few seconds, press the Pause button ▮▮, then click ▶ again to watch the rest of the video

4. Click the VIDEO TOOLS PLAYBACK tab if necessary, click the Start list arrow in the Video Options group, then click Automatically as shown in FIGURE N-7

   The video will now start as soon as the slide appears in the slide show, without the presenter having to click it first. The video image is a little small for the slide, so you resize and reposition it.

5. Drag the lower left corner of the selected video object to match the size and location shown in FIGURE N-8

   The video is a bit long, so you decide to remove a segment from the beginning of the video.

6. Click the Trim Video button in the Editing group on the VIDEO TOOLS PLAYBACK tab

   The Trim Video dialog box opens, as shown in FIGURE N-9, where you can drag the green start point and red end point markers to shorten the video from the beginning or the end. You want to move the start point marker to the point where the bird starts to chirp.

QUICK TIP

To adjust the time more precisely, click the up and down Start Time arrows, or type a number in the Start Time text box.

7. Drag the green Start point marker ▮ to approximately the 00:04.660 position on the timebar, then drag the red End point marker to approximately the 14.91 position

   The video will start and end at the points you set. You decide to preview the movie in Slide Show view.

8. Click OK, click the Slide Show button 🖵 on the status bar, view the slide until the video finishes playing, then press [Esc]

   The current slide plays automatically, from the start point you set, as soon as the slide appears. You decide to preview the slide show as your audience will see it.

QUICK TIP

To start the slide show from the beginning using the keyboard, press [F5]. To start the slide show with the current slide, press [Shift][F5].

9. Click the Slide Show tab, click the From Beginning button in the Start Slide Show group, press [Spacebar] to view the slide show, clicking the Play button below the audio object on Slide 3 and viewing the video object as it plays on Slide 4, then save your changes

   The sound plays after you click the audio object on Slide 3, and the movie plays as soon as Slide 4 appears.

FIGURE N-7: Setting the video to start automatically

FIGURE N-8: Resized video in new location

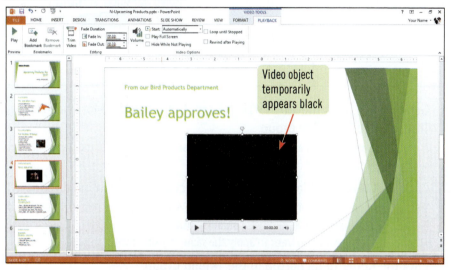

FIGURE N-9: Trim video dialog box

Video courtesy of Michele Miller

Formatting sound and video objects

You can change the way a sound or video object appears on a slide. For example, you can adjust its color or brightness, just as you can with a picture. You can also apply a style, such as a frame, or a shape, border, or effect, as well as crop and rotate the object. For example, **FIGURE N-10** shows a video with a beveled black oval. To copy formatting from one object to another, click the object whose formatting you want to copy, click the Format Painter button in the Clipboard group on the HOME tab, then click the second object.

FIGURE N-10: Applying styles to objects

Video courtesy of Michele Miller

Polishing and Running a Presentation

Set Slide Transitions and Timing

Learning Outcomes
• Add slide transitions
• Add slide timings

There may be times when you want to run a presentation automatically, without manually controlling when each slide appears. For example, you might want the presentation to run unattended at a booth or kiosk. You might also want to customize how slides appear in a slide show. To do this, you can set slide transitions and timings in PowerPoint. A **transition** is a special effect that determines how a slide appears as it enters or leaves the screen, such as a fade or a dissolve transition. A **timing** is the number of seconds a slide remains on the screen before advancing to the next one. **CASE** *Jihong wants to concentrate on her message instead of running the slide show. You decide to set the transitions and timings, and add an audio transition to the last slide.*

STEPS

1. **Go to Slide 1, click the TRANSITIONS tab, then click the More button ⯆ in the Transition to This Slide group**

   A gallery shows transition effects in three categories: Subtle, Exciting, and Dynamic Content. You decide to add an Exciting transition to Slide 1.

2. **Click the Cube transition in the Exciting section, as shown in FIGURE N-11**

   You see a preview of the Cube transition on Slide 1. When a slide has a transition applied to it, or has a video like the one you inserted in Slide 4, a small transition icon ⯐ appears under the slide number in the Thumbnails pane. Now you want to apply the same transition to all the slides.

   > **QUICK TIP**
   > To adjust the timing or transition for an individual slide, select the slide, then adjust the settings as desired.

3. **Click the Apply To All button in the Timing group**

   The transition you applied to Slide 1 is now applied to all slides in the presentation. The star transition icon appears under every slide in the Thumbnail pane. You now want to set the slide show to advance automatically after a set amount of time.

   > **QUICK TIP**
   > To remove a transition for the current slide, click the More button on the Transition to This Slide gallery, then click None.

4. **In the Timing group, click the Advance Slide After up arrow until 00:08.00 appears, then click the Apply To All button**

   Each slide will remain on the screen for 8 seconds before automatically advancing to the next one. But you can override these settings during the presentation by pressing [Spacebar] or any other slide advance technique, because the On Mouse Click option is still selected.

5. **Click the Slide Sorter button ⊞ on the status bar, then adjust the zoom using the status bar controls so you can see all the slides**

   The slide timing and transition icons appear beneath each thumbnail.

6. **Click Slide 7, click the Sound list arrow in the Timing group, click Drum Roll, compare your screen to FIGURE N-12, then click the Preview button in the Preview group**

   The Drum Roll sound plays during the transition to Slide 7. Finally, you decide to view the entire presentation with the transitions and timings you have set. Instead of using Slide Show view, you decide to use Reading view, which lets you see a presentation in full screen but also gives you status bar controls that are useful for reviewing a presentation.

7. **Click Slide 1, click the Reading View button 🔲 on the status bar, allow the presentation to play for the first three slides, then use [Spacebar] to advance the remaining slides**

   The slide transitions, timing, animation, and sounds play in the slide show until the end, then you return to Slide Sorter view. You decide to remove the slide timings so it's a little easier to work with the presentation.

8. **In Slide Sorter view, click Slide 1, press and hold [Shift], click Slide 7, click the Transitions tab if necessary, click the After check box in the Timing group to deselect it, then save your changes**

FIGURE N-11: Applying the cube transition

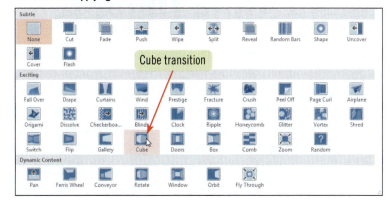

FIGURE N-12: Timing and a transition applied to a slide in Slide Sorter view

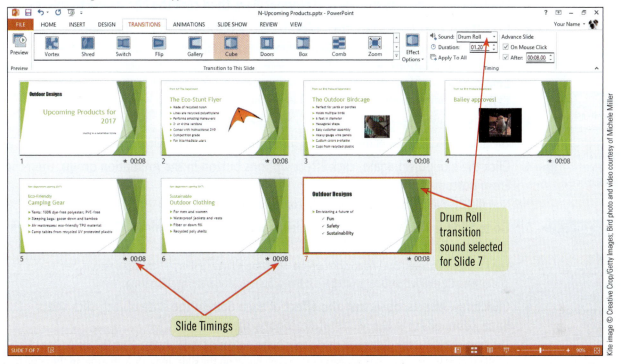

Using slide masters

There may be times when you want to make a design change to all the slides in your presentation, such as changing the alignment or font size of text, or adding a logo to every slide. Instead of making the change on each slide, you can change the slide master. A **slide master** contains the layouts, design elements, and other formatting for a presentation. Every slide you create is based on a slide master. A slide master has a number of supporting **layouts**, or arrangements of slide placeholders, such as a Title slide layout, which has placeholders for a presentation title and subtitle, or a Title and Content layout, which has placeholders for a slide title and for slide content. You can customize a slide master, or any supporting layout, and save it for future use. See **FIGURE N-13**. To modify a slide master, click the VIEW tab, then click the Slide Master button in the Master Views group. Click to select a master in the thumbnail pane, then use the buttons on

the SLIDE MASTER tab to apply a theme, change its background, or add placeholders. To create a new slide master, click the Insert Slide Master button in the Edit Master group, then customize the new slide master or one of its supporting layouts.

FIGURE N-13: Modifying the Title and Content layout master by adding a logo

Polishing and Running a Presentation

Animate Slide Objects

Once you have added text and graphics to a presentation, you can add interest to them by applying animations. **Animation effects** are movements or changes in appearance that you can apply to any text placeholder or graphic, including clip art, photos, and illustrations. For example, you can have a graphics "fly in" from the top or bottom of the slide, or "bounce out." You can also call attention to a slide object by having it "grow," "pulse," or "spin." Use animations to control how any object enters, exits, or becomes emphasized on a slide during the slide show. Once you have animated an object, you can use the Animation Painter to apply those same settings to other objects. **CASE** *You decide to animate the graphic on Slide 2 and the bulleted text in Slide 5. Then you copy the text animation to the text in Slide 6.*

STEPS

1. **Double-click Slide 2 to display it in Normal view, then click the kite image to select it**

2. **Click the ANIMATIONS tab, then click the More button ▼ in the Animation group**
   A gallery opens, showing animation effects in three categories: Entrance, Emphasis, and Exit. See FIGURE N-14. **Entrance animations** determine how a selected placeholder or other object appears on the slide, **Emphasis animations** show various ways you can emphasize an object that's already on the slide, and **Exit animations** determine how an object leaves the slide.

3. **In the Entrance category, click the Fly In animation effect**
   The slide shows a preview of the kite "flying in" from the bottom of the slide.

4. **Click the kite object again, click Effect Options button in the Animation group, then click From Bottom-Right**
   Now the kite flies in from the bottom-right corner of the slide.

5. **Go to Slide 5, click the bulleted list placeholder, click the Animation More button, then click More Entrance Effects**
   The Change Entrance Effect dialog box opens, showing a larger gallery of entrance effects. See FIGURE N-15. The effects are divided into four categories: Basic, Subtle, Moderate, and Exciting.

6. **Click a few effects, observing the effect of each one on the slide object, click the Basic Zoom effect in the Moderate category, then click OK**
   The preview behind the dialog box shows each bullet appearing individually. After the dialog box closes, a small number in an orange box appears next to each bullet on the slide, indicating its order in the animation sequence, as shown in FIGURE N-16. You decide to have the bullets appear all at the same time, instead of individually.

7. **Click the Effect Options button in the Animation group; in the Sequence category click All at Once, then click the Preview button in the Preview group**
   The animation previews, and the numbers next to each bullet change to "1"s, indicating that all the bullets appear at the same time. Now you decide to copy the animation effect to the bulleted list placeholder on Slide 6.

8. **Click the bulleted list placeholder on Slide 5, click the Animation Painter button in the Advanced Animation group, go to Slide 6, then click the bulleted list placeholder**

9. **Save your work, go to Slide 1, then click the Slide Show button on the status bar and view the slide show, pressing [Spacebar] to play the effects and end the show**

FIGURE N-14: Selecting an animation

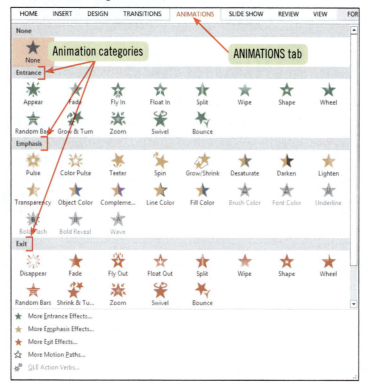

FIGURE N-15: Change Entrance Effect dialog box

FIGURE N-16: Animation order numbers

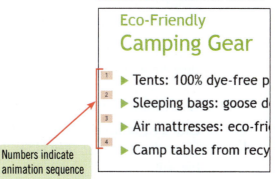

Adding animations using the Animation pane

You can add more than one animation to an object and control when each animation occurs using the Animation pane. Select an object to which you've applied one animation, then click the Add Animation button in the Advanced Animation group and select another animation. Click the Animation Pane button in the Advanced Animation group. The Animation Pane opens to the right of the slide, and lists the two animations in order. Click the list arrow to the right of a selected animation to see options for changing that animation's timing or behavior. See **FIGURE N-17**. Drag an animation up or down in the list to change its order. To delete an animation effect, click its list arrow, then click Remove.

FIGURE N-17: Using the Animation Pane

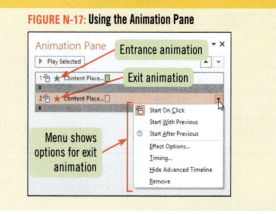

Use Speaker Notes and Slide Show Commands

Learning Outcomes
- Add speaker notes
- View slides in Notes Page view
- Use Presenter view

When you show your presentation to others, you might need to use notes to remind yourself of important points you want to make. You can add **speaker notes** to any slide using the **Notes pane**, which appears below the slide window in Normal view. Then you can view your slides and notes in **Notes Page view**, print a copy of your slides with their notes, and refer to them during the presentation. Or you can run your presentation in **presenter view** and preview how it would appear if you were using two monitors: one that the audience sees, and one that only you can see, containing your notes. **CASE** *Jihong asks you to mention the company's "going green" initiative, so you insert notes about it, and then run the presentation.*

STEPS

1. **Go to Slide 1, click the VIEW tab, then click the Notes button in the Show group**

   The Notes pane appears below the slide, with the prompt text "Click to add notes." Although the pane appears to be small, it can hold multiple lines of text.

2. **Click in the Notes pane, then type Our sustainability strategy: Recycling, energy efficiency, and green packaging, as shown in FIGURE N-18**

3. **Enter the following slide notes:**

Slide 2	Note the use of recycled materials
Slide 3	Note that 90% of this product is biodegradable
Slide 5	Emphasize eco-friendly materials

4. **Click the Notes Page button in the Presentation Views group, then press [↑] and [↓] to view the slides and the notes**

   Notes Page view shows a reduced image of your slides with your notes below it. See **FIGURE N-19**, which shows the notes for Slide 1. Next you'll view the presentation in Presenter view.

5. **Click the Normal button ▤ on the status bar, go to Slide 1, click the Slide Show button ▣ on the status bar, then move the mouse pointer toward the lower-left corner of the slide**

   Six faint white icons appear in the lower-left corner of the slide, as shown in **FIGURE N-20**.

6. **Click the far-right icon ⊙, then in the shortcut menu click Show Presenter View**

   Your presentation appears in Presenter view, as shown in **FIGURE N-21**. The current slide, as it appears to the audience, appears on the left side of the screen, and a thumbnail of the next slide, Slide 2, appears on the right. Your notes for Slide 1 appear below the thumbnail, and navigation controls appear near the bottom of the screen.

7. **Click the Advance to the next slide button ◉, note that the Next slide thumbnail shows the animation for this slide, then click ◉ to observe the rest of the slide show**

   The Slide 2 text appears, and a thumbnail of the next event, the animated kite, appears on the right.

8. **Click the See all slides button ▦ below the slide image to display all the slides, click Slide 1, click the Pen and laser pointer tools button ◪, then click Pen**

9. **Move the mouse pointer over the slide, draw a circle around the subtitle slide text "Looking to a sustainable future", click END SLIDE SHOW at the top of the screen, click Discard, then save your work**

   If you click Keep, your annotations become drawing objects in the presentation file.

FIGURE N-18: Speaker notes

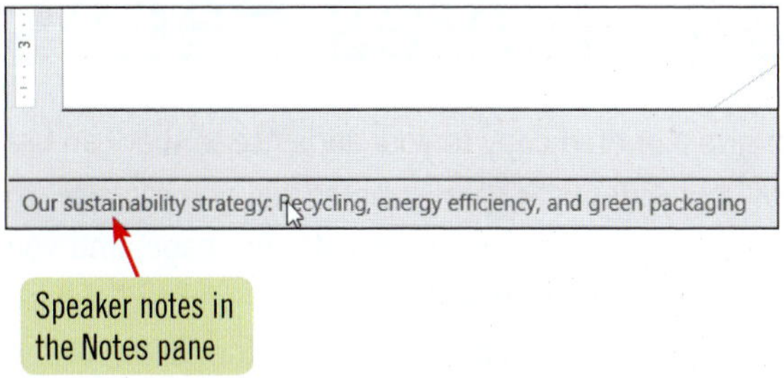

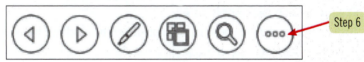

Our sustainability strategy: Recycling, energy efficiency, and green packaging
Speaker notes in the Notes pane

FIGURE N-19: Notes Page view

Outdoor Designs
Upcoming Products for 2017
Our sustainability strategy: Recycling, energy efficiency, and green packaging

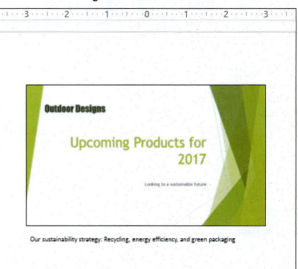

FIGURE N-20: Slide show icons

Step 6

FIGURE N-21: Presenter view

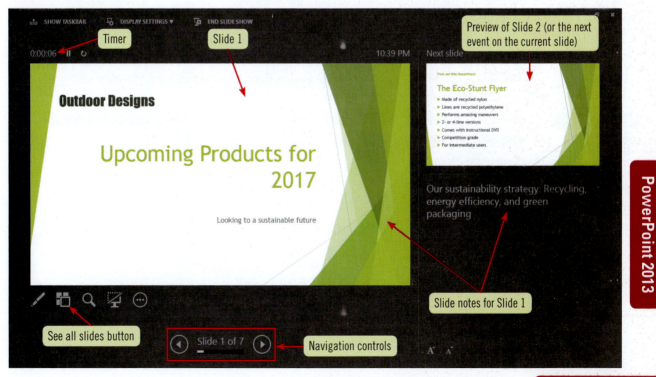

SHOW TASKBAR
DISPLAY SETTINGS
END SLIDE SHOW
Timer
Slide 1
Preview of Slide 2 (or the next event on the current slide)
0:00:06
10:39 PM
Next slide
Outdoor Designs
Upcoming Products for 2017
Looking to a sustainable future
The Eco-Stunt Flyer
Made of recycled nylon
Lines are recycled polyethylene
Performs amazing maneuvers
2- or 4-line versions
Comes with instructional DVD
Competition grade
For intermediate users
Our sustainability strategy: Recycling, energy efficiency, and green packaging
Slide notes for Slide 1
See all slides button
Slide 1 of 7
Navigation controls

PowerPoint 2013

Print Handouts and Notes Pages

Learning Outcomes
- Print handouts
- Print Notes pages
- Add headers and footers

When you give a presentation, you may also want to give a printed copy to your audience so they can use it to take notes. You may also want a printed copy of your slides with speaker notes that you can refer to during the presentation. You can print **handouts**, which contain one or more slides per page, and you can include blank lines for audience members to use for notes. **Notes pages** contain a thumbnail of each slide plus any speaker notes you added in the Notes pane, as well as header and footer information. Before printing any document, it is always a good idea to preview it. **CASE** *You want to add information at the top of every handout page, so you print handout pages for Jihong to review. Then you print Notes pages she can refer to during the presentation. Note: Many schools limit printing in order to conserve paper. If your school restricts printing, skip Steps 5 and 7.*

STEPS

1. **Click the FILE tab, click Print, click the Full Page Slides list arrow; in the Handouts section click 2 Slides, then click the Next Page button ▶ to see the handout pages**

   You see a preview of the handouts showing two slides per page. The date appears in the **handout header**, the area at the top of every page. You want to add the presentation name to the header.

2. **Click Edit Header & Footer at the bottom of the center section, then click the Notes and Handouts tab in the Header and Footer dialog box if necessary**

3. **Click the Header check box to select it, click the Header text box, type Upcoming Products, then click Apply to All**

   The text you typed now appears in the upper-left corner of all the handout pages. See **FIGURE N-22**.

   > **QUICK TIP**
   > If you do not have a color printer selected, the preview will appear in grayscale, showing shades of gray.

4. **Click the Color list arrow, then click Pure Black and White**

   Using the Pure Black and white option is the most economical way to print because it prints object outlines and does not print colors or background shading, saving toner.

   > **QUICK TIP**
   > To select all, current, or a range of slides to print, click Print All Slides, then select the option you want.

5. **If your school allows printing, click the Print button in the Print section to print the handouts (if you don't print, click the Back button ⬅ to return to the HOME tab)**

   You return to the HOME tab. Next, you print the Notes pages.

6. **Click the FILE tab, click Print, click the 2 Slides list arrow, click Notes Pages, compare your screen to FIGURE N-23, then click ▶ to see the notes pages**

   You see a preview of the Notes pages, with the header information you entered. Each notes page contains one slide as well as any speaker notes. The preview shows that the pure black-and-white setting you chose for the handouts also applies to the notes pages.

   > **QUICK TIP**
   > To select another printer, click the selected printer in the Printer section, then click a different printer.

7. **If your school allows printing, click the Print button in the Print section to print the handouts (if you don't print, click ⬅ to return to the HOME tab)**

8. **Save your changes**

FIGURE N-22: Preparing to print handouts with headers

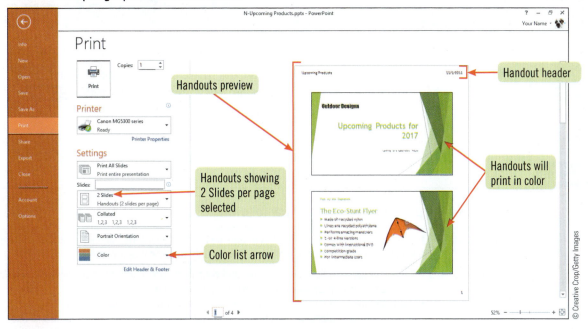

FIGURE N-23: Preparing to print Notes pages with headers

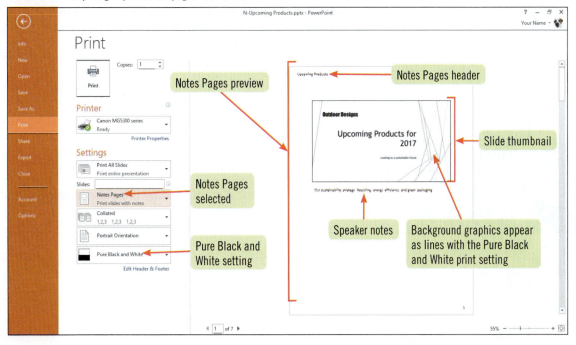

© Creative Crop/Getty Images

Printing presentation slides

You might want to print each of your presentation slides on a separate page, adding header and footer information such as the date and slide number. Click the FILE tab, click Print, click the Notes Pages (or the previously selected print option) list arrow, then click Full Page Slides. The first slide appears in the preview area. To add a header and footer, click Edit Header & Footer, click the Date and time check box to select it, and select the Update automatically or Fixed option. Click the Slide number check box to print the slide number on each slide, and click the Footer check box to select it and then enter footer text. If you don't want the header or footer information to print on the title slide, select the Don't show on title slide check box. Then click Apply to put the header and footer information on the current slide only, or click Apply to All to have the information appear on all presentation slides. Click the Next Page button ▶ to view the slides with the header and footer information you added. When you return to your presentation slides, you'll see the header and footer information on the slide or slides you specified.

Design Effective Presentations

Learning Outcomes
• Follow effective presentation guidelines
• Evaluate a presentation

As you create presentations, make sure they are effective—that is, make sure they communicate your presentation goals to the audience. To accomplish this, make sure that your text and graphics are appropriate in both content and appearance. To do this, follow some simple guidelines. **CASE** ▸ *Jihong asks you to use the guidelines to review the completed presentation.*

DETAILS

As you create a presentation, consider the following:

Content	• Make sure your text, graphics, and design are right for your target audience's age and interests. • Keep your content brief: For a live audience, only supply content highlights.
Design	• Keep your presentation design simple and consistent. Don't add too many design elements, which can clutter your slides and interfere with your message. • Use templates or themes to ensure consistency throughout the presentation. • Use appropriate colors: greens and blues are good for many business presentations. Use strong colors like bright yellow sparingly.
Text	• Use a maximum of two fonts in your presentation—one for headings and one for bulleted text. • Use sans serif fonts. A **serif** is a small decorative stroke at the tops and bottoms of letters, and "sans" means "without." **Sans serif fonts** include Trebuchet, Arial, and Helvetica. Sans serif type is easier to read from a distance. • Keep text short, and try to follow the 6 x 6 rule for most slides: use a maximum of six lines of text per slide, and six words per line. • If you're presenting to a large group, make sure text is at least 24 points and contrasts with the background for visibility.
Graphics	• Use images, tables, charts, and diagrams to clarify and illustrate your points, but in general, use one graphic, or a maximum of two graphics, per slide.
Transitions and Animations	• Don't use too many transitions or animations—these can distract the audience's attention from your presentation content if overused.

See **FIGURE N-24** for an example of a slide that does not follow the above rules for creating effective presentations.

STEPS

1. Go to **Slide 1**, click the **Reading View button** on the status bar, then press **[Spacebar]** to move through the presentation, evaluating each slide against the guidelines in this lesson

Content	The slide content directly addresses the target audience, the Outdoor Designs sales force. The bullets present the most important product highlights.
Design	The design uses a theme, creating a clear, consistent design. The green color is appropriate for the company name and goals.
Text	The presentation uses two fonts, Trebuchet and Impact, both sans serif fonts. Slides 2 and 3 do exceed the recommended 6 lines of text, but the font size is 24 pt and contrasts well with the background, so these will be acceptable in Jihong's presentation setting.
Graphics	There is only one graphic per slide, and they are simple and clear.
Transitions and Animations	There is only one type of transition, and animations are used sparingly.

2. Click the **INSERT tab**, click the **Header & Footer button** in the Text group, click the **Footer check box** to select it, click in the **Footer text box**, type your name, then click **Apply to All**

3. Click the **Slide Sorter View button** on the taskbar, compare your screen to **FIGURE N-25**, save your changes, then submit your finished presentation to your instructor

FIGURE N-25: The final presentation

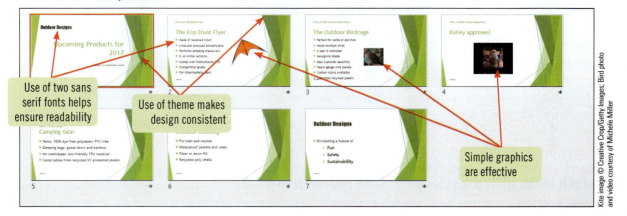

Sharing a presentation

You can share you presentations with others in several different ways, including via email, the web, or a network location. To share your presentation, open it, click the FILE tab, then click Share. To save to your SkyDrive (you must have a SkyDrive account, which gives you free online storage), click Save to the Cloud, click the name of your SkyDrive, then navigate to the SkyDrive folder in which you want to save the file. To share using email, click Email, and choose from one of the format options. To share your presentation online, click Present Online, which creates a link others can use to watch your slide show using their web browsers. You need a Microsoft account to use this free service. You can also publish slides to a slide library or on a social networking site. If you want viewers to be able to watch your presentation at any time, record a video of your presentation in Windows Media Video (.wmv) format, playable in the Windows Media Player. Click the FILE tab, click Export, click Create a Video, then click Create Video.

Practice

Concepts Review

Label the PowerPoint window elements shown in FIGURE N-26.

FIGURE N-26

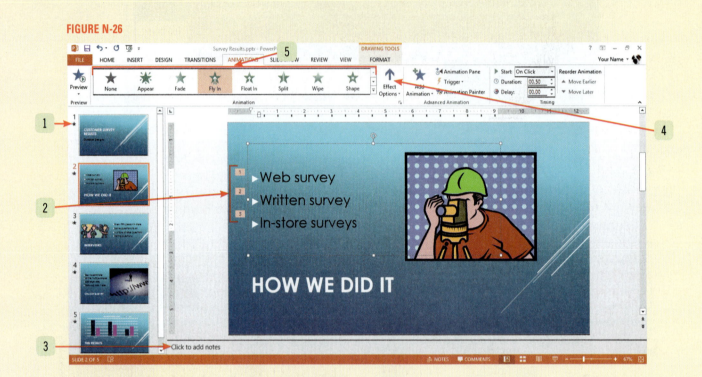

Match each term with the statement that best describes it.

6. **Animation Painter**
7. **Transition**
8. **Crop**
9. **Timing**
10. **Sound clip**
11. **Serif**

a. Audio file that you can insert on a slide
b. To cut off part of a picture
c. A small, decorative stroke at the top and bottom of letters
d. Transfers animation settings to another object
e. The number of seconds a slide remains on the screen
f. A special effect that determines how a slide enters or leaves the screen

Select the best answer from the list of choices.

12. **Movements or changes in appearance that you can apply to slide text or graphics are called:**
    a. Transitions.
    b. Animation effects.
    c. Handouts.
    d. Sounds clips.

13. **Which animation type calls attention to an object that's already on a slide?**
    a. Entrance animation
    b. Emphasis animation
    c. Exit animation
    d. Transitions

14. What should you use in presentations to ensure readability?

a. Serif fonts

b. Sans serif fonts

c. Lots of bright yellow

d. Text under 22 pt in size

15. Which PowerPoint view lets you display your slides and also preview the next slide?

a. Slide Show view

b. Notes Page view

c. Normal view

d. Presenter view

Skills Review

1. Add pictures.

a. Start PowerPoint, open the file N-2.pptx from the location where you store your Data Files, then save it as **N-Gekkos**.

b. Play the slide show in Reading View to get an idea of the content.

c. Go to Slide 4, then insert the picture gary.jpg from the location where you store your Data Files, using the Pictures icon in the right placeholder.

d. Resize the picture by dragging its corners so it fills the right side of the slide, then drag it as necessary to reposition it.

e. Crop the picture to remove the object on the right side.

f. Use the PICTURE TOOLS FORMAT tab to align the picture vertically to the middle of the slide area.

g. Drag the picture so it's approximately centered in the white area.

2. Add sound.

a. On Slide 4, insert an online audio file from Office.com, using the search text **reptile**. Insert one of the sound files titled Dragon fire.

b. Verify the inserted sound object is set to play when you click it during the slide show. (*Hint*: Select the sound object if necessary, display the AUDIO TOOLS PLAYBACK tab, then set the Start option to On Click in the Audio Options group.)

FIGURE N-27

c. With the sound object still selected, use the Change Picture command on the AUDIO TOOLS FORMAT tab to replace the speaker graphic. Search using the term **lizard** at Office.com Clip Art and select the image shown in **FIGURE N-27** or another one you like.

d. Drag the sound file object to the purple area near the top of the slide. Compare your screen to **FIGURE N-27**.

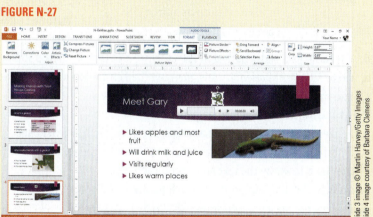

Slide 3 image © Martin Harvey/Getty Images
Slide 4 image courtesy of Barbara Clemens

3. Add video.

a. Go to Slide 5, then insert the WMV file gary_exploring.wmv from the location where you store your Data Files.

b. Play the video.

c. Set the video to play automatically, as soon as the slide appears. (*Hint*: Use the VIDEO TOOLS PLAYBACK tab.)

d. Use the VIDEO TOOLS PLAYBACK tab to trim the video so it runs from about the 1 second mark to the 7.5 second mark.

e. Center the video horizontally on the slide. (*Hint*: Use the Align Center command.)

f. Save the presentation, go to Slide 1, then view the presentation in Slide Show view; on Slide 4, click the Play button on the audio file to play it (be sure to point to the sound file first, to see the button), and watch the Slide 5 video start automatically.

Skills Review (continued)

4. Set slide transitions and timings.

   a. Go to Slide Sorter view and apply the Switch transition to all the slides, select Slide 1, then view the presentation in Reading view.

   b. Adjust the slide timing so each slide stays on the screen for 5 seconds before automatically moving to the next one.

   c. View the slide show in Slide Show view.

   d. Remove the timing setting, ensuring that the slides will now advance when you click the mouse button during the presentation.

   e. In Slide Sorter view, select Slide 7, then apply the Chime transition sound. (*Hint*: Click the Sound list arrow in the Timing group, then click Chime.)

   f. Preview the sound transition on the slide.

5. Animate slide objects.

   a. Go to Slide 3 in Normal view, then animate the gekko picture with the Zoom entrance animation effect. (*Hint*: You'll need to click More Entrance Effects in the Animations gallery.)

   b. Set the Effect Options so the vanishing point is the slide center instead of the object center.

   c. Go to Slide 2, and apply the Grow & Turn animation to the bulleted list. (*Hint*: The Grow & Turn animation is under More Entrance Effects, and is in the Moderate category.)

   d. Select the bulleted list, then use the Animation Painter to copy the animation effect to the bulleted list on Slide 3.

   e. View the slide show in Slide Show view, pressing [Spacebar] as necessary to view the slide objects, and clicking the Play button on the audio object on Slide 4.

6. Use speaker notes and slide show commands.

   a. Go to Slide 1 in Normal view, and display the Notes pane.

   b. Enter the following slide notes:

Slide 1	Ask audience if they see gekkos
Slide 2	The chirp can sound like a click
Slide 6	Don't try to capture them!

   c. Save your work, then view the presentation in Presenter view from Slide 1 and observe the slide notes. (*Hint*: Recall you can display Presenter view by first going to Slide Show view and clicking the far-right icon.)

   d. Use the See all slides button in Presenter view to display all the slides.

   e. Go to Slide 1 in Presenter view, then use the Pen tool to draw a line under "A Hawaiian Adventure."

   f. End the slide show, discarding your annotation.

7. Print handouts and notes pages.

   a. Preview the presentation as handouts, showing two slides per page. View the preview of all the handout pages.

   b. Edit the Notes and Handouts header so it includes the text **About Gekkos** and apply it to all the pages. Preview the pages to verify the text appears on each one.

   c. Change the handout print color to Pure Black and White.

   d. Preview the presentation Notes pages and view the preview of each page, verifying that you can see the slide notes on Slides 1, 2, and 6.

   e. Print the handouts if desired, then save your work.

8. Design effective presentations.

   a. Add your name to the footer of all slides. (Notice that it will appear on the right side of the slides.)

   b. View the presentation in Slide Show view from the beginning, using a command on the SLIDE SHOW tab.

   c. Evaluate the presentation content and design.

   d. Save your changes, submit your finished presentation to your instructor, then exit PowerPoint.

Independent Challenge 1

You are taking a course at a local teachers college. To practice your in-class speaking and presentation skills, you have been assigned to create a presentation on any scientific topic, using information you obtain on the web. The presentation audience will include adults without a scientific background. You have decided the purpose of your presentation will be to

Independent Challenge 1 (continued)

educate the audience on the basics of solar flares, which are powerful eruptions on the sun. You have researched this topic on the web and created the basic text in PowerPoint, and now you want to polish and run your presentation.

a. Start PowerPoint, open the file N-3.pptx from the location where you store your Data Files, then save it as **N-Solar Flares**.

b. Play the slide show in Slide Show view.

c. Go to Slide 8 and insert the picture telescopes.jpg from the location where you store your Data Files. Enlarge it so it fills the right side of the slide attractively, and reposition it as necessary.

d. Crop out the legs of the telescope tripod in the lower portion of the picture, then readjust its size and placement as necessary.

e. Go to Slide 2 and insert the video flare.mp4 from the location where you store your Data Files. Resize and reposition it to fill the right side of the slide, then preview the video.

f. Trim off approximately the first 3 seconds of the video, then set it to play automatically. (*Hint*: On the VIDEO TOOLS PLAYBACK tab, use the Start option.)

g. Insert the online audio clip titled Large Explosion on Slide 2, then move it to the lower-left corner of the slide. (*Hint*: Use the search text **explosion**.)

h. Play the slide show in Slide Show view, and as the video on Slide 2 begins to play, click the sound clip object to play the explosion sound.

i. Add the following speaker notes:

Slide 2	Video is from NASA
Slide 8	These are great for an eclipse

j. Apply the transition of your choice to all the slides.

k. Animate the picture on Slide 7 using the Dissolve In entrance effect. (*Hint*: Look in the More Entrance Effects dialog box.)

l. View the presentation in Presenter view, observing your speaker notes, and evaluating the presentation for effectiveness.

m. Preview the Notes Pages for the presentation.

n. Preview the handouts, 9 slides (Horizontal) per page, add your name to all pages of the handout header, set them to print in Pure Black and White, then print the handouts, if desired.

o. Add your name to the footer of all slides (notice that it will appear on the right side of the slides), save your changes, submit your finished presentation to your instructor, then exit PowerPoint.

Independent Challenge 2

As a new marketing associate for Tour the World Travel Agency, you often create PowerPoint presentations for company representatives to use when selling tours to organizations. Sylvia Alvarez, the marketing director, has asked you to create a presentation for a tour to Alaska. She has given you the basic text and some graphics, and she has asked you to polish the presentation.

a. Start PowerPoint, then open the file N-4.pptx from the location where you store your Data Files, then save it as **N-Alaska Tour**.

b. View the presentation in Slide Show view.

c. On Slide 3, insert the picture gull.jpg from the location where you store your Data Files, using a command on the Insert menu. Remove the picture's background (but leave the white wave behind the gull). Then crop, resize, and reposition the picture so it's to the right of the slide text.

d. On Slide 4, insert the two picture files whales1.jpg and whales2.jpg from the location where you store your Data Files. Resize them so they're approximately 3 1/2" wide. Position one of the pictures below the bulleted list. Position the other one to the right of the bulleted list, then align it vertically in the middle of the slide.

e. On Slide 5, insert the two picture files glacier1.jpg and glacier2.jpg. Resize them to about 3 1/2" wide, and position them both to the right of the bulleted list. Select both pictures and align them with each other. (*Hint*: Select both pictures using [Shift][Click], then use the Align Center command.)

Independent Challenge 2 (continued)

f. On Slide 3, insert the online audio of Surf and Gulls. (*Hint*: Use the search text **gulls**.) Move the sound object to the lower-left corner of the slide, and set it to start playing automatically when the slide appears in the slide show.

g. Insert the transitions of your choice to all slides, then set the slide timings so each slide remains on the screen for 7 seconds.

h. Remove the slide timings, and verify that during the show, the slides will advance only when the presenter clicks the mouse or presses an appropriate key.

i. Animate the pictures and the bulleted list placeholder on Slide 4 using the animation effect of your choice. Use the Animation Painter to copy the bulleted list animation effect to the bulleted list placeholder on Slide 5.

j. Add the following speaker notes:

Slide 3	Most airlines fly to Seattle
Slide 6	Emphasize guide certification
Slide 7	Direct them to our website

k. View the presentation in Notes Page view and in Presenter view, evaluating the presentation for effectiveness.

l. Preview the presentation as handouts, 3 slides to a page, and add the footer **Tour the World Travel**, followed by your name, to the footer for all pages of the Notes and Handouts. (*Hint*: Use both tabs in the Header and Footer dialog box.) Print the handouts and Notes pages if desired, using Pure Black and White.

FIGURE N-28

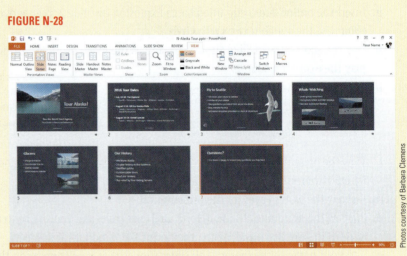

Photos courtesy of Barbara Clemens

m. View the presentation in Slide Show view once more to view the slide footers.

n. Save your changes, compare your presentation to **FIGURE N-28**, submit your final presentation to your instructor, then exit PowerPoint.

Independent Challenge 3

You own a restaurant called The Best Table. You've created a presentation outlining your menu offerings to show at a meeting of your local Chamber of Commerce, which is showcasing local restaurants to tour companies. You've developed the slide text, but now you need to polish the presentation and make it eye-catching. You decide to do this using graphics, transitions, sound, and animations.

a. Start PowerPoint, open the file N-5.pptx from where you store your Data Files, then save it as **N-Best Table**.

b. On Slide 2, insert two food pictures you might have that relate to the slide content. If you don't have suitable pictures, insert clip art. Crop, resize, reposition, or align them however you wish. If you like, remove the pictures' backgrounds.

c. On Slides 3, 4, and 5, add a single picture that relates to a food item mentioned; use clip art if necessary. Resize, reposition, and align them as necessary.

d. Add the Dish Rattle online audio clip to Slide 7. Set it to start automatically when the slide appears during the slide show. Preview the sound.

e. Change the picture on the sound file to an appropriate one of your choice, using Office.com Clip Art, using search text you choose. Resize and reposition it so it's placed attractively on the slide.

f. Apply slide transitions to each slide: Use a transition in the Subtle category for Slides 1 through 6. (*Hint*: Click Slide 1 in the Thumbnail pane, press and hold [Shift], click Slide 6, then apply the transition). Apply a transition from the Exciting category to Slide 7.

Independent Challenge 3 (continued)

g. On Slide 2, apply the Peek In entrance animation to the bulleted list, then apply the effect options of your choice to it.

h. Use the Animation Painter to copy the animation to the bulleted lists on Slides 3, 4, 5, and 6. (*Hint*: When you copy the Slide 2 animation, double-click the Animation Painter button, click the bulleted list on each slide, then press [Esc].)

i. Add any speaker notes you choose to three of the slides, save the presentation, then view it in Presenter view, evaluating it for effectiveness. Add an annotation to any slide, but don't save it when you end the slide show.

j. Add a header that reads **The Best Table** to all pages of the notes and handouts only.

k. View the presentation in Presenter view, observing your speaker notes.

l. Preview the Notes pages and Handouts, printing them if you wish.

m. Add your name to the footer of all slides, save your changes, submit your finished document to your instructor, then close the presentation and exit PowerPoint.

Independent Challenge 4: Explore

You are doing volunteer work at your local animal shelter. The director knows you've been studying PowerPoint, so she asks you to create a short presentation they can show to groups of potential dog adopters to emphasize safety.

a. Open the file N-6.pptx and save it as **N-Dog Safety**.

b. Insert at least three pictures in the presentation, on any slides you like, using your own photos. Change slide layouts as necessary if you want to use placeholders to insert pictures. (*Hint*: To change a slide layout, click the Layout button in the Slides group on the HOME tab.) Check the photo's file extension and verify that it's a file type you can use in PowerPoint, such as JPG, GIF, WMF, TIF, or BMP. If you don't have suitable pictures, then choose online pictures from Office.com clip art. Crop, resize, and position them appropriately. Delete background where necessary.

c. Add sound to at least one of the slides. Substitute a picture on the sound file, and then format the sound object with a picture style. (*Hint*: Use the AUDIO TOOLS FORMAT tab.)

d. Have the audio file fade in (use the AUDIO TOOLS FORMAT tab), and have it play On Click during the slide show.

e. Add a video clip to any slide. It can be a video of your own or a video from the Bing Video Search. (*Hint*: In the Insert Video dialog box, enter an appropriate search term in the Bing Video Search text box, then press Enter. Have the video start On Click when the slide appears in the slide show.)

f. Add a text box to any slide, then resize, reposition, and format it as you wish. (*Hint*: Use the INSERT tab and then the DRAWING TOOLS FORMAT tab.)

g. Go to the slide master. (*Hint*: On the VIEW tab, use the Slide Master button in the Master Views group.) Add a graphic to the Title and Content layout that you want to appear in the lower-left corner on every slide that uses that layout. (*Hint*: With the slide master visible, use the INSERT tab to insert an online graphic and position it in the lower-left corner of the slide master. Then click the SLIDE MASTER tab and click the Close Master View button to close the master.)

h. On Slide 2, apply an entrance animation to the bulleted list. Then add an Emphasis animation to the same object. (*Hint*: Use the Add Animation button in the Advanced Animation group.) Open the Animation Pane, select the second animation, then use the Start list arrow in the Timing group to have it start "After Previous"—that is, after the entrance animation. Click the Preview button in the Preview group to see the two animations play in sequence.

i. Copy the animation effects to the other bulleted lists in the presentation.

j. Review each slide and align objects to each other as necessary.

k. Preview the slide handouts, using the 6 Slides Horizontal setting, and print them if desired. Make any adjustments necessary to make the design effective.

l. Add your name to the footer of all slides, save your work, then play the presentation in Slide Show view. Submit your presentation to your instructor, then exit PowerPoint.

Visual Workshop

Create the presentation shown in **FIGURE N-29** below. Create a new, blank presentation and save it as **N-Company Benefits**. Use the Ion Boardroom theme, the first variation. Increase the font sizes of the subtitle to 28 pt and the bulleted lists to 32 pt. On Slide 1, insert a sound file using the search term "relax," add an appropriate picture to the sound object, and have it play automatically when the slide appears. On Slide 2, insert an online picture using the search term **medicine**, and delete the picture's background. (*Hint:* If necessary, try using the Mark Areas to Keep and Mark Areas to Remove tools.) On Slide 3, insert an online picture using **401K** as the search text. Add the text **Employee Orientation** followed by your name to the footer of Slides 2 and 3, then submit the presentation to your instructor.

FIGURE N-29

Integrating Office 2013 Programs

CASE ▶ Jihong Chen, assistant sales manager for Outdoor Designs, needs you to insert an Excel chart into a presentation she developed, create slides from a Word outline, and insert a screenshot into a slide. She also has a letter for the shareholders; she needs you to paste a linked chart into the letter, and then send it out as a mail merge form letter.

Unit Objectives

After completing this unit, you will be able to:

- Insert an Excel chart into a PowerPoint slide
- Create PowerPoint slides from a Word document
- Insert screen clips into a Word document
- Insert text from a Word file into an open document

- Link Excel data to a Word document
- Update a linked Excel chart in a Word document
- Insert merge fields into a Word document
- Perform a mail merge

Files You Will Need

O-1.pptx	O-12.xlsx
O-2.docx	O-13.accdb
O-3.pptx	O-14.pptx
O-4.docx	O-15.docx
O-5.docx	O-16.docx
O-6.xlsx	O-17.docx
O-7.accdb	O-18.docx
O-8.pptx	O-19.xlsx
O-9.docx	O-20.accdb
O-10.docx	O-21.xlsx
O-11.docx	O-22.docx

©HelenStock/Shutterstock

Insert an Excel Chart into a PowerPoint Slide

When you want to show a simple chart to your audience in PowerPoint, you can enter the data and select a chart type using an Excel spreadsheet within PowerPoint. When you create a chart in PowerPoint, you **embed** data into the presentation, meaning that the chart is part of the presentation but that you can edit it using Excel spreadsheet tools. Once you've created an embedded chart, you can edit and format it using the CHART TOOLS DESIGN and CHART TOOLS FORMAT tabs in PowerPoint. **CASE** *Jihong has given you a presentation she created for the quarterly sales meeting and a hard copy of sales figures. You need to insert a chart comparing sales, so you decide to embed the chart directly in PowerPoint.*

STEPS

1. **Start PowerPoint, open the file O-1.pptx from the location where you store your Data Files, then save it as O-Projections**

2. **Move to Slide 2, then click the Insert Chart icon in the content placeholder**
   The Insert Chart dialog box opens, shown in **FIGURE O-1**.

3. **Verify the Clustered Column chart style is selected, as shown in FIGURE O-1, then click OK**
   An Excel spreadsheet with sample data opens on top of a chart based on the sample data, as shown in **FIGURE O-2**. The CHART TOOLS DESIGN tab is active. You replace the sample data in the spreadsheet with figures from Jihong's report.

4. **Replace the data in the spreadsheet with the data in the following table (including the commas):**

	A	B	C	D
1		Q4 2014	Q4 2015	Projected Q4 2016
2	Northeast	530,000	633,000	678,000
3	Midwest	439,000	428,000	459,000
4	Southeast	356,000	399,000	402,000
5	West	512,000	526,000	599,000

   As you enter the data in the spreadsheet, the chart in the slide updates automatically.

5. **Click the Close button on the spreadsheet window**
   The chart with the Outdoor Designs data appears on the slide. The embedded data is saved as part of the presentation. You receive word that one of the projection numbers has changed, so you need to edit the chart data.

6. **Click the chart to select it if necessary, then on the CHART TOOLS DESIGN tab click the Edit Data button in the Data group**
   The spreadsheet reopens.

7. **Click cell D5, type 587,000, press [Enter], click the spreadsheet window Close button, click the chart title, then press [Delete]**

8. **On the CHART TOOLS DESIGN tab, click Style 2 in the Chart Styles group, click the Change Colors button in the Chart Styles group, then click Color 3 (the third row of colors)**
   Your completed chart appears as shown in **FIGURE O-3**.

9. **Save your changes to the presentation**

FIGURE O-1: Choosing a chart style in the Insert Chart dialog box

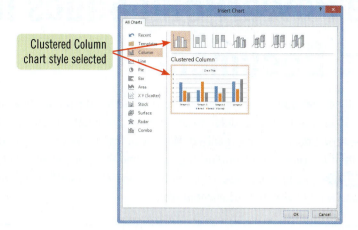

Clustered Column chart style selected

FIGURE O-2: Spreadsheet with sample data on top of chart

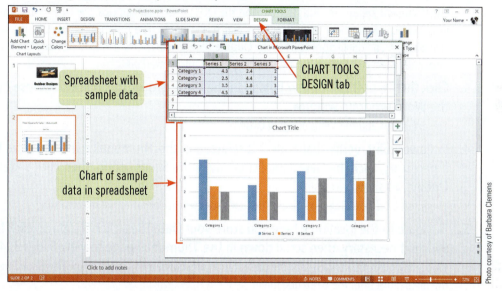

Spreadsheet with sample data

CHART TOOLS DESIGN tab

Chart of sample data in spreadsheet

Photo courtesy of Barbara Clemens

FIGURE O-3: Completed chart

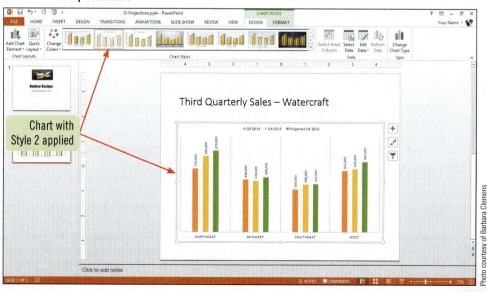

Chart with Style 2 applied

Photo courtesy of Barbara Clemens

Create PowerPoint Slides from a Word Document

Learning Outcomes
- Insert slides from a Word outline
- Reset a slide's theme

You can use an outline that you have created in Word as a starting point for a new PowerPoint presentation, or you can use it to add slides to an existing presentation. The Word Outline view makes it easy to see how a document is organized. When you insert a Word outline into PowerPoint, lines that are formatted as Level 1 in the outline appear as slide titles, and lower-level text appears as bulleted text. **CASE** *Jihong wants you to incorporate one of her outlines as new slides in the presentation. First, you want to view the document in Word.*

STEPS

1. **Start Word, then open the file O-2.docx from the location where you store your Data Files**

2. **Click the VIEW tab, then click the Outline button in the Views group**

   The document appears in Outline view, and the OUTLINING tab appears. See **FIGURE O-4**. The text appears in a hierarchical structure using headings and subheadings. The insertion point is in the first slide title, "Division 3," and the Outline level in the Outline Tools group shows "Level 1." Because the text is organized into outline levels, it will be just right for importing into PowerPoint.

3. **Click the Close Outline View button in the Close group, then click the Close button on the Word program window**

   The document and the Word program close.

4. **In PowerPoint, verify that Slide 2 is selected in the Thumbnail pane, click the HOME tab if necessary, click the New Slide list arrow in the Slides group, then click Slides from Outline, as shown in FIGURE O-5**

   The Insert Outline dialog box opens. The new slides will appear after the selected slide.

5. **Navigate to the location where you store your Data Files, click O-2.docx, click Insert, click Slide 3 if necessary, then scroll down in the Thumbnail pane to view Slides 3, 4, and 5**

   Three new slides are inserted into the presentation, as shown in **FIGURE O-6**. The new slides are formatted in the theme font from the Word document.

6. **Verify that Slide 3 is selected in the Thumbnail pane**

   The slide title, "Division 3", was formatted as Level 1 in the Word outline, and it appears as the slide title in the first imported slide.

7. **With Slide 3 selected, press and hold [Shift], click Slide 5, release [Shift], then click the Reset button in the Slides group**

   The newly added slides are formatted in the theme of the presentation.

8. **Click the INSERT tab, click the Header & Footer button in the Text group, click the Footer check box to select it, click the Footer text box, type your name, then click Apply to All**

9. **Click the SLIDE SHOW tab, click the From Beginning button in the Start Slide Show group, view the presentation, save your changes, then close the presentation**

FIGURE O-4: Viewing a Word document in Outline view

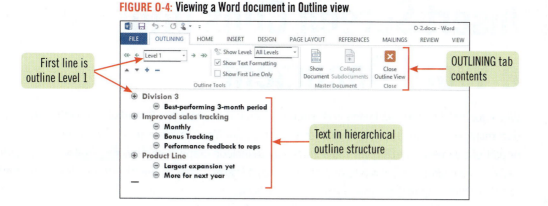

First line is outline Level 1

OUTLINING tab contents

Text in hierarchical outline structure

FIGURE O-5: Inserting slides from a Word outline

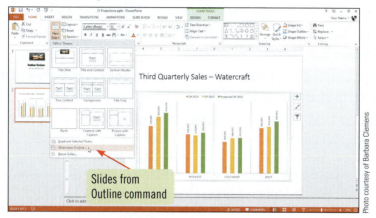

Slides from Outline command

Photo courtesy of Barbara Clemens

FIGURE O-6: PowerPoint slides created from Word outline text

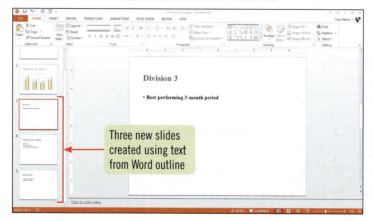

Three new slides created using text from Word outline

Using outlines in Word and PowerPoint

If you want to create an outline in Word that you can use as the basis for a PowerPoint presentation, it is best to use Word outline levels in your text. Start a new document in Word, click the VIEW tab, then click the Outline button in the Views group. As you type your outline text, use the Outline Level list arrow in the Outline Tools group to apply a level for each line. Use the Level 1 style for slide titles, Level 2 for the first level of indented text, and so on. In Normal view, use the Heading styles, which correspond to the Level styles in Outline view. The styles determine the structure of the outline when it is imported into PowerPoint.

You can adjust the outlining structure by clicking the Promote, Demote, and Move Up or Move Down buttons. You can change the view by clicking the Expand or Collapse buttons in the Outline Tools group. When the outline is complete, save and close the Word document.

You can also save a PowerPoint presentation in outline format and then open it in Word. To save a PowerPoint outline, click the FILE tab, click Save As, click Browse, click the Save as type list arrow, then click Outline/RTF (*.rtf). Next, open the document in Word, then reformat the text using Word commands.

Insert Screen Clips into a Word Document

Learning Outcomes
• Insert a screen clip into a document
• Center a screen clip in a document

When you need to place an image from another open document into a PowerPoint presentation or Word document, you can use the PowerPoint Screenshot feature. You can take a screenshot of an entire window or part of a window, which gives you a quick way to include graphics or data. **CASE** ▶ *Jihong wants to include a screenshot from a PowerPoint presentation as a logo in a letter to shareholders. You use the Screenshot tool to capture a clip of the slide as it plays in Normal view.*

STEPS

1. **In PowerPoint, open the file O-3.pptx from the location where you store your Data Files**

2. **Start Word, open the file O-4.docx from the location where you store your Data Files, then save it as O-Shareholder Letter**

3. **Press [Ctrl][Home] to make sure the insertion point is at the top of the document, press [Enter] to insert a new line, then press [↑] to move up a line**

4. **Click the INSERT tab, then click the Screenshot button in the Illustrations group**

   Thumbnails of open programs that are not minimized to the taskbar appear in the list, as shown in **FIGURE O-7**. To insert a full screen, you would click a thumbnail in the Available Windows section. You decide to capture just part of the image in Slide Show view. When you use the Screen Clipping option, Word automatically switches to the previous window, which is the first thumbnail shown in the Available Windows section. If you have multiple programs open and maximized or in restore down mode, be sure that the window from where you want to capture a clip is the first thumbnail. In this case, the slide you want to clip is the only one, but you only want to use part of the slide, so you use screen clipping.

5. **Click Screen Clipping; when the + pointer appears, drag a selection box around the image starting at the upper-left corner, as shown in FIGURE O-8, then release the mouse button**

   The Screen Clipping feature switches to the PowerPoint Slide View screen, where you can select any area on the screen. When you release the mouse button, Word inserts the captured screen image into the document. The inserted image is selected, and the PICTURE TOOLS FORMAT tab appears in the Ribbon. You can use this tab to adjust the image's size and apply effects to it. The image of the Outdoor Designs logo is too large for the letter, so you decide to resize it.

6. **On the PICTURE TOOLS FORMAT tab, click the Shape Height text box in the Size group, type 2, then press [Enter]**

   The image would look better if it were centered.

7. **Click the HOME tab, then click the Center button ≣ in the Paragraph group**

   The image is centered on the page, as shown in **FIGURE O-9**. You can adjust the image and apply styles and effects to it as you would any photograph.

8. **Save your changes to the Word document, close the PowerPoint presentation, then exit PowerPoint**

FIGURE O-7: Screenshot options

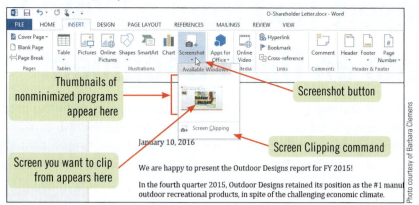

Thumbnails of nonminimized programs appear here

Screenshot button

Screen Clipping command

Screen you want to clip from appears here

FIGURE O-8: Capturing a screen clip

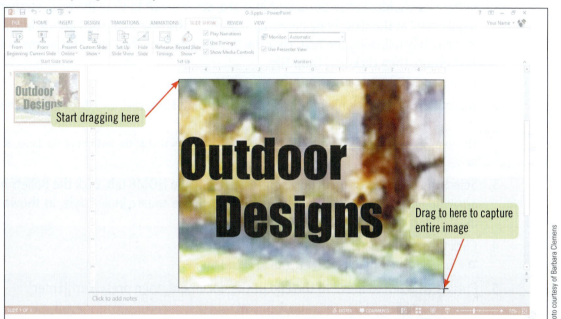

Start dragging here

Drag to here to capture entire image

Photo courtesy of Barbara Clemens

FIGURE O-9: Screen clip inserted and centered in a Word document

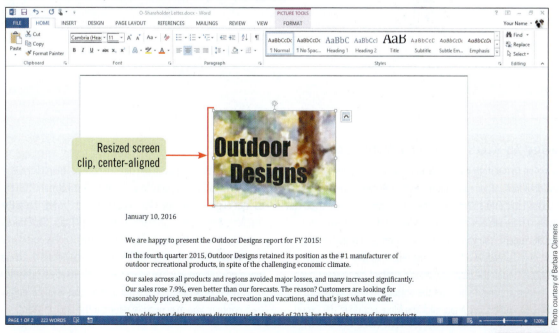

Resized screen clip, center-aligned

Photo courtesy of Barbara Clemens

Insert Text from a Word File into an Open Document

As you work, you might want to combine two files into one, or insert another document into the current one. Although you can easily copy and paste information between two or more open documents, it is sometimes easier to insert the contents from a file without having to open it first. **CASE** ▶ *Jihong wants you to include strategic highlights from a document she created in the letter to shareholders that you have been working on.*

STEPS

1. **In the Shareholder Letter document in Word, scroll down to view the text "strategic highlights:" in the sixth body paragraph, position the insertion point on the blank line immediately following the text, click the INSERT tab, click the Object list arrow in the Text group, then click Text from File**

   The Insert File dialog box opens.

2. **Navigate to the location where you store your Data Files, click O-5.docx as shown in FIGURE O-10, then click Insert**

   The contents of the file, consisting of five lines of text, are inserted at the bottom of the letter, as shown in **FIGURE O-11**.

3. **Select the five lines of text you just inserted, click the HOME tab, click the Bullets list arrow ⌄ in the Paragraph group, then point to the square bullet style, as shown in FIGURE O-12**

4. **Click the square bullet style**

   The strategic highlights text is formatted in a bulleted list.

5. **Press [Ctrl][End] to move to the end of the document, then press [Ctrl][Enter]**

   A new page is inserted at the end of the document.

6. **Save your changes to the document**

Placing an Access table in a Word document

In addition to inserting a Word file into a Word document, you can insert data from other applications, such as Access. You can insert an Access table into a Word document by various methods. You can copy the entire table or individual records and paste them into a Word document. You can also use the Export feature in Access to export objects, such as a table, query, report, or form. To export from Access, open the database, enable content if necessary, open the Navigation pane, then select the object you want to export. Click the EXTERNAL DATA tab, click the More button in the Export group, click Word, choose the desired options, then click OK. Note that Access always exports to a new Rich Text Format (RTF) file; you cannot export to an open Word document. In Word, insert the RTF file using the Object command on the INSERT tab. Click the Create from File tab and locate the file. The inserted Access object in Word is a standard table; it does not link back to the Access database. So any modifications you make to a table in Word affect only the Word document. Depending on the number of fields and the length of their content, you may need to reformat the table in Word.

FIGURE O-10: Insert File dialog box

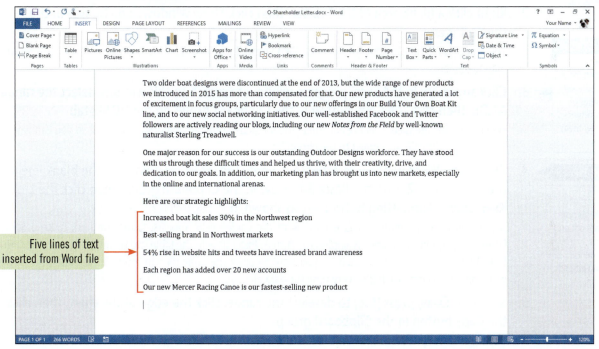

FIGURE O-11: File text inserted into letter

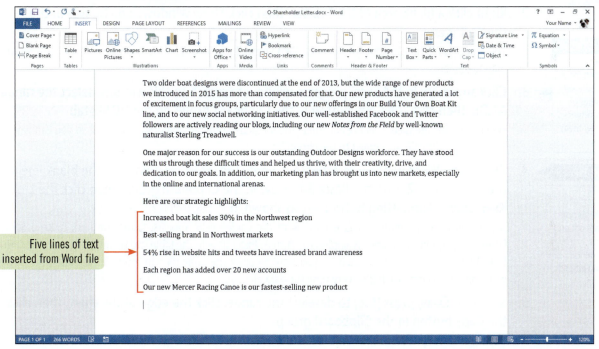

Two older boat designs were discontinued at the end of 2013, but the wide range of new products we introduced in 2015 has more than compensated for that. Our new products have generated a lot of excitement in focus groups, particularly due to our new offerings in our Build Your Own Boat Kit line, and to our new social networking initiatives. Our well-established Facebook and Twitter followers are actively reading our blogs, including our new *Notes from the Field* by well-known naturalist Sterling Treadwell.

One major reason for our success is our outstanding Outdoor Designs workforce. They have stood with us through these difficult times and helped us thrive, with their creativity, drive, and dedication to our goals. In addition, our marketing plan has brought us into new markets, especially in the online and international arenas.

Here are our strategic highlights:

Increased boat kit sales 30% in the Northwest region

Best-selling brand in Northwest markets

Five lines of text inserted from Word file → 54% rise in website hits and tweets have increased brand awareness

Each region has added over 20 new accounts

Our new Mercer Racing Canoe is our fastest-selling new product

FIGURE O-12: Formatting bulleted text

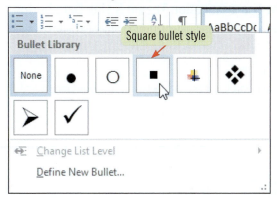

Link Excel Data to a Word Document

Learning Outcomes
• Link an Excel range to a Word document
• Link an Excel chart to a Word document

Linking data shares updated information between files and programs. A **link** displays information from a **source** file (which is the original file containing the data) in the **destination** file (the location to which that data is copied or moved). In a Word document, linked data looks just like inserted or embedded data. However, you can edit the linked data in its original program by right-clicking it and clicking Edit Data. **CASE** ▶ *Jihong wants to add data from the survey to the shareholder letter. You decide to link the Excel spreadsheet to the shareholder letter so if Jihong updates any of the data, the changes will be updated automatically in the letter.*

STEPS

TROUBLE
If you have other windows open, close them, then repeat Step 2.

QUICK TIP
You can also drag the Word and Excel title bars to the left and right sides of the screen, respectively, to view them side by side.

QUICK TIP
Whether you are pasting a chart or copied cells, you can select a paste option that includes source or destination formatting, and embed or link options.

1. **Start Excel, open the file O-6.xlsx from the location where you store your Data Files, then save it as O-Survey Results**

   The worksheet contains data and a chart.

2. **Right-click a blank area of the taskbar, then click Show windows side by side in the shortcut menu**

   The Word and Excel program windows are tiled vertically, so you can switch between them while viewing both documents.

3. **Click anywhere in the Excel program window to switch to this window, select the range A1:D6, then click the Copy button in the Clipboard group on the HOME tab**

   When windows are tiled, clicking anywhere in an inactive program window activates it so you can work in the window. The cells are copied to the clipboard.

4. **Click in the Word window to activate it, verify the insertion point is in the blank line at the top of page 2, click the Paste list arrow in the Clipboard group, then click the Link & Keep Source Formatting button 🔲, as shown in FIGURE O-13**

   Before you click the button, a Live Preview of the copied cells appears. Using the Link & Keep Source Formatting option automatically applies the current Excel style to the table and permits automatic updating from Word or Excel, which is useful if you want to paste the same data in multiple files and not have to worry about updating each file every time the data changes.

5. **Switch to Excel, press [Esc] to deselect the range, click the edge of the chart, then click the Copy button in the Clipboard group**

   The chart object is copied to the clipboard.

6. **Switch to Word, click the Maximize button 🔲 on the program window title bar, verify that the insertion point is under the table, press [Enter] twice, click the Paste list arrow, then click the Use Destination Theme & Link Data button**

   The chart appears in the Shareholder letter document as a linked chart object in the current Word theme, as shown in **FIGURE O-14**.

7. **Save your changes**

   In the next lesson, you'll test the link between the Word report and the Excel workbook.

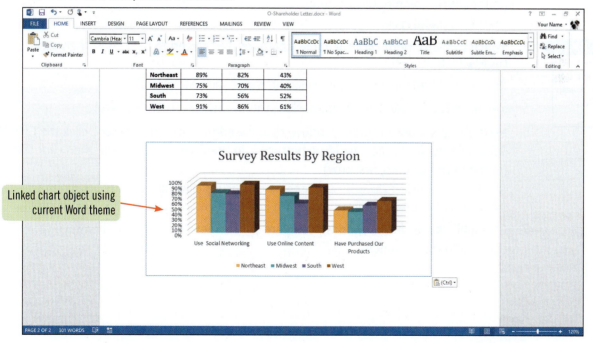

FIGURE O-14: Excel chart pasted as a link in Word

Update a Linked Excel Chart in a Word Document

Learning Outcomes
- Edit a source file
- Update a linked file

Linked files save time and help ensure accuracy in your documents, because when you update a source file, linked objects in destination files can be updated automatically. You can also update a linked object manually by right-clicking it and clicking Update Link, or by selecting the linked object and pressing [F9]. The [F9] key updates links in any Office application. **CASE** ▸ *Jihong just received updates to the survey data for the West region. You make the changes in Excel, and view the updated results in the linked Word document.*

STEPS

1. **Right-click a blank area of the taskbar, then click Show windows side by side in the shortcut menu**

2. **Switch to Excel, edit the data in the Survey Results workbook to match that in the following table, then click an empty cell:**

Cell	Data
B6	85
C6	89
D6	65

   The chart columns in Excel and in Word change as you enter new figures, as shown in **FIGURE O-15**. However, the linked table in Word does not update automatically, which you'll fix in a moment.

3. **Maximize the Excel program window, select the range A1:D6, click the Fill Color button list arrow ▾ in the Font group, then click the Dark Blue, Text 2, Lighter 80% color (in the fourth column, second row)**

   The cells are shaded in blue.

4. **Switch to Word, right-click the table, compare your screen to FIGURE O-16, then click Update Link**

   The table is updated with the content and format changes you made in Excel.

5. **Switch to Excel, save your changes, close the worksheet, then exit Excel**

6. **Maximize the Word program window, click the edge of the chart object, click the CHART TOOLS DESIGN tab, click the More button ▾ in the Chart Styles group, then click Style 4 (in the fourth column, first row)**

   The chart design style is changed. Because you selected to paste the chart with the destination style, any style changes you make in the future to the chart in Excel will not be reflected in the Word document.

7. **Click a blank area in the window, compare your screen to FIGURE O-17, then save your changes to the document**

FIGURE O-15: Viewing updated chart data from a linked file

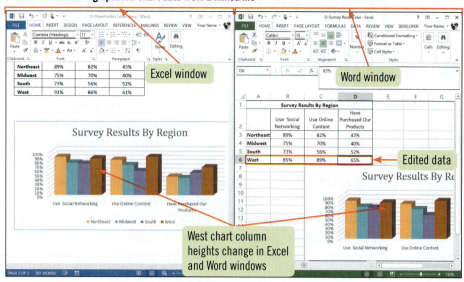

FIGURE O-16: Updating data in Word

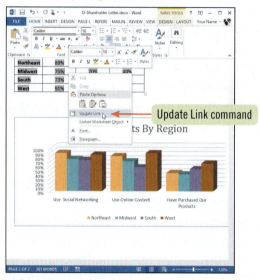

FIGURE O-17: Updated objects in Word

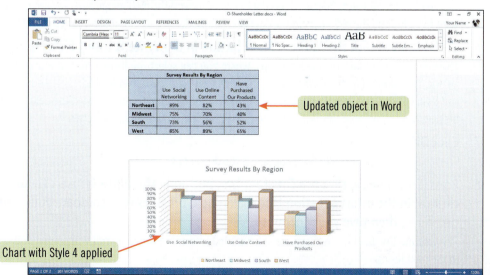

Learning Outcomes
• Start a mail merge
• Insert merge fields

Insert Merge Fields into a Word Document

A **form letter** is a document that contains standard body text and a custom heading containing the name and address for one of many recipients. The letter, or **main document**, is usually created in Word; the data for the custom heading, also known as the **data source**, is usually stored in a table, a worksheet, or a database such as Access. From these two files—the main document and the data source—you can print your merged documents, or create a third file, a **merged document**, consisting of multiple personalized letters. This process is called **mail merge**. Before performing a mail merge, you add **merge fields** to the main document, which are placeholders to indicate where the custom information from the data source should appear. **CASE** ▶ *Jihong asks you to send the shareholder letter to the company's four principal investors, and she gives you a file containing their names and addresses. First, you insert merge fields.*

STEPS

TROUBLE
If the Word document is closed, click Yes to update the data when you reopen it.

1. **In Word, press [Ctrl][Home], then click the blank line below the date**

2. **Click the MAILINGS tab, click the Start Mail Merge button in the Start Mail Merge group, compare your screen to FIGURE O-18, then click Letters**

   The document is now identified as a main document in a Letter mail merge and is ready for you to add merge fields, such as names, addresses, and salutations, from the data source. You can also perform a mail merge for email messages, address labels, envelopes, or a catalog or directory.

3. **Click the Select Recipients button in the Start Mail Merge group, then click Use an Existing List**

   The Select Data Source dialog box opens, with the My Data Sources folder as the default data source location. Your data source is in your Data Files folder. You can select from a variety of data sources, such as an Outlook address book, data from an Excel spreadsheet, or a Word document or an HTML file that contains a single table. Your data source is an Access database.

4. **Navigate to the location where you store your Data Files, click O-7.accdb, then click Open**

   The Select Data Source dialog box closes. Although the Access database file is designated as the data source, Access does not need to be open in order to use the data.

QUICK TIP
To modify individual records or to add or delete data source fields in a recipient list, select the data source file in the Mail Merge Recipients dialog box, then click Edit.

5. **Click the Edit Recipient List button in the Start Mail Merge group**

   The Mail Merge Recipients dialog box opens, as shown in **FIGURE O-19**. Here you can view the records in the data source file and select, filter, and sort data so you can send the mail merge letter to specific recipients. You want to include all the recipients in the database, so you do not need to make changes to this dialog box.

6. **Click OK, then click the Address Block button in the Write & Insert Fields group**

   The Insert Address Block dialog box opens, where you can select the format for the address block and preview it. The address block is created using the Title, First Name, Last Name, Address 1, Address 2, City, State, and Postal Code fields from the Access database file. Word automatically arranged the fields as shown in the Preview window because this is a common format for fields in a mail merge letter.

TROUBLE
If you see an actual address instead of the <<Address-Block>> field, click the Preview Results button in the Preview Results group to deselect it.

7. **Click OK**

   The block field, <<AddressBlock>>, appears in the document.

8. **Press [Enter] twice, click the Greeting Line button in the Write & Insert Fields group, click OK in the Insert Greeting Line dialog box, press [Enter], compare your screen to FIGURE O-20, then save your changes**

   The greeting line field <<GreetingLine>> is inserted into the document. You will complete the mail merge in the next lesson.

FIGURE O-18: Selecting the Letters Mail Merge option

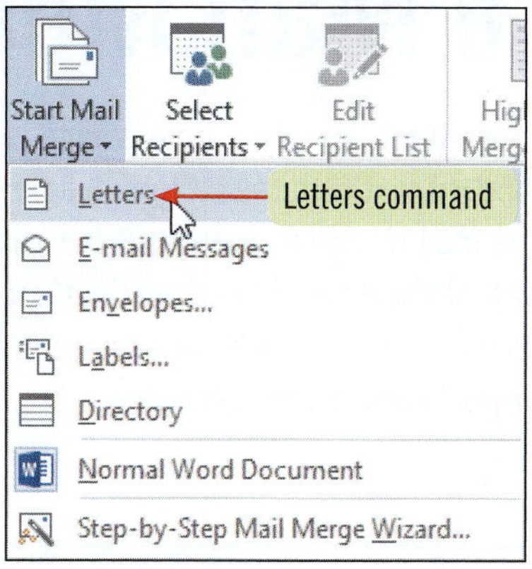

Letters command

Letters
E-mail Messages
Envelopes...
Labels...
Directory
Normal Word Document
Step-by-Step Mail Merge Wizard...

FIGURE O-19: Mail Merge Recipients dialog box

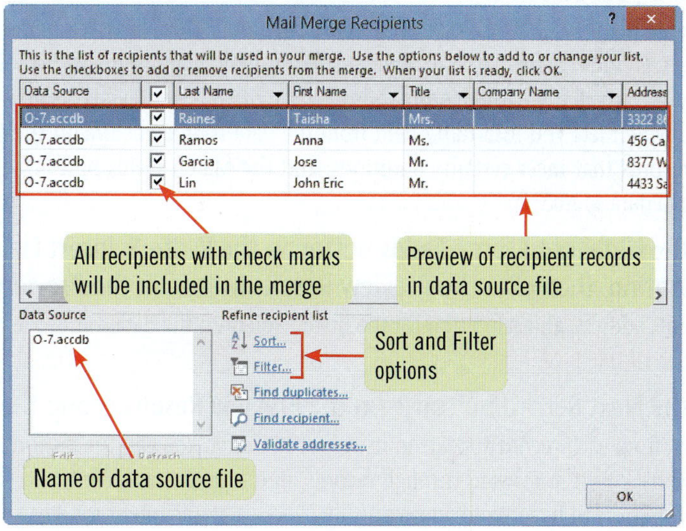

Mail Merge Recipients

This is the list of recipients that will be used in your merge. Use the options below to add to or change your list. Use the checkboxes to add or remove recipients from the merge. When your list is ready, click OK.

Data Source		Last Name	First Name	Title	Company Name	Address
O-7.accdb	✓	Raines	Taisha	Mrs.		3322 8
O-7.accdb	✓	Ramos	Anna	Ms.		456 Ca
O-7.accdb	✓	Garcia	Jose	Mr.		8377 W
O-7.accdb	✓	Lin	John Eric	Mr.		4433 Sa

All recipients with check marks will be included in the merge

Preview of recipient records in data source file

Data Source

O-7.accdb

Refine recipient list

Sort...
Filter...
Find duplicates...
Find recipient...
Validate addresses...

Sort and Filter options

Name of data source file

OK

FIGURE O-20: Viewing inserted merge fields

AddressBlock and GreetingLine merge fields inserted

Perform a Mail Merge

After you set up a main document, specify a data source, and insert merge fields, you are ready to merge, or combine, the standard text with the custom heading information to create personalized documents. You can preview the mail merge to ensure all the information will appear properly in the final document. **CASE** *Now that the main document—the shareholder letter—has merge fields inserted, you are ready to preview and then merge it with the data source to create the final mail merge letters. You also want to print one of the merged letters for Jihong's review.*

STEPS

1. **Click the Highlight Merge Fields button in the Write & Insert Fields group, then compare your screen to FIGURE O-21**

   The merge fields <<AddressBlock>>, which includes all the necessary name and address fields from the data source, and <<GreetingLine>> are shaded in gray, making it easy to see where merged data will be inserted into the letter. Other commands in the Write & Insert Fields group include the Insert Merge Field button, which lets you insert any field from the data source document; the Rules button, which lets you select records that meet certain conditions; and the Match Fields button, which lets you match or map fields in a data source.

2. **Click the Highlight Merge Fields button in the Write & Insert Fields group to turn off highlighting, then click the Preview Results button in the Preview Results group**

   The name, address, and salutation for the first recipient in the data source file replace the fields in the document. See **FIGURE O-22**.

3. **Click the Next Record button ▶ in the Preview Results group three times**

   The data from each record appears in its respective letter. You can use buttons in the Preview Results group to move backward or forward through records, find a particular record, and check for errors. You can click Check for Errors to have Word automatically check each document for errors.

4. **Click the Finish & Merge button in the Finish group, as shown in FIGURE O-23, then click Print Documents**

   The Merge to Printer dialog box opens, where you choose the records you want to print.

5. **Click the Current record option button, then click OK**

   The Print dialog box opens. The fourth record in the merge letter is set to print.

6. **In the Print dialog box, click OK if your lab allows printing, or click Cancel**

7. **Save your changes, close the document, then exit Word**

Using mail merge to send personalized email messages

While it is easy to send an email message to several recipients at once using the carbon copy (CC) feature in Outlook, you are limited to sending the same message to everyone. Using mail merge to create the email message enables you to personalize messages, ensuring that only the recipient's email address appears in the To: text box in the email message. The steps for creating an email mail merge are basically the same as for a letter mail merge. The main document can be a Word document, and the data source file can be your Outlook contact list. When you click the Start Mail Merge button to begin the mail merge, click E-Mail Messages. Next, click the Select Recipients button, click Choose from Outlook Contacts, then follow the prompts to choose the correct address book and import the contacts folder. When you are ready to merge the final document, click the Finish & Merge button in the Finish group, then click Send Email Messages. Note that you cannot add a recipient to the Cc (carbon copy) or Bcc (blind carbon copy) fields. If you want to receive a copy of the email message, add your email address to the Mail Merge Recipients list.

FIGURE O-21: Viewing highlighted merge fields

Highlight Merge Fields button

Merge fields are highlighted

FIGURE O-22: Previewing merged file

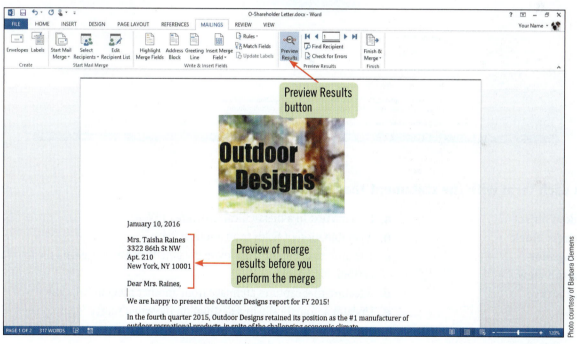

Preview Results button

Preview of merge results before you perform the merge

FIGURE O-23: Printing merged letters

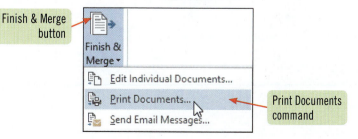

Finish & Merge button

Print Documents command

Integration 2013

Practice

Put your skills into practice with SAM! If you have a SAM account, go to www.cengage.com/sam2013 to access SAM assignments for this unit.

Concepts Review

Label the elements of the Word window shown in FIGURE O-24.

FIGURE O-24

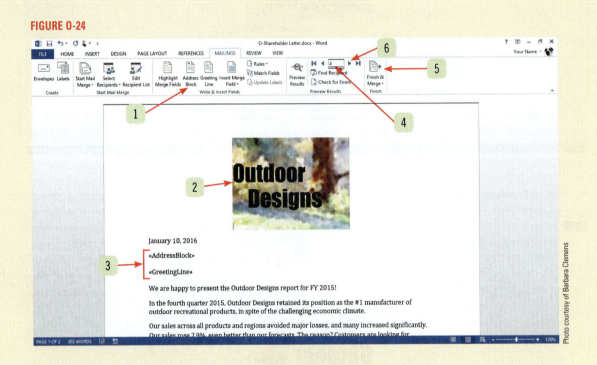

Photo courtesy of Barbara Clemens

Match each term with the statement that best describes it.

7. Linked object

8. Address block

9. Screenshot

10. Outline view

11. Mail merge

a. Presents text in a hierarchical structure in Word

b. A combination of fields from a source file

c. The process of combining a main document and a source data file to create custom documents

d. A feature that captures an image from another program window

e. Updates automatically in a destination file when source file is updated

Select the best answer from the list of choices.

12. **When you create a chart in PowerPoint, which of the following describes the chart?**
    a. It cannot be formatted.
    c. It cannot be edited.
    b. It is a linked object on the slide.
    d. It is an embedded object on the slide.

13. **Which of the following indicates a merge field?**
    a. << AddressBlock >>
    c. "" AddressBlock ""
    b. --AddressBlock--
    d. [[AddressBlock]]

14. **Receiving a prompt to update data in a document indicates that:**
    a. The document has been published to the Web.
    c. The document contains a linked object.
    b. The document has an embedded object.
    d. The document is a mail merge source document.

15. **When you insert a Word outline into a PowerPoint presentation, the Level 1 outline headings become what in PowerPoint?**
    a. Bulleted text
    c. Graphics
    b. Slide titles
    d. Charts

Skills Review

1. **Insert an Excel chart into a PowerPoint slide.**
   a. Start PowerPoint, open the file O-8.pptx from the location where you store your Data Files, then save it as **O-Theater Techs**. (*Hint*: Throughout this exercise, maximize windows as necessary.)
   b. Move to Slide 2, then use the content placeholder to insert a 3-D pie chart. (*Hint*: Click Pie on the left side of the dialog box, then click the 3-D Pie option.)
   c. Enter the following data in the spreadsheet:

	A	B
1		# supplied 2015
2	Stage Managers	250
3	Set Designers	98
4	Costume Designers	86
5	Propmasters	77
6	Sound Engineers	94

   d. Widen columns as necessary to view all the data, then close the spreadsheet.
   e. Reopen the spreadsheet, edit the number of Set Designers to **107**, then close the spreadsheet.
   f. With the chart selected, apply Chart Style 2 and change the chart colors to Color 2.
   g. Save your changes.

2. **Create PowerPoint slides from a Word document.**
   a. Start Word, then open the file O-9.docx from the location where you store your Data Files.
   b. View the document in Outline view.
   c. Close the document, and exit Word.
   d. In PowerPoint, insert the file O-9.docx after Slide 2 using the Slides from Outline command.
   e. Select the new slides, then use a button in the Slides group on the HOME tab to reset the new slides to the presentation theme.
   f. Add your name to the slide footer (*Hint*: Use the INSERT tab and open the Header and Footer dialog box), apply it to all slides, move to Slide 1, then save your changes.

Skills Review (continued)

3. Insert screen clips into a Word document.

  a. Start Word.

  b. Open the file O-10.docx from the location where you store your Data Files, then save it as **O-Theater Techs Services**.

  c. Verify the insertion point is at the top of the page, then use the Screenshot button on the INSERT tab to select Screen Clipping.

  d. In PowerPoint, drag to select the hammer on Slide 1.

  e. Apply the Compound Frame, Black style to the clip.

  f. Change the Shape Height of the clip to **.75"** in the Size group, save your changes in Word, then switch to PowerPoint and close the program.

  g. In the Word document, use a command on the HOME tab to center the logo horizontally, and then save your changes.

4. Insert text from a Word file into an open document.

  a. Position the insertion point at the beginning of the line that starts "Our approval ratings," then insert the file O-11.docx from the location where you store your Data Files as Text from File. (*Hint*: Click a list arrow on the INSERT tab.)

  b. Select the three lines of text you just inserted from the file, then format them as a bulleted list using a hollow bullet style.

  c. Save your changes.

5. Link Excel data to a Word document.

  a. Start Excel, open the file O-12.xlsx, then save it as **O-Theater Techs Approval Ratings**.

  b. Show Word and Excel side by side.

  c. Switch to Excel, then select and copy the range A2:D4.

  d. Switch to Word, press [Ctrl][End], insert a blank line, use the Paste list arrow to insert the copied range, using Link & Keep Source Formatting option.

  e. Switch to Excel, then copy the chart.

  f. Switch to Word, insert a blank line after the inserted cells, use the Paste list arrow to insert the copied chart using the Use Destination Theme & Link Data option.

  g. Save your changes.

6. Update a linked Excel chart in a Word document.

  a. In Excel, change cell B4 to **97** and cell D4 to **92**.

  b. Switch to Word, then update the document with data from the linked file. (*Hint*: Right-click a cell in the table, then click Update Link, if necessary.) Verify the chart in both the Word document and the Excel workbook were updated.

  c. In Excel, select the range B2:D2, then format the text in white and the cell fill in black.

  d. In the Word document, update the linked table, verify that the formatting updates to show your latest changes, then save the file.

  e. Switch to Excel, save and close the worksheet, exit Excel, then maximize the Word window.

7. Insert merge fields into a Word document.

  a. Move to the top of the document, then insert two blank lines below the date.

  b. Start a letters mail merge.

  c. Designate file O-13.accdb as the selected recipient list from the location where you store your Data Files.

  d. Open the Mail Merge Recipients dialog box, then accept the defaults and close the dialog box.

  e. Insert an address block, then insert two blank lines in the document.

  f. Use a command on the MAILINGS tab to insert a greeting line that uses just the first name, then insert one line after this line. (*Hint*: In the Insert Greeting Line dialog box, click the Greeting line format name list arrow, scroll down the list of greetings, then click "Joshua.")

  g. Save your changes.

Skills Review (continued)

8. Perform a mail merge.

   a. Use a command on the MAILINGS tab to highlight the merge fields, then turn off highlighting.

   b. Preview your mail merge results, reviewing each record in the merge.

   c. Preview the document, and verify the letter content fits on one page. If it doesn't, drag the chart's sizing handle to make it smaller. (*Hint*: If the chart moves to the top of the page, position the mouse pointer over the edge of the chart and drag it to the bottom of the page.)

   d. Compare your screen to **FIGURE O-25**.

   e. Finish the mail merge using the Print Documents command, printing the current record if your lab allows it.

   f. Save and close the document and exit Word.

FIGURE O-25

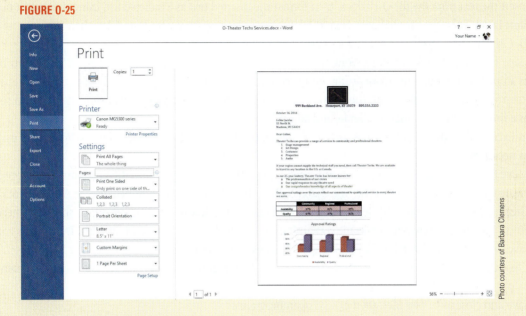

Photo courtesy of Barbara Clemens

Independent Challenge 1

You are working as a managerial trainee at ChildPlay, a nonprofit organization that supplies musical instruments and instruction to elementary and high school students in schools that don't have music programs. You're working on a fundraising presentation that you will give at a meeting of a charitable organization. You also need to send personalized form letters to donors who have already made contributions to the organization.

   a. Start PowerPoint, open the file O-14.pptx from the location where you store your Data Files, then save it as **O-ChildPlay Presentation**. (*Hint*: Throughout this exercise, maximize windows as necessary.)

   b. On Slide 2, insert a pie chart using the 3-D Pie style.

   c. In the spreadsheet, enter the following data, and if necessary, select only that data to display in the chart. (*Hint*: Drag the blue line up to cell B5.)

	A	B
1	Age Groupings	Number
2	4 to 5	332
3	6 to 8	773
4	9 to 11	634
5	12+	843

   d. Close the spreadsheet, then choose Chart Style 3.

   e. Following Slide 2, insert slides from the outline contained in the file O-15.docx, then run the slide show from the beginning to view the new slides.

Independent Challenge 1 (continued)

f. Add your name to the footer of all slides except the title slide (*Hint*: Use a check box in the Header and Footer dialog box), then save your changes, close the file, and exit PowerPoint.

g. Start Word, open the file O-16.docx from the location where you store your Data Files, then save it as **O-ChildPlay Letter**. Replace the Your Name text at the end of the letter with *your* name.

h. Move the insertion point to the top of the page, insert a blank line and move the insertion point to the blank line, open the file O-17.docx, return to the letter, then use the Screen Clipping feature to insert the image from the O-17.docx file at the top of the page. Center the image, then resize it to one inch in height. Close the file O-17.docx.

i. Move the insertion point to the space below the third line of body text (after "our goals are:"), insert a blank line, insert the text from the file O-18.docx, then format the inserted text as a bulleted list, using the default bullet style.

j. Start Excel, open the file O-19.xlsx from the location where you store your Data Files, then save it as **O-ChildPlay Data**, then add your name to the footer.

k. Copy the range A1:B5, switch to Word, then paste the data after the paragraph that begins "As a contributor," as a link keeping the source formatting. Adjust column widths as necessary.

l. Return to Excel, copy the chart, then paste it in the letter after the paragraph that begins "As you can see…" as a link, using the destination theme, and adjust its height to 2.5".

m. In Excel, adjust the amount for the State Foundation on the Arts to **$60,000**. Return to Word, and update links as necessary.

n. Move to the top of the first page of the document, place the insertion point on the blank line below the date, then create a letters mail merge that uses file O-20.accdb as the data source file and includes the Address Block and Greeting Line fields, using the field formats of your choice. Preview the results, and adjust spacing as necessary.

o. Finish the merge by creating a new file containing all records (*Hint*: Use the Edit Individual Documents command), save the new file as **O-ChildPlay Merged Letters**, then print the third record if your lab allows it.

p. Close the merged document, save the O-ChildPlay Letter document, preview it, compare your document to **FIGURE O-26**, then close it.

q. Save and close any open files, then exit all open programs.

FIGURE O-26

©Chad Baker/Ryan McVay/Getty Images

Independent Challenge 2

You and your business partner, chef Dana Rossi, are planning to open a new bakery called Y&R Bakery in Fort Worth, Texas. You need to apply for a start-up loan to get the business going. Your first task is to write a cover letter that will accompany your loan request to several banks. You also want to prepare a PowerPoint presentation of a few menu items that potential lenders can view on your website.

a. Start Word, then write a letter that you can send to banks along with the loan package. You will add recipient information in a future step; for now, write the body of the letter, including the name and location of your new restaurant, why you are applying for the loan, why the business will be successful, and how much you would like to borrow.

b. Save the letter as **O-Bakery Loan Letter** in the location where you store your Data Files. (*Hint*: Throughout this exercise, maximize windows as necessary.)

c. Start Excel, open the file O-21.xlsx from the location where you store your Data Files, then save it as **O-Bakery Sales Comparison**. This chart shows the success of similar bakeries in a comparable city.

d. Change the chart style, chart layout, or individual chart elements as desired, then copy the chart object.

e. In Word, insert the chart, keeping source formatting and linking data.

f. Start a letters mail merge, then create a new recipient list with at least three entries. To create the list, click the Select Recipients button in the Start Mail Merge group, then click Type a New List. Enter names and addresses in the New Address List dialog box, clicking New Entry as needed. When the list is complete, click OK, then save the file where you store your Data Files as **O-Bakery Loan List**.

g. Above the letter body text, insert Address Block and Greeting Line fields, using the options of your choice. Insert blank lines as appropriate.

h. Insert a blank footer and add your name, left-aligned. Add a graphic to the top of the letter if desired.

i. Preview the mail merge, compare your screen to FIGURE O-27, adjust fonts as necessary, complete the merge, printing the first record if your lab allows it, then save and close the document.

j. Start PowerPoint, create a presentation that contains a title slide with the name of your restaurant and a slogan, plus four slides that highlight menu items, then save it as **O-Bakery Menu** in the location where you store your Data Files.

FIGURE O-27

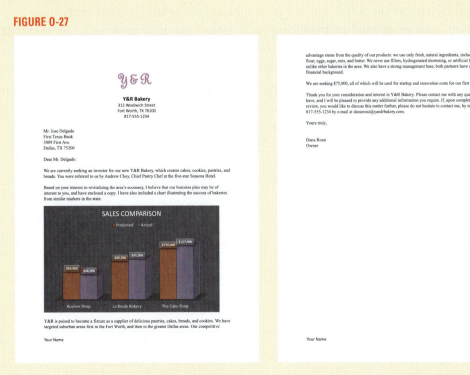

Independent Challenge 2 (continued)

k. Apply a theme and transitions, insert clip art and photographs as desired, then add your name to the slide footer.

l. Create a new blank presentation, and on the title slide, change the slide layout to Blank. Copy, paste, and arrange some of the clip art you previously inserted, then insert a screen clipping of that collage into the first slide of the bakery menu presentation. Add styles or effects to the new image as desired. Do not save the new presentation.

m. Save and close any open files, then exit any open programs.

Independent Challenge 3

The Helping Hand food bank in Denver, Colorado, is organizing its annual Thanksgiving Day Fun Run, which generates proceeds for the benefit of local food pantries. The organization's president, Edward Dimaya, has asked you to create a PowerPoint presentation that includes information about the event, including financial information, for potential sponsors and participants.

a. Start PowerPoint, create a new, blank presentation using any theme and variation you like, customizing the title slide with appropriate text and clip art, then save it as **O-Fun Run Presentation** in the location where you store your Data Files. (*Hint*: Throughout this exercise, maximize windows as necessary.)

b. Add another slide that lists important dates, including deadlines for individual registration and group registration, and the date of the event itself, then add your name to the footer of all slides except the title slide.

c. Use the Slides from Outline command to insert content from the file O-22.docx into the presentation, after the second slide.

d. Adjust formatting as needed for the newly added slides. Insert clip art and/or photographs as desired.

e. At the end of the presentation, add a new slide with a title-only layout titled **Financials**, start Excel, then create a worksheet and a chart in the style of your choice that show the amount of income for the last three years and three expense categories (such as Equipment, Traffic Control, and Security).

f. Add a chart title, and format it as you wish.

g. Save the worksheet as **O-Fun Run Financials** where you store your Data Files, then copy the chart you created.

h. In PowerPoint, paste the Excel chart you copied, linked with either source or destination formatting.

i. Open the Excel file, change one of the expense figures, then update the link chart in PowerPoint.

j. Start Word, then create an informal confirmation letter to runners who have registered for the event. Write at least two short paragraphs for the letter body text, confirming that the recipient is registered for the event. Add your name at the end of the letter. Save the document as **O-Fun Run Confirmation Letter**.

k. Find an image to use as the organization's logo, display it on the screen in another program, then capture it using Screen Clipping and insert it at the top of the letter.

l. Start a mail merge. Create a Mail Merge Recipients list in Word with at least three records. (*Hint*: Use the Type a New List command.) Include fields for Title, First Name, Last Name, Address 1, City, State, and ZIP Code. Save the data as **O-Fun Run Registrations**.

m. Below the heading at the top of the document, insert address block and greeting line fields. Preview your results and adjust spacing as necessary.

n. Finish the mail merge by merging to the printer, then print the second letter if your lab allows printing.

o. Close any open files, then exit all programs.

Independent Challenge 4: Explore

Think of an organization you either work for now or would like to work for, in either a paid or volunteer position. You'll create a letter, which could be an appeal for donations, a thank-you letter, or some kind of business communication for an event. In the content, you'll include a place for a table of names and email addresses and include text that introduces the table. (For example, your table might be a list of names and email addresses of participants or others who have volunteered to help out.) You'll create a table in Access with this information, then export it to an RTF document that you'll insert into your Word letter.

a. Start Word, then save a new document as **O-My Letter** in the location where you store your Data Files. (*Hint*: Throughout this exercise, maximize windows as necessary.)

b. Type the letter text, including the table introduction. Add clip art or photographs as desired. Include your name as the signer of the document.

c. Start Access, then open a blank desktop database named **O-My Database**. Create a table containing fields for First Name, Last Name, and Email Address, giving the table an appropriate name, and add at least three records.

d. Export the Access table to an RTF file named **O-My Export**. (*Hint*: Use a command on the EXTERNAL DATA tab, in the Export group. Do not save export steps. Save the file in the same location as your other files for this exercise.) Close the database and exit Access.

e. In the Word document, insert the exported RTF file in the appropriate location using the Text from File command. Delete the ID column, then format the inserted table any way you wish. (*Hint*: You may wish to use the Header Row check box in the Table Style Options group.)

f. Make any final formatting changes, then save and close the letter.

g. Open a new Word document, and type a short email message to the four participants, reminding them of the date or another relevant fact about your organization, perhaps an upcoming event. Save the file as **O-My Email text**.

h. Start a mail merge, using the E-mail Messages selection, and use O-My Database as the data source.

i. Use the Insert Merge Field button to insert each recipient's email address at the top of the message.

j. Finish the merge, using the Edit Individual Documents command. Rather than sending the email messages, save the merged document as **O-My Electronic Messages**.

k. Save and close all documents and programs.

Visual Workshop

Using the skills you learned in this unit, create the PowerPoint slides shown in FIGURE O-28. The spreadsheet is an embedded object from a spreadsheet you create from within PowerPoint. For the worksheet data, list the capacities in GB in column A, and the prices shown for each one in column B. The storage device graphic on the third slide is a screen clip; to capture it, with the PowerPoint presentation on the screen, open a File Explorer window (if you are using Windows 7, open a Windows Explorer window) showing the contents of your Computer window. Return to PowerPoint and select the Screen Clipping command. Your computer contents will differ from the figure, depending on the computer drives you have in, and connected to, your computer. (*Hints:* The text on the first slide is bolded and enlarged, and the numbers on the chart are enlarged. To make your chart agree with the one shown, click the chart's vertical axis and click the Increase Font Size button in the Font group on the HOME tab until the font is 20 point. Click the number label on any bar, then click the Increase Font Size button until the size is 18 point.) Save the presentation as **O-Computer Talk** in the location where you store your Data Files.

FIGURE O-28

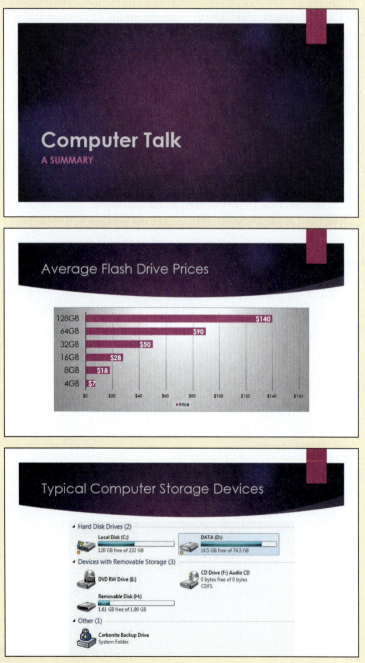

Working in the Cloud

CASE > In your job for the Vancouver branch of Quest Specialty Travel, you travel frequently, you often work from home, and you also collaborate online with colleagues and clients. You want to learn how to work in the Cloud so that you can access and work on your files anytime and anywhere. (*Note*: OneDrive and Office Online are dynamic Web pages, and might change over time, including the way they are organized and how commands are performed. The steps and figures in this appendix reflect these pages at the time this book was published.)

Unit Objectives

After completing this unit, you will be able to:

- Explore Office 365 and the Cloud
- Manage and Share Files
- Explore Office Online
- Complete a Team Project

Files You Will Need

CLOUD-1.docx

Explore Office 365 and the Cloud

The term **cloud computing** refers to the process of working with files and apps online. You may already be familiar with Web-based e-mail accounts such as Gmail and outlook.com. These applications are **cloud-based**, which means that you do not need a program installed on your computer to run them. Office 365 has also been designed as a cloud-based application. When you work in Office 365 you can choose to store your files "in the Cloud" so that you can access them on any device connected to the Internet. **CASE** *You review the concepts related to working in the Cloud with Office 365.*

DETAILS

- ### What is Office 365?

  Microsoft Office 365 delivers a subscription-based service from the Cloud. Various services are available, but most plans include access to the Microsoft Office programs such as Word, Excel, PowerPoint, OneNote, Outlook, and so on. **FIGURE CLOUD-1** shows some of the subscription options available on the Microsoft website. These programs are stored in the Cloud, instead of on your computer, until you need to use them. A subscription to Microsoft Office 365 is a less expensive alternative to purchasing Microsoft Office 2013 and includes access to email, calendars, conferencing, file sharing, and website design.

- ### How Does Office 365 work in the Cloud?

  When you launch an Office application such as Word or Excel, you might see your name and maybe even your picture in the top right corner of your screen. This information tells you that you have signed in to Office 365, either with your personal account or with an account you are given as part of an organization such as a company or school. **FIGURE CLOUD-2** shows the user information that appears in Word when you click the list arrow next to your name in the top right corner of the screen. When you are signed in to Office 2013 and click the FILE tab in an application such as Word or Excel, you see a list of the files that you have used recently on your current computer and on any other connected device such as a laptop, a tablet, or even a Windows phone. The file path appears beneath each filename so that you can quickly identify its location. Office 365 also remembers your personalized settings so that they are available on all the devices you use.

- ### How Do I Get a Microsoft Account?

  If you have been working with Windows and Office 2013, you probably already have a Microsoft account. You also have an account if you use outlook.com, OneDrive, Xbox LIVE, or have a Windows phone. A Microsoft account consists of an email address and a password. If you wish to create a new Microsoft account go to https://signup.live.com/ and follow the directions provided.

- ### What is OneDrive?

  OneDrive (formerly called SkyDrive) is an online storage and file sharing service. When you are signed in to your computer with your Microsoft account, you receive access to your own OneDrive, which is your personal storage area in the Cloud. Every file you save to OneDrive is synced among your computers and your personal storage area on OneDrive.com. The term **synced** (which stands for synchronized) means that when you add, change or delete files on one computer, the same files on your other devices are also updated.

- ### What is Office Online?

  Office Online provides users with limited versions of Microsoft Word, Excel, PowerPoint, and OneNote that you can access online from your Web browser. An Office Online program does not include all of the features and functions included with the full Office version of its associated program. However, you can use Office Online from any computer that is connected to the Internet, even if Microsoft Office 2013 is not installed on that computer. You can also use the programs in Office Online free of charge.

FIGURE CLOUD-1: Office 365 subscription services

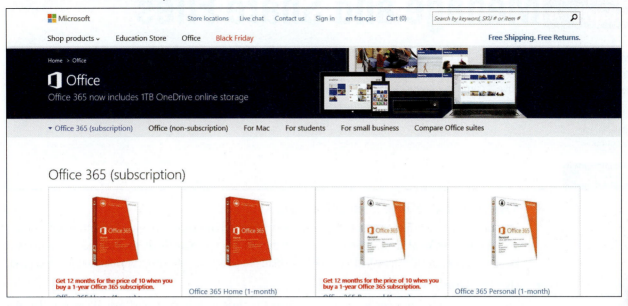

FIGURE CLOUD-2: Viewing Windows account options in Word

Manage and Share Files

Learning Outcomes
- Explore ways to save files to OneDrive
- Identify file management options

OneDrive works like the hard drive on your computer. You can save and open files, create folders, and manage files. You can access the files you save on OneDrive from any of your connected devices and from anywhere you have a computer connection. You can also share files with other users. **CASE** ▶ *You explore the various ways in which you can manage and share files in the Cloud using OneDrive.*

DETAILS

- ### Save Files to OneDrive from Office 2013

  You can choose to store files on your personal OneDrive when you are signed into your Microsoft account. To save a file directly from Word, Excel, or PowerPoint, click the FILE tab, click Save As, then select OneDrive as the save location. You can save files into a folder on OneDrive in the same manner you save files to folder on your computer.

- ### Use the OneDrive App

  You can use the OneDrive App from the Start screen to upload a file to your OneDrive. When you click the OneDrive app, all the folders stored on your OneDrive appear as tiles. To upload a file, right click the folder to show the Apps bar at the bottom of the screen, as shown in **FIGURE CLOUD-3**. From this bar, you can create a new folder, or click the More button at the far right of the bar, then click Add Files. Note that in Windows 8, the Start screen displays a SkyDrive app tile. The files and folders you access from the SkyDrive file are identical to the files on your OneDrive contents. Only the interface and Apps bar layout are different. When you install Office 365, a OneDrive tile accesses a synced version of the OneDrive contents on your computer. When you click this tile, you open a File Explorer window showing the synced files and folders on your computer.

- ### Work with Files from the website

  When you access OneDrive from Internet Explorer, you can do more file management tasks than you can with the OneDrive App, including renaming and moving files. When you go to the onedrive.com website, your personal OneDrive will open if you are signed into your Microsoft account. If you are not signed in, the login page appears where you can enter the email address and password associated with your Microsoft account. Once you have accessed the website, you can open a file, download a file to your computer, share it, embed it, and perform other actions such as renaming and deleting. **FIGURE CLOUD-4** shows the lists of file management tasks you can perform. To show this list, right click a file or folder on OneDrive.

- ### Share Files

QUICK TIP
If you share a folder, you are granting access to all the files in that folder.

  To share files and folders on your OneDrive, access OneDrive from the website, right-click the file or the folder you wish to share, then click Share. When prompted, type the email address of the person with whom you wish to share the folder, type a personal message if you wish, then click Share. The person with whom you have shared the file or folder will receive an email message containing a link to the shared file or folder. You can also choose to connect with one of the social media sites listed to post the link to the file, or you can get the link and include it in another email or on a website. To share a file from Word, Excel, or PowerPoint, first save it to OneDrive, then click the FILE tab, click Share, verify that Invite People is selected, then complete the same steps to enter an email address and message.

Co-authoring documents

You can work on a document, presentation, or workbook simultaneously with a partner. Save the file to your OneDrive, click the FILE tab, click Share, then click Invite People. Enter the email addresses of the people you want to work on the file with you and then click Share. Once your partner has received, opened, and started editing the document, you can start working together. You will see a notification in the status bar that someone is editing the document with you. When you click the notification, you can see the name of the other user and their picture if they have one attached to their Windows account. When your partner saves, you'll see his or her changes in green shading which goes away the next time you save.

FIGURE CLOUD-3: Options for working with files on the OneDrive app

Click the More button
to add files

FIGURE CLOUD-4: Options for working with files on the OneDrive website

Cloud Computing Team Project

CLOUD-1

Open in Word

Open in Word Online

Download

Share

Embed

Rename

Delete

Move to

Copy to

Version history

Properties

How to disable default saving to OneDrive

You can specify how you want to save files from Office 2013 applications. By default, files are saved to locations you specify on your OneDrive. You can change the default to be a different location. In Word, PowerPoint, or Excel, click the FILE tab, then click Options. Click Save in the left sidebar, then in the Save sec- tion, click the Save to Computer by default check box. Click OK to close the Options dialog box. The Save options you've selected will be active in Word, PowerPoint, and Excel, regard- less of which application you were using when you changed the option.

Explore Office Online

Learning Outcomes
- Create a presentation with PowerPoint Online
- Open a presentation from PowerPoint Online

When you are signed in to OneDrive on your Web browser, you have access to Office Online. Office Online consists of scaled-down versions of four Microsoft Office 2013 programs: Word, Excel, PowerPoint, and OneNote. You can work in Office Online to create and edit documents even if you don't have Office 2013 installed on your computer. Each Office Online programs uses a similar interface to its corresponding Office 2013 version. From OneDrive, you can also open the document in the full Office application if the application is installed on the computer you are using. **CASE** *You create a PowerPoint presentation in PowerPoint Online, and then open the presentation in the full version of PowerPoint.*

STEPS

1. **Open a Web browser, go to onedrive.com, then sign in to your personal OneDrive if necessary. Click Create at the top of the OneDrive window, click PowerPoint presentation, then review the Ribbon and its tabs to familiarize yourself with the commands you can access from PowerPoint Online**

   TABLE CLOUD-1 summarizes the commands that are available.

2. **Click the DESIGN tab, click the More Themes list arrow ▼ to show the selection of designs available, then select the Quotable design**

   A limited number of designs are available on PowerPoint Online.

3. **Click Click to add title, type QST Vancouver, click Click to add subtitle, then type Your Name**

4. **Click the INSERT tab, click New Slide in the Slides group, then click Add Slide to add the default Title and Content slide layout**

5. **Type QST Tours for the slide title, then enter Hornby Island Kayaking and Pender Island Fishing as two bullet points as shown in FIGURE CLOUD-5**

   You can make limited formatting changes to slide text in PowerPoint Online.

6. **Select the two lines of bulleted text, click the HOME tab, click the Font Size list arrow in the Font group, then click 32**

7. **Click on a blank area of the slide, click OPEN IN POWERPOINT at the top of the window, then click Yes in response to the message**

QUICK TIP
The presentation is automatically saved as Presentation1 on OneDrive.

8. **Click the FILE tab, click Save As, save the document as CLOUD-QST Tours to your computer, then exit PowerPoint and close the Web browser**

Exploring other Office Online Programs

Three other Office Online programs are Word, Excel, and OneNote. You can also create an Excel survey and a Plain text document. To familiarize yourself with the commands available in an Office Online program, create a new file and then review the commands on each tab on the Ribbon. If you want to perform a task that is not available in the Office Online program, open the file in the full version of the application.

FIGURE CLOUD-5: Completed slide in PowerPoint Online

TABLE CLOUD-1: Commands on PowerPoint Online

tab	category/group	options
FILE	Info	• Open in PowerPoint and previous versions
	New	• Create a new blank presentation
	Open	• Open an existing presentation
	Save As	• Download: use to download a copy of the presentation to your computer
	Print	• Create a printable PDF of the presentation that you can then open and print
	Share	• Share with people and embed the presentation in a blog or website
	About	• Try Microsoft Office, Terms of Use, and Privacy and Cookies
	Help	• Help with PowerPoint Online questions, Give Feedback to Microsoft
HOME	Undo	• Undo and Redo
	Clipboard	• Copy, Paste, Format Painter
	Delete	• Delete a slide
	Slides	• Add a new slide, select a slide layout, duplicate a slide, hide a slide
	Font	• Change the font, size, style, and color of selected text
	Paragraph	• Add bullets and numbering, indent text, align text, and change text direction
	Drawing	• Add and arrange text boxes and shapes, apply Quick Styles, modify shape fill and outline, duplicate shapes
INSERT	Slides	• Add new slides with selected layout
	Images	• Add pictures from your computer or clip art
	Illustrations	• Add shapes or SmartArt
	Links	• Add links to objects
	Text	• Add text boxes
	Comments	• Add comments
	Symbol	• Add symbols
DESIGN	Themes	• Apply a limited number of themes, variants and format backgrounds
TRANSITIONS	Transitions to This Slide	• Apply a limited number of transition effects to slides and chose to apply the effect to all slides
ANIMATIONS	Animation	• Apply a limited number of animation effects to a slide element and modify existing timings
VIEW	Presentation Views	• View slides in Editing View, Reading View, and Slide Show View, and show notes and comments

Cloud

Team Project

To explore how you can work with OneDrive and Office Online programs, you will work with two other people to complete a team project to plan a special event of your choice, such as a class party, a lecture, or a concert. Follow the guidelines provided below to create a Word document, a PowerPoint presentation, and an Excel workbook.

    a. Share email addresses among all three team members, then set up a time (either via email, an online chat session, Internet Messaging, or face to face) to choose an event and identify who is responsible for the Word document, Excel spreadsheet, and PowerPoint presentation.

    b. Individually, complete the tasks listed below for the file you are responsible for. You need to develop appropriate content, format the file attractively, and then share the file with the other team members.

    c. Go to **onedrive.com**, sign in if necessary, create a folder called **Cloud Project**, then work in Office Online to create the file you are assigned.

Word Document – Event Responsibilities Table

In Office Online, create a new Word document. Include a title with the name of your project and a subtitle with the names of your team members. Create and format a three-column table with up to ten rows and the headings "Task," "Person Responsible," and "Deadline," and then complete it with appropriate tasks such as "Contact the caterers" or "Pick up the speaker." Close the file, rename the file **Cloud Project_Responsibilities**, then move the file from the Documents folder to the Cloud Project folder. You will share the document with your team members and receive feedback in the next section.

Excel Workbook – Budget

In Office Online, create a new Excel workbook. Create a budget that includes expected revenues from the event (ticket sales, donations, etc.) and expenses (advertising costs, food costs, transportation costs, etc.) Calculate totals and the net profit. Format the budget attractively. Close the file, rename the file **Cloud Project_Budget**, then move the file from the Documents folder to the Cloud Project folder. You will share the workbook with your team members and receive feedback in the next section.

PowerPoint Presentation – Special Event Description

In Office Online, create a new PowerPoint presentation. Create a presentation that consists of three to five slides including the title slide that states the purpose of the event, and the location, time, and cost. Format the presentation using the theme of your choice. Close the file, rename the file **Cloud Project_Presentation**, then move the file from the Documents folder to the Cloud Project folder. You will share the presentation with your team members and receive feedback.

    d. You need to share your file, then add feedback to the other two files. For example, if you created the Excel budget, you can provide the person who created the PowerPoint presentation with information about the cost breakdown. If you created the Word document, you can add information about the total revenue and expenses contained in the Excel budget to your description.

    e. From OneDrive on your Web browser, open the file you created in the Office Online version of the program, click the **FILE tab**, click **Share**, then click **Share with People**. Enter the email addresses of the other two team members, then enter the following message: **Here's the file I created for our team project. Please make any changes, provide suggestions, and then save it. Thanks!** Click the **Share button**.

    f. Allow team members time to add information and comments to your file, then save a final version.

    g. Assign a team member to open **CLOUD-1.docx** from the location where you save your Data Files, then save it to your Cloud Project folder as **Cloud Project_Summary**. Read the directions in the document, then enter your name as Team Member 1 and write a short description of your experience working with OneDrive and Office Online programs to complete the team project. Share the file with your team members and request that they add their own names and descriptions.

    h. When all team members have finished working on the document, save all the changes. Make sure you store all four files completed for the project in the Cloud Project folder on your OneDrive, then submit them to your instructor on behalf of your team.

Integrating Word, PowerPoint, Excel, and Access 2013

CASE ▶ This appendix contains three Integrated Projects that cover tasks you can perform to integrate content from two or more Microsoft Office 2013 applications. Each Integrated Project presents a new case scenario that encourages you to apply your skills and knowledge in a realistic, professional context.

Unit Objectives

Integrated Project 1

- Use the Office Clipboard to integrate content
- Create PowerPoint slides from a Word outline
- Export a Word document as a PDF file

Integrated Project 2

- Import Excel data into an Access table
- Export Access data to an Excel spreadsheet

Integrated Project 3

- Use the Paste options to paste, embed, and link content
- Embed an Excel worksheet in PowerPoint
- Edit an embedded object
- Link an Excel chart to a PowerPoint presentation
- Update a linked object
- Paste Access data into a PowerPoint presentation

Files You Will Need

IntProjects

Project1
Coaching.jpg
Flyer.docx
Healthy
Employees.jpg
Outline.docx
Productivity.jpg

Project2
GCC Inventory.xlsx

Project3
Event Details.xlsx
Event.jpg
Funding Sources.xlsx
Sponsor.docx
Sponsors.accdb
Teamwork.jpg

©HelenStock/Shutterstock

Integrated Project 1: Word and PowerPoint

Integrated Project 1: In this project, you work with Word and PowerPoint to copy and paste multiple items from the Office Clipboard, insert slides in a PowerPoint presentation from a Word outline, and export a Word document as a file in the Portable Document Format (PDF). **CASE** ▸ *As the marketing and promotions manager for a corporate wellness services company, you are preparing a presentation and accompanying handout for a meeting with a potential client next week. You have an outline with key points for the presentation that you can use as the basis for your slides, and have already prepared a draft of a flyer summarizing the benefits of your on-site wellness programs.*

STEPS

1. Create a blank PowerPoint presentation and then save it as **Health** to the drive and folder where you are storing your files.

2. Apply the Wisp theme to the presentation, and then select the second variant with the tan background, orange arrow, and green accent bar.

3. Make the following changes to Slide 1:
   a. Use **Improving Your Health** as the presentation title.
   b. Add the subtitle **Presented by: First Last** using your first and last names.
   c. Insert the photo **Healthy Employees** from the location where you store your Data Files.
   d. Resize the image to a height of 3.52" and width of 5.28".
   e. Center the photo above the title.
   f. Apply the Beveled Oval, Black picture style to the photo.

4. Import the Word document **Outline** from the location where you store your Data Files into the open presentation to create slides from an outline. Resize the bulleted text on Slides 2 through 5 to 28 points.

5. On Slide 4 ("Benefits of Healthy Employees"), make the following changes:
   a. Change the layout to Two Content.
   b. In the placeholder, insert the photo **Productivity** from the location where you store your Data Files.
   c. Resize the Productivity image to a height of 3" and width of 4.09".
   d. Apply the Bevel Perspective picture style to the image.
   e. Move the image to the lower-right corner of the slide.

6. To the right of the bulleted list on Slide 4 ("Benefits of Healthy Employees"), insert and format a shape as follows:
   a. Insert a Bent Arrow shape with a height of 4.08" and a width of 1.54".
   b. Apply the Intense Effect - Green, Accent 6 style to the shape.
   c. Click the Rotate button in the Arrange group on the DRAWING TOOLS FORMAT tab.
   d. Click Rotate Right 90° to rotate the shape.
   e. Position the arrow so that it points from the list to the image.

7. On Slide 5 ("Ways We Can Help"), insert a photo as follows:

   a. Insert the photo **Coaching** from the location where you store your Data Files.
   b. Resize the image to a height of 2.5" and a width of 3.75".
   c. Use the Smart Guides to align the image with the top of the content placeholder and the right margin of the slide.

8. On Slide 5 ("Ways We Can Help"), select the Coaching image then format it as follows:

   a. On the PICTURE TOOLS FORMAT tab in the Adjust group, click the Color button.
   b. In the Recolor section of the Color gallery, click Sepia to recolor the image.
   c. Apply the Reflected Rounded Rectangle picture style to the image.

9. On Slide 6 ("Where to Start"), make the following changes:

   a. Change the slide layout to Comparison.
   b. Insert **Health Assessment** in the left heading placeholder.
   c. Insert **Wellness Campaign** in the right heading placeholder.
   d. Add content as follows to the two other placeholders:

Health Assessment	Wellness Campaign
Provides a baseline for comparison	Encourages involvement from all employees
Educates employees on the need for wellness	Boosts morale through friendly competition
Offers benefits to everyone	Creates internal and external motivation

© 2016 Cengage Learning

10. Insert a new Slide 7 as follows:

    a. Use the Title and Content slide layout.
    b. Insert **Launching a Wellness Campaign** as the slide title.
    c. Insert a bulleted list with the following text:

       Determine activity

       Promote sign-ups

       Kick off event

       Collect results

       Announce winners

11. On Slide 7 ("Launching a Wellness Campaign"), select the bulleted list and then perform the following tasks:

    a. Convert the bulleted list to a Continuous Cycle SmartArt graphic.
    b. On the SMARTART TOOLS DESIGN tab in the SmartArt Styles group, click the Change Colors button to display the Change Colors gallery.
    c. In the Colorful group, click the Colorful - Accent Colors option to change the colors of the SmartArt graphic.

12. Insert a new Slide 8 as follows:

    a. Use the Title Slide layout.
    b. Insert **Questions?** as the slide title.
    c. Insert **Email:** followed by your email address as the subtitle.

13. Copy the image from Slide 1 ("Improving Your Health") and paste the image in the same location on Slide 8 ("Questions?").

14. Apply the Blinds transition effect with a duration of 01.00 to all slides.

15. Save the presentation and then run it in Slide Show view. When you are finished, exit the slide show. **FIGURE 1-1** shows the completed presentation in Slide Sorter view.

FIGURE 1-1: Completed Health presentation

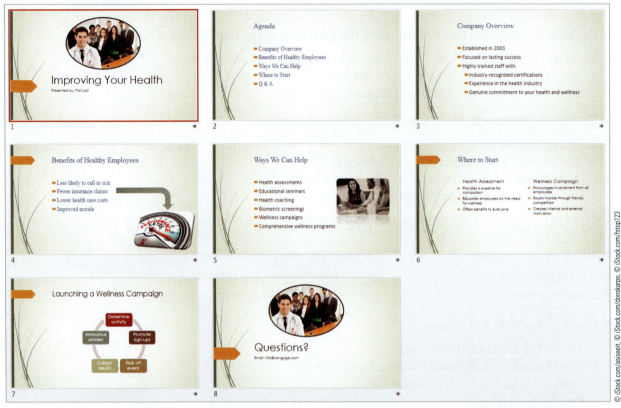

16. Open the Word document Flyer from the location where you store your Data Files, and then save the document as Wellness Flyer.

17. Update the document content as follows:
    a. Replace the {Company Name} placeholder in the subtitle with *your school name*.
    b. Below the "Your Personal Consultant" heading on page 2, replace the contact information with your contact details.

18. In the blank paragraph below the line separator on page 2, insert the text Your Next Steps to Launching a Wellness Campaign, and then apply the Heading 1 style.

19. In the Health presentation, display the Office Clipboard, and then copy items as follows:
    a. On Slide 4 ("Benefits of Healthy Employees"), copy the Productivity image to the Office Clipboard.
    b. On Slide 5 ("Ways We Can Help"), copy the Coaching image to the Office Clipboard.
    c. On Slide 7 ("Launching a Wellness Campaign"), copy the SmartArt graphic to the Office Clipboard.

20. **In the Wellness Flyer document, display the Office Clipboard, and then paste and format items as follows:**
   a. Paste the SmartArt graphic below the new heading at the end of the Wellness Flyer document, then resize the SmartArt graphic to a height of 5".
   b. Paste the Productivity image in the blank paragraph below the "EVERYONE COUNTS!" sidebar on page 1 of the flyer.
   c. With the Productivity image selected, click the Reset Picture button on the PICTURE TOOLS FORMAT tab in the Adjust group to reset the image to its original format.
   d. Paste the Coaching image on the blank line above the caption at the top of page 2 of the flyer.
   e. Using the same technique as in Step 20c, reset the Coaching image to its original format.

21. **Apply the Wisp theme to the Word document so it matches the theme of the presentation.**

22. **Save the Wellness Flyer document.** FIGURE 1-2 shows the completed flyer.

FIGURE 1-2: Completed Wellness Flyer document

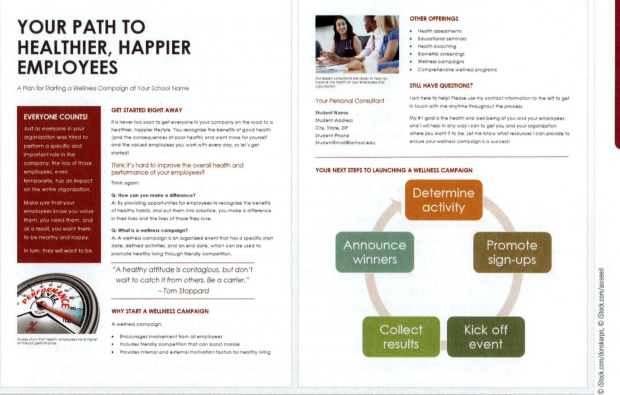

23. **Export the final flyer as a Portable Document Format (PDF) file as follows:**
   a. Click the FILE tab on the ribbon, then click Export.
   b. Click the Create PDF/XPS button, then navigate to the location where you store your Data Files.
   c. Use **Wellness Flyer PDF** as the filename.
   d. Click Publish.

Integrated Project 2: Excel and Access

Integrated Project 2: In this project, you work with Excel and Access to create Access tables from Excel worksheets, and then export Access data to an Excel workbook. **CASE** ▶ *Green Cleaning Company is a corporate cleaning service that uses environmentally friendly products to clean offices and other business sites. As the company's scheduling director, you need to manage your inventory of cleaning products efficiently to meet the demands of your growing business. You have been using an Excel workbook to manage your customer list and track inventory usage and now want to switch to Access to perform the same tasks. You also want to continue using Excel to analyze the details of each cleaning product in inventory.*

STEPS

1. **Create a blank desktop database named GCC. When the new database opens, close TABLE 1.**

2. **Use the Import Spreadsheet Wizard to add a table to the database as follows. The data you need to import is contained in the Customer List worksheet in the GCC Inventory workbook, which is an Excel file located where you store your Data Files.**
   a. On the ribbon, click the EXTERNAL DATA tab, then in the Import & Link group, click the Excel button to open the Get External Data – Excel Spreadsheet dialog box.
   b. Click the Browse button, navigate to the location where you store your Data Files, then double-click the **GCC Inventory** file.
   c. If it is not already selected, click the Import the source data into a new table in the current database option button, then click OK. In the first Import Spreadsheet Wizard dialog box, select Customer List if it is not already selected, then click Next.
   d. Click the First Row Contains Column Headings check box.
   e. Click Next, then click each column and remove spaces in the following field names: CustomerID, CompanyName, FirstName, LastName, and CustomerSince.
   f. Click the ZIP field, then set its Data Type to Short Text.
   g. Click Next, click the Choose my own primary key option button, then select CustomerID if it is not already specified as the primary key.
   h. Click Next, type **Customers** as the table name, then click Finish to create the table.
   i. Click Close to close the wizard without saving the import steps.

3. **Applying the same techniques you learned in Step 2, use the Import Spreadsheet Wizard to add a second table to the database as follows. The data you need to import is contained in the Inventory worksheet in the GCC Inventory workbook, which is an Excel file located where you store your Data Files.**
   a. Import all columns from the Inventory worksheet in the **GCC Inventory** Excel workbook into a new table.
   b. Remove spaces from the ProductID field.
   c. Change the Data Type for the QOH and Reorder fields to Integer.
   d. Specify ProductID as the primary key.
   e. Import the data into a new table named **Products** and do not save the import steps.

4. **Applying the same techniques you learned in Step 2, use the Import Spreadsheet Wizard to add a third table to the database as follows. The data you need to import is contained in the Product Usage worksheet in the GCC Inventory workbook, which is an Excel file located where you store your Data Files.**

   a. Import only the Customer ID, Product ID, Date, and Quantity columns from the Product Usage worksheet in the **GCC Inventory** Excel workbook into a new table. (*Hint*: In the third step of the wizard, select each field you are not importing, then select the Do not import field (Skip) check box.)
   b. Remove spaces from the CustomerID and ProductID fields.
   c. Change the Data Type property for the Quantity field to Integer.
   d. Do not specify a primary key.
   e. Import the data to a new table named **Usage** and do not save the import steps.

5. **Define the one-to-many relationships between the database tables as follows. (*Hint*: If field lists other than those for the three tables you created appear in the Relationships window, click the Clear Layout button in the Tools group on the RELATIONSHIP TOOLS DESIGN tab to remove them.)**

   a. Define a one-to-many relationship between the primary Customers table and the related Usage table.
   b. Define a one-to-many relationship between the primary Products table and the related Usage table.
   c. Enforce referential integrity for each relationship.
   d. Save the layout of the Relationships window.

6. **Use the Form button to create a form named CustomerForm that includes all the fields in the Customers table. (This form also includes three fields from the Usage table.) Use the Form button to create a second form named ProductForm that includes all the fields in the Products table. (This form also includes three fields from the Usage table.) In both forms, update labels as appropriate to insert spaces between words in field names containing more than one word.**

7. **Using the ProductForm, add a new product record to the database with the data shown in TABLE 2-1.**

TABLE 2-1: New product record

Field Name	Value
ProductID	EC-51487W
Description	Wood Floor Polish
Brand	Earthscape Cleaners
Cost	10.43
Retail	25.03
QOH	20
Reorder	10

© 2016 Cengage Learning

8. Using the CustomerForm, add a new customer record to the database with the data shown in TABLE 2-2.

TABLE 2-2: New customer record

Field Name	Value	Field Name	Value
CustomerID	CLAY-092015	State	OK
CompanyName	Cleveland University	ZIP	59668
FirstName	Zachary	Phone	(539) 900-3721
LastName	Axson	Email	ZacAxs7276@clevelanduniversity.com
Address	7293 Lincoln Rd	CustomerSince	9/1/2015
City	Turley		

9. In the CustomerForm, add the products shown in TABLE 2-3 to the Cleveland University customer record.

TABLE 2-3: Products for Cleveland University

ProductID	Date	Quantity
GC-88925F	9/1/2015	2
EC-51487W	9/1/2015	1

10. Create a query in Design view using the Products and Usage tables as follows. FIGURE 2-1 shows the results of the completed query.

   a. On the ribbon, click the CREATE tab, then in the Queries group, click the Query Design button.
   b. In the Show Table dialog box, double-click Products, double-click Usage, then click Close to display the field lists for the two tables.
   c. Add fields from the Products field list to the design grid in the following order: Description, Brand, Cost, Retail, QOH, and Reorder.
   d. Add the Quantity field from the Usage field list to the design grid.
   e. On the QUERY TOOLS DESIGN tab, in the Show/Hide group, click the Totals button, click Group By in the Quantity column, click the list arrow, then click Sum to add the Total row to the query grid. The query will calculate the sum of the Quantity field values.
   f. Specify criteria to limit the results to those products with a quantity on hand (QOH) less than the specified reorder level.
   g. Click the Quantity field in the design grid, then on the QUERY TOOLS DESIGN tab, in the Show/Hide group, click the Property Sheet button to open the Property Sheet for the field.
   h. Click the blank cell for the Caption property, type **Current Use**, then close the Property Sheet.
   i. Save the query as **CurrentNeed** and then run the query.

11. Export the CurrentNeed query to a new Excel workbook as follows:

   a. Click the EXTERNAL DATA tab on the ribbon, then in the Export group, click the Excel button to open the Export – Excel Spreadsheet dialog box.
   b. Click the Browse button, then navigate to where you store your Data Files.
   c. Type **Current Needs Export** in the File name text box, then click the Save button.
   d. Click the Export data with formatting and layout check box, then click OK.
   e. Click Close to export the data without saving the export steps.

© 2016 Cengage Learning

FIGURE 2-1: Results of the CurrentNeed query

CurrentNeed

Description	Brand	Cost	Retail	QOH	Reorder	Current Use
All Purpose Flc	Better Way Prc	$10.17	$24.41	64	67	43
All Purpose Flc	GreenCleen	$16.30	$39.12	12	69	39
Antiseptic Soa|	EcoKonshis	$13.11	$31.46	4	59	42
Antiseptic Soa|	GreenCleen	$7.66	$18.38	34	59	49
Carpet Deodor	SafeOne Eco Cl	$11.83	$28.39	30	71	51
Carpet Stain Re	Earthscape Cle	$5.56	$13.34	52	57	46
Carpet Stain Re	Well-4-All	$8.53	$20.47	22	29	48
Floor Wax	EcoKonshis	$8.69	$20.86	15	48	49
Floor Wax	Well-4-All	$2.83	$6.79	67	71	33
Garbage Pail D	Better Way Prc	$15.90	$38.16	18	52	49
Garbage Pail D	EcoKonshis	$1.59	$3.82	24	65	44
Garbage Pail D	Well-4-All	$20.00	$48.00	38	67	45
Laundry Soap	Better Way Prc	$15.16	$36.38	18	54	49
Laundry Soap	Earthscape Cle	$14.52	$34.85	39	40	45
Laundry Soap	Well-4-All	$19.82	$47.57	39	51	43
Leather Cleane	Better Way Prc	$8.71	$20.90	22	29	47
Leather Cleane	Earthscape Cle	$19.79	$47.50	21	35	43
Leather Cleane	SafeOne Eco Cl	$6.85	$16.44	14	51	41
Spot Cleaner	Better Way Prc	$6.07	$14.57	51	57	55
Spot Cleaner	GreenCleen	$2.55	$6.12	14	31	45
Spot Cleaner	SafeOne Eco Cl	$18.33	$43.99	24	36	48
Spot Cleaner	Well-4-All	$12.03	$28.87	33	55	33
Stain Remover	Earthscape Cle	$17.66	$42.38	20	59	45
Stain Remover	EcoKonshis	$17.09	$41.02	24	62	40
Stain Remover	SafeOne Eco Cl	$6.21	$14.90	52	63	47
Toilet Bowl Cle	EcoKonshis	$3.16	$7.58	45	60	17
Toilet Bowl Cle	GreenCleen	$7.12	$17.09	19	27	52
Vinyl Cleaner	EcoKonshis	$8.59	$20.62	32	50	47
Vinyl Cleaner	Well-4-All	$15.80	$37.92	8	61	47
Wood Floor Po	Better Way Prc	$12.84	$30.82	65	69	53
Wood Floor Po	EcoKonshis	$2.14	$5.14	31	75	39
Wood Floor Po	Well-4-All	$11.01	$26.42	20	61	46

Record: 1 of 32 | No Filter | Search

Field caption specified in Design view

32 records

12. Open the exported Excel workbook, and then make the following changes to the CurrentNeed worksheet:

a. Change the heading in cell G1 to **August**.
b. In cell H1, insert **Order** as the column heading, and in cell I1, insert **Amount** as the column heading.
c. Apply the Accounting number format to the range C2:D33.
d. Apply the Heading 3 style to the range A1:I1.
e. AutoFit all column widths.
f. Sort the worksheet data in ascending order by Brand.
g. In cell H34, insert **Total**.
h. Apply the Total style to the range H34:I34.

13. Create a formula in cell H2 as follows to determine the ordering need if the reorder level is larger than the amount of product used in August. If not, determine how much product to order to cover two months of use minus the quantity on hand.

a. In cell H2, type **=IF(** to begin a formula using the IF function.
b. Type **F2 > G2,** to test whether the reorder level (column F) is larger than the actual usage in August (column G).
c. Type **F2 - E2 + G2,** to calculate a value if this condition is true. In that case, you need to order enough product to cover the difference between the reorder level (column F) and quantity on hand (column E) plus a current month of use (column G).
d. Type **2 * G2 - E2)** to enter the last part of the function, which calculates a value if the condition is false. In that case, you need to order enough product to cover the difference between two months of current use (column G) and the quantity on hand (column E).
e. Use the fill handle to copy the complete formula in cell H2 to the range H3:H33.

14. Create a formula in cell I2 to determine the total order cost for the first product as follows:

   a. Multiply the order quantity (column H) and the product cost (column C).
   b. Use the fill handle to copy the formula in cell I2 to the range I3:I33.
   c. Resize column I to display all of its data.

15. In cell I34, use the SUM function to calculate the total order amount.

16. Save the Excel workbook. **FIGURE 2-2** shows the completed Current Needs Export workbook formatted to show row 1 and rows 17–34 in the CurrentNeed worksheet.

FIGURE 2-2: Completed Current Needs Export workbook

	A	B	C	D	E	F	G	H	I
1	Description	Brand	Cost	Retail	QOH	Reorder	August	Order	Amount
17	Vinyl Cleaner	EcoKonshis	$ 8.59	$20.62	32	50	47	65	$ 558.35
18	Wood Floor Polish	EcoKonshis	$ 2.14	$ 5.14	31	75	39	83	$ 177.62
19	All Purpose Floor Cleaner	GreenCleen	$16.30	$39.12	12	69	39	96	$ 1,564.80
20	Antiseptic Soap Spray	GreenCleen	$ 7.66	$18.38	34	59	49	74	$ 566.84
21	Spot Cleaner	GreenCleen	$ 2.55	$ 6.12	14	31	45	76	$ 193.80
22	Toilet Bowl Cleaner	GreenCleen	$ 7.12	$17.09	19	27	52	85	$ 605.20
23	Carpet Deodorizer	SafeOne Eco Cleaners	$11.83	$28.39	30	71	51	92	$ 1,088.36
24	Leather Cleaner	SafeOne Eco Cleaners	$ 6.85	$16.44	14	51	41	78	$ 534.30
25	Spot Cleaner	SafeOne Eco Cleaners	$18.33	$43.99	24	36	48	72	$ 1,319.76
26	Stain Remover	SafeOne Eco Cleaners	$ 6.21	$14.90	52	63	47	58	$ 360.18
27	Carpet Stain Remover	Well-4-All	$ 8.53	$20.47	22	29	48	74	$ 631.22
28	Floor Wax	Well-4-All	$ 2.83	$ 6.79	67	71	33	37	$ 104.71
29	Garbage Pail Deodorizer	Well-4-All	$20.00	$48.00	38	67	45	74	$ 1,480.00
30	Laundry Soap	Well-4-All	$19.82	$47.57	39	51	43	55	$ 1,090.10
31	Spot Cleaner	Well-4-All	$12.03	$28.87	33	55	33	55	$ 661.65
32	Vinyl Cleaner	Well-4-All	$15.80	$37.92	8	61	47	100	$ 1,580.00
33	Wood Floor Polish	Well-4-All	$11.01	$26.42	20	61	46	87	$ 957.87
34								Total	$25,636.25
35									

CurrentNeed

Total order amount

Integrated Project 3: Word, PowerPoint, Excel, and Access

Integrated Project 3: In this project, you integrate Word, Excel, and Access content in a PowerPoint presentation. You import an outline from Word, embed data from an Excel worksheet, link data to an Excel chart, and copy and paste Access data. You also update all of the content you integrate into the presentation to see how these different types of integration tasks handle editing and updating content. **CASE** ▶ *As the sponsorship team leader for the 2016 Valley East Walk for Cancer Research and Treatment, you are preparing a presentation for recruiting walk sponsors. The presentation should provide up-to-date information on available sponsorship opportunities and show how the funds raised for this event contribute to cancer research and treatment. You started an outline for the presentation in Word, have an Access database with information about the sponsorship opportunities, and have Excel workbooks with the details about the event and fund allocations from the 2015 walk. You will use information from all of these sources in the final presentation.*

STEPS

1. **Open the Sponsor Word document located where you store your Data Files and save the document as Sponsor Outline. Make the following changes to the document:**
   a. In the first paragraph, move the text "for Cancer Research and Treatment" to a new paragraph directly below "2016 Valley East Walk."
   b. Assign the Heading 2 style to the new paragraph.
   c. Assign the Heading 2 style to the seven sponsorship type paragraphs beginning with "Presenting Sponsor" and ending with "Table Sponsors (25)."
   d. Add a new paragraph between "Presenting Sponsor" and "Gold-Level Sponsor" with the text **Valley East Hospital**.
   e. Assign the Heading 3 style to the new paragraph.
   f. Save and close the Sponsor Outline document.

2. **Create a new PowerPoint presentation as follows:**
   a. Use the Vapor Trail theme and select the third variant with the white background and pink and blue images.
   b. Save the presentation as **Sponsors** in the location where you store your Data Files.
   c. Import the **Sponsor Outline** Word document into the open presentation.
   d. Delete Slide 1.

3. **Change the slide layouts in the presentation as follows:**
   a. Slide 1 ("2016 Valley East Walk"): Title Slide layout
   b. Slides 2 ("Event Details") through 4 ("Sponsorship Opportunities"): Two Content layout
   c. Slide 5 ("Remaining Opportunities"): Title Only layout
   d. Slide 6 ("Thank You!"): Title Slide layout

4. **On Slide 2 ("Event Details"), insert an image as follows:**
   a. In the first placeholder, insert the **Event** image in the location where you store your Data Files.
   b. Resize the image to a height of 4" and a width of 5.66".
   c. Position the image to the left of the remaining placeholder using the Smart Guides to align the top edge of the image with the top edge of the placeholder.
   d. Apply the Rotated, White picture style to the Event image.

5. **On Slide 2 ("Event Details"), embed data from an Excel workbook as follows:**

    a. Click the second placeholder to select it, then press the DELETE key to delete the placeholder.

    b. Open the **Event Details** workbook in the location where you store your Data Files, then copy the data in the range A1:B4.

    c. On Slide 2 ("Event Details") in the Sponsors presentation, display the Paste Options menu, then embed the Excel worksheet data.

    d. Resize the embedded object so it is about 2.0" tall and 5.74" wide.

    e. Position the embedded object to the right of the image.

    f. Close the Event Details workbook.

6. **On Slide 2 ("Event Details"), edit the embedded worksheet to change the registration time in cell B2 from 8:30 AM to 8:00 AM.**

7. **On Slide 3 ("How 2015 Funds Were Allocated"), increase the width of the title placeholder so that the title appears on a single line. Save the presentation.**

8. **Open the Funding Sources Excel workbook from the location where you store your Data Files, and then save it as 2015 Funding. Format the contents as follows:**

    a. Change the theme to Ion Boardroom.

    b. For the range A1:B1, apply the Heading 1 cell style.

    c. For the range A2:A5, apply the 20% Accent 1 cell style.

    d. For the range A6:B6, apply the Total cell style.

    e. For the range B2:B6, apply the Accounting number format.

9. **Insert a chart as follows:**

    a. Create a 3-D pie chart based on data in the range A1:B5.

    b. Use **2015 Fund Allocation** as the chart title.

    c. Click the Chart Elements button, point to Data Labels, click the Data Labels arrow, then click More Options.

    d. In the Format Data Labels task pane, click the Value check box to remove the check mark, click the Percentage check box to insert a check mark, scroll down, then click the Outside End option button to add percentage data labels to the outside end of the pie chart segments.

    e. Position the chart below the worksheet data so the upper-left corner aligns with the upper-left corner of cell A8.

    f. Save the workbook. **FIGURE 3-1** shows the completed workbook.

FIGURE 3-1: Completed 2015 Funding workbook

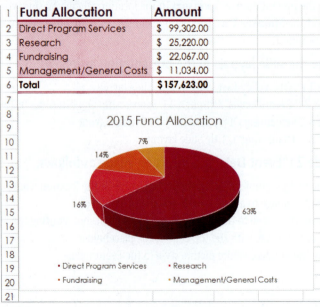

10. **Link the Excel worksheet data and chart to the PowerPoint presentation as follows:**

   a. In the 2015 Funding workbook, copy the range A1:B6.
   b. On Slide 3 ("How 2015 Funds Were Allocated") of the Sponsors presentation, click the first content placeholder to select it, then press the DELETE key to delete it.
   c. Use the Paste Special command to paste a link to the Excel worksheet data you copied.
   d. Resize the linked object so it is 2.4" tall and 5.5" wide.
   e. Move the linked object to the left of the remaining placeholder.
   f. Click the remaining placeholder on the slide to select it, then press the DELETE key to delete the placeholder.
   g. Copy the chart object in the 2015 Funding workbook.
   h. On Slide 3 ("How 2015 Funds Were Allocated") of the Sponsors presentation, paste the chart as a link keeping the source formatting.
   i. Resize the chart object so it is about 3.5" tall and 5.8" wide and then position it to the right of the linked worksheet object.
   j. Middle-align the worksheet and the chart.

11. **Test the link as follows:**

   a. In the 2015 Funding workbook, change the value in cell B4 to **45,000**.
   b. Save and close the workbook.
   c. On Slide 3 ("How 2015 Funds Were Allocated") of the Sponsors presentation, verify that the linked data in the worksheet and the chart have been updated.

12. **On Slide 4 ("Sponsorship Opportunities") of the Sponsors presentation, insert the Teamwork image into the remaining placeholder and apply the Soft Edge Oval picture style.**

13. **Open the Sponsors Access database and then open the RemainingOpportunities query in Datasheet view to run the query. Review the results to verify that all seven opportunities, including the Presenting Sponsor opportunity, are listed, and then close the query.**

14. **Create a new form based on the Sponsors table:**

   a. Include all fields from the Sponsors table except the ID field.
   b. Save the form as **SponsorsForm**.
   c. Change the title to **Sponsors Form**.
   d. Change the labels for ZipCode and SponsorType to add a space between the words.

15. **Use the SponsorsForm to enter the following sponsor record. Note that Sponsor Type 1 indicates a presenting sponsor. FIGURE 3-2 shows the completed Sponsors form with the new record.**

Field	Value
Company	Valley East Hospital
Address	100 Hospital Drive
City	Martinsburg
State	WV
Zip Code	25403
Phone	304-675-1549
Sponsor Type	1

© 2016 Cengage Learning

FIGURE 3-2: Completed Sponsors form

Sponsors Form

Company	Valley East Hospital
Address	100 Hospital Drive
City	Martinsburg
State	WV
Zip Code	25403
Phone	304-675-1549
Sponsor Type	1

16. Save and close the SponsorsForm. Run the RemainingOpportunities query and verify that the Presenting Sponsor item is no longer in the results.

17. Select all the records in the RemainingOpportunities query, right-click the selection, then click Copy on the shortcut menu to copy the records to the Office Clipboard.

18. On Slide 5 ("Remaining Opportunities") of the Sponsors presentation, insert the copied records as follows:

   a. Use the Paste Options menu to paste the records using the destination theme.
   b. Delete row 1 of the new table, which contains the RemainingOpportunities text.
   c. Increase the font size of all the text in the table to 24 points.
   d. Apply the Themed Style 1 - Accent 5 table style.
   e. On the TABLE TOOLS DESIGN tab in the Table Style Options group, click the Header Row check box to format row 1 as the header row.

19. On Slide 5 ("Remaining Opportunities"), change the number of remaining refreshment sponsors from 2 to 1.

20. On Slide 6 ("Thank You!"), click the subtitle placeholder, press the DELETE key to delete the placeholder, then save the presentation. FIGURE 3-3 shows the completed Sponsors presentation in Slide Sorter view.

FIGURE 3-3: Completed Sponsors presentation

© iStock.com/Jorgenmac, © iStock.com/esenkartal

SAM Projects

Introduction

With SAM Projects—SAM's hands-on, live-in-the-application projects—students master Microsoft Office skills that are essential to academic and career success. SAM Projects engage students in applying the latest Microsoft Office 2013 skills to real-world scenarios. Immediate grading and feedback allow students to fix errors and understand where they may need more practice.

This appendix provides the printed instructions for eight SAM Projects that correspond to this text, two for each application (Word, Excel, Access, and PowerPoint). The first project per application was created by an instructor currently teaching an Introduction to Computing course. These projects and their authors are identified below:

- Word Project: created by Brad West, Associate Professor, Sinclair Community College

- Excel Project: created by Diane Smoot, Ph.D., Associate Professor, Harris-Stowe State University

- Access Project: created by Emily H. Shepard, Instructor, Central Carolina Community College

- PowerPoint Project: created by Barbara M. Waxer, Instructor & Trainer, Santa Fe Community College

The second project per application is a SAM Capstone Project. The Capstone Projects cover key learning objectives from all the chapters for the specific application.

To complete the projects in this appendix, you must log into your SAM account. Go to sam.cengage.com for more information or contact your instructor.

Due to Microsoft software and version updates, SAM Project files may differ slightly. The content and directions contained in this Appendix are accurate at the time of printing.

©HelenStock/Shutterstock

Creating a Resume
GETTING THE JOB YOU WANT

PROJECT DESCRIPTION

Created by Brad West, Associate Professor, Sinclair Community College
Now that you have mastered Office 2013, you are ready to apply for a job that will utilize your skills. You have already organized an outline that you will use to enter your information into your partially completed resume. After you complete the resume and proofread it, you will format it appropriately.

GETTING STARTED

- Download the following file from the SAM website:

  ○ **SAM_Word2013_SE_P1a_*FirstLastName*_1.docx**

- Open the file you just downloaded and save it with the name:

  ○ **SAM_Word2013_SE_P1a_*FirstLastName*_2.docx**

  ○ *Hint*: If you do not see the **.docx** file extension in the Save file dialog box, do not type it. Word will add the file extension for you automatically.

- To complete this Project, you will also need to download and save the following support file from the SAM website:

  ○ **support_SAM_W13_SE_P1a_resume_outline.docx**

- With the file **SAM_Word2013_SE_P1a_*FirstLastName*_2.docx** still open, ensure that your first and last name is displayed in the footer. If the footer does not display your name, delete the file and download a new copy from the SAM website.

PROJECT STEPS

1. Replace "Student Name" with your name.

2. Replace "Student Contact Information" with the address from the Resume Outline in **support_SAM_W13_SE_P1a_resume_outline.docx** available for download from the SAM website. Insert a tab, then insert the phone number, another tab, and the email address.

   ○ *Hint*: Each time you paste text from the support file, use the **Keep Text Only** option.

3. Replace "Insert Duties from Job 1 Here" with the duties from **Job 1** in the Resume Outline.

4. Replace "Insert Duties from Job 2 Here" with the duties from **Job 2** in the Resume Outline.

5. Run the Spelling & Grammar check. Correct all spelling mistakes, but ignore the punctuation error.

6. Change the document margins to **Normal**.

7. Change the document theme to **Depth**.

8. Change the document theme colors to **Blue**.

9. In the address line of the document, set a center tab stop at **3.5"** and a right tab stop at **6.5"**.

10. On the lines that begin with "Associate of Applied…", "Binder Clips…", and "Burgers!…", set right tab stops at **6.5"**.

11. Apply the **Title** style to your name at the top of the resume.

12. Apply the **Heading 1** style to "OBJECTIVE", "EDUCATION", "QUALIFICATIONS", "RELATED EXPERIENCE", and "OTHER EXPERIENCE".

13. Apply the **Heading 2** style to "Intern" and "Team Leader".

14. Apply **bold** to "Binder Clips" and "Burgers!".

15. Change the case of "OBJECTIVE", "EDUCATION", "QUALIFICATIONS", "RELATED EXPERIENCE", and "OTHER EXPERIENCE" to **Capitalize Each Word**.

   ○ *Hint*: Use the **Change Case** tool.

16. Create a bulleted list that begins with "Entered and updated account information in Access database for over 300 clients" and ends with "Greeted visitors and presented appropriate company information". Create a second bulleted list that begins with "Took cash, credit card, and debit card payments at cash register" and ends with "Closed register and prepared cash and transaction reports, investigated and rectified errors as appropriate".

17. Change the style of the bullets used in both bulleted lists to the arrow style:

   ➢

Save your changes, close the document, and exit Word. Follow the directions on the SAM website to submit your completed project.

Going Green
COMPLETING A TRIFOLD BROCHURE

PROJECT DESCRIPTION

You are helping to promote programs about *Going Green* hosted by the public library. The head librarian has created a document with specific Green Tips, as well as information on other green-related programs. You will format the text as a trifold brochure that presents the information in columns with bulleted lists. You will add formatting, a table, a photo, and a clip art image to enhance the text.

GETTING STARTED

- Download the following file from the SAM website:
  - **IF_Word2013_CS_UD-F_P1a_*FirstLastName*_1.docx**
- Open the file you just downloaded and save it with the name:
  - **IF_Word2013_CS_UD-F_P1a_*FirstLastName*_2.docx**
  - *Hint*: If you do not see the **.docx** file extension in the Save file dialog box, do not type it. Access will add the file extension for you automatically.
- With the **IF_Word2013_CS_UD-F_P1a_FirstLastName_2.docx** still open, ensure that your first and last name is displayed in the footer. If the footer does not display your name, delete the file and download a new copy from the SAM website.

PROJECT STEPS

1. Change the page orientation of all pages in the document to **Landscape**. (*Hint*: Click the **PAGE LAYOUT** tab, click the **Orientation button** in the Page Setup group, then click **Landscape**.)

2. Change all of the document margins to **0.7"**.

3. Change the document theme to **Organic**.

4. On page one, **center-align** the heading starting "Common-Sense Tips...", and then format it using **24 pt. Arial Black** font and the **Green, Accent 1, Darker 25%** font color (5th column, 5th row in the Theme Colors palette).

5. Add a **bottom paragraph border** to the heading starting "Common-Sense Tips..." using the **Orange, Accent 5, Darker 25%** font color (9th column, 5th row in the Theme Colors palette) and a **3 pt.** width. (*Hint*: To apply the border, select the "Common Sense Tips..." heading, open the Borders and Shading dialog box, click the bottom edge of the preview diagram, set the weight, color, and style of the border by choosing the appropriate options, then click OK. To match the Final Figure, use the **thin top line, thick bottom line** border style.)

6. Move the insertion point before the "G" in "GO" and insert a **Continuous** section break. (*Hint*: Click the Page Layout tab, then click the **Breaks down arrow** in the Page Setup group, then click **Continuous**.) Create **3 columns** of equal width using the default settings. (*Hint*: Click the columns button in the Page Setup group, then click **Three**.) Change the Apply setting to **This point forward**. (*Hint*: Click the launcher in the Page Setup group to open the Page Setup dialog box, click the **Apply to down arrow**, click **This point forward**, then click **OK**.)

7. Apply a **Dropped** Drop Cap to the "G" in "GO". (*Hint*: Click the **Insert tab**, click **Drop Cap** in the Text group, then click **Drop**.) **Justify** the text in the first paragraph.

8. Format the heading "At home..." using the **Heading 1** style, a **14 pt.** font, **bold**, and **Small caps**. (*Hint*: To apply small caps formatting, click the **Home tab**, click the **Font group launcher** to open the Font dialog box, click the small caps check box, then click **OK**.)

9. Use the **Format Painter** to apply the formatting from Step 8 to the following headings:

    a. "At work..."

    b. "In your community..."

    c. "While on the go..."

    d. "Additional Resources..."

10. Format the text under the heading "At Home..." as a **bulleted list**. (*Hint*: The list should contain exactly 13 list items.) Then, complete the following:

    a. Decrease the list indent by one level.

    b. Change the bullets to **check marks**. (*Hint*: Use Wingdings Character Code 252.)

    c. Apply the **Orange, Accent 5** font color (9th column, 1st row in the Theme Colors palette) to the check mark bullets. (*Hint*: The font color of the text should remain black.)

11. Use the **Format Painter** to apply the list formatting from Step 10 to the text under the following headings:

   a. "At work…" (*Hint*: The list should contain exactly seven list items. Stop before the text "You can make the world…Reduce Reuse Recycle".)

   b. "In your community…" (*Hint*: The list should contain exactly 5 list items.)

   c. "While on the go…" (*Hint*: The list should contain exactly 4 list items.)

12. At the bottom of the second column, select the image of the recycle symbol, apply **Square** text wrapping. If necessary, adjust the position and size of the image so that the top side aligns with the text beginning with "You can make…".

13. At the bottom of the third column under the heading "Additional Resources", insert a table with **2 columns** and **5 rows** and then enter the data shown in Table 1. If necessary, remove the hyperlinks from the text in column 1. (*Hint*: To remove a hyperlink, right click the hyperlink, then click **Remove Hyperlink**.)

Table 1: Additional Resources

URL	Comments
www.greenamerica.org	Tips for home
www.gowireless.org	Tips for e-waste
www.kidsbegreen.org	Tips for kids
http://corporatekindness.org	Tips for work

© 2015 Cengage Learning.

14. Change the font size of all text in the table to **9 pt.,** then apply the **Grid Table 4 – Accent 5** table style.

15. On page two, insert **column breaks** before the following headings: (*Hint*: To insert a column break, click before the heading, click the **Page Layout tab**, click **Break**, then click **Column**.)

   a. "Other Upcoming Programs"

   b. "Go Green Tips"

16. At the top of the first column on page two, **center-align** the heading "Greendale Public Library…environmentalist C. J. Clover" and then format it using **16 pt.** font, the **Orange, Accent 5, Darker 25%** font color (9th column, 5th row in the Theme Colors palette), and **bold** formatting.

17. Move the insertion point before the text "C.J. Clover" in the paragraph of text below the heading you just formatted. Insert an Online Picture by searching Office.com for the **woman waterfall** photograph shown in Figure 1. If the **woman waterfall** image is not available, insert another related image of your choice.

Figure 1: Woman Waterfall Photograph

© 2015 Cengage Learning

18. Format the Online Picture using the following parameters:

   a. Set the width to **1.3"**.

   b. Apply **Tight** text wrapping so that the text wraps to the right of the image.

   c. Apply the **Simple Frame, White** picture style.

19. At the bottom of column 1, **center-align** the text that begins with "To reserve your spot..." and ends with "...number of people in your reservation" and then format it using **bold**, and **Green, Accent 1, Lighter 60%** paragraph shading (5th column, 3rd row in the Theme Colors palette).

20. Format the heading "Other Upcoming Programs" using **14 pt. Arial Black** font and the **Green, Accent 1** font color (5th column, 1st row in the Theme Colors palette).

21. Format the heading "This Green Planet" using the **Orange, Accent 5, Darker 25%** font color (9th column, 5th row in the Theme Colors palette), **All caps,** and **Orange, Accent 5, Lighter 80%** paragraph shading (9th column, 2nd row in the Theme Colors palette). (*Hint*: To apply **All caps**, select the heading text, right-click to open the context menu, select Font, then check All caps from the open dialog box.)

22. Use the **Format Painter** to apply the formatting from Step 21 to the following headings:

   a. "Living Green!"

   b. "Kids - Eating Green"

23. Under the heading "This Green Planet", **right-align** the text that starts with "Thursday…" and apply **bold**.

24. Use the **Format Painter** to apply the paragraph formatting from Step 23 to the other instances of date, time, and place under the following headings:

    a. "Living Green!"

    b. "Kids - Eating Green"

25. In column 3, **center-align** the title "Go Green Tips", then format the title using **36 pt. Arial Black** font and the **Green, Accent 1, Darker 25%** font color (5th column, 5th row in the Theme Colors palette).

26. Recolor the clip art under the title using the **Green, Accent color 1 Dark** (2nd color, 2nd row in the Recolor gallery), and then resize the clip art so that it is **2.5"** wide.

27. **Center-align** the three paragraphs starting with "Join us" and ending with "Greendale Public Library!" and then format them using **14 pt.** font, the **Orange, Accent 5, Darker 25%** font color (9th column, 5th row in the Theme Colors palette), and **1.15** line spacing.

28. Check the Spelling & Grammar in the document to identify and correct any spelling errors. (*Hint*: Ignore all grammatical errors and all proper nouns. You should find and correct at least 1 additional spelling error.)

Save your changes, close the document, and exit Word. Follow the directions on the SAM website to submit your completed project.

Water Works
CREATING CHARTS USING REAL-WORLD DATA

PROJECT DESCRIPTION

Created by Diane Smoot, Ph.D., Associate Professor, Harris-Stowe State University

Now that you have mastered Office 2013, you are ready to make an impact. In conjunction with the faculty at your school, a student club called Water Works is analyzing worldwide flood trends with the goal of improving the accuracy of flood forecasting techniques. You decide to join and will assist Water Works in its research.

You have already gathered data from reputable environmental sources, such as the World Resources Institute and the Dartmouth Flood Observatory. You will use Excel to create charts to visually represent this data in an approachable and memorable way.

GETTING STARTED

- Download the following file from the SAM website:

    - **SAM_Excel2013_SE_P1a_*FirstLastName*_1.xlsx**

- Open the file you just downloaded and save it with the name:

    - **SAM_Excel2013_SE_P1a_*FirstLastName*_2.xlsx**

    - *Hint*: If you do not see the **.xlsx** file extension in the Save file dialog box, do not type it. Excel will add the file extension for you automatically.

- With the file **SAM_Excel2013_SE_P1a_*FirstLastName*_2.xlsx** still open, ensure that your first and last name is displayed in cell B6 of the Documentation sheet. If cell B6 does not display your name, delete the file and download a new copy from the SAM website.

PROJECT STEPS

1. Open the *European Floods* worksheet. Add a header to the worksheet using the **Header and Footer Elements** as described below:

    a. In the right header section, insert the **Current Date** element. (*Hint*: This element will appear as &[Date].)

    b. In the left header section, insert the **File Name** element. (*Hint*: This element will appear as &[File].)

    Return to viewing the worksheet in Normal view.

2. Select the range **A1:F2** and create a **2D Clustered Bar Chart**. Resize and reposition the chart so that the upper-left corner of the chart appears in cell **A5** and the lower-right corner of the chart appears in cell **F20**.

3. Change the title of the 2D Clustered Bar Chart to **Number of Major Flood Events by Decade**.

4. Add a **vertical axis** title to the chart and insert **Decade** as the title.

5. Add a **horizontal axis** title to the chart and insert **Number of Major Flood Events** as the title.

6. Add **data labels** to the chart using the **Outside End** option.

7. Change the fill color of the Chart Area to **Olive Green, Accent 3, Lighter 40%** (7th column, 4th row in the Theme Colors palette).

8. Change the fill color of the Plot Area to **Olive Green, Accent 3, Lighter 80%** (7th column, 2nd row in the Theme Colors palette).

9. Insert a **text box** in the worksheet as described below. (*Hint*: Use the Text Box button in the Insert Shapes section of the Chart Tools Format tab.)

   a. Insert the text **Europe** in the text box.

   b. Move the text box to the approximate position shown in Figure 1. (*Hint*: The text box control should line up with the 1950-1959 data bar.)

Figure 1: European Floods Worksheet

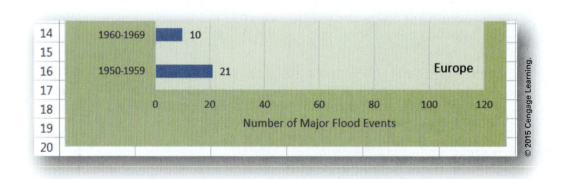

© 2015 Cengage Learning.

10. Switch to viewing the *High-Low Magnitude Floods* worksheet. Select the range **A3:C24**. Using the Recommended Charts option, create a **Clustered Column Chart**. Resize and reposition the chart so that the upper-left corner is located in cell **E3** and the lower-right corner is located in cell **P24**.

11. Change the style of the chart to **Chart Style 14**.

12. Change the title of the chart to **Worldwide Low- and High-Magnitude Floods**.

13. Reposition the chart legend using the **Top** positioning option.

14. Update the **vertical** axis in the chart as described below:

    a. Change the **Maximum** bounds of the axis to **225** and the **Minimum** bounds of the axis to **0**. (*Hint*: The Minimum bounds value will change when you update the Maximum bounds value, so update the Maximum bounds value first.)

    b. Update the **Major** units of the axis to **25**.

15. Add a **vertical axis** title to the chart and insert **Number of Floods** as the title.

16. Add **Primary Major Vertical Gridlines** to the chart.

17. Add a **horizontal axis** title to the chart and insert **Year** as the title.

18. Change the color of the Chart Area to **Blue, Accent 1, Lighter 80%** (5th column, 2nd row in the Theme Colors palette).

19. Change the color of the Plot Area to **Dark Blue, Text 2, Lighter 60%** (4th column, 3rd row in the Theme Colors palette).

    Confirm that your worksheet matches Figure 2.

Figure 2: High-Low Magnitude Floods Worksheet (Columns E–P)

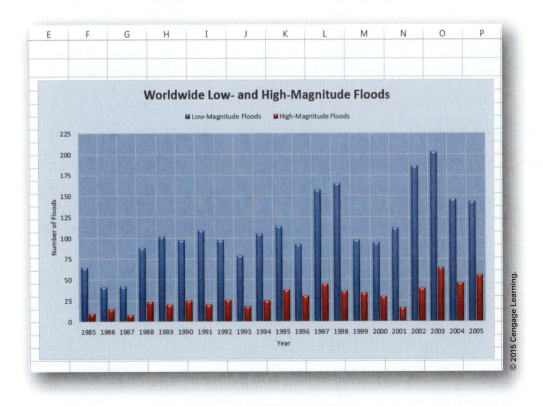

Save your changes, close the workbook, and exit Excel. Follow the directions on the SAM website to submit your completed project.

Microsoft Office 2013 Illustrated Fundamentals Excel

Units G-I: SAM Capstone Project 1a

SpringLeaf Designs
FORMATTING, FORMULAS, AND CHARTS

PROJECT DESCRIPTION

Christy Chen works at SpringLeaf Designs, a Seattle-based company that makes jewelry and accessories out of recycled materials. Christy has created a workbook to analyze costs and profits by product line. She has also compiled sales forecasts for the next five years. She has asked you to complete the data entry and analysis and to format the worksheets so they have a consistent and professional look.

GETTING STARTED

- Download the following file from the SAM website:

    ○ **IF_Excel2013_CS_UG-I_P1a_*FirstLastName*_1.xlsx**

- Open the file you just downloaded and save it with the name:

    ○ **IF_Excel2013_CS_UG-I_P1a_*FirstLastName*_2.xlsx**

    ○ *Hint*: If you do not see the **.xlsx** file extension in the Save file dialog box, do not type it. Excel will add the file extension for you automatically.

- With the file **IF_Excel2013_CS_UG-I_P1a_*FirstLastName*_2.xlsx** still open, ensure that your first and last name is displayed in cell B6 of the Documentation sheet. If cell B6 does not display your name, delete the file and download a new copy from the SAM website.

PROJECT STEPS

1. Switch to the *Sheet1* worksheet. Make the following formatting changes:

    a. **Merge and center** the range F3:I3. Apply the **Heading 2** cell style to the merged cell and change the fill color to **Blue, Accent 5, Lighter 60%** (9th column, 3rd row in the Theme Colors palette). Replicate these formatting steps for range C3:E3.

    b. Make the fill color of the range B19:I19 **White, Background 1, Darker 35%** (1st column, 5th row in the Theme Colors palette).

    c. Add a **Thick Box Border** around the range B2:I19.

    d. Add a **Left Border** to the ranges C3:C19 and F3:F19.

2. Make the following formatting changes to the range C4:I4:

   a. Change the font to **Verdana**.

   b. Change the font color to **Blue-Gray, Text 2** (4th Column, 1st row in the Theme Colors palette).

   c. Change the font size to **10 pt**.

   d. Apply **bold** formatting.

   e. **Center align** cell contents.

   f. Apply **text wrapping**.

3. Apply **bold** formatting to the ranges B19:C19 and E21:E23.

4. **Italicize** text in the ranges B6:B8, B10:B12, and B15:B16.

5. Add a comment to cell F4 with the text: **Average selling price listed. Prices vary slightly by store location and channel.** Remove any existing text from the comment box, including the user name, before entering the new comment.

6. In cell F6, type a formula to calculate the average selling price per beaded earring unit. (*Hint*: The average selling price for the beaded earrings is calculated by dividing the total Sales values in cell C6, by the number of Units Sold value in cell D6.) Copy the formula from cell F6 to the ranges F7:F8, F10:F13, and F15:F18.

7. Apply the **Currency** Number format to the range F6:F18. (*Tip:* The **Currency** Number format should have 2 decimal places displayed by default. If it doesn't, update the range to display 2 decimal places.)

8. Select the range D6:D18 and use the **Quick Analysis** tool to create a formula that calculates the total number of units sold. The formula will use the **SUM** function and should appear in cell D19.

9. Enter a formula in cell E6 to calculate the percentage of total sales accounted for by beaded earrings. The formula will divide beaded earring sales in C6 by total sales in C19. (*Hint*: Use an absolute reference to the total sales in cell C19, and a relative reference to beaded earring sales in cell C6.) Copy the formula from cell E6 to the ranges E7:E8, E10:E13, and E15:E18.

10. Apply the **Percentage** Number format with no decimal places to the range E6:E18.

11. Based on range I6:I18, enter a formula in cell I21 that uses the **MAX** function to identify the highest average unit profit across SpringLeaf Design's product lines.

12. Based on range I6:I18, enter a formula in cell I22 that uses the **MIN** function to identify the lowest average unit profit across SpringLeaf Design's product lines.

13. Based on range I6:I18, enter a formula in cell I23 that uses the **AVERAGE** function to calculate SpringLeaf Design's average profit per unit across product lines.

14. Add a **Thick Box Border** around range E21:I23.

15. Use conditional formatting to apply **Solid Fill Blue Data Bars** to the range I6:I18.

16. Find and replace the misspelled word **Cufs** with the correctly spelled word **Cuffs**.

17. Rename *Sheet1* **Sales Analysis** and apply the **Green, Accent 6** tab color (10th column, 1st row of the Theme Colors palette) to the sheet tab.

18. Go to the *Forecast Data* worksheet. Move the contents of cell G10 to cell G9.

19. Fill the range E3:G3 with a number series based on the contents of range C3:D3. (*Hint*: You can ignore the error message in cells E3:G3.)

20. Format the range C4:G9 with the **Accounting** Number format with no decimal places. (*Hint*: Depending on how you complete this action, the number format may appear as **Custom** instead of **Accounting**.)

21. Make the following changes to the column widths and row heights:

    a. Change the width of the column B to best fit (using AutoFit) its contents.

    b. Change the width of columns C through F to **9.0 characters**.

    c. Change the height of row 2 to **40 pt**.

22. Enter a formula in cell C10 using the **SUM** function to total the values in range C4:C9. Copy the formula from cell C10 to the range D10:G10.

23. Add a **Thick Box Border** cell border around range B2:H10.

24. Insert a **3-D Pie** chart based on the range B4:C9 to graph 2016 Sales by product line. Apply chart **Style 7** and enter the text **2016 Sales by Product** as the chart title. Reposition the chart so the upper-left corner is in cell B13.

25. Select the range B3:G9 and use the **Quick Analysis** tool to create a **Clustered Column** chart showing the sales forecasted through 2020 for SpringLeaf Design's product line. (*Tip:* The data should be grouped by product in your chart.) Apply chart style **Style 8** to the chart and enter the text **Sales Forecast** as the chart title. Resize and reposition the chart so that the upper-left corner is in cell J2 and the bottom-right corner is in cell P10.

26. Insert a header in the worksheet. Using the Header & Footer Elements, display the worksheet name in the center header section and the current date in the right header section.

27. Hide the gridlines in the worksheet.

28. Go to the *Forecast Chart* worksheet. Make the following changes to the Stacked Bar chart:

    a. Change the data labels to the **Center** position.

    b. Reposition the chart legend to appear in the **Right** position.

Save your changes, close the workbook, and exit Excel. Follow the directions on the SAM website to submit your completed project.

Zombie Apocalypse
CREATING QUERIES FOR QUICK ACCESS TO DATA

PROJECT DESCRIPTION

Created by Emily H. Shepard, Instructor, Central Carolina Community College

The only place you used to be able to find zombies was in horror movies or on television. Since the Zombie Apocalypse began in Boston, Massachusetts, finding a zombie is the least of the world's problems. You are a member of the Shepards (named after the group's founder, Emily Shepard), a group of survivors attempting to end the zombie plague. Your group combats the zombies by finding zombie herds before they become major threats and by administering the experimental zombie vaccine (as it becomes available) in neighboring towns.

You are responsible for tracking your team's efforts in an Access database. You've already generated a few tables of records regarding medics, missions, zombie herds, and cities that your group supports. Because time is of the essence, you've decided to create queries to allow you to more rapidly access and update table data.

GETTING STARTED

- Download the following file from the SAM website:

  - **SAM_Access2013_SE_P1a_*FirstLastName*_1.accdb**

- Open the file you just downloaded and save it with the name:

  - **SAM_Access2013_SE_P1a_*FirstLastName*_2.accdb**

  - *Hint*: If you do not see the **.accdb** file extension in the Save file dialog box, do not type it. Access will add the file extension for you automatically.

- Open the **_GradingInfoTable** table and ensure that your first and last name is displayed as the first record in the table. If the table does not contain your name, delete the file and download a new copy from the SAM website.

PROJECT STEPS

1. Create a new query in Query Design View based on the *KnownHerds* table as described below:

   a. Add the fields **HerdID**, **HerdSize**, **Active**, **FirstEncounterDate**, **FirstEncounterLocation**, and **HerdNotes** to the query in that order.

b. Add a **descending** sort order on the *FirstEncounterLocation* field.

c. Save the query with the name **Known Herds Query**.

Run the *Known Herds Query* query to confirm it works, and then close the query.

2. Create a new query in Query Design View based on the *City* table as described below:

a. Add the **City**, **State**, **Population**, **VaccinatedPopulation**, **LastReview**, and **MissionSecurityCost** fields (from the *City* table) to the query in that order.

b. Add a **descending** sort order on the *State* field.

c. Save the query with the name **City Query**.

Run the *City Query* query to confirm it works, and then close the query.

3. Create a new parameter query in Design View based on the *VaccinationMissions* and *Medics* tables as described below:

a. Add the **VMissionID** field from the *VaccinationMissions* table to the query.

b. After the *VMissionID* field, add the **MedicFirstName** and **MedicLastName** fields (in that order) from the *Medics* table to the query.

c. After the *MedicLastName* field, add the **VMTeamSize**, **VMCasualties**, **VMCasualtyNumber**, and **VMLocation** fields (in that order) from the *VaccinationMissions* table to the query.

d. Add the criterion **[Enter Vaccination Mission Location]** (including brackets) to the *VMLocation* field.

e. Save the query with the name **Vaccination Parameter Query**.

Run the *Vaccination Parameter Query* query to confirm it works, and then close the query. (*Hint*: If you enter **NCRAL** as the parameter value, the query should return 6 records.)

4. Create a new query in Query Design View based on the *ReconMissions* table with the following options:

a. Add the fields **RMissionID**, **RMLocation**, **RMEndDate**, and **NewHerd** from the *ReconMissions* table to the query in that order.

b. Add an **ascending** sort order on the *RMLocation* field.

c. Add a criterion to select only those records where the *RMEndDate* field is **greater than 5/8/2014**.

d. Save the query with the name **Recent Recon Query**.

Run the *Recent Recon Query* query to confirm it works, and then close the query. (*Hint*: If you entered the criterion correctly, the query should display 9 records.)

5. Create a copy of the *Medic Query* query, using the name **Living Medic Query**. In Query Design View, modify the *Living Medic Query* query as described below:

   a. Modify the query to show only records where the *Deceased* field is equal to **False**.

   b. Save the query.

   Run the *Living Medic Query* query to confirm it works, and then close the query. (*Hint*: If you modified the criterion correctly, the query should return 9 records.)

6. Create a copy of the *Medic Query* query and name it **Expert Deceased Query**. In Query Design View, modify the *Expert Deceased Query* query as described below:

   a. Modify the query to show only records where the *DateDeceased* is **greater than or equal to 4/20/2014** and the *SecurityLevel* is **equal to Expert**.

   b. Save the query.

   Run the *Expert Deceased Query* query to confirm it works, and then close the query. (*Hint*: If you modified the criterion correctly, the query should return 2 records.)

7. Create a copy of the *Recon Query* query and name it **New or Large Recon Query**. In Query Design View, modify the *New or Large Recon Query* query as described below:

   a. Add criteria to the query so that it will return records with an *RTeamSize* value **greater than 10** or a *NewHerd* field value of **True**.

   b. Save the query.

   Run the *New or Large Recon Query* query to confirm that it works, and then close the query. (*Hint*: If you entered the criteria correctly, the query should return 9 records.)

8. Create a copy of the *Recon Query* query and name it **Recon N Location Query**. In Query Design View, modify the *Recon N Location Query* query as described below:

   a. Using a wildcard criterion, modify the query so that it only returns records with *RMLocation* field values that begin with the letter **N**.

   b. Save the query.

   Run the *Recon N Location Query* query to confirm that it works, and then close the query. (*Hint*: If you entered the criterion correctly, the query should return 6 records.)

9. Create a copy of the *Vaccination Query* query and name it **Containment Vac Query**. In Query Design View, modify the *Containment Vac Query* query as described below:

   a. Modify the query to show only records where the *Specialty* field value is equal to **Containment**.

   b. Hide the **Specialty** field, so that it does not appear in the query results.

   c. Save the query.

   Run the *Containment Vac Query* query to confirm it works, and then close the query. (*Hint*: Your query should return 3 records when run and, if you switch back to Query Design View, the *Specialty* field should still be available in the query.)

10. Create a copy of the *Vaccination Query* query and name it **Vaccination Sort Query**. In Query Design View, modify the *Vaccination Sort Query* query as described below:

    a. Modify the query to sort records first in **ascending** order by the values of the *Specialty* field and then in **descending** order by the values of the *TotalVaccinations* field.

    b. Save the query.

    Run the *Vaccination Sort Query* query to confirm it works, and then close your query.

11. Create a copy of the *Vaccination Query* query and name it **High Vaccination Query**. In Query Design View, modify the *High Vaccination Query* query as described below:

    a. Add a criterion to select only those records where the value in the *AdministeredVaccinations* field is **greater than or equal to 20**.

    b. Sort the query in **descending** order by the *AdministeredVaccinations* field values.

    c. Save the query.

    Run the *High Vaccination Query* query to confirm it works, and then close the query. (*Hint*: If you entered the criterion correctly, the query should return 8 results.)

12. Open the *Vaccination Mission Query* query in Design View, and then hide the **VMTeamSize** and **VMCasualties** fields in the query. Save the query, and then run it to confirm the query works as expected before closing it. (*Hint*: The *VMTeamSize* and *VMCasualties* fields should not appear in the query results, but they should still be available when viewing the query in Design View.)

13. Open the *City Resource Query* query in Design View and update it as described below:

    a. Delete the criterion associated with the *Security* field.

    b. Move the **VaccinatedPopulation** field so that it is the last field in the query (after the *WaterAccess* field).

    c. Add an **ascending** sort order on the *MedicalFacilities* and *WaterAccess* fields.

    d. Save the query.

Run the *City Resource Query* query to confirm that it matches Figure 1, and then close the query.

Figure 1: City Resource Query

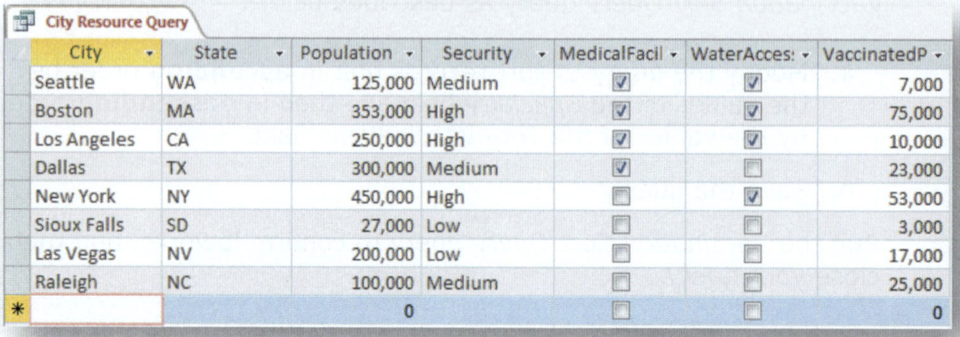

City	State	Population	Security	MedicalFacil	WaterAcces:	VaccinatedP
Seattle	WA	125,000	Medium	✓	✓	7,000
Boston	MA	353,000	High	✓	✓	75,000
Los Angeles	CA	250,000	High	✓	✓	10,000
Dallas	TX	300,000	Medium	✓	☐	23,000
New York	NY	450,000	High	☐	✓	53,000
Sioux Falls	SD	27,000	Low	☐	☐	3,000
Las Vegas	NV	200,000	Low	☐	☐	17,000
Raleigh	NC	100,000	Medium	☐	☐	25,000
		0		☐	☐	0

© 2015 Cengage Learning.

14. Use the **Form** button to create a simple form based on the *Medic Query* query, and then save the form as **Medic Form** and close the form.

15. Using the Report Wizard, create a new report based on the *Recon Query* query with the following options:

    a. Include the **RMissionID**, **RTeamSize**, **RMLocation**, **RMEndDate**, **HerdEncountered**, **NewHerd**, and **HerdID** fields (in that order) from the *Recon Query* query in the report.

    b. Group the report by the default **HerdID** field, but use no additional grouping in the report.

    c. Use no additional sorting in the report.

    d. Use a **Stepped** layout and **Landscape** orientation for the report.

    e. Name the report **Recon Report**, and then preview the report to confirm it matches Figure 2.

Save and close the report.

Figure 2: Recon Report in Print Preview View

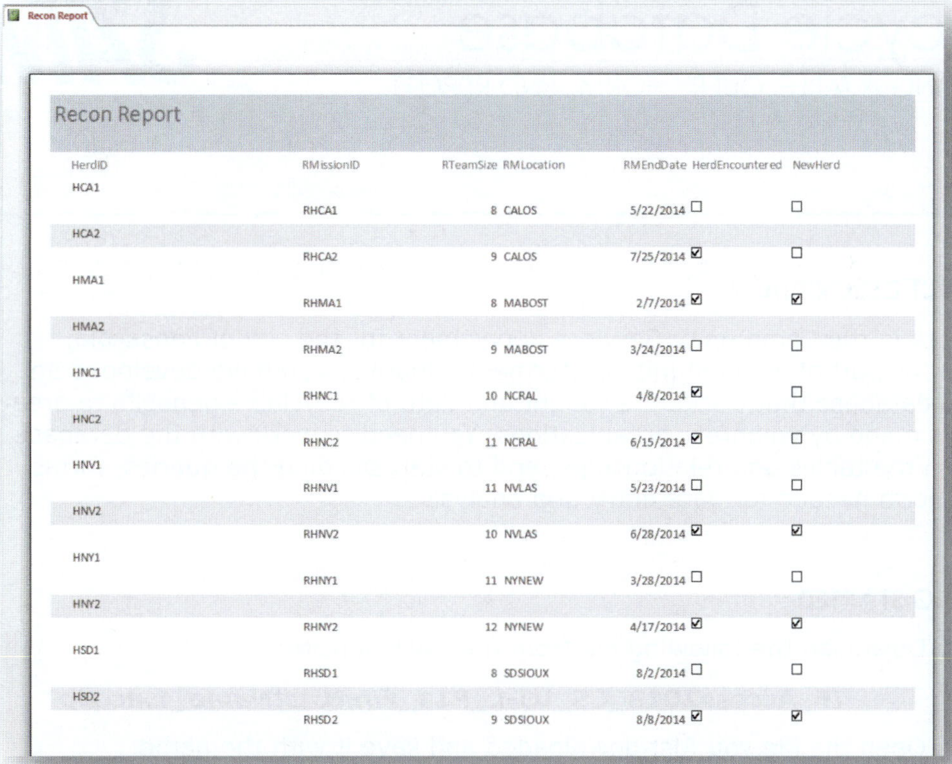

Recon Report

HerdID	RMissionID	RTeamSize	RMLocation	RMEndDate	HerdEncountered	NewHerd
HCA1						
	RHCA1	8	CALOS	5/22/2014	☐	☐
HCA2						
	RHCA2	9	CALOS	7/25/2014	☑	☐
HMA1						
	RHMA1	8	MABOST	2/7/2014	☑	☑
HMA2						
	RHMA2	9	MABOST	3/24/2014	☐	☐
HNC1						
	RHNC1	10	NCRAL	4/8/2014	☑	☐
HNC2						
	RHNC2	11	NCRAL	6/15/2014	☑	☐
HNV1						
	RHNV1	11	NVLAS	5/23/2014	☐	☐
HNV2						
	RHNV2	10	NVLAS	6/28/2014	☑	☑
HNY1						
	RHNY1	11	NYNEW	3/28/2014	☐	☐
HNY2						
	RHNY2	12	NYNEW	4/17/2014	☑	☑
HSD1						
	RHSD1	8	SDSIOUX	8/2/2014	☐	☐
HSD2						
	RHSD2	9	SDSIOUX	8/8/2014	☑	☑

Save and close any open database objects. Compact and repair your database, and then exit Access. Follow the directions on the SAM website to submit your completed project.

Recycle Database

CREATING A TABLE, QUERY, FORM, AND REPORT

PROJECT DESCRIPTION

You work in the Community Services department for the city of Pensacola, Florida. As part of a community betterment initiative, you have developed an Access database that tracks the weight and date of recyclable deposits to area landfills made by volunteer organizations. You need to work with the database to finish the tables and relationships, and to start building the queries, forms, and reports needed for data entry and analysis.

GETTING STARTED

- Download the following file from the SAM website:

    - **IF_Access2013_CS_UJ-L_P1a_*FirstLastName*_1.accdb**

- Open the file you just downloaded and save it with the name:

    - **IF_Access2013_CS_ UJ-L_P1a_*FirstLastName*_2.accdb**

    - *Hint*: If you do not see the **.accdb** file extension in the Save file dialog box, do not type it. Access will add the file extension for you automatically.

- Open the **_GradingInfoTable** table and ensure that your first and last name is displayed as the first record in the table. If the table does not contain your name, delete the file and download a new copy from the SAM website.

PROJECT STEPS

1. Create and save a new table in Design view with four fields as follows:

    a. Add a field with the name **AwardNo** with an **AutoNumber** data type.

    b. Add a field with the name **ClubNo** with a **Number** data type.

    c. Add a field with the name **AwardName** with a **Short Text** data type.

    d. Add a field with the name **AwardDate** with a **Date/Time** data type.

    e. Set **AwardNo** field as the table's primary key.

    Save the table with the name **ClubAwards**, but do not close it.

2. With the *ClubAwards* table still open in Table Design view, change the field size of the *ClubNo* field to **Integer**. Save and close the table.

3. Open the *Clubs* table in Table Design view. Add another field to the *Clubs* table using the field name **ClubEmail** and a Hyperlink data type.

4. Save the *Clubs* table, switch to Datasheet view and widen the ClubEmail column. Enter the ClubEmail field data shown in Table 1. After entering the data, save and close the *Clubs* table. (*Note*: The ClubStreet, ClubCity, ClubState, ClubZip, and ClubPhone fields are not shown in Table 1.)

Table 1: ClubEmail Data

Club No	ClubName	FName	LName	ClubEmail
1	Access Users Group	Arlene	Millen	millen@hug.net
2	Boy Scouts Troop 6	Jordan	Mahring	mahring@bsatroop6.org
3	Great Plains 4-H Club	Yaneth	Smith	ysmith@greatplains.org
4	Lions of Bellview	John	Harmon	info@lions.org
5	Junior League	Earl	Hutchison	hutch@juniorleague.org
6	Girl Scouts Troop 12	Brittany	Langguth	blangguth@girlscouts.org
7	Oak Hill Liberty	Amanda	Wang	wang@liberty.com

© 2015 Cengage Learning.

5. Open the Relationships window and add the *ClubAwards* table. Link the *Clubs* table to the *ClubAwards* table using the common **ClubNo** field in a **one-to-many** relationship and be sure to **enforce referential integrity** on the relationship, as shown in Figure 1.

6. With the Relationships window still open, add the *Awards* table. Link the *Awards* table to the *ClubAwards* table using the common **AwardName** field in a **one-to-many** relationship and be sure to **enforce referential integrity** on the relationship, as shown in Figure 1. Save and close the Relationships window.

Figure 1: Relationships

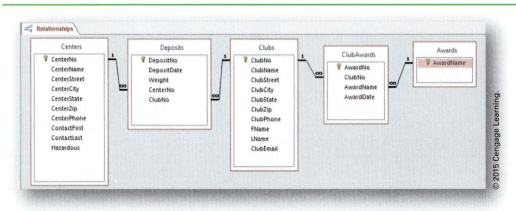

© 2015 Cengage Learning.

7. Create a new query in Query Design view using the *Centers*, *Deposits*, and *Clubs* tables with the following options:

   a. Select the following fields in the following order for the query: The **CenterName** field from the *Centers* table, the **ClubName** field from the *Clubs* table, the **DepositDate** field and **Weight** field from the *Deposits* table.

   b. Add an **ascending sort** order on the CenterName, ClubName, and DepositDate fields.

   c. Add criteria so that only those records with a DepositDate field value **less than 1/1/2015** and a Weight field value **greater than 100** are selected. (*Hint*: The records returned by the query will fulfill both criteria.)

   d. Save the query with the name **Large 2014 Deposits**.

   Run the query and check it against Figure 2, and then close the *Large 2014 Deposits* query.

Figure 2: Large 2014 Deposits Query

CenterName	ClubName	DepositDate	Weight
Advanced Disposal Service	Junior League	3/5/2014	150
Escambia County Landfill	Boy Scouts Troop 6	4/19/2014	105
Escambia County Landfill	Lions of Bellview	4/4/2014	115
Escambia County Landfill	Oak Hill Liberty	8/20/2014	205
Perdido Landfill	Access Users Group	3/6/2014	200
Perdido Landfill	Boy Scouts Troop 6	2/20/2014	200
Rolling Hills Trash	Access Users Group	8/21/2014	105
Rolling Hills Trash	Girl Scouts Troop 12	2/13/2014	200
Rolling Hills Trash	Junior League	2/8/2014	150
Rolling Hills Trash	Junior League	3/2/2014	150
Rolling Hills Trash	Lions of Bellview	2/28/2014	125

© 2015 Cengage Learning.

8. Create a new query in Query Design view using the *Centers*, *Deposits*, and *Clubs* tables with the following options:

   a. Select the following fields in the following order for the query: The **ClubName** field from the *Clubs* table, the **DepositDate** and **Weight** fields from the *Deposits* table, and the **CenterName** field from the *Centers* table.

   b. Add an **ascending sort** order on the ClubName field, and a **descending sort** order on the DepositDate field.

c. Add criteria so that only those records with a *ClubName* field value of **Boy Scouts Troop 6** or those with a *CenterName* field value equal to **Rolling Hills Trash** are selected. (*Hint*: The records returned by the query will fulfill either criteria.)

d. Save the query with the name **Boy Scouts Or Rolling Hills**.

Run the query, check it against Figure 3, and then close it.

Figure 3: Boy Scouts Or Rolling Hills Query

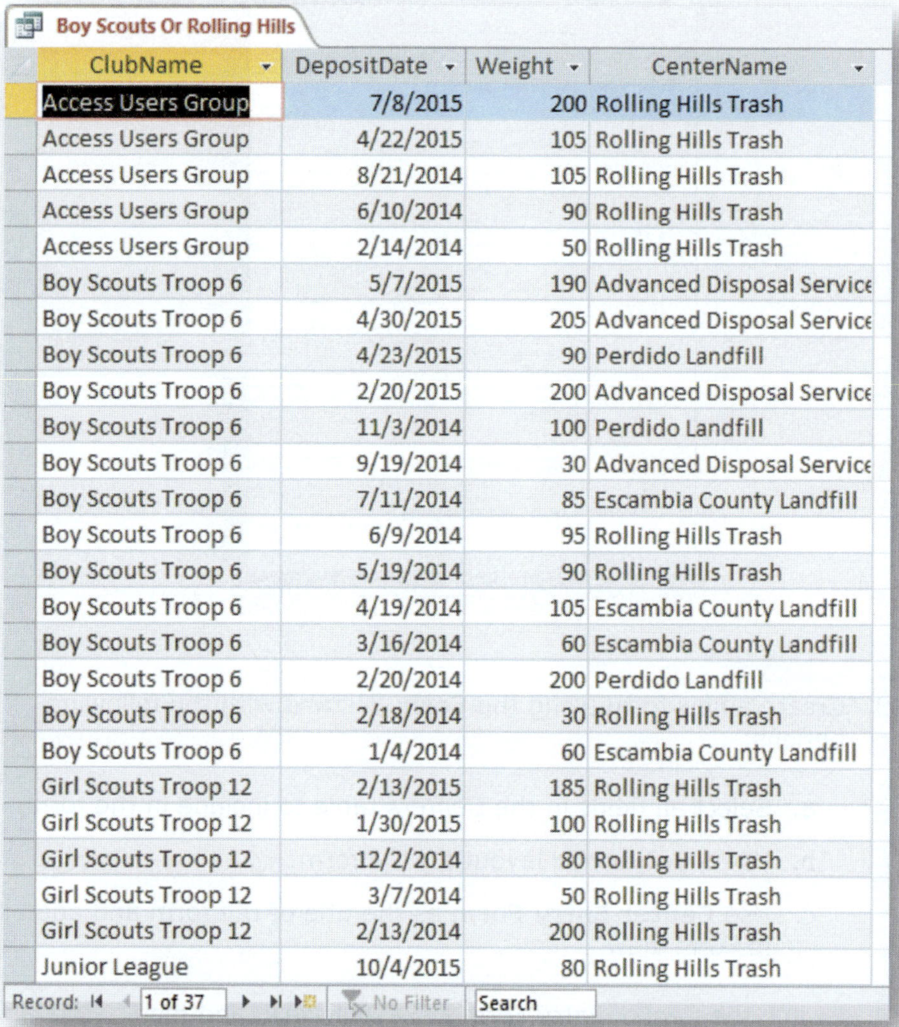

ClubName	DepositDate	Weight	CenterName
Access Users Group	7/8/2015	200	Rolling Hills Trash
Access Users Group	4/22/2015	105	Rolling Hills Trash
Access Users Group	8/21/2014	105	Rolling Hills Trash
Access Users Group	6/10/2014	90	Rolling Hills Trash
Access Users Group	2/14/2014	50	Rolling Hills Trash
Boy Scouts Troop 6	5/7/2015	190	Advanced Disposal Service
Boy Scouts Troop 6	4/30/2015	205	Advanced Disposal Service
Boy Scouts Troop 6	4/23/2015	90	Perdido Landfill
Boy Scouts Troop 6	2/20/2015	200	Advanced Disposal Service
Boy Scouts Troop 6	11/3/2014	100	Perdido Landfill
Boy Scouts Troop 6	9/19/2014	30	Advanced Disposal Service
Boy Scouts Troop 6	7/11/2014	85	Escambia County Landfill
Boy Scouts Troop 6	6/9/2014	95	Rolling Hills Trash
Boy Scouts Troop 6	5/19/2014	90	Rolling Hills Trash
Boy Scouts Troop 6	4/19/2014	105	Escambia County Landfill
Boy Scouts Troop 6	3/16/2014	60	Escambia County Landfill
Boy Scouts Troop 6	2/20/2014	200	Perdido Landfill
Boy Scouts Troop 6	2/18/2014	30	Rolling Hills Trash
Boy Scouts Troop 6	1/4/2014	60	Escambia County Landfill
Girl Scouts Troop 12	2/13/2015	185	Rolling Hills Trash
Girl Scouts Troop 12	1/30/2015	100	Rolling Hills Trash
Girl Scouts Troop 12	12/2/2014	80	Rolling Hills Trash
Girl Scouts Troop 12	3/7/2014	50	Rolling Hills Trash
Girl Scouts Troop 12	2/13/2014	200	Rolling Hills Trash
Junior League	10/4/2015	80	Rolling Hills Trash

Record: 1 of 37 — No Filter — Search

© 2015 Cengage Learning.

9. In Datasheet view of the *Boy Scouts Or Rolling Hills* query find *Junior League* in any record in the *ClubName* field, and change the value to **Junior League of Pensacola**. Widen the ClubName field to see the entire entry, then save and close the *Boy Scouts Or Rolling Hills* query.

10. Use the **Form Tool** to create a new form based on the *Clubs* table. Save the form with the name **Club Entry Form** and open it in Form view.

11. Navigate to the record for ClubNo 4, Lions of Bellview, and change the FName value from John to **Sherry**. Change the LName value from Harmon to **Timbrook**.

12. Enter a new record in the Club Entry Form as shown in Figure 4.

Figure 4: Club Entry Form

Club Entry Form	
Clubs	
ClubNo	8
ClubName	Optimists Club
ClubStreet	2030 Peachtree Drive
ClubCity	Pensacola
ClubState	FL
ClubZip	32514
ClubPhone	(555) 988-7777
FName	Camilo
LName	Watkins
ClubEmail	cwatkins@coldmail.com

Record: ◄ ◄ 8 of 8 ► ►I ►* No Filter Search

© 2015 Cengage Learning.

13. Create a new form using the **Form Wizard** with the following options:

   a. Select all fields in the *Centers* table to include in the form.

   b. Use a **Columnar** layout for the form.

   c. Use **Center Entry Form** as the title of the form and open it in Form view.

14. Switch the *Center Entry Form* to Layout view, and modify the labels in the first column so that there is a space between the words, as shown in Figure 5. (*Hint*: You will modify 9 labels in the form.)

15. Switch to the *Center Entry Form* to Form view and enter the new record shown in Figure 5.

Figure 5: Center Entry Form

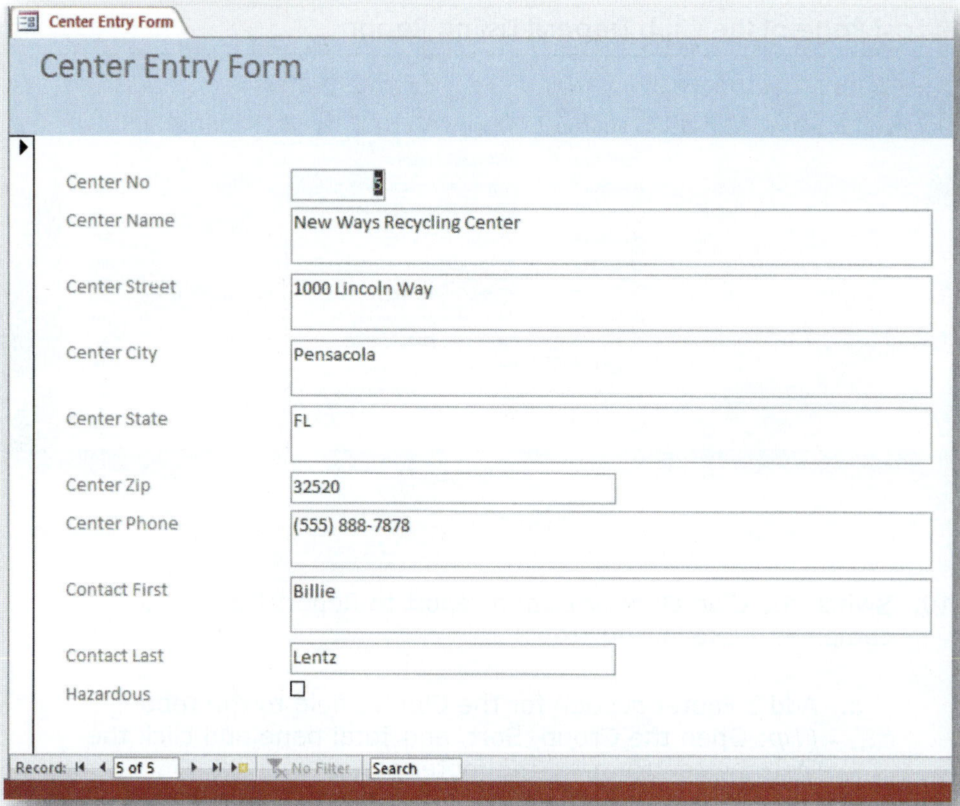

© 2015 Cengage Learning.

16. Navigate to the first record in the *Center Entry Form* (which has a Center No field value of 1) and edit the Center Street value from 13009 Bumper Road to **13008 Brentwood Drive**. Save and close the *Center Entry Form*.

17. Create a new report using the **Report Wizard** with the following options:

   a. Select the following fields in the following order for the report: the **ClubName** field from the *Clubs* table, **CenterName** field from the *Centers* table, and the **DepositDate** field and **Weight** field from the *Deposits* table.

   b. View the data by Clubs, do not add any additional grouping levels.

   c. Sort the report in **ascending order** by the DepositDate field.

   d. Use a **Stepped** layout and **Portrait** orientation.

   e. Title the report **Club Deposit Listing**.

   Preview the report.

18. Switch the *Club Deposit Listing* report to Layout view, and resize and position the DepositDate column, as shown in Figure 6. (*Note*: Figure 6 shows only a portion of the last page of the report.)

Figure 6: Last Page of the Club Deposit Listing Report

© 2015 Cengage Learning.

19. Switch the *Club Deposit Listing* report to Report Design view and complete the following steps:

   a. Add a Footer section for the ClubNo field to the report. (*Tip*: Open the Group, Sort, and Total pane and click the More button to make the footer option available.)

   b. Add a text box control to the ClubNo Footer section directly below the Weight text box in the Detail section.

   c. In the Unbound text box in the ClubNo Footer section, enter the expression **=Sum([Weight])** to subtotal the weight for each ClubNo.

   d. Change the label in the ClubNo Footer section to read **Subtotal:**

20. **Bold** the new Subtotal: label as well as the text box with the =Sum([Weight]) expression in the ClubNo Footer section. Save the report, preview the last page of the report, and then close the *Club Deposit Listing* report.

Save and close any open objects in your database. Compact and repair your database, close it, and exit Access. Follow the directions on the SAM website to submit your completed project.

Gamitopia EdTech

ENHANCED SKILLS

PROJECT DESCRIPTION

Created by Barbara M. Waxer, Instructor & Trainer, Santa Fe Community College

Your company, Gamitopia EdTech, has received a federal grant to create classroom-based gaming systems that help students identify their interests and develop 21st century learning skills—a trend called "gamification." Because gamification is new and not well understood, you will first educate parents and the community about how it works and the benefits it offers to students.

You will introduce the first game, which is aimed at high school freshmen, at a state school board meeting, where your team will demonstrate the game for board members and other attendees. While your team finishes the game, you will complete an informative presentation on gamification using tables, charts, animation, and graphics in PowerPoint.

GETTING STARTED

- Download the following file from the SAM website:

    - **SAM_PPT2013_SE_P1a_*FirstLastName*_1.pptx**

- Open the file you just downloaded and save it with the name:

    - **SAM_PPT2013_SE_P1a_*FirstLastName*_2.pptx**

    - *Hint*: If you do not see the **.pptx** file extension in the Save file dialog box, do not type it. PowerPoint will add the file extension for you automatically.

- To complete this Project, you will also need to download and save the following support file from the SAM website:

    - **support_SAM_P13_SE_P1a_brain.jpg**

    - *Hint*: Opening an image may alter its file size. If you open an image support file, delete the file and download a new copy from the SAM website.

- With the file **SAM_PPT2013_SE_P1a_*FirstLastName*_2.pptx** still open, ensure that your first and last name is displayed in the presenter notes on Slide 1. If the presenter notes do not display your name, delete the file and download a new copy from the SAM website.

PROJECT STEPS

1. Apply the **fourth** variant of the **Slice** theme to the presentation.

2. On Slide 1 ("Gamification and Education"), select the text "Gamification and Education: Top Things to Know" and apply the WordArt style **Fill - White, Text 1, Shadow** (1st column, 1st row in the WordArt Style gallery).

3. On Slide 2 ("What is Gamification?"), select the text "What is Gamification?", change the font to **Georgia**, and then **bold** the text.

4. With Slide 2 still displaying, move the round trophy picture down and to the left so that it is vertically centered across from the middle of the badge picture and positioned to the immediate right of the progress bar picture.

5. With Slide 2 still displaying, select all three pictures, and then group them.

6. On Slide 3 ("Hours Spent Playing Video, Mobile, & Computer Games"), select the text box "3 Billion" (in the blue sphere) and complete the following:

   a. Apply the animation **Grow & Turn** (10th option in the Entrance section of the Animation gallery).

   b. Apply the animation timing **Start After Previous**.

   c. Set the animation delay to **01.00** seconds.

7. With Slide 3 still displaying, insert a new text box and complete the following:

   a. Type **Globally per week** in the new text box.

   b. **Bold** the text.

   c. Resize the text box to a width of **2.5"**.

   d. Position the text box so that it is centered immediately above the blue sphere.

8. On Slide 4 ("What Leads to Learning?"), convert the bulleted list to a numbered list.

9. On Slide 5 ("Results"), change the chart data in cell B3 to **28**, and change the chart data in cell B5 to **32**.

10. On Slide 6 ("Learning Impacts"), use the content placeholder to insert a table with **2 columns** and **5 rows**, and then enter the data shown in Table 1.

Table 1: Data for Slide 6

Activity	Retention
Read	10%
Listen with visuals	30%
Observe action	50%
Perform action	90%

11. On Slide 7 ("Brain Food"), in the content placeholder, type the following bulleted list items:

    Confidence
    Motivation
    Deeper learning

    a. Change the font size of the list items to **32 pt.**

    b. Apply the animation **Wipe** (6th option in Entrance section of the Animation gallery) using the animation timing **Start After Previous**.

12. On Slide 8 ("Brain Science"), complete the following:

    a. Convert the bulleted list to the SmartArt graphic **Vertical Box List** (2nd column, 2nd row in the List section of the Choose a SmartArt Graphic gallery).

    b. Apply the SmartArt style **Moderate Effect** (4th column, 1st row in the SmartArt Styles gallery).

13. With Slide 8 still displaying, insert the picture **support_SAM_P13_ SE_P1a_brain.jpg** available for download from the SAM website. Move the picture so that its right edge touches the right side of the slide, and then apply the **Send to Back** option.

14. Move Slide 8 to become the new Slide 7.

15. Apply the transition **Reveal** (7th option in the Subtle section of the Transition to This Slide gallery) to all slides in the presentation. Set the duration to **02.00** seconds.

16. On the new Slide 8 ("Brain Food"), apply the transition **Peel Off** (8th option in the Exciting section of the Transition to This Slide gallery) only to this slide.

17. Add a footer to all slides except the title slide.

    a. Type the footer text:

       Gamitopia EdTech

    b. Include the **slide number**.

Save your changes, close the presentation, and exit PowerPoint. Follow the directions on the SAM website to submit your completed project.

Off-Grid Solar Solutions
CREATING A POLISHED PRESENTATION

PROJECT DESCRIPTION

Your company has won a state contract to provide low-cost solar energy kits through a technology transfer program. You will introduce your company's products to the governor and heads of several state agencies to prepare them for the media outreach events.

Your goal is to briefly outline the products and services of Off-Grid Solar Solutions by taking advantage of the graphics and features in PowerPoint.

GETTING STARTED

- Download the following file from the SAM website:

    o **IF_PPT2013_CS_UM-N_P1a_*FirstLastName*_1.pptx**

- Open the file you just downloaded and save it with the name:

    o **IF_PPT2013_CS_UM-N_P1a_*FirstLastName*_2.pptx**

    o *Hint*: If you do not see the **.pptx** file extension in the Save file dialog box, do not type it. PowerPoint will add the file extension for you automatically.

- To complete this Project, you will also need to download and save the following support files from the SAM website:

    o **support_IF_P13_CS_UM-N_P1a_sun.png**

    o **support_IF_P13_CS_UM-N_P1a_solarkits.docx**

    o *Hint*: Opening an image may alter its file size. If you open an image support file, delete the file and download a new copy from the SAM website.

- With the file **IF_PPT2013_CS_UM-N_P1a_*FirstLastName*_2.pptx** still open, ensure that your first and last name is displayed in the presenter notes on Slide 1. If the presenter notes do not display your name, delete the file and download a new copy from the SAM website.

PROJECT STEPS

1. Apply the second variant of the **Wisp** theme to all the slides in the presentation.

2. Open the Slide Master. On the Title and Content Layout, change the font size of the "Click to edit Master text styles" bullet text to **24 pt.**, then close the Slide Master.

3. On Slide 1 ("Off-Grid Solar Solutions"), select the text "Easy & Affordable Solar Kits," change the font to **Georgia**, then **bold** the text.

4. On Slide 1, insert the picture **support_IF_P13_CS_UM-N_P1a_ sun.png** available for download from the SAM website. Move the sun picture to the left of the arrow-in-circle picture, then use Smart Guides to align it with the top of the arrow-in-circle picture.

5. On Slide 1, select the gray gear and green circle shapes, then align the shapes using **Align Center** and **Align Middle**. Next, deselect the shapes, select the green circle and the gray gear shapes in that order, then apply the merge shape command **Combine**.

6. On Slide 1, resize the green gear so that it is **1.6"** high and **1.5"** wide. Move the green gear to the right of the arrow-in-circle picture, then use Smart Guides to align it to the top of the arrow-in-circle picture.

7. Display Slide 2 ("What We Do"), then insert three new slides from an outline using the file **support_IF_P13_CS_UM-N_P1a_solarkits. docx**, available for download at the SAM website.

8. In the Thumbnails pane, select Slides 3, 4, and 5, then **reset** them.

9. Move Slide 5 ("Supernova Class") so that it becomes the new Slide 4.

10. On Slide 6 ("Why Go Green?"), select the title text, change the font color to **Olive Green, Text 2, Darker 25%** (4th column, 5th row in the Theme Colors gallery), then change the font size to **54 pt**.

11. On Slide 6, **underline** the word "Why" in the title text.

12. On Slide 6, convert the bulleted list to the SmartArt graphic **Basic Block List** (1st row, 1st column in the List section of the Convert to SmartArt gallery).

13. On Slide 6, apply the SmartArt style **Intense Effect** (1st row, 5th column in the SmartArt Styles gallery) to the SmartArt.

14. With Slide 6 still displaying, insert a new slide with the **Title and Content** layout. Type **Advantage...Green** in the title placeholder of the new slide.

15. On Slide 7 ("Advantage...Green"), use the content placeholder to insert a table with **3 columns** and **5 rows**, then enter the values shown in Table 1.

Table 1: Slide 7 Table

Item	Savings	Return on Investment
Programmable Thermostat	$180	157%
LED Bulbs	$24	134%
Passive Solar Wall	$180	102%
Solar Garden Lights	$176	75%

© 2015 Cengage Learning.

16. On Slide 7, apply the table style **Medium Style 1 – Accent 5**. Align the table on the slide using the **Align-Middle** command.

17. On Slide 8 ("Go Green to Get $Green$"), apply the picture effect **Tight Reflection, touching** (1st row, 1st column in the Reflection Variations section of the Reflection gallery) to the round battery recycling and house pictures.

18. On Slide 8, group all four of the green pictures.

19. On Slide 8, select the picture group, then apply the animation **Zoom** (11th option in the Entrance section of the Animation gallery) and the animation timing **Start After Previous**.

20. On Slide 8, select the title text box, then add the animation **Float In** (4th option in the Entrance section of the Animation gallery).

21. On Slide 8, open the Animation pane, select the Parallelogram animation, then move it to the top of the list. Apply the animation timing **Start With Previous** to the Parallelogram animation. Close the Animation pane.

22. Apply the transition **Uncover** (10th option in the Subtle section of the Transition to This Slide gallery) to all the slides in the presentation.

23. On Slide 8, apply the transition **Airplane** (10th option in Exciting section of the Transition to This Slide gallery) to this slide only.

24. Add the **slide number** to all the slides in the presentation.

25. Add a footer with the text **Technology Transfer Program** to all the slides in the presentation.

26. Check the Spelling in the presentation to identify and correct any spelling errors. (*Hint*: You should find and correct at least 2 spelling errors.) Run the slide show to the end.

Save your changes, close the presentation, and exit PowerPoint. Follow the directions on the SAM website to submit your completed project.

Capstone Projects

CASE ▶ You work at The Right Fit, a fitness center based in San Diego. Your manager, Joanne Kleinen, needs you to use Word, Excel, Access, and PowerPoint to create and modify files that address specific company-related needs.

Unit Objectives

You will create projects using

- Microsoft Word
- Microsoft Excel
- Microsoft Access
- Microsoft PowerPoint

Files You Will Need

CS-1.docx	CS-6.pptx
CS-2.docx	CS-7.pptx
CS-3.xlsx	shoe.png
CS-4.xlsx	weight.png
CS-5.accdb	bike.avi

©HelenStock/Shutterstock

Microsoft® product screenshots used with permission from Microsoft® Corporation.

Word Capstone Project 1

As the manager of The Right Fit, a state-of-the-art gym and fitness facility in San Diego, Joanne Kleinen plans to organize a Community Wellness Day on Saturday, May 20, 2016, in partnership with two other local businesses and students in the Health and Wellness program at Pacific College in San Diego. She has written the text for a two-page proposal that describes her plans for the day. Now she needs you to format the headings with styles, apply a theme and a style set, search and replace selected text, format a table, insert a citation and generate a list of works cited, and insert a header and footer. When you finish all the required tasks, the two-page proposal should look like **FIGURE CS-1**.

STEPS

TROUBLE

The spelling errors in the data file are deliberate. You will correct them in a later step.

1. Open CS-1.docx, save it as CS-Community Wellness Day Proposal, apply the Title style to the first line in the document, then apply the Subtitle Style to the second line. Center align both lines of text, then in line 2, replace the text Your Name with your name. Apply the Heading 1 style to these headings: Introduction, Free Training Sessions from Local Businesses, Community Wellness Day Schedule, and Awards Ceremony

2. Apply the Quotable theme, then apply the Lines (Simple) Style set

3. Go to the top of the document, find every instance of the text Mason County College and replace each occurrence of it with Pacific College

4. Scroll to the table, add a new blank row at the bottom of the table, enter the text 3:00 - 4:00 in the first cell, Beginning Stretching in the second cell, and The Real You Dance Studio in the third cell, then format the table with the Grid Table 4 - Accent 6 table style

5. Go to the top of the document, use the Find command to locate the text Weeder, then insert a footnote following the comma with the text Frank Weeder became famous in the 1990s for his patented fitness and diet program that helped millions get fit

6. Find the text our responsibility, insert a citation after the quotes using the MLA style and the following source information: Author: Lucy Ortega, Title: The Lucy Ortega Fitness Book, Year: 2015, City: New York, Publisher: Get Fit Now Press, Medium: Print. Apply italic formatting to the book title in the first paragraph

7. Insert a page break above the Pacific Sight Pilates heading at the bottom of page 1, insert a header starting on page 2 containing the text Community Wellness Day Proposal centered and bold, then add a footer containing the page number centered

8. Generate a list of Works Cited at the bottom of page 2

9. Check and correct spelling errors in the document (do not correct "The Right Fit" or any proper names), then save and close the document

Community Wellness Day Proposal

Submitted by Your Name, The Right Fit

Introduction

This proposal discusses plans to organize a Community Wellness Day on Saturday, May 20, 2016. Three local businesses The Right Fit, Pacific Sight Pilates, and The Real You Dance Studio, will participate in Community Wellness Day, along with students in the Health and Wellness program at Pacific College in San Diego. The purpose of Community Wellness Day is to celebrate fitness and to encourage all members of the community to develop a strategy for keeping fit and staying healthy. As Lucy Ortega, best-selling author of *The Lucy Ortega Fitness Book*, states, "As fitness professionals, helping others to get fit and stay fit is not just our passion; it is our responsibility." (Ortega)

This proposal provides information on the following: local business involvement, Community Wellness Day Schedule, and Awards Ceremony.

Free Training Sessions from Local Businesses

Three local business have committed to offering free training sessions on Community Wellness Day. Their goal is to raise awareness of the programs they offer and inspire our citizens to lead more active and healthy lifestyles.

The Right Fit

Founded in 2008 by Francis Weeder[1], The Right Fit has earned a solid reputation for promoting a wide range of fitness activities and events in the community. In 2010, The Right Fit sponsored a 5K run to raise funds for various health charitable causes and has since become an annual event attracting thousands of runners. For Community Wellness Day, The Right Fit will offer two free classes, open its gym ar[...] and conduct free fitness evaluations throughout the [...]

---

[1] Frank Weeder became famous in the 1990s for his pate[...] helped millions get fit.

Community Wellness Day Proposal

Pacific Sight Pilates

Under the ownership of Aurora Parker, Pacific Sight Pilates is a 9,000 square foot studio that offers eighteen Pilates classes every week. On Community Wellness Day, Pacific Sight Pilates will offer classes aimed at beginners.

The Real You Dance Studio

As one of San Diego's oldest dance training centers, The Real You Dance Studio was established in the 1950s and is still going strong today. The studio's mandate has expanded to include all dance levels in its state-of-the-art studio. On Community Wellness Day, The Real You will provide free beginning dance lessons.

Community Wellness Day Schedule

Free sessions at the three fitness venues will be held throughout the day, and the 5K Run will begin at 10:00 at Lincoln Middle School. The Healthy Food Fest kicks off at noon and features healthy cuisine from local restaurants. The schedule, included below, is organized so that everyone can attend at least one class at each of the three venues. Students in the Health and Wellness program at Pacific College will assist staff at all events.

Time	Event/Session	Location
10:00 – 12:00	5K Run	Lincoln Middle School
11:00 – 12:00	Cross Training for Beginners	The Right Fit
2:00 – 3:00	Low Impact Aerobics	The Right Fit
2:00 – 3:00	Yoga for Beginners	Pacific Sight Pilates
2:00 – 3:00	Beginning Ballroom Dancing	The Real You Dance Studio
3:00 – 4:00	Beginning Pilates	Pacific Sight Pilates
3:00 – 4:00	Beginning Tap Dance	The Real You Dance Studio
3:00 – 4:00	Beginning Stretching	The Real You Dance Studio

Awards Ceremony

The Community Wellness Day culminates in an awards ceremony for students in the Health and Wellness program at Pacific College. This ceremony will honor outstanding students in the program and will showcase their contributions to the Community Wellness Day events.

Works Cited

Ortega, Lucy. *The Lucy Ortega Fitness Book*. New York: Get Fit Now Press, 2015. Print.

2

Word Capstone Project 2

Each season, The Right Fit schedules fitness classes in its San Diego facility. Joanne Kleinen, the facility manager, saves time by modifying the previous season's schedule to include new classes, and to remove classes no longer offered. Joanne asks you to open the fitness schedule for Fall 2015 and then modify the schedule so it includes information about the winter classes. When you finish all the required tasks, the schedule should look like FIGURE CS-2.

STEPS

1. Open CS-2.docx, save it as CS-Winter Fitness Schedule, change the margins to the Moderate setting, change Fall to Winter in the title, then change the font of the title text to TW Cen MT and the font size to 28 pt, then remove italics

2. Change the Theme colors to Blue Warm

3. In the blank line below the title, create a table consisting of two columns and three rows; using FIGURE CS-2 as a guide, enter the text for column 1 (Level 1, Level 2, Level 3), bold the text, then adjust the width of the columns so the table appears as shown in the figure

4. In the new table, fill cell 1 in column 2 with Blue-Gray, Accent 1, Lighter 80%; fill cell 2 with Blue-Gray, Accent 1, Lighter 40%; then fill cell 3 with Blue-Gray, Accent 1, Darker 50%

5. In the table containing the schedule, insert a new column to the right of column 1, enter the text for the new column shown in FIGURE CS-2 ("Sunday," etc.), then modify the fill colors to match the figure

6. Select the text below the Fitness Class Prices heading, format this selected text as a numbered list, change the line spacing to 2, then insert a left-aligned tab stop at the 2.5" mark on the ruler. Add a second tab stop at the 5" mark on the ruler, then change the numbered list formatting to a bulleted list with the solid black circle bullet

7. Insert the clipart of a snowflake shown in the figure from Office.com (look for a red version of the snowflake shown in the figure). Change the text wrapping to Square, apply the Metal Oval shape style, and change the Color to Blue, Accent Color 3, Light. Using FIGURE CS-2 as a guide, place the image in the position shown in the figure

8. Add the footer as shown in the figure; be sure to center align the footer text

9. View the completed document in Print Preview, save and close the document, then submit the completed document to your instructor

The Right Fit Winter Fitness Classes

Level 1	
Level 2	
Level 3	

Time	Sunday	Monday	Tuesday	Wednesday	Thursday	Friday	Saturday
8 a.m.	Tai Chi	Aerobics 1		Aerobics 1		Circuit Training	Tai Chi
9 a.m.		Aqua Aerobics 1	Step Aerobics 2	Step Aerobics 2	Yoga 1	Yoga 1	Aqua Aerobics 1
10 a.m.		Yoga 2	Pilates 2	Yoga 2	Pilates 2	Yoga 2	Pilates 2
5 p.m.	Yoga 1	Indoor Cycling 2	Indoor Cycling 2	Yoga 1	Indoor Cycling 2	Yoga 1	
6 p.m.		Cross Training 3	Yoga 3	Cross Training 3			
7 p.m.		Pilates 2	Yoga 3	Pilates 2	Yoga 3	Yoga 3	

Fitness Class Prices

- Level 1 Classes $12.00/class $30.00/week

- Level 2 Classes $15.00/class $35.00/week

- Level 3 Classes $18.00/class $45.00/week

Your Name, *The Right Fit*, 680 Palm Drive, San Diego, CA 92103 (619)555-6688
www.therightfitsandiego.com

Excel Capstone Project 1

Joanne Kleinen, manager of The Right Fit, needs to provide a sales analysis for the last two years of exercise classes to Chase Blackwell, the owner of The Right Fit. Chase wants to see the total sales that each class generated for each year, the amount each class increased or decreased (both in dollar amounts and as a percentage), and the profit generated by each class. He also wants Joanne to identify the highest and lowest class sales, the largest increase, the average growth, and the average sales per class. Joanne has already entered some of the labels and values in the worksheet, and now she wants you to complete it and add a chart. When you finish all the required tasks, the worksheet and chart should look like **FIGURE CS-3**.

STEPS

1. Open **CS-3.xlsx**, and save it as **CS-Classes Sales Analysis**. Enter the following labels in the range D4:F4: **Sales Growth, % Increase, Total Sales**

2. Enter a formula in cell **D5** that calculates how much the Aerobics classes sales increased in 2016 over 2015, copy this formula to cells **D6:D15**, then format cells **B5:H15** as **Currency**, with no decimals

> **QUICK TIP**
>
> To calculate the percentage increase, divide the Aerobic sales growth value by the 2015 Aerobic sales value.

3. Enter a formula in cell **E5** that calculates the percentage the Aerobics classes sales increased in 2016, format cell **E5** so the result appears as a **percentage**, then copy the formula in **E5** to cells **E6:E15**

4. Enter a formula in cell **F5** that calculates the total sales for Aerobic classes for 2015 and 2016, then copy the formula to cells **F6:F15**

> **QUICK TIP**
>
> The formula should subtract the Instructor Fee for Aerobics from the Total Sales for Aerobics.

5. In cell **H5**, enter a formula that calculates the profit for Aerobics classes, then copy the formula to cells **H6:H15**

6. Add the label **Total** in **A16**, use **AutoSum** to calculate the 2016 Sales total in cell **B16**, then copy this formula to cells **C16, D16, F16, G16,** and **H16**

7. Enter appropriate formulas in cells **B19:B23**, using functions where appropriate. In cell **B24**, enter a complex formula that calculates the Instructor Bonus Pool. To do this, you will first need to add the cells of any 2015 or 2016 classes whose values are greater than $10,000, then multiply this total by 5 percent (or .05)

8. Enter a formula in cell **B25** that calculates the adjusted Total Profit, which is the Total Profit less the Instructor Bonus Pool

9. Insert a line sparkline in cell **I5** for the data range **B5:C5**, apply the **Sparkline Style Accent 2 Darker 50%** style, then add markers (same style). Copy the sparkline in cell **I5** to the range **I6:I15**

10. Format the worksheet so it looks like the figure (do your best to match the colors and font sizes shown), then add a footer with your name in the left section, the filename in the middle section, and the page number in the right section

11. Create a **Stacked column chart** that shows the 2015 and 2016 Classes Sales. Move the chart to a separate chart sheet named **Classes 2015-2016**. Apply **Quick Layout 8** to the chart. Change the title to **The Right Fit Classes, 2015-2016**, then format it as shown in the figure. Apply **Style 2** to the chart, change the vertical axis title to **SALES**, then change the horizontal axis title to **CLASSES**. Enhance the chart by applying the **Intense Effect-Blue Accent 1 shape style** to the chart title and the **Intense Effect-Red Accent 2 shape style** to the axis titles

12. Change the orientation of the worksheet to **Landscape**, save your changes, then print and close the workbook

The Right Fit
Classes Sales Analysis, 2015-2016

	2015	2016	Sales Growth	% Increase	Total Sales	Instructor Fees	Profit	Trend
Aerobics	$3,233	$5,688	$2,455	76%	$8,921	$1,200	$7,721	
Hydro Training	$2,144	$7,632	$5,488	256%	$9,776	$1,200	$8,576	
Aqua Aerobics	$6,587	$5,644	-$943	-14%	$12,231	$1,575	$10,656	
Indoor Cycling	$3,277	$9,855	$6,578	201%	$13,132	$2,200	$10,932	
Weight Training	$5,987	$8,755	$2,768	46%	$14,742	$1,200	$13,542	
Cross Training	$6,755	$8,643	$1,888	28%	$15,398	$1,500	$13,898	
Tai Chi	$7,643	$8,976	$1,333	17%	$16,619	$2,200	$14,419	
Kickboxing	$7,654	$10,987	$3,333	44%	$18,641	$2,500	$16,141	
Strength and Flexibility	$8,755	$10,667	$1,912	22%	$19,422	$2,400	$17,022	
Pilates	$10,988	$12,025	$1,037	9%	$23,013	$2,000	$21,013	
Yoga	$10,876	$12,550	$1,674	15%	$23,426	$2,200	$21,226	
Total	$75,914	$103,438	$27,523		$175,321	$20,175	$155,146	

Analysis	Amount
Lowest class sales amount	$2,144
Highest class sales amount	$12,550
Largest sales increase	$6,578
Average growth %	64%
Average sales per class	$15,938
Instructor bonus pool	$3,404.65
Adjusted profit	$151,741.35

Your Name

Excel Capstone Project 2

Joanne Kleinen, manager of The Right Fit, needs you to prepare a workbook that provides information about the 5K run that The Right Fit recently sponsored. The first sheet in the workbook needs to show the budget for the event, including a listing of the budgeted costs, the actual costs, and the difference between them. Joanne wants you to use conditional formatting to highlight which costs were over and which were under budget. Joanne also wants you to include a pie chart that shows all of the actual costs expended for the event. The second sheet needs to show the top 10 fundraisers, the donations they raised, and the date that the amounts are due. To complete this worksheet you need to convert the data to a table and sort it to identify the top 10 fundraisers. You will also apply conditional formatting and use a date function.

STEPS

1. Open CS-4.xlsx, then save it as CS-5K Race. Notice that this workbook contains two worksheets named Budget and Fundraisers

QUICK TIP
The formula should subtract the Municipality Fees Actual Amount Spent from the Municipality Fees Budgeted Amount.

2. In the Budget worksheet, enter a formula in cell D5 that calculates the variance between the Budgeted Amount and the Actual Amount Spent for Municipality Fees, then copy this formula to cells D6:D12

3. Enter Total as a label in cell A13, enter a formula in cell B13 that calculates the total budgeted expenses, then copy this formula to cells C13 and D13

4. Apply conditional formatting to cells D5:D13, specify to apply a Green Fill with Dark Green Text to any value that is greater than zero, then specify to apply a Light Red Fill with Dark Red Text to any value that is less than zero

5. Enter your name in cell B32, then enter a function in cell B33 that returns today's date

6. Format the other cells in the Budget worksheet so the title, labels, and number formats look like those in FIGURE CS-4A. Apply the number formats, borders, shading, and cell styles shown. Use your best judgment in matching the figure

7. Insert a 3D pie chart that shows the actual amounts spent for the 5K run. Apply Quick Layout 6 and Style 10 to format the chart. Change the chart colors and apply other formatting so the chart matches the one shown in FIGURE CS-4A. Position and format the chart to match the figure

8. Open the Fundraisers sheet. Type your name in cell A3. Apply the Accounting number format with no decimals to cells C5:C35. Enter a formula in cell E5 that calculates the date that is 10 days after the date in cell D5. Copy the formula in cell E5 to E6:E35

9. Convert the range A4:E35 to a table, choose Table Style Light 14, sort the table from largest to smallest by the Donations Raised column, then use Conditional Formatting to apply the 3 Traffic Lights (Rimmed) icon set to the values in the Donations Raised column

10. Apply the Top Ten number filter to the Donations Raised column so only the top 10 fundraisers are displayed

11. Add a Total row to the table, click cell C36, click the C36 down arrow, click Sum to insert a formula that adds up the Donations raised for the top 10 fund-raisers, then delete the value in cell E36

12. Edit cell A2 so it reads 5K Run, Top Ten Fundraisers and Donation Amounts, then format cells A1:A3 so they match the formatting in FIGURE CS-4B

13. Save your changes, close the workbook, exit Excel, then submit the workbook to your instructor

FIGURE CS-4A: Completed Budget worksheet with chart

The Right Fit
5K Run, Budget vs. Actual

Cost	Budgeted Amount		Actual Amount Spent		Variance	
Municipality Fees	$	3,800.00	$	3,750.00	$	50.00
Runner Premiums	$	3,000.00	$	2,950.00	$	50.00
Management Fees	$	2,950.00	$	3,120.00	$	(170.00)
Transportation	$	800.00	$	705.00	$	95.00
Water Stations	$	575.00	$	425.00	$	150.00
Emergency Services	$	1,000.00	$	2,012.00	$	(1,012.00)
Temporary Staff	$	1,765.00	$	1,425.00	$	340.00
Promotion	$	2,750.00	$	2,550.00	$	200.00
Total	$	**16,640.00**	$	**16,937.00**	$	**(297.00)**

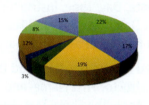

5K Run Actual Expenses

■ Municipality Fees ■ Runner Premiums ■ Management Fees ■ Transportation
■ Water Stations ■ Emergency Services ■ Temporary Staff ■ Promotion

Prepared by: Your Name
Today's Date: 2/17/2013

FIGURE CS-4B: Completed Top 10 Fundraisers worksheet

The Right Fit
5K Run, Top Ten Fundraisers and Donation Amounts
Your Name

Last Name	First Name	Donations Raised		Date Registered	Donations Due
Hannah	Ed	● $	12,655	3/6/2016	3/16/2016
Knowles	Phil	● $	10,860	2/14/2016	2/24/2016
Brennan	Roy	● $	10,245	2/20/2016	3/1/2016
Victor	Morales	● $	9,755	1/15/2016	1/25/2016
Bishop	Oliver	● $	9,040	2/4/2016	2/14/2016
Schnitzer	Iris	● $	8,745	3/12/2016	3/22/2016
Sullivan	Mallory	● $	7,895	1/18/2016	1/28/2016
Brochu	Joe	● $	7,645	3/1/2016	3/11/2016
Rowe	Peter	● $	7,565	1/14/2016	1/24/2016
Rosen	Albert	● $	6,665	2/24/2016	3/5/2016
Total		$	**91,070**		

Access Capstone Project 1

Joanne Kleinen, manager of The Right Fit, needs to create a database to manage information about the programs offered at the fitness center. For instance, the database is needed to manage information about classes and instructors. Joanne needs your help. She asks you to create the database, add tables containing information about classes and instructors, add fields to each table and set their data types, enter data into the tables using Datasheet view and a form, relate the two tables, and create queries and a report.

STEPS

1. Create a new database with the name CS-The Right Fit

2. Create a table named Classes, then add the following fields/data types to it: Class ID, Class, Fee, Sessions, Start Date, Day, Time, Instructor ID. Set the data type to Short Text for all fields except for Start Date, Sessions, and Fee, then apply appropriate data types for each. Verify the Class ID field is set as the primary key field

3. Create a second table named Instructors, then add the following fields to it: Instructor ID, Instructor Last Name, Instructor First Name, and Full Time?. Apply the Yes/No data type to the Full Time? field. Apply the Short Text data type to the remaining fields. In Design view, verify the Instructor ID field is set as the primary key field

4. In the Instructors table, add the following description to the Full Time? field: Yes if Instructor works more than 32 hours per week. Save your changes, then close both tables

5. View the Classes table in Datasheet view, then enter the records shown in FIGURE CS-5A into it

6. Create a new form based on the Instructors table, then save the form as Instructors. Use the form to enter the records shown in FIGURE CS-5B, then close it

7. Create a one-to-many relationship between the Instructor ID field in the Instructors table and the Instructor ID field in the Classes table. Enforce referential integrity, then save the relationship

8. Create a query using the Query Wizard that includes the following fields from the Classes table: Class, Day, and Time. Then add the Instructor Last Name field from the Instructors table. Save the query as Classes Schedule, then print it in Datasheet view

9. Modify the Classes Schedule query so it shows only the classes taught by instructor Murray, save the query as Murray's Classes, then close it

10. Using FIGURE CS-5C as your guide, create a report based on the Classes Schedule query. Include all fields. Specify to view the data by Classes, then specify to group the report by Instructor Last Name. Sort the report in ascending order by Class. Choose the Stepped layout, then specify Portrait orientation. Save the report as Classes by Instructor. Apply the Slice theme. Move and resize columns as necessary to match the figure and to make sure all the field names and data are visible. Add your name to the report header in parentheses as shown, then save, print, and close the report

11. Close all open objects, then close the database

FIGURE CS-5A: Data to enter in the Classes table

Class ID	Class	Fee	Sessions	Start Date	Day	Time	Instructor ID
C-111	Aerobics	$150	10	1/2/2016	Sat	8:30-9:30 AM	I-201
C-112	Aqua Aerobics	$175	10	1/4/2016	Mon	7:00-8:00 PM	I-202
C-113	Hydro Training	$125	10	1/6/2016	Wed	7:00-8:00 PM	I-201
C-114	Indoor Cycling	$125	8	1/7/2016	Thurs	5:00-6:00 PM	I-202
C-115	Cross Training	$140	9	1/8/2016	Fri	7:00-8:00 PM	I-202
C-116	Pilates	$125	10	1/2/2016	Sat	10:00-11:00 AM	I-203
C-117	Yoga	$150	12	1/4/2016	Mon	6:00-7:00 PM	I-203
C-118	Tai Chi	$125	10	1/6/2016	Wed	5:00-6:00 PM	I-203
C-119	Kickboxing	$150	12	1/6/2016	Wed	4:00-5:00 PM	I-201
C-120	Weight Training	$125	10	1/2/2016	Sat	3:00-4:00 PM	I-202

FIGURE CS-5B: Data to enter in the Instructors table

Instructor ID	Instructor Last Name	Instructor First Name	Full Time?
I-201	Murray	Claudette	Yes
I-202	Martineau	Robert	Yes
I-203	Williams	Marcia	No

FIGURE CS-5C: Classes by Instructor report

Classes by Instructor (Your Name)

Instructor Last Name	Class	Day	Time
Martineau			
	Aqua Aerobics	Mon	7:00-8:00 PM
	Cross Training	Fri	7:00-8:00 PM
	Indoor Cycling	Thurs	5:00-6:00 PM
	Weight Training	Sat	3:00-4:00 PM
Murray			
	Aerobics	Sat	8:30-9:30 AM
	Hydro Training	Wed	7:00-8:00 PM
	Kickboxing	Wed	4:00-5:00 PM
Williams			
	Pilates	Sat	10:00-11:00 AM
	Tai Chi	Wed	5:00-6:00 PM
	Yoga	Mon	6:00-7:00 PM

Access Capstone Project 2

Community Wellness Day celebrates and promotes good health by conducting five community events, each of which needs sponsorships from local businesses. Joanne Kleinen, manager of The Right Fit, has already created a database in Access that contains two tables; one with information about the events and one with information about the sponsors. Joanne wants you to use the database to pull information on the status of the sponsors for each event. She wants you to create queries to show the events and sponsors to date, as well as sponsors who have contributed more than $200. You also need to create a report that shows the status of the event sponsors to date so she can see how close each event is to meeting its sponsorship targets. When you finish all the required tasks, your finished queries should look like FIGURE CS-6A and FIGURE CS-6B and your finished report should look like FIGURE CS-6C.

STEPS

1. Open the Data File CS-5.accdb, save it as CS-Community Wellness Day, enable the content, then take a moment to open and look at the Events table and the Sponsors table

2. Close both tables, set up a one-to-many relationship between the Event ID field in the Events table and the Event ID field in the Sponsors table, enforce referential integrity, then save the relationship

3. Create a query using the Query Wizard that contains the Event Name field from the Events table and the Sponsor and Amount Sponsored fields from the Sponsors table. Specify to show Detail (not Summary) in the Query Wizard. Save the query as Events and Sponsors. View the query in Design view. Sort the records in ascending order by Event Name and descending order by Amount Sponsored. View the query in Datasheet view. Compare your screen to FIGURE CS-6A. Save your changes

4. Create a new query based on the Events and Sponsors query named Gold Sponsors. In Query Design view, specify to show all the sponsors who have sponsored more than $200. Sort the query results in descending order by the Amount Sponsored field. View the query results in Datasheet view, then compare your screen to FIGURE CS-6B. Save your changes

5. Close all open objects, then create a new report using the Report Wizard. Include the Event Name field and Sponsorship Needed field from the Events table, and the Sponsor field and Amount Sponsored field from the Sponsors table. Specify to view the data by Events, and specify no other grouping levels. Sort the report by the Amount Sponsored field in descending order. Include the Sum summary option for the Amount Sponsored field and specify to show Detail and Summary. Specify the Block layout and Portrait orientation. Save the report as Events and Sponsors (your name)

6. Make formatting changes to the report so it matches FIGURE CS-6C. You will need to format field labels and field values, resize fields so all text is visible, and move the Sum label and Sum field value. Use your best judgment in formatting the report so it matches the figure

7. Use Conditional Formatting to apply dark green bold text formatting to any value in the Amount Sponsored field that is greater than $200

8. Save and close the report, close all open objects, exit Access, then submit the database to your instructor

FIGURE CS-6A: Events and Sponsors query

Event Name	Sponsor	Amount Sponsored
5K Run	The Right Fit	$500.00
5K Run	Wildwood Fun Land	$250.00
5K Run	Brenda's Bistro	$225.00
5K Run	Harvey's Auto Shop	$100.00
5K Run	Holistic Health Services	$75.00
5K Run	Tidy Up Cleaning Services	$75.00
5K Run	Otis-Beasley Contractors	$75.00
Awards Ceremony	Fernpath Mall	$500.00
Awards Ceremony	Pete and Joe's Pizzeria	$100.00
Awards Ceremony	Hannah's House of Fish	$100.00
Awards Ceremony	Fit and Ready Sporting Goods	$100.00
Awards Ceremony	Dazzle Me Day Spa	$75.00
Free Pilates Classes	Butchie's BBQ House	$255.00
Free Pilates Classes	Green Brick Carpentry	$100.00
Free Pilates Classes	Golden Mule Community Services	$50.00
Free Pilates Classes	Flying Koala Teas	$50.00
Free Yoga Classes	The Real You Dance Studio	$100.00
Free Yoga Classes	Jessie's Tea House	$50.00
Free Yoga Classes	Seize the Day Personal Trainers, Inc.	$50.00
Healthy Food Fest	The Laughing Lizard Grocers	$250.00
Healthy Food Fest	Burns and Gregor Medical Center	$250.00
Healthy Food Fest	Molly's Good Cookin' Caterers	$100.00
Healthy Food Fest	The Happy Dolphin Spa	$100.00
Healthy Food Fest	Organic Matter Foods	$100.00
Healthy Food Fest	For Your Health	$100.00
Healthy Food Fest	Take Me Away Travel Services	$100.00
Healthy Food Fest	Healthy Haven Spices	$75.00
Healthy Food Fest	Backyard Grillers Caterers	$50.00
Healthy Food Fest	Pacific Sight Pilates	$50.00

FIGURE CS-6B: Gold Sponsors query

Event Name	Sponsor	Amount Sponsored
5K Run	The Right Fit	$500.00
Awards Ceremony	Fernpath Mall	$500.00
Free Pilates Classes	Butchie's BBQ House	$255.00
Healthy Food Fest	The Laughing Lizard Grocers	$250.00
Healthy Food Fest	Burns and Gregor Medical Center	$250.00
5K Run	Wildwood Fun Land	$250.00
5K Run	Brenda's Bistro	$225.00

FIGURE CS-6C: Top part of Events and Sponsors (your name) report

Events and Sponsors (Your Name)

Event Name	Sponsorship Needed	Amount Sponsored	Sponsor
Free Pilates Classes	$500.00	$255.00	Butchie's BBQ House
		$100.00	Green Brick Carpentry
		$50.00	Golden Mule Community Services
		$50.00	Flying Koala Teas
Summary for 'Event ID' = Event-01 (4 detail records)			
	Sum	$455.00	
Free Yoga Classes	$1,000.00	$100.00	The Real You Dance Studio
		$50.00	Jessie's Tea House
		$50.00	Seize the Day Personal Trainers, Inc.
Summary for 'Event ID' = Event-02 (3 detail records)			
	Sum	$200.00	
Healthy Food Fest	$12,750.00	$250.00	The Laughing Lizard Grocers
		$250.00	Burns and Gregor Medical Center
		$100.00	Molly's Good Cookin' Caterers
		$100.00	The Happy Dolphin Spa
		$100.00	Organic Matter Foods
		$100.00	For Your Health
		$100.00	Take Me Away Travel Services
		$75.00	Healthy Haven Spices
		$50.00	Backyard Grillers Caterers
		$50.00	Pacific Sight Pilates
Summary for 'Event ID' = Event-03 (10 detail records)			
	Sum	$1,175.00	

Capstone Projects

PowerPoint Capstone Project 1

The Right Fit is a state-of-the-art gym and fitness facility in San Diego. Its manager, Joanne Kleinen, has been asked by the owners of the company to put together a PowerPoint presentation to describe the facility to potential investors. Joanne has entered text for the presentation slides, and now she needs you to enhance the presentation with a theme, images, a SmartArt diagram, and other elements. When you finish all the required tasks, the six-slide presentation should look like FIGURE CS-7.

STEPS

1. Start PowerPoint, open the file CS-6.pptx from the location where you store your Data Files, then save it as CS-Company Overview

2. Apply the Ion theme, apply the second variant, then view the presentation in Slide Show view and Slide Sorter view

3. On Slide 1, bold the two lines in the subtitle, then add your name where indicated

4. Add two more bulleted items on Slide 4, Ellipticals and Strength Machines, as shown in FIGURE CS-7

5. Insert the picture weight.jpg from the location where you store your Data Files on the title slide, move and resize it so it fits in the area above the presentation title, crop the right side of the picture to remove the two rounded white objects, align it horizontally in the center of the slide, remove the picture's background, then adjust its size and position to match FIGURE CS-7

6. Insert the clip art of the runner (search using the keyword fitness) on Slide 3, resize and position it as shown in FIGURE CS-7, then apply the Perspective Diagonal Upper Right shadow effect

7. On Slide 6, create the SmartArt diagram shown in FIGURE CS-7 using the Vertical Curved List layout, use the Change Colors button to apply the Dark 2 Fill colors to the object, then on Slide 4, convert the bulleted list to SmartArt using the Vertical Accent List layout

8. Insert the online sound Just drums on Slide 5 (use the search term exercise), have it play automatically when the slide appears in the slide show, change the sound object's picture to shoe.png from the location where you store your Data Files, move and resize it as shown in FIGURE CS-7, then use the Trim Audio button to reduce the clip's length to about 10 seconds

9. Insert a footer with the text The Right Fit that appears on all presentation slides except the title slide (the footer will appear on the right side of the slides)

10. View the entire slide show from the beginning, evaluate the presentation's effectiveness, preview (and if desired print) a copy of the presentation as a handout with six slides (horizontal) to the page, then save and close the presentation

PowerPoint Capstone Project 2

Each year in the fall, The Right Fit recruits students enrolled in recreation and sports programs at local colleges to work part-time at the facility as personal trainers, fitness instructors, and receptionists. The manager, Joanne Kleinen, has decided to bring all the recruits together for an orientation session that includes a PowerPoint presentation. Joanne has completed most of the presentation and now asks you to add some enhancements including interesting animation, video, and transition effects. When you finish all the required tasks, the six-slide presentation should look like FIGURE CS-8.

STEPS

1. Start PowerPoint, open the file CS-7.pptx from the location where you store your Data Files, then save it as CS-Staff Orientation

2. Go to Slide 2, draw a triangle shape, add the text The Right Fit to the shape, change the font size to 36 pt bold text, change its shape style to Colored Fill - Green, Accent 6, then size and position it as shown in FIGURE CS-8

3. Apply the Float In entrance animation effect to the triangle shape, then apply the Float Down effect option; for the Slide 2 bullets, apply the Float Up animation effect (in the Moderate category); then copy the animation effect to the other bulleted lists in the presentation

4. On Slide 3, insert the movie clip bike.avi from the location where you store your Data Files, position and size it as shown in FIGURE CS-8, have it play automatically in the slide show, trim the clip so it's about four seconds long, then verify that the clip runs in Slide Show view (it will play after the bullet animation)

5. On Slide 5, change the slide layout to the Two Content layout (use the Layout button in the Slides group), then use a content placeholder button to insert the table shown in FIGURE CS-8 (Hint: All the table text is bold 20-point; the table has Wide cell margins and is 2.5" in height.)

6. Add the following text in the Notes pane on Slide 1: Welcome students and ask them to introduce themselves, then view the presentation in Notes Page view

7. Apply the Uncover transition effect to all slides, have the Slide 5 transition accompanied by the Applause online sound, and apply a slide timing of 10 seconds to Slide 6

8. Go to Slide 1 in Slide Show view, go to Presenter view and view each slide, evaluating the presentation for effectiveness; on Slide 5, after the animations play, use the Pen tool to circle the text Celebrate your successes, then, when asked at the end of the slide show, discard your annotation

9. Type your name where indicated on Slide 1, preview the presentation as a handout with six slides to the page (horizontal), add your name to the handout footer, print the handout if desired, then save and close the presentation

Slide 3 image courtesy of Barbara Clemens

Glossary

Absolute cell reference In Excel, a cell reference that does not change when the formula is copied and pasted to a new location. For example, the formula "=$B$5*C5" in cell D5 does not change to "=$B$6*C6" when you copy the formula to cell D6. *See also* Relative cell reference.

Accessories Simple Windows application programs (apps) that perform specific tasks, such as the Calculator accessory for performing calculations. *Also called* Windows accessories.

Active cell In an Excel worksheet, the current location of the cell pointer.

Active window The window that you are currently using, if multiple windows are open, the window with the darker title bar.

Address A sequence of drive and folder names that describes a folder's or file's location in the file hierarchy; the highest hierarchy level is on the left, with lower hierarchy levels separated by the ▶ symbol to its right.

Address bar In a window, the area just below the title bar that shows the file hierarchy, or address of the files that appear in the file list below it; the address appears as a series of links you can click to navigate to other locations on your computer.

Adware Software installed with another program that generates advertising revenue for the program's creator by displaying targeted ads to the program's user.

Alignment The horizontal or vertical position of numbers or text, relative to the page margins. Text can be right-, center-, left-, top-, or bottom-aligned, or justified between the margins. *See also* Justified text.

Alt text Alternate text in a Web page that describes a picture or other element that has not yet loaded; you can add alt text to an element so that a user can read it while the element loads or if it is missing.

Analog signal A continuous wave signal (sound wave) that can traverse ordinary phone lines.

Animation effects Movements or changes in appearance that you can apply to any text placeholder or graphic, including clip art, photos, and illustrations.

Animation Painter A tool that copies animation settings from one object so that you can apply them to another.

App An application program; Windows 8 apps are designed to occupy the full screen and are available on the Start screen and at the Windows store. Desktop apps, such as Microsoft Office, open in resizable windows, and are available from many software companies.

App window The window that opens after you start an app, showing you the tools you need to use the program and any open program documents.

Anti-spyware software Software that detects and removes spyware.

Antivirus software Software that searches executable files for the sequences of characters that may cause harm and disinfects the files by erasing or disabling those commands. *Also called* virus protection software.

Application software Software that enables you to perform specific computer tasks, such as document production, spreadsheet calculations, database management, and presentation preparation. *Also called* application program or app.

Area chart A line chart in which each area is colored or patterned to emphasize the relationships between pieces of charted information.

Architecture The design and construction of a computer. *Also called* configuration.

ASCII (American Standard Code for Information Interchange) The number system that personal computers use to represent character data.

Attachment A file sent along with an email message.

Argument A value, cell reference, or text used in an Excel function. Commas or a colon separate arguments and parentheses enclose them; for example, AVERAGE(A1,10,5) or SUM(A1:A5).

Arial A popular sans serif font, often used for headlines.

Ascending order A way to sort records in a database table or data in a spreadsheet, in which fields are ordered numerically from 0–9 or alphabetically from A–Z.

Audio files *See* Sound clips.

AutoCorrect A feature that automatically corrects certain words as you type after you press [Spacebar].

AutoCorrect Options button A button that appears after Office makes an automatic text or formatting correction that contains a menu of options you can choose from.

AutoFit A feature that automatically resizes a table column to fit the longest entry when a column boundary is double-clicked.

AutoNumber data type In Access, a data type that assigns a unique sequential number to each record.

AVERAGE function Calculates the average value of the arguments.

Axis titles Labels in a chart that identify the values for each axis in the chart.

Backstage view Commands and tools to help you work with your files, which are available when you click the FILE tab in any Office app.

Backup A duplicate copy of a file that is stored in another location.

Bar chart A chart that displays worksheet data as a series of horizontal bars.

BD-R A Blu-ray disc on which you can record data once.

BD-RE A Blu-ray disc on which you can record data as on a BD-R, and then delete or re-record data on it as needed.

Bibliography A list of citations from works referenced in a document that is usually placed at the end of the document.

Binary digit (bit) The representation of data as a 1 or 0.

BIOS Stands for basic input/output system, the set of instructions stored in ROM that the computer uses to check its components to ensure they are working and to activate the software that provides the basic functionality of the computer when you turn on the computer.

Bitmap A graphic that displays a picture image as a matrix of pixels on a grid.

Bits per second (bps) The unit of measurement for the speed of data transmission.

Blog Web log, or a personal commentary on a website.

Bluetooth A wireless technology standard that allows electronic devices to use short range radio waves to communicate with one another or connect to the Internet; the radio waves can be transmitted around corners and through walls.

Blu-ray A disc used for storing high-definition video that stores 25 GB of data per layer.

Bold A font style that makes text appear in thicker type; used to emphasize text in a document, spreadsheet, database, or presentation.

Boot process The set of events that occurs between the moment you turn on the computer and the moment you can begin to use the computer.

Boot up The act of turning on the computer.

Border A window's edge; you can drag to resize the window.

Bridging A technique that uses multiple routers to increase the range of a Wi-Fi signal.

Broadband connection A high-speed connection to the Internet.

Browser A program, such as Microsoft Internet Explorer, designed to access the Internet.

Bullet A small graphic, usually a dot, used to identify items in a list.

Button A small rectangle you can click in order to issue a command to an application program.

Byte A series of eight bits.

CMOS *See* Complementary metal oxide semiconductor memory.

Cable Plastic-enclosed wires that attach a peripheral device to a computer port.

Cache memory Special high-speed memory chips on the motherboard or CPU that store frequently-accessed and recently-accessed data and commands. *Also called* RAM cache or CPU cache.

Calculated field In Access, a field that displays a value that is the result of a formula that contains field values and mathematical operators.

Canvas In the Paint accessory program, the area in the center of the program window that you use to create drawings.

Caption property In Access, a label that appears in a form, report, or in Datasheet view in place of the actual field name.

Card A removable circuit board that is inserted into a slot in the motherboard to expand the capabilities of the motherboard.

Case sensitive Describes a program's (app's) ability to differentiate between uppercase and lowercase letters; usually used to describe how an operating system evaluates passwords that users type to gain entry to user accounts.

Category axis *See* X-axis and Horizontal axis.

CD (compact disc) An optical storage device that can store 700 MB of data.

CD-R (compact disc recordable) A CD that on which you can record data with a laser that changes the reflectivity of a dye layer on the blank disk, creating dark spots on the disk's surface that represent the data; once the data is recorded, you cannot erase or modify it.

CD-ROM (compact disc read-only memory) A CD that contains software or music when you purchase it, but you cannot record additional data on it.

CD-RW (compact disc rewritable) A CD on which you can record data as on a CD-R, and then delete or re-record data on it as needed.

Cell The intersection of a row and a column in an Excel worksheet or a Word table.

Cell address In Excel, a row letter followed by a column number that specifies the location of a cell.

Cell pointer The dark border that surrounds the active cell in an Excel worksheet.

Cell range *See* Range.

Cell reference The address of a cell in an Excel worksheet that defines its location in the worksheet by column letter and row number (for example, A1), and that can be used in formulas and functions.

Center-aligned text Text that is placed evenly between the margins.

Central processing unit (CPU) *See* Microprocessor.

Channel The medium, such as telephone or coaxial cable, over which a message is sent in data communications.

Charms bar A set of buttons that appear on the right side of the Windows 8 screen that let you find and send information, change your machine settings, and turn off your computer. When you display the Charms bar, the time and date appear on the left side of the screen.

Chart A graphic representation of selected worksheet data.

Chart area A chart object that is the background behind the chart.

Chart layout In Excel, a predefined arrangement of chart elements that you can apply to any chart.

Chart objects Individual components of a chart, such as the chart background or legend, which you can move or resize independently.

Chart sheet A worksheet in an Excel workbook that contains a chart.

Chart style A predefined set of chart colors and fills that you can apply to any chart.

Check box A square box that you click to add a check mark (also known as selecting) or remove a checkmark (also known as deselecting) to turn an option on or off.

Chip An integrated circuit embedded in semiconductor material.

Circuit A path along which an electric current travels.

Circuit board A rigid piece of insulating material with circuits on it that control specific functions.

Click To quickly press and release the left button on a mouse or other pointing device. *Also called* single-click.

Client A computer networked to and dependent on a server.

Client/server network A network with a server and computers dependent on the server.

Clip A media file, such as a piece of art, an animation, video, or photograph, available through the Clip Art task pane.

Clip art Ready-to-use electronic artwork

Clipboard A temporary storage space on your computer's hard disk containing information that has been cut or copied. *See also* Windows Clipboard, Office Clipboard.

Clock speed The pulse of the processor measured in megahertz or gigahertz.

Close button A button that when clicked quits a program or removes a window from the desktop. The Close button usually appears in the upper-right corner of a window.

Cloud computing When data, applications, and resources are stored on servers accessed over the Internet or a company's internal network rather than on user's computers.

Cloud storage File storage locations on the World Wide Web, such as Windows OneDrive or Dropbox.

Color scales In Excel, shading patterns that use two or three colors to show the relative values of a range of cells.

Column chart A chart that displays worksheet data as a series of vertical columns.

Column separator In Access in Datasheet view, the border between two field names that you can drag or double-click to adjust the width of the column.

Column sparkline A miniature column chart that fits in one cell that includes a bar for each cell in a selected range.

Command An instruction to perform a task, such as opening a file or deleting text.

Command button In a dialog box, a button that carries out an action. A command button usually has a label that describes its action, such as Cancel or Help. If the label is followed by an ellipsis (...), clicking the button displays another dialog box.

Compact disc *See* CD.

Compact disc read-only memory *See* CD-ROM.

Compact disc recordable *See* CD-R.

Compact disc rewritable *See* CD-RW.

Complementary metal oxide semiconductor (CMOS) memory A chip installed on the motherboard powered by a battery whose content changes every time you add or remove hardware on your computer system and that is activated during the boot process so it can identify where essential software is stored. *Also called* semipermanent memory.

Complex formula A formula in Excel that contains more than one mathematical operator (for example, +, –, *, or /).

Computer An electronic device that accepts input, processes data, displays output, and stores data for retrieval later.

Computer accessibility Technology that allows people with physical impairments or disabilities to use computers.

Computer system A computer, its peripheral devices, and software.

Conditional formatting In Excel and Access, formatting that is applied to cells in a spreadsheet or fields in a form or report when specified criteria are met.

Context sensitive Help Onscreen guidance tools that appear in the form of text descriptions or instructions when the mouse points to a particular screen element, to describe the function of the element or provide instructions on how to perform a particular task.

Contextual tab A tab that only appears when a particular type of object is selected.

Control An object on an Access form or report that is composed of the field label and the field value text box and that displays data, performs calculations, or is used for decoration. Examples include fields, text boxes, and graphic images.

Controller card A card that plugs into a slot on the motherboard and connects to a port to provide an electrical connection to a peripheral device. *Also called* expansion card or interface card.

Copy A command that copies selected text in a document to the Windows and Office Clipboard; copied text is also left in its original location.

COUNT function In Excel, a pre-written formula that calculates the number of values in the argument list.

CPU *See* Microprocessor.

CPU cache *See* Cache memory.

Criteria In Access, conditions or qualifications that determine whether a record is chosen for a filter or query. In Excel, specified conditions that determine whether a row in a table is displayed.

Cropping handles Dark lines that appear on the corners and edges of a selected graphic after you click the Crop button on the PICTURES TOOLS FORMAT tab; drag cropping handles to include or exclude areas of the graphic.

CSS (Cascading Style Sheets) In web design, the language and techniques for styling HTML pages.

Cut A command that removes selected text or objects from a document and places them on the Windows and Office Clipboard, usually to be pasted into another location.

Data The words, numbers, figures, sounds, and graphics that describe people, events, things, and ideas.

Data bars In Excel, colored bars that make it easy to identify the large and small values in a selected range of cells and also highlight the relative value of cells to each other.

Data bus The path between the microprocessor, RAM, and the peripherals along which communication travels.

Data communications The transmission of data from one computer to another or to a peripheral device via a channel using a protocol.

Data file A file created by a user, usually with software, such as a report that you write with a word processing program.

Data marker A bar, area, dot, slice, or other symbol in a chart that represents a single data point or value that originates from a worksheet cell.

Data series In a chart, a sequence of related numbers that show a trend, such as sales amounts of various months, quarters, or years.

Data source The database file that stores the variable information for a form letter or other mail merge document.

Data table In Excel, a grid in a chart that contains the chart's underlying worksheet data, and which is usually placed below the x-axis.

Data type A specific category of data in a database field, such as text, dates, or numbers.

Database An organized collection of data related to a particular topic or purpose and stored electronically in a file.

Database management program A program used to store, organize, display, and retrieve information, such as names and addresses, product inventories, and employee data.

Database object In Access, one of seven program components that you can create and modify to store, retrieve, and work with data. Tables, objects, queries, reports, macros, forms, pages, and modules are objects you can create in Access.

Datasheet view A view in Access that displays records in a grid format, making records easy to compare, sort, and edit.

Default In an app window or dialog box, a value that is automatically set; you can change the default to any valid value. *Also* default setting.

Design view In Access, the view that shows the structure of a table, form, query, or report. Use this view to modify the design by editing or moving controls or to modify table structure by adding, deleting, or editing fields and field properties.

Desktop apps Application programs (apps), such as Microsoft Office, that open in resizeable windows that you can move and resize to view alongside other app windows. *Also called* traditional apps.

Desktop computer A personal computer designed to sit compactly on a desk.

Desktop publishing program A program that lets you create printed documents combining text and graphics.

Destination file When linking and embedding data between documents, the target file or program.

Detail section In Access, the section of a form or report that displays the field labels and data for each record.

Device A hardware component that is part of your computer system, such as a disk drive, a pointing device, or a touch screen device.

Device driver System software that handles the transmission protocol between a computer and its peripheral devices. *Also called* driver.

Dialog box A window in which you enter information needed to carry out a command. Clicking most dialog box launchers and some buttons on the Ribbon opens a dialog box in which you must select options before the Office program can carry out the command.

Dialog box launcher *See* Launcher.

Digital signal A stop-start signal that your computer outputs.

Digital subscriber line *See* DSL.

Display *See* Monitor.

Display resolution The number of pixels that a monitor displays. *See* Pixels per inch (PPI).

DNS server A computer responsible for directing Internet traffic.

Document window The portion of an application program's (app's) window in which you create the document; displays all or part of an open document.

Document production software Word processing software or esktop publishing software that assists you in writing and formatting documents, including changing the font and checking the spelling.

Documents folder The folder on your hard drive used to store most of the files you create or receive from others; might contain subfolders to organize the files into smaller groups.

Dots per inch (DPI) Determines quality of a printer's output. A higher number generally indicates higher quality.

Double-click To press and release the left mouse button or pointing device twice quickly.

Draft view In Word, a view that displays the text and some graphic elements in a document without showing exactly how all the elements in the document will print.

Drag To point to an object, press and hold the left button on the pointing device, move the object to a new location, and then release the left button.

Drag and drop To use a pointing device to move or copy selected text or data or a file or folder directly to a new location instead of using the Clipboard.

Drive A physical location on your computer where you can store files.

Drive name A name for a drive that consists of a letter followed by a colon, such as C: for the hard disk drive.

Driver *See* Device driver.

Dropbox A free online storage site that lets you transfer files that can be retrieved by other people you invite. *See also* Cloud storage.

DSL (digital subscriber line) A high-speed connection over phone lines.

Dual-core processor A CPU that has two processors on the chip.

DVD An optical storage device that can store up to 15.9 GB of data.

DVD+R, DVD-R A DVD on which you can record data once.

DVD+RW, DVD-RW A DVD on which you can record data as on a DVD-R, and then delete or re-record data on it as needed.

DVI (digital video interface) port A port that digitally transmits video.

Edit To modify the contents of a file.

Email An electronic message sent from one person to another over the Internet.

Embed The process of inserting data from one program into another program and being able to edit the data using the tools of the program in which it was originally created.

Embedded object A separate copy of a file that is inserted in a file in a different program and that you can edit using the tools of the program in which it was created.

Emphasis animation An animation that determines how a slide object will be visually emphasized on a slide during the slide show.

Encrypt Access security feature that compacts and scrambles a database file so that it is difficult for unauthorized users to decipher.

Endnote A note or citation that corresponds to a number or symbol in a document and appears at the end of the document. *See also* Footnote.

End-of-cell mark In Word, the mark in each cell in a table; all text entered in the cell is entered to the left of the end-of-cell mark.

End-of-row mark In Word, the clipmark at the end of each row in a table.

Entering text In Word, the act of typing text in a document.

Entrance animation An animation that determines how a slide object first appears on a slide during the slide show.

Ergonomic Designed to fit the natural placement of the body to reduce the risk of repetitive-motion injuries.

Ethernet port A port used to connect computers in a LAN or sometimes directly to the Internet; it allows for high-speed data transmission.

Executable file A file that contains the instructions that tell a computer how to perform a specific task, such as the files that are used during the boot process.

Exit animation An animation that determines how a slide object leaves the slide.

Expansion card *See* Controller card.

Expansion port The interface between a cable and a controller card. *Also called* port.

Expansion slot An electrical connector on the motherboard into which a card is plugged. *Also called* slot.

Expression In Access, a combination of fields, values, and mathematical operators (similar to a formula in Excel).

Field A specific category of information in a database such as name, address, or phone number. Usually organized in the smallest possible unit to facilitate organization, such as last name and first name.

Field description In a database table in Access, a descriptive comment that explains the purpose of a field, to help the person entering data into it.

Field list A list that contains all the fields in a database table; used to add fields to forms or reports.

Field name In an Access table, column headings in a table that indicate the type of information entered for each field value text box.

Field properties In Access, settings and characteristics that determine the way data is stored, displayed, or manipulated in a field, such as the length of a text field or the number of decimal places in a number field.

Field value In Access, the data entered in a field for a particular record.

File An electronic collection of data that has a unique name, distinguishing it from other files.

File Explorer A Windows accessory that allows you to navigate your computer's file hierarchy and manage your files and folders.

File extension A three- or four-letter sequence, preceded by a period, at the end of a filename that identifies the file as a particular type of document; for example, Word documents file extension .docx.

File hierarchy A logical structure for folders and files that mimics how you would organize files and folders in a filing cabinet.

File list A section of a window that shows the contents of the folder or drive currently selected in the Navigation pane.

File management The process of organizing and keeping track of files and folders on a computer.

Filename A unique, descriptive name for a file that identifies the file's content.

File properties Details that Windows stores about a file, such as the date it was created or modified.

FILE tab Tab on the Ribbon that contains commands and tools that let you work with the whole document. For instance, you use the FILE tab to open, save, print, and close documents. The FILE tab is present in all Office programs.

Fill handle A small square that appears on the lower right corner of a selected worksheet cell that you can drag to the right or down to copy the cell's contents into adjacent cells.

Filter A command that displays only the data that you want to see in an Excel worksheet or an Access database table based on criteria you set.

Filter drop-down list In an Excel table, a menu that appears when you click the filter list arrow in a column heading that let you apply a filter or a sort order to the data in table.

Firewall Hardware or software that prevents other computers on the Internet from accessing a computer or prevents a program on a computer from accessing the Internet.

FireWire A standard for transferring information between digital devices developed by Apple Computer company and the Institute of Electrical and Electronics Engineers (IEEE); was standardized as IEEE 1394 interface.

Firmware *See* Read-only memory (ROM).

Firmware update Allows ROM to be re-programmed with bug fixes or new features.

First line indent In a document, when the first line of text in a paragraph is indented from the left margin by a specified amount of space.

Flash memory Memory that is similar to ROM except that it can be written to more than once. *Also called* solid state storage.

Flash memory card A small, portable card encased in hard plastic to which data can be written and rewritten.

Flat panel monitor A lightweight monitor that takes up very little room on the desktop and uses LCD technology to create the image on the screen.

Floating image An image that can be dragged to any location on a page, and to which text wrapping has been applied.

Folder An electronic container that helps you organize your computer files, like a cardboard folder on your desk; it can contain subfolders for organizing files into smaller groups.

Folder name A unique, descriptive name for a folder that helps to identify the folder's contents.

Font A set of characters in a particular design; for example, Arial or Times New Roman.

Font effects Special enhancements to fonts such as small caps, shadow and superscript that you can apply to selected text in a document, spreadsheet, database, or presentation.

Font size The size of a font, measured in points. One point measures 1/72".

Font style Attribute that changes the appearance of text when applied; bold, italic, and underline are common font styles.

Footer Text that appears just above the bottom margin of every page in a document, or on every slide, handout, or notes page in a presentation.

Footnote A note or citation that corresponds to a number or symbol in a document, and which is placed at the bottom of the document page. *See also* Endnote.

Foreign key In Access, where two tables that have a one-to-many relationship, the primary key in the second table that is shared by the first table.

Form A database object that is used to enter, edit, or display records in a database one at a time.

Formatting To enhance the appearance of text in a document, spreadsheet, database, or presentation without changing the content. Also refers to the process of preparing a disk so it can store information.

Form controls In Access, elements in a form that make it possible to enter data; such as text boxes, scroll bars, or check boxes. A common type of form control consists or a field label and a field value text box.

Form letter A merged document that contains standard body text and a custom header for each recipient.

Formula An equation that calculates a new value from existing values. Formulas can contain numbers, mathematical operators, cell references, and built-in equations called functions. *See also* Function.

Formula AutoComplete In Excel, a feature that helps you enter a formula in a cell by suggesting a listing of functions as you type letters and providing syntax information to help you write the formula correctly.

Formula bar In Excel, the area below the Ribbon where you enter or edit a formula or data in the selected cell.

Forum Electronic gathering places where anyone can add questions and answers on computer issues.

Function A prewritten formula you can use instead of typing a formula from scratch. Each function includes the function name, a set of parentheses, and function arguments separated by commas and enclosed in parentheses. *See also* Formula.

Gadget An optional program you can display on your desktop that presents helpful or entertaining information, such as a clock, current news headlines, a calendar, a picture album, or a weather report.

GB *See* Gigabyte.

Gesture An action you take with your fingertip directly on the screen, such as tapping or swiping, to make a selection for perform a task.

GHz *See* Gigahertz.

Gigabyte (GB) 1,073,741,824 bytes, or about one billion bytes.

Gigahertz (GHz) One billion cycles per second.

Graphic Interchange Format (GIF) File format for graphics that is often used for line art and clip art images.

Graphical user interface (GUI) A computer environment in which the user manipulates graphics, icons, and dialog boxes to execute commands.

Graphics card A card installed on the motherboard that controls the signals the computer sends to the monitor. *Also called* video display adapter or video card.

Graphics display A monitor that is capable of displaying graphics by dividing the screen into a matrix of pixels.

Graphics processor A processor that controls the signals the computer sends to the monitor. *Also called* built-in graphics card.

Graphics software Software that allows you to create illustrations, diagrams, graphs, and charts.

Gridlines Horizontal and vertical lines connecting to the x-axis and y-axis in a chart that make it easier to identify the value of each data series.

Group In a Microsoft app window's Ribbon, a section containing related command buttons.

Group footer The part of an Access report that contains the chosen group field name and appears at the end of each group of records.

Group header The part of an Access report that contains the Group field name; used when the information in a report is grouped by a chosen field or fields.

Grouping A way of organizing information in an Access report by a field or field values to make spotting trends or finding important information easier.

GUI *See* Graphical user interface.

Handheld computer A small computer designed to fit in the palm of your hand and that generally has fewer capabilities than personal computers.

Handout header The area at the top of every PowerPoint handout page page.

Handouts In PowerPoint, hard copies of a presentation that you can print and distribute to an audience.

Hanging indent A type of paragraph indent in a Word document in which the second and subsequent lines of text in a paragraph indent further than the first line by a set amount of space.

Hard copy A printed copy of computer output.

Hard disk drive (HDD) A magnetic storage device that contains several magnetic oxide-covered metal platters that are usually sealed in a case inside the computer. *Also called* hard disk or hard drive.

Hard drive *See* Hard disk drive (HDD).

Hard page break A page break inserted manually in a Word document to cause the text following the page break to begin at the top of a subsequent page.

Hardware The physical components of a computer.

HDMI (high-definition multimedia interface) port A port that digitally transmits video and audio.

Header Text that appears just below the top margin of every page in a document.

Header row In Excel, the row at the top of a table that contains column headings.

Headphones Worn over one's ears, allow you to hear sounds generated by your computer. *See also* Speakers.

Highlighted Describes the changed appearance of an item or other object, usually a change in its color, background color, and/or border; often used for an object on which you will perform an action, such as a desktop icon.

Highlighting When an icon is shaded differently, indicating it is selected. *See also* Select.

HOME tab The tab on the Ribbon that contains the most frequently used commands in the active Office 2013 program (app).

Horizontal axis In an Excel chart, is the horizontal line at the base of a chart that shows categories. *Also called* x-axis or category axis.

HTML (HyperText Markup Language) The primary code language used to create web pages.

I/O *See* Input and output.

Icon A small image that represents an item, such as the Recycle Bin on your computer; you can rearrange, add, and delete desktop icons.

IEEE 1394 interface *See* FireWire.

Inactive window An open window you are not currently using; if multiple windows are open, the window(s) with the dimmed title bar.

Indent A set amount of space between the edge of a paragraph and the right or left margin.

Information management software Software that keeps track of schedules, appointments, contacts, and "to-do" lists.

Infrared technology A wireless technology in which devices communicate with one another using infrared light waves; the devices must be positioned so that the infrared ports are pointed directly at one another.

Inkjet printer A printer that sprays ink onto paper and produces output whose quality is comparable to that of a laser printer.

Inline graphic A graphic that is part of a line of text and moves with it when the text moves.

Input The data or instructions you type into the computer.

Input and output (I/O) The flow of data from the microprocessor to memory to peripherals and back again.

Input device A hardware peripheral, such as a keyboard or a mouse, that you use to enter data and issue commands to the computer.

Insertion point In a Word document or a filename, a blinking vertical line indicating the point where text will be inserted when you type.

Interface card *See* Controller card.

Internet The largest network in the world.

Italic A font style that makes text appear slanted; used to emphasize text in a document.

Joint Expert Photographic Experts Group (JPEG) File format that is often used for photographs because it uses and compresses color so well.

Justified text Text aligned equally between the right and left margins.

K *See* Kilobyte.

KB *See* Kilobyte.

Keyboard The most frequently used input device; consists of three major parts: the main keyboard, the keypads, and the function keys.

Keyboard shortcut A keyboard alternative for executing a menu command (for example, [Ctrl][X] for Cut).

Keywords Words that you type into a search engine text box, task pane, or dialog box that relate to a particular topic, and which the program will use to search its database for related topics, images, sound files, or other items.

Kilobyte (KB or K) 1,024 bytes, or approximately one thousand bytes.

Label Descriptive text used to identify worksheet data in Excel, and titles or brief descriptions in Access.

LAN *See* Local area network.

Landscape Layout orientation for a document that specifies to print the page so it is wider than it is long.

Laptop computer *See* Notebook computer.

Laser printer A printer that produces high-quality output quickly and efficiently by transferring a temporary laser image onto paper with toner.

Launch To start a program that was previously closed.

Launcher Small arrow located to the right of a group name on the Ribbon that when clicked opens a dialog box or task pane where you can enter additional information to complete a task. *Also called* a dialog box launcher.

Layout In PowerPoint, an arrangement of placeholders and formatting that can hold a particular type of content.

Layout view In Access, a view in which you can see data in a form or report, and also make simple formatting changes.

LCD (liquid crystal display) A display technology that creates images by manipulating light within a layer of liquid crystal.

LED (light emitting diode) monitor A flat-panel monitor that uses LEDs to provide backlight.

LED printer Similar to a laser printer, produces high-quality output quickly and efficiently by using light to transfer a temporary image onto paper with toner.

Left indent In Word, a set amount of space between the left margin and the left edge of an entire paragraph.

Legend Area in a chart that explains what the labels, colors, and patterns of the chart represent.

Library A window that shows files and folders stored in different storage locations; default libraries in Windows 8 include the Documents, Music, Pictures, and Videos libraries.

Line chart A graph of data mapped by a series of lines. Because line charts show changes in data or categories of data over time, they are often used to document trends.

Line sparkline A miniature line chart that fits in one cell and is ideal for showing a trend over a period of time.

Link (1) Verb: To paste content from one file (the source file) into another (the destination file) and maintain a connection with the source file. (2) Noun: Text or an image that you click to display another location, such as a Help topic, a website, or a device

Liquid crystal display *See* LCD.

List box A box that displays a list of options from which you can choose (you may need to scroll and adjust your view to see additional options in the list).

Live Preview A feature that allows you to preview how a formatting option will look on the page before actually choosing that option.

Live tile Updated, "live" content that appears on some apps' tiles on the Windows Start screen, including the Weather app and the News app.

Load To copy and place an app into your computer's memory in preparation for use.

Local area network (LAN) A network in which the computers and peripheral devices are located relatively close to each other, generally in the same building, and are usually connected with cables.

Lock screen The screen that appears when you first start your computer, or after you leave it unattended for a period of time, before the sign-in screen.

Log in/log on To sign in with a user name and password before being able to use a computer.

Log off To close all windows, programs, and documents, then display the Welcome screen.

Magnetic storage device Uses various patterns of magnetization to store data on a magnetized surface.

Mail merge The process of combining a Word form letter that contains field names with data from a data source to create a third document that contains multiple personalized letters or labels.

Main document In a Word mail merge, the document that stores the standard body text for a form letter or other document.

Mainframe computer A computer used by larger business and government agencies that provides centralized storage, processing, and management for large amounts of data.

Malware A broad term that describes any program that is intended to cause harm or convey information to others without the owner's permission.

Margin In a document, the amount of space between the edge of the page and the text in your document.

MAX function Calculates the largest value in the argument list.

Maximize button On the right side of a window's title bar, the center button of three buttons; use to expand a window so that it fills the entire screen. In a maximized screen, this button turns into a Restore button.

Maximized window A window that fills the desktop.

MB *See* Megabyte.

Megabyte (MB) 1,048,576 bytes, or about one million bytes.

Megahertz (MHz) One million cycles per second.

Memory A set of storage locations on the main circuit board that store instructions and data.

Memory capacity The amount of data that the device can handle at any given time.

Menu A list of related commands.

Menu bar A bar near the top of the program window that provides access to most of a program's features through categories of related commands.

Merge To combine information from a data source, such as an Access database table, with standard text contained in a Word document to create personalized form letters or other mail merge documents. *See also* Mail merge.

Merge fields Field names from a specified data source that act as placeholders for variable information in a form letter or other mail merge document.

Merged document A file or printout that contains all the personalized letters in a mail merge document.

MHz *See* Megahertz.

Microphone Used to record sound or communicate with others using audio or video conferencing software.

Microprocessor A silicon chip, located on the motherboard, that is responsible for executing instructions to process data. *Also called* processor or central processing unit (CPU).

Microsoft Access Database management program created by Microsoft Corporation you can use to store, organize, retrieve, and display information, such as names, addresses, product inventories, and employee data.

Microsoft Community Website A Microsoft Help feature that lets you search forums (electronic gathering places where anyone can add questions and answers on computer issues), Microsoft help files, and even on-screen video demonstrations about selected topics. (Formerly the Microsoft Answers website.)

Microsoft Excel Spreadsheet program created by Microsoft Corporation you can use to manipulate, analyze, and chart quantitative data.

Microsoft Office 365 A subscription-based service that includes use of the Microsoft Office apps suite and many services optimized for working in the cloud.

Microsoft Office Web Apps A set of scaled-down versions of Microsoft Office applications that run over the Internet. *See also* Office Online.

Microsoft OneNote A software program you can use to capture and store information such as website addresses, graphics, notes written by your or others, or text pulled from a report.

Microsoft Outlook An email program and information manager created by Microsoft Corporation that comes with Microsoft Office that you use to send and receive email, schedule appointments, maintain to do lists, and store contact information.

Microsoft PowerPoint Presentation graphics program created by Microsoft Corporation you can use to develop materials for presentations, including electronic slide shows, computer-based presentations, speaker's notes, and audience handouts.

Microsoft Publisher A desktop publishing program created by Microsoft Corporation that comes with Microsoft Office 2013 Professional that lets you create printed documents combining text and graphics, such as newsletters, brochures, letterheads, business cards, and other publications.

Microsoft SkyDrive A Microsoft website where you can obtain free file storage space, using your own account, that you can share with others; you can access SkyDrive from a laptop, tablet computer, or smartphone. *See also* OneDrive.

Microsoft Windows 8 An operating system developed by Microsoft Corporation.

Microsoft Word A word processing program created by Microsoft Corporation you can use to create text-based documents such as letters, memos, and newsletters.

MIN function Calculates the smallest value in the argument range.

Minimize button On the right side of a window's title bar, the left-most button of three buttons; use to reduce a window so that it only appears as an icon on the taskbar.

Minimized window A window that is visible only as an icon on the taskbar.

Mini notebook computer *See* Subnotebook computer.

Mini toolbar In Word, a group of buttons that appears on screen when text is selected that contains commonly used buttons for formatting text.

Modem Stands for modulator-demodulator; a device that converts the digital signals from your computer into analog signals that can traverse ordinary phone lines, and then converts analog signals back into digital signals at the receiving computer.

Monitor The TV-like peripheral device that displays the output from the computer.

Motherboard The main circuit board of the computer on which processing tasks occur.

Mouse A pointing device that has a rolling ball on its underside and two or more buttons for clicking commands; you control the movement of the pointer by moving the entire mouse around on your desk.

Mouse pointer A small arrow or other symbol on the screen that you move by manipulating the pointing device. *Also called* a pointer.

Move To change the location of a file, folder, or other object by physically placing it in another location.

MP3 player A hand-held computer that is used primarily to play and store music, but that can also be used to play digital movies or television shows, allow you to listen to FM radio stations, and access the Internet and email.

Multifunction printer (MFP) Combines several devices into one. Most MFPs can print, scan, copy, and fax documents.

Multimedia authoring software Software that allows you to record digital sound files, video files, and animations that can be included in presentations and other documents.

My Documents folder The folder on your hard drive used to store most of the files you create or receive from others; might contain subfolders to organize the files into smaller groups.

Name box In Excel, displays the name or reference of the currently selected cell in the worksheet.

Navigate To move around in your computers' folder and file hierarchy.

Navigate down To move to a lower level in your computers' folder and file hierarchy.

Navigate up To move to a higher level in your computers' folder and file hierarchy.

Navigation bar Bar containing buttons at the bottom of the Access program window that let you move among records in a table.

Navigation pane In Windows, a pane in a window that contains links to folders and libraries; click an item in the Navigation pane to display its contents in the file list or click the ◢ or ▷ symbols to display or hide subfolders in the Navigation pane. In Access, a pane to the left of the database window that displays all the objects in the database. In Word, a pane to the left of the document window that helps you to find specific text in a document and navigate a document.

Netbook A type of subnotebook computer that is primarily designed to allow users to access the Internet and check email. *See also* Slate computer.

Network Two or more computers that share data and resources and which are connected to each other and to peripheral devices.

Network interface card (NIC) The card in a computer on a network that creates a communications channel between the computer and the network.

Network software Software that establishes the communications protocols that will be observed on the network and controls the "traffic flow" as data travels throughout the network.

NIC *See* Network interface card.

Node Any device connected to a network.

Nonvolatile memory *See* Read-only memory.

Normal style In Word, a built-in style that is the default paragraph style for any new, blank Word document, and that is defined as 11-point Calibri.

Normal view In PowerPoint, a view that displays the presentation in two areas: a thumbnail pane on the left that shows small versions of the presentation slides, and on the right, the Slide pane; Normal view may also show the Notes pane with speaker notes below the Slide pane.

Notebook computer A small, lightweight computer designed for portability. *Also called* laptop computer.

Notes pages Pages you can create in PowerPoint that contain a miniature version of each slide plus speaker notes added in the Notes pane.

Notes Page view A PowerPoint view in which you can see your slide and any notes you have made.

Notes pane In PowerPoint in Normal view, the area below the Slide pane into which text can be typed to remind the presenter of key points to make to an audience; to display the Notes pane, click the Notes button in the Show group on the VIEW tab.

Notification area An area on the right side of the Windows 8 taskbar that displays the current time as well as icons representing apps; displays pop-up messages when a program on your computer needs attention.

Number format A format applied to numbers in cells that represents different number types, such as currency, decimal, date, or percent.

Object A graphic or other item or set of items that can be moved and resized as a single unit. In Excel, the components of a chart are called objects. In Access, objects are a collection of principal program components that you can create and modify, including tables, queries, forms, reports, pages, macros, and modules. In PowerPoint, each graphic or text element is an object. In Word, any item that is embedded or linked to the document is called an object.

Office 365 A cloud-based application that delivers various subscription-based services, such as Microsoft Office programs.

Office Clipboard A storage area for storing cut and copied items that can hold up to 24 items at once, and which is accessible from any Office app. *See also* Windows Clipboard.

Office Online Formerly called Office Web Apps, this provides users with limited versions of Microsoft Word, Excel, PowerPoint and OneNote that can be accessed anywhere via web browser.

OneDrive Formerly called SkyDrive, this is an online storage and file sharing service.

OneNote A software program used to capture and store information such as web addresses, graphics, notes written by you and others, or text pulled from a report.

One-to-many relationship In Access, the most common type of relationship that is defined for two tables, where the primary key field in one table is associated with multiple records in a second table.

Operating environment An operating system that provides a graphical user interface, such as Microsoft Windows and the MAC OS.

Operating system A computer program that controls the complete operation of your computer and the programs you run on it. Windows 8 is an example of an operating system.

Optical character recognition (OCR) Software that translates a scanned text document into text that can be edited in a word processing program.

Optical storage device Uses laser technology to store data in the form of tiny pits or bumps on the reflective surface of a spinning polycarbonate disc. To access the data, a laser illuminates the data path while a read head interprets the reflection.

Option button A small circle in a dialog box that you click to select an option.

Order of operations The order in which Excel calculates a formula; the order of precedence is exponents, multiplication and division, addition and subtraction. Calculations in parentheses are evaluated first.

Outline view In Word, a view that shows only the headings in a document. In PowerPoint, a view that shows only slide text in the Thumbnail pane, in an indented format.

Output The result of the computer processing input.

Output device A device, such as a monitor or printer, that displays output.

Page break The point at which text in a document flows to the top of a new page.

Page footer The part of an Access report that contains the current date and page number and appears at the bottom of each page.

Page header The part of an Access report that contains the field labels and appears at the top of every page of the report.

PAGE LAYOUT tab In Word, the tab on the Ribbon that contains commands to lay out and format a document.

Pages per minute (ppm) The unit of measurement for the speed of laser and inkjet printers.

Paint A graphics program (app) that comes with Windows 8.

PAN *See* Personal area network.

Pane A section of a divided window.

Paragraph In Word, any text that ends with a hard return.

Password A special sequence of numbers and letters that users can use to control who can access the files in their user account area; by keeping the password private, helps keep users' computer information secure.

Paste A command in the Clipboard group on the HOME tab that copies information from the Windows Clipboard or Office Clipboard into a document at the location of the insertion point.

Path An address that describes the exact location of a file in a file hierarchy; shows the folder with the highest hierarchy level on the left and steps through each hierarchy level toward the right. Locations are separated by small triangles or by backslashes.

PC *See* Personal computer.

Peer-to-peer network A network in which all the computers essentially are equal, and programs and data are distributed among them.

Peripheral device The components of a computer that accomplish its input, output, and storage functions.

Permanent memory *See* Read-only memory.

Personal area network (PAN) A network in which two or more devices communicate directly with each other.

Personal computer (PC) A computer typically used by a single user in the home or office for general computing tasks such as word processing, working with photographs or graphics, email, and Internet access.

Pharm To break into a DNS server and redirect any attempts to access a particular website to a spoofed site.

Phish To send emails to customers or potential customers of a legitimate website asking them to click a link in the email and then verify their personal information; the link leads to a spoofed site.

Photo editing software Software that allows you to manipulate digital photos.

Photos app A Windows 8 app that lets you view and organize your pictures.

Pie chart A circular chart that displays data in one data series as slices of a pie. A pie chart is useful for showing the relationship of parts to a whole.

Pixel A small square of color that comprises a digital image.

Pixels per inch (PPI) The number of pixels that a monitor can fit within one square inch. Higher PPI generally produces higher quality images. *See* Display resolution.

Placeholder A slide area that can hold text, graphics, and other slide content.

Play button In PowerPoint, the video control button that appears in Slide Show view; when clicked, the video for the current slide plays.

Plot area In a chart, the area behind the data markers.

Point A unit of measurement used to measure characters; a point equals 1/72 of an inch; also to position the mouse pointer in a particular location on your screen.

Pointer The typically arrow-shaped object on the screen that follows the movement of the mouse or pointing device. The shape of the pointer changes depending on the program and the task being executed. *Also called* a mouse pointer.

Pointing device A device that lets you interact with your computer by controlling the movement of the mouse pointer on your

computer screen; examples include a mouse, trackball, touchpad, pointing stick, on-screen touch pointer, or a tablet.

Pointing device action A movement you execute with your computer's pointing device to communicate with the computer. The five pointing device actions are point, click, double-click, drag, and right-click.

Port *See* Expansion port.

Portrait Layout orientation for a document that specifies to print the page so that it is longer than it is wide.

Poster frame An image that acts as a video's preview image on a slide; can be an image from the video or an image inserted from another source.

Power button The physical button on your computer that turns your computer on.

ppm *See* Pages per minute.

Presentation graphics app Software designed for creating on-screen slide shows, 35mm slides, overhead transparencies, and other business presentation materials.

Presenter view A PowerPoint view that lets you preview how your presentation would appear if you were using two monitors: one that the audience sees, and one that only you can see, containing your notes.

Preview pane A pane on the right side of a window that shows the actual contents of a selected file without opening a program; might not work for some types of files.

Primary key field In Access, a field that ensures that each record is unique in a table.

Printer The peripheral computer component that produces a hard copy of the text or graphics processed by the computer.

Print Layout view A view in Word that displays layout, graphics, and footnotes exactly as they will appear when printed.

Print Preview A view that shows exactly how a document will look when it is printed and contains options specific to previewing the printed document.

Processing Modifying data in a computer.

Processor *See* Microprocessor.

Program A set of instructions written for a computer, such as an operating system program or an application program to perform a task. *Also called* an application or app.

Program window (or app window) The window that opens after you start a program, showing you the tools you need to use the program and any open program documents.

Programming language Software used to write computer instructions.

Properties Characteristics of a specific computer element (such as the mouse, keyboard, or desktop display) that you can customize; in Access, those characteristics of a specific field, section, object, or control that you can customize.

Protocol The set of rules that establishes the orderly transfer of data between the sender and the receiver in data communications.

PS/2 port A port through which a keyboard or a mouse is connected.

Quad-core processor A CPU with four processors on the chip.

Query A database object that extracts data from one or more tables in a database according to set criteria.

Quick Access toolbar A small toolbar on the left side of a Microsoft application program window's title bar, containing icons that you click to quickly perform common actions, such as saving a file; available to use no matter what tab is currently active.

Random access memory (RAM) The storage location that is part of every computer that temporarily stores open apps and document data while a computer is on. When you turn the computer off, all information in RAM is lost.

Range A selected area of adjacent cells in an Excel worksheet. *Also called* a cell range.

Reading view A view in PowerPoint that displays the presentation full-screen, but also includes title and status bars.

Read Mode view In Word, view that displays the active document in a magnified view that is optimal for reading on screen.

Read-only memory (ROM) A chip on the motherboard that is prerecorded with and permanently stores the set of instructions that the computer uses when you turn it on. *Also called* nonvolatile memory or permanent memory.

Receiver The computer or peripheral at the message's destination in data communications.

Record A collection of related fields that contains all information for an entry in a database such as a customer, item, or business.

Record source In Access, the table or query from which a report gets its data.

Recycle Bin A desktop object that stores folders and files you delete from your hard drive(s) and that enables you to restore them

Reference mark The mark next to a word in a document that indicates a footnote or endnote is associated with the word, and that is linked to the footnote or endnote.

Relate The process of specifying a relationship between two tables in Access.

Relational database A database that contains multiple tables that are related to each other and can share information. Access is a relational database management program.

Relative cell reference In Excel, a cell reference that changes when copied to refer to cells relative to the new location. For example, the formula "=B5*C5" in cell D5 changes to "=B6*C6" when you copy the formula to cell D6. *See also* Absolute cell reference.

Removable storage Storage media that you can easily transfer from one computer to another, such as DVDs, CDs, or USB flash drives.

Repaginate In Word, the automatic process of renumbering pages in a document, which can occur if you change the margin settings or add or delete text.

Replace A command in the Clipboard group on the HOME tab that lets you search for a word or format in a document, spreadsheet, presentation, or database and insert another word or format in its place.

Report A summary of database information designed specifically for printing.

Report footer Information or images that appear at the bottom of the last printed page of a report.

Report header Area of a report that contains the report name and appears only at the top of the first printed page of a report.

Report view In Access, the default view when you open a report from the Navigation pane. Report view looks similar to Print Preview, except that it displays the report in a continuous flow, without page breaks. You cannot edit in Report view.

Report Wizard In Access, a series of dialog box that automatically creates a report based on settings you specify.

Resolution *See* Display resolution.

Restore Down button On the right side of a maximized window's title bar, the center of three buttons; use to reduce a window to its last non-maximized size. In a restored window, this button changes to a Maximize button.

Ribbon In many Microsoft app windows, a horizontal strip near the top of the window that contains tabs (pages) of grouped command buttons that you click to interact with the app.

Ribbon Display Options button In an Office app, a button located on the right end of the title bar that provides commands for hiding or displaying the Ribbon.

Rich Text Format (RTF) The file format that the WordPad app uses to save files.

Right-click To press and release the right button on the pointing device; use to display a shortcut menu with commands you issue by left-clicking them.

Right indent In Word, when text in a paragraph is indented from the right margin.

Router A device that controls traffic between network components and usually has a built-in firewall.

Row selector In Access, the small box to the left of each record that when clicked selects the entire record.

Royalty free Describes images that do not require the payment of a fee for use.

RTF *See* Rich Text Format.

Scanner A device that captures the image on a photograph or piece of paper and stores it digitally.

Scatter chart A chart that shows the relationship between two kinds of related worksheet data.

Screen size The diagonal measurement from one corner of the screen to the other.

ScreenTip A concise description of a button or other screen element that appears when you point to the item.

Scroll To adjust your view to see portions of the program window that are not currently in a window.

Scroll arrow A button at each end of a scroll bar for adjusting your view in a window in small increments in that direction.

Scroll bar A bar that appears at the bottom and/or right edge of a window whose contents are not entirely visible; you click the arrows or drag the box in the direction you want to move. *See also* Scroll box.

Scroll box A rectangle located in the vertical and horizontal scroll bars that indicates your relative position in a file and that you can drag to view other parts of the file or window. *See also* Scroll bar.

Scroll wheel A wheel on a mouse that you roll to scroll the page on the screen.

Search criteria Descriptive text that helps identify the application program (app), folder, file, or website you want to locate when conducting a search.

Search engine An online tool that allows you to enter keywords or terms; the engine then presents a list of sites that match those terms.

Search Tools tab A tab that appears in the File Explorer window after you click the Search text box; lets you specify a specific search location, limit your search, repeat previous searches, save searches, and open a folder containing a found file.

Security The steps a computer owner takes to prevent unauthorized use of or damage to the computer.

Select To change the appearance of an item by clicking, double-clicking, or dragging across it, to indicate that you want to perform an action on it. *See also* Highlighting.

Selection bar In Word, the area to the left of the left margin. You can select entire lines of text in the selection bar using the pointer.

Selection box A dashed-line rectangle surrounding a selected placeholder in PowerPoint.

Select pointer The mouse pointer shape that looks like a white arrow oriented toward the upper-left corner of the screen.

Select query A commonly used query in which records are collected and displayed in a datasheet and can be modified.

Semipermanent memory *See* Complementary metal oxide semiconductor memory.

Sender The computer that originates the message in data communications.

Serial value A number used in an Excel worksheet that represents a date or time used in calculations; a date that is formatted in General format will appear as a serial value.

Server A computer on a network that acts as the central storage location for programs and provides mass storage for most of the data used on the network.

Sheet tab In Excel, a tab at the bottom of the worksheet window that displays the name of a worksheet in a workbook.

Shortcut A link that you can place in any location that gives you quick access to a file, folder, or program located on your hard disk or network.

Shortcut menu A menu that appears when you right-click an item.

Shut down To exit the operating system and turn off your computer.

Sign in To select a user account name when a computer starts up, giving access to that user's files. *Also called* log in.

Simple database A database that contains just one table.

Single-click *See* Click.

Single-core processor A CPU with one processor on the chip.

SkyDrive A large storage space on the Internet (or in the cloud) that you and others can access from any location for storing files. To set up your own SkyDrive, you must first obtain a Microsoft account, which is a set of free online services from Microsoft Corporation. *See also* OneDrive.

Slate computer A thin computer primarily used to read electronic books, view video, and access the Internet, and that does not have an external keyboard or a mouse; instead users touch the screen or use a stylus to accomplish tasks.

Slide In PowerPoint, an on-screen page for use in a slide show.

Slide Master Contains the layouts, design elements and other formatting attributes for a presentation.

Slide pane In Normal view in PowerPoint, an area of the program window that displays the text and graphics of a presentation slide; these objects can be edited in the Slide pane.

Slider An item in a dialog box that you drag to set the degree to which an option is in effect.

Slide show A full-screen display of slides, containing text and graphics, on a computer.

Slide Show view A view in PowerPoint that displays presentation slides in full-screen and also displays all slide transitions and animation effects.

Slide Sorter view A view in PowerPoint that shows thumbnails of every slide in a presentation at a reduced size so you can reorder slides easily.

SmartArt Ready-made conceptual diagrams that you can insert in an Office document and customize to create striking visuals to illustrate a process, hierarchy or relationship.

Smartphone A handheld computer used to make and received phone calls, maintain an address book, electronic appointment book, calculator, and notepad, send email, connect to the Internet, play music, take photos or video, and perform some of the same functions as a PC, such as word processing.

Snap feature For desktop application programs (apps), the Windows 8 feature that lets you drag a window to the left or right side of the screen, where it "snaps" to fill that half of the screen; also, for Windows 8 apps, the feature that lets you position one of two open apps so it occupies one- or two-thirds of the screen.

Soft page break Page breaks that are automatically inserted by Word at the bottom of a page.

Software The intangible components of a computer system, particularly the programs that the computer needs to perform a specific task.

Solid state drive (SDD) Based on flash memory and intended as a replacement for a traditional hard disk drive. Though still more expensive than hard drives, SSDs use less power while offering much faster data access and increased reliability.

Solid state storage *See* Flash memory.

Sort Change the order of, such as the order of files or folders in a window based on criteria such as date, file size, or alphabetical by filename.

Sound clips Sound or music files that you either create yourself or obtain from outside sources; you can insert sound clips in any PowerPoint slide so they will play during the slide show. *Also called* audio files.

Source file When linking or embedding data between two files, the original file.

Sparkline A miniature chart that fits in one cell and illustrates trends in a selected range, usually adjacent to the sparkline.

Speaker notes In PowerPoint, notes that accompany slides; used to help the speaker remember important information that should not appear on the slides themselves.

Speakers Allow you to hear sounds generated by your computer. Can be separate peripheral devices, or can be built into the computer case or monitor.

Specifications The technical details about a hardware component.

Spell check The feature in document production software that helps you avoid typographical and grammatical errors.

Spin box A text box with up and down arrows; you can type a setting in the text box or click the arrows to increase or decrease the setting.

Split form In Access, a form that displays the underlying datasheet at the bottom and the data entry form above it.

Spoof To create a website that looks exactly like another legitimate site on the web but steals the information people enter.

Spreadsheet Another word for a workbook or worksheet.

Spreadsheet program (or app) A computer-based data analysis tool that displays numerical data in a row and column grid format, and which can perform numeric calculations.

Spyware Software that track a computer user's Internet usage and sends this data back to the company or person that created it, usually without the computer user's permission or knowledge.

Standalone computer A personal computer that is not connected to a network.

Standard colors A group of ten colors that appear below the Theme Colors in any Office color palette that contain basic hues such as red, orange, green, and blue.

Start screen The screen you see after you sign in to Windows 8; contains controls, such as tiles, that let you interact with the Windows 8 operating system.

Status bar Area at the bottom of an Office program window that displays information such as the current page or record number, and important messages, such as the status of the current print job.

Strong password A string of at least eight characters of upper and lowercase letters and numbers.

Style In Word, a defined set of formatting characteristics for a character or paragraph; can include the font, font size, font style, paragraph alignment, spacing of the paragraph, tab settings, and anything else that defines the format of the paragraph.

Style set A group of professionally coordinated styles that look great together and can be applied to a document to instantly change its overall appearance.

Subfolder A folder within another folder for organizing sets of related files into smaller groups.

Subnotebook computers Notebook computers that are smaller and lighter than ordinary notebooks. *Also called* ultraportable computer and mini notebook.

Subtitle placeholder On a slide with the Title layout, the placeholder below the Title placeholder; contains the placeholder text "Click to add subtitle."

Suite A collection of programs (sometimes called applications) that share a common user interface and are distributed together. Microsoft Office 2013 is a software suite.

SUM function In Excel, the function used to calculate the total of the arguments.

Summary information In an Access report, displays statistics about one or more fields in a database including statistics on the sum, average, minimum, or maximum value in any numeric field.

Supercomputer The largest and fastest type of computer used by large corporations and government agencies for processing a tremendous volume of data.

Synced When files that are added, changed or deleted on one computer, the same files on other devices are also updated.

Synchronous dynamic RAM (SDRAM) RAM that is synchronized with the clock speed of the CPU's bus to allow faster access to its contents.

System resource Any part of the computer system, including memory, storage devices, and the microprocessor, that can be used by a computer program.

System software A collection of programs and data that helps the computer carry out its basic operating tasks.

T

Tab (Ribbon) In an Office 2013 app, an area on the Ribbon that contains groups of related commands for completing a specific type of task. In a Word document, a set position where text following a tab character aligns.

Tab indicator An icon on the ruler used to align text differently, such as to the right or center of a tab stop.

Table In Access, a collection of related records. In Word and PowerPoint, information displayed in a grid containing rows and columns. In Excel, A range of cells containing fields and records that you can analyze, sort, and filter separately from other cells in a worksheet.

Table style In Word or Excel, a predefined set of formatting attributes such as shading, fonts, and border color, that specifies how a table looks.

Tablet A computer designed for portability that includes the capability of recognizing ordinary handwriting on the screen.

Tab selector In Word, button on left end of horizontal ruler that displays the type of tab stop that will be inserted on the ruler when the ruler is clicked. By default, the tab selector displays the Left tab icon. Click the tab selector to display the type of tab you want to insert.

Tab stop A location on the ruler where the insertion point moves to when the Tab key is pressed.

Taskbar The horizontal bar at the bottom of the Windows 8 desktop; displays icons representing apps, folders, and/or files on the left, and the Notification area, containing the date and time and special program messages, on the right.

TB *See* Terabyte.

Telecommunications The transmission of data over a comparatively long distance using a phone line.

Template A presentation that contains colors, graphics, and fonts, as well as content guidance.

Temporary memory *See* Random access memory.

Terabyte (TB) 1,024 GB, or approximately one trillion bytes.

Text box Text object that automatically wraps text and can be resized or moved.

Text placeholder A designated area on a PowerPoint slide for entering text, such as titles, subtitles, and body text.

Text wrapping style The settings for how text flows in relation to a graphic.

The cloud The Internet.

Theme A predesigned set of formatting specifications for fonts and colors that you can apply to an Office 2013 file to achieve a coordinated overall look throughout the document, workbook, presentation, or database.

Themes gallery In PowerPoint, thumbnails of the themes installed on the computer.

Thumbnail pane In Normal view in PowerPoint, the left pane, which shows miniature versions (thumbnails) of each presentation slide.

Thumbnails Small representations of clip art images that appear in the Clip Art task pane during a search. In PowerPoint, small representations of presentation slides that appear on the Slides tab to the left of the slide window.

Tile A shaded rectangle on the Windows 8 Start screen that represents an app. *See also* App and Application software.

Times New Roman Type of serif font traditionally used in newspapers.

Timing The amount of time a slide remains on the screen during a presentation.

Title bar The shaded top border of a window that displays the name of the window, folder, or file and the app name. Darker shading indicates the active window.

Title placeholder An area on a slide with the Title slide layout, which contains the text "Click to add title."

Title slide layout The slide layout usually used for the first slide in a presentation; contains a Title placeholder and a Subtitle placeholder.

Toner A powdery substance used by laser printers to transfer a laser image onto paper.

Toolbar In an application program, a set of buttons, lists, and menus you can use to issue program commands.

Total row In Excel, an extra row at the bottom of a table that can be used to display subtotals and other calculations.

Touch pad A touch-sensitive device on a laptop computer that you drag your finger over to control the pointer; buttons for clicking commands are located in front of the touch pad.

Touch pointer A pointer on the screen for performing pointing operations with a finger if touch input is available on your computer.

Touchscreen A display that shows you output and allows you to touch it with your finger or a stylus to input commands.

Trackball A pointing device with a rolling ball on the top side and buttons for clicking commands; you control the movement of the pointer by moving the ball.

Track pad *See* Touch pad.

Traditional apps Application programs (apps), such as Microsoft Office, that open in windows that you can move and resize to view alongside other app windows. *Also called* desktop apps.

Transition The way a slide first appears in a slide show and replaces the previous slide.

Translucency The transparency feature of Windows Aero that enables you to locate content by seeing through one window to the next window.

Trim To edit the start or end frames of a video to determine its length.

Ultraportable computer *See* Subnotebook computers.

Universal Serial Bus port *See* USB port.

URL An address on the web.

USB (Universal Serial Bus) port A high-speed port to which you can connect a device with a USB connector to have the computer recognize the device and allow you to use it immediately.

USB connector A small, rectangular plug attached to a peripheral device and that you connect to a USB port.

USB flash drive A removable storage device for folders and files that you plug into a USB port on your computer; makes it easy to transport folders and files to other computers. Also called a pen drive, flash drive, jump drive, keychain drive, or thumb drive.

User account A special area in a computer's operating system where users can store their own files and preferences.

User Interface The collection of buttons and tools you use to interact with a software program.

Utility software A type of system software that helps analyze, optimize, configure, and maintain a computer. Examples include anti-virus software, backup tools, and disk tools that allow you to analyze a hard drive or compress data to save space.

Value axis The vertical line that defines the left edge of a chart, and usually measures values. *Also called* the vertical axis or y-axis.

Vertical axis The vertical line that defines the left edge of a chart, and usually measures values. *Also called* the value axis or y-axis.

VGA (video graphics array) port A port that transmits analog video.

Video card *See* Graphics card.

Video display adapter *See* Graphics card.

Video editing software Software that allows you to edit video by clipping it, adding captions or a soundtrack, or rearranging clips.

View A preset configuration that determines which elements of a file are visible on-screen in an Office program (app); does not affect the actual content of the document. In Windows, a set of appearance choices for folder contents, such as Large Icons view or Details view.

View buttons Buttons at the far right of the status bar that you use to change your view of the document.

Virtual memory Space on the computer's storage devices that simulates additional RAM.

Virus A harmful program that instructs a computer to perform destructive activities, such as erasing a disk drive; variants are called worms and Trojan horses.

Virus protection software *See* Antivirus software.

Voice recognition software Allows you to input data and commands by speaking into a microphone.

Volatile memory *See* Random access memory.

WAN *See* Wide area network.

Web *See* World Wide Web.

Web browser *See* Browser.

Web Layout view A view that shows how a document will look if you save it as a Web page.

Website creation and management software Software that allows you to create and manage websites and to see what the web pages will look like as you create them.

Welcome screen An initial startup screen that displays icons for each user account on the computer.

Wide area network (WAN) A network that connects one or more LAN.

Wi-Fi *See* Wireless fidelity.

WiMAX (Worldwide Interoperability for Microwave Access) A standard of wireless communication defined by the IEEE that allows computers to communicate wirelessly over many miles; signals are transmitted from WiMAX towers to a WiMAX receiver in a device.

Window Rectangular-shaped work area on a screen that might contain icons, the contents of a file, or other usable data.

Window control icons The set of three buttons on the right side of a window's title bar that let you control the window's state, such as minimized, maximized, restored to its previous open size, or closed.

Windows 8 apps Apps (application programs) for Windows 8 that have a single purpose, such as Photos, News, or OneDrive.

Windows 8 UI The Windows 8 user interface. *See also* User interface.

Windows accessories Application programs (apps), such as Paint or WordPad, that come with the Windows 8 operating system.

Windows Clipboard A temporary storage area in your computer's memory for cut and copied items. *See also* Office Clipboard.

Windows desktop An electronic work area that lets you organize and manage your information, much like your own physical desktop.

Windows Search The Windows feature that lets you look for files and folders on your computer storage devices; to search, type text in the Search text box in the title bar of any open window, or click the Office button and type text in the Search programs and files text box.

Windows Website A link in the Windows Help app that lets you find Windows 8 resources such as blogs, video tours, and downloads. the title bar of any open window, or click the Office button and type text in the Search programs and files text box.

Win/Loss sparkline A miniature chart that shows either a bar (representing a gain) or a bar (representing a loss for a selected cells.

Wireless fidelity The term created by the nonprofit Wi-Fi Alliance to describe networks connected using a standard radio frequency established by the Institute of Electrical and Electronics Engineers (IEEE); frequently referred to as Wi-Fi.

Wireless local area network (WLAN) A LAN connected using high frequency radio waves rather than cables.

WLAN *See* Wireless local area network.

Word processing program (or app) A program (app) used to create and manipulate text-based documents, such as memos, newsletters, or term papers.

Word size The amount of data that is processed by a microprocessor at one time.

Word wrap In Word, a feature that automatically pushes text to the next line when the insertion point meets the right margin.

Workbook In Excel, a collection of related worksheets saved in a single Excel file.

Worksheet An Excel spreadsheet comprised of rows and columns of information that is used for performing numeric calculations, displaying business data, presenting information on the Web, and other purposes.

Workstation A computer that is connected to a network.

Worldwide Interoperability for Microwave Access *See* WiMAX.

World Wide Web (Web) A huge database of information that is stored on network servers in places that allow public access.

Wrap *See* Word wrap.

X-axis The horizontal line in a chart that contains a series of related values from the worksheet. *Also called* the horizontal or category axis.

Y-axis The vertical line in a chart that contains a series of related values from the worksheet. *Also called* the vertical or value axis.

Zoom slider Located to the right of the View buttons, used to set the magnification level of your document.

Index